Professional Stage

Module F

Management and Strategy

ACCA Textbook

229X/J00

British Library Cataloguing-in-Publication Data

A catalogue record for this book is available from the British Library.

Published by Foulks Lynch Ltd
Number 4
The Griffin Centre
Staines Road
Feltham
Middlesex
TW14 0HS

ISBN 0 7483 4229 X

Acknowledgements

We are grateful to the Association of Chartered Certified Accountants, the Chartered Institute of Management Accountants and the Institute of Chartered Accountants in England and Wales for permission to reproduce past examination questions. The answers have been prepared by Foulks Lynch Ltd.

CONTENTS

PREFACE

This Textbook is the ACCA's official text for paper 12, Management and Strategy, and is part of the ACCA's official series produced for students taking the ACCA examinations. It has been produced with direct guidance from the examiner specifically for paper 12, and covers the syllabus and teaching guide in great detail giving appropriate weighting to the various topics.

This Textbook is, however, very different from a reference book or a more traditional style textbook. It is targeted very closely on the examinations and is written in a way that will help you assimilate the information easily and give you plenty of practice at the various techniques involved. Particular attention has been paid to producing an interactive text that will maintain your interest with a series of carefully designed features.

- **Introduction with learning objectives**. We put the chapter into context and set out clearly the learning objectives that will be achieved by the reader.
- **Definitions**. The text clearly defines key words or concepts. The purpose of including these definitions is **not** that you should learn them - rote learning is not required and is positively harmful. The definitions are included to focus your attention on the point being covered.
- **Brick-building style**. We build up techniques slowly, with simpler ideas leading to exam standard questions. This is a key feature and it is the natural way to learn.
- **Activities**. The text involves you in the learning process with a series of activities designed to arrest your attention and make you concentrate and respond.
- **Conclusions**. Where helpful, the text includes conclusions that summarise important points as you read through the chapter rather than leaving the conclusion to the chapter end. The purpose of this is to summarise concisely the key material that has just been covered so that you can constantly monitor your understanding of the material as you read it.
- **Self test questions**. At the end of each chapter there is a series of self test questions. The purpose of these is to help you revise some of the key elements of the chapter. The answer to each is a paragraph reference, encouraging you to go back and re-read and revise that point.
- **End of chapter questions**. At the end of each chapter we include examination style questions. These will give you a very good idea of the sort of thing the examiner will ask and will test your understanding of what has been covered.

Complementary Revision Series, Lynchpins and Audio Tapes

Revision Series - The ACCA Revision Series contains all the relevant current syllabus exam questions from June 1994 to December 1999 with the examiner's own official answers, all updated in January 2000.

What better way to revise for your exams than to read and study the examiner's own answers!

Lynchpins - The ACCA Lynchpins, pocket-sized revision aids which can be used throughout your course, contain revision notes of all main syllabus topics, all fully indexed, plus numerous examples and diagrams. They provide invaluable focus and assistance in keeping key topics in the front of your mind.

Audio Tapes - Our 'Tracks' audio tapes are fully integrated with our other publications. They provide clear explanations of key aspects of the syllabus, invaluable throughout your studies and at the revision stage.

FORMAT OF THE EXAMINATION

	Number of marks
Section A: 1 compulsory mini case study	50
Section B: 2 (out of 3) questions of 25 marks each	50
	100

Time allowed: 3 hours

Questions will be set in a practical context and will require candidates to analyse scenarios and offer solutions to problems posed within the case study.

Occasionally one of the optional questions may be linked into the main case study, which could help in reducing the amount of reading within the question paper. There will generally be financial data within the compulsory case study and this should be assessed in order to evaluate past strategies or comment on proposed strategies. This case study will focus mainly on core material whereas it is likely that the optional questions will concentrate on the more specialist areas of the syllabus.

All the answers should be based upon the case scenarios and should not be a repetition of the academic theories. Theoretical models should be used to support and justify the candidate's practical analyses and arguments. Although covered within the syllabus, a detailed knowledge of UK legislation on matters such as health and safety and employment legislation is not required, but these aspects could be considered as examples of good practice.

SYLLABUS

Professional stage - Module F Paper 12: MANAGEMENT AND STRATEGY

Introduction

This paper draws on the topics introduced in paper 4 and examines them in greater detail. The paper looks at the theoretical background of management with the express purpose that the student will draw on this knowledge in order to improve their own management competence within their organisation. It aims to broaden the student's knowledge regarding management and organisations beyond that possible from working in one situation alone.

Chapter reference

(1) STRATEGIC MANAGEMENT AND BUSINESS PLANNING — 1-12

(a) Competitive advantage

(i) its meaning in different markets and industries

(ii) of nations and the implications of this for organisational success

(iii) the different approaches used by organisations and management in different countries and the lessons which can be applied to the UK

(iv) the effect on organisations of working in an international environment, the key aspects of that environment and methods of entry into it.

(b) The future for nations, industries, organisations and the workforce (including management)

(i) scanning the environment of the organisation and the context in which it is set for changes, developments and opportunities

(ii) forecasting trends and developments in relevant areas through the use of relevant quantitative and qualitative analysis

(iii) future basing (ie anticipating long term prospects for the business and its likelihood of survival) and other scenario building techniques.

(c) Strategic management and business planning

(i) the purpose of strategic management and business planning and the relationship between the two

(ii) the methods which organisations use to plan for the future (including the role of information technology)

(iii) the effects which the external environment may have on strategy and plans

Chapter reference

(iv) methods of gaining support and commitment for strategies

(v) formulating and evaluating plans with an awareness of the various techniques available to managers

(vi) understanding and managing the risk of a proposed business plan for the plan itself and for all the aspects of business which it will influence

(vii) reviewing strategy for the effect it will have on the organisation and the local and global community.

(2) MANAGING OPERATIONS AND SERVICES 13-18

(a) Determining the work to be undertaken

(i) estimating time and resources needed to undertake work

(ii) calculating the cost of services to be provided

(iii) determining whether there are any reasons for the work being problematic or where contingencies are likely to occur.

(b) Planning resource allocation

(i) setting work objectives in line with organisational strategy so that the former contributes to the latter

(ii) designing/modifying methods of achieving work objectives which are consistent with ethos, strategy, practices

(iii) allocating available resources in an optimum way to achieve and exceed targets set

(iv) formulating and evaluating work plans including an awareness of assignment and allocation techniques

(v) evaluating previous resource allocations to improve present performance

(vi) the importance of time management.

(c) Monitoring and maintaining services

(i) the different concepts of quality

(ii) monitoring and evaluating the implementation of work plans using methods which are consistent with organisational ethos and strategy, the concepts of quality

(iii) methods of assessing, analysing and interpreting information on service delivery and other non-financial targets, resource utilisation and costs.

Chapter reference

(d) Marketing

(i) the purpose and functioning of marketing and the different roles which it may play for the organisation

(ii) analysing market needs and identifying marketing opportunities and/or improvements in services

(iii) obtaining a competitive advantage

(iv) the impact of the global market.

(3) HUMAN RESOURCES MANAGEMENT 19-22

(a) Recruitment, selection, employment and dismissal

(i) the purpose of personnel specifications in the recruitment and selection of staff and the different forms which these may take

(ii) identifying the competences and attributes required to meet and to develop the service as a whole through a number of different methods

(iii) specifying personnel requirements in relation to the work to be undertaken, overall resources and the strategy, objectives and ethos of the organisation

(iv) evaluating and determining the benefits and costs of additional/new personnel

(v) identifying and evaluating suitable methods of recruitment

(vi) the range of selection methods which are available, the different circumstances where they may be of use, their costs and benefits and best practice within each

(vii) methods of motivating/supporting personnel within the work place

(viii) staff appraisal and the assessment of personnel (including self) in relation to organisational direction, strategy, ethos, objectives and aims

(ix) the legal and organisational policies and procedures regarding the warning and dismissal of personnel and the role of specialists/specialist departments in the process

(x) the role of employee groups and joint employer/employee groups/ committees in promoting the welfare of personnel

Chapter reference

(xi) awareness of the legislation which affects recruitment, selection, employment and dismissal and the ways in which anti-discriminatory practice can be promoted

(xii) the management of change - both organisational and personal.

(b) Human resources development

(i) the role which individual and team development can play in the growth and development of the organisation

(ii) traditional versus progressive views regarding an organisation's human resources and their development

(iii) the relationship between human resource development and the structure and functioning of organisations

(iv) the ways in which individuals and teams can be encouraged to grow and develop and the manner in which this can contribute to the organisation through career paths

(v) the internal and external factors which may affect an individual's/team's development

(vi) the different concepts and models of competence and the 'competent manager' and the ways in which these might enhance development

(vii) methods of encouraging and supporting development.

(4) MANAGEMENT OF THE WORKING ENVIRONMENT 23

(a) The main principles of current legislation in relation to the management of the working environment, the ways in which these principles can be applied effectively.

(b) Monitoring, interpreting and applying good practice and legislation related to the work environment for the different needs of its users (such as staff and clients whether they are able bodied or with limiting abilities).

(c) The role and purpose of health, safety and security requirements/procedures/ guidelines.

(d) The roles and responsibilities in relation to the working environment and those within it and methods for improving practice.

(5) THE ACCOUNTANT AS AN EFFECTIVE COMMUNICATOR 24, 27

The skills of communication which are necessary for effective accountants

(i) seeking and clarifying information and views from others including reflecting back information and viewpoints to the giver

Chapter reference

(ii) isolating the key aspects of information and summarising for others' use

(iii) presenting information clearly to others both orally and in writing

(iv) negotiating and agreeing with others

(v) promoting new ideas to others to gain their support

(vi) giving and receiving constructive criticism to improve future performance

(vii) advising others in one's area of responsibility/expertise

(viii) encouraging others to offer information, suggestions etc.

(6) STRATEGIC IMPLICATIONS OF INFORMATION TECHNOLOGY 25-28

This section covers future developments of the system and the ways in which the user may monitor the latest best practice.

(a) Monitoring new developments/good practice in system design, operation, evaluation

(i) structured methods
(ii) documentation
(iii) testing and evaluation
(iv) quality assurance.

(b) Sources and access to relevant specialist knowledge (eg computer programming)

(i) accredited suppliers
(ii) accredited contractors.

(c) Current good accounting practice and latest developments in accounting systems

(i) sources of information
(ii) future developments.

(d) Information technology as a strategic resource including

(i) criticality of information technology to the organisation in terms of funding, expenditure levels, strategic advantage

(ii) formulation, organisation and control of information strategy and activities

(iii) responsibility accounting for information technology

Chapter reference

(iv) organisational positioning of the information systems department including centralisation versus decentralisation, information centres, end-user computing.

(e) The management of information systems development, including

(i) role, composition and significance of the steering committee
(ii) role of senior information technology management
(iii) criteria likely to influence project selection
(iv) use of project planning and control techniques
(v) information technology project appraisal.

(f) Liaison between the information technology managers and the accountant to identify the needs of the organisation.

THE OFFICIAL ACCA TEACHING GUIDE

Paper 12 - Management and Strategy

		Syllabus Reference	Chapter Reference
Session 1	***Introduction***		

BLOCK 1 - Strategic Management & Business Planning

Session 2	***What is Strategy? - 1***	1c(i)	1

Definitions of Strategy
- the different levels of strategy - corporate, business, operational, functional
- alternative definitions of strategy (eg, Hofer & Schendel, Ansoff, Andrews and, especially, Mintzberg)
- Drucker's analysis of and approach to making strategic decisions
- Johnson & Scholes' characteristics of strategic decisions
- gaining competitive advantage (Ohmae and Porter)

Session 3	***What is Strategy? - 2***		2

The Strategic Management Process
- define strategic management
- the purpose of strategic management and business planning, and the relationship between the two
- Mintzberg's strategy making in three modes - entrepreneurial, adaptive and planned
- 'rational' models of strategic management
- 'emergent strategy' and 'crafting strategy'
- the locus of strategy formulation and strategy implementation
- Japanese approach of 'pursuing a vision'

Session 4	***Building a Strategy***	1c(ii)	3, 4

Establishing Strategic Intent
- the importance of the mission statement
- characteristics of a good mission statement
- Mintzberg's definition of goals and objectives
- developing of goals and objectives
- the role of mission statement, goals and objectives in shaping a vision of the future

Strategic Options
- strategic options which an organisation might pursue
- implementing the strategies through internal or external growth

The Ideas of Professor Michael Porter
- the five forces model
- the meaning of 'competitive advantage'
- generic strategies for gaining competitive advantage

Session 5	***Some Strategic Planning Tools***	1c(v)	5

Other Planning Tools
- product portfolio analysis (Boston Matrix etc)
- Ansoff's product/market growth vector
- Gap Analysis
- Life Cycle Analysis

		Syllabus reference	*Chapter reference*
	Strategy Evaluation ♦ use of decision trees, ranking and scoring methods to formulate and evaluate strategy ♦ the impact of strategies on the organisation and the community ♦ linking strategies to possible scenarios		
	Analysing Risk ♦ sensitivity analysis using computer spreadsheets ♦ using risk analysis to assess uncertainty ♦ value of decision matrices in choosing alternative strategies ♦ importance of stakeholder and political risk analysis		
Session 6	***The Impact of Strategy on the Organisation***	1c(vii)	6, 7
	Understanding the Organisation ♦ internal appraisal of the organisation ♦ Porter's value chain analysis ♦ influence of structure and systems on strategy		
	Organisation Culture ♦ the major influences on culture ♦ levels of culture ♦ the concept of excellence ♦ cultural influence on strategy ♦ identifying key strengths and weaknesses		
BLOCK II 'No Man is an Island'			
Session 7	***The World in which we Live***	1a	8
	The Global Environment ♦ key aspects of the international business environment ♦ the effect of an international environment on organisations ♦ alternative ways to enter foreign markets ♦ recent trends and developments in global business strategy		
	The Competitive Advantage of Nations ♦ Porter's determinants of national competitive advantage ♦ the implications for company strategy and national economics		
	The Impact of the Global Market ♦ national marketing and global marketing ♦ 'global companies win out' Porter ♦ risks of global markets ♦ effects of cultural differences ♦ assessing opportunities and threats ♦ some key strategic issues		
Session 8	***The Business Environment***	1b	9
	Forecasting Trends and Developments ♦ role of forecasting in strategic decision making ♦ the techniques available ♦ the use of scenario building		

	Syllabus reference	Chapter reference

Understanding the Environment
- key influences on the organisation
- effect of the external environment of corporate strategies and plans
- a framework for environmental analysis
- the concept of boundary management

Scanning & Monitoring the Environment
- identifying current and emerging changes
- the role of monitoring specific trends
- information sources

BLOCK III - Implementing Planning

	Syllabus reference	Chapter reference
Session 9 ***Building the Framework***	1c(ii)	10

A Framework for Strategy Implementation
- real work begins after strategies are formulated
- different skills needed for successful strategy
- implementation
- problems which can arise
- key implementation issues
- developing a framework

Matching Strategy with Structure
- different types of organisation structure
- effect of decentralised and centralised decision making
- advantages and disadvantages
- Mintzberg's structural configurations
- influences on organisational design

	Syllabus reference	Chapter reference
Session 10 ***Operational Planning***	1c(vi)	11

Translating Strategic into Operational Plans
- the process by which strategic plans are translated into operating plans and policies
- the importance of active participation in the planning process
- a methodology for effective resource allocation
- budgets as tool for control

Planning at the Tactical/Operational Level
- simple aids to planning
- analysis risk
- the role of computer packages

	Syllabus reference	Chapter reference
Session 11 ***Some Problems of Change***	1c(iv)	12

The Dynamics of Change
- why change is a challenge to management
- the role of force field analysis as a way of understanding change
- factors affecting an individual's responses to change
- why people may resist change

	Syllabus reference	*Chapter reference*

Managing Change

- ways of overcoming resistance
- key issues in successful change management
- how organisations can create readiness for change
- gaining support and commitment
- the role of the leader

The Change Process

- Lewin's 3-step model of change
- alternative models of change management
- implementing change through power politics
- a simple framework for the management of change

Strategy Review and Strategic Issue Management

- the importance of reviewing progress
- a framework for strategy review
- the importance of strategic issue management

BLOCK IV - Planning and the individual

	Syllabus reference	Chapter reference
Session 12 ***Setting Employee Goals***	2b(i),(ii), (iii),(iv)	13

Setting Work Objectives

- the role of individual work objectives in ensuring the achievement of the organisations goals
- the hierarchy of objectives
- top down versus bottom up strategy setting
- management by objectives, its advantages and disadvantages
- setting objectives using Management by objectives

Planning for the Achievement of Objectives

- setting priorities
- the role of policies and procedures
- formulating and evaluating work plans
- allocating available resources
- assessing and analysing resource allocation
- the importance of time management

	Syllabus reference	Chapter reference
Session 13 ***The Work to be Undertaken***	2a 2b(v),(vi)	14

Project Management

- the project life cycle
- the objectives of project management
- breaking projects down into manageable units

Estimating Resource Requirements

- the importance of accurate estimates
- use of work breakdown structure to identify resource needs
- estimating direct and indirect costs
- why estimates may be inaccurate
- calculating total project costs

		Syllabus reference	*Chapter reference*

Planning the Timescale
- estimating the time needed
- Gantt charts, network analysis and critical path analysis
- use of resource histograms and resource smoothing
- parallel scheduling

Session 14/15	***Marketing***	2d	15, 16

The Role and Purpose of Marketing
- the marketing concept
- the characteristics of a market orientated organisation
- marketing in not-for-profit organisations
- the main activities of the marketing function
- Promoting the corporate image

Analysing Market Needs and Identifying Opportunities
- the objectives of market analysis
- a framework for analysing the market
- analysing buyer behaviour
- market segmentation
- methods of consumer and market research
- developing new products and services
- selection and control of distribution channels
- integration of pricing into the marketing activities

Session 16	***Maintaining Services Pt1***	2c	17

The Concept of Quality
- quality management (the ideas of Demming, Crosby, Juran, Feigenbaum, Ishikawa and Taguchi)
- the difference between 'quality control' and 'quality assurance'
- the role of standards (eg, BS5750/IS9000)
- total quality management

The Pursuit of Excellence
- the characteristics of a successful organisation (eg, Peters & Waterman, Goldsmith & Clutterbuck)
- the role of quality
- have we reached the end of sustainable excellence?

Session 17	***Maintaining Services Pt2***	2c,d(iii)	17, 18

Monitoring and Maintaining Quality
- barriers to quality
- a total quality programme
- assessing the quality of services
- the role of quality audits, assessments and reviews
- continuous improvement

Pursuit of Competitive Advantages
- the strategic role of marketing
- sustainable competitive advantage
- gaining positional advantage
- sources of competitive advantage
- tactics of competitive advantage (defensive, offensive, flanking, market niches)

		Syllabus reference	*Chapter reference*

BLOCK V - Human Resource Management

Session 18	***The Concept of Human Resource Management***	3b	19

An Overview of Human Resource Development

- the role and purpose of Human Resource Management (HRM) and Human Resource Development
- the integration of HRM into strategic planning
- the main areas covered by a human resource plan and the formulation of personnel policies and procedures

The Task of Human Resource Development

- traditional views of human resources and their development compared with the more modern approach
- the relationship between human resource development and the structure and functioning of the organisation
- the role of individual and team development in the growth and development of the organisation
- the objectives, purpose and role of career management
- internal and external factors that might affect an individual's, or a team's, performance

Session 19	***Recruitment and Selection***	3a(i)-(vi)	20

Recruitment

- the process by which personnel requirements are determined
- different forms of employment
- the use of cost/benefit analysis in evaluating and determining the benefits of additional/new personnel
- the purpose of job and personnel specifications in the recruitment and selection of staff
- the different forms that personnel specifications can take
- suitable methods of recruitment

Selection

- the use of application forms and CVs as part of the selection process
- the role of the interview in the selection process and describe the different types of selection interviews
- the use of psychometric tests
- other methods of selection
- the usefulness of references

Session 20	***Motivation, Appraisal & Discipline***	3a(vii), (viii)	21

Motivation

- Schien's models of motivation
- the needs, expectancy and goal theories of motivation with reference to Maslow, Herzberg, McLelland, Vroom, Porter & Lawler, Latham and Locke
- methods of improving motivation

		Syllabus reference	*Chapter reference*

Appraisal

- the purposes of staff appraisal and the appraisal process
- outline the role of the assessment centre in assessing participants' competences
- identify the importance of congruence between an organisation's appraisal system and its objectives, strategy and culture

Session 21	***A Legal Framework***	3a(ix),(x) (xi)	22

- contracts of employment, termination of employment, unfair dismissal, redundancy and maternity rights
- equal opportunities (eg, equal pay, sex discrimination, race relations)
- promotion of non-discrimination
- managers' responsibilities for developing good practice

BLOCK VI - Managing the Working Environment

Session 22	***Legal Background***	4	23

Legislation and the Working Environment

- the reasons for health, safety and security requirements
- outline the principal legislation affecting employers and employees
- how managers can keep up to date

Applying Good Practice

- the key elements of a health and safety programme
- the role of education and training
- the role of managers, supervisors, advisors etc
- essentials of a safety policy
- good housekeeping and prevention policies

Office Design

- the effect of environment of work performance
- different needs of various groups
- some guidelines for good design
- good office practice
- management responsibilities and the role of the office manager

BLOCK VII - Accountant as Communicator

Session 23	***Gaining and Using Information***	5(i)-(viii)	24

Seeking and Clarifying Information

- the communication process both oral and written
- effective ways to gain information
- clarifying information
- good listening
- summarising information

Presentation and Persuasion

- presenting information in writing and verbally
- use of visual aids
- persuading others to your point of view

	Syllabus reference	*Chapter reference*
Negotiation ♦ different types of negotiating situation ♦ various stages of negotiation ♦ strategies and tactics ♦ effective negotiation skills		
BLOCK VIII - Information Technology (IT)		
Session 24 — Evolution of IT Applications	6a,b,c	25
Phases of Development ♦ the phases of development of information systems applications ♦ Nolan's six stages of evolution ♦ implications of the evolutionary process		
The Importance of IT ♦ the criticality of IT spending ♦ use of McFarlan's Strategic Grid to analyse the importance of IT to a business ♦ the forces which drive an organisation round the Strategic Grid		
Formulating an Information Systems Strategy ♦ why is it important? ♦ the elements of a strategy ♦ developing the strategy ♦ linking information systems planning to business goals ♦ liaison between IT managers and users ♦ the contribution of the accountant		
Session 25 — IT and Strategic Advantage	6d	26
Using IT to Support Strategic Decision Making ♦ examples of strategic planning packages ♦ their limitations ♦ effect of IT on management processes in future		
Using IT to Gain a Strategic Advantage ♦ IT as a strategic weapon ♦ how information technology permiates the value chain ♦ other frameworks to help identify options to use IT strategically		
Session 26 — Managing Information Systems	5a(i)-(v)	27
Deploying Information Systems Resources ♦ centralisation or decentralisation, the pressures for and against ♦ end user computing ♦ the role of the information centre ♦ factors influencing the positioning of IT resources		
Information Systems Departments ♦ challenges facing Information Systems departments ♦ key issues facing department structure ♦ the role of the IT Director ♦ the role of steering committees		

		Syllabus reference	Chapter reference
Session 27	***Controlling IT***		28

Control and Responsibility Accounting

- the main issues concerning control of IT
- measuring and evaluating the value of information systems
- the role of responsibility accounting
- the control architecture of responsibility accounting

Management of Information Systems Development

- a framework
- the steering committee its role and composition
- the role of senior IT management
- project selection
- planning and controlling projects
- appraising IT

Session 28

A review of some of the major concepts

1 STRATEGIC MANAGEMENT AND BUSINESS PLANNING: WHAT IS STRATEGY?

INTRODUCTION & LEARNING OBJECTIVES

The task of this chapter is to look at the terms which will be encountered and some of the definitions of strategy. There are many ways in which to interpret strategy and the aim is to familiarise students with some of the main writers and their interpretations of the meaning of strategy.

When you have studied this chapter you should be able to do the following.

- Define strategy.
- Classify the different levels of strategy
- Understand that different companies have different planning needs.
- Appreciate what is required for effective strategic planning.
- Make a case for strategic planning.
- Know the influence of some management writers on the formulation of strategy.

1 ALTERNATIVE DEFINITIONS OF STRATEGY

1.1 Concept

Definition Strategy: a course of action, including the specification of resources required, to achieve a specific objective.

This definition, although stated in a single sentence, provides a framework which can be expanded, shaped, applied and developed further.

Because of the rapid technological and social changes affecting an organisation's environment, there is a need for strategies to achieve agreed goals and objectives, giving a sense of purpose and direction to the organisation.

In military terms, 'strategy' refers to the important plan. Where the objective is to defeat the enemy, the strategy will be to deploy the resources available in a manner which is likely to achieve the aim.

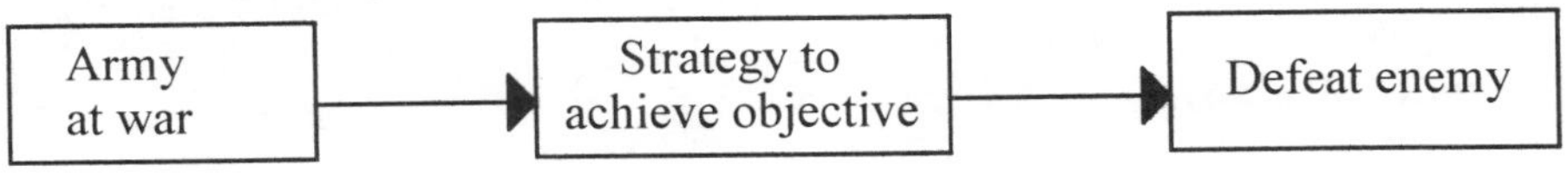

1.2 A wider view

We view strategy as the organised development of resources to achieve specific objectives against competition from rival organisations. It is the use of all the entity's resources, financial, manufacturing, marketing, technological, manpower etc, in the pursuit of its objectives.

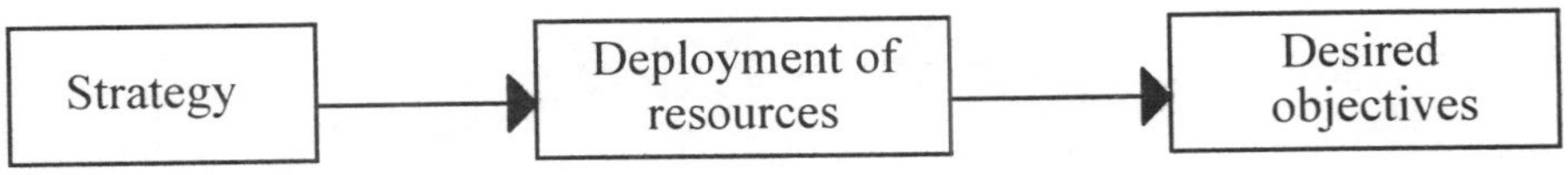

It is a set of policies adopted by senior management which guides the scope and direction of the entity. It takes into account the environment in which the company operates.

'**Scope**' used in this context relates to size and range, and '**direction**' describes product/market positioning. In simple terms, an entity's '**environment**' relates to the uncontrollable factors that influence it. All three terms will be discussed in more depth later.

1.3 Activity

Consider carefully the above explanation of strategy and then try to relate it to either a strategy that you have read about or one from your own organisation. Your example should bring out, or emphasise, the importance of the following words included in the explanation: entity objectives, resources, scope, direction and environment.

1.4 Activity solution

Although the example of strategy given here was implemented by IBM over a decade ago, it is still considered to be a classic example of competitive strategy, and one that exemplifies our explanation of strategy.

In August 1981, **IBM** launched a massive attack on the $1.4 billion US personal computer market, which had been planned in scrupulous detail to take market leadership away from the market creator, Apple. The strategy was in response to the falling main-frame computer market of which IBM was market leader, and the fast developing personal computer market in which the company did not then have a presence. IBM's strategy was based on a simultaneous three-pronged thrust.

First, at the core of the IBM's new PC architecture was an Intel 16-bit microprocessor providing speed and memory size with much superior processing power than obtained from the market's existing 8-bit microprocessor based products.

Second IBM publicised its PC specifications well ahead of its product launch and permitted Microsoft, the supplier of its PCs' basic operating systems to license its software to other manufacturers, a strategy which very soon made the IBM microcomputer equipment, and the software produced for it, *de facto* the industry standard.

Third, IBM launched a massive $40 million advertising campaign which it supported with 800 carefully selected computer retailers, at the same time using its experience, goodwill and enormous sales force to penetrate the office segment. Within one year IBM had secured 16% of the PC market. The second wave of the IBM attack, a massive 20% price reduction, took place in the following year, April 1983, securing for it another 10% share, and leadership, of the market.

When implementing this strategy IBM was attempting to respond to its changing business environment by using its considerable resources and distinctive competence to outmanoeuvre its opponents in order to achieve its objective of gaining a superior position in a new market, and to achieve specific financial objectives. Explained simply the company was involved in the process of planning a way by which it could utilise its resources to achieve specific results in a hostile and dynamic business environment.

1.5 Alternative views of strategy

There is no one specific definition of a strategy and writers have discussed the lack of consensus over what a strategy actually is. However, it is generally agreed that a strategy is some sort of future plan of action. There are many ways of viewing the creation of a strategy and the diagram below sets out some of the vantage points from which the strategy may be created.

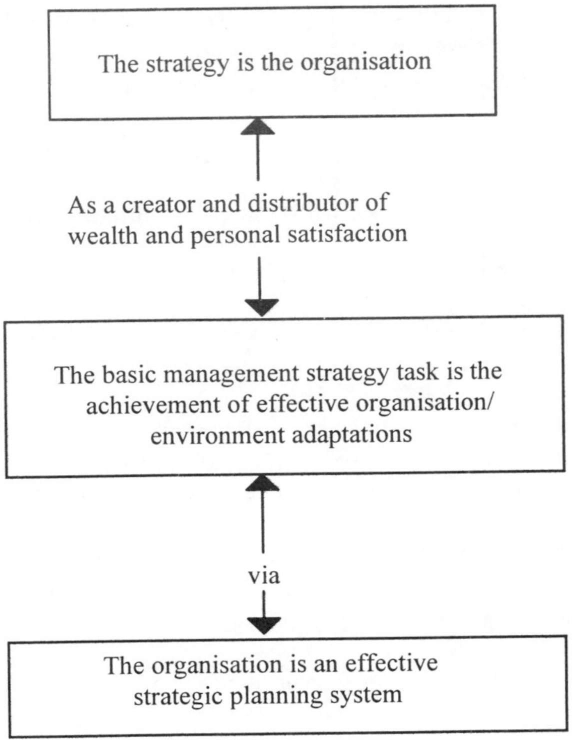

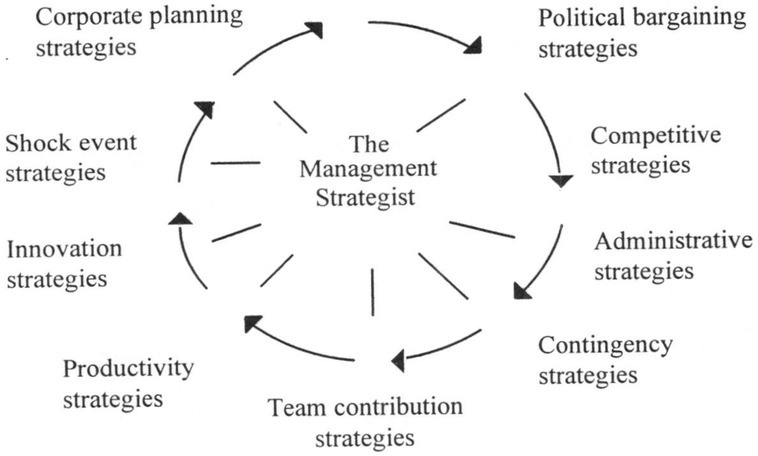

1.6 The strategy is the organisation

The view that the organisation is the fundamental strategy is supported by both Henry Mintzberg and Igor Ansoff:

"The one goal all of the players may share is the need for a common playing field", H Mintzberg, **Power in and around Organizations**

"For over one hundred years, the firm has been the principal and successful instrument (strategy) of social progress... it is a breeder of wealth", H. I. Ansoff, **Implementing Strategic Management**

The organisation is, therefore, seen as a creator and distributor of wealth and the wealth both sustains the organisation and provides satisfaction (by way of payment) to the people working within the organisation.

1.7 Adaptation to its environment - Hofer and Schendel

Definition A strategy is the mediating force or 'match' between the organisation and the environment. (Hofer and Schendel)

Harrison also supports the proposition that strategy is the achieving of the match between the organisation and its environment. It is viewing the internal capabilities of the organisation and, in the light of these, identifying the opportunities or threats that exist externally.

By using the organisation as a strategy for the fulfilment of needs, it must continue to grow and devolve thereby creating more wealth from its environment. The organisation will only be efficient, however, if it controls its wealth and its interaction with the environment providing that wealth.

1.8 The organisation viewed as a multi-decision making system - Andrews

According to Andrews, a successful organisation is achieved by a system of plans, decisions and actions.

Definition The Corporate Strategy is the pattern of decisions in a company that determines and reveals its objectives, purpose or goals, and produces the principal policies and plans for achieving those goals. K Andrews, **The Concept of Corporate Strategy**

Andrews also argues that the strategy should define the range of business the company will pursue, the kind of economic and human organisation it is or intends to be, and the nature of economic and non-economic contributions it intends to make to its stakeholders.

The pattern of decisions means an interdependence of purposes, policies and action which is crucial to the strategy and the organisation's ability to identify competitive advantages.

Mintzberg also supported this view:

Definition Strategy is a pattern in a stream of decisions.

This view of strategy is the basis on which practical strategists make plans and decisions.

Mintzberg also suggests various definitions of strategy, covering the five Ps: a plan, a ploy, a pattern, a position and a perspective.

Strategy as a plan which can be defined and followed.

Strategy as a ploy which can be seen as a move in a competitive business game.

Strategy as a pattern of consistent behaviour, giving the impression of a logically thought out strategy.

Strategy as a position is a means of identifying where an organisation places itself in an environment or market.

Strategy as a perspective consists not just of a chosen position but of a unique way of perceiving the world. In this respect Mintzberg is suggesting that the organisation's strategy is similar to the individual's personality.

1.9 Plans for problems

Management strategy can also be categorised into attempts to help to provide particular sets of plans to meet the needs of particular types of problems. These plans would be in response to changes in the environment and would aim to promote better decision-making.

The study of management strategy might therefore proceed through a series of related sub-systems as shown on the wheel of the diagram.

Political bargaining strategies

The design and implementation of political bargaining strategies are described by Ansoff

"If the firm is to play a more effective role in the shaping of its future (it may develop a societal strategy)... In bargaining processes, which involve mutual give and take... the firm needs to formulate a bargaining strategy"

On the same theme, Mintzberg:

"Strategic decisions of large organisations inevitably involve social as well as economic consequences, inextricably intertwined – and, thus the orientation of basic strategies to suit personal interests is the ultimate pay off, reserved for the most powerful of influencers"

The theory and practice of strategic management are very much concerned with the political arena of the organisation, and the use of political bargaining strategies, by stakeholders, to achieve beneficial exchanges.

2 THE DIFFERENT LEVELS OF STRATEGY

2.1 Corporate strategy

All organisations should carry out some form of corporate strategy activity. The need for involvement increases with the complexity of the organisation and the uncertainty and turbulence of its environment.

Corporate strategy consists of strategic planning at a corporate level and is not confined to one particular area - marketing, personnel, production/operational and financial implications are all taken into consideration. It is primarily concerned with the determination of ends such as what business or businesses the firm is in or should be in and how integrated these businesses should be with one another. It covers a longer time period and has a wider scope than the other levels of corporate planning.

Johnson and Scholes identify three levels of corporate strategy

(a) **Corporate strategy** – what business or businesses the firm is in or should be in and how integrated these businesses should be with one another.

(b) **Business strategy** – how each business attempts to achieve its mission within its chosen area of activity.

(c) **Functional strategy** – how the different functions of the business support the corporate and business strategies.

They claim that corporate strategy is concerned with the scope of an organisation's activities and the matching of these to the organisation's environment, its resource capabilities and the values and expectations of its various stakeholders.

A number of students complain that the formulation of corporate strategy is too far removed from their likely level of activity, but an understanding is essential for all management in that:

(a) Through the means-end chain, lower-level objectives are inexorably linked to higher-level strategies. An appreciation of these strategies and how they are formulated can be an effective guide to action.

(b) The principles of corporate strategy are equally appropriate for the smaller organisation.

(c) Whatever the level on which a manager operates within an organisation, he or she can have some influence over that organisation's corporate strategy.

2.2 Business strategy

Business strategy is concerned with how each business attempts to achieve its mission within its chosen area of activity. Here strategy is about which products or services should be developed and offered to which markets and the extent to which the customer needs are met whilst achieving the objectives of the organisation. It includes corporate planning at the tactical level and consists of the allocation of resources for complete operations. It is means-oriented and is mainly administrative and persuasive in its endeavours.

2.3 Functional strategy

Functional strategy examines how the different functions of the business (marketing, production, finance etc) support the corporate and business strategies. Such corporate planning at the operational level is means-oriented and most activities are concerned only with the ability to undertake directions.

However, despite the points evaluated above, the boundaries between the three categories are very indistinct and much depends upon the circumstances prevailing and the kind of organisation. Overall, corporate planning is concerned with the scope of an organisation's activities and the matching of these to the organisation's environment, its resource capabilities and the values and expectations of its various stakeholders.

3 STRATEGIC DECISIONS

3.1 Drucker's analysis

Drucker, in his book **Managing for Results,** discusses business strategies and states that whatever a company's programme it must decide:

(a) what opportunities it wants to pursue and what risks it is willing and able to accept;

(b) its scope and structure, and especially the right balance between specialisation, diversification and integration;

(c) between time and money, between building its own or buying, ie using sale of a business, merger, acquisition and joint venture to attain its goals;

(d) on an organisation structure appropriate to its economic realities, its opportunities and its programme for performance.

There are three kinds of opportunities

(a) **Additive** – exploitation of existing resources.

(b) **Complementary** – involving structural changes in the company.

(c) **Breakthrough** – changing the fundamental economic characteristics of the business.

Risks can be placed in four categories

(a) those that must be accepted;

(b) those that can be afforded;

(c) those that cannot be afforded; and

(d) those the company cannot afford to miss.

The right opportunities will not be selected unless the company attempts to maximise opportunities rather than to minimise risk. Quantitative techniques can be used to evaluate the likely outcomes of different decisions.

3.2 Characteristics

In their book, **Exploring Corporate Strategy**, Johnson and Scholes outline the characteristics of strategic decisions. They discuss the following areas:

(i) Strategic decisions are likely to be affected by the **scope of an organisation's activities**, because the scope concerns the way the management conceive the organisation's boundaries. It is to do with what they want the organisation to be like and be about.

(ii) Strategy involves the **matching of the activities of an organisation to its environment**.

(iii) Strategy must also **match the activities of an organisation to its resource capability.** It is not just about being aware of the environmental threats and opportunities but about matching the organisational resources to these threats and opportunities.

(iv) Strategies need to be considered in terms of **the extent to which resources can be obtained, allocated and controlled** to develop a strategy for the future.

(v) **Operational decisions will be affected** by strategic decisions because they will set off waves of lesser decisions.

(vi) As well as the environmental forces and the resource availability, the strategy of an organisation will be **affected by the expectations and values of those who have power** within and around the organisation.

(vii) Strategic decisions are apt to affect the long-term direction of the organisation.

Johnson and Scholes argue that what distinguishes strategic management from other aspects of management in an organisation is the complexity. There are three reasons for this:

- it involves a high degree of uncertainty;
- it is likely to require an integrated approach to management; and
- it may involve major change in the organisation.

4 JUSTIFICATION FOR STRATEGY

4.1 Short-term freewheeling opportunism

Opponents of structured long-term strategic planning argue that in instigating explicit long-term strategy managers are putting their organisations into what is effectively a strait-jacket, resulting in a serious loss of flexibility rendering difficult the exploitation of opportunities on a more free- wheeling basis. The arguments imply certain weaknesses in the disciplined approach, such as its inflexibility, forecasting inaccuracy, complexity and bureaucratic nature.

The characteristics of **free-wheeling opportunism** are as follows.

(a) Essentially it concentrates on finding, evaluating and exploiting short-term product-market opportunities instead of adhering to the rigidity of a predetermined strategy.

(b) It encourages a non-corporate philosophy, and managers who have vested interests will try to exert pressure for the acceptance of their own ideas even if they are incompatible with existing corporate aims.

(c) It is perceived by some managers to be dynamic, exciting and innovative. Furthermore because of its unstructured approach, strategy arising from it is seen to bear the stamp of individual managers.

4.2 The arguments against long-term strategy

(a) Setting corporate objectives

A criticism frequently levelled at the practice of spelling out corporate objectives is that the exercise descends into the formulation of empty platitudes which offer no positive directional indicators for decision making. Those executives responsible for decision making need to know not merely the overall direction in which the organisation is supposed to be heading, but also which evaluative standards to apply in order to judge competitive strategies, with the standards expressed in meaningful terms such as market share and sales volume. Corporate strategy can be viewed from so many different angles and interests that it may be necessary to apply a whole range of evaluative standards, some of which may be in conflict, for instance, a strengthening of liquid resources may be accompanied by a lower return on capital employed. An individual measure will have to be weighted according to its significance in the problem situation under review, although it is not possible to carry out such evaluation with any sort of mathematical precision.

(b) The difficulties of forecasting accurately

The development of a forecasting capability, and the development of models which relate environmental changes to corporate performance are significant aspects of strategic planning. While the general level of practice concerning environmental issues is still quite primitive, the state of the art is rapidly advancing.

There are difficult problems associated with trying to accurately forecast for the long term.

- The fact that it is a long-term period.
- The complexity of the environment that needs to be forecast.
- The rapidity and novelty of environmental change.
- The interrelationships between the environmental variables involved.
- The limitations of the data available.
- The amount and complexity of the calculations involved.

(c) Short-term pressures

The pressures on management are for short term results and ostensibly strategy is concerned with the long term eg, 'What should we be doing now to help us reach the position we want to be in, in five years time.' Often it is difficult to motivate managers by setting long term expectations.

(d) Rigidity

Operational managers are frequently reluctant to specify their planning assumptions because the situations which their plans are designed to meet may change so rapidly that they can be made to look foolish. Even if a plan is reasonably accurate, the situation might change for reasons other than those forecast. Executives are often held prisoners by the rigidity of the planning process, because plans have to be set out in detail long before the period to which they apply.

The rigidity of the long-term plan, particularly in regard to the rationing and scheduling of resources, may also place the company in a position where it is unable to react to short-term unforeseen opportunities, or serious short-term crisis.

(e) Stifling initiative

If adherence to the strategy becomes all-important, it discounts flair and creativity. Operational managers can generate enthusiasm or dampen down potential trouble spots and quick action may be required to avert trouble or improve a situation by actions outside the strategy. If operational managers then have to defend their actions against criticisms of acting '**outside the plan**', irrespective of the resultant benefits, they are likely to become apathetic and indifferent.

(f) **The cost**

The strategic planning process can be costly, involving the use of specialists, sometimes a specialist department, and taking up management time. The process generates its own bureaucracy and associated paper or electronic data flow. Personal authorities are, to a greater or lesser extent, replaced by written guidelines.

(g) **Lacks dynamism**

The process might be inhibitive in that it programmes activities and events and removes the excitement and exhilaration of spontaneity and the unexpected.

(h) **Why start now?**

A general attitude particularly shown by managers in small growing companies is that they have managed quite successfully in the past without formalised strategic planning systems. So why start now?

(i) **Management distrust of techniques**

The strategic planning process involves the use of management techniques, not least forecasting, modelling, cost analysis and operational research. This can produce adverse reactions for two reasons. Firstly, senior management may distrust, 'laboratory techniques untested in their ambit of activity', and secondly they might distrust the recommendations of younger specialist people who are, 'on balance heavy on academic learning but light on practical experience'.

(j) **The clash of personal and corporate loyalties**

The adoption of corporate strategy requires a tacit acceptance by everyone that the interests of departments, activities and individuals are subordinate to the corporate interests. Department managers are required to consider the contribution to corporate profits or the reduction in corporate costs of any decision. They should not allow their decisions to be limited by departmental parameters.

It is only natural that managers should seek personal advancement. As a company is the primary vehicle by which this can be achieved, a cleavage of loyalty may occur. A problem of strategic planning is identifying those areas where there may be a clash of interests and loyalties, and in assessing where an individual has allowed vested interests to dominate decisions.

4.3 The case for long-term strategy

Notwithstanding the points raised in answering the previous question, planning long term corporate strategy can be justified in the following ways:

(a) Certain action which is fundamental to the corporate operations is **irreversible** in the short term at least. It is difficult to imagine managers making decisions which have a degree of permanency without first going through some form of formalised strategic planning.

(b) The bigger an organisation grows the bigger are the **risks** involved in top management decisions. Strategic planning helps to identify these risks and either prevent or mitigate their effects.

(c) The business environment is dynamic and the rate of change is escalating. Integral to the strategic planning process is **environmental appraisal** which often uses sophisticated forecasting techniques requiring expert interpretation and evaluation of strategic options.

(d) Some companies have undoubtedly managed quite successfully without strategic planning. However it is probable that they **could have performed much better**. Even an upward sloping profit line can be criticised if it prevents the occurrence of an even steeper profit line. Strategic planning ensures that performance is targeted rather than merely assessed against loose expectations.

(e) Corporate planning is concerned with the **long term**, and the long term is an essential dimension in the overall survival pattern of a company. The planning disciplines concentrate management's attention on long-term matters, but not at the exclusion of short-term considerations. Free-wheel planning is apt to focus only on the short term and there is evidence to suggest that this is perilous.

(f) Strategic planning requires the clarification of **corporate objectives**. The process aids in the formulation of organisational goals and objectives and the strategy formulation process can be used to evaluate whether or not the tentative objectives established are achievable, given the organisation's resources and the nature of the changes occurring in its environment, and, if not, what other objectives could be achieved.

(g) The systematic survey of the environment involved in strategic planning can only improve the basis of **information** on which trends are identified, projections made and evaluative criteria produced.

(h) Strategic planning quantifies long-term **resource** problems and produces a basis upon which resources can be **planned and rationed** between programmes.

(i) The systematic survey of the corporate environment and of the company's internal strengths and weaknesses, acts as **'an early warning system'**. The process will, hopefully, identify product/market threats and resource weaknesses in time for the company to bring in preventive or remedial measures.

(j) Strategic planning helps to **integrate** long, medium and short plans and to harmonise the activities of different departments and functions. The planning process results in people from different functions working together in teams, and the plan itself clarifies the contribution made by the different functions to the achievement of overall objectives.

(k) The emergent plan should reflect the **'corporate' nature** of the company, instead of merely being an aggregation of the plans of individual departments.

(l) Strategic planning demands a logical, deliberate and analytical approach to decision making. It requires the generation of **alternative strategies**, and the evaluation of the probable results of their execution.

(m) The plans formulated can be used as **yardsticks** against which actual performance can be judged and remedial needs identified.

(n) The planning process is **continuous** and not conducted as a **'one-off'** ad hoc exercise. This requires the maintenance of an information system which will continuously provide up-to-date data for on-going decision making and control purposes.

(o) The strategy spells out in definite terms the **responsibility and authority** of each executive and management activity. This tends to boost morale, and produces better results since most groups and individuals perform better if they know what is expected of them and how they contribute to the overall progress of the company.

(p) Strategic planning, when carried out imaginatively and conducted in the right atmosphere of **communication, participation and incentive**, helps to develop a climate conducive to creative thinking, initiative and innovation.

5 GAINING COMPETITIVE ADVANTAGE

5.1 Kenichi Ohmae

In the real world, many decisions are taken without any formal kind of textbook analysis of the problem to be solved. This may well occur when the success of the whole enterprise depends upon the quality of the critical decisions made. Kenichi Ohmae, after explaining in his book **The mind of the strategist** that some of Japan's most outstanding strategists had little or no formal business education, goes on to write:

'But they have an intuitive grasp of the basic elements of strategy. They have an idiosyncratic mode of thinking in which company, customers and competition merge in dynamic interaction out of which a comprehensive set of objectives and plans for action eventually crystallises.'

The success of the strategy depends on the interplay of these elements, the three C's - company, customers and competition. Ohmae calls this the strategic triangle.

Ohmae argues that a good business strategy is one where an organisation can gain significant ground on its competitors at an acceptable cost. Unlike some other management theorists he also believes that, instead of reacting to the environment, the organisation should shape the environment whilst directing the strategy towards the competition. The ways that organisations can do this include:

(a) Identifying the key factors for success and concentrating resources on these activities

(b) Achieving relative superiority by exploiting the competitor's actual or potential weaknesses or the organisation's own strengths

(c) Challenging assumptions about particular markets eg, ATMs (Automated Teller Machines) and telephone banking challenge the assumptions about branch networks in banks

(d) Altering the markets or finding new ways of exploiting them.

5.2 Michael Porter

Professor Porter of Harvard Business School, who has been influential in the development of competitive strategy, argues that rather than being a continuation of one's own company products and markets, a strategy has to be viewed primarily in the context of the industrial competitive situation. He says that the thrust of business strategy formulation is to identify the competitive advantage that the business holds and to build on that, denying any existing or potential competition the opportunity to meet it.

According to his views rigorous strategic formulation involves analysing the competitor's likely strategy before developing your own.

6 CHAPTER SUMMARY

We have seen that there are many different definitions of strategy ranging from the simple to the complex. However, most of these definitions interpret a strategy as being some sort of future plan of action.

The levels of strategy can be classified as corporate, business and functional. The corporate strategy is the most general level of strategy in an organisation. The business strategy relates to how an organisation approaches a particular market or activity. The operational and functional strategies are those made at operational levels eg, personnel policy, pricing strategies.

Johnson and Scholes' characteristics of strategic decisions could be used as the basis of the following definition of strategy:

Strategy decisions cover the direction and scope of an organisation over the long term. Ideally, the strategy should match the organisation's resources to its changing environment and in particular its markets and customers so as to meet stakeholder expectations.

7 SELF TEST QUESTIONS

7.1 Give a simple definition of strategy (1.1)

7.2 What are the five P's of strategy according to Mintzberg? (1.8)

7.3 List the three different types of strategy (2.1)

7.4 Name Drucker's three kinds of opportunities (3.1)

7.5 What are the characteristics of strategic decisions? (3.2)

7.6 According to Michael Porter, what does strategy formulation involve? (5.2)

8 EXAMINATION TYPE QUESTION

8.1 Strategic planning

Your managing director has attended a conference at which a speaker said that long-term strategic planning was obsolete. He is naturally concerned about this comment.

Draft a report to your managing director stressing the benefits of long-term strategic planning and examining the case for its abolition.

9 ANSWER TO EXAMINATION TYPE QUESTION

9.1 Strategic planning

REPORT

To: Managing director

From: Accountant

Date: X/X/19XX

Subject: Long-term strategic planning

A definition of long-term planning is 'The formulation, evaluation and selection of strategies; involving a review of the objectives of an organisation, the environment in which it is to operate, and an assessment of the strengths, weaknesses, opportunities etc. for the purpose of preparing a long-term strategic plan of action which will attain the objective set.'

Strategic management provides the necessary organisational setting; McNamee describes this as 'that type of management through which an organisation tries to obtain a good fit with its environment'.

The case for abolition

(a) Strategic planning has a high opportunity cost. Board level management are intimately involved (they could be involved with the business operationally, eg. by selling).

(b) There is no statutory requirement for strategic planning.

(c) Any plans of action which are formulated using detailed quantitative techniques are likely to be rendered useless by drastic changes in the business environment. One can't plan for chaotic and turbulent change, since plans quickly become outdated and useless. This factor in the modern business environment explains why some commentators have referred to long-term strategic planning as 'obsolete'.

(d) Argenti has demonstrated an absence of correlation between corporate planning systems and success. One should remember, though, that **all** businesses have strategic plans, which are required for any company taking a bank loan, for instance. Similarly, shareholders (particular institutionalised shareholders) will require strategic plans.

(e) Corporate entrepreneurial agility could be hindered by the shackles of fixed corporate planning.

(f) Critics of strategic planning have argued that the process tends to treat all businesses in the same way, as profit seekers. This may stifle managerial style.

The benefits of strategic planning

(a) Effective strategic planning is substantially dependent on a detailed knowledge of the environment.

(1) The remote environment (eg. the European economies)

(2) The immediate environment of the industry, as described by variables such as:

- power structure;
- number of players;
- length and intensity of distribution channels;
- customer and supplier behaviour;
- various stakeholder interests and intents.

Companies have found – from their strategic planning – the best ways to distribute resources. The decentralised SBU (strategic business unit) is a good example of this philosophy. Significantly, companies in adopting such structures are likely to enjoy competitive advantage.

The flexibility implied by strategic planning is important. There is no single 'best' way of carrying it out.

Qualitative plans are more likely to succeed than the more fragile quantitative plans mentioned above. The former may be employed to identify key strategic variables and to define important management issues. The plans are also more likely to enable a unidirectional approach to be taken by the company.

In answer to Argenti's point above studies have empirically demonstrated that successful companies tend to have more focused non-changing strategies (implying strategic planning).

(b) Strategic management accounting systems may be developed (to run in parallel with strategic planning) as decision–making aids.

(c) The sense of strategic direction, as represented by goals, and their resultant (probably largely qualitatively expressed) strategies, may be significant in acting as a set of codified rules for management to follow at an operational level. The codification results in systematic corporate questions – the continual 'reinventing of the wheel' is rendered less necessary.

Conclusion

A company-specific strategic planning system will result in substantial competitive advantage. Arguably, most companies will require such systems, in order to proactively cope with their turbulent business environments.

SIGNATURE

2 THE STRATEGIC PROCESS

INTRODUCTION & LEARNING OBJECTIVES

The objectives of this chapter are to explain the strategic management and business planning process.

To do this we will be looking at the relationship between the two and also examining some of the most important models.

Managerial decision-making receives considerable attention from researchers and practitioners. It is a useful way of viewing what managers actually do in the process of co-ordinating the organisational effort towards achieving the desired objectives.

All of the basic ideas on strategic planning are discussed and we will look in detail at the process of strategy making from the point of view of Mintzberg.

There are many models of strategic planning and this chapter tries to explain the rational models and, at the opposite extreme, the visionary model and many strategies which lie in between these two.

When you have studied this chapter you should be able to do the following:

- Define strategic management
- Outline the purpose of strategic management and business planning.
- Explain the relationship between strategic management and business planning.
- Describe the characteristics of entrepreneurial, adaptive and planned strategies.
- Relate rational models of strategic planning to specific situations.
- Describe the process of crafting a strategy
- Explain emerging strategies
- Understand the approach of pursuing a vision

1 STRATEGIC MANAGEMENT

1.1 The nature of management

The term management can have many meanings, depending in part on whether it is the process of management, the managers or the body of knowledge that is being referred to.

If it is the process that is being considered then this is normally understood to mean the successful utilisation of the company's resources which include men, materials, money and machines.

Definition A useful short definition of management is given by Kast and Rosenzweig 'A process of integrating human and material resources into a total system for objective accomplishment'.

Definition The definition given by Koontz, is 'the process of designing and maintaining an environment in which individuals work together in groups and accomplish efficiently selected aims'.

Therefore, management is concerned with achieving organisational goals through people.

Brech shows management functioning at two levels.

(a) Strategic management involves risk taking, handling uncertainty and making decisions on objectives, the direction of the firm and innovation. It is ends-oriented and involves:

'Judgement and decision in determining plans.'

Such a process is often referred to as entrepreneurship.

(b) Tactical and operational management is concerned with decisions designed to achieve the objectives set out by the entrepreneurial determination of the kind of business to be operated. It is means-oriented and is termed administration by some writers.

There are two components:

- 'Development of data procedures to assist control of performance and progress against plans.'

  This is the control process of management which is further examined later in this text.

- 'Guidance, integration, motivation and supervision of the personnel composing the enterprise and carrying out its activities.'

  Leadership is the term often attached to these processes which are fully explored later in this text.

Management is not a new concept and important writers in the past include Plato and Machiavelli. However, rapid technical development and consequent upheaval of values has led to an increasing search for effective ways to manage.

Mintzberg feels that management is best described in terms of various roles identified with a particular position and that these include:

(a) **Interpersonal roles** - figurehead, leader and liaison person.

(b) **Informational roles** - monitor, disseminator and spokesman.

(c) **Decisional roles** - entrepreneur, disturbance handler, resource allocator and negotiator.

1.2 Strategic management

Decisions about products, locations, structure, personnel and other resources are all major or strategic decisions. They will generally make an impact on the performance of the organisation. How these decisions are made and how they are implemented can be defined as the process of strategic management

Definition Strategic management is concerned with deciding on a strategy and planning how that strategy is to be put into effect

Johnson and Scholes

Strategic management is concerned with ensuring that the strategy is implemented. It can be described as having three elements:

(a) Strategic analysis - seeking to understand the strategic position of the organisation;

(b) Strategic choice - about the formulation of possible courses of action, their evaluation and the choice between them;

(c) Strategy implementation - planning how the strategy can be put into effect.

1.3 Strategic analysis

The aim of strategic analysis is to form a view of the main influences on the present and future well-being of the organisation. This will obviously affect the strategy choice. This analysis would cover the following areas:

- The environmental variables eg, political, economic, social and technological as well as competitive factors and how they will affect the organisation and its activities.
- The resource availability and its relative strengths and weaknesses.
- The aspirations and expectations of the groups which have an interest in the organisation eg, shareholders, managers, owners, employees and unions.
- The beliefs and assumptions that make up the culture of the organisation will have an effect because they are the means of interpreting the environment and resource influences.

Strategic analysis provides the basis for the next element in the strategic management, that of strategic choice.

1.4 Strategic choice

There are three parts to this element:

(a) Generation of strategic options eg, growth, acquisition, diversification or concentration.

(b) Evaluation of the options to assess their relative merits and feasibility.

(c) Selection of the strategy or option that the organisation will pursue. There could be more than one strategy chosen but there is a chance of an inherent danger or disadvantage to any choice made. Although there are techniques for evaluating specific options, the selection is often subjective and likely to be influenced by the values of managers and other groups with an interest in the organisation.

1.5 Strategy implementation

The implementation process can also be thought of as having several parts.

(a) Resource planning and the logistics of implementation. The process will address the problems of the tasks that need to be carried out and also the timing of them. There may need to be changes in the mix of resources required to implement the strategy and decisions will need to be taken about who is to be responsible for the changes.

(b) The organisational structure may need to be changed, eg, from hierarchical to matrix or from centralised to decentralised.

(c) The systems employed to manage the organisation may be improved. These systems provide the information and operational procedures needed in the organisation. It may be that a new information management system is required to monitor the progress of the strategy. Staff may need to be retrained or new staff recruited.

2 STRATEGIC MANAGEMENT AND BUSINESS PLANNING

2.1 Planning

Definition **Planning** is 'the establishment of objectives, and the formulation, evaluation and selection of policies, strategies, tactics and action required to achieve them'.

Planning comprises long-term/strategic planning and short-term operation planning. The later is usually for a year.

Planning can take place at three levels, defined by Anthony as follows

(a) **strategic** – deciding on the objectives of the organisation, on changes in these objectives, on the resources used to attain these objectives and on the policies that are to govern the acquisition, use and disposition of these resources

(b) **tactical** – ensuring that the resources are obtained and used effectively and efficiently in the accomplishment of the organisation's objectives

(c) **operational** – ensuring that specific tasks are carried out effectively and efficiently.

Anthony, rather confusingly, refers to these levels as **strategic planning, management control and operational control**. He quotes examples of planning at the different levels:

Strategic Planning	*Management Control*	*Operational Control*
Choosing objectives	Formulating budgets	
Organisational planning	Planning staff levels	Controlling hiring
Policy setting:	Formulating:	Implementing policy
- personnel	- personnel practices	Implementing policy
- financial	- working capital plans	Implementing policy
- marketing	- advertising programme	Implementing policy
- research	- research projects	Implementing policy
Factory acquisition	Plant rearrangement	Production schedules

Strategic planning is primarily concerned with determining the organisation's future and is sometimes opportunistic rather than systematic (for example, exploiting the situation of a competitor's failure).

Management control, often referred to as tactical planning and primarily concerned with the allocation of resources for complete operations, is means-oriented as is operational control which involves the management of individual tasks. Mental activity related to management control is considered by Anthony to be administrative and persuasive whereas operational control is only concerned with the ability to undertake directions.

2.2 Business decisions

As every accountant knows, much of any professional person or manager's time is concerned with decision-making. Decisions have to be taken on routine matters like whether to have a cup of coffee or not, whether to make a telephone call, when to call the next production, marketing or budget meeting, what items to discuss, through to decisions which have the most important consequences for the organisation, like, shall we go ahead with project X, acquire Company Y or invest in portfolio Z?

This profusion of decisions faces everyone in the business firm and it becomes particularly pronounced for the chief executive of the firm.

Decisions and problems are related and should always be regarded as linked from the point of view of decision making. However, we have first of all to define these terms.

(a) **A problem**

A problem is a departure from the norm, from what is expected, and it is, therefore, generally regarded in management terms as:

- Something unexpected.

- Necessitating a choice.
- Unpleasant, or at least adverse.
- In some way an obstacle to carrying out a plan.

(b) **A decision**

A decision is a commitment to a course of action, and may be considered as:

- Needing action.
- Requiring a choice.
- Demanding use (and therefore allocation) of resources.

If these definitions are examined, the problem and the decision are clearly linked. If there is no plan (or norm), there is no problem. Planning itself is a continuous process of making decisions, and its problems are usually dealt with on a subjective basis.

2.3 Example

The problem.

In November 1978 **Chrysler** reported its record quarterly loss. Worse was to come. In the first half of 1979 the price of oil rocketed. The already reducing car sales swung towards small cars where Chrysler was poorly positioned. At the same time interest rates shot up. By November 1981 Chrysler looked destined for the mortuary. It was down to $1 million cash and its cash spending was running at $50 million per day.

The decision.

Only three years later, in 1984, Chrysler made profits of $2.4 billion, more than it had earned in its previous fifty-eight years of history combined. How it was done was down to its President, Lee Iacocca, who achieved this remarkable turnaround by:

(a) Reducing the company's cost base to a level where the company could be competitive. Production break-even point was lowered from 2.3 million cars in 1979 to 1.1 million in 1983.

(b) Radically improving product quality. (In 1980 rust warranty claims alone on one model cost the company $109 million.)

(c) Turning the company into a marketing- and engineering-led organisation, where teamwork was important. (Previously Chrysler was a financially driven collection of individuals.)

(d) Investing heavily in developing a range of new products with customer appeal. (A $6.5 billion Five-year Product Investment Plan was formulated in 1980 and spending continued even in the years when the company looked a terminal case. By the mid-1980s Chrysler was considered to be ahead of its American competitors in computer-aided design, in the use of corrosion-resistant body panels, and in speed of reaction.)

2.4 Classifying problems

First, problems will be examined within their categories. The usual classification of problems is as follows.

(a) **Operating problems**

These problems will, as a general rule, concern matters such as the allocation of resources, job-sequencing (placing work in a specific order in which it is to be dealt with) and/or choice between relatively straightforward alternatives which are familiar. In the usual way, these problems are solved by decisions which are 'programmable' (ie, reached through well-established routines, possibly a manual of some kind.) There are 'decision rules'.

(b) **Planning problems**

Because planning is a continuous operation, the problems here are generally identified against very subjective standards (ie, through management experience). Incidentally, decisions for this problem category are not usually programmable, and are therefore called 'non-programmable' solutions.

(c) **Controlling problems**

This category deals with the establishment of the standards by which (a) and (b) are to be assessed. Usually, these problems are coped with by accountants because of their familiarity with quantifying techniques.

Before going on, however, it is worth considering another way of categorising problems. We may also say that individual problems could be:

(a) **Truly unique**

This is a completely exceptional situation which has not occurred before (and has a high probability of not occurring again).

(b) **Unique to a specific enterprise**

The problem has not arisen previously in a given organisation, eg consideration of an offer to merge with another organisation. Note that whilst this is not unusual in general terms, it is unusual as far as the specific organisation is concerned.

(c) **Generic**

This type of problem occurs when a particular event is identified which causes the need for a decision to be made but which is really only the symptom of a more serious problem. The **real** problem is a generic one and may not be perceived immediately - so that much time and effort is expended in the organisation in dealing with the relatively small problems which are really symptoms of the larger issue.

Sometimes, too, a problem may occur again and again unless 'generic solutions' are adopted to tackle the real issue in (c). Thus, a problem may occur which is the early sign of future occurrences. A major radiation leak, for instance, occurred in Russia in 1986 - and this was regarded as an early manifestation of future problems.

The use of these categories assists executives to make correct decisions. Incorrect classification therefore results in wrong decisions being made.

2.5 Classifying decisions

We shall now examine the classifications for decisions. We could, for instance, place them in the three categories adopted for problems: operating, planning and controlling. These are decisions taken to solve the respective problems in these categories.

As a rule though the following method is adopted.

(a) **Strategic decision**

Definition A course of action including the specification of resources required to achieve a specific objective.

(b) **Tactical decision**

Definition Planning the most efficient deployment of resources in an agreed strategy.

(c) **Operational control**

Definition The management of daily activities in accordance with strategic and tactical plans.

2.6 Strategy, tactics and operational control

The following table depicts the three different types of decision-making.

Example:	*Army*	*Industry*
Main objective Secondary objective	Defeat enemy Preserve our forces	25% return on capital Increase market share
Strategy	Attack through border. Use 24,000 infantry.	Sell on the basis that a 20% increase in sales and production capacity will reduce unit cost by 25%. Use £10m capital.
Tactics	Send ¾ troops in first. Hold ¼ reserve. 12,000 infantry to seize ports at night. 6,000 to sever communications and 6,000 in reserve.	Drop selling process now by 5%. Offer 5% bulk buying discounts.
Operational control	Monitor progress towards ports. Redeploy if opposition stiffer than expected.	Monitor sales progress. Ensure machines and labour are ready to take up 20% unused capacity.

2.7 Activity

Consider your own position. You are now following a course of study which leads you to the final qualifying examination of ACCA. Use the approach adopted in the above table to indicate your:

(a) Main objectives.
(b) Secondary objectives.
(c) Strategy.
(d) Tactics.
(e) Operational control.

2.8 Activity solution

You will deal with this problem according to your own views and perceptions. However one response is as follows:

Main objective	:	a successful professional career.
Secondary objective	:	to qualify with ACCA.
Strategy	:	to pass the examinations.
Tactics	:	to attend a part-time course of study.
Operational control	:	to sit progress tests, monitor results and revise areas of weakness.

2.9 The link between planning and decision-making

Planning and decision-making are closely linked. The existence of a plan is the result of certain decisions having been taken, and at the same time the plan provides a framework for other decisions.

If there is an effective plan, each executive knows what is expected and why. If on the other hand an executive does not know what targets have been allocated there will be no criteria against which alternative courses of action can be evaluated. Without planning there is a danger that the various departments will be run without adequate co-ordination, and may be under-performing, pursuing different objectives, or optimising their own performance at the expense of the organisation as a whole.

Too often, management consists of managing short-term problems, of trying to find ways out of immediate difficulties, of muddling through from one crisis to the next. Planning forces attention on the longer term, gives the company a direction, and should help to avoid some of the difficulties. It should at least help to predict future difficulties before they reach crisis proportions, so that there is more time to consider possible solutions.

To take a very simple analogy, managing a business is like a planned car journey. Before setting out you decide where you are going and what route you will take. You may hear on your car radio about difficulties ahead and change your route to avoid encountering a traffic jam. However, eventually you will probably resume your normal course in order to reach your specified destination, although naturally you are quite free to change your mind half-way there.

3 RATIONAL MODELS OF STRATEGIC PLANNING

3.1 Rationality

A rational process is considered to be one 'based on reasoning', one that is not subjective but objective, one that is logical and sensible. Using rational behaviour, policy is formed by firstly defining the goal and then selecting the means to achieve the goal by rational analysis.

Cause and effect are seen to be interlinked and an element of predictability is expected. In many problem-solving situations an assumption is made that the goals or objectives can be measured or assessed in quantitative terms. Rationality in this sense is based on the choice the decision-maker makes with reference to clear-cut alternatives. The following areas are present:

- Complete knowledge of environmental factors;
- Ability to order the preferences using some yardstick of utility, mainly with money as the common denominator;
- Ability to choose the alternative that returns the best outcome.

These provisions provide the framework for the techniques that are available and applicable under relatively closed systems. They are closed because they give neither weight to the environment of the decision-maker nor to the complexity of the act of choice.

There is also the problem that a decision may be rational from the individual's point of view but not from the standpoint of the organisation. Because organisations involve co-operative effort it is not likely that each individual can maximise personal objectives all the time. The rationality of organisational behaviour should be concerned with group objectives, not with what the individual would do in that situation.

3.2 Bounded rationality

This assumes that the decision-maker does not have the knowledge assumed in the last section, and must therefore deal with a limited picture of any given problem. In such a case the person must make a choice based on their own knowledge. Another individual or outside agency with more complete knowledge may query the rationality of the choice, as indeed the person who originally made the choice may think it was stupid with the benefit of hindsight.

3.3 Logical incremental view

Charles Lindblom suggested that managing strategies through logical, planning mechanisms was not realistic. Because of the complexity of organisations and the environments in which they operate, it would be difficult for managers to consider all the strategic options and measure them against preset, unambiguous objectives.

He argued that strategic choice takes place by comparing possible options against each other and considering which would give the best outcome. Lindblom called this strategy building through 'successive limited comparisons'.

Another writer, J B Quinn in his book **Strategies for Change**, wrote that the management process could best be described as logical incrementalism. This is the situation where managers have a view of where they want the organisation to be in the years to come but try to move towards that objective in an evolutionary way. They do this by attempting to develop a strong, secure but flexible core business whilst also continually experimenting with 'side issues'.

Quinn's studies recognised that such experiments could not be the sole responsibility of the top managers but they should be encouraged to come from the lower levels of the organisation.

This process is seen as having benefits to the organisation. Continual testing and gradual strategy implementation provide improved quality of information to help decision-making.

4 MINTZBERG'S VIEWS

4.1 Strategy development

Mintzberg's studies of organisations illustrated several patterns of strategic change as shown in the diagram below:

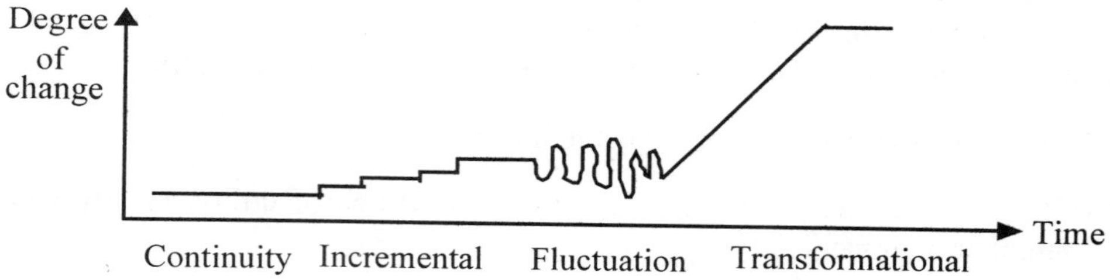

Most organisations that he studied were inclined to change incrementally with their strategies being formed gradually or through piecemeal change. He noticed a tendency towards 'momentum' of strategy, where, once an organisation had adopted a particular strategy then it tended to develop from and within that strategy, rather than fundamentally changing direction. There were periods of continuity in which the established strategy remained unchanged and periods of fluctuation where the strategies did change but in no clear direction. Global or transformational change was infrequent, tending to occur at times of crisis in organisations when performance had declined significantly.

4.2 Intended and emerging strategies

We tend to visualise a strategy as being formulated, perhaps through some planning process, resulting in a clear expression of direction which then comes about or is actually realised. It is conceived of as a deliberate, systematic process of development and implementation. However, in many organisations which attempt to formulate strategies in systematic ways, the intended strategies do not become realised, or only a part of what was intended actually happens.

Mintzberg states that strategies can emerge rather than be due to a deliberate planning process.

"One idea leads to another, until a new pattern forms. Action has driven thinking and a new strategy, has emerged... Out in the field, a salesman visits a customer. The product isn't right, and together they work out some modifications. The salesman returns to the company and puts the changes through; after two or three more rounds, they finally get it right. A new product emerges, which eventually opens up a new market. The company has changed strategic course."

The figure below shows that the actual outcome, the organisation's realised strategy, can come about through a planned, deliberate formulation and implementation. The realised strategy can also come about from a pattern in a stream of decisions (emergent strategy).

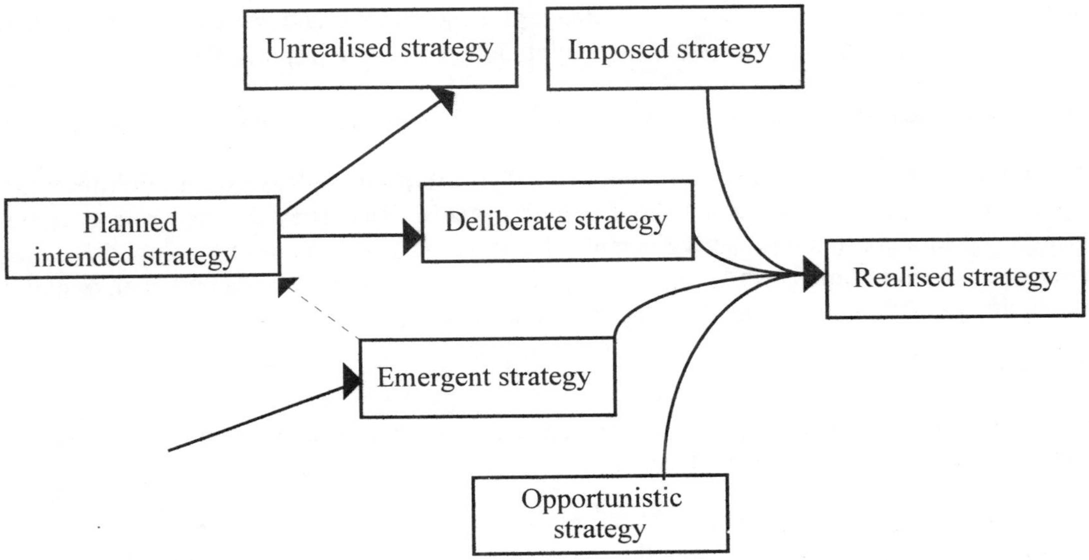

4.3 Modes of strategy making

It must be realised at the outset that there is no one best way of managing the strategy of an organisation. A flexible, reactive style may suit a small firm in a rapidly changing environment, whereas a large company may need to take a long term view and plan accordingly. Strategies may come about in different ways and Mintzberg has identified various kinds of strategies, from very deliberate to mostly emergent.

Planned strategy: precise intentions are formulated and articulated by a central leadership, and backed up by formal controls to ensure surprise-free implementation in an environment that is controllable or predictable. These strategies are extremely deliberate.

Entrepreneurial (opportunistic) strategy: intentions exist as the personal, unarticulated vision of a single leader, and so are adaptable to new opportunities. An organisation may take advantage of changes in the environment or recognise new skills in an opportunistic manner or a firm may be set up by an entrepreneur because of an opportunity in the market place. These strategies are relatively deliberate but can emerge too.

Ideological strategy: intentions exist as the collective vision of all the members of the organisation, controlled through strong, shared norms; the organisation is often proactive towards its environment. These strategies are rather deliberate.

Umbrella strategy: a leadership in partial control of the organisation's actions defines strategic targets or boundaries within which others must act. This strategy can be called deliberately emergent in that the leadership purposefully allows others the flexibility to manoeuvre and form patterns within the boundaries.

Process strategy: the leadership controls the process aspects of the strategy, leaving the actual content of the strategy to others. Again, strategies are partly deliberate (concerning process) and partly emergent (concerning content) and deliberately emergent.

Disconnected strategy: members are loosely coupled to the rest of the organisation and produce patterns in the streams of their own actions in the absence of the central intentions of the organisation at large. The strategies can be deliberate for those who make them.

Consensus strategy: through mutual adjustment, various members converge on patterns that pervade the organisation in the absence of central intentions. These strategies are rather emergent in nature.

Imposed strategy: the external environment dictates patterns in actions, either through direct imposition or through implicitly pre-empting organisational choice. Government policies may have an impact on the strategy; this has been the case for those public utilities recently privatised. Recession and threat of a takeover may force a strategy of cost cutting and retrenchment. Technological developments may cause an organisation to develop new products to replace those which have become obsolescent.
These strategies are organisationally emergent although they may be internalised and made deliberate.

Another mode of strategy making is sometimes called **adaptive** because it fits the description that managers give of how strategies come about in their organisations. They see their role as strategists as being involved in a continual proactive pursuit of a strategic goal, countering competitive moves and adapting to their environment whilst not rocking the boat too much. Incremental change may be seen as an adaptive process in a continually changing environment.

4.4 Crafting a strategy

Mintzberg likens the management of a strategy to a potter crafting clay. The clay is thrown and by shaping the clay on the wheel, the potter gives it shape through a gradual process.

> "The crafting image captures the process by which effective strategies come to be. The planning image, long popular in the literature, distorts those processes and thereby misguides organisations that embrace it unreservedly."

According to Mintzberg there are five activities involved in strategic management.

(i) **Manage stability**: managers should know when to change and not assume perpetual environmental change. A large proportion of managers' time should be spent effectively implementing the strategies, not planning them.

(ii) **Detect discontinuity**: strategic managers must be able to recognise the changes which are significant to their organisation.

(iii) **Know the business**: including an awareness and understanding of the operations in the organisation.

(iv) **Manage patterns**: managers should have the ability to detect emerging patterns and help them take shape; knowing which emergent strategies to nurture.

(v) **Reconcile change and continuity**: requires a combination or bringing together of the future, present and past; understanding that an obsession with either change or continuity can be counterproductive.

5 EASTERN PERSPECTIVES ON STRATEGY

5.1 Introduction

Most of this text is concerned with models of strategic thinking that have been formulated in Western economies, above all in Britain and the United States. However, it would be misleading to suppose that these provided the only possible frameworks for strategy formulation. Increasingly, authorities on strategy have looked to alternatives emerging from Pacific Rim countries, and especially from Japan.

The study of comparative management styles is based on an analysis of similarities and differences between management and business systems from different countries. The subject embraces general aspects of management style and culture, but also focuses on specific areas of strategic activity, such as the management of joint ventures between partners from different countries.

5.2 Approaches to comparative management

R D Robinson (in **International Business Management** 1978) argues that there are three broad approaches to the study of this subject.

- The **universalist approach** holds that few major differences exist among managers from different social and cultural backgrounds. Management theories and practices can easily be transferred from one culture to another.

- The **economic cluster approach** is to say that economic similarities and differences among nations, or groups of nations, constitute the most important basis for management tasks.

- The **cultural cluster approach** emphasises differences in attitudes and behaviour as determinants of management activities in different cultures.

It is this last approach which has come to prominence in recent years, particularly as the spread of multinational corporations has increased the need for organisations to understand how best to manage employees from different cultures.

5.3 Asian management systems

The economies of East Asia and South East Asia - Japan, China, Taiwan, South Korea, Hong Kong and the ASEAN countries - have recently been among the most dynamic in the world. Although this is partly attributable to their general political and economic policies, these countries have also benefited from the competitive activity of their business organisations. Japanese, Chinese and Korean management systems have all proved to be highly competitive in their different ways.

A common feature of these management approaches has been their tradition of holding together an organisation as a dynamic group. This suits the collectionist norms of Asian cultures.

The traditional model of management and competitiveness in the West has been based on Max Weber's study of the Protestant ethic in the rise of capitalism. Weber argued that at connection exists between the religious and cultural beliefs by which an individual is surrounded and the attitude to economic activity held by that individual. His analysis led to a view of strategic management activity based on individualism, mastery over the world, **laissez faire** economic principles, and the supremacy of market mechanisms.

Analysts studying comparative management have seized on Weber's ideas by trying to show how the different religious and cultural values held in Asian countries have been translated into different styles of management. These commentators have emphasised certain aspects of a 'Confucian' ethic which are believed to underlie much management theory and practice in Japan and other Eastern nations.

- While the Protestant ethic is highly conscious of rights, the Confucian ethic instead emphasises obligation. Individuals should be conscious of their group responsibilities.

- Western approaches to management emphasise adversarial relations, while Eastern approaches are based instead on a fiduciary community. This emphasis on trust implies that **laissez faire** principles are unwelcome; leadership and intervention by the government are the norm.

5.4 Pursuing a vision

The development of strategies can also be seen as the outcome of the influence of visionary leaders, especially where the organisation is dominated by a charismatic leader. These are generally organisations where the leader founded the company.

There may be managers or other staff who may not be as dedicated to cause and effect strategies but may have very high intuitive skills and can identify new possibilities and ideas. These executives have a 'feel' for what makes sense in volatile environments where forecasting is useless.

Kenichi Ohmae, in his book **The Mind of the Strategist**, argues that strategy making is essentially a creative process, needing strategic vision. Japanese companies which have been successful had a strategic thinker rather than a strategic planning process. This thinker should have a perceptive grasp of the basic elements of strategy.

Ohmae's objective was to show how outstanding strategists, who in Japan often lack formal business education, develop the ideas that solve problems and create opportunities for their organisations. His explanation is a set of concepts and approaches which can help anyone to develop this valuable mental agility.

The process of analysis should be a combination of intuition and rationality. Intuition and insight, in Ohmae's view, are more effective keys to successful strategy then rational analysis, though this has a place in the process. He defines creative insight as:

Definition The ability to combine, synthesise or reshuffle previously unrelated phenomena in such a way that you get more out of the emergent whole than you have put in.

Ohmae maintains that if creativity cannot be taught, it can certainly be consciously cultivated. The book is divided into three sections:

(i) The art of strategic thinking.

(ii) Building successful strategies.

(iii) Modern strategic realities.

The first part of his book, **the art of strategic thinking**, explores the basic mental processes involved in the development of strategy. Strategic thinking involves:

- flexible thinking;
- keeping details in perspective;
- focusing on key factors and the essentials of a business; and
- avoiding wrongly-focused perfectionism.

This process includes dissecting a problem or situation into its constituent parts; asking the right solution-oriented questions; constructing 'issue diagrams' and 'profit diagrams' to achieve the right diagnosis. Ohmae identifies the 'four routes to strategic advantage':

(i) strategy based on an organisation's key factors for success in its capability to increase market share and profitability;

(ii) strategy based on exploiting any relative superiority;

(iii) strategy based on aggressive initiatives which challenge accepted assumptions; and

(iv) strategy based on 'strategic degrees of freedom' (SDF), the development of innovations such as new markets or products.

All four routes are illustrated with case studies drawn from Japanese industry. An example of aggressive initiative challenging assumptions is that of Toyota's Taiichi Ohno questioning the need to stockpile large quantities of parts for the production line. This questioning eventually led to the introduction of 'Just in Time' and a revolution in production systems worldwide. Ohmae argues that if, instead of accepting the first answer, a person persists in asking 'why' four or five times, the fundamental problems and bottlenecks will be explored.

Strategies based on strategic degrees of freedom also require the recognition of changes in the consumers' objective function. For example, the preference for compact physical size in stereo equipment over performance measured by power output was capitalised on by Sony. Honda, and other car companies, perceived that customers were switching from speed and prestige to convenience, economy and utility.

In the second section of the book, **building successful strategies**, Ohmae states that responsiveness to changing customer objectives lies at the root of his system for constructing a business strategy. His three points of the strategic triangle are shown below:

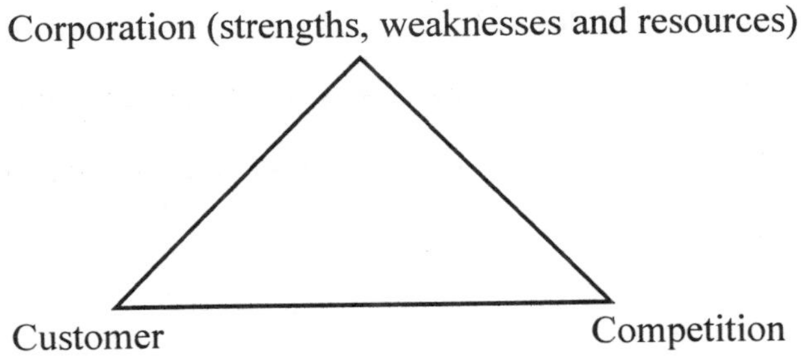

Corporate strategy, he argues, implies an attempt to alter a company's strength relative to that of its competitors in the most efficient way.
This section of the book goes on to analyse competitive advantage by price, volume and cost and their effect on profitability. If an organisation can charge more for a product which is a better design, they may be able to achieve a higher profit performance that their competitors.

In the final section, on **modern strategic realities**, Ohmae set his planning process against five 'key economic trends' which had an impact on business strategies in the following decade. When he wrote the book (1982) they were:

- continuing low growth;
- market maturity and strategic stalemate;
- uneven distribution of resources, such as oil;
- growing international complexities; and
- irreversible inflation.

A strategist should be able to see beyond the present; the strategic realities of the 1990's which are likely to influence business strategies include the following:

- a shift from labour intensive to capital intensive industries;
- a shift in the fixed to variable cost ratio;
- a shift from steel to electronics based industries;
- a shift from international to local financial management;
- a shift from multinational to multi-local companies.

6 CHAPTER SUMMARY

Strategy calls for a mixture of both technical mastery and intuitive insight. Science and art need to work together. Strategists should not reject analysis and techniques; indeed these are essential ingredients, but should be used only to stimulate the innovative process. Strategic concepts, and the techniques, structure and terminology surrounding them, should be a means to an end and not an end in themselves.

We started by defining strategic management and then considered the need for planning, before examining a typical strategic planning process.

The next section covered the ingredients that are essential for strategic planning if it is to be effective, looking at the levels of planning - strategic, tactical and operational.

We looked at a number of models of strategic planning, from the rational through to the visionary, concentrating on Mintzberg's modes of strategic planning.

7 SELF TEST QUESTIONS

7.1 Define strategic management (1.2).

7.2 Distinguish between a problem and a decision (2.2).

7.3 List the three different types of problem (2.4).

7.4 List three different types of decision (2.5).

7.5 Outline the three areas present in the rational process of strategic planning (3.1).

7.6 Ohmae thinks the process of analysis should be a combination of what? (5.4).

8 EXAMINATION TYPE QUESTION

8.1 Corporate planning

What is corporate planning, and why is it carried out? Describe and show the relationship between its different components at strategic, tactical and operational levels. **(20 marks)**

9 ANSWER TO EXAMINATION TYPE QUESTION

9.1 Corporate planning

Planning can take place at three levels, defined by Anthony as:

(a) **Strategic** - 'deciding on the objectives of the organisation, on changes in these objectives, on the resources used to attain these objectives and on the policies that are to govern the acquisition, use and disposition of these resources'.

(b) **Tactical** - 'assuring that the resources are obtained and used effectively and efficiently in the accomplishment of the organisation's objectives'.

(c) **Operational** - 'assuring that specific tasks are carried out effectively and efficiently'.

Argenti argues that corporate planning should be distinguished from other forms of planning where managers make decisions *ad hoc* ie, as and when opportunities arise. With corporate planning, management select a strategic framework on which to evaluate and select individual strategies continuously. Corporate planning therefore takes a holistic and structured approach which often affects the long-term direction of an organisation and is invariably complex in nature.

Corporate strategy consists of strategic planning at a corporate level and is not confined to one particular area - marketing, personnel, production/operational and financial implications are all taken into consideration. It is primarily concerned with the determination of ends such as what business or businesses the firm is in or should be in and how integrated these businesses should be with one another. It covers a longer time period and has a wider scope than the other levels of corporate planning.

Business strategy is concerned with how each business attempts to achieve its mission within its chosen area of activity. It includes corporate planning at the tactical level and consists of the allocation of resources for complete operations. It is means oriented and is mainly administrative and persuasive in its endeavours.

Functional strategy examines how the different functions of the business support the corporate and business strategies. Such corporate planning at the operational level is means oriented and most activities are concerned only with the ability to undertake directions.

However, despite the points evaluated above, the boundaries between the three categories are very indistinct and much depends upon the circumstances prevailing and the kind of organisation. Overall, corporate planning is concerned with the scope of an organisation's activities and the matching of these to the organisation's environment, its resource capabilities and the values and expectations of its various stakeholders.

All organisations, both large and small, should carry out some form of corporate planning activity. The need for involvement increases with the complexity of the organisation and with the uncertainty and turbulence of its environment.

An understanding of corporate planning is essential for all management because, through the means-end chain, lower level objectives are inexorably linked to higher level strategies. An appreciation of these strategies and how they are formulated can be an effective guide to action. Moreover, whatever the level at which a manager operates within an organisation, he or she can have some influence over that organisation's corporate strategy.

3 BUILDING A STRATEGY

INTRODUCTION & LEARNING OBJECTIVES

One year Chris Evert's goal was to win Wimbledon and be ranked first in the world. She did both and experienced that marvellous feeling of accomplishment that you get when you achieve a hard-won victory. But, she said it only lasted about 30 minutes. Then it was back to reality and on to the next goal. We are, all of us, always chasing goals. Goals are continuous and changing targets - there to be achieved. And, of course, it is no different for organisations.

Every organisation needs to be clear about its goals. As the environment changes and presents new challenges, organisations need to review and reassess their goals. Some organisations will discover that their goals are no longer relevant and they are drifting. Others will find that their goals are clear, relevant, and effective. Still others will discover that their goals are no longer even clear and that they have no firm direction. The purpose of developing a clear set of goals for an organisation is to prevent it from drifting into an uncertain future.

When you have studied this chapter you should be able to do the following:

- Describe the 'mission statement' and its place in the hierarchy of objectives.
- Describe organisational goals and how they are established.
- Describe corporate objectives and their relation to planning strategy.
- Describe the relationships between strategy, tactics and operational planning.
- Discuss the setting of organisational objectives.
- Outline the role of the mission statement, goals and objectives in shaping a vision of the future.

1 MISSION STATEMENT

1.1 Hierarchy of objectives

Most writers agree with the idea that there is a hierarchy of objectives, just as there is a hierarchy of managers. At each higher level in the hierarchy the objectives are more relevant to a greater proportion of the organisation's activities so that the objectives at the top of the hierarchy are relevant to every aspect of the organisation. The following diagram illustrates the hierarchical relationship of missions, goals, objectives, strategy, tactics and operational plans.

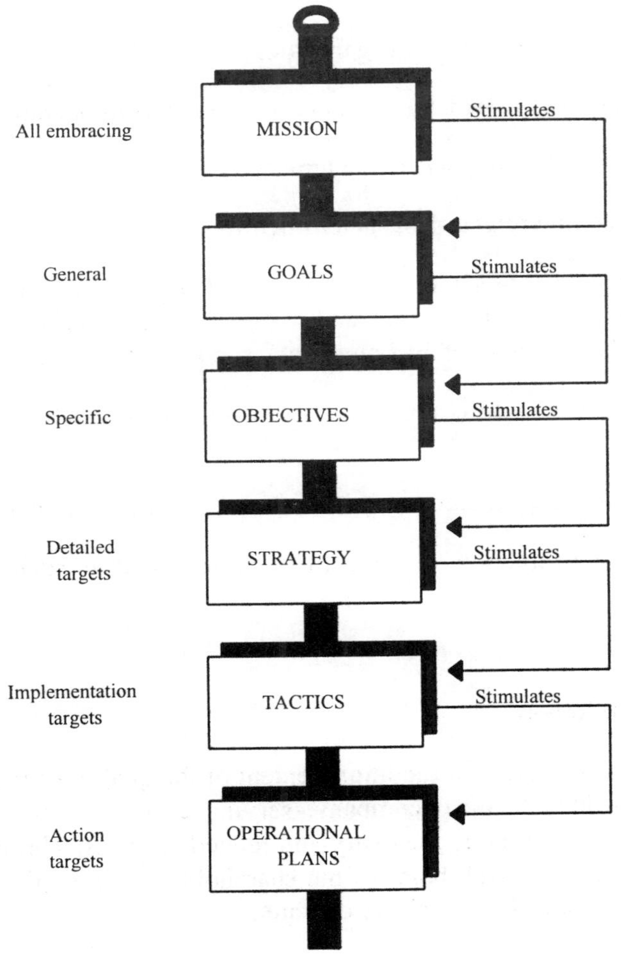

Hierarchy of objectives

The topmost statement of organisational objectives is usually termed 'the mission'. This is where we start.

1.2 The importance of the mission statement

Definition A statement in writing that describes the basic purpose of an organisation, that is, what it is trying to accomplish.

Mission - the *raison d'êtr* of an organisation which is central and overriding. If it is subject to change there can be considerable disturbances within the organisation. It is normally very general and visionary. It should be viewed as where the organisation is conceived to be throughout time rather than where it currently is or where it wants to get to at any one moment in time.

1.3 Characteristics of a good mission statement

A mission statement can be viewed as a statement primarily directed towards the employees of an organisation which should assist in the attainment of the objectives of the organisation. In short, a 'Mission statement' will have some or all of the following characteristics:

- It is usually a brief statement of no more than a page in length. (Some companies have produced very effective mission statements comprising of a single sentence, although there are also successful company credos that extend into several pages, for example the statement written by William Hewlett for Hewlett-Packard, *'What is the HP Way?'*, which is relatively lengthy.)

- It is a very general statement of entity culture.
- It states the aims (or purposes) of the organisation.
- It states the business areas in which the organisation intends to operate.
- It is open-ended (not stated in quantifiable terms).
- It does not include commercial terms, such as **profit**.
- It is not time-assigned. (For example, the credo of J.C.Penny Company, *'The Penny Idea'* was formulated in 1913; that of Johnson and Johnson, *'Our Credo'* in the 1940s; and some missions are carved on stone or etched on plaque, such as that found at Lever House.)
- It forms a basis of communication to the people inside the organisation and to people outside the organisation.
- It is used to formulate goal statements, objectives and short-term targets.
- It therefore guides the direction of the entity's strategy and as such is part of management information.

Example

ICI PLC (From 1991 Annual Report)

The chemical industry is a major force for the improvement of the quality of life across the world. ICI aims to be the world's leading chemical company, serving customers internationally through the innovative and responsible application of chemistry and related sciences. Through achievement of our aim, we will enhance the wealth and well-being of our shareholders, our employees, our customers and the communities which we serve and in which we operate'

1.4 Mission statements with an external orientation

A mission's goals do not have to be 'internal'. Some of the most effective are directed outside the company, on customers, or competitors. Federal Express Corporation's U.S. operation has a short but powerful mission statement: *'Absolutely, Positively Overnight*!' Everyone in the company knows what that statement means. Almost nothing more has to be said to ensure that every action of every person is aimed at total customer satisfaction. Another short credo that says it all belongs to PepsiCo. PepsiCo's mission has long been simply to *'Beat Coke'*, a mission it has yet to achieve. Honda, faced with the prospect of Yamaha dethroning it as the world's leading motorcycle maker, penned the memorable mission, *'We will crush, squash, slaughter Yamaha!'*. It did! But like that of Federal Express most mission statements place an emphasis on serving the customer. Here is another example of such:

The mission of our company, as William Hesketh Lever saw it, is to make cleanliness commonplace, to lessen work for women, to foster health and to contribute to personal attractiveness so that life may be more enjoyable for the people who use our products.

Plaque: Lever House

Mission statements like these will prompt people to think **first** about the customer, and will provide a gauge against which employees can judge their efforts to satisfy customers. It will equip employees with a strong inner compass for navigating their actions. It will stamp the culture of the organisation. Mission statements are like visions or dreams. We should not forget that in a memorable speech, Dr. Martin Luther King, Jr., said, **"I Have a Dream"** - he did not say **"I have a strategic plan."**

In isolation, however, missions can be self-destructive. Concentrating single-mindedly on their mission, many entities lose their way when the strived-for goal is achieved. Having landed a man on the moon, NASA drifted. It has yet to find a new mission as compelling as its first one.

1.5 The search for a mission

According to Peter Drucker there are a number of fundamental questions that an organisation will need to address in its search for purpose. These are :

- What is our business?
- What is value to the customer?
- What will our business be?
- What should our business be?

Although seemingly simple these questions are among the most difficult the strategist will need to solve. Successful planners will raise these questions and seek to answer them correctly and thoroughly. The mission of an organisation is generally influenced by five key elements:

- The history of the organisation.
- The current preferences of the organisation's management and owners.
- The environmental factors influencing the organisation.
- The organisation's resources.
- The organisation's distinctive competence.

Producing a formal mission intent is not an easy task. It will relate to a lot of factors and people, including in many cases, shareholders, customers, employees and the public. The organisation's mission acts as an 'invisible hand' that guides widely dispersed management to work independently, and yet collectively towards the achievement of the organisational goal.

To summarise these points, a 'Mission Statement' for an organisation should incorporate a number of different factors. These include:

- The business domain in which the organisation will operate.
- The organisation's raison d'être (or reason for existence).
- The stakeholder groups the organisation will serve.

The top level of management should be responsible for the preparation of a statement of corporate mission. Consequently, the mission statement should incorporate the broad aims of the executive management.

1.6 The relevance of a mission for strategic planning

A statement of corporate mission is inextricably linked with the organisation's goals and objectives, although it is important to draw a distinction between these three aspects of the strategic planning process. Whilst the organisational objectives comprise the specific targets of the company and the goals comprise its broad aims, the mission encapsulates the reason that the entity exists in terms of the service and utility provided to meet specific needs of society. Refer back to the diagram which illustrates the hierarchy of objectives in an organisation and you will see this relationship again.

Before setting about the preparation of a strategic plan the management should consider the mission of an organisation. Many commentators have suggested that consideration and determination of the mission and its articulation into a statement of corporate mission constitutes the first stage in the strategic planning process and that therefore it is central to the whole planning process.

Johnson and Scholes have suggested that 'the mission of an organisation is the most generalised type of objective and can be thought of as an expression of its raison d'être'. On the other hand, some commentators believe that the mission statement is the end product of the process of strategic planning and this illustrates the confusion which often exists between the organisation's mission and its goals and objectives.

1.7 Effect on employees

A statement of corporate mission will provide all managers involved in the decision making process within the organisation with a clear indication as to what constitutes the raison d'être of the organisation. The existence of a mission statement should assist those responsible for the formulation of strategic plans since it will focus upon critical issues which will help to ensure that strategic plans are prepared in accordance with desired norms within the organisation.

Mission statements can provide motivation to the employees of the organisation in the sense that they tell people what is important from the standpoint of executive management. A mission statement will clearly specify the business domain in which the company is to operate thereby facilitating planning activities. Decision making processes within an organisation should be improved as a result of the clarification of the overall direction of the company which is contained within a corporate mission statement.

A mission statement will also aid staff, both existing and newly appointed in their appreciation of the company's philosophies as well as providing a clear indication as to the expectations and attitudes which exist within the company.

1.8 Activity

Think about the organisation you are currently employed in, or one that you have been employed in, or one that you know of, and then draft a 'Mission Statement' that would be appropriate for it.

2 GOAL STATEMENTS

2.1 Characteristics

Definition Goals are long-run, open-ended attributes or ends a person or organisation seeks and are sufficient for the satisfaction of the organisation's mission.

In short, goals will have all or some of the following characteristics:

- They are mainly narrative statements derived from the mission.
- More than one goal statement is required to satisfy the organisation's mission.
- Goal statements are set in advance of the objectives. (They decouple the organisation's mission from the detailed, time-assigned objectives.)
- They are open-ended (not stated in quantifiable terms).
- In the main they have no time-assigned basis.

John Naber who had won four gold medals and one silver for swimming in the 1976 Olympics said he used goal setting extensively during his training. He set very specific goals for each event, including daily, weekly, monthly and quarterly objectives, some of which involved improving his time by thousandths of a second. But those goals were just a step towards him achieving a larger dream - the dream of winning the gold medal and being the world champion.

2.2 Clarifying the meaning of 'goal'

The distinction between goals, objectives and targets is a common cause of confusion. Some writers assign different meanings to the same terms, others use them interchangeably and almost all disagree on their relative values and significance. Some examples will serve to exemplify the distinction.

(a) Lorange, P., 'Corporate Planning, An Executive Viewpoint'

'Objectives, as referred to in this book, are more general statements about a direction in which the firm intends to go, without stating specific targets to be reached at particular points in time. A goal, on the other hand, is much more specific, indicating where one intends to be at a given point in time. A goal thus is an operational transformation of an objective; typically a general objective often gets transformed into one or more specific goals.'

(b) Vancil, R., 'Strategy Formulation in Complex Organisations'

'One of John F. Kennedy's **objectives** in 1960 was to re-establish and maintain this (USA) country's position as a leader in the fields of science and technology. One of his **goals** was to land a man on the moon and return him safely before the end of the decade.'

However as mentioned previously, in this text we adhere to the view that goals will be a narrative transformation of the mission statement (or mission), and typically a goal will be transformed into one or more specific objectives. Thus we categorise objectives into five components:

- **Mission**, the primary raison d'être set in advance of strategy.
- **Goals**, the secondary and mainly narrative objectives derived from the mission and also set in advance of strategy.
- **Corporate objectives** which are time-assigned aims derived from the goals and also set in advance of strategy.
- **Strategic targets** which are time-assigned and derived from the strategy.
- **Standards of performance** (often identical with targets) assigned to particular individuals.

In this respect we are close to the opinions of writers such as:

(a) Mintzberg, H., ('Power in and Around Organisations'):

- **Mission**: An organisation's mission is its basic function in society...
- **Goals**: An organisation's goals are the intentions behind its decisions or actions.
- **Objectives**: Objectives are goals expressed in a form in which they can be measured.

(b) Hofer, C., and Schendel, D., ('Strategy Formulation: Analytical Concepts'):

'We consider goals to be the ultimate, long-run, open-ended attributes or ends a person or organisation seeks, while we consider objectives to be the intermediate-term targets that are necessary but not sufficient for the satisfaction of goal.'

There is no reason for you to be worried about the confusion of terms. Your examiner will also be aware that they are frequently used interchangeably by writers and practitioners. What is important though is that if needs be you clarify the ways in which you are using them.

3 OBJECTIVES

3.1 Characteristics

Definition Objectives are time-assigned targets derived from the goals, and are set in advance of strategy.

In short, objectives have all or some of the following characteristics:

- They are mainly statements expressed in quantitative terms ('closed') derived from the goals.
- More than one objective may be required to satisfy a goal.

- Objectives are set in advance of strategy.
- They are time-assigned.

One thing which is clear is that objectives must be capable of being quantified, otherwise progress towards them cannot be measured. For a local authority, for instance, to state a goal as 'to improve the welfare of old age pensioners in the Borough' is not precise enough. The goal needs to be translated into objectives which state how it is going to measure the achievement - in terms perhaps of the number of places made available in old people's homes by *x* date, the number of meals-on-wheels served in *x* period, the number of patients treated in geriatric wards - so that several targets may make up its overall objective.

In other words, for objectives to be of use in practice, they must have three components:

- Attribute chosen to be measured, eg, profit, return on capital, output.
- Scale by which it is to be measured, eg, £, %, tonnes.
- Target, ie, the level on the scale which it is hoped to achieve, eg, £1m, 12%, 350,000 tonnes.

As well as being **explicit** objectives need to be realistic and attainable. Ideally, existing performance statistics should be used to measure objectives, if a new system of data collection or processing has to be instituted in order to measure progress towards objectives, extra cost will be incurred.

3.2 Example:

Let us take a hypothetical example for a private-sector company and use it to see the hierarchical structure at work.

Mission Statement (extract)

.... and we will enhance the wealth and wellbeing of our shareholders, ...

Goal Statements

1 We will provide our shareholders with a return on their investment which is commensurate with their expectations.

2 We will protect the security of our shareholders' investments.

3 We will endeavour to increase the capital value of our shareholders' investment.

Objectives

- **Goal 1: Shareholders' return on investment**
    - To realise a return on investment of 25% during the next *x* years.
    - To achieve a growth in sales turnover of x % in *y* years.
    - To maintain net profit margins.
    - That the return to shareholders should grow in line with the growth in net profit. .....
- **Goal 2: Security of shareholders' investments**
    - To maintain the quality of existing assets by investing not less than 8% of sales annually for the next *x* years, and to make new investment at rates of return applicable to the risk involved to meet the company's targeted return on capital employed.
    - To ensure that loans should not exceed 45% of capital employed unless required for exceptional circumstances of a short-term nature.
    - To maintain a match between foreign currency assets and liabilities. .....

- **Goal 3: Growth in shareholders's investments**
  - To achieve a price-earnings multiple of x by y date. .....

4 SHAPING A VISION

4.1 Role of the mission statement

If all the information generated through the strategic analysis could be condensed into a unifying, understandable, communicable and viable strategic vision, it could take the form of a mission statement.

The purpose of the mission statement is to communicate to those making the strategic decisions the broad ground rules that the organisation has set for itself in conducting its business. A good mission statement will include:

- A statement of beliefs and values.
- The needs that the organisation will satisfy.
- The markets where the organisation will trade.
- How those markets will be reached.
- The technologies the organisation will use.
- The organisation's attitude to growth and financing.

Good mission statements or visions are exciting and inspiring. A well-crafted statement that is understood and believed can be a powerful force for change. As a vision it can provide the framework for exercising initiative, influencing attitudes from the top to the bottom of the organisation.

5 CHAPTER SUMMARY

Goals are determined within the overall mission of the organisation. The organisation's mission can be formal (say, in writing) or informal, and represents its basic purpose or raison d'être. That is what the organisation wants to be, or to accomplish. Defining the mission of the organisation is important because it affects everything else. The *'Mission Statement'* if produced, is part of the management information system.

Having established the organisation's mission and its goals within the mission (relating these to the expectations of the various coalitions) the strategist can then set about translating them into objectives and strategic imperatives. Objectives need to be attainable, explicit, and measurable. Once the set of objectives are decided management is ready to move on to the detailed work of strategy formulation and budgeting.

6 SELF TEST QUESTIONS

6.1 List at least eight characteristics of a *'Mission Statement'* (1.3).

6.2 Peter Drucker discussed the fundamental questions that an organisation will need to address in its search for purpose. What are they? (1.5).

6.2 Define the term 'goal', and list the characteristics of goals (2.1).

6.3 Explain the confusion between the two terms 'goals' and 'objectives' (2.2).

6.4 Define the term 'objective' and list the characteristics of objectives (3.1).

7 EXAMINATION TYPE QUESTION

7.1 Corporate mission

The managing director of TDM plc has recently returned from a conference entitled 'Strategic planning beyond the 90's'. Whilst at the conference, she attended a session on 'corporate mission statements'. She found the session very interesting but it was rather short and she has asked the following questions:

(a) 'What does corporate mission mean? I don't see how it fits in with our strategic planning process.'

(b) 'Where does our mission come from and what areas of corporate life should it cover?'

(c) 'Even if we were to develop one of these mission statements, what benefits would the company get from it?'

Prepare a report which answers the managing director's questions.

(25 marks)

8 ANSWER TO EXAMINATION TYPE QUESTION

8.1 Corporate mission

To: The Managing Director
From: The Management Accountant
Subject: Corporate mission statements

The meaning of corporate mission

The corporate mission embodies the overall purposes of an organisation. A corporate mission statement is formulated to express the company's philosophy and should answer fundamental questions such as: Why does the company exist? Who will be served by and benefit from the company? What products or services will be provided? The majority of mission statements are presented using general, rather than detailed, concepts.

Corporate mission and strategic planning

In order to prepare an effective strategic plan, the management must first address the organisation's mission. There is a certain amount of controversy regarding the point in the planning process at which the mission statement is best formulated. One view is that the mission statement is of such a fundamental nature that the strategic plan cannot be prepared without reference to it. Another view, expressed by Argenti, is diametrically opposed. He postulates that the mission statement is the end result of the strategic-planning process. These opinions demonstrate how difficult it can be to differentiate between an organisation's mission and its objectives. The *mission* is a wide-ranging statement which presents the organisation's *raison d'être* in terms of its ability to satisfy some of society's needs whilst its *objectives* are the company's broad goals.

Areas to be covered

The mission statement is likely to be formulated by the company's board of directors. Although it will not be quantitative in nature it will usually highlight several areas:

(a) the kinds of products and services the company aims to provide;
(b) the customers to be served;
(c) the markets in which the company anticipates operating;
(d) an overview of the company philosophy and the broad expression of its policies;
(e) the company's attitude towards matters encompassing social obligations;
(f) the manner in which management wishes the firm to be perceived by the public.

Benefits from developing a mission statement

The usefulness of a mission statement may be summarised as follows.

(a) All staff will gain an understanding of the firm's purpose and philosophy.

(b) Expectations and attitudes within the firm will be expressed in terms of a long-range vision.

(c) The organisation will benefit from a unanimity of purpose which should result in decisions advantageous to the purposes of the company.

(d) The boundaries within which the company operates will be clearly laid down. This will assist in developing co-ordinated plans.

(e) An unambiguous statement regarding the overall direction of the company should lead to enhanced allocation of resources.

Conclusion

The company would gain several benefits from the formulation of a mission statement. It would greatly assist the decision-makers and those responsible for implementing the firm's policies. The mission statement also has an important role to play in helping management focus on fundamental issues in terms of strategic planning and will ensure that strategic plans do not conflict with the basic purpose of the organisation.

4 STRATEGIC OPTIONS

INTRODUCTION & LEARNING OBJECTIVES

In this Chapter we classify the strategies by using as a guide the ideas of Patrick McNamee **('Strategic Planning and Marketing')**, who in part follows a classification developed by Porter **('Competitive Strategy: Techniques for Analysing Industries and Competitors')**.

McNamee uses a two stage methodology to show the development of new strategies. The first stage is to decide upon a **fundamental strategy**.

The second stage uses Porter's classification of **generic strategies**:

(a) High volume, low cost
(b) Differentiation
(c) Focus

When you have studied this chapter you should be able to do the following:

- Describe the strategic options which an organisation might pursue.
- Explain what is involved in a recovery strategy.
- Describe non-growth strategies.
- Describe corrective strategies.
- Discuss neutral strategy.
- Give examples of growth, both internal and external.
- Explain different risk policies and describe different risk-reducing strategies.
- Describe reduction strategy.
- Describe the principal aims of the generic strategies.
- Explain the importance to strategic planning of the competitive perspective.
- Appreciate the difficulties of identifying and studying competitors.
- Explain Porter's five competitive forces.
- Discuss the meaning of competitive advantage.
- Discuss the aims of cost-leadership strategy, and explain different approaches.
- Explain the place of product and service differentiation.
- Appreciate why companies pursue a strategy of market-focus.

1 STRATEGIC OPTIONS WHICH AN ORGANISATION MIGHT PURSUE

1.1 Types of fundamental strategy

It is assumed (following McNamee) that there are seven fundamental strategies, each one of which will comprise the heart or base of a company's new strategic initiative. Each is planned to meet specific objectives or needs and encompasses other secondary strategies. The seven are:

(a) Recovery
(b) Non-growth
(c) Corrective
(d) Neutral
(e) Growth
(f) Risk reducing
(g) Reduction

We will examine each strategy in the following sub-sections. Which strategy an organisation will choose depends in large measure on an evaluation of the organisation's current position. This idea of a **position audit** is described fully in a later chapter.

1.2 Recovery strategy

Definition 'Corporate recovery is about the management of firms in crisis, firms that will be come insolvent unless appropriate management actions are taken to effect turnaround in their financial performance. They are failing companies which, if not already on the brink of insolvency, will be within two or three years if specific turnaround strategies are not adopted.'

S Slatter **(Corporate Recovery)**

Distinction between symptoms and causes of decline

You should be careful to distinguish between symptoms and causes of decline. Symptoms are indications that the company is sick or ailing. They spell out the problems of the company and give warning 'tell-tale' signs that it has severe problems - even of crisis proportions. Symptoms send out danger signals, but they do **not** provide a prescription for management action. What is important - if a company is going to adequately deal with its significant difficulties - is for management to find out the fundamental causes of the company's problems. The medical analogy is apt - pain is a symptom of affliction or virus, not its cause. The causes of the pain needs to be established before a doctor can dispense the appropriate medicine or treatment.

Symptoms of decline

The symptoms of decline are usually easier to detect than its causes simply because there are clear financial and non-financial measures which have proved to be good indicators of failure or pending failure. By this stage in your studies you should already be aware of many such indicators and their implications, and the following list of symptoms indicating corporate failure will serve as a reminder.

- Decreasing profitability - indicated by reductions of: earnings per share, profits (adjusted for inflation) before tax, return on investment, profit as a percentage of sales.
- Fall in volume of sales/production/assets.
- Declining market share - local/domestic/world volume.
- Increase in debt - normally expressed in terms of the company's gearing ratio, its debt-to-equity ratio.
- Decrease in liquidity with the use of indicators such as current ratio, quick ratio, debtor lead-time, creditor days, inventory turnover, decreasing bank balances, etc.
- 'Running down' of plant and equipment signalled by time between failures, downtime as a percentage of total time available, time between maintenance overhauls, number of significant machine failures.
- Reduction in R&D effort shown by percentage of R&D expenditure to sales, and extent of new product innovation.
- Employee worry indicated by staff lost to competitors (particularly senior managers), and increases in other management and labour turnovers and a rise in the percentage of absenteeism.
- Accounting practices - by the use of generally unacceptable accounting practices, and undue delays in publishing annual financial statements.

This is by no means an exhaustive list of symptoms and is one you should try to add to. Usually a single indicator does not suggest the need for a turnaround strategy; rather it is a combination of adverse symptoms which highlights the danger and provides the impetus. The extent to which a measure indicates failure is difficult to determine although there are some established 'bench-marks'. One 'rule of thumb' approach often used by companies is to compare their results against industry and inter-company statistics.

Causes of decline

There is no hard-and-fast definition of what constitutes a turnaround situation. The following factors however are the principal causes of corporate decline:

- Ineffective management: this can be due to one man rule, neglect of core business, lack of management depth or an inadequate board. The board's inadequacy may be because of insufficient specialist knowledge and experience, conflict between members, a lack of communication between members or the apathy of non-executive directors

  Example

  The US. multinational, United Brands Inc, undertook a diversification programme in the late 1960s and early 1970s that detracted management attention from its two core businesses, Fyffes bananas and Morrell meat. The diversification programme, which took the company into such involvements as Baskin-Robbins Ice Cream (later sold to J.Lyons), became an alternative for the primary business, not a supplement. Eventually, severe difficulties emerged in the core business and the company experienced heavy losses, with the unhappy outcome that the company chairman, Eli Black, took his own life by throwing himself off the top of New York's Pan Am Building.

- Poor financial control:
- Lack of competitiveness:
- Poor marketing effort:
- High cost structure: may be due to insufficient volume and scale, low experience or operating inefficiencies.
- The use of outdated technology.
- Poor financial policy:
- Problems with large investment projects: such as the acquisition of losers, paying too much for acquisitions, and poor control of acquisitions.
- Poor industrial culture, including industrial stoppages (or 'strikes').
- Over trading.

Facets of a successful recovery strategy

A successful recovery strategy constitutes a number of generic turnaround strategies used in combination. Slatter refers to ten generic strategies and these provide a good basis for dealing with the problems outlined above - as appropriate, of course, to a company's particular situation and needs. His list of generic strategies is:

- Change of management
- Strong central financial control
- Organisational change and decentralisation
- Product-market reorientation

- Improved marketing
- Growth via acquisitions
- Asset reduction
- Cost reduction
- Investment
- Debt restructuring and other financial strategies.

A classic example of a product-market orientation is the story of a company that once was called Interstate Department Stores. This once very successful retailer was struggling in the savage discount department store wars in USA. Interstate was stuck with chains like Topps and others that were failing. Then it acquired Toys R US in an embryonic state, allowed itself to go into liquidation, and emerged as strictly a toy retailer. The rest is history. The recovery had been achieved.

1.3 Non-growth strategy

It is possible that non-growth strategies are adopted because of the prevailing socio-political economic climate. Some large companies are confronted by anti-monopoly legislation or are constrained by public opinion. They might for instance, have too large an effect on a particular local population: for instance, a company, might face pressure to abandon plans to modernise a certain factory with the consequent reduction in the labour-force, since that would cause too serious an increase in the unemployment rate in the locality, where that factory is the main employer. In addition, there is a debate about the quality of life, as opposed to continued economic growth, which calls into question some of the fundamental philosophies of large companies. Thus the company cannot always be guided by purely economic motives.

Apart from the external pressures, there may be internal reasons for deciding on a non-growth strategy. It might be that once the company gets above a certain size, management problems rise out of proportion to the growth in size. Owner-managers might prefer to keep their firms at a size which they personally could control comfortably, rather than have to appoint other managers or raise outside capital with perhaps the eventual risk of losing control of their organisations. Also, some managers with a loyal, dedicated and high calibre work force would be reluctant to grow if that meant that the quality of the new employees would not match the old, or if the door might be opened to disruptive elements. Furthermore, the production system might be such that growth led to diseconomies of scale.

A company might pursue a non-growth strategy if it saw its non-economic objectives as more important than its economic objectives (given a certain minimum level of profit), although a non-growth strategy does not imply a lack of attention to economic objectives. Strictly speaking, a non-growth strategy means no growth in **earnings**. This does not necessarily mean no growth in **turnover** - if margins are falling, turnover will need to increase to maintain the same level of earnings. Capital equipment will have to be kept up-to-date, but there will be no net increase in investment - all the earnings can therefore be paid out as dividends to the shareholders.

Or there could even be negative growth, by paying out dividends larger than current earnings, so that shareholders are effectively receiving a refund of their capital investment, and there is a net fall in assets employed. A negative growth strategy can be employed in pursuit of an objective to increase the percentage return to the shareholders - if the company pulls out of the least profitable areas of its operations first, it will increase its overall return on investment, although the total investment will be less. You will recall that we discussed earlier whether growth should be an objective in its own right. The foregoing reinforces the point made that growth is simply one way of achieving a target return to the shareholders; it is possible that the same target can also be reached by a policy of no growth or negative growth.

It is emphasised that pursuing a negative growth strategy is not the same as simply allowing the company to run down. The negative growth strategy consists of an orderly, planned withdrawal from less profitable areas, and while the shareholders' dividend may eventually decline their return can rise since the capital invested also falls. If the company simply runs down, their return will also fall.

1.4 Corrective strategy

A non-growth strategy certainly does not mean that the company can afford to be complacent (although the pressures on management and the risks they have to take will be less than with a growth strategy). A company pursuing a non-growth strategy will be concerned with **correcting** its overall strategic structure to achieve the optimum. This involves seeking a balance between different areas of operations and also seeking the optimum organisation structure for efficient operation.

Thus although there is no overall growth (or negative growth occurs) the company will shift its product-market positions, it will employ its resources in different fields and it will continue to search for new opportunities. In particular it will aim to correct any weaknesses it has discovered during its appraisal. For this reason the term **corrective strategy** is also used.

A non-growth strategy is bound to be a corrective strategy, but a corrective strategy can also be used in conjunction with, or as one component of, a growth strategy. Often companies pursuing a growth strategy need to correct one significant problem or a number of different problems.

Example

Walt Disney is the market leader for the 'G' movies (for general audiences). However in this new wide-open, sexually liberated world, no one other than tiny tots wants to see a G movie anymore. PG or R movies are where the big sales are. Disney Studios required a corrective 'product-shift' strategy. They ventured into adult movies and these were failures. The Disney name turned off teenagers and adults looking for something a little more risqué than what Disney was known for. Then Disney Studios came up with a corrective strategy that was to prove successful. They created an adult label called Touchstone Pictures and soon were producing successful adult films such as Down and Out in Beverly Hills and Three Men and a Baby

1.5 Neutral strategy

Definition 'A neutral strategy could be described as one where there is no significant deviation from the past strategy ie, the goals achieved, the organisation's activities and its current competitive position have been historically satisfactory and similar achievements in the future would be considered satisfactory.'

P McNamee **(Management Accounting, Strategic Planning and Marketing)**

(a) **Circumstances that might favour a neutral strategy**

- The environment: this could be where the environment does not encourage change or where no change is anticipated in the company's current and future environments are considered to be fairly stable.
- The competition: the company has a good competitive position and any attempt to **'rock the boat'** may bring more dangers than advantages.
- The company's resources and competence: the company may have little choice because it only has the resources required for the same strategies as it pursued in the past.
- The goals of the company; where past goals, and the achievement of them, are satisfactory, and it is thought that similar performance will be obtained from the same strategy.
- The culture of the organisation; this is the easiest strategy to implement. It is doubtful that it will be resisted.

The points made above seem to suggest that if a strategic formula appears successful the best way forward is not to **'tinker'** and to limit the number of changes. In other words, to quote an old American expression (excuse the poor grammar) 'if it ain't broke leave it alone'. However many would say that this is a dangerous supposition. The rate of change occurring today, in some respects is accelerating exponentially, shifting so fast it is difficult to make even short-term predictions accurately. Change is like the croquet game in Alice in Wonderland, a business world in which, like Alice, every time we turn around the game has changed. 'The pace of change in the nineties', said Jack Welch, chairman of the American GE, 'will make the eighties look like a picnic. Simply doing what worked in the eighties .... will be too slow.' A view also held by Iacocca, then president of Chrysler who said, 'I have to take risks every day. I'd rather not, but the world doesn't give me that option. 'They are both in good company - a lot of other senior executives are saying the same things. There is obviously a place for neutral strategy but the other view is also important. As another experienced executive said, 'The time to change is when you don't have to; when you're on the crest of the wave, not when you're in a trough.'

1.6 Growth strategy

(a) The dimensions of growth

Growth is measured in three basic dimensions:

- the actual growth rates of the performance measures expressed in quantitative measures, such as return on investment, earnings per share, dividend yield, etc;
- an increase in the number of markets served; and/or
- an increase in the number or range of products which the organisation offers.

Growth strategies are classified as two items - conservative growth and high growth - because they have different characteristics.

(b) Conservative growth strategy

A conservative growth strategy implies that the organisation's growth rate is:

- similar to the industry average; or related products;
- similar to its own historical performance.

An alternative implication is that the organisation continues to serve the same or related markets with similar or related products. Conservative growth can thus be achieved by greater internal efficiency or a gradual development of products and/or markets.

(c) The circumstances which favour a conservative growth strategy

A company will tend to follow a conservative strategy for the following reasons.

- The environment
  - The current and future environments are thought to be fairly stable.
  - There is a moderate growth in the economy or a moderate growth is projected.
  - There are no obvious opportunities in the environment which would justify large investment.
  - There are no significant threats in the environment requiring large defensive investment.

- Threat of entry
  - The industry has high entry barriers.
  - The company has obtained strong brand differentiation.
  - The company has patent protection etc.
- There are no strong threats of substitutes.
- The power of the buyers in the industry is not regarded as a threat.
- The power of suppliers in the industry is not considered threatening.
- Rivalry within the industry
  - The modest growth in the economy satisfies the expectations of the major companies in the industry.
  - Competitors are not jostling for competitive advantage.
  - Attempts at high growth may upset the relatively comfortable equilibrium within the industry provoking fierce competitive reaction with consequent depressed returns for all competitors.
- The company's resources and competence

  The company's growth may be limited by the resources (finance, management, space, plant, etc) it has available to support strategy.
- The goals of the company

  If the policy makers have set modest goals in the past and have been largely satisfied with this level of achievement, then such targets are likely to persist in the future thus reducing the need for significant strategic change.
- The culture of the organisation

  Conservative growth does not involve significant organisational change and therefore does not result in employee resistance or any other forms of cultural difficulty. If a company is not accustomed to change or if the policy makers favour a strategy of conservative growth (perhaps because they are adverse to risk) an aggressive strategy of high growth might be inappropriate.

(d) **High growth strategy**

The use of resources to achieve high growth objectives are the most common form of business strategy and are present in most companies, at least to the extent of specific product/market involvement(s). Attacking with a new market entry; defending a market from competitive attack; funding at high cost long range research for major technological innovation; and diversifying into high margin markets are all examples of high growth strategy.

A high growth strategy implies that the organisation's growth rate is:

- significantly greater than the industry average; or
- significantly in excess of its own historical performance.

Alternatively the organisation wishes to adjust its previously accepted measures of performance, or diversify into new areas.

High growth can be achieved by:

- Using the same policies as conservative growth but setting higher targets. In addition it is more likely that new related products are developed. This strategy is described as **concentric diversification.**
- Sales of unrelated products.

High growth can be achieved by **internal** expansion, although more often it is achieved by **external** product-market expansion and diversification.

(e) **The circumstances which favour a high growth strategy**

- The environment
  - The current and future business environments are thought to be dynamic.
  - There is a healthy growth in the economy, or a healthy growth is forecast.
  - There are obvious opportunities in the environment which if they are to be exploited require large investment.
  - There are significant threats in the environment which if they are to be prevented, or if the effects of their occurrence are to be mitigated require large investment.
- Competition

  In business conflict companies invariably adopt a combination of sub-strategies which straddle a number of individual strategic manoeuvres. For example, in a typical market offensive, sub-strategies are used for, product quality, price, credit, distribution, sales force deployment, advertising, promotion and after-sales servicing, all of which relate back to the central high growth theme.

  By analysing the key competitive forces in its markets (perhaps by using Porter's suggested framework) a company will be able to estimate the magnitude of the competitive task it faces, and the need for combat. Combat, whether offensive or defensive, can be costly, and a keen sense of judgement is required to balance intent with resources. The forces referred to are listed in the following sub-sections.
- Threat of entry
  - There are strong threats of new rivals.
  - The industry has low entry barriers.
  - The company needs to build, or reinforce, its brand differentiation.
  - The company does not have patent protection.

  Example

  When the Reagan Administration in 1988 agreed to help Japan develop a new fighter plane, it stumbled into a hornet's nest. Critics of the FSX project warned that Japan would use American technology to design and build its own commercial industry to compete with US. manufacturers. Now with military sales flagging, Japanese aircraft and engine companies are gearing up in the civilian aerospace business itself. The Japanese are putting the building blocks in place for a bigger, more sophisticated aerospace industry.
- There are strong threats of substitutes.
- The power of buyers is weak, and there are opportunities for high-margin growth.

- The power of suppliers is weak and they are vulnerable.
- Rivalry within the industry

  - It is thought that the high growth expected in the economy will increase the combative nature of the market.

  - Competitors are expected to be jostling for competitive advantage.

- The company's resources and competence

  The company has sufficient resources (finance, management, space, plant, etc) to sustain high growth strategy. Because it has :

  - under-utilised assets,
  - a low gearing ratio,
  - under-utilised financial resources,
  - under-utilised human resources.

- The goals of the company

  The policy makers have ambitious aspirations and are prepared to set tough goals, regardless of the economic and business environment.

- The company has a growth-oriented culture.

1.7 Risk reducing contingency strategy

A company faces risk because of its lack of knowledge of the future. When it evaluates a project, it will at best be able to forecast that 'if event A happens we shall have such and such a return, but if event B happens we shall lose £xm.' The extent of the risk it faces can be revealed by the use of performance-risk gap analysis, where forecasts of the outcome in *n* years' time take into account not only the likely returns but also the risk - ie, the probability of achieving various returns less than the likely level.

Using the terminology above - event A being favourable to the company and event B unfavourable - there are four basic ways in which a company can reduce its risk:

(a) It can attempt to influence events so that event A happens and event B does not. For instance if the company thought that a Conservative government was likely to be more favourable to it than a Labour government it could give money to the Conservative party to back their campaign. If it anticipated legislation which would seriously affect some aspect of its operations it could lobby Members of Parliament to try and avert the threat and it could try and influence public opinion on the matter.

(b) If it seemed fairly likely that event B was going to happen, the company could attempt to mitigate the effect that this would have. We considered the flexibility objective, and ways of achieving it, previously. The company can aim for internal flexibility - the building up of funds to help it through the difficulty - or external flexibility - the 'not putting all one's eggs in one basket' approach. External flexibility could be achieved by operating in different markets (with negatively correlated demand forces) and/or by using different technologies. If event B was 'a decline in demand at home' a possible strategy to mitigate the effect of that threat would be to expand export activity. If event B was 'a general downturn in the world economy' a possible strategy would be to stockpile cash to see the company through the crisis until the next upswing.

(c) If event B seemed a fairly remote possibility, but its happening would have serious consequences for the company, contingency plans should be prepared. For instance, there might be plans to cope with such events as the sudden deaths of key personnel; the merger of two competitors into one large unit; a breakthrough in technology by the company's competitors. Because of the speed of events these days and the magnitude of the effect which events such as technological breakthrough can have, no corporate strategy is complete without contingency plans. Nevertheless, they are only one part of the risk-reducing strategy.

(d) Whatever the company does to prepare for particular unfavourable events it must be recognised that the whole future is uncertain and the company must put itself in a position where it can take advantage of new (unforeseen) opportunities and avoid unforeseen threats. Contingency plans can only be prepared against events which have been predicted, even though they may be thought unlikely to happen. To avoid being taken totally by surprise, a company must have a constant 'ear to the ground' to catch hints of potentially threatening or promising developments at an early stage. (It is equally bad to miss an opportunity as to fail to forecast a threat - an opportunity rapidly becomes a threat if a company fails to take advantage of it and its competitors are quicker off the mark!)

This is probably best achieved by both formal and informal information collection methods. Thus the company will keep abreast (as far as it can) of what its competitors are doing and someone will have an eye on general economic trends, the opinions of political commentators and the progress of scientific research at the **pure** as well as the **applied** stage, in addition to any more specific research work the company may itself be engaged in.

While we are on the subject of risk, it should be remembered that although it is desirable for a company to reduce its risk, some risk is inevitably involved in any business. In fact there are different ways of looking at risk:

(a) **Risk which is inevitable in the nature of business;** this risk should be minimised as outlined above.

(b) **Risk which an organisation can afford to take.** In general, high returns involve higher risk, and a company which is in a strong position might be prepared to take a higher risk in the hope of achieving a high return. But it should still try to minimise such risk (surely no company is complacent enough to indulge in risky projects for the excitement of it) and it should ensure that it can afford to take the risk - that is, if the project was a total failure, how would the company stand?

(c) **Risk which the company cannot afford to take.** A company cannot afford to commit its last penny (and perhaps an overdraft as well) to a risky project. In the event of failure it would be left in an extremely vulnerable position and could even face winding up.

(d) **Risk which an organisation cannot afford not to take.** Sometimes a company is forced to take a risk because it knows that its competitors are going to act and if it does not follow suit it could be left seriously behind. For instance, competitors might be known to be investigating the commercial applicability of a new technology which, if successful, could render the existing products obsolete within five years. Then the company might decide that it too must gain know-how in this field, despite the risk of research coming to nothing and resources having been spent in vain, because the consequences of being left behind would be far worse.

For example, after 48 years of extremely profitable operations, Caterpillar Tractor made the mistake of putting too much faith in its own forecasts. In 1975 Cat's thinking was 'The world's infrastructure is crumbling, so it will need more roads, more construction, more bridges, more dams.' Caterpillar then proceeded to invest $2 billion in new capacity. But the world said, 'Let the infrastructure crumble, we don't have the money', and the heavy-machinery market dropped by 30 per cent. The moral of the story: be cautious, move slowly, be flexible, have contingency plans ready.

Atari, unwilling to invest in the video game superboom, lost $500 million and dwindled from 7,000 employees to a few hundred in 7 years. The moral of the story: there are some risks that a company cannot afford not to take.

Xerox tried to compete head-on against IBM in the computer field, and took its focus off its golden goose copier business and as a result lost 20 per cent of the copier market. Other investments that will haunt the company are its billion-dollar purchase of an insurance and financial services business and its disastrous SDS acquisition of the 1960s. The moral of the story: there are risks an organisation cannot afford to take.

1.8 Reduction strategy

(a) **Deliberate curtailment**

A reduction strategy involves the curtailment of some activities. A company could therefore be said to be adopting a reduction strategy when there is a planned cutback or retrenchment in the overall level of its business activities, and thus when one or more of the following policies ensues:

- Reduction in the range of markets served.
- Cutback in the range of products offered.
- Decline in the volume or absolute value of sales.
- Reduction in geographical scope;
- Decrease in the total assets of the company.

We considered 'non-growth strategies' previously and the implications of 'reduction strategies' are very similar. Divestment is the main approach and we will consider this at a later stage.

(b) **The circumstances which favour a reduction strategy**

Companies have frequently been forced to make strategic withdrawals from products and markets in the face of untenable product, social, political or technological conditions. Causes for reduction strategy include the following:

- The environment
  - There are reductions in the market.
  - The effects of general economic recession.
  - The company is forced to withdraw from a market as a direct or indirect result of political pressures.
  - The company is forced by social pressures to withdraw from the market place.

Ralph Nader conducted a successful campaign in the 1960s against General Motors' Chevrolet Corvair on safety grounds which forced General Motors to eventually withdraw the car from the market.

- The competition
  - The company can no longer compete effectively with its products or services in terms of cost, price, quality and delivery against its opponents' product and service offerings.
  - The company is forced to retreat from the market due to the superiority of competitive technology and the lack of internal-technological resources.

During the 1970s, the AM radio stations in the US were gradually forced out of the mainstream of radio broadcasting as the low quality signal made it impossible for AM stations to match the stereo quality sound of FM radio stations. By the late 1970s the FM stations had moved from the beautiful music format through progressive rock to the pop chart, forcing AM stations to withdraw into the less lucrative low audience markets for news, sports and talk shows.

- The company's resources and competence
    - It experiences poor operating results.
    - It has inadequate resources to sustain its current strategic structure.
    - It has an incompatible, or ineffective product/market portfolio.

2 INTERNAL OR EXTERNAL GROWTH

2.1 Growth by acquisition versus internal growth

Companies make mergers or acquisitions as one means of achieving growth; to put up more effective barriers to the entry of new firms by acquisition in their own industry; in order to diversify; to cut costs by economies of scale; to obtain skills; to obtain liquid resources (the acquiring company can defray the purchase price by the issue of additional equity capital, particularly where the price earnings ratio is high) etc. A company might wish to be acquired because the owner wants to retire to obtain additional cash; in order to use the larger company's R & D facilities to assist its expansion; to provide more extensive career opportunities for the owner/directors, etc.

Among factors to be considered when deciding whether to grow internally or make an acquisition are:

(a) **Timing**

If analysis of the proposed product-market area shows that time is of the essence, acquisition of a company already in the field is indicated as this can generally be achieved very much more quickly (except in the case of the relatively small number of industries where the lead time for product development is of the order of weeks or a few months rather than years, or where start-up synergy is large enough to allow a quick start.)

(b) **Start-up cost**

If the cost of entering a new area will be high it might be better to acquire.

(c) **Synergy**

If the new area has relatively little synergy with the old, acquisition might be better.

(d) **Structure of the new industry**

If the competitive structure of the new industry would not admit another member, or if barriers to entry are high, acquisition is the only way. If there are no attractive acquisition opportunities in the area, internal growth is the only way.

(e) **Relative cost and risk**

Acquisition is often more costly than internal development because one has to pay the owners of the acquired company for the risks they have already taken. On the other hand, if the company decides on internal growth it has to bear such risk itself, so that there is a trade-off between cost and risk.

(f) **Relative price-earnings ratio**

If the price-earnings ratio is significantly higher in the new industry than the present one, acquisition may not be possible because it would cause too great a dilution in earnings per share to the existing shareholders. On the other hand, if the present company has a high price-earnings ratio it can boost earnings per share by issuing its own equity in settlement of the purchase price.

(g) **Asset valuation**

If the acquiring company believes that the potential acquisition's assets are under- valued it might acquire in order to undertake an **asset stripping** operation, ie, selling off or using the company's assets rather than operating it as a going concern.

2.2 Activity

List all the possible motives you can think of for a company attempting to acquire the ownership of more, or all, of another company.

2.3 Activity solution

Among possible aims are to:

(a) **General**:

- obtain joint synergy,
- buy management talent,
- buy time while the strategy of the acquiring company develops.

(b) **Marketing**:

- preserve the balance of market power;
- control spheres of influence of potential competitors;
- break into a new market (perhaps export or beachhead);
- take advantage of joint marketing synergies (for example by the way of rationalisation of distribution, advertising, sales organisation and sales costs in general);
- reposition markets and products;
- obtain the reputation or prestige of the acquired company;
- take over 'problem child' products;
- obtain a critical mass position.

(c) **Manufacturing**:

- acquire technical know-how;
- amalgamate manufacturing facilities to obtain synergies (economies of scale, group technology, shared research, rationalisation of facilities and working capital, and so on);
- extend manufacturing involvement (for example the provision of field maintenance services).

(d) **Procurement of supplies:**

- control spheres of supply influence;
- safeguard a source of supply for materials;
- obtain operating cost synergies;
- share the benefits of the suppliers' profitability.

(e) **Financial:**

- acquire property;
- acquire 'cash cow' organisations;
- obtain direct access to cash resources;

- acquire assets surplus to the needs of the combined businesses and dispose of them for cash;
- obtain a bigger asset backing;
- improve financial standing (market price and earnings per share);
- speculative gain purposes;

2.4 Distinction between merger and acquisition

A merger involves two companies, often of similar size, who decide that it would be to their mutual advantage to join forces.

An acquisition involves a company gaining control of another company for its own benefit, possibly against the wishes of the other company (though of course in the case of a public company the shareholders must consent) . Usually it is a larger company gaining control of a smaller company.

Mergers and acquisitions are often made to achieve diversification but equally a company might choose to merge with or take over another in its own industry. The same considerations apply. The failure rate for mergers and acquisitions shows that there are considerable risks, and the operation should therefore be carefully planned.

Certainly most studies suggest that, in general, mergers are risky. For instance, Porter, of the Harvard Business School, concluded a study of merger behaviour among thirty-three big U.S. firms from 1950 through 1980. As a group, they subsequently unbundled (or unloaded) 53 percent of all their acquisitions during this period and sold off a huge 74 percent of their acquisitions in unrelated new fields (those purchases that were to have made them safe by positioning them in "guaranteed" growth sectors, according to the press releases). Similarly, when consultants McKinsey & Co made an extensive study in 1986 of mergers between 1972 and 1983 that involved the two hundred largest public corporations, they determined that a mere 23 percent were successful (as measured by an increase in value to shareholders).

2.5 Practical experience of acquisitions

In addition to these two studies there have been other analyses into the practical success - or otherwise - of acquisitions. The main conclusions seem to be:

(a) **Plan the acquisition carefully**

This might seem an obvious admonition, but there is considerable evidence that companies do not plan carefully enough before they make an acquisition. Part of the trouble is probably what has been called 'tunnel vision' - once the company has spotted an attractive opportunity it closes its eyes to all others before it has carried out a full evaluation. General guidelines for a company pursuing a strategy of acquisition are:

- Determine the reasons for the acquisition.
- Identify the potential candidate company or companies.
- Investigate candidate(s).
- Evaluate candidate(s).
- Select acquisition target.
- Plan post-acquisition policy.
    - control systems,
    - integration,
    - legal formalities.
- Set terms of the bid:
    - range of acceptable prices,
    - acquisition 'package'.

- Plan the detail of the bid or strike:
  - timing,
  - price and package,
  - good press,
  - smooth transfer of control.
- Make bid.

(b) **Horizontal acquisitions**

Companies buying in their traditional business area - are the most successful, and most acquisitions are of this type.

(c) **When diversifying, buy a fairly large market share in the new industry**

Ansoff suggests that one of the criteria on which companies should select the industry into which they will diversify should be the size of the share they would be able to afford in that industry. The exception to the 'buy big' creed would be where the company already owns a fair market share and is doing a 'topping up' operation.

(d) **Don't be over-optimistic**

Many companies think that they can buy a company which is not doing well and 'turn it round'. Experience has shown that this seldom works, and a company should be very sure that there is untapped potential before adopting this strategy. Another interesting observation is that theoretical synergy (especially in production and marketing) is often not realised in practice.

2.6 Selecting the acquisition

There should of course be a thorough analysis of the potential of any company which it is proposed to acquire in order to assess the contribution it could make to the corporate objectives. The analysis will, like the analysis of the firm itself, cover strengths, weaknesses, opportunities and threats, but taking into account the effects of any changes which would be introduced following the take-over. Among points the company must determine are:

(a) How the proposed acquisition has performed in its industry.

(b) Whether past performance trends would be likely to continue (here, recent competitive activity must be taken into account).

(c) How the industry as a whole has performed.

(d) Whether, if it is an attractive industry, acquisition is indeed preferable to internal growth.

(e) What resources the parent company would have to commit to the acquisition, over and above the purchase price.

(f) The fit of the proposed acquisition with the existing business - do they complement each other's strengths and overcome each other's weaknesses?

(g) How would the combined company stand with regard to anti-monopoly legislation?

If there are rivals in the take-over bid the buying company should assess the consequences of the other company being bought by one of its rivals. If it is a conglomerate acquisition the consequences may be no more serious than the need to continue the search for another candidate; but in a horizontal acquisition the consequences of losing to a competitor could be disastrous. In other words, buying a company might prove to be one of the **risks the company cannot afford not to take**.

If at all possible, the acquiring company should insist on access to the about-to-be-acquired company to examine production facilities, accounts, management skills etc. This **audit of diligence** should be possible in the case of an agreed acquisition and if the request is not granted it could indicate an attempt to hide something.

2.7 Activity

Write out a **detailed** checklist of information a company would need about another company that it is targeting for acquisition.

2.8 Activity solution

Information checklist*

General information

(a) Name of the company and address of its registered office and principal locations.

(b) Names of directors and senior managers together with their ages and length of service.

(c) Main business objectives sub-analysed by product/markets if these are published.

(d) The general standing and reputation of the company. Facts can be determined by examining product/market growth rates, etc.

(e) The style of management and the prevailing culture - some hints on these can be obtained from published organisation structures and the stability of tenure of senior executives.

Ownership

(a) The capital structure and voting rights.

(b) The disposition of shares including institutional shareholders and whether it is a closed company.

(c) Details of any shares held by trustees.

(d) Details of any significant disposals of shares by major shareholders or directors.

Financial information for the past few years

(a) Turnover and profit trends, noting any exceptional items.
(b) Liquidity trends.
(c) Capital expenditure on each class of asset.
(d) Trends in the stock market price and price-earnings ratio.
(e) Capital expenditure commitments.
(f) Accounting policies and any audit qualifications.
(g) Capital gearing including any significant changes.
(h) Prospects and problems mentioned in the chairman's statements.

Market and product information

(a) The main fields of activity and approximate market shares.
(b) Any comments on research and the development or introduction of new products.
(c) Overseas and any other territorial expansion during recent years.
(d) Product reputation and the company's reputation for fair dealing.
(e) The nature and extent of competition.
(f) Distribution channels.

Management

(a) The quality of senior and second-tier management.

(b) The ages, qualifications and, if possible, contractual terms for all key managers (those considered important for the continuance of the company).

3 THE IDEAS OF PROFESSOR MICHAEL PORTER

3.1 The five forces model

The key text dealing with competitive analysis is Professor Michael Porter's work 'Competitive Strategy: Techniques for Analysing Industries and Competitors' and this provides a useful guide. Porter's five forces model is used to gain insights into the competitiveness of the firm's industry. These forces are illustrated below, and explained in the following subsections:

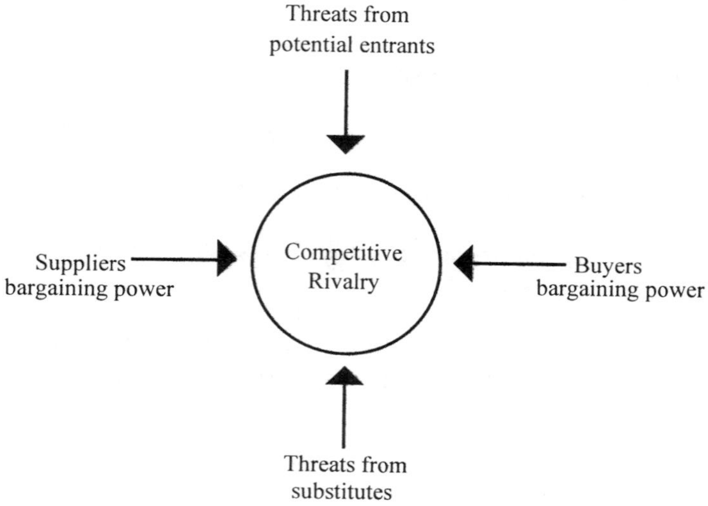

3.2 Threats from potential entrants

(a) By increasing the extent of competition.

New competitors to an industry may make it more competitive in three ways.

- Expanding capacity without necessarily increasing market demand.
- Their need to penetrate the market to achieve **critical mass** and then build market share, which may include product and marketing innovations.
- Increasing costs as they bid for factors of production.

(b) Barriers to entry.

It is in the interests of existing competitors to deter new entrants. There are seven main barriers to entry.

- Economies of scale.
- Brand (or product) differentiation
- Capital requirements.
- Switching costs.
- Access to distribution channels.
- Cost disadvantages independent of scale.
- Government regulation (including legal barriers).

Economies of scale

Many industries, such as cement and chemicals, offer increasing returns in manufacture, and companies benefit by being able to lower unit costs by increasing output volume. Thus potential entrants would be at a considerable cost disadvantage, unless they can immediately set up their operations on a scale large enough to reap similar economies. (This scale is termed the **'critical mass'**.) In any case, it might take several years and a heavy investment programme to construct and equip the necessary factories to put them on a competitive footing.

For example, Avon, the cosmetics company, sells part of its line direct to housewives, so any company intending to compete on a similar footing would have to:

- recruit and train an efficient sales force skilled in **'party-selling'**;
- establish warehouses to maintain buffer stocks;
- hire a design team to develop a competitive product range;
- manufacture and distribute the volume and quality of products required.

Brand (or product) differentiation

Some brands generate a greater consumer loyalty than others and consumers will not be easily lured away by competing products even though they are similar or close substitutes. The cost for a new entrant attempting to penetrate the market in such a situation is likely to be high. The task will involve persuading entrenched consumers to trial their products, perhaps by offering special inducements, such as free samples or gifts. Although the exercise is costly, there is no guarantee of success, particularly as the defending company will combat entry tactics.

Products can be differentiated in terms of: price, quality, brand image, features, distribution, exclusivity, packaging, value.

For example, Proctor and Gamble in the US uses its enormous $500 million media advertising budget to buy and maintain its high market share and deter other companies entering or trying to increase their shares in the markets dominated by P&G products.

Lucas Industries has built up a strong reputation for reliability of supply and quality over the years with the result that almost all British manufactured cars use Lucas lighting. This reputation and market position is sufficient to deter potential competitors.

Capital requirements

This also relates to economies of scale. For example the long-lead, high-cost, high-risk business cycle of the pharmaceutical industry, where the number of successful products reaching the market is relatively small, but development costs are between £25m to £50m per product has deterred all but the largest new companies from entering the market. (In fact with the exception of Janssen and Syntax no totally new company to this market has succeeded, from start up, in becoming medium-sized in the last forty years.)

Switching costs

These are one-off costs facing a company which switches from one supplier's product to another's. Switching costs may include costs of certification, product redesign, costs and time in assessing a new source, or even the cultural problems of severing a relationship.

For example, In the mid-1970s, FFW-Fokker indicated to British Aerospace (BAe) that it would not tolerate their planned HS-146 aircraft in direct competition against their own existing F28 short-haul jet airliner. Fokker had over 40% of the total cost of both their F-17 and F-28 aircraft supplied by British companies, and indicated that this would be at risk if the

HS-146 project continued. BAe correctly considered the threat was not credible since cost-shifting (re-design, re-tooling and re-certification for both aircraft using non-British equipment) would be prohibitive to Fokker.

Access to distribution channels

One of the biggest dilemmas facing the producer is obtaining shelf or floor space in retail outlets. In order to sell brands the producer must not only persuade the retailer to stock them, but to give them a fair share of shelf/floor space and to feature them periodically. Shelf and floor space is limited (consider here how much **High street'** space an electric dish-washing machine takes to display), and already faced with a bewildering array and assortment of similar products (for example a large Sainsbury store carries some 7,000 products) retail management are not anxious to accept new products, particularly from new entrants lacking a proven track record in the market.

Although BIC, by using its competence in plastics technology, took the initiative by creating the volume market for disposable razors and lighters in the US, it was new to the market and needed to divide its resources between promotion and establishing a national distribution network. BIC did not have the resources to win a battle on two-fronts and leadership went to Gillette.

Cost disadvantages independent of scale

Established companies may have costs advantages not available to potential entrants, not matter what their size and cost levels. Critical factors include: proprietary product technology, favourable locations, learning or experience curve, favourable access to sources of raw materials and government subsidies.

Government regulation (including legal barriers)

Legal restrictions still prevent companies from entering into direct competition with most nationalised industries, while many governments have permitted the establishment of quasi-nationalised bodies controlling marketing operations in milk, eggs, agriculture, etc. Patents and copyright offer inventors some protection against new entrants. Governments also licence the right to produce certain categories of products.

Japanese companies use the complexity of the distribution and legal system in Japan to deter potential entrants in the domestic market. Disney spent five years negotiating the licensing agreement for its Tokyo theme Park. Coca-Cola, which now has a 60 percent share of the Japanese soft-drink market suffered a full decade of red tape, and ROLM, as a small firm, succeeded in Japan but only after senior officers made twenty odd trips, just to conclude the first, tiny sale.

3.3 Threats from substitutes

These are alternative products that serve the same purpose, eg, gas central heating systems in competition with solid fuel systems. (One of the starkest examples of substitution, and a rapid one at that, was the way in which gas-fired central heating overtook electrical central-heating after the OPEC oil crisis of 1973/74, one result of which was the insolvency of at least one major British company.) The main threat posed by substitutes, though, is that they limit the price that a company can charge for it's products. There is also a danger that the threat of a substitute may not be realised until it is too late to arrest their entry. Substitute products that warrant most attention are those that are:

(a) subject to an environment improving their price-performance trade-off with the industry's product, or

(b) produced by industries earning high profits and who have the resources available to bring them rapidly into play.

For example, in 1978 the producers of fibreglass insulation enjoyed unprecedented demand as the result of high energy costs and severe winter weather in US. But the industry's ability to raise prices was impeded by the plethora of insulation substitutes, including cellulose, rock wool, and styrofoam.

3.4 Threats from the bargaining power of buyers

The power used by buyers in an industry make it more competitive in three ways.

(a) Forcing down prices.
(b) Bargaining for higher quality or improved services.
(c) Playing competitors against each other.

All three of these at the expense of industry profitability.

Porter purports that the power of the industry's buyer groups depends on the characteristics of its market situation and of the relative importance of its purchases from the industry compared with its overall business. He suggests that buyers are particularly powerful in seven situations.

- Purchases are large relative to sellers.
- Purchases represents a significant proportion of the buyers' costs.
- Purchases are undifferentiated.
- Buyers earn low profits.
- Buyers have the potential for backward integration.
- The buyer's product is not strongly affected by the quality of the suppliers' product.
- The buyer has full information.

3.5 Threats from the power of suppliers

Suppliers can exert bargaining power over companies within an industry in two main ways.

(a) Threatening to raise their prices.
(b) Threatening to reduce the quality of their goods and services.

The effect of this power will be to squeeze profitability out of an industry unable to recover cost increases by raising its own prices.

Porter suggests that suppliers are particularly powerful in six situations.

- There are few suppliers.
- There are few substitutes for their products.
- The industry supplied is not an important customer.
- The supplier's product is an important component to the buyer's business.
- The supplier's product is differentiated.
- Suppliers can integrate forward.

3.6 Rivalry and competition among competitors

Conflict among existing competitors takes some form of offensive strategy, which we discuss later in this chapter. Tactics commonly used to implement such strategy include product innovations and improvements, price competitions, advertising battles and increased customer services. Rivalry occurs because one or more companies feels threatened or sees a market opportunity to improve its position, although competitive moves by the initiator company usually results in counter-defensive strategies from its competitors. This interactive pattern of offensive and defensive strategies may not leave the initiating company and the industry better off, and on the contrary may leave all the companies in the industry worse off than before.

Porter suggests that there are seven main determinants relating to the strength of internal competition and rivalry within an industry.

- Many equally balanced competitors.
- Slow rate of industrial growth.
- Lack of differentiation.
- Capacity can only be increased by large amounts.
- High fixed costs in the industry.
- There are many diverse competitors.
- There are high exit barriers.

3.7 Competitive strategy options

Porter's major contribution to the options available to industries was to point out that there are only two routes to superior performance. The organisation either becomes the lowest cost producer in their industry or they differentiate their product/service in ways that are valued by the buyers to the extent that they will pay a premium price to get those benefits. Organisations can either choose to apply either of these strategies to a broad market or to a narrow focused market. Porter called these strategies 'generic'

4 GENERIC STRATEGIES

4.1 The meaning of 'competitive advantage'

Definition Competitive advantage is anything which gives one organisation an edge over its rivals in the products it sells or the services it offers.

Porter states that a firm may possess two kinds of competitive advantage: low cost or differentiation. Competitive advantage is a function of either providing comparable buyer value more efficiently than competitors (low cost), or performing activities at comparable cost but in unique ways that create more buyer value than competitors and, hence, command a premium price (differentiation).

Organisations can either choose to apply either of these strategies to a broad market or to a narrow focused market. Porter called these strategies 'generic', and he identified three generic strategies for competitive advantage.

(i) Cost leadership: the lowest cost producer in the industry.

(ii) Differentiation: the exploitation of a product or service that is believed to be unique in the industry as a whole.

(iii) Focus: a restriction of activities to only a segment of the market by either providing goods or services at a lower cost to that segment or by providing a differentiated product or service for that segment.

4.2 High volume/low cost

The first generic strategy is to achieve overall cost leadership in an industry. For companies competing in a 'price-sensitive' market, cost leadership is the strategic imperative of the entire organisation. It is vitally important for these companies to have a thorough comprehension of their costs and cost drivers. They also need to fully understand their targeted customer group's definition of quality, usually denoted in terms of design specifications, contractual requirements, delivery arrangements, and so on. Their essential task is to supply precisely the required quality of goods and services at the lowest possible cost. Of particular importance will be for the company to attain a cost level that is low relative to its competitors.

For companies not competing on price, cost leadership is still vitally important. Companies competing in the industry through product and service differentiation will need to focus on cost effectiveness and quality to maintain or enhance the value perceived by their target customers. Customers will select products and suppliers that provide value which equals or exceeds their actual and perceived cost both at the time of purchase and over the product's life. Price remains a function of value, although not to the same extent as for an undifferentiated market.

Cost leadership must be a goal of every organisation, regardless of their specific market orientation. It enables companies to:

(a) **Defend market share**

Cost leadership enables the company to defend itself against powerful buyers, because buyers only have power to drive the price down to the level of the next most efficient competitor.

(b) **Defend supply**

In the same way a low-cost position enables the company to cope with any price increases imposed by powerful suppliers.

(c) **Build entry barriers**

The factors that lead to a low cost position, such as scale of economies, the use of advanced manufacturing technologies, quality systems and synergies provide the company with substantial entry barriers.

(d) **Weaken threat of substitutes**

The dangers of substitutes are reduced in a low-price market.

(e) **Defend market share against rivals**

Having a low-cost position yields the company above-average profits in its industry despite strong competitive pressures. Its cost-leadership position also provides the company with a strong defensive position against rivalry from existing or potential competitors.

(f) **Increase market share**

Cost leadership allows the company to provide its targeted customer group with the best price to quality relationship, by having (i) the resources to vigorously innovate and continuously improve the quality of its products and services, and (ii) the ability to price its products more aggressively than its competitors.

(g) **Enter new markets**

A cost leadership position enables the company to successfully penetrate new domestic and foreign markets often by brand extension or 'brand stretch' strategy. Its low cost and high quality position permits it to be selective when targeting markets.

(h) **Reduce the cost of capital**

The benefits described above allow the company to maintain a strong financial position and to generate superior returns to its shareholders. These in turn reduce the company's costs of capital of both borrowed funds and the cost of raising funds from the equity market.

Achieving a low cost position thus protects the company against all five of the competitive forces highlighted by Porter. However attaining a low overall cost position requires sustained commitment throughout the organisation; from senior executives to line employees.

4.3 Differentiation

The second strategy is one of differentiating the company's products or services, in other words creating an offering that is perceived to be **unique** in the market. It is an obvious defensive competitive response for a company faced by a strong low-cost competitor. The strategy is to gain advantage through differentiating the product from lower priced ones on the basis of some non-price factor such as:

(a) Quality (Marks and Spencer in clothing and other products).
(b) Features (Sony in domestic 'brown furniture' items).
(c) Style (Jaguar in automobiles)
(d) Brand image (Mars in chocolate, drink, and ice-cream)
(e) Dealer network (Caterpillar Tractor in construction equipment).
(f) Customer service (Littlewoods in mail-order shopping)
(g) Technology and performance (IBM in computers of all sizes)
(h) Packaging (After Eight in mint chocolates)
(i) Uniqueness (Coca Cola in taste).

For example, Caterpillar's strategy was to offer a broad product range of high- quality machines at premium prices, using a dedicated dealer network. All parts were standard worldwide. Superior service was an important peg in the strategy. Caterpillar guaranteed 48-hour delivery of parts anywhere in the world and did not charge for the parts if it failed to meet this deadline: '48-hour parts service anywhere in the world - or Cat pays'.

Ideally, the company differentiates along several dimensions. Marks and Spencer, for example, is known for its extensive and localised branch network, for the high quality of its customer services and for its extremely high-quality durable products linked to the reputation of the St. Michael brand.

For similar reasons discussed for cost-leadership, a highly differentiated market position will protect the company against the five competitive forces in its industry. Its 'uniqueness', brand loyalty and resulting lower sensitivity to price, will protect it against new entrants, the power of buyers, the power of suppliers, the effects of new substitutes entering the market and rivalry within its markets. However differentiation does have its downside. The customer perception of 'exclusivity' is often incompatible with high market share. Also a lowering of price sensitivity will only be achieved within a price range. Although customers perceive the superiority of the offerings they might not be willing to pay prices significantly higher than the industrial average.

4.4 Focus

The third, and last generic strategy is for the organisation to differentiate its offerings by focusing them on a particular buyer group, market segment or geographical region. Focus can relate to:

(a) End-use specialism (Lucas Lighting in automobile electronics).
(b) Customer size specialism.
(c) Specific customer specialism (Burton Group with its fashion focus eg, Top Shop).
(d) Geographical specialism.
(e) Product or product-line specialism (The Tie Rack which specialises in one item of clothing).
(f) Product-feature specialism ('Howard Paper' in its narrow range of industrial-grade papers).
(g) Quality - price specialism (Rolls Royce in luxury automobiles).
(h) Service specialism.

For example, Tetra-Pak is the international leader in packaging liquids for human consumption, with worldwide sales of $1.9 billion. It does not sell packaging for non-edible use eg, motor oil or washing powder, since its packaging must be clearly identified with liquid foods and drinks only. Involvement with customers is active, not passive. Rather than just leasing machines and selling packaging, Tetra-Pak management will contribute to raising machine efficiency, and feed in market research and creative ideas to help with customers' selling and marketing.

Within its narrow targets the company can attempt to build a low-cost and/or differentiated position. As we have discussed in the context of cost leadership and product differentiation the focused position will provide the company with protection against each of the five competitive forces.

5 CHAPTER SUMMARY

Fundamental strategies are formulated to deal with problems or to achieve goals. Fundamental strategies can be oriented between a range of crisis recovery to 'high-growth and high-risk' investments.

In spite of the increased role of quality and other non-price factors in today's markets, price still remains an important element. Cost leadership therefore provides the company with the capability to sustain an advantage against all its competitors and to protect its market share and position against the different competitive forces in the market. By pursuing rigorous strategies towards the aim of cost leadership not only will the company achieve both defensive and aggressive flexibility but will obtain many other benefits, such as achieving a higher-than-average return which in turn will help reduce its costs of capital. The resultant higher financial returns will also allow the cost-leader to strengthen its competitive position through continuous product innovation, improvements in quality and the enhancement of its customer services.

Porter identified the five forces which affect a company's strategic options. A strategy of differentiation of the company's products and services is a competitive response to the pressures exerted by a low-cost competitor. The strategy, if correctly executed, will also protect the company against the five competitive forces in the market and will enable it to remain flexible in both defensive and offensive dimensions. A strategy of market focus will enable a company to concentrate resources and to strengthen both its cost and differentiation positions within the narrow market area.

6 SELF TEST QUESTIONS

6.1 List the seven fundamental strategies identified by McNamee (1.1).

6.2 List the symptoms of corporate failure (1.2).

6.3 List the possible causes of corporate decline (1.2).

6.4 Define 'neutral strategy' (1.5).

6.5 Explain the circumstances that might favour a conservative growth strategy (1.6).

6.6 Explain the circumstances that might favour a high-growth strategy (1.6).

6.7 Explain the different ways of looking at risk (1.7).

6.8 Explain the circumstances that might favour a reduction strategy (1.8).

6.9 Itemise Porter's five competitive forces (3.1).

6.10 List 7 barriers to entry of a market (3.2).

6.11 List 6 situations in which buyers are particularly powerful (3.5).

6.12 Describe the advantages of cost leadership (4.1).

6.13 List ways by which a company can differentiate its offerings (4.3).

6.14 Explain 'market focus' strategy (4.4).

7 EXAMINATION TYPE QUESTION

7.1 Classes of strategy

(a) It is recognised in most industrialised, commercial and institutionalised organisations that there are three principal classes of strategy:

- growth;
- corrective; and
- contingency.

You are required to:

(i) explain and compare the three classes **(5 marks)**

and

(ii) describe the methods that may be used to secure the objectives of a growth strategy. **(10 marks)**

(b) The profits of C Accessories Ltd have risen over the past twenty years by an average of 10% per annum although, because the company is a major supplier of components to the automotive industry, there have been peaks and troughs. During the period of growth in the automotive industry, C Accessories Ltd's increased profits came from increased sales. More recently such increased sales and profits have stemmed mainly from obtaining a bigger share of a somewhat reducing market.

In recent years many new products have been introduced: currently there are thirty products, as against fifteen five years ago. Over the twenty year period the number of customers has fallen from fifteen to five, one of whom takes a little over half of C Accessories Ltd's output.

You are required to critically appraise the company's present strategy and recent development, and state your views on its future. **(10 marks)**

(Total: 25 marks)

8 ANSWER TO EXAMINATION TYPE QUESTION

8.1 Classes of strategy

(a) (i) A company pursuing a growth strategy is aiming to expand earnings, probably through an increase in turnover and increased investment in the company. Variables which may be used to measure growth include return on capital employed, profit, sales, earnings per share, manpower.

A corrective strategy aims at correcting the balance of the company's operations so as to reduce risk and 'correcting' the organisation structure of the company in order to produce the most efficient operation.

A contingency strategy is designed to ensure that action can be taken quickly if an unexpected event occurs. It consists of saying 'if event E happens we shall take action A'. For instance, a company might have a contingency strategy which it could put into effect in the event that its demand forecasts turn out to be 20% wrong.

Selecting a growth strategy primarily concerns decisions about the firm's product-market posture. A corrective strategy also involves decisions about organisation and resources.

(ii) Growth may be achieved by market penetration, product or market development, or diversification. The first of these involves improvements to existing products and/or intensified marketing in order to sell more in the same markets; the other options involve developing new products or new markets or both. The firm pursuing a growth strategy should not, however, forget the importance of dropping some of its least profitable lines as well as developing new ones, especially if resources are scarce. Turnover might fall as a result of such divestment but earnings or return on capital employed can rise.

The same appreciation of the importance of the growth in profits rather than in turnover must guide the use of pricing policy as a means of pursuing a growth strategy. Cutting prices to increase sales might not be the right method.

A growth strategy will probably necessitate an active research department to develop new products, new markets, and new applications for existing products. It is possible, however, to buy know-how or to manufacture under licence in order to achieve internal growth. As an alternative to internal growth an acquisition or merger might be sought - either to strengthen the company's position in its own industry or to achieve diversification.

Firms which decide to diversify can often achieve rapid growth by taking advantage of the most profitable opportunities, although the risks increase the further away the firm moves from its original business.

A growing company can often take advantage of economies of scale or synergy to achieve higher return on capital.

(b) It is of course easy to criticise with hindsight, but it does appear that C Ltd has not been operating to a strategy. If they have it has been an inappropriate one. Nevertheless, one must recognise that recent years have been difficult for the automotive industry, which is very competitive. It is likely that whatever strategy a company adopted it might have been in difficulties.

Recent development of C Ltd

The overall drop in the number of customers was probably inevitable due to mergers in the industry and may itself pose no serious threat. Nevertheless, the dependence on a single customer is worrying as it makes C Ltd very vulnerable to a change in its fortunes. Is the return it is getting sufficient compensation for the loss in flexibility?

The large number of products seems to suggest that while new product innovation has been good, there has been little attention to divestment. It would be interesting to see a breakdown of the returns from various products. Even if all are profitable the company would be able to increase its overall return on invested capital if it dropped the less profitable lines. Its objectives should probably be 'profit' or 'ROI' rather than simply 'market share' or 'turnover' - we are not told what its objectives actually are.

Future of C Ltd

First of all it is useful to summarise the strengths and weaknesses, opportunities and threats of C Ltd, as far as they can be deduced from the information given.

Strengths	*Weaknesses*
Good, innovative research and development dept. Well established company - good reputation.	Over-dependence on one customer. Cumbersome product range (needs pruning).
Opportunities	*Threats*
	Declining overall market. Peaks and troughs in trade.

It looks as though C Ltd needs to consider either new markets for components of a similar type or a product-market diversification. It should build on its strength in having (apparently) a good R&D department. A company cannot long continue to grow in a declining market even when it is increasing its market share. Nevertheless, it should enlarge that share as far as possible, by competitive pricing, trade advertising etc. We are not told whether the declining market is national or international but C Ltd could attempt to increase exports.

The company must discover in more detail **why** its sales have held up despite the declining market, and try and build on those strengths. It must examine the causes of failure amongst its competitors and try and avoid the same pitfalls.

The company appears to have a very good chance of survival in the short to medium term because it is so well-established (though it should try to overcome its dependence on one customer) but whether it can survive as a worthwhile concern in the long term depends on its ability to find a new 'mission' for itself.

5 STRATEGIC PLANNING TOOLS

INTRODUCTION & LEARNING OBJECTIVES

There are a number of planning tools, or methods, which might help the company to establish the attractiveness of different products in order that the correct balance of capital investment and revenue funding between them can be achieved. In the first part of this chapter the ones that we will look at are:

- the 'Boston Consulting Group (BCG)' portfolio
- Ansoff's product-market vector
- the product life cycle
- business process re-engineering

The last part of this chapter will concentrate on the various methods of screening, assessing and analysing strategic options. The methods we are covering include:

- decision trees
- ranking and scoring
- scenario setting
- sensitivity analysis
- risk analysis

When you have studied this chapter you should be able to do the following:

- Explain the Boston Consulting Group's (BCG) growth-share matrix theory.
- Construct a BCG growth-share matrix from data which is provided.
- Interpret a BCG growth-share matrix.
- Interpret a product-market vector (Ansoff's).
- Demonstrate a general knowledge of the product life-cycle concept.
- Understand the basic elements of business process re-engineering.
- Interpret a chart of strategic options using ranking or scoring methods.
- Construct a decision tree.
- Explain the importance of stakeholder and political risk analysis.

1 THE PRODUCT MARKET PORTFOLIO

1.1 Introduction

Whilst there are companies which produce a single product or service, most organisations are multi-product or consider diversification into other products. Within a multi-divisional company, there may be some products at maturity, some at the design stage, and others in decline. Each of these may be in different markets, and different countries. This is a complex planning process, and the Product Market Portfolio (PMP), developed by the Boston Consulting Group (1972), is a technique developed to try and handle it.

The product market portfolio is a useful tool for strategic planning, in that it allows the planners to select the optimal strategy for individual units whilst aiming for overall corporate objectives. Although the technique was developed to analyse a multi-product situation, it also provides useful information for a one-product organisation (or useful information for a part of the organisation which produces just one product). Indeed, as a first step, the technique requires an assessment of each product of an organisation in isolation from other products. The first example in the next section shows the application of the technique for one product.

1.2 The growth-share matrix

This is illustrated by reference to the following simplified example:

Year	*Company*	*Product*	*Sales* £	*Sales units*	*Market growth* %
19X8	A	Widgets	500	100	12
19X8	B	Widgets	400	80	12
19X8	C	Widgets	100	10	12
19X9	A	Widgets	750	150	15
19X9	B	Widgets	500	100	15
19X9	C	Widgets	220	22	15

The three key pieces of information displayed in this table are analysed below:

(a) **Growth rate of market**

It is usually easier to penetrate a growing market than a static or declining market. Equally, existing products will have difficulty in maintaining market share in a static or declining market.

The market growth rate is plotted, net of inflation, on the vertical axis of the growth-share matrix beyond. It is plotted on an **arithmetic** scale.

(b) **Product's relative market share**

This is the market share relative to the largest competitor. It is found by:

relative market share = unit sales ÷ sales of largest competitor

Applying this to the data above:

Year	*Company*	*Sales units*	*Relative market share*
19X8	A	100	1.25
19X8	B	80	0.80
19X8	C	10	0.10
19X9	A	150	1.50
19X9	B	100	0.67
19X9	C	22	0.15

It is believed that relative market share is a better indicator of relative competitive position than absolute share. For example, a 30% share of a market where the largest competitor has 20% is very different to the same 30% where the largest competitor has 65%.

Relative market share is plotted on the horizontal axis using a **log** scale in the growth-share matrix.

(c) **Money value of product sales**

This is plotted in the display by the relative size of the circle. The results of this analysis for the two years are shown below:

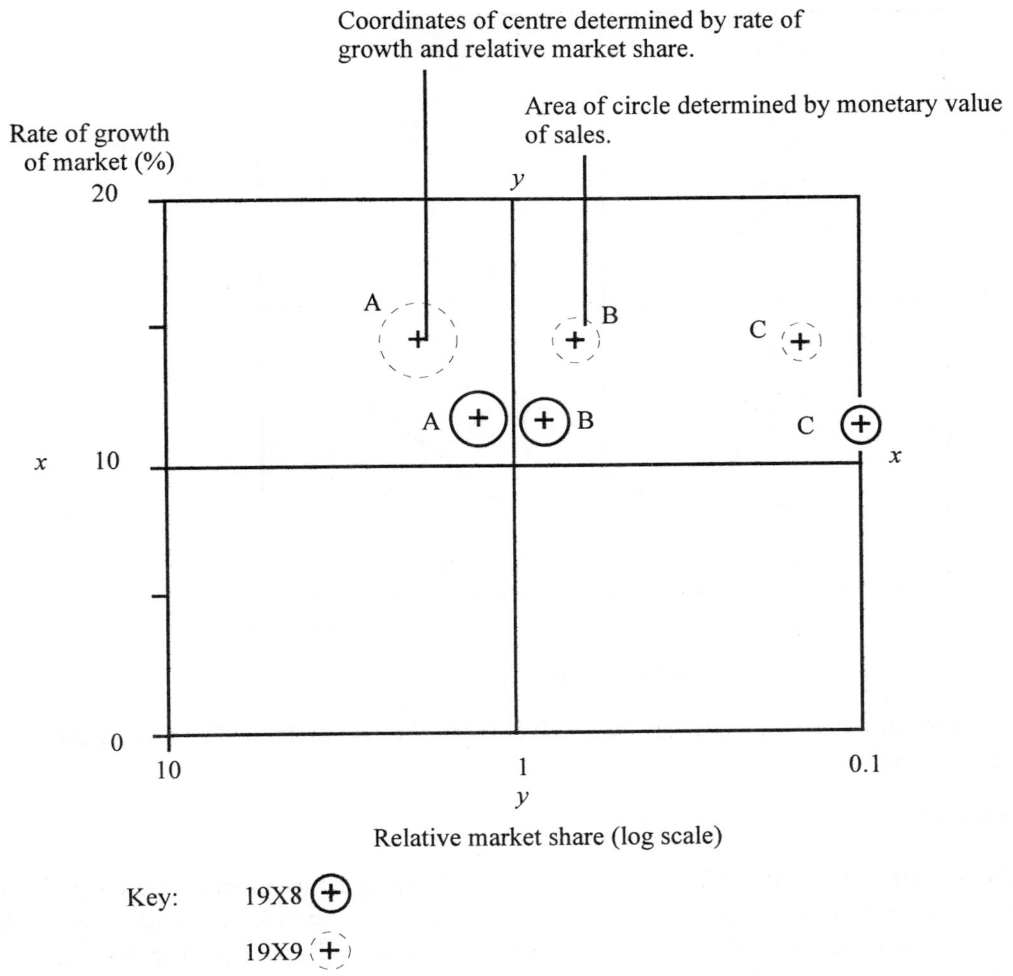

1.3 Interpretation of matrix

You will note that the matrix is divided into four quadrants. These are defined fairly arbitrarily by setting the growth rate divider at 10%, and the market share divider at 1.0, ie, joint market leaders. Thus, in terms of market shares, companies to the left are market leaders, and those to the right are market followers. The growth rate divider at 10% is harder to justify. It becomes more acceptable when other products are shown on the matrix which have a range of market growth rates.

As a generalisation, the cash characteristics of the products are defined by the quadrants into which they fall:

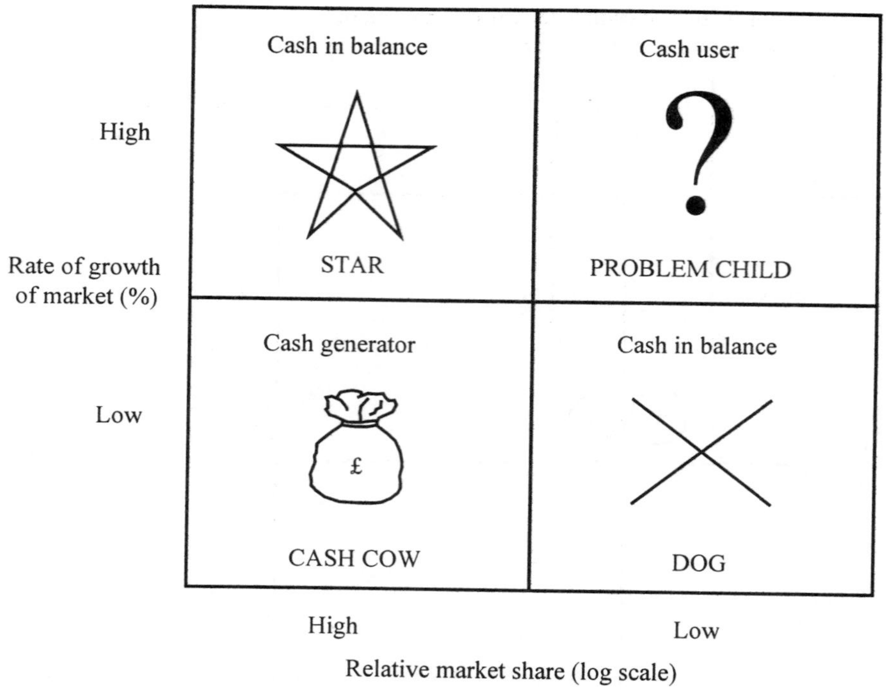

The characteristics of the product depends where it is located in the matrix. The characteristics of each quadrant are described below:

(a) **Cash cow**

This type of product has a high relative market share in a low growth market and should be generating substantial cash inflows. The period of high growth in the market has ended, (the product life cycle is in the maturity or decline stage), and consequently the market is less attractive to new entrants and existing competitors. Cash cow products tend to generate cash in excess of what is needed to sustain their market positions.

(b) **Star**

A star product has a high relative market share in a high growth market. This type of product may be in a later stage of its product life cycle.

A star may be only cash neutral despite its strong position, as large amounts of cash may need to be spent to defend an organisation's position against competitors. Competitors will be attracted to the market by the high growth rates. Failure to support a star sufficiently strongly, may lead to the product losing its leading market share position, slipping eastwards in the matrix and becoming a problem child. A star, however, represents the best future prospects for an organisation. As the growth rate for a star slows, it will drop vertically in the matrix into the cash cow quadrant and its cash characteristics will change.

(c) **Problem child**

Low market share in a high growth market. Substantial net cash input is required to maintain or increase market share. The planner is faced with three choices:

- do nothing - but cash continues to be absorbed;
- invest to gain market share; or
- sell off.

(d) **Dog**

The dog product has a low relative market share in a low growth market. Such a product, tends to have a negative cash flow which is likely to continue. It is unlikely that a dog can wrest market share from competitors. Competitors, which have the advantage of having larger market shares, are likely to fiercely resist any attempts to reduce their share of a low growth or static market. Consequently, in the view of the Boston Consulting Group, a dog product is 'essentially worthless' and should be liquidated.

In the example of widgets, the market is in a stage of high growth. Company A is market leader and has increased its market dominance in the last year. All the companies need to spend heavily - company A to maintain its position and companies B and C to increase their market share.

The next sections deal with the further stages in the technique. Each organisation will determine the product-market position for **all** of its products (ie, its portfolio) and determine a strategy on the future direction of the portfolio.

1.4 Strategic movements

A product's place in the matrix is not fixed for ever. The rate of growth of the market, though normally outside the control of the planners, should be taken into account in determining strategy. Stars tend to move vertically downwards as the market growth rate slows, to become cash cows. The cash that they generate can be used to turn problem children into stars, and eventually cash cows.

The ideal progression is illustrated below:

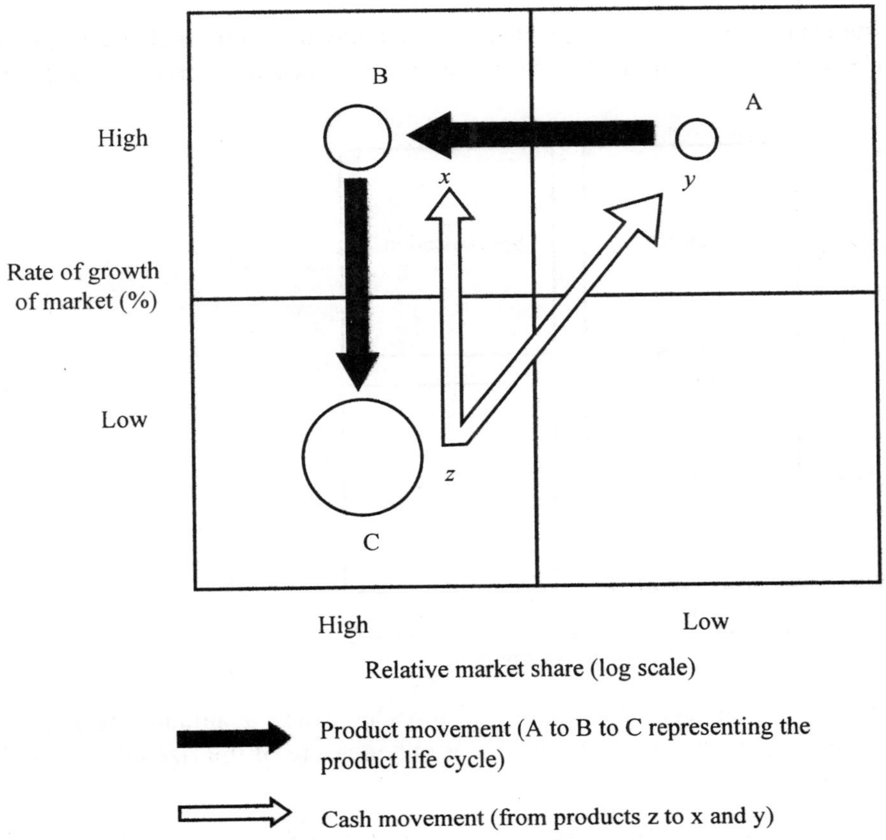

1.5 Strategic management of the market portfolio

The strategies for the **overall** portfolio are concerned with balance. Strategies would be to have:

(a) Cash cows of sufficient size and/or number which can support other products in the portfolio;

(b) Stars of sufficient size and/or number which will provide sufficient cash generation when the current cash cows can no longer do so;

(c) Problem children which have reasonable prospects of becoming future stars;

(d) No dogs, and if there are any, there would need to be good reasons for retaining them.

In deciding which strategy to adopt, numerous factors other than those in the matrix display need to be considered, eg:

(a) risk attached to the strategy; and
(b) nature of the products/markets.

Nevertheless, the matrix position provides a good and objective indication of the competitive position of the products.

1.6 Limitations of the approach

Although companies marketing industrial products have found the BCG's product-market portfolio strategy to be of use, in other industries the concept has not been so successful. The experience curve strategies appear relevant in commodity markets where costs and price are critical. However there are few markets which exactly fit this pattern because almost all products have features which allow companies to differentiate their offerings from competitors. In most cases, while the product may be similar the values attached to them by customers are different.

The limitations of the BCG's approach may be summarised as follows:

(a) **The matrix uses only two measures**

The two measures are growth and market share. These may be too limited as a basis for policy decisions. The Boston Consulting Group has now developed a further matrix to meet this criticism:

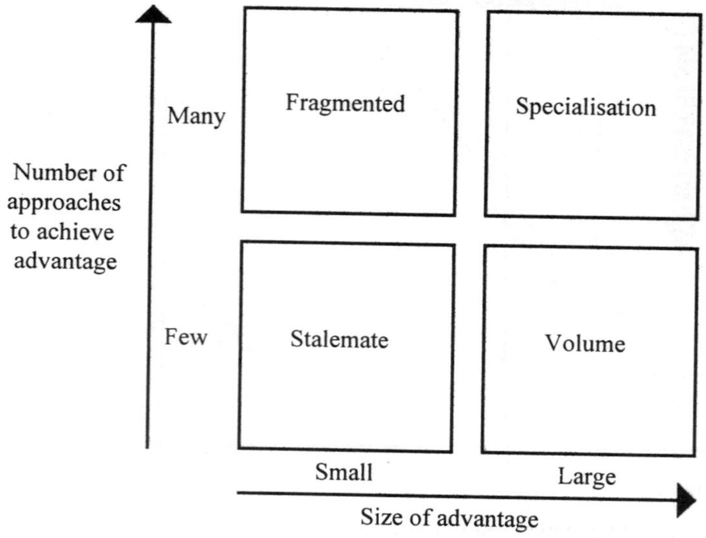

The vertical axis now indicates the number of ways in which a unique advantage may be achieved over competitors, and the horizontal axis is a measure of the size advantage that may be created over competitors.

The new matrix makes the exercise much more a matter of qualitative judgement.

(b) **Encourages companies to adopt holding strategies**

The strategic principles involved advocate that companies with large market shares in static or low growth markets (ie, cash cows) adopt holding or harvesting strategies rather than encouraging them to try and increase the **total demand** of the markets in which their products are selling. Compliance with these strategic tenets has lead to devastating results for some companies.

There are a number of dangers in assuming that a product is a **'cash cow'**. (BCG defines a cash cow as a product occupying a strong position in a static or slow growing market.) First management may be tempted to pull back on investment, by treating the product as in **'safe-water'**, and second make assumptions about future cash flow that may be unrealistic. Radios, for example, form a product line, which was treated by a number of manufacturers as a cash cow. Convinced that every product had its **'product life cycle'** they treated the radio as a product that had passed its peak and the radio business as a candidate for cash milking. Japanese radio manufacturers were not prepared to treat the radio-line in this way, and by creating new markets, expanded the total demand for radios. The result was a flood of innovative products which included: **radio-cassette, stereo radio-cassette, ultra-thin radio, 'Walkman with radio', radio-in-pocket with calculator, radio-in-TV** and **digital clock radio**. All successful products.

Yamaha destroyed the dominance of the well-established US musical instrument manufacturers who concentrated on milking their mature products for profit rather than on planning how to defend their market shares.

(c) **Implies only those with large market shares should remain**

There are many examples of businesses with a low market share continuing to operate profitably. Sometimes this is because the market is not unitary, but fragmented, and the small competitor has found itself a particular market niche; on other occasions large companies may prefer smaller competitors to preserve the impression of competition.

The link between profitability and market share may be weak because:

- low share competitors entering the market late may be on the steepest experience curve;
- low share competitors may have some inbuilt cost advantage;
- not all products have costs related to experience; and
- large competitors may receive more government attention and regulation.

(d) **Implies that the most profitable markets are those with high growth**

Again this is not always so, due to:

- high entry barriers, especially in high technology industries; and
- high price competition.

Both of these problems are typified by the microcomputer business. Despite impressive rates of growth, a number of companies have been unable to make profits because of the high levels of initial investment followed by extreme price competition from low-cost late entrants.

The US company Republic Gypsum is a small one-plant manufacturer of wallboards with only a 2% share of the US plasterboard market. It is a lot smaller than the majors with US Gypsum holding 37% and National Gypsum 27%. Republic concentrates on a small geographical niche centred on Oklahoma and North Texas, and meets local prices and absorbs high freight costs by using its own trucking fleet. Its competitors use contract freight carriers at high cost. In

1982 Republic achieved 94% plant utilisation, against 70% for the rest of the industry, and reported a 13.5% operating margin after depreciation, triple that of US Gypsum and almost quadruple that of National Gypsum.

(e) **Not all dogs should be condemned**

A very large number of small but successful businesses are 'dogs', and according to the BCG concept are ripe for reinvestment or liquidation. However this would not always be the case. Dog products are often used not with the primary aim of maximising the profit from the product itself, but to provide economies of scale in manufacturing, marketing and administration to sustain the **overall** business. Furthermore the BCG portfolio theory does not seem to take into account the need for competitive strategy. A company might, for example, launch a product to act as a 'second front' to support the thrust of its main offering, although the product, by definition, is a dog.

The Clorox company's purpose of introducing **'Wave'** into the US domestic bleach market was to try and deflect Proctor and Gamble's attack on the market brand leader, Clorox, by creating a **'second front'**, rather than to generate substantial profits from Wave.

Despite these criticisms, in certain circumstances the model provides a useful method by which a company can (a) attempt to achieve overall cost leadership in its market(s) through aggressive use of directed efficiency; (b) focus its expenditures and capital investment programmes; and (c) plan for an appropriate balance of resources between conflicting product-market claims. Also the information and analysis required to construct the matrix will provide meaningful indicators. It should, however, not be used in a rigid, stereotype manner. The model ought to be used as a means to an end, not as representing the end objective in itself.

2 ANSOFF'S PRODUCT-MARKET GROWTH VECTOR

2.1 Search for opportunities

Growth in the size of an organisation can be measured in many ways - profit, turnover, earnings per share, manpower etc - but the real aim of a growth strategy is growth in **profits.** The pursuit of size or increased turnover is not an end in itself but is only worthwhile if it leads to higher profits. If an organisation has decided that it does need growth in order to achieve its economic objectives, its search for new opportunities must be particularly active (although it would still need new opportunities even if pursuing a non growth strategy).

2.2 The mix

Ansoff describes the product-market mix as a combination of current and new products in current and new markets. The four areas are shown in the diagram below with the organisation's strategic options.

	Existing product	*New product / service*
Existing market	Internal efficiency Market penetration	Product or service development
Existing product	Market development	Diversification

Improvements in internal efficiency are not something about which strategic decisions are taken. They should be constantly sought as part of the day-to-day running of the firm and so are covered in the operations plan (which is one of the sub-plans which elaborate the strategy).

2.3 Market penetration

This is a strategy by which a company seeks to increase the sales of its present products in its existing markets. (We have already considered strategies for internal efficiency.)

Kotler suggests that market penetration involves aggressive marketing effort, and proposes three main ways a company can penetrate a market. These are:

(a) The company can try to stimulate customers to increase their current rate of usage. Strategies might include:
- increasing unit of customer purchase;
- speeding up the rate of product improvement or obsolescence;
- suggesting new uses for the product; and
- offering customers price incentives for increased use.

(b) The company can increase its efforts to attract non-users by using promotional incentives, advertising, pricing up or down, etc.

(c) The company can increase its efforts to swing competitors' customers by brand differentiation, and stepping up promotion, etc.

Market penetration strategy would be contemplated for the following reasons:

(a) When the overall market is growing, or can be induced to grow it may be relatively easy for companies entering the market, or those wishing to gain market share, to do so relatively quickly. (Some companies established in the market may be unable or unwilling to invest resources in an attempt to grow to meet the new demand). In contrast, market penetration in static, or declining, markets can be much more difficult to achieve.

(b) Market penetration strategy would be forced on a company that is determined to confine its interests to its existing product/market area but is unwilling to permit a decline in sales even though the overall market is declining.

(c) If other companies are leaving the market for whatever reasons, penetration could prove easy - although the good sense of the strategy may be in doubt.

(d) A company which holds a strong market position and is able to use its experience and competence to obtain strong distinctive competitive advantages may find it relatively easy to penetrate the market.

(e) A market penetration strategy requires a relatively lower level of investment with a corresponding reduction in risk and senior management involvement.

2.4 Product development

This strategy has the aim of a company increasing sales by developing products for its existing market. For our purposes new-product development is a generic term which incorporates innovative products and modifications and improvements to existing products. Therefore, product development strategy of the company could:

(a) develop new product features through attempting to adapt, modify, magnify, minify, substitute, rearrange, reverse or combine existing features.

(b) create different quality versions of the product.

(c) develop additional models and sizes.

A company might show a preference for product development strategy for the following reasons.

(a) It holds a high relative share of the market, has a strong brand presence and enjoys distinctive competitive advantages in the market.

(b) There is growth potential in the market. (You may remember that the Boston Consulting Group, for instance, recommend companies to invest in growth markets.)

(c) The changing needs of its customers demand new products. Continuous product innovation is often the only way to prevent product obsolescence.

(d) It needs to react to technological developments.

(e) The company is particularly strong in R&D.

(f) The company has a strong organisation structure based on product divisions.

(g) For offensive or defensive motives, for example responding to competitive innovations in the market.

However product development strategy does have its downside and there are strong reasons why it might not be appropriate for a company. For example, the process of creating a broad product line is expensive and potentially unprofitable, and it carries considerable investment risk. Empirical research reveals that companies enjoying high market share may benefit in profit terms from relatively high levels of R&D expenditure, while companies in weak market positions with high R&D expenditure fare badly.

There are reasons why new-product development is becoming increasingly difficult to achieve.

(a) In some industries there is a shortage of new product ideas.

(b) Increasing market differentiation causes market segments to narrow with the effect that low volumes reduce profit potential which in turn increases the risk of the investment involved.

(c) A company typically has to develop many product ideas in order to produce one good one. This makes new-product development very costly.

(d) Even when a product is successful it might still suffer a short life cycle with rivals quick to 'copycat' in the market but with their own innovations and improvements.

(e) There is a high chance of product failure.

2.5 Market development

Market development strategy has the aim of increasing sales by repositioning present products to new markets. (Note: this strategy is also referred to as **'market creation'**.)

Kotler suggests that there are two possibilities.

(a) The company can open additional geographical markets through regional, national or international expansion.

(b) The company can try to attract other market segments through developing product versions that appeal to these segments, entering new channels of distribution, or advertising in other media.

For example, during 1992 Kellogg's undertook a major television and promotion campaign to reposition Kellogg's Corn-Flakes (traditionally regarded as a breakfast cereal) to provide afternoon and evening meals. In the same way the malt drink, Horlicks had previously repositioned from a once-a-day product ('a night meal') to become a through-the-day 'relaxing drink'.

Market development strategy would be contemplated for the following reasons:

(a) The company identifies potential opportunities for market development including the possibilities of repositioning, exploiting new uses for the product or spreading into new geographical areas.

(b) The company's resources are structured to produce a particular product or product line and it would be very costly to switch technologies.

(c) The company's distinctive competence lies with the product and it also has strong marketing competence. (Coca-Cola provides a good example of a company that pursues market development strategies, as does the fast-food restaurant chain of McDonalds.)

2.6 Growth by diversification

We have already seen from our study of Ansoff's product-market growth matrix that diversification is a strategy that entails the deployment of a company's resources into new products and new markets. The company thus becomes involved in activities which are different from those in which it is currently involved. Diversification strategy means the company selectively changes the product lines, customer targets and perhaps its manufacturing and distribution arrangements.

Because of the extent of the change there is clearly more risk involved than in a strategy of product-market expansion (ie, remaining within the existing product-market scope), so we must consider the reasons why companies nevertheless diversify. Ansoff suggests three main reasons:

(a) Objectives can no longer be met without diversification. This would be identified by the momentum line (status-quo) forecast and gap analysis. The reason for the dissatisfaction with the present industry might be either due to poor return caused by product decline, with little opportunity for technological innovation in the same field, or due to lack of flexibility, eg, unavoidable dependence on a single customer or a single product line.

(b) The company has more cash than it needs for expansion. Whether it prefers to invest this outside the business or to seek opportunities for diversification will depend on the relative rates of return obtainable (in general the return from operations exceeds the return from outside investments, but of course more risk is involved) and management preference (management have to balance the internal flexibility achieved by keeping reserves in liquid form with external flexibility offered by diversification).

(c) Companies may diversify even if their objectives are being or could be met within their industry, if diversification promises to be more profitable than expansion.

Steiner adds more possible reasons:

(d) To avoid the company depending only on product-line.

(e) For the company to make greater use of an existing distribution system.

More reasons put forward by other writers are:

(f) For the company to expand horizontally into other industries and use the synergy obtainable to strengthen its existing products.

(g) For the company to compete at all points with a competitor. If a competitor is obtaining synergy from its product-market mix which provides it with some form of competitive advantage, the company might be compelled to also diversify to achieve the same advantageous mix.

(h) To take advantage of downstream opportunities such as by-products, etc.

If a company is unable to reach a decision about the relative merits of expansion and diversification due to lack of quantifiable information, it might continue to search for diversification opportunities short of actually committing resources. In other words it delays the decision until better information is available, as has already been advocated.

A company may diversify by itself developing a new product-market area (organically), or by acquiring or merging with a company already operational in the proposed new field. The former implies an active research department initiative. The latter can lead to quicker entry into the new area (time is often of the essence) and to **start-up** economies, but is not without its own difficulties.

3 GAP ANALYSIS

3.1 The concept of gap analysis

Definition The comparison of an entity's ultimate objective with the sum of projections and already planned projects, and identifying how the consequent gap might be closed.

Having obtained data about its current position and decided its objectives the firm must determine the **gap** between its predicted and desired performance. The company will already have available various statistics about its past and present performance - sales, profit margin, return on capital employed, turnover ratios, etc, and it can use these to extrapolate from the past and present data to predict what its future position would be if it made no effort to change the situation. The extrapolation would use **momentum lines** (conceptual projections of the anticipated consequences of pursuing an existing strategy without any major directional changes), and the method employed is sometimes referred to as **status-quo forecasting**.

3.2 Strategic gap

A strategic gap is the shortfall between the targeted performance and the projected momentum line at a specific point of time ahead. The concept is useful because it focuses attention on the magnitude of the task facing planners and the time span available to them.

An example of a simple strategic gap is shown below. Although the momentum line can be generated in many ways and from a variety of sources, in this case the profits for the last five years have been plotted and a momentum line derived from the trend. The term **simple** is used because the gap represents **one** point of time ahead, and therefore both lines which link the objective and the projected performance at that point in time with the current time are straight lines. For this reason regression formulae can be used to plot the momentum line.

Example of strategic gap

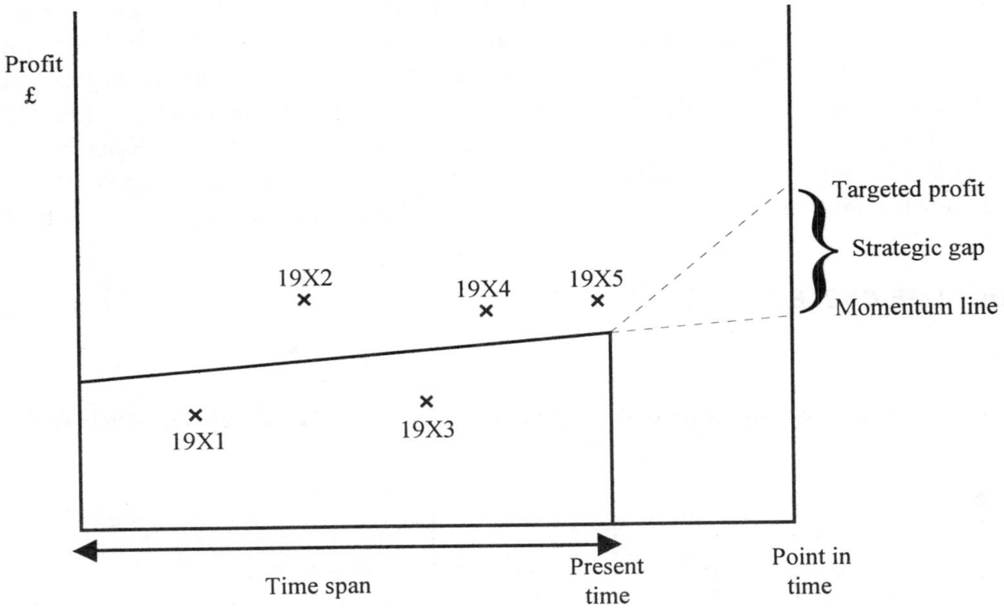

3.3 The value of the momentum line

In a business world of rapidly changing customer needs and technology, intense competition, and formidable environmental uncertainty, a large question-mark must be placed firstly on the sense of a company spending time and resources on projecting the momentum line of the existing strategy knowing that there is an odds-on chance that the strategy will be changed or added to anyway, and secondly the ability of analysts to plot the company's long-term strategic position with any success. What then is the value of attempting to plot the momentum line, which is based on the assumption that the company is going to behave in the future, exactly as it did in the past? In pondering this question some reasons can be found as to why this is indeed a valuable exercise.

(a) The most important reason is that the whole point of making the forecast is to establish the need for any **new** strategies. It would destroy the purpose of the momentum line if it included new strategies.

(b) A forecast that included new activity of which the company has no experience would be more inaccurate than one dealing with only those activities the company has hitherto pursued.

(c) Any forecast for a company consists of a complex mix of individual assumptions, bias, opinions, separate forecasts and calculations, and it is perhaps sensible to keep this complexity within bounds. Simple momentum lines derived from linear regression remove a lot of the complexity.

(d) Sometimes a company that is facing threat takes vigorous action to avoid it without first estimating the consequences of not avoiding it. It must sometimes be the case that standing still is preferable to change, for the sake of change, and the momentum line shows what the consequence of a **zero change** (or **'neutral') strategy** might be.

(e) In order to project the momentum line, analysts have to review the salient features of the company's recent performance. In doing so they may discover, or re-discover, a number of indicators that could have a profound effect on the formulation of future strategy.

(f) The examination of the company's recent past may place into perspective the size, and speed of the changes, and associated problems which would help indicate the extent and difficulty of the changes that would be required by the company immediately, or in the medium-term future.

3.4 The analysis aspect

Companies are faced with a chicken and egg situation. Which comes first? Targets or strategy? A strong body of opinion favours the approach we have just discussed, that is it inclines towards a company developing an aspirational set of targets and then attempting to generate strategies capable of reaching them. There is another school which conclude that targets and ratios ought not to dictate the structure of the strategic plan: their function is to assist in direction and control. Alternative strategies should be formulated against the background of available corporate expertise, available and potential resources and the envisaged operating environment. Targets should emerge logically from the selected strategy.

4 THE PRODUCT LIFE-CYCLE

4.1 Introduction

The product life-cycle concept suggests that all products have a similar life-cycle, which is illustrated below:

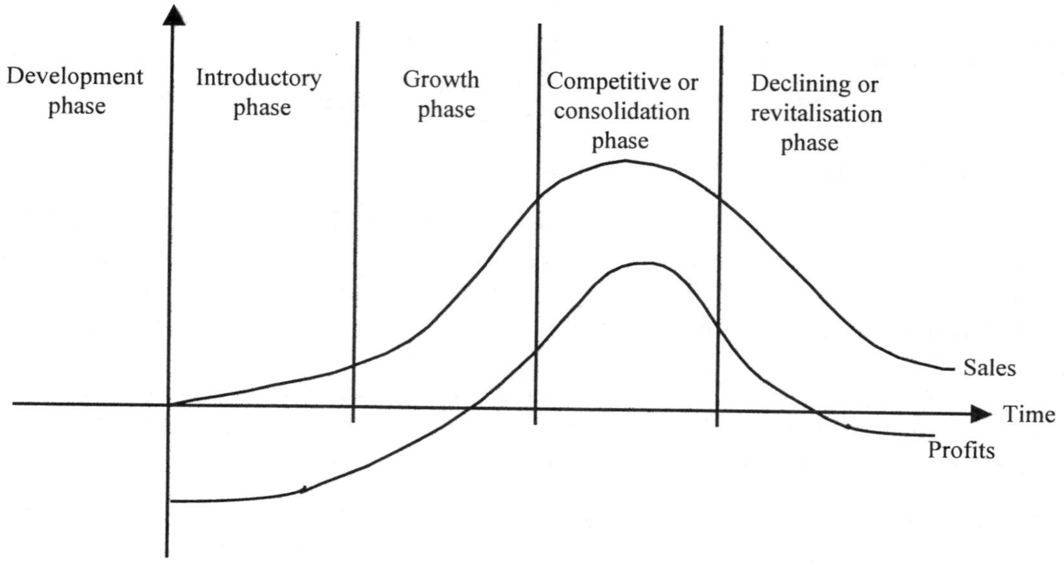

The length of the cycle will vary with the type of product and technology; eg long for aircraft, short for fashion garments.

The characteristics of the various **phases** are as follows:

(a) **Development**

The product is being designed and developed; market research may be undertaken to determine the potential market.

(b) **Introductory**

The product is launched; losses are made; few companies are in the field; design changes are being made. (For this last reason it does not always pay to be an innovator: it may be better to wait until someone else has ironed out all the snags.)

(c) **Growth**

The product becomes more widely known and sales begin to take off, prompted by active marketing. Good profits can be made and more companies enter the industry. The rate of growth and length of the growth phase depends on factors such as novelty value of the product; usefulness of the product; availability of substitutes; rate of growth of consumer incomes and proportion spent on luxuries/necessities; expenditure on advertising etc.

(d) **Competitive or consolidation**

Sales have reached saturation points. There is no room for new companies in the industry and there is stiff competition among the existing ones. This is a time for looking at cost reduction: profit margins are falling. There is a tendency for companies to merge which both achieves cost reduction and puts up further barriers to the entry of new companies because they would be too small to compete. Some companies will drop out of the market altogether.

(e) **Decline or re-vitalisation**

Sales of the product fall off, and the decline will continue unless the product can be revitalised by the new technology, by advertising (likely to be of limited use only), by finding a new use for the product or by some other means. For instance, the introduction of colour television revitalised the television market.

Andrew Liver Salt, first sold in 1884 by Phillips Scott & Turner, grew steadily through the 1920s and 1930s, slowed down in the 1940s and by the mid-1950s had begun to decline in volume terms.

A company is in a weak position if all its products are at the same phase of the life cycle. If they are all in the growth phase there are problems ahead: if they are all in one of the other phases there are immediate difficulties.

Companies try to overcome this problem by introducing new products which are growing as the old products are declining and by having products with life-cycles of different lengths. This is illustrated below. (The example is entirely invented and is not based on actual data.)

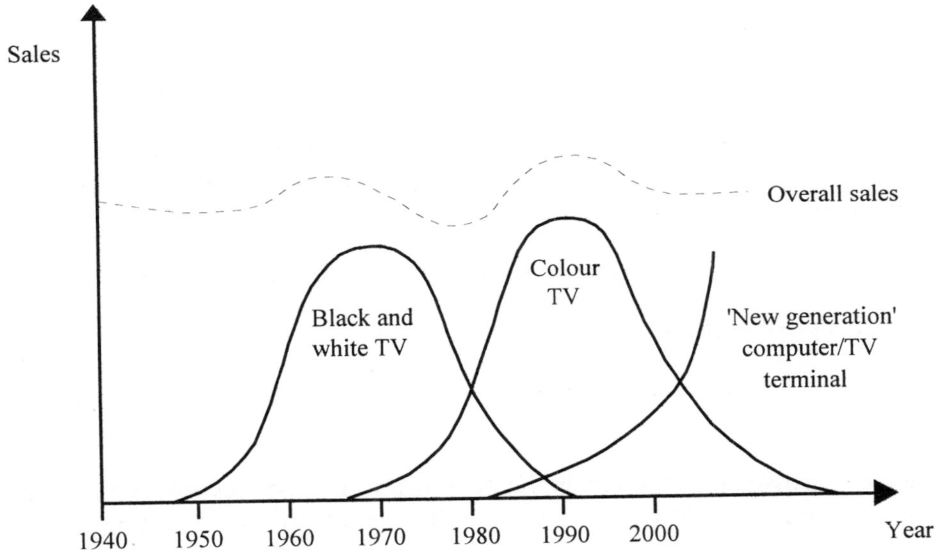

In any particular instance the industry analysis will show the company whether it can hope to get the right balance of life-cycle within its own industry or whether it will have to think of diversifying.

4.2 Life-cycle analysis

The **'Product Life Cycle'** concept commonly known as the S-curve, is valid for most products, markets, economies, industries, technologies, popular movements, fashions and companies. Although the basic concept of the life cycle is well covered in most study texts which deal with marketing management or new product development policy, and the concept is highly valued as a predictive technique, one has to search quite hard to find an explanation on how the curve is actually projected.

The first task is to project the shape of the S curve, using historic and forecasting data. The two shapes most widely referred to are the logistic and Gompertz curves; however, as in most concepts there are many variations. Once the basic shape has been projected (in terms of **'relative'** duration between development, growth and useful life) the next task is to project the financial parameters. If a cash flow basis is applied, the projection parameters will be:

(a) Maximum net outflow during development.

(b) Maximum net outflow immediately prior to take-off.

(c) Maximum net positive cash flow at the height of sales volume (after achieving maximum growth).

(d) Maximum net positive cash flow immediately prior to decline.

(e) Level of positive net cash flow at the point at which a decision may need to be taken to discontinue the product.

Having established the shape and financial parameters which provides the data required to plot the vertical axis on a graph, the final task is to forecast the duration of each stage required for the horizontal, or time axis. The techniques of intuitive and technological forecasting are available to help project time-spans involved, - however this is an extremely difficult aspect of life-cycle forecasting and depending upon the shape and time spans involved the later parts of the life curve may, perhaps, be calculated in broad terms only.

A product life is influenced by many factors, such as, technological innovation, customer behaviour, government fiscal policies (ie, the incidence and rates of Value Added Tax), the activities of competitors and much more. It is these factors which need to be forecast in order for the life cycle curve to be projected with any confidence of accuracy.

5 BUSINESS PROCESS RE-ENGINEERING

5.1 Introduction

Business process re-engineering (BPR) has been described as 'a new management approach reflecting the practical experiences of managers and providing a source of practical feedback to management science. It represents a response to:

- failure of business processes to meet customers' needs and deliver customer satisfaction
- the challenge of organisational politics
- the yawning gap between strategic intent in the boardroom and the day-to-day practice of the business
- disappointments following the application of information technology to businesses during the 1980s'. (Birchall and Lyons in *Creating Tomorrow's Organisation,* Pitman)

This last point is an important one. There is evidence that many companies have failed to benefit as they had expected from their investment in information technology. Often the reason has been that senior managers have failed to align their IT strategy with corporate objectives.

BPR is on of a number of techniques that have been advocated to overhaul existing business processes and practices with a view to improving organisational performance.

BPR, as the name suggests, places emphasis on processes as a change mechanism. Consideration of processes may challenge preconceived ideas on the most appropriate structure.

5.2 How BPR works

BPR is not confined to manufacturing processes and has been applied to a wide range of administrative and operational activities. Indeed, to overcome the barrier of an inappropriate title many commentators prefer to use the terms business process re-design, business process re-structure or simply business process improvement.

In each case the idea is to ask radical questions about why things are done in a particular way, and whether alternative methods could achieve better results. Often the focus has been on staffing levels, the implication being that more staff are employed than are strictly needed to achieve the desired outcomes. However, this is a by-product of the technique and is not a main purpose of BPR.

Steve Smith (in *The Quality Revolution*, Management Books 2000) cites the example of a health insurance company where processing of an application for health insurance used to take 28 days and called for input from seven members of staff. After re-engineering, processing takes only seven days and is completed by a single member of staff. The point is that only 45 minutes of work is needed on each application; the rest of the 28 days was occupied by the file being in transit

5.3 The role of the accountant

The accountant contributes to planning a BPR exercise above all by providing the information required to evaluate alternatives. As mentioned above, the primary purpose of BPR is to investigate different ways in which defined outcomes can be achieved. The effects of each method on costs and profitability will be a key criterion in determining the best option, and the management accountant is well placed to provide such information.

Accountants will work closely with operational managers to achieve this. By looking at their existing processes, and helping to formulate alternatives, the management accountant will inform himself or herself in detail about what is involved. The task then is to translate this information into financial form. The methods of reporting on processes may themselves need to be revised as a result: often adoption of BPR has gone hand in hand with a move to activity based costing.

As the term suggests, BPR is concerned with how processes are to work in practice. In implementing a BPR programme, managers will be concerned to have the appropriate information to enable them to manage new processes. Accountants can help by reconsidering the form in which reports are presented. In many cases, the required change will be from an emphasis on transactions processing to an emphasis on decision making and control. Underlying all of this should be a focus on customer needs.

Once the appropriate information has been determined, it is equally important to ensure that it is presented appropriately. If the new emphasis is on support for decision making it is essential that managers can appreciate the information and digest it rapidly. User friendliness is an important criterion, and too much detail is as unhelpful as too little.

5.4 Advantages and disadvantages of BPR

Advantages of BPR include the following.

- BPR revolves around customer needs and helps to give an appropriate focus to the business.
- BPR provides cost advantages that assist the organisation's competitive position.
- BPR encourages a long-term strategic view of operational processes by asking radical questions about how things are done and how processes could be improved.
- BPR helps overcome the shortsighted approaches that sometimes emerge from excessive concentration on functional boundaries. By focusing on entire processes the exercise can streamline activities throughout the organisation.
- BPR can help to reduce organisational complexity by eliminating unnecessary activities.

Criticisms of BPR include the following.

- BPR is sometimes seen (incorrectly) as a means of making small improvements in existing practices. In reality, it is a more radical approach that questions whether existing practices make any sense in their present form.

- BPR is sometimes seen (incorrectly) as a single, once-for-all cost-cutting exercise. In reality, it is not primarily concerned with cost-cutting (though cost reductions often result), and should be regarded as ongoing rather than once-for-all. This misconception often creates hostility in the minds of staff who see the exercise as a threat to their security.

- BPR requires a far-reaching and long-term commitment by management and staff. Securing this is not an easy task, and many organisations have rejected the whole idea as not worth the effort.

6 STRATEGY EVALUATION

6.1 Introduction

This section is concerned with how specific options can be evaluated and considers the following

(a) The **screening** of options
(b) Methods of assessing specific options against different measures

(i) The **return** which a strategy is expected to produce.
(ii) The degree of **risk** which a strategy would imply.
(iii) The extent to which the strategy appears **feasible.**

6.2 Screening options

The options available include:

- **Scoring** methods which rank options against a set of predetermined factors concerning the organisation's strategic situation.

- **Decision trees** which also assess specific options against a list of key strategic factors.

- **Scenarios** which attempt to match specific options with a range of possible future outcomes and are particularly useful where a high degree of uncertainty exists.

6.3 Scoring methods

Scoring methods are a systematic way of analysing **specific** options for their suitability or fit with the picture gained from the strategic analysis.

Ranking is a simple scoring method where each option is assessed against a number of key factors. The illustration below is an example of how such a ranking might be performed. More sophisticated approaches to ranking assign weightings to each factor in recognition that some will be of more importance in the evaluation than others. The method can also be combined with sensitivity analysis to test out the likely impact on the company if the assumptions about each factor should change.

	Options	Desire for small company	Need to control quality	Need for high margins	Threat of competition	Dependent on supplier	Rank
1	Do nothing (ie current strategy)	✓	✓	✓	X	X	C
2	Seek new suppliers	✓	✓	?	X	X	C
3	More customers of same type	X	✓	✓	X	✓	A
4	Expand nationally	X	X	✓	✓	✓	A
5	Expand product range	✓	X	✓	X	✓	B
6	Seek new outlets	X	X	X	X	✓	A
7	Diversify	?	X	?	X	X	B

✓ = Favourable influence X = Unfavourable influence ? = Uncertain or irrelevant

A = Appear most suitable B = Moderately suitable C = Appear least suitable

The ranking process shown in the chart is used to group the various options into three categories (A, B and C) in relation to their suitability. It should be noted that each strategic factor might not carry the same weight or importance. The need for growth to counter competition was in fact of overriding importance, so options 4 and 6 were identified as most suitable despite their lack of fit with other factors.

6.4 Decision trees

The decision tree approach ranks options by the process of progressively eliminating others. This elimination process is achieved by identifying a few key elements which future developments are intended to incorporate such as growth, investment and diversification. For example, in the diagram below choosing growth as an important aspect of future strategies would automatically rank options 1 – 4 more highly than 5 – 8. At the second step the need for low investment strategies would rank options 3 and 4 above 1 and 2, and so on.

The greatest limitation of decision tree analysis is that the choice at each branch on the tree can tend to be simplistic. Nevertheless, as a starting point for evaluation, decision trees can often provide a useful framework.

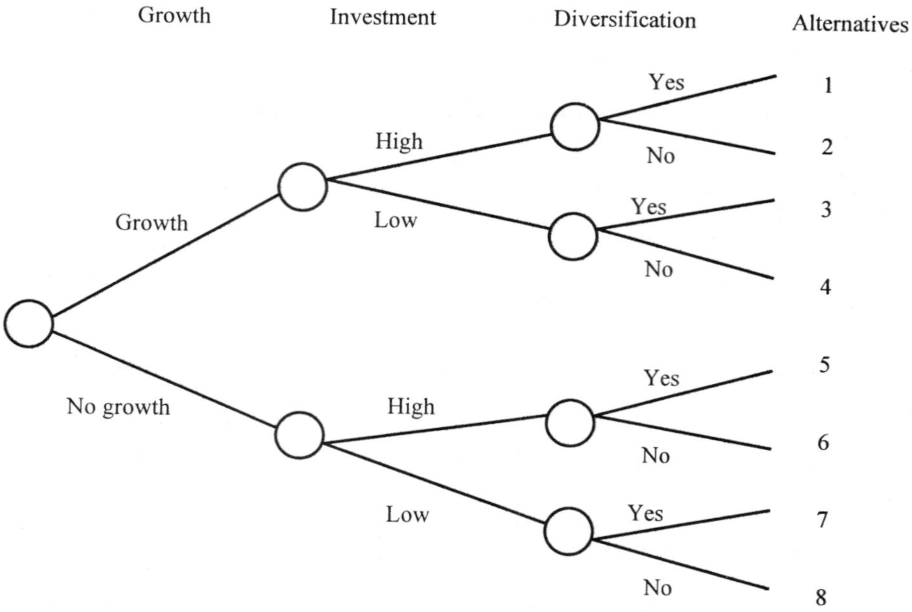

6.5 Scenarios

Scenario planning attempts to match specific options with a range of possible future situations (or scenarios). The approach is essentially used as a means of addressing some of the less well structured or uncertain aspects of evaluation. To construct a scenario:

First use the industry scenarios and develop a set of assumptions about the task environment. At 3M, for example, the general manager of each business unit is required annually to describe what his or her industry will look like in 15 years.

Second, for each strategic alternative, develop a set of optimistic, pessimistic, and most likely assumptions about the impact of key variables on the company's future financial statements. Forecast three sets of sales and cost of goods sold figures for at least five years into the future. Look at historical data from past financial statements and make adjustments based on the environmental assumptions listed above. Do the same for other figures that can vary significantly. Plug in expected inventory levels, accounts receivable, accounts payable, R & D expenses, advertising and promotion expenses, capital expenditures and debt payments.

Third, construct detailed pro forma financial statements for each of the strategic alternatives. Using a spreadsheet program, list the actual figures from this year's financial statement in the left column. To the right of this column, list the optimistic figures for year one, year two, year three, year four and year five. Go through this same process with the same strategic alternative, but now list the pessimistic figures for the next five years. Do the same with the most likely figures. Once this is done, develop a similar set of optimistic (O), pessimistic (P). and most likely (ML) pro forma statements for the second stage alternative. This process will generate six different pro forma scenarios reflecting three different situations (O, P and ML) for two strategic alternatives. Next, calculate financial ratios and common-sized income statements, and balance sheets to accompany the pro formas.

The result of this detailed scenario construction should be anticipated net profits, cash flow, and net working capital for each of three versions of the two alternatives for five years into the future.

6.6 The impact of strategies on the organisation and the community

Johnson and Scholes, in their book Exploring Corporate Strategy, have outlined a set of evaluation criteria based on three categories: suitability; feasibility; and acceptability. These categories emphasise how an organisation's circumstances might influence the broad types of strategy they should follow.

(i) **Suitability**

Suitability is an evaluation criterion for assessing the extent to which a proposed strategy actually fits the situation identified in the strategic analysis, and how it would sustain or improve the competitive position of the organisation. The strategic analysis would include the major opportunities and threats which face the organisation, its particular strengths and weaknesses and any expectations which are an important influence on strategic choice.

Suitability is a useful criterion for screening strategies, asking the following questions about strategic options:

- Does the strategy exploit the company strengths, such as providing work for skilled craftsmen or environmental opportunities eg, helping to establish the organisation in new growth sectors of the market?
- How far does the strategy overcome the difficulties identified in the analysis? For example, is the strategy likely to improve the organisation's competitive standing, solve the company's liquidity problems or decrease dependence on a particular supplier?
- Does the option fit in with the organisation's purposes? For example, would the strategy achieve profit targets or growth expectations, or would it retain control for an owner-manager?

(ii) **Feasibility**

An assessment of the feasibility of any strategy is concerned with whether it can be implemented successfully. The scale of the proposed changes needs to be achievable in resource terms. At the evaluation stage there are a number of questions which need to be asked when assessing feasibility. These include:

- Can the strategy be funded?
- Is the organisation capable of performing to the required level eg, quality or service?
- Can the necessary market position be achieved, and will the necessary marketing skills be available?
- Can the organisation cope with competitive reactions?
- How will the organisation ensure that the required skills at both managerial and operative level are available?
- Will the technology (both product and process) be available to compete effectively?
- Can the necessary materials and services be obtained?

(iii) **Acceptability**

Acceptability is strongly related to people's expectations, and therefore the issue of 'acceptable to whom?' requires the analysis to be thought through carefully. Some of the questions that will help identify the likely consequences of any strategy are as follows:

- How will the organisation perform in profitability terms? The parallel in the public sector would be cost/benefit assessment.
- How will the financial risk (e.g. liquidity) change?
- What effect will it have on capital structure (gearing or share ownership)?

- Will the function of any department, group or individual change significantly?
- Will the organisation's relationship with outside stakeholders eg, suppliers, government, unions, customers) need to change?
- Will the strategy be acceptable in the organisation's environment eg, higher levels of noise?

7 ANALYSING RISK

7.1 Introduction

An assessment of the return likely to accrue from specific options is a key measure of the **acceptability** of an option. There are different ways in which the returns can be reviewed.

Profitability analyses a useful evaluation measure in the anticipated return on capital employed x years after a new strategy is implemented. Care must be taken to establish whether this measure is to be applied to the whole company or simply to the extra profit related to the extra capital required for a particular strategy.

When new strategies involve significant sums of capital investment then there are better measures of the relationship between capital expenditure and earnings. One such measure is that of payback which assesses the period of time required to pay back the invested capital.

The payback period is calculated by finding the time at which the cumulative net cash flow becomes zero.

Discounted cash flow (DCF) analysis is the most widely used investment appraisal technique and is essentially an extension of the payback period type. Once the net cash flows have been assessed for each of the preceding years they are discounted progressively to reflect the fact that the funds generated early are of more real value than those in later periods.

Cost/Benefit analysis attempts to put a money value on all the costs and benefits of a strategic option – including intangibles. One of the difficulties of cost/benefit analysis is deciding on the boundaries of the analysis.

Despite difficulties with cost/benefit analysis it is an approach which is valuable if its limitations are understood. Its major benefit is in forcing people to be explicit about the variety of factors which should influence strategic choice.

7.2 Analysis

The techniques for analysing risk may be classified as follows:

Single decisions	*Multiple decisions*
Pay-off matrix - maximum rule - minimax regret rule - expected values	Decision trees - expected values - sensitivity analysis

7.3 Pay-off matrix

The pay-off matrix is a tabular layout specifying the result of each possible outcome.

Example

A company has three variations of a new product A, B and C, of which it can only introduce one. The level of demand for **each** course of action might be low, medium or high. If the company decides to introduce product A, the net income that would result from the levels of demand possible are estimated at £20, £40 and £50 respectively. Similarly, if product B is chosen, net income is estimated at £80, £70 and -£10, and for product C, £10, £100 and £40 respectively.

Construct a pay-off matrix to present this information concisely.

Outcome (demand)	*Decision (action to introduce)*		
	A £	B £	C £
Low	20	80	10
Medium	40	70	100
High	50	(10)	40

The pay-off matrix shows the net income (£S) resulting from the introduction of products A, B and C, if demand is low, medium or high.

Note: A realistic assumption might be that the company is obliged to meet whatever level of demand arises (for fear of incurring customer *bad will* and, thus, less sales of its other products). This would justify the fall in net income at higher levels of demand in the case of product B in particular, where it appears that there are considerable diseconomies of scale.

7.4 Decision-making criteria

In the example above, it is by no means clear which decision is going to produce the most satisfactory result, since each product gives the most desirable outcome at one level of demand.

There are three techniques for choosing between A, B and C in this situation:

(a) maximin rule;
(b) minimax regret rule;
(c) maximisation of expected values.

7.5 Maximin rule

Select the alternative which maximises the minimum pay-off achievable. In the example above, the minimum pay-offs are: A £20, B £–10, C £10; on this criteria, A is chosen.

Note that this pessimistic approach seeks to achieve the best result if the worst happens.

7.6 Minimax regret rule

Select the alternative which minimises the loss through not selecting another alternative.

If the company in our example had chosen to introduce product A and subsequently demand had been high, the company would have felt no regret (ie, it was the best decision possible for that particular outcome). However, if the outcome had been medium demand and the company had chosen to introduce product A, the net income would have been £40, whereas if the product C had been chosen the net income would have been £100. Thus, the company has **lost the opportunity** to make an extra £60 net income and this can be termed the maximum extent of its regret (or opportunity cost).

You should be able to see that the maximum possible regret in respect of B occurs if demand is high (maximum regret £60), and in respect of C if demand is low (maximum regret £70). On this criteria, A and B score equally; both are preferable to C.

7.7 Expected values

The fundamental weakness of both the maximin and minimax regret rules is that they take no account of the relative likelihood of each of the possible outcomes occurring. For instance, in Example 1, if there was a 98% chance that demand would be medium and only a 2% chance of it being low or high there would be a strong temptation to choose product C (pay-off £100 when outcome is medium demand).

In order to have a rational basis for decision-making, it is therefore necessary to have some estimate of the **probabilities** of the various outcomes and then to use them in the decision criterion. Such probabilities may be **objective** or **subjective**. Objective probabilities are mathematically derived (eg, the probability of an unbiased tossed coin coming down heads is fifty per cent) or based on historical experience (eg, in a manufacturing concern, the probability of a given proportion of units proving defective can be accurately derived from past experience). Subjective probabilities, on the other hand, are someone's best estimate made without the benefit of experience (eg, in launching a new product, the probability of success will probably have to be subjectively estimated).

The third decision criterion is the **maximisation of expected value**, where the expected value of a particular action is defined as the *sum of the values of the possible outcomes, each multiplied by their respective probabilities.* Calculation of expected values is of course a familiar process in discounted cash flow (DCF) analysis.

7.8 Decision trees

So far, only a single decision has had to be made. However, the implementation of a strategic plan can consist of a rather long, drawn-out structure involving a whole sequence of actions and outcomes. Where a number of decisions have to be made sequentially, the complexity of the decision-making process increases considerably. By using **decision trees**, however, highly complex problems can be broken down into a series of simpler ones while providing, at the same time, opportunity for the decision-makers to obtain specialist advice in relation to each stage of their problem.

A **decision tree** is a way of applying the expected value criterion to situations where a number of decisions are made sequentially. It is so called because the decision alternatives are represented as **branches** in a **tree** diagram.

Having analysed the costs of various options and the likely impact on unit production costs, there are four different decision rules which could be applied.

(i) The **optimistic** decision rule would choose the best of the best outcomes for each options.

(ii) The **pessimistic** decision rule would take the entirely opposite view, In this case the best of the worst outcomes for each option is chosen.

(iii) The **regret** decision rule would favour options which minimise the lost opportunity which might occur by choosing a particular option.

(iv) The **expected value** rule introduces the **probability** that each outcome would occur. This can then be used to weigh the outcomes for each option and, then, compare the options on this basis.

7.9 Sensitivity analysis

Sensitivity analysis allows each of the important assumptions underlying a particular option to be questioned and changed. It seeks to test how sensitive the predicted performance or outcome is to each of these assumptions. Sensitivity analysis asks what would be the effect of performance if, for example, market demand grew at only 1% or as much as 10%. Its use has grown with the availability of computer spreadsheet packages which are ideally suited to this type of analysis.

The process helps management to assess the risks of making a particular strategic decision and the degree of confidence it may have in a given decision. By changing the value of different variables in the model, a number of different scenarios may be produced, allowing a full picture to emerge of how the achievement of planning targets would be affected by different values for each variable eg, wages, introduction of new machinery or sales price.

7.10 Heuristic models

Heuristic models are a means of identifying satisfactory 'solutions' in a systematic way. Where the situation is complex, when there are many options available to an organisation and many different requirements to be fulfilled, the various options are *searched* until one is found which satisfies all the criteria. This is not necessarily the best option. With the advent of cheap and powerful computers, heuristic modelling is becoming useful as an evaluation technique since the search process can be undertaken quickly even when many criteria need to be met and several hundred options exist.

7.11 Stakeholder and political risk

The objectives of an organisation should be derived by balancing the often conflicting claims of the various stakeholders (or coalitions) in the organisation. These stakeholders consist of coalitions of people within the organisation, and external groups. The organisation has responsibilities to all these groups and should formulate its strategic goals to give each a measure of satisfaction. The difficulty is balancing the conflicting interests and differing degrees of power. For example there might be conflicts of interest between a company's shareholders and its employees. If the strategy of the organisation is to truly reflect the interests of its stakeholders the strategic planner will need to consider, and be influenced by, factors relating to them. These are:

- Composition and significance of each group.
- Power that each group can exert.
- Legitimate claims that each group may have on the organisation.
- Degree to which these claims conflict and significant areas of concern.
- Extent to which the organisation is satisfying claims.
- Overall mission of the organisation.

In practice the assessment of the *political risk* inherent in various strategies can be an important deciding factor between strategies. For example, a strategy of market development might require the cutting out of wholesalers, hence running the risk of backlash which could jeopardise the success of the strategy.

Other political risk factors would include a substantial issue of new shares which might be unacceptable to unions, government or other customers. The understanding of these softer measures of risk is invariably important during strategy evaluation. It would be unwise to proceed with options which are likely to be undermined by the political activity of either consumers or other organised groups.

8 CHAPTER SUMMARY

The best known approach to portfolio analysis was developed by the Boston Consulting Group (BCG), who used a 2 x 2 matrix to plot the attractiveness of products. Their theory was based on the 'experience curve' and on a product life cycle view of markets and led to the positioning of products or businesses in one of the four quadrants. Limitations to BCG's portfolio analysis have subsequently been discovered.

The product life cycle is an important concept in marketing that provides insights into a market's dynamics. In this chapter we focused on a general description of the stages involved in a product's life. Later we will consider the marketing implications of the different stages.

Ansoff's product-market mix looks at existing and new products facing existing and new markets to show the resultant strategies and attendant risk levels. It is used to analyse the products/services offered by the organisation and the markets it sells to. The level of risk that a company undertakes, the incidence and rate of change and the way in which resources are distributed can all be controlled through analysis of this mix.

9 SELF TEST QUESTIONS

9.1 Describe the three key pieces of information which are required to draw up a BCG growth-share matrix (1.2).

9.2 Describe a 'cash cow' product (1.3).

9.3 Describe a 'star' product (1.3).

9.4 Describe a 'problem child' product (1.3).

9.5 Describe a 'dog' product (1.3).

9.6 Discuss the limitations of the BCG growth-share matrix (1.6).

9.7 Draw Ansoff's four areas in the product-market mix (2.2).

9.8 Describe the stages of the product life-cycle (4.1).

9.9 List four influences on a product's life (4.2).

9.10 Briefly describe three screening options (6.2).

9.11 Describe a decision tree (7.8).

10 EXAMINATION TYPE QUESTIONS

10.1 Megaweb Industries

Megaweb Industries is a large diversified group which operates in several industries including civil engineering, chemicals, commercial heaters and heavy electrical control gear. Each area is organised as a strategic business unit. Corporate management is finalising policy with regard to Heataweb Ltd, its commercial heater division. At present Heataweb produces a range of commercial heaters and hearing equipment, but the market is now virtually static, with only a slight growth rate, and its brand, promotional budget and geographical spread are dwarfed by three other competitors, one of which, the market leader, enjoys a market share at least three times as large as Heataweb's. On a Boston Consulting Group's growth/share matrix, this business would be called a dog. Heataweb has two manufacturing sites and Megaweb's corporate management has decided to close one site and concentrate all manufacturing into the other. A decision has not yet been reached on which site to close.

You are required to:

(a) discuss the **financial criteria** for deciding the site closure policy for Heataweb; **(10 marks)**

(b) enumerate the operational factors which corporate management should consider in deciding which site should be retained; **(8 marks)**

(c) explain what is meant by 'dog' in relation to a growth-share matrix, and describe the main issues to be examined before classifying a product as 'dog', and then formulating strategy appropriate for this category of product. **(7 marks)**

(Total: 25 marks)

10.2 The product life cycle

You are required to explain the product life-cycle concept and why it is important to a company planning for the development of new products. Illustrate your answer using examples with which you are familiar.
(25 marks)

11 ANSWERS TO EXAMINATION TYPE QUESTIONS

11.1 Megaweb Industries

(a) **Financial criteria** which should be used to decide the site closure policy for Heataweb will include the following:

1. **Rental costs**

   These vary quite considerably between different locations. Consideration should be given as to which location is cheaper. Contractual conditions for renting or leasing should also be evaluated and compared.

2. **Rateable value**

   Rates can be a major cost. Consideration should be given as to which of the two locations is cheapest. Local grants, etc, would need to be taken into account.

3. **Labour costs**

   Labour costs may be relevant. The North/South divide, a popular catch phrase used by the media, does represent a considerable difference in labour costs. Heataweb would be advised to consider and compare for each location.

   - differentiation in local pay rates;
   - the extent of competition for local labour;
   - the quality of labour available;
   - the scarcity of labour.

4. **Site valuation**

   A number of questions will be pressing:

   - Which site has the largest resale value?
   - Does the company own one site and rent/lease the other?

   The questions will provide important answers if the company is considering liquidating its investment held in property, or in comparing long-term operating costs.

5. **Cost of moving key personnel**

   It is assumed that although with the rationalisation envisaged there will be staff surplus (leading to redundancy) key personnel will move from the closing site to the one remaining. The cost of compensating staff for the disruption and inconvenience caused would need to be costed.

6. **Cost of transporting products to other market**

   The cost of transporting products to the market area of the closed site will need to be evaluated. For example, it may be advisable for Heataweb to close the site with the **smallest** market size (growth trends taken into account).

7. **Productivity**

The level of productivity, taking into account labour relations, union militancy, etc, compared between the two sites would be a further financial factor to be considered. Labour flexibility, versatility, training levels, etc, are also relevant factors.

8. **Level of technology**

The level and quality of technology (newness etc,) and the costs of increasing the level of technology in one site to meet the combined output of both would need to be costed.

9. **Level of specific (attributable) fixed cost**

Both sites would need to be compared in terms of the level of fixed cost specific to each that would be **avoided** if the site was closed. There might well be a significant difference between the two.

10. **Contribution analysis**

It can be expected that the level of all costs will differ between sites, variable as well as fixed. A **contribution analysis** taking into account sales and variable costs, including additional costs arising from the need of extra transport to the market, will provide useful data about the **financial worth** of each site.

(b) **Operational factors** that Heataweb's corporate management should consider in deciding which site should be retained are enumerated below:

1. **Labour factors**

Questions will include:

- Is one location more attractive to work and live near?
- Unemployment levels?
- Productivity levels?
- Skill levels?
- Labour problems?
- Industrial relations and organisational climate?

2. **Level and quality of plant and technology**

3. **Expansion possibilities**

Does either site present problems in terms of factory expansion? Local planning regulations and local government policy will need to be considered.

4. **Premises**

Which site has the superior premises in terms of carrying out the work required? Also local services, proximity to supply, energy supplies, etc. will need to be considered.

5. **Effect of move on customers**

Will the company lose customers because of the move? Also because of increased transport costs? Comparisons should be made between the two sites.

6. **Opposition to the move - internal**

To what extent, and in what ways, will the move be resisted by managers and employees within each site?

7. **Opposition to the move - external**

   To what extent, and in what form will the move be resisted by pressure groups, etc.? Such pressure and resistance will mostly be centred on the site gaining the additional work.

8. **Proximity to market**

   Considerations here will take into account the nearness of the market and the quality of communication links including motorways and rail links.

9. **Production systems**

   Systems are extremely important and should be considered when the value of a production unit is evaluated. The quality of production planning, material control, quality control, performance control and budgetary control systems should be included within this analysis.

10. **Preferences of senior management**

   Decision makers are often influenced by a number of factors which have indirect influence on operational performance. Costs of housing, local amenities and natural aspects of each site are likely to be considered in the final analysis.

(c) A **dog** is part of the terminology used in the work of the Boston Consulting Group (BCG) that has come to be widely recognised in business and national economic strategy. The BCG theory can in part be explained by displaying a 'growth-share' matrix, as shown below:

Rate of market growth	Relative market share: High	Relative market share: Low
High	Star	Problem child
Low	Cash cow	Dog

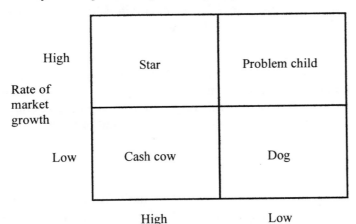

As can be seen products will fall into one of four categories - 'cash cow', 'star', 'problem child' and 'dog'.

The cash characteristics of each quadrant in the matrix are illustrated in the diagram below:

High	Cash in balance 0	Cash users
Low	Cash generators +	Cash in balance or loss -
	High	Low

'Dog' products are illustrated in the bottom right quadrant as having low relative market shares in low growth markets. The situation may have been caused by **high inflation rates, slumping market growth rates** or a **rapid shift** in patterns of consumption. It is probable that a 'dog' product faces poor future prospects with estimates of low profits or losses.

Relatively recent update in the BCG theory has suggested that there are two main categories of **Dog**:

(i) **Cash Dog**. In some markets it is extremely difficult for a product to increase its relative market share, and anyway there may be no conclusive advantages to leadership, or large growths in market share. The product may be earning a net cash inflow although not to the same levels as **Cash Cows**. The product may have developed a niche in the market. In this case it may be wise to continue marketing this product.

(ii) **Genuine Dogs**, however, due perhaps to slumping growth rates, very high inflation rates and rapidly changing patterns of consumption, have very weak competitive positions, adverse cash balances with very little prospect of becoming profitable. For such products liquidation, either immediate or gradual is likely to be the appropriate strategy.

11.2 The product life cycle

Many products pass through a number of stages in their history until they eventually decline in the face of outside competition or a change in consumer tastes. As illustrated below, it is very important to consider carefully when to start developing new products in order to achieve a steady rate of growth in both turnover and profits for the whole company.

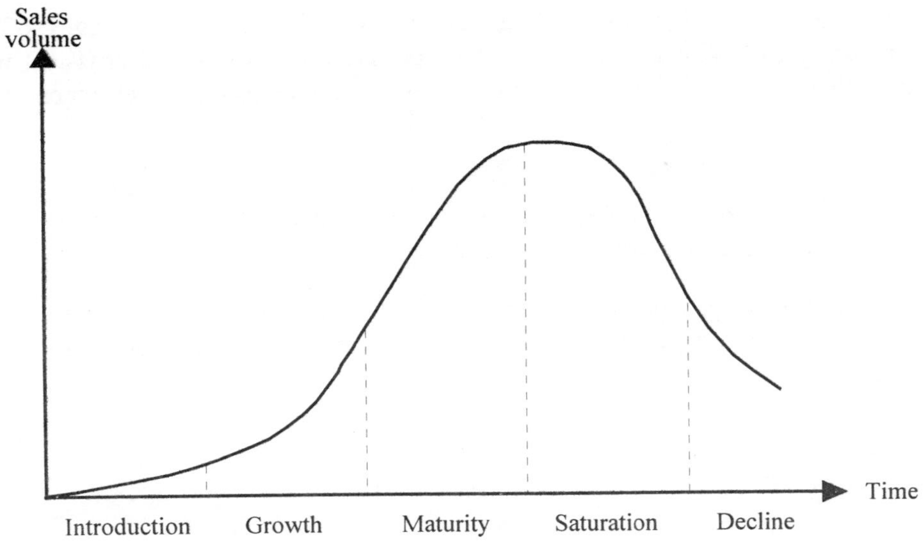

It should be noted that periods are only shown in the diagram as being of equal size for convenience. For example, product development may take three years but the product may be in decline for four years after market introduction. If this were the case, the product development of the second product would need to be started before market introduction of the first.

Some products have much longer life cycles than others - basic foodstuffs have much longer lives than more fashionable products such as clothes, although perhaps the days of the white loaf are numbered. The time required to develop a product also varies tremendously - forty years so far have been spent developing the fast breeder nuclear reactor and it is still not commercially viable. Conversely, it now takes about four years to develop a new car although the Mini took fifteen years.

It should also be realised that within an industry different products will have reached different stages which might not be typical of the industry as a whole. It is commonly believed that the electrical domestic appliance market has reached the maturity stage. However, although refrigerators are already in 90% of homes, microwave ovens have less than 15% ownership and it is consequently hardly surprising that the Japanese have decided to focus on this segment in order to enter the industry globally.

Marketing activities will change as a product passes through its life cycle. For example, strategic issues at the development stage of a grocery product would be concerned with such questions as 'What business are we in?' whilst marketing research would be concerned with new product testing. Marketing mix considerations would be at the planning stage although sales training would be taking place.

During the market introduction of the product the overall strategic decision would be whether to continue or to cancel. Marketing research would be directed at customer and consumer reactions which could lead to modifications to the product or to the pricing policy which could initially have been based on skimming or a penetration price. Promotion would be concentrating on the 'creation of demand' while the sales force would be dealing with unforeseen problems and gaining new distribution outlets.

In the growth stage the company can take risks with over-capacity and even with quality in order to establish a market position - profit margins will permit production inefficiencies. Strategic issues would include how to deal with private brands and marketing research would be focusing on brand share information. Price falls are likely and new variants would be introduced as a result of new product development. Promotion would be building up brand loyalty as the sales force battled for shelf space. Distribution would have to cope with the surge of demand as new outlets stocked up.

During maturity and saturation efficient use of plant and close attention to production costs become much more important. Strategy will be concerned with the introduction of new products and the relation of these to existing products. Marketing research will be looking for signs of market saturation and stagnation. Price will remain steady if no private brands exist; otherwise it will fall, particularly as large outlets pressure for special terms. 'Below the line' promotional expenditure will rise if private brands exist.

The decline stage will raise the question 'Do we wish to remain in business?' and how much will depend on the forecasts provided by marketing research. Prices would continue to fall and there would be greater promotional expenditure in an attempt to maintain sales.

It can therefore be seen that the product life cycle concept is not only a useful tool for analysing demand but is also valuable in managing the marketing mix during the introduction of a product and throughout its life cycle.

6 THE IMPACT OF STRATEGY ON THE ORGANISATION

INTRODUCTION & LEARNING OBJECTIVES

The first part of the chapter is devoted to an important initial stage of planning strategy - the **Position Audit**. Companies find that a useful procedure is to start with understanding the company's present position, and then to extrapolate this into the future while adjusting it for factors which are expected to produce deviations from trends.

A comparison can be made between the company's objectives and the extrapolated results, or momentum line. This shows the difference between the company's aspirations and expectations. The second part of the chapter deals with the concept of gap analysis.

We look briefly at the **Corporate Appraisal**. This stage of the strategic planning model draws on the data obtained about: objectives, current position, extrapolated position, gaps and environmental forecasts and considers the significance and implications of the company's consequential strengths, weaknesses, opportunities and threats. The appraisal involves conducting a **competence and competitive profile** of the company, its competitors and its industry and outside industries. The information when formatted would provide strategic planners with useful, probably essential, information.

One way of gaining a deeper insight into consumer needs is through value chain analysis. The value chain breaks down the firm into its strategically important activities in order to understand the behaviour of costs and the existing or potential sources of differentiation. Value activities are the technologically and physically distinct activities that an organisation performs.

When you have studied this chapter you should be able to do the following:

- Describe what an internal appraisal involves.
- Calculate a simple strategic gap.
- Know what a corporate appraisal involves.
- Discuss Porter's value chain analysis.
- Begin to understand the influence of structure and systems on strategy.

1 INTERNAL APPRAISAL OF THE ORGANISATION

1.1 Activating the problem solving process

Corporate problems are generated through the need to change existing conditions and circumstances, but the responsible executives can only begin to analyse and rectify those areas of concern drawn to their attention.

The decision process is triggered off by someone feeling that existing circumstances and conditions need to be changed and that he or she, or somebody else, should do something about it. The earlier and more positively management can identify a problem the better the chances of arriving at an acceptable solution. Monitoring devices are at their most effective when they are able to distinguish between important and insignificant signals. When immediate and drastic remedial action is called for, the signal should be strong enough to draw management's attention to the need for action, but when the problem context is more subtle the signal may be too weak to capture attention until the situation has assumed crisis proportions.

Operational and control problems will be signalled in a standardised format using standardised documentation within a management information system, so that data required for the solution of a problem will be readily available from internal sources and in a form suitable for immediate diagnosis.

With **strategic** problems it is quite possible for management to have become aware of the existence of the problem without any monitoring devices, such as by chance or through the intuition of individual managers.

The action taken on receipt of a signal indicating the existence of a problem depends primarily on the executives who receive the signal. Their reactions will depend on:

(a) Whether they consider the signal to be a genuine problem indicator, and, if so, what should be done about it.

(b) Their experience and status in the organisation. They may not be sufficiently experienced to recognise whether or not the problem merits priority treatment or should be ignored.

(c) The length of time which has elapsed between the first intimation that a problem existed and the results of the subsequent collection and analysis of relevant data.

(d) The validity of the signal.

1.2 Activity

Managers usually become aware of strategic problems without resorting to formal structured corporate audits. Use your own knowledge and experience to list how managers develop a 'feeling' (on an informal basis) that they are, or might be, facing a problem, or problems which could be of a strategic dimension.

1.3 Activity solution

The list includes:

(a) Gut feeling that something is wrong.

(b) Various stimuli, such as an increasing labour turnover, or a lengthening stock turnover period.

(c) Market signals, or 'ear twitchers', such as an increase in customer complaints, or adverse customers' reactions to marketing-mix changes made by the company, for example, price increases.

(d) Field reports from the sales force.

(e) Trade feedback.

(f) Press and media articles, such as reports about the company's competitors and their activities.

(g) Public relations activities, advertising and general promotion of the company's competitors.

(h) From internal operating control reports, such as departmental budget reports.

1.4 The formal, periodic, systematic audit approach

Managers responsible for strategic planning will pick up problem signals by such unstructured and informal ways. However, many companies, although aware of the value of intuitive and 'freewheeling' management, also recognise its limitations, and have adopted more formal approaches. A company in this category sees that there is an essential need for a system that investigates and appraises its operational performance from time to time (some do this on an annual basis) to ensure that it is effective and that its strategic structure **fits** with its changing environment and that it is dealing adequately with existing weaknesses and using the full potential of any strengths it possesses. The investigation and appraisal system is often referred to as **Position Audit**.

1.5 Position Audit

A Position Audit is an important (some would say essential) part of the strategic planning process. The carrying out of a Position Audit focuses the attention of those responsible for the formulation of strategic plans upon the question of 'where are we now?' In other words it is an examination of the organisation's **current** situation.

Definition A Position Audit is part of the planning process which examines the current state of the entity in respect of:

(a) resources of tangible and intangible assets and finance;
(b) products, brands and markets;
(c) operating systems such as production and distribution;
(d) internal organisation;
(e) current results;
(f) returns to stockholders.

The primary purpose of the Position Audit is to identify, through systematic analysis and review, the entity's current state and to isolate its strengths and weaknesses. Drucker provides us with a good explanation of the purpose of this analytical approach in his book 'Managing for Results': 'The basic business analysis starts with an examination of the business as it is now, the business as it has been bequeathed to us by the decisions, actions and results of the past. We need to see the hard skeleton, the basic stuff that is the economic structure. We need to see the relationship, and inter-relationship of resources and results, of efforts and achievements, of revenues and costs'.

A company's operational environment is composed of those dimensions which directly or indirectly influence corporate success or failure. Most external factors are beyond the control of the company, whereas **internal** dimensions are generally within its management ambit. The essential purpose of a strategic Position Audit is to collect and analyse all the relevant and available information about the company and its **current** operations which will provide strategic planners with information on:

(a) The competitive strengths and weaknesses of the company's current strategic position;

(b) The consequences of the company continuing its present strategy;

(c) The internal resources which are available for implementing any strategic change that may be required.

1.6 The detailed audit

It is not possible to provide a definitive list of the aspects that should be analysed in a strategic position audit. This must depend on the particular situation, circumstances and forces at work in the operational environment of a given organisation. However, the analytical audit approach should utilise a systematic set of questions that takes the auditor into the main areas of a company's structure and operations. For illustrative purposes, a typical position audit questionnaire form is contained in the example shown below.

POSITION EVALUATION QUESTIONNAIRE FORM

A Corporate dimension

1. Is the rate of corporate profits and profitability acceptable?

2. Are corporate resources used to their optimum effectiveness?

3. What is the nature and significance of the key factors which:

   - have shaped past corporate performances?
   - will determine the shape of the corporate future?

4. What are the actual and potential problem situations?

5. Is optimal allocation of resources between business units and products currently achieved?

6. Are acceptable operational standards and targets in use for monitoring and control purposes?

7. How does the company's operational efficiency compare with that of its major competitors?

8. How adaptable is the organisation to change?

9. Are contingency strategies available?

10. Is the company securing an adequate return on its investment in research and development?

B Market dimension

For each market the company operates in:

11. What is the speed of technological change affecting the market?

12. Is the market susceptible to the trade cycle?

13. What are the prospects of government intervention in the market?

14. What are the prospects for market growth?

15. Is the market susceptible to substitutes:
    - that the company can introduce?
    - that competitors can introduce?

16. What is the size and nature of barriers to market entry?

17. What are the prospects of new competitors entering the market?

18. What is the product life cycle position for each of the company's main products in the market?

19. What is the company's image in the market?

20. What is the company's absolute, and relative market share?

C Marketing dimension

21. Are distribution methods and channels adequate?

22. Is the market information and intelligence system adequate?

23. Is the balance between market segments optimum?

24. What are the competitive strengths or weaknesses of the company's products in terms of:
    - after-sales service?
    - quality?
    - specification?
    - packaging?
    - price?
    - standardisation?
    - guarantees?

25. What is the rate of new product development? How does this compare against main competitors?

26. Are the advertising and sales promotions effective, in terms of:
    - campaigns?
    - size of budget?
    - quality of advertising agency?
27. How adaptable is the company to customers' special requirements?
28. Does the company have adequate patent protection?
29. Is the company's sales force effective, in terms of:
    - technical expertise?
    - structure?
    - geographical location?
    - size of budget?
30. Does the company maximise the advantages of its brand names and other goodwill?

D Manufacturing dimensions

31. Is the geographical location of plant and equipment optimum?
32. Is the capacity of production facilities optimum?
33. Is the correct balance obtained between various items of plant with different optimum operational levels?
34. What is the age of plant, and the associated threat of obsolescence?
35. Are production methods, plant layout, and organisation efficient and effective?
36. Is the workforce skill and balance adequate?
37. Are quality assurance systems adequate?
38. Are inventory levels optimum?
39. What is the capacity for expansion?
40. Are the costs of manufacture competitive?

E Financial dimensions

41. Is financial performance satisfactory, in terms of:
    - return on capital employed?
    - residual income?
    - profit margin ratio?
    - sales turnover?
    - growth in sales turnover?
    - price/earnings (P/E) ratio?
    - gearing ratio?
    - interest cover?
    - dividends policy?
    - profit stability?

42. Is the financial structure satisfactory, in terms of:

- level of debtors?
- level of creditors?
- liquidity?
- investment management?

43. Are financial resources managed effectively, in terms of:

- cash at bank?
- borrowing capacity?
- cash flow?
- shareholding in other companies?

44. What is the company's financial reputation with the public? Does it need to be improved?

45. Are there alternative avenues for investing surplus funds?

46. What methods are used for financing growth? Are they the best ways?

47. Are management accounting techniques used in the evaluation of operational alternatives?

48. Are reporting procedures suitable?

49. Are resources, such as computer systems, used in the management of finance adequate?

50. Are financial projections used for evaluating current operational and investment plans and programmes? Are they accurate?

F Procurement dimension

51. Are sources of material and components reliable?

52. How do external costs compare against in-plant manufacture?

53. Are quality assurance procedures adequate?

54. Are alternative sources of supply researched and evaluated?

55. Is knowledge of new sources of supply obtained? Are these new sources researched and evaluated?

56. Are the company's negotiating skills satisfactory?

57. Are there advantages in the company owning, or part owning, its supplier(s)?

58. Are research programmes conducted by the company's major suppliers?

59. Do contingency plans exist in case of supplier default?

60. Do special relationships exist with certain suppliers? Are the benefits of these relationships maximised?

G Personnel dimension

61. Is the decision making structure effective?

62. Is the balance of experience, skills and qualifications adequate, in terms of:

- corporate and senior management?
- middle management?

- junior management?
- supervisory management?

63. How effective are the company's training schemes?

64. Is management succession planned?

65. Are the levels of staff turnover satisfactory?

66. Are industrial relations satisfactory?

67. What impact has government regulations had on the company, and likely to have in the future?

68. How effective is personnel policy, in terms of:

    - pay and conditions?
    - working environment and conditions?
    - recruitment?
    - redundancy?
    - pensions?

69. Are there particular labour problems?

70. What is the level of productivity? Could it be improved?

H Information technology (IT)

71. Is the location and capacity of IT in use optimum?

72. What methods are used for the acquisition of IT facilities?

73. Is there an overall IT strategy?

74. What actual and potential IT problems exist?

75. Is the IT security policy adequate?

76. What is the age of IT equipment, and the associated threat of obsolescence?

77. Are IT methods, and organisation structure efficient and effective? Is the IT staffing skills and balance adequate?

78. Are IT quality assurance systems adequate?

79. What is the IT capacity for expansion?

80. Are the IT costs satisfactory?

I Systems dimension

Are the following control systems adequate and complied with:

81. Security?

82. Stock control?

83. Quality control?

84. Working capital control?

85. Capital investment control?

86. Customer-credit control?

87. Production control?

88. Plant maintenance control?

89. Budgetary control?

90. Internal audit?

J Objectives dimension

91. What is the company's mission (if mission exists)? When was the mission last reviewed?

92. What are the company's objectives? What system exists for reviewing the objectives?

93. Which coalitions or power groupings influence the objectives?

94. Are the legitimate claims of coalitions being met?

95. Are the expectations of coalitions realised?

96. Are the changing values and expectations of different coalitions taken into account when plans are formulated?

97. What are the company's perceived 'social responsibilities'? Are they achieved?

98. In what ways are objectives communicated and used in the company? Are these ways effective?

99. Are existing objectives still valid?

The questionnaire indicates the comprehensive nature of the audit. The audit would cover all aspects of the company and would not just concentrate on one or two activities that seem to be problematic. Activities are interrelated and a problem in one may be caused by troubles in another.

The data obtained from the Position Audit will be input into the **'Corporate Appraisal'** stage which we examine later.

2 CORPORATE APPRAISAL

2.1 The concept

To assist in closing the gap between its predicted and desired performance, the organisation's strengths, weaknesses, opportunities and threats need to be ascertained. The work involved draws on the data obtained about objectives, current position, extrapolated position, gaps and environmental forecasts, and is sometimes called **corporate appraisal**.

Definition 'A critical assessment of the strengths and weaknesses, opportunities and threats **(SWOT analysis)** in relation to the internal and environmental factors affecting an entity in order to establish its condition prior to the preparation of the long term plan.

The factors involved in SWOT analysis are wide ranging and include decision variables which strengthen or constrain the operational powers of the company, such as the size of its markets, the competitive forces in the markets, opportunities for new products, availability of skilled labour, control of vital raw materials and access to additional capital.

2.2 Competence and competitive profile

The appraisal process will raise serious questions and may produce surprises. The findings need to be compiled into a presentation format which will take the form of what Ansoff refers to as a **Competence and Competitive Profile**. If correctly formatted and presented, the document will be a succinct summary of the appraisal and will concentrate management's attention on main areas for resolution. The company profile provides details of current and projected corporate resources in terms of capacity, location, costs, operational flexibility, relevant details of past operational performances and trends, by activities, divisions and cost centres, as well as a survey of the major influences and pressure points impacting on the operational environment, such as target markets, market shares, competitive activities, product mix, technological factors, economic trends and assumptions.

Many analytical tools have been developed over recent years to aid this process. They include:

(a) financial ratio analysis;

(b) product-market matrix displays;

(c) product-life cycle analysis.

Here we consider the overall corporate appraisal without delving into the individual techniques that might aid its process. The following table adapted from Ansoff's **Corporate Strategy** shows how a company's skills, facilities, etc, can be analysed both in relation to competitors in its own industry and more widely. Ansoff suggests that in assigning the relative ratings some companies might use a simple two-valued strength or weakness classification. Others would prefer to rank the capabilities as outstanding, average or weak.

	Facilities	Personnel	Organisational skills	Management skills
Finance & general management	Data processing equipment.	Depth of GM and Fin. skills to cope easily.	Divisional structure. Planning & control.	(a) Investment management control. (b) Centralised. Decentralised.
Research & Development	Special equipment test facilities.	Special technical skills.	Product development industrial & consumer products.	Cost-performance optimisation
Operations	Machine shop automated products.	Machine operation. Close tolerance work.	Mass production. Batch & jobbing. Quality control.	Tight scheduling. Cost control.
Marketing	Warehousing Retailing	Types of selling expertise.	Direct sales. Retail. Industrial service.	Industrial marketing. Consumer marketing.

The competence profile will serve three separate uses for assessment.

(a) **Assessment of internal strengths and weaknesses.**

The competence profile can be used to assess the company's internal resources and to determine the areas in which the company is either very good or very poor. The facts and figures required for the assessment would be obtained from the company's Position Audit.

(b) **Assessment of competitiveness**

A part of the appraisal will conduct a competence profile of each of the company's main competitors. Superposition of the company's competence profile with the respective competitive profiles measures the company's competitiveness and determines those areas where the company excels or is deficient.

(c) **Assessment of external opportunities and threats**

Another part of the appraisal will conduct a competence profile of the company's industry and outside industries. Superposition of these profiles measures the attractiveness, or otherwise, of the company's present industry and other industries. It will also measure the company's 'fit' with its existing industry, and its 'fit' with other industries thus indicating the chances of a successful entry.

3 PORTER'S VALUE CHAINS

3.1 Concept of value

The concept of value should be continually assessed from the point of view of the final consumer or user of the product or service. This may be overlooked by organisations which are distanced from their final users by intermediaries such as distributors, leaving them out of touch with the realities of their markets. The consumers' idea of value may change over time, perhaps due to competitive offerings giving better value for money becoming available.

3.2 Value chain

According to Porter, the business of an organisation is best described by way of a value chain in which total revenue minus total costs of all activities undertaken to develop and market a product or service yields value.

All organisations in a particular industry will have a similar value chain which will include activities such as obtaining raw materials, designing products, building manufacturing facilities, developing co-operative agreements, and providing customer service.

An organisation will be profitable as long as total revenues exceed the total costs incurred in creating and delivering the product or service.

It is therefore necessary that organisations should strive to understand their value chain and also that of their competitors, suppliers, distributors, etc.

The value chain, shown in the diagram below, displays total value and consists of value activities. Value activities are the physically and technologically distinct activities that an organisation performs.

The value chain

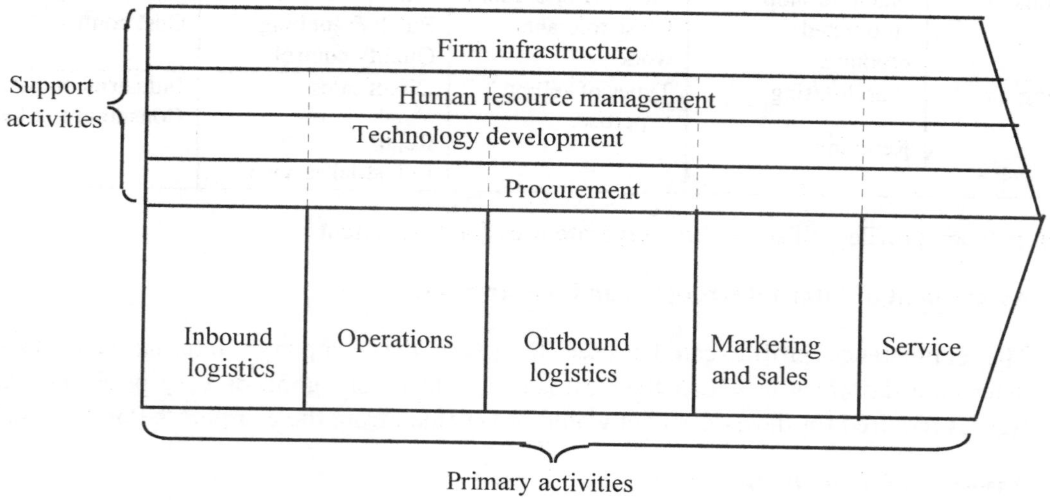

This schematic representation of the value chain clearly shows its constituent parts. The primary activities, in the lower half of the value chain, show in sequence the activities performed by the organisation in converting raw material inputs to finished products and the transfer of the product or service to the buyer and any after-sales service. These are grouped into five main areas.

(a) Inbound logistics are the activities concerned with receiving, storing and handling raw material inputs.

(b) Operations are concerned with the transformation of the raw material inputs into finished goods or services. The activities include assembly, testing, packing and equipment maintenance.

(c) Outbound logistics are concerned with the storing, distributing and delivering the finished goods to the customers.

(d) Marketing and sales are responsible for communication with the customers eg, advertising, pricing and promotion.

(e) Service covers all of the activities which occur after the point of sale eg, installation, repair and maintenance.

Each of these may be a source of advantage. Alongside all of these primary activities are the secondary, or support, activities of procurement, technology, human resource management and corporate infrastructure. Each of these cuts across all of the primary activities, as in the case of procurement where at each stage items are acquired to aid the primary functions. At the inbound logistics stage it may well be raw materials, but at the production stage capital equipment will be acquired, and so on.

To study the internal structure of the organisation using the value chain, each section must list, from the customers' viewpoint, those activities which are strategically significant in adding real value to the product or service. The value chain will differ significantly between organisations, and even between Strategic Business Units (SBUs) within one organisation.

3.3 Value systems

The company's value chain does not exist in isolation. There will be direct links between the inbound logistics of the firm and the outbound logistics of its suppliers, for example. An understanding of the value system, and how the organisation's value chain fits in to it will therefore aid in the strategic planning process.

The value system

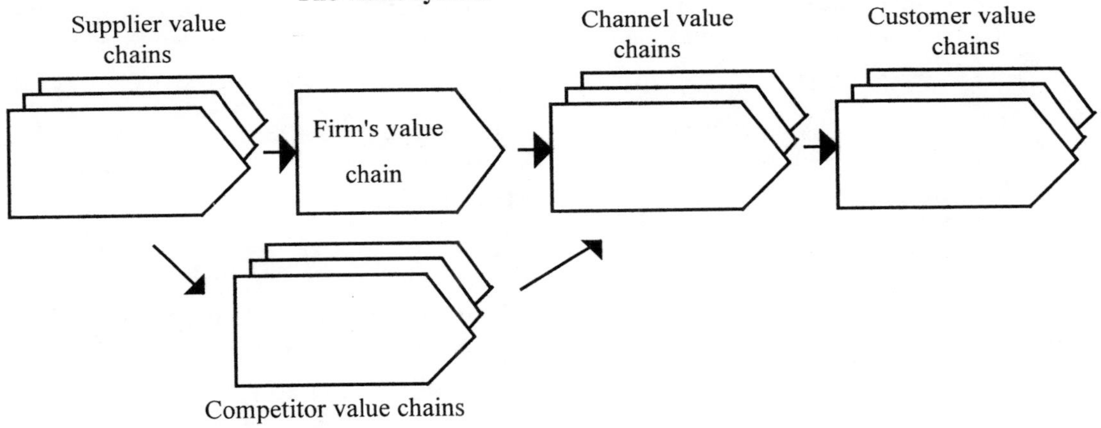

4 INFLUENCE OF STRUCTURE AND SYSTEMS ON STRATEGY

4.1 Resources

One of the notable features of value analysis is that it recognises that an organisation is much more than a random collection of machinery, money and people. These resources are of no value unless they are organised into structures, routines and systems which ensure that the products or services which are valued by the final consumer are the ones which are produced. The organisation must assess how the resources are utilised and linked to competitive advantage. An analysis of resource utilisation can be undertaken, comprising the following steps:

(i) **Identify the value activities**

This stage should include an assignment of costs and added value and an identification of the critical activities. These are the various value activities which underpin the production and delivery of its products or services, including the supply and distribution chains. It is important for the organisation to identify the value activities which are critical in terms of its competitive advantage. For example, for one organisation the low price of its product to the consumer may be underpinned by a low cost supply of parts and a low mark-up by the distributor. By strengthening and building on the key activities the organisation is likely to achieve success.

(ii) **Identify the cost or value drivers**

The factors which sustain the competitive position are called the cost drivers or value drivers. In the example of a low cost supply, the factors may be related to physical proximity of the suppliers and could disappear with geographical expansion.

(iii) **Identify the linkages**

An organisation's value activities and the linkages between them are the source of competitive advantage. There may be important links between the primary activities. To recap, these are: inbound logistics, operations, outbound logistics, marketing and sales and services. For example, good communications between sales, operations and purchasing can help cut stocks; the purchase of more expensive or more reliable machinery and equipment may lead to cost savings and quality improvements in the manufacturing process.

Choices will have to be made about the relationships and how they influence value creation and strategic capability. Holding high levels of finished goods might ease production scheduling problems and give a faster customer response time but will probably add to the overall cost of operations. An assessment as to whether the added value of high stocks is greater than the added cost needs to be made.

Linkages between the organisation's support activities may also create value. These activities, according to Porter, are the firm's infrastructure, human resource management, technological development and procurement. The extent to which human resource management has been involved in new technologies has brought about successful implementation of new production and office systems.

Because of the linkages it is important that the organisation's activities are not dealt with in isolation. Competitors can often imitate the separate activities of an organisation but it is more difficult to copy the linkages within and between value chains.

4.2 Structure of organisations

The structure of an organisation is a skeleton on which the flesh can be hung. Structure itself will not ensure the success of the strategy, although an inappropriate choice of structure could impede success. The relevance of organisation structures on the strategic planning process is viewed in two main ways by writers.

One view is that the structure of an organisation is influenced by many environmental factors and the personalities of the top management. Thus the objectives in a strategic plan must be developed within the existing organisational framework. Examples are:

(a) **Environmental**

The structure of an organisation located in a South American country will be influenced by the social/cultural background of the local employees. These influences may be dramatically different to the factors bearing on a North American organisation.

(b) **Top management**

Top management may have particular views on an appropriate leadership style. In one organisation, the view of good leadership may be 'task based'. This view is derived from the scientific management theories of Taylor. The primary concern would be achieving high levels of efficiency and people in the organisation are just a factor of production.

The organisation structure is thus regarded as on a par with an analysis of the environment. Both should be analysed at an early stage in the strategic planning process. In particular, the objectives set for a strategic plan can only be established after taking into account the 'environment' within the organisation.

As is often the case, the truth is somewhere in the middle. Ideally the structure should reflect the plan and not vice versa, but to attempt to change existing structures without care can lead to tremendous difficulties. A pragmatic approach will often be best.

5 CHAPTER SUMMARY

A company needs to understand its present position before strategy can be planned. Although managers maintain awareness of their individual positions on an informal and intuitive basis, the position of the overall organisation is more complex. Many organisations therefore conduct a periodic, formal, systematic and comprehensive analytical audit which is focused on current operational aspects, and which is sometimes called a Position Audit. The data obtained from this audit can be used to assess the company's strengths and weaknesses, to extrapolate the company's position forward in time, and to evaluate the feasibility of intended strategic changes.

The objectives of a Corporate Appraisal are to bring together all the strands of data concerning the company's objectives, present position, extrapolated position, strategic gaps and environmental forecasts and to profile the company's strengths, weaknesses, opportunities and threats. The profile will be conducted for the company's internal, competitive, and industry 'fit' positions. The information provides important, if not vital, information for strategic management, about the company's position, the extent of strategic change required and when, the resources that are available and the direction the organisation ought to be aiming for. By highlighting the company's strengths, weaknesses, opportunities and threats the profiles produced also provide management with ideas as to how gaps might best be closed.

Sometimes an internal appraisal of an organisation may not be thorough because the individual areas or activities are treated in isolation. Porter argues that competitive advantage arises out of the way in which firms organise and perform activities (referred to as value activities). Consumers purchase value for money, which they measure by comparing one organisation's product or service with similar offerings by competitors. The organisation can create value by carrying out its activities more efficiently than its rivals or it can combine its activities in such a way as to provide a unique product or service.

6 SELF TEST QUESTIONS

6.1 Define 'Position Audit' (1.5).

6.2 List 10 main areas that would be investigated in a 'Position Audit' (1.6).

6.3 Define 'Corporate appraisal' (2.1).

6.4 Describe the three types of assessment which use the competence profile (2.2).

6.5 What are the four support activities in Porter's value chain? (3.2).

6.6 Describe the primary activities in the value chain (3.2).

6.7 List the three steps in analysing resource utilisation (4.1).

7 EXAMINATION TYPE QUESTION

7.1 Strengths And Weaknesses

In ascertaining an organisation's strengths and weaknesses, management often concentrate on certain key areas. You are required to specify and describe five key areas and explain the way that an assessment of this type may be conducted. **(25 marks)**

8 ANSWER TO EXAMINATION TYPE QUESTION

8.1 Strengths And Weaknesses

When conducting a survey of the strengths and weaknesses of an organisation, invariably there is a tendency for management to concentrate on certain aspects of the operation. This is not to say however, that the extent of the survey will be identical in each area on every occasion. Neither does it imply that other areas of investigation should automatically be eliminated. A strengths and weaknesses appraisal is part of the work of a position audit.

(a) **Financial resources**

As with internal appraisal, this consists of constructing a series of accounting ratios to measure profitability, growth and liquidity, and then comparing them with earlier results and also with results of other firms in similar circumstances. Such an exercise will indicate the firm's strengths and weaknesses both in terms of former occasions and current competitiveness.

(b) **Profitability**

This involves a series of analyses each with the aim of identifying the organisation's operational position. For example, it might include an analysis of sales and profit involving sales mix, pricing strategy, discount facilities, and an assessment of the returns on total assets employed. Costs obviously have important implications for profitability and therefore, determination of operational costs and internal efficiency is also required.

(c) **Effectiveness of functional departments within the organisation**

This is normally done by defining the specialist knowledge available, specialist activities undertaken, the significant factors on which the company depends, including the areas of vulnerability.

During the exercise these issues will be raised in connection with all the functional activities and in addition, it is necessary to ascertain specific details for each function. For example, the plant utilisation rate, the proportion of bad debts, the extent of production delays due to failure of supplies etc.

(d) **Product range**

Frequently companies have an extensive product range which needs frequent reviewing to ensure that it is well balanced and relevant to current market needs. This involves the determination of the profit contribution of each product in relationship to the resources it utilises. It is also necessary to pay particular attention to market trends to ascertain whether in the product mix, certain products need upgrading whilst others require phasing out. In addition, there is the need to establish the position regarding the introduction of new products, both in terms of frequency and timing, to ensure the company's competitive position is maintained. All these various activities add up to an extensive marketing research assignment.

(e) **Human resources of the organisation**

Any such appraisal must ensure that personnel are suitably motivated and adequate facilities are available for appropriate staff development. One technique which many companies have adopted in one form or another, is management by objectives (MBO). This includes establishing key tasks for a job, agreed performance standards and providing suitable encouragement for such standards to be achieved and is followed by a subsequent stage in which a review is conducted involving the managers and their superiors to compare actual performance against the standards agreed. It also provides from time to time, an assessment of the potential of each manager.

Whatever form of management style the organisation uses it is essential that a thorough assessment of the human resources of the organisation is carried out with the main purpose of ensuring that the manpower resources of the company match both the current technical and social skills requirements, and also those that it is anticipated will be required in the future.

In addition, it is necessary to ensure that the organisational structure is the most suitable for present day needs. With rapid technological, economic, political and sociological changes, an organisation can rapidly become out of date. Conducting frequent organisational appraisals should avoid this happening.

Therefore, it can be seen that an appraisal of the firm's strengths and weaknesses is a considerable task with a notable contribution required from the accountant. The exercise involves considerable analysis and invariably leads to certain criticisms of the existing arrangements. Such criticisms, even if only implied, may not always be readily acceptable but must be carried out, and carried out authentically, if the company is to obtain the maximum benefit from an appraisal of its strengths and weaknesses.

7 CULTURE OF THE ORGANISATION

INTRODUCTION & LEARNING OBJECTIVES

Managers' perceptions of the world, like everyone else's, are coloured by their background and experience, and this can critically affect the decision-making process in the organisation.

Their view of the competition will be influenced by remarks made by customers, by their advertisements, reported and rumoured performance, as well as comments made by ex-employees and other managers. This information may then be interpreted by management to fit a stereotype of a particular competitor, based on some past experience where the organisation either 'won' or 'lost' some battle with the competition.

Strong shared values and beliefs can be a tremendous driving force in the organisation. However, these values are deep-rooted and cannot be changed easily. They tend to be a stabilising force keeping the status quo in the organisation and may cause problems if they do not support the preferred organisational strategy.

This chapter considers the main issue of organisational culture. This topic has been paramount in management thinking over the past decade and the business pages of newspapers constantly carry company references to:

- 'Going back to care'.
- 'Promoting a corporate image'.
- 'Developing a customer based culture' etc.

The existence of culture and the process of changing and developing an organisation's culture affects every aspect of every management position. It therefore touches each chapter in this text.

When you have studied this chapter you should be able to do the following:

- Define and explain culture.
- Assess the management of culture and its effect upon individuals.
- Describe the types of culture.
- Discuss the concept of excellence.
- Outline the cultural influence on strategy.

1 CULTURE AND ORGANISATION

1.1 Introduction

The term culture has its origins in the work of social anthropologists who used the term to refer to 'the complex whole which includes knowledge, belief, art, law, morals, custom and the many other capabilities and habits acquired by a person as a member of a society'. The term was used to refer to total societies, the external environment of the organisation. However, since the mid-1970s the concept of culture has been increasingly applied to organisations. Each organisation is seen as possessing its own distinctive culture, which not only provides a basis for understanding organisational behaviour but also is a key determinant of organisational success.

1.2 The definition of organisational culture

There is no shortage of definitions of organisational culture. It has been described, for example, as 'the dominant values espoused by an organisation', 'the philosophy that guides an organisation's policy toward employees and customers', 'the basic assumptions and beliefs that are shared by members of an organisation'. More simply culture has been referred to as the 'way things are done around here'. Despite the variety it is possible to distil the common characteristics and recognise the common features of the definitions.

In every organisation there has evolved, over time, a system of beliefs, values, symbols, myths and practices which are shared by members of the organisation. Culture refers to the shared understandings and meanings that members have concerning an organisation. Rather as individuals have distinctive personalities, organisations have their own particular culture. Some will be friendly, relaxed and informal whilst others will be highly formal, aloof and hostile. This raises the important issue of whether there is a 'right' culture for an organisation, and we shall address this question later.

1.3 Major influences on culture

A problem stemming from the definitions of culture we have looked at is that they do not provide a structured approach to analysing the culture of an organisation. However, Robbins suggests that we can identify ten key characteristics which influence an organisation's culture:

(a) Individual initiative - the degree of responsibility, freedom and independence that individuals have.

(b) Risk tolerance - the degree to which employees are encouraged to be aggressive, innovative and risk-taking.

(c) Direction - the degree to which the organisation creates clear objectives and performance expectations.

(d) Integration - the degree to which units in the organisation are encouraged to operate in a co-ordinated manner.

(e) Management contact - the degree to which managers provide clear communication, assistance and support to their subordinates.

(f) Control - the degree of rules and regulations, and the amount of direct supervision, that are used to oversee and control employee behaviour.

(g) Identity - the degree to which members identify with the organisation as a whole rather than with their particular work group or field of professional expertise.

(h) Reward system - the degree to which reward allocations (ie, salary increases, promotions) are based on employee performance criteria.

(i) Conflict tolerance - the degree to which employees are encouraged to air conflicts and grievances openly.

(j) Communication patterns - the degree to which organisational communications are restricted to the formal hierarchy of command.

These ten characteristics provide a framework for analysing the culture of any organisation.

Morse and Lorsch identify seven elements that affect an organisation's culture:

(a) structural orientation (eg, centralised, or satellite branches?);
(b) distribution of influence (eg size of the business);
(c) character of superior/subordinate relationships (eg, how is management carried out?);
(d) relations between staff (eg, good in small, skilled teams);
(e) time orientation (eg, do we take a short or long term view?);
(f) goal orientation (eg, people working only for money); and
(g) management style (eg, 'X' or 'Y').

1.4 Types of culture

A different approach is adopted by Handy in his book **Understanding Organizations**. He cites Harrison's four basic classifications of the types of culture one might expect to find in an organisation ie, the power culture, the role culture, the task culture and the person culture.

(a) **The power culture**

Here there is one major source of power and influence. This is most likely to be the owners of the organisation (in a small firm the original founders, in a large firm the major shareholding individuals). In this type of culture there are few procedures and rules of a formal kind. The major decisions are taken by key individuals; others use broad guidelines or knowledge of what has happened previously to decide what should be done. This suggests that this kind of organisation can be very adaptive to changing conditions though this is, of course, dependent on the abilities of the key decision makers. The power culture tends to be found in small organisations where the pattern of communication is simpler than in large ones. Examples: entrepreneur heading small company.

(b) **The role culture**

In this version of culture there is a formality of organisational structure, procedures and rules which determine what is to be done. In other words, it is a bureaucratic organisation. It is a 'role culture' in that people act in terms of the roles specified by the job descriptions.

The structure determines the authority and responsibility of individuals and these boundaries are not to be crossed by any individual. Individual personalities are unimportant; it is the job that counts. This is a feature of many large bureaucracies. People describe their job by its duties, **not** by its purpose.

This kind of culture is best suited to an environment which is relatively stable and a large-sized organisation. Although it can adapt, this ability is restricted and a 'role culture' will have problems in surviving a dramatic change. Examples: civil service, ICI.

(c) **The task culture**

Task culture is best seen in teams established to achieve specific tasks ie, project teams where the emphasis is on the execution of a particular task. People describe their positions in terms of the results they are achieving.

Note: the life of the team lasts for the duration of the task and it ceases to exist after completion. This type of culture is often found in rapidly changing organisations where groups are established on a short-term basis to deal with a particular change. Structurally this culture is often associated with the matrix structure. Examples: market research organisations, entertainment industry, computer software design.

(d) **The person culture**

Less common than any of the other cultures, the person culture is characterised by the fact that it exists to satisfy the requirements of the particular individual(s) involved in the organisation. If there is a small, highly participatory organisation where individuals undertake all the duties themselves, one will find the person culture. More commonly, a key individual heads a support team of different skills. Examples: barrister in chambers.

Handy's classification, like Robbins', gives a means of analysing the specific features of the culture of any organisation.

1.5 Are cultures uniform?

We are perhaps mistaken to speak of **an** organisational culture. Though it may well be that an organisation possesses a dominant culture it is not always shared by all members. Groups form in organisations eg, departments and informal work groups who create distinctive shared understandings of their own. This leads to the existence of **sub-cultures** which, though they may share the core features of the whole organisation, are nonetheless distinct. For example a Research and Development department may well have its unique culture as a result of its specialist role, its qualified staff and its geographical separation from other employees.

At the extreme, organisations may be faced with the existence of **counter-cultures** where the aim is to undermine the dominant culture. Examples of this might be in groups which seek to undermine management control, groups who practise vandalism and sabotage, or groups who are simply alienated and apathetic.

In the light of these observations it is important to remember that most writers on organisational culture are referring to the **dominant culture** and tend to ignore or underplay the existence of sub-or-counter cultures.

1.6 Culture and organisational effectiveness

An initial point that should be made here is that until the late 1970s organisations were, for the most part, seen as rational means of co-ordinating and controlling a group of people. Effectiveness was to be achieved by a purely rational approach. Just as decisions needed to be taken on the most rational basis, so organisational problems of size and structure had to have rational solutions. The idea that factors such as myths and symbols, values and beliefs can affect organisational effectiveness is relatively new and increasingly influential.

A simple distinction can be drawn between strong and weak cultures. A strong culture is marked by the organisation's core values being both intensely held and widely shared. On the other hand, weak cultures show a lack of uniformity and limited commitment. Some writers, noticeably Peters and Waterman in their book **In Search of Excellence**, have suggested that a strong organisational culture is a key factor in determining organisational effectiveness.

2 THE CONCEPT OF EXCELLENCE

2.1 The importance of cultural factors

Following the impact of Peters and Waterman's much acclaimed book there has been an increasing emphasis placed on the importance of cultural factors in developing standards of quality and excellence.

This culture needs to exist at all levels within the company, not just at senior management level. Peters and Waterman show that employees tend to welcome the norms associated with this definite culture or else they leave.

Peters and Waterman suggest from their analysis of 'excellent' organisations that there is a common set of shared values which are to be found in all of them. The study looked at organisations in the United States which had performed consistently well, in terms of innovation and return on investment, over a twenty year period. These are listed below:

Excellent companies

Amdahl	Intel
Amoco	IBM
Avon	Johnson & Johnson
Boeing	K-mart
Bristol-Myers	Levi Strauss
Caterpillar	Marriott

Chesebrough-Pond's	McDonald's
Dana Corp.	Maytag
Data General	Merck
Delta Airlines	3M
Digital Equipment	Nat. Semiconductor
Disney Productions	Procter & Gamble
Dow Chemical	Raychem
DuPont	Revlon
Eastman Kodak	Schlumberger
Emerson Electric	Texas Instruments
Fluor	Wal-Mart
Hewlett Packard	Wang Labs

However, some five years after the above list was produced, Fortune magazine carried an article suggesting that several of the companies no longer qualified for the term 'excellent companies'.

2.2 Shared values

Peters and Waterman recognised that a clear, coherent culture was evident in excellent companies. This culture varies between organisations and is expressed distinctly in different companies:

(a) IBM bases its culture on service;
(b) McDonald's is based on consistent quality.

The main aspects of culture in 'excellent' companies are:

(a) **A bias for action** - an urgency to produce and complete results rather than analyse obstacles to action. A positive attitude of 'what can we do now' rather than a negative attitude of 'what is preventing us'.

(b) **Hands-on, value driven** - showing a commitment to the organisational values.

(c) **Close to the customer** - a continuous pursuit to understand the customer's needs and improve the quality offered. Peters and Waterman see improving quality as a motivating force for workers as well as affording opportunities for employees to be innovative. Their concern for quality and customer needs must exist in all functions at all levels.

(d) **Stick to the knitting** - no evidence of conglomerate diversification.

(e) **Autonomy and entrepreneurship** - teams and individuals are encouraged to establish their own targets for improvement. An element of competition is regarded as invigorating. This self-improvement drive encourages innovation and a customer satisfaction based culture.

(f) **Simple form, lean staff** - uncomplicated structures without large numbers of employees at head office.

(g) **Productivity through people** - staff must be treated as intelligent contributors, who are individually valuable and capable of 'extraordinary effort'. Sir John Harvey-Jones in his experience at ICI states that he never ceased to be surprised at the exceptional results that motivated people were capable of achieving.

(h) **Simultaneous tight-loose properties** - tight controls and detailed rules were replaced by common understanding and acceptance of the main guiding values of the organisation. Clearly this philosophy affects a company's recruitment, training and promotion standards and is not attainable overnight. Rather there is a steady change in the balance between control and trust.

(Source: In Search of Excellence, Peters and Waterman, (1982))

2.3 Activity

Peters and Waterman state that staff are capable of exceptional loyalty and effort if the organisation culture is attuned to this. How could this occur?

2.4 Activity solution

Peters and Waterman list three basic requirements:

(a) The tasks must be obviously worthwhile eg, creating satisfied customers, so engendering pride in staff.

(b) Staff individuals are treated as winners. Positive attitudes and contributions are highlighted.

(c) The organisation of work allows staff to satisfy the two desires of being highly regarded in their own right and also as a welcomed member of a successful group.

3 CULTURAL INFLUENCE ON STRATEGY

3.1 Matching objectives

Peters and Waterman's arguments are very persuasive and supported by much evidence, but can we conclude that a strong culture is always desirable? The first point that needs to be made is that the content of the culture must match the objectives and the environment of the organisation. A strong innovative culture, for example, will only work well if the company wishes to innovate and is operating in a dynamic environment. Strong cultures will always be more difficult to change than weak ones. A strong culture might be based on values that are not compatible with organisational effectiveness; for example, certain loyalties may restrict the process of change. Problems clearly can arise in a merger or acquisition situation where two conflicting organisational cultures are brought together.

Though a strong culture may be a liability we should not forget the potential benefits. A strong culture increases commitment to the organisation and the consistency of behaviour of its members. Having a clear mission and agreed values about the means of pursuing it removes ambiguities and can replace the need for more formal controls. An **appropriate** culture, as Peters and Waterman suggest, can be a crucial factor in determining levels of performance, both for the organisation and for the individual.

3.2 Culture and developing strategy

There are many factors which influence the expectations that people are likely to have of an organisation, as shown in the diagram below:

Influences on strategy

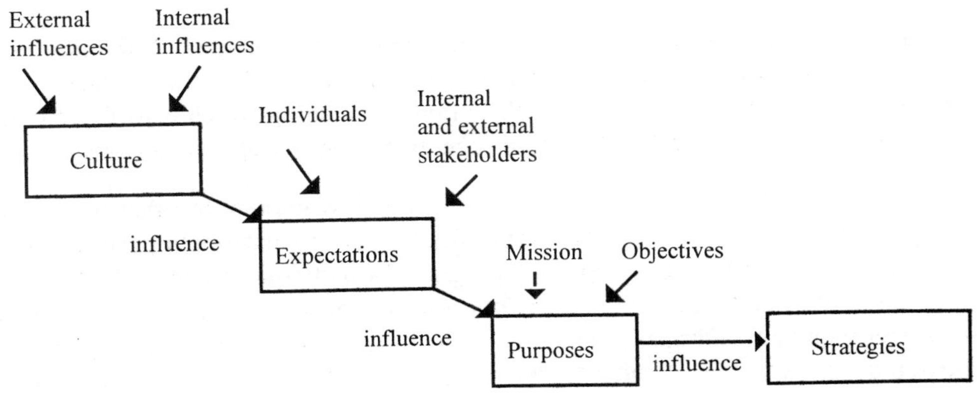

The significance of these factors in the strategic development must be analysed carefully. There are three main questions which must be addressed:

(a) Which factors inside and outside the organisation have most influence on people's expectations?

(b) To what extent do current strategies reflect the influence of any one factor or combination of factors?

(c) How far would these factors help or hinder the pursuit of new strategies?

3.3 The growth and maintenance of organisational culture

The origins of the culture of an organisation are logically sought in the influence, style and goals of the founders of the organisation. Founders begin with an original idea, unconstrained by previous ways of doing things and therefore able to impose their vision of how and why things should be done. They play a major role in establishing custom and traditions. The influence of founders and the early members of the organisation often lasts well beyond their life span.

There are many examples of founders of organisations such as Henry Ford at the Ford Motor Company and David Packard at Hewlett Packard who have had profound and lasting effects on their organisation's culture. If we take the example of Thomas Watson at IBM we can see that though he died in 1956 his influence is still felt in the research and development policies, the mode of dress of employees and the compensation policies adopted by the company today.

We can distinguish three main sources of the maintenance of culture:

(a) **Top management** - because of their power and influence, top managers have a considerable influence in either sustaining or modifying organisational culture. Their behaviour will be observed by other employees and they will establish norms of behaviour that will filter throughout the organisation.

(b) **Selection** - the selection/rejection decision can be taken on the basis that a potential recruit will or will not help in maintaining the existing culture.

(c) **Socialisation** - organisational socialisation is the process of indoctrination into the culture of the organisation. Frequently this is done by some form of induction training but in many organisations there are also informal practices which serve a similar function. Typically the new employee is told 'how things are done around here' both in the training situation and as words of advice from superior and colleagues.

Culture is often transmitted through the medium of stories, myths, rituals, material symbols and the special language (eg, acronyms and jargon) that are unique to the particular organisation.

3.4 The management of culture

Organisational cultures will exist, be they weak or strong, planned or unplanned. Sub-cultures and/or counter-cultures are frequently present. The culture of any organisation will be the product of complex human interaction over time. All of these factors make culture something which is difficult to manage or formulate. In essence, you cannot start with a clean sheet in any organisation at any stage.

However, the implications of studies such as those of Peters and Waterman are that there is a clear need to manage organisational culture. It is so intrinsically tied to organisational performance that it would be foolish to ignore it. Culture develops in the light of a particular set of circumstances, at a certain time and in the light of certain conditions. Times and circumstances change and an old culture may well impede rather than help an organisation cope with change. In such cases management would need to intervene to modify the culture by altering those factors which sustain the present culture.

The argument is that if culture can be learned, it can also be unlearned and replaced by a new, more appropriate culture. Thus, management might seek to change culture by appointing people who are sympathetic to the new culture, introduce new training and socialisation devices and change the stories, myths, rituals, language and material symbols that are part of the traditional culture.

Cultures take a long time to develop, and once socialised, people are likely to be very resistant to changes in their culture. Some critics have said that the timescale of managing cultural change makes it an impractical proposition. Employees may well have chosen to work in an organisation because they find it compatible with their own norms and values and any attempts to change culture will lead to aggression, apathy, absenteeism or a high labour turnover.

Robbins suggests the following list of activities which can be undertaken to accomplish cultural change:

(a) Have top management become positive role models, setting the tone through their behaviour.

(b) Create new stories, symbols and rituals to replace those currently in vogue.

(c) Select, promote and support employees who espouse the new values that are sought.

(d) Redesign socialisation processes to align with new values.

(e) Change the reward system to encourage the acceptance of a new set of values.

(f) Replace unwritten norms with formal rules and regulations that are tightly enforced.

(g) Shake up current sub-cultures through extensive use of job rotation.

(h) Work to get peer group consensus through utilisation of employee participation and the creation of a climate with a high level of trust.

4 CHAPTER SUMMARY

Culture is an important influence on every aspect of a company's operations. Despite this, many practising managers are unable to define and explain the concept. This is because they are not attuned to looking at the organisation as being in a state of constant flux; instead they see change as a temporary occurrence between periods of stability. Peters and Waterman explain the need to develop an overall set of values which staff naturally adopt in their day to day thinking. Within this, they have autonomy to operate in their own way, ie, they are encouraged to try and make mistakes rather than not try at all.

The management of culture is problematic and is always likely to be a long-term process. Conditions have to be favourable, and even then, cultural change has to be seen as a long-term process to be accomplished in years rather than months. Despite the difficulties, the management of culture is now seen as a major responsibility, not only of top management who set the culture for the whole organisation, but also of all managers with responsibilities for sub-groups in the organisation.

Though the term culture is normally applied to large groups eg, societies and organisations, it should be remembered that it has major and profound impacts on the individual, both employer and employee.

Increasingly, the concept of culture is used to highlight other managerial problems, in particular the problems of one culture eg, the Japanese establishing businesses in other cultures such as European societies. This raises issues of both national and organisational culture.

5 SELF TEST QUESTIONS

5.1 Define culture (1.2).

5.2 List Robbin's ten aspects of culture (1.3).

5.3 Explain Harrison's four classes of culture (1.4).

5.4 What are the common values of excellence? (2.2).

6 EXAMINATION TYPE QUESTION

6.1 Cultures in 'excellent' organisations

What, according to Peters and Waterman, are the characteristics of the culture of the 'excellent' organisation? Comment on the possible drawbacks of a strong organisational culture. **(20 marks)**

7 ANSWER TO EXAMINATION TYPE QUESTION

7.1 Cultures in 'excellent' organisations

Peters and Waterman identified the following core values that were associated with 'excellent' organisations:

(a) **A bias for action** - the excellent companies get on with it. They are analytical in their decision making but this does not paralyse them as it does with some companies.

(b) **Close to the customer** - they get to know their customers and provide them with quality, reliability and service.

(c) **Autonomy and entrepreneurship** - leaders and innovators are fostered and given scope.

(d) **Productivity through people** - they really believe that the basis for quality and productivity is the employee. They do not just pay lip service to the notion 'people are our most important asset'. They do something about it by encouraging commitment and getting everyone involved.

(e) **Hands-on, value driven** - the people who run the organisation get close to those who work for them and ensure that the organisation's values are understood and acted upon.

(f) **Stick to the knitting** - the successful organisations stay reasonably close to the businesses they know.

(g) **Simple form, lean staff** - the organisation structure is simple and corporate staff are kept to the minimum.

(h) **Simultaneous loose-tight properties** - they are both centralised and decentralised. They push decisions and autonomy as far down the organisation as they can get, into individual units and profit centres. But, as Peters and Waterman state, 'they are fanatic centralists around the few core values they hold dear'.

Though Peters and Waterman stress the positive benefits of having a strong organisational culture there are also potential drawbacks:

(a) Strong cultures are difficult to change.

(b) Strong cultures may stress inappropriate values.

(c) Where two strong cultures come into contact, eg, in a merger, then conflicts can arise.

(d) A strong culture may not be attuned to the environment eg, a strong innovative culture is only appropriate in a dynamic, shifting environment.

Despite these problems it is still possible to agree with Alan Sugar, Chairman of Amstrad, who said in 1987 'It is essential to retain a strong corporate culture and philosophy, otherwise the business can drift and become confused and lost in direction'.

8 THE WORLD IN WHICH WE LIVE

INTRODUCTION & LEARNING OBJECTIVES

The market for many goods and services today has become much more international, if not global. The concept of 'excellence' has generated a preoccupation with high performance and 'world class' organisational standards.

There has been growing attention to the development of international companies in the past few decades. Before 1992 some large companies saw a threat to their future expansion by the development of trade barriers around Europe. This led Japanese companies to establish production units in the UK (Nissan in the North East is an example) and other companies to take over a company already established within the community (Nestle's take-over of Rowntree is an example here).

There has also been a growing concern that international companies are in a position to abuse their power by acting as if they were independent of local laws and customs. We must remember that many multinationals have an income greater than many nations. The oil companies are very conscious of their possible vulnerability in this area of criticism.

When you have studied this chapter you should be able to do the following:

- Explain the global environment.
- Outline the key aspects of an international business environment.
- Discuss the effect of an international environment on organisations.
- Describe the alternative ways to enter foreign markets.
- Discuss recent trends and developments in global business strategy
- Outline the competitive advantage of nations.
- Discuss the impact of the global market.
- Analyse the effects of cultural differences.

1 THE GLOBAL ENVIRONMENT

1.1 Likely aspects of the international business environment

Even companies not marketing internationally also need to appraise the international economic environment. A company is essentially a resource-conversion engine that consumes material, labour, machines and funds. The necessary resources are often obtained from overseas sources, even if indirectly. How well the company buys depends on how well it grasps the workings of the international commodity and currency-exchange markets. Appraisal of the international environment by multinationals and other companies is largely a matter of forecasting the character of, and estimating the rate of change within, its various segments: geographical regions, countries, etc. This often involves assessment of all, or some of, the relevant factors.

(a) Comparable rates of inflation in different countries.

(b) Comparable gross national products (GNP).

(c) Comparable wage levels, and labour availability and quality.

(d) Nature and extent of exchange controls in specific countries (including selective monetary controls and discriminatory exchange rate policies).

(e) Extent of protectionism against imports (quotas and trade control regulations).

(f) Levels of corporate, personal, excise and indirect **taxes** in different countries.

(g) Development of international trading communities such as the European Community (EC), the Pacific Rim and North American blocks and the problems and opportunities of trading with companies within them.

(h) Exchange rates between different currencies, and the movement of these rates.

(i) Nature, and extent, of the comparative advantages obtained by operating in different countries.

(j) Political stability in the country or region.

(k) Extent of counter-trade (where both seller and buyer is dependent on co-operative participation and where they support each other).

In order to sell the F16 fighter plane to Belgium, Holland, Norway and Denmark, the General Dynamics Corporation agreed to arrangements which offset purchase costs against local manufacture of components and partial assembly in all four of the countries involved.

One of the most significant developments to occur in business over the past quarter of a century has been its increasing internationalisation. International trade, has of course, always existed; what is new is its scale and penetration. This is evidenced by a number of factors.

(a) The standardisation and integration of operations between subsidiaries in different countries eg, car manufacturing.

(b) The growth and power of multinationals, so that today they form some of the largest economic units in the world.

(c) The interdependence of the world economy.

1.2 Multinational companies

(a) Characteristics

Companies often develop businesses in several international markets and get involved in overseas ventures. A company may export to one country, licence to another, own a subsidiary in a third and have a joint-ownership venture in a fourth. Sooner or later it will create an international division, and have one, or a number, of overseas subsidiary companies to handle its international activities. The international division will be organised according to particular needs, by geographical region, product-group or matrix. A major disadvantage of the international divisional concept is that the corporate management may regard it as just another division and never get involved enough to appreciate its cultural and economic differences, and plan for global marketing.

While it is not practical to attempt a definitive identikit of a modern multinational company (MNC) because of the variety of organisational structures, industries, products, management philosophies, investments, sales volumes, relationships between parent companies and host governments, it is possible to draw up a set of characteristics which most possess.

- They comprise overseas subsidiaries which are complete industrial and/or commercial organisations covering research and development, manufacturing, selling and after-sales activities.

- There is involvement in numerous countries, which may be at different stages of economic and political development.

- The formulation of a universally accepted and understood corporate policy for the guidance and direction of the overseas subsidiaries in pursuit of declared aims and objectives.

(b) **Motives of multinationals**

The driving force behind the growth and expansion of MNCs is the belief that vertically integrated companies linked by a global strategic plan should possess a distinct competitive advantage over under-capitalised and technologically-backward local companies in the exploitation of any potentially profitable overseas markets. The reasons why MNCs possess this distinctive advantage are reasonably clear.

- Effectiveness in mobilising, directing and controlling the resources at their disposal.
- Better opportunities of achieving economies of scale because of their larger production base and market horizons.
- Able to draw on a wealth of corporate experience in strategic planning, forecasting, market research, finance, production and marketing (particularly in the fields of product positioning, pricing, advertising and promotional budgeting, and distribution).
- Ability to keep in close and constant touch with their overseas subsidiaries by the use of high capacity cable, distributed database systems, satellite communications, and efficient airline systems.

  For example, Unilever have categorically stated that one of their prime objectives is to invest capital wherever profitable opportunities exist, and if these opportunities occur more frequently overseas, then so be it.

(c) **International sourcing**

Another motive for overseas investment has been the attempt to secure and protect supplies of key raw materials, prompted by the prominence given to the threats of world-wide shortage of natural resources, and/or their politicisation. Moves by MNCs have been counter-balanced since the early 1970s by host countries who have become increasingly reluctant to allow foreign countries to control the extraction and processing of their prized indigenous raw materials.

The comparatively lower labour costs of many overseas countries has also been an incentive to MNCs to transfer the manufacture of their products to selected areas of the world.

For example, in May 1990 Japanese car giant Toyota began building a £700 million assembly plant at Burnston, just outside Derby. It was planned that on completion the plant would cover 2 million square feet and produce 100,000 cars a year, at full capacity. The Toyota factory is significant, not just for the size of the investment, but for the way in which it highlights the plight of the British automotive industry over the past 25 years. While Ford, British Leyland and General Motors were putting their workers on short-time, the Japanese were investing heavily and planning their assault on Europe from the bastion of Britain.

2 THE EFFECT OF AN INTERNATIONAL ENVIRONMENT ON ORGANISATIONS

2.1 The complexity of international operations

Operational activities conducted on an international scale are far more complex than those confined to the domestic field.

- Communication with subsidiaries is more difficult; documentation procedures tend to lengthen the delivery chain; while the lack of immediate and close contact with overseas customers tends to escalate trivial complaints over such matters as quality and reliability into major issues.
- Where the MNC is a leader in its industry, the problems of the industry tend to hit the MNC more heavily than a smaller company. Industrial problems are often compounded by oil price

rises, sluggish development of the home market, industrial disputes, inflation, high interest rates, and world recession.

- Restrictions are imposed by host governments. Whereas the MNC will be principally concerned with prospective return on its capital invested, the host government will be concerned with:

  - number of local people employed, and wage rates paid;
  - contribution of the MNC to the local GNP;
  - percentage of control exercised by nationals;
  - imposition of taxes, currency movement;
  - transfer pricing;
  - environmental pollution; and
  - degree to which the MNC can assist in strengthening the home industrial base.

- The co-ordination and control of activities of a heterogeneous group of overseas companies operating in countries with a diverse range of cultures and languages; at different stages of industrial, commercial and social development; and with no apparent common purchasing behavioural patters; raises unique problems. There is no **folklore** to which companies can refer, and central management has to develop its own set of rules, procedures and principles. We discuss this problem more fully in the following sub-sections.

- Exchange rate fluctuations; transfer of capital into and out of subsidiaries; and cross border transfer pricing.

- The split between centralised and decentralised control ie, the degree of independence to be given (or taken by) overseas subsidiaries.

- Deployment of limited resources for investment, and the reconciliation of potentially divisive needs and demands of overseas companies and countries.

- Reconciliation of conflicting pressures from overseas markets which are subject to different cultures, political climates, language, geography, time zones, buying behaviour patterns, buying power and susceptibility to advertising and promotion campaigns.

- The growing complexity of the legal environments affecting MNCs. Basically, a government can only effectively legislate for the activities of those of its citizens and companies living or operating within its boundaries. At law, most countries appear to regard MNCs and their overseas affiliates as part of a unitary enterprise, but the plain fact is that the national governments accord anti-trust measures and restrictive practices different levels of priority. The regulations of the European Community are a minefield for MNCs. We shall briefly examine the problems later.

2.2 Distinction between 'top-down' and 'bottom-up' strategic planning

It is also important to recognise the distinction between 'top-down' and 'bottom-up' strategic planning.

- *'Top-down'* planning, or policy making, takes place when the central planners draft the strategy covering all the operational divisions, and then hives off the relevant sections for transmission to the divisions, who are required to prepare their local strategy within the parameters laid down centrally.

- *'Bottom-up'* planning refers to the process whereby divisions prepare their own strategies (perhaps using predictions and observations generated centrally and locally), and then put them forward to the central planners for aggregation into, what might be optimistically termed, the global strategy.

Many multinationals, with strong overseas divisions, expect the latter to first develop their own strategies and then submit them to the head-office where their individual impact can be assessed on the aggregate global plan. Financial resources are usually limited, so there will be competition among subsidiaries for resource allotment. Regular discussions and consultation between central and subsidiary company planners are vital if there is to be harmony and goodwill. Management incentives will also play a very important part.

3 ALTERNATIVE WAYS TO ENTER FOREIGN MARKETS

3.1 Ways of going international

There are a number of **entry strategies** that a firm can adopt in order to develop international markets and these include:

(a) **Exporting** - goods are produced domestically and transferred overseas for sale in exchange for currency or by barter. Barter, or countertrade as it is often called, is employed when dealing with developing countries who have products to exchange but no foreign currency - it accounts for approximately 20% of the world trade.

Negotiations for the sale of goods can be conducted through local **agencies** working on a commission basis or through local **distributors** who purchase the goods from the exporter and then sell them on to the local users. In both cases some degree of exclusivity is normally given in exchange for the local organisations agreeing to certain conditions such as not representing competitors, carrying out a certain amount of local marketing or undertaking the local servicing of products.

Alternatively the company may set up a **local sales office** or form a foreign sales subsidiary to sell, or sell and service, its goods.

(b) **Licensing** - this is where a licensor in one country provides certain resources to licensees in other countries in order that the latter can produce and market products similar to those the licensor has been producing in his own country. The resources provided include technical know-how, managerial skills and/or patent and trade mark rights and in exchange the licensor receives from the licensee a percentage of the licensed goods sold and/or a lump sum down payment.

Doz identifies three reasons why companies enter into licensing agreements rather than engage in exporting or overseas production:

- so as not to upset the fragile equilibrium of existing oligopolies. Pilkington has profited considerably from licensing its float glass process to its international competitors rather than run the risk of their developing their own process;
- where the innovating company lacks interest in active foreign investment. This was the case when RCA licensed the overseas manufacture of its TV tubes;
- where a company feels there are excessive risks or difficulties in entering foreign markets on its own. Corning took this view with its optical fibre products.

A particularly contained form of licensing is **franchising** which is defined by Daft as where:

'... the franchiser provides foreign franchisees with a complete package of materials and services, including equipment, products, product ingredients, trademark and trade name rights, managerial advice and a standardised operating system.'

Fast food chains such as Kentucky Fried Chicken and McDonald's are good examples of franchising operations. As with licensing, the franchising route offers easy access to international markets - Bass has recently become the largest hotel operator in the world by acquiring the Holiday Inns franchise system of 1,268 hotels with 234,000 rooms.

(c) **Overseas production** - which can be achieved by **direct investment** in manufacturing facilities in a foreign country, either totally or partially through a **joint venture** when two or more firms come together to operate in a way that is of value to all concerned. Such activities are becoming more attractive as the rate of environmental change accelerates - AT&T and Phillips have recently formed a joint venture involving private branch exchange technology and expertise in office automation.

Alternatively, the company may set up an overseas **manufacturing subsidiary** which may be wholly owned or may have some form of local equity participation. In some countries local participation is mandatory - Zambia insists that its state holding companies own at least 51% of any foreign company's subsidiaries.

Companies can either set up the overseas subsidiary from scratch or merge with or acquire an existing operation. **Greenfield development** is often employed by companies handling products which are highly technical in design or method of manufacture as well as by those desiring direct involvement in the development of new markets and wishing to dispense with intermediate agents. It is also the only method available when breaking into new ground or when there are no suitable companies willing to be acquired or involved in other ways.

Although the final cost may be greater its spread over time is more favourable and realistic. Moreover, it minimises disruption and avoids the behavioural problems associated with acquisitions and mergers.

Acquisitions and mergers are preferred to 'Greenfield development' when

- Time is of the essence
- The cost of upgrading internal competencies is greater than acquisition costs
- There is no knowledge/resources on which internal development could be based
- An additional firm operating in the market may create a situation of over supply

Problems associated with acquisitions and mergers involve finding the right firm which is agreeable to a deal, negotiating a fair price and integrating activities in the post acquisition phase.

3.2 Activity

A large UK manufacturer of confectionery wishes to expand into European markets. However, the UK style of chocolate is not widely appreciated in Europe. What mode of entry would you suggest for the manufacturer?

3.3 Activity solution

The company would probably manufacture overseas, maybe buying an overseas company with existing expertise and available brands.

4 RECENT TRENDS AND DEVELOPMENTS IN GLOBAL BUSINESS STRATEGY

Within a multi-domestic industry, international business is really a collection of domestic industries, where competitive advantage in one country is more or less independent of competition in the others. For this type of industry, many of the activities involved in production, marketing and servicing need to be tailored to the particular requirements of the country. This tailoring is critical to competitive advantage.

In global industries the competitive advantage in one country is strongly influenced by its position in others. Rivals battle it out worldwide and competitive advantage may be gained by operating and organising on a global basis.

In some respects a global industry will react to the same forces as a national industry eg. it will be subject to the same five main competitive forces that we considered earlier. However, there are clear differences for a company operating internationally in a global industry compared to a national company competing in the same industry. There are five differences that can be readily identified as having an influence on strategy.

- Differing views and policies of governments.
- Differing availability and costs of labour and raw materials.
- Varying cost structures in different countries creates multi-choice situations of production and distribution.
- Different circumstances in foreign markets.
- Differences in competition encountered in foreign countries.

The nature of success in the global markets is a subject of concern for both business leaders and politicians. Organisations in the West have been accused of ignoring the threat coming from Japan and other nations such as Korea and Taiwan. The outcome of this apathy has been the decline of established manufacturing industries such as radio, television, shipbuilding, motor cycles, cameras and steel, especially in the US and in the UK.

Long term investment in capital and human resources is needed to compete globally. Western organisations have been criticised for being too limited in their vision and driven by short term profit mentality in their respective stock markets.

The global success of Japanese organisations is based on a number of strategies which are long term in their design and delivery. They are concerned with: obtaining market share; internally generated growth rather than by acquisition; and innovation linked to constant new product development.

5 THE COMPETITIVE ADVANTAGE OF NATIONS

5.1 Porter's determinants of national competitive advantage

Michael Porter, in his book *The competitive advantage of nations*, tries to isolate the national attributes that further competitive advantage in an industry.

His study argues that, for a country's industry to be successful, it needs to have the attributes and relationships shown in the diagram below. He calls this the 'diamond'.

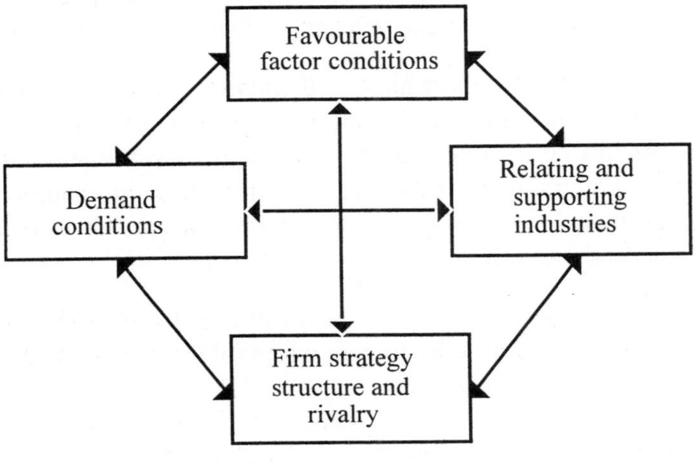

(a) **Favourable factor conditions -** factors include the following:

(i) Physical resources such as land, minerals and weather;
(ii) Capital;

(iii Human resources such as skills, motivation, price and industrial relations;
(iv) Knowledge which can be used effectively;
(v) Infrastructure.

Porter also found that countries which had factor disadvantages were forced to innovate to overcome these problems. This innovation has been the basis of competitive advantage eg, where nations experienced high energy costs they were forced to develop energy-efficient products and processes which were subsequently demanded worldwide.

(b) **Demand conditions** - there must be a strong home market demand for the product or service. This determines how industries perceive and respond to buyer needs and creates the pressure to innovate. A compliant domestic market is a disadvantage because it does not force the industry to become innovative and excellent.

(c) **Relating and supporting industries -** the success of an industry can be due to its suppliers and related industries. Sweden's global superiority in its pulp and paper industries is supported by a network of related industries including packaging, chemicals, wood-processing, conveyor systems and truck manufacture. Many of these supporting industries have also achieved leading global positions.

(d) **Firm strategy, structure and rivalry** -organisational goals can be determined by ownership structure. Smaller companies may have slightly longer time horizons to operate in because their shares are not traded as much as larger organisations. They might also have different return on capital requirements.

Porter found that domestic competition was vital as a spur to innovation and also enhanced global competitive advantage. Conversely, where governments have encouraged mergers to get the critical mass required to be a global player, these national monopolies have not, on the whole, been successful in establishing a global position.

5.2 The implications of company strategy and national economics

There are a vast number of environmental factors that shape business strategy, but these can mainly be grouped into four major forces:

(a) **Competition**

One of the most important characteristics of competition is that it is global. Practically all advanced countries are experiencing competition from abroad. There are few protected industries or regulated monopolies left in the world and even such areas as telecommunications, airlines, and stock market exchanges are becoming privately owned.

Competition is no longer limited to the more advanced countries of the world and there is a big rise in multinational companies in places like Brazil, India, Korea and Taiwan. In fact, in many sectors of the world's economy, it is multinational companies from the less developed nations that are dominant. This is particularly so in the areas of agriculture, cut diamonds, textiles, and other low value-added products or commodities. Korea and Taiwan have demonstrated their global competitiveness in products such as consumer electronics.

Global competition is often based on strategic considerations. Competitors from abroad are often willing to sacrifice some profit in order to gain a foothold in a large domestic market and are also willing to engage in cross subsidisation.
These facts, therefore, suggest that managing competition in domestic markets is a greater challenge today than it used to be. Organisations, therefore, need a global strategy with emphasis on obtaining and keeping their share of the global market.

(b) **Markets**

One of the characteristics of markets is that customers are becoming global in their orientation. It is not only the industrial and business customers who procure their products or services from global sources, so do the ordinary consumers. Examples of this are consumer electronics, garments, cars, appliances, and even foods and beverages all of which carry a mixture of domestic and foreign brand names in most countries of the world. The customer, therefore, has expectations of quality, service, and affordability based on world standards. Domestic products such as cars and television sets may not be considered reliable or user friendly once the customer has experienced products from abroad.

In many business markets it is not unusual to find that customers are becoming competitors and are deciding to make the product themselves rather than buy it.

Markets are becoming more and more fragmented, especially consumer markets. This is due to diversity demographics, such as age and income distribution. Fragmented markets create opportunities for niche and encourages competition from abroad.

(c) **Government regulations**

There has been a big change over the years in the formation of regional economic alliances such as the European Community (EC) and the freedom of world trade through GATT (General Agreement on Trade and Tariffs) negotiations. Such changes have softened national geographic boundaries for products and services.

Countries less developed like India and China have made significant demands upon the multinationals. This has caused a significant change in corporate strategy, structure and even corporate culture. IBM and General Motors for example, have accepted strategic alliances as the only way of doing business in some countries, despite having strong preferences toward wholly owned subsidiaries.

Currency exchange rules and regulations and the floating of hard currencies such as the US dollar and the British pound have also had a dramatic impact on the cash flow and pricing decisions by businesses.

It has become important, therefore, for enterprises to utilise the tools and processes of a political economy, by lobbying through political action committees (PACs), legislative reforms, and government intervention.

(d) **Technology**

Technology is available worldwide, especially in areas such as electronics and mechanics. Technical barriers across national borders are easily overcome and it is as easy for a less developed country to produce high quality electronic products such as personal computers and television sets as it is for an advanced country.

A new generation of technologies are providing a sharp experience curve. It is possible for competitors around the world to offset capacity advantages with a relatively small production volume.

It encourages local production through transfer of technology to other countries to gain cost advantages in local manufacturing and local assembly.

Life spans of technologies are also getting shorter and shorter. It is, therefore, becoming necessary to recover capital as soon as capacity is installed. It is less and less desirable to think local first and global second when a business is about to invest in technology as that technology will rapidly become obsolete. Instead, businesses, must think globally in relation to product design, manufacturing capacity, and marketing issues.

The international dimensions of environmental forces are powerful and it is becoming necessary, therefore, to incorporate them in corporate planning and strategy.

6 THE IMPACT OF THE GLOBAL MARKET

6.1 National and global marketing

Marketing provides the means whereby consumers are made aware of the product or service and are able to purchase it.
International marketing involves the marketing of goods and services outside an organisation's home country. Multinational marketing is a complex form of international marketing that involves an organisation engaged in marketing activities in many foreign countries.

International marketing varies widely. At one end of the spectrum, a company may limit itself to one or more foreign markets, manufacture goods domestically, and market them to foreign countries with little or no adaptation of the domestic marketing plan. At the opposite end, a multinational firm has a global orientation, operates in many countries, uses foreign manufacturing and marketing subsidiaries to cater for individual markets.

There are several reasons why countries and individual organisations go international. The opportunities arise from comparative advantage, economic trends, demographic conditions, competition in the domestic market, the stage in the product life cycle and tax structures.

(a) Comparative advantage exists where countries have different rates of productivity for different products because of resources, specialisation, mechanisation or climate. Because of this, countries can benefit by trading goods in which they have relative production advantages for those in which they have relative disadvantages.

(b) Economic trends vary by country. As a way of minimising the effects of inflation, recession and unemployment, organisations may market their goods or services in countries with favourable economic conditions.

(c) Demographic conditions may offer opportunities by allowing a firm in a country with a small or stagnant population to find new markets by entering foreign markets with under-satisfied market segments.

(d) Competition in the domestic market may become intense and force the organisation into international expansion.

(e) Different stages of the product life cycle may encourage organisations to export to prolong the product's life. International marketing can also help to dispose of discontinued merchandise or seconds without spoiling the domestic market for full price, first quality goods.

(f) Tax advantages may accrue where countries entice new business from foreign companies by offering tax incentives in the form of reduced property, income or import taxes for a limited time period.

7 THE RISK OF GLOBAL MARKETS AND CULTURAL DIFFERENCES

Most of the problems experienced by organisations operated overseas are caused by the more diverse and volatile environmental conditions encountered when operating simultaneously in many different countries. Of particular importance are:

7.1 Cultural differences affecting internal management

Most management writings contain themselves to organisations based in America and Britain although there is an increasing interest in Japanese organisations. Although international variations exist at the present time it is implied that organisations all over the world are converging so that their national and cultural differences are becoming less and less important.

Such are the views of the *convergers* who feel that the operations required of an organisation depend on universal technologies and structures and an increasing reliance on multinational corporations.

These views are strongly contested by the *culturalists* who, according to Paton,

'...maintain that societal differences based on national history and geography provide organisations with their key values, while the basic processes and structures of organisations depend crucially on the skills and capabilities generated by national educational and class systems.'

Both schools of thought have some validity – certain tasks have to be carried out utilising specific technologies but the management of these technologies can be modified to suit the culture of the operators as the Japanese have amply demonstrated. Moreover, large scale industrialisation is a pre-requisite of capitalism and has been actively encouraged by Western nations since the start of the Industrial Revolution. Alternative technologies are available and may be better suited to the environments of developing nations or to post-industrial countries like Britain.

Specific problem areas have been identified by various researchers, notably the Aston Group which investigated international variations in organisational structure and Hofstede who looked at cultural differences in work related attitudes. These include

(i) **Leadership** – in some countries such as those in Latin America, leaders are expected to take a strong personal interest in employees and appear at private social functions such as weddings etc, whereas in other countries such as Germany such social contact is discouraged.

In other countries, notably in Asia and Africa, public criticism is intolerable as the loss of self respect brings dishonour to the employee and his family.

(ii) **Motivation** – the incentives for effective performance must match the culture. It is pointless offering individual bonuses to workers where there are strong group and company loyalties, as in Japan, or where loyalty to an individual's superior is paramount as in Turkey and the Near East.

(iii) **Structure** – research by Maurice showed that French firms are bureaucratic with orders and procedures set from above whereas German work organisation relies more on the professional expertise which derives from the trained knowledge and skill of the more junior employees.

7.2 Sociological-cultural constraints

The factors that make up these constraints include:

(i) attitude towards managers – Alistair Mant quotes the cultural tradition within the UK that industry is still on the wrong side of the respectability line, and this in turn dictates irrelevant assumptions about education;

(ii) views about subordinates and authority;

(iii) group co-operation;

(iv) relations between management and unions;

(v) the view of achievement;

(vi) flexibility of the class structure;

(vii) attitudes towards wealth and material gain;

(viii) recognition of the relationships in economic life – demand, price, wages, training, absenteeism and turnover; (one of the problems with Eastern Airlines was the failure of the unions to recognise basic economic facts of life);

(ix) attitudes towards risk;

(x) attitudes towards change – one of the problems that plagues the survival plans for some of the older industries in Europe is the failure of operatives to see the need for change, and be prepared to move according to these needs; this is seen in the reluctance of coal miners to leave South Wales for Nottinghamshire where there is still work for them, or for traditional newspaper workers in the UK to see that survival depended upon adopting new technology.

7.3 Cultural differences affecting marketing

There are numerous examples of a company's international marketing efforts failing because they did not take account of the local culture particularly regarding

(i) **Linguistics** – some brand names have unfortunate connotations in the local language.

(ii) **Graphics** – a triangle by the roadside is a cautionary sign in Europe, but represents a helicopter landing point in the USA and a birth control clinic in India. Care in the use of colours is also important, for example in China the colour white connotes death.

(iii) **Life style** – French housewives like to cook and avoid convenience food, the Japanese cosmetic market is problematic because perfume is hardly used, suntans are considered ugly and bath oil is impractical in communal baths.

7.4 Problems affecting business negotiations

These include differences regarding

(i) **Body language** – eye contact, posture and gesture, social distance and acceptability of touch vary from country to country.

(ii) **Receptiveness of proposals** – the Japanese tend to conceal sentiments, rely on group decisions, allow long breaks in discussions for contemplation and rarely say 'no' for fear of offending others.

(iii) **Linguistic ability** – Englishmen are often at a disadvantage when negotiating with foreigners because of their poor command of foreign languages. Whilst the negotiations can often be conducted in English the foreigners can have discussions amongst themselves in virtual secrecy.

(iv) **Personal ethics** – many Westerners find it very difficult to establish rapport with Asian and African contacts by presenting gifts, which are not considered bribes by the recipients, or by employing flattery in asking for advice and opinion when none is considered necessary.

7.5 Problems affecting financial control

There are several specific problems of financial management when operating internationally

(i) **Currency management** – operating in a variety of currencies provides opportunities for gains or losses through exchange rate fluctuations and lending/borrowing at the most favourable rates.

(ii) **Remittance of profits** – profits may be repatriated by means of dividends, management fees, loan interest or repayments and transfer pricing. Many countries impose restrictions on, or tax heavily, some or all of these methods.

(iii) **Transfer pricing** – in a multinational situation, transfer pricing can serve a variety of purposes including:

- maximising post-tax profits by transferring profits from high to low tax regimes;
- artificially altering a subsidiary's reported profits;
- transferring funds in the face of restrictions;
- imposing financial controls.

7.6 Legal-political constraints

There are six factors that can be recognised:

(a) the relevant legislation in which the organisation must work; obvious examples of this are labour laws about recruitment and job retention, and about employment costs; in Europe for example, the hiring of people is plagued with a plethora of legislation about equal opportunities, race relations and job security; in addition, there is the problem of employment costs, which increase the cost of employing people still further;

(b) defence policy and national security – this has considerable impact on the use of labour resources and funds available for technological advance; in the West, much of the advancement in the electronic and aerospace industry has been as a result of government patronage;

(c) foreign policy;

(d) political stability – in this context, the student should not think purely in terms of some despot in a banana republic; the stability in local government in the UK has had considerable effects on the working environment.

(e) political organisation;

(f) flexibility of law and legal changes.

7.7 Economic constraints

This embraces such things as:

(a) the extent to which the banks help or hinder organisational growth or development (banks in USA and Japan have a greater acceptance of commercial risk than in UK);

(b) fiscal policy in general and all the resulting ramifications;

(c) economic stability and levels of inflation.

8 ASSESSING OPPORTUNITIES AND THREATS

8.1 Opportunities of global competition

The opportunities available to an international company arise from different sources, such as the following.

(a) An inherent national advantage used to gain comparative advantage abroad (eg, low labour costs in Taiwan and Korea relative to other countries);

(b) Production economies of scale. In some industries such as steel and car manufacture the minimum efficiency production unit is too great for solely national demand so exporting from a central base will out-compete national producers;

(c) Operating worldwide may allow necessarily high fixed costs incurred nationally for logistical needs to be recouped eg. specialised cargo ships;

(d) Marketing economies of scale.

(e) Choices in location. It may be cheaper to produce parts in one country, assemble them in another, and it may be more effective to locate fundamental R&D in a third country. The global company can choose the most advantageous locations for different parts of the business.

(f) Experience curve advantages. Organisations can gain opportunities from sharing resources and experiences across countries.

(g) Differentiate with multinational buyers. Where the organisation's customers are multinational, there may be opportunities to organise on a global scale to service them eg, consider the trend for accountancy practices to go global to give a better service to their multinational clients.

8.2 Activity

Describe an organisation or industry which chooses advantageous locations for different parts of its business.

8.3 Activity solution

An example of an industry which locates different areas of its business to take advantage of particular skills or low wages is the computer industry. R&D may be concentrated in the US, the microchips and printed circuit boards are constructed in the Pacific Rim and the machines are assembled in various countries, such as the UK.

An example of an organisation is Ford. The components for car manufacture are made in many countries eg, gears in Germany, some models are assembled in Spain, others in the UK and the engine design is in the US.

8.4 Threats to global competition

The scope for global competition is limited by the following factors:

(a) National tastes and needs can be markedly different eg. the German beer trade is strongly regionalised in taste, the opportunities for an imported or licence manufactured standardised beer being poor;

(b) Lead times may be critical and only a national company on the spot can provide the service dictated;

(c) Access to established distribution channels may be blocked;

(d) Terms of trading may require local ownership or provision of local sales and servicing organisations;

(e) Government impediments through tariffs, subsidies to national producers, tax regulations etc.

8.5 Experiences

These threats can be very powerful and, in some industries, outweigh the general environmental factors that are encouraging globalisation. These factors include a narrowing of national differences in taste and culture, acceptance of free trade concept and reduced global distribution and communication costs.

There are companies who have tried to go 'global' and failed.

ITT (USA) went global in the 70's and found that various countries would not swap R&D information and the company was forced to withdraw from the market where it had been leader. There is a general comment that American companies are bad at international management and tend to compensate by strong centralisation.

KAO (Japanese soap manufacturer) failed in its attempts to become global. The reason given for this failure was that while everything in Japan sold on performance and quality, which works well with high technology products, it fails with products sold on 'image' eg, personal care products.

8.6 Strategic issues

Porter's strategic recommendations for the competitive organisation are:

- Sell to the most sophisticated and demanding buyers because they will set a standard for the organisation.
- Seek out buyers with the most difficult needs which then become part of the firm's R&D programme.
- Establish norms of exceeding the toughest regulatory hurdles or product standards: these provide targets that will force improvement.
- Source from the most advanced and international home-based suppliers: those with competitive advantage already will challenge the firm to improve and upgrade.
- Treat employees as permanent instead of demoralising hire-and-fire approach.
- Establish outstanding competitors as motivators.

The challenge facing the global company is how to respond to the particular needs of individual countries whilst at the same time not jeopardising the advantages of being part of a global company. There are a few branded products that are marketed in the same way across the world eg, Coca-Cola and Marlboro, but these tend to be the exceptions. Most global organisations adapt either the marketing approach or the product to the particular requirements of each country eg, Unilever's global shampoo brand, Timotei, is promoted with the same healthy image worldwide, but the product is changed to suit the different ways that nationalities wash their hair. Schweppes tonic water is marketed as a mixer for alcoholic drinks in the UK but as a soft drink in France.

Organisations need to develop global strategies in marketing but create local autonomy for managers to adopt strategies for local markets. International companies achieve their best success in using a country as a 'lead subsidiary' ie, specialise in that nation's strengths. For example:

(a) Phillips use Taiwan as lead company in everything related to black and white TVs.
(b) Ericsson use Australia as lead country globally for R&D.

9 CHAPTER SUMMARY

In this chapter we have looked at the global environment and the effect it has on organisations. One of the most significant developments to occur in business over the past twenty to thirty years has been the increasing internationalisation. The growth and power of multinationals is evidence of this, as is the interdependence of the world economy. The characteristics and motives of multinationals were discussed and the distinction between top-down and bottom-up strategic planning, as it applies to companies with overseas divisions, was also covered.

If an organisation has decided to enter an overseas market, the manner it does so is of crucial importance. The ways to enter foreign markets include exporting, licensing and overseas production. There is no uniformity in this approach since countries vary greatly and require individual analysis and planning. Some companies, eg. Coca-Cola, McDonald's, have established a consistent global image which is seen as a great strength whilst others have eschewed this common approach and sought to be flexible, adapting to each local area.

Michael Porter's theory of the competitive advantage of nations takes as its key a 'diamond' of factors that makes some nations (and consequently their industries) more competitive than others. The four points of this diamond are:

(i) Factor conditions;
(ii) Demand conditions;
(iii) Related and supporting industries; and
(iv) Company strategy, structure and rivalry.

The main environmental factors that affect global business strategy are competition, markets, government regulations and technology. These factors are so powerful that it is becoming necessary for organisations to incorporate them into their corporate planning and strategy.

10 SELF TEST QUESTIONS

10.1 List four factors which are relevant in the appraisal of the international environment (1.1).

10.2 Draw up a set of characteristics which a multinational might possess (1.2).

10.3 What concerns might a host country have when dealing with a multinational? (2.1).

10.4 Distinguish between top-down and bottom-up strategic planning (2.2).

10.5 Describe the entry strategies available to an organisation (3.1).

10.6 When are acquisitions and mergers preferable to Greenfield developments? (3.1).

10.7 What global strategies are Japanese organisations identified with? (4).

10.8 Draw Michael Porter's diamond showing the attributes and relationships needed for a country's industry to be successful (5.1).

10.9 What are the views of the convergers? (7.1).

10.10 Describe the cultural differences in work-related attitudes (7.1).

10.11 Outline five factors that contribute to sociological-cultural constraints (7.2).

10.12 Describe the cultural differences which may affect marketing (7.3).

10.13 List the problems which may affect business negotiating (7.4).

10.14 Outline three factors which may limit the scope for global competition (8.4).

11 EXAMINATION TYPE QUESTIONS

11.1 Multinational

The acquisition of a local company by a multinational conglomerate from abroad must take account, not only of differing tax regimes, currency controls and tariff and quota systems, but also of the cultural background developed within that local company.

Required

(a) Discuss to what extent a foreign parent should permit a local subsidiary to retain its practices which are due to local cultural factors and which might conflict with group practices. **(12 marks)**

(b) Discuss how the integration of expatriate and locally recruited personnel can be engendered. **(6 marks)**

(c) Discuss how a subsidiary can be encouraged to respond to local opportunities whilst having regard to the wider interests of its parent company. **(7 marks)**

(Total: 25 marks)

11.2 Tempco

John Adams is the managing director of Tempco, a medium-sized company manufacturing and marketing central heating and air-conditioning control systems. The company is a strategic business unit, owned entirely by a major UK conglomerate company. Tempco both manufactures and installs building control systems and has a strong reputation within the European market. About 70% of Tempco's sales are focused on the industrial and business sectors with the remainder going to the household consumer. Exports to continental Europe are about 40% of the total sales.

In the past few years the market within Europe has been very difficult. The recession has curtailed new building programmes and competition is becoming increasingly price dictated. Adams believes that future growth will not be strong in Europe but that the Pacific Rim areas offer the most attractive opportunities. Adams favours targeting South East Asia and feels that an investment led rather than export led entry mode is most attractive.

Adams has the approval of the headquarters management team (and the financial support) to develop an entry strategy into one or more of the South East Asian markets. He is however faced with a number of difficult choices including whether to set up Tempco's own 'greenfield site' (literally starting with a greenfield, that is, with no prior manufacturing facility), whether to acquire a local company operating in the sector or whether to make a strategic alliance with a local producer.

John Adams has asked you, as a member of his staff, to prepare a briefing paper for presentation to the main board of the parent company outlining the merits and de-merits of differing entry strategies.

Requirements:

Write a briefing paper for John Adams. The briefing paper should cover the following areas:

(a) the case in support of direct investment as a strategy for entry into the South East Asia market; **(7 marks)**

(b) the key factors which should be considered when making the choice between:

(i) a joint venture with local interests or a wholly owned subsidiary; and **(9 marks)**

(ii) a 'greenfield' investment versus the take-over of an indigenous firm. **(9 marks)**

(Total: 25 marks)

12 ANSWERS TO EXAMINATION TYPE QUESTIONS

12.1 Multinational

(a) Most multinational conglomerates have their own 'international' culture which is adapted to the host country they are operating in. The overseas company should identify with the multinational and this is usually done through standardised policies, procedures and operating instructions, thus allowing for consistency of operation as far as possible around the world.

Long-term strategic planning and decision-making will usually be carried out by the multinational headquarters. These plans and decisions will then be reviewed by each country, who will adopt the most appropriate 'local' tactics to achieve the objectives formulated. This means in practice that multinationals build a degree of flexibility into their planning process to allow for local conditions.

Headquarters should remember that local cultures will produce attitudes, desires, expectations, beliefs and customs which may have a significant effect on the way the organisation is managed and functions. A country's nationals cannot change practices of a life time, nor would it be appropriate to do so, as the organisation would be 'out of step' with business practices in operation in the host country, which would cause trading problems.

For example, local management will be familiar with local customs, suppliers, customers, government regulations and employment practices, none of which can be ignored by the multinational.

Where an acquisition or a merger attempts radically to change the approach taken by the host countries management, serious problems can occur. Employees may feel resentment and concern and communication barriers may be constructed. This can lead to demotivation and alienation.

It will take time and considerable effort to find the right balance between a multinational and local culture, but without this balance the operation will not be working at its most efficient and effective.

(b) The integration of expatriate and locally recruited personnel has always been a challenge to multinationals. Many multinationals appoint expatriate managers to senior positions in the overseas company, in order to ensure that the 'corporate' line is followed, and local managers are trained in the appropriate manner.

The selection of expatriate managers is a key feature, as they are required not only to have good technical skills but also to develop diplomatic and advanced social skills in order to avoid or resolve potential areas of conflict. Managers are encouraged to mix and live in an integrated fashion with the 'locals' in order to facilitate their understanding of the culture. Usually expatriate managers' appointments last a defined number of years and can be seen as part of their management development programme.

Multinationals have developed various programmes which are specifically designed to integrate expatriate and local personnel. These programmes can cover such topics as language training, skills training and international management courses. Often local management are trained at the multinational's headquarters which facilitates identification with the corporate culture.

Multinationals tend to use local personnel as far as possible through all levels of the organisation, providing training where required.

There is potential for unity providing that it is based upon the sharing of tactical and managerial knowledge, the development of human and material skills and equity of treatment.

(c) There are various ways in which a subsidiary can be encouraged to respond to local opportunities whilst having regard to the wider interests of its parent company.

The subsidiary could be organised as a profit centre; employees would then be responsible for the subsidiary's performance. This should motivate staff to perform efficiently and effectively as results will be directly linked to local effort rather than getting lost in the multinational's performance. This will make it an identifiable part of the organisation, and can encourage local pride in achievements.

In addition, pay could be linked to profit or another performance measure, with bonuses being paid or shares being issued to staff.

Locally generated profits could be used to the benefit of local employees and inhabitants, for example the provision of sports facilities.

It may be appropriate to exploit local opportunities by using the international expertise, as well as inputs from the appropriate resources of the multinational.

12.2 Tempco

Management Briefing Paper

Market Entry Strategies for South East Asia

Prepared by: Date:

Ref:

Introduction

This briefing paper is intended to outline the issues facing Tempco in putting together a market entry strategy for the South East Asia region. The first phase of the strategy is to decide whether the market entry will be made through exports from the UK or through a direct investment in a manufacturing base in the region. The second phase is to make the choice between ownership models - wholly owned subsidiary or joint venture, and production models - start up from scratch or takeover of an existing manufacturing facility within the region. The features of each of these option choices are reviewed in the paper.

Investment led or export led?

The culture of most emerging and developed markets expects that suppliers have a demonstrable commitment to the market. Although exporting without direct investment is low risk it also has a lower likelihood of successful market entry. Whereas historically investment followed trade it is clear in the final quarter of the twentieth century that trade follows investment. This change can be seen in the UK with the investment led entry of the Japanese automobile companies followed by investment from many of their Japanese suppliers. The predominant view (Drucker, Ohmae) is that a business cannot hold a leadership position within a major market unless it also manufactures there.

A prime requirement therefore is to have direct representation through investment within the South East Asian market. In addition to creating market standing and demonstrating long-term commitment we can identify four other advantages for Tempco:

- assistance in avoiding regional trade barriers;
- placing decision-making nearer to the market so creating flexibility and speed of response;
- possible access to cheaper labour;
- access to local finance.

Joint venture or local subsidiary?

The advantages of using a strategic alliance/joint venture is that expansion can be achieved more rapidly with a manufacturing plant already in operation. This expansion will also require less initial capital outlay. In addition there are associated advantages:

- if the choice of partner is made carefully there will be a provision of market expertise which will prove invaluable in an area where trading customs and culture and the general external environment will be considerably different from that experienced in Europe. By having host country alliances it is possible that sales prospects will improve.

- indigenous pride will not be affronted and governments, who may be critical buyers or influencers, will be more likely to place orders with a joint venture company than with an exclusively foreign supplier. In some countries the only practical method of access is with a joint venture. There is often a reluctance to permit 100% foreign ownership of manufacturing plants based on the argument that there will be no long-term benefit to the industrialisation of the host country.

A major attraction of operating a wholly owned subsidiary is that control is total. There is no split in responsibilities such as might occur with a joint venture. There is a lack of flexibility with decision-making in a joint venture whereas with a wholly owned subsidiary decision-making only involves one major stakeholder. Involvement in a joint venture might result in working with an organisation which may have local knowledge but does not have the manufacturing expertise or quality standards which might be considered essential.

With a wholly owned subsidiary there are no conflicts of interest. With joint venture partners there may be differences in corporate objectives:

- on dividend payout policy. The host country partner in a joint venture may be looking for a reinvestment policy whereas the foreign partner may wish to repatriate a larger level of profits
- there may be arguments about trading areas whereby the domestic partner is looking for trade in third country markets which could involve moving into territories already covered by the other partner
- there could be disputes concerning pricing strategies, particularly inter-company transfers which might be used to minimise tax liabilities
- some policies, like the international standardisation of products or parts, and the rationalisation of facilities or supply routes, are difficult to manage in joint ventures because of differing objectives, skills, experiences and cultures;
- finally the sharing of competitive information concerning markets and technologies may be unattractive to either partner.

Working independently of a partner avoids these issues.

Greenfield site or local acquisition?

The attractions of developing a 'greenfield site' include:

- locational advantage - we can site ideally near markets or supplies and where there are good communication links - helpful for just-in-time logistical systems;
- the factory can include the latest technology, customised for the company;
- the labour does not arrive with the culture of past industrial and company practices and any associated inflexibility;
- there may be good incentives from the government to develop in certain geographic areas in exchange for employment and technological transfer;
- the past reputation of the indigenous company may not be an attraction, particularly if our image or target segments need to be different.

However there are benefits from buying an existing company in the host country. These can be summarised as follows:

- the factory can be on stream more quickly;
- it could be cheaper than building from the bottom up;
- the purchased company may have a good reputation which will benefit Tempco;
- it is possible to, if required, hide our identity in markets which could be xenophobic;
- there may be access to local knowledge.

Conclusion

Investment led entry by whatever means requires a high level of management commitment in terms of both time and finance. The strategic consequences of the entry methods reviewed have major implications for Tempco and a final decision can only be made on the basis of an in-depth analysis of the local environment.

9 THE BUSINESS ENVIRONMENT

INTRODUCTION & LEARNING OBJECTIVES

We shall now consider some of the most basic forces that affect the structure, conduct, and performance of company strategic planning systems. These forces make up the business environment. They have a great impact on the company, while the reverse is seldom true. They are the 'uncontrollables', to which companies adapt through setting the 'controllable' factors, their strategies.

The key point about the environment is that it keeps changing, but the rate and impact of the change is uncertain, and disputed. Recent researches document how economic, social and technological changes show an 'accelerative thrust', with the crucial implication that companies need to invest more to keep abreast by using strategies that are flexible and versatile, and finely tuned to their environments.
This chapter examines the nature of the business environment, environmental management, forecasting systems, and their implications for the planning of strategy.

When you have studied this chapter you should be able to do the following:

- Analyse the role of forecasting in strategic decision making.
- Describe the techniques available.
- Discuss the use of scenario building.
- Outline the effect of the external environment on corporate strategies and plans.
- Identify current and emerging trends.
- Describe the sources of information.

1 THE ROLE OF FORECASTING IN STRATEGIC DECISION MAKING

Trying to forecast the environment is just about the most difficult of managerial tasks - second only perhaps to laying off staff, which of course is often the result of failure to see into the future. It was H.L.Mencken who said that he never made forecasts - especially about the future. He had a point, but one that is not sympathetic to the problems of many companies who operate in extremely difficult environments.

Management attempting to cope with all the complexities of doing business in today's rapidly changing environment must guard against being caught in the potentially damaging trap of failing to recognise and adapt to environmental changes early enough. This trap is all too familiar to many companies which have lost market and cost leadership through failure to innovate, as well as multitudes of smaller firms. For this reason forecasting should not be looked upon as an expensive illusion of academics, rather it is the work of hard-nosed business managers.

Textbooks traditionally divide forecasting techniques into three: statistical (or quantitative) techniques, intuitive (or qualitative) techniques, and causal models, but the balance between quantitative and qualitative is a fine one. It is hardly surprising given the complexities and dynamism of business environments that companies make mistakes and fail to achieve objectives. The point is do they do so because they ignore the basic realities of the market-place? Do planners still exhibit the urge to apply mathematical formulae and simulation to business strategic planning without taking full account of the qualitative factors in play? In other words is there a danger of management science outgunning the intuition, pure logic, hunch, and reason that derives from human ability and experience, even if the end game-plan appears irrational when matched against the output from computer driven algorithms? This is a balancing-act that needs to be addressed. The role that any technique plays in strategic planning must be supportive. A technique is used as a means to an end, and is not the end itself. Results must be tempered with reasoning. Quantitative output needs to be balanced against qualitative judgements.

2 THE TECHNIQUES AVAILABLE

2.1 Statistical models

The statistical approach to forecasting is concerned with the projection of **time series.**

Definition Time series analysis involves the identification of short and long term patterns in previous data and the application of these patterns for projections.

A variety of methods is available including:

- moving averages
- exponential smoothing
- correlation analysis
- sensitivity and key factor analysis
- risk analysis
- multiple regression analysis

Where there are numerous short and long term factors at work, forecasting becomes very difficult. If the series of data being analysed is very regular, some simple procedure such as **exponential smoothing** may be sufficient. On the other hand, more complex patterns may require techniques of **regression analysis, risk analysis** and **multiple regression**. By using relatively simple mathematics, it may be possible to calculate to a *'level of confidence'* the volume of demand, etc. Trend analysis is a particularly useful tool for companies who have to forecast demand which is influenced by seasonal fluctuations, or where demand is strongly influenced by the business cycle.

2.2 Intuitive forecasting methods

All forecasting techniques involve judgement. For example, statistical techniques require judgements about the amount of past data that is relevant, and how this data should be weighted, while casual models involve judgements about what are the critical variables in the situation. In both cases, judgements have to be made regarding the reliability of the data, the stability of the relationships between the variables over time, and the accuracy of the predictions. Therefore what distinguishes intuitive techniques is the relative emphasis they place on judgement, and the value of such techniques lies not in their statistical sophistication but in the method of systematising expert knowledge. Intuitive forecasting techniques include the use of *think tanks, Delphi methods, scenario planning, brain-storming, derived demand analysis, and social and political forecasting.*

(a) **A think tank** comprises a group of experts who are encouraged, in a relatively unstructured atmosphere, to speculate about future developments in particular areas and to identify possible courses of action. The essential features of a think tank are: the relative independence of its members, enabling unpopular, unacceptable or novel ideas to be broached; the relative absence of positional authority in the group, which enables free discussion and argument to take place; and the group nature of the activity which not only makes possible the sharing of knowledge and views, but also encourages a consensus view or preferred **'scenario'**. Think tanks are used by large organisations, including government, and may cross the line between forecasting and planning. However, the organisations that directly employ, or fund them, are careful to emphasise that their think-tank proposals do not necessarily constitute company or government policy.

Think tanks are useful in generating ideas and assessing their feasibility, as well as providing an opportunity to test out reaction to ideas prior to organisational commitment.

(b) **The Delphi technique** is named after the *Oracle of Apollo at Delphi*, renowned for somewhat ambiguous predictions. The method was pioneered at the Rand Corporation in 1950 to assess the timing and likelihood of new technology, and it since has gained considerable recognition as a valuable planning tool with a great variety of applications. Delphi seeks to avoid the group pressures to conformity that are inherent in the *'think tank'* method. It does this by **individually**, systematically and sequentially interrogating a panel of experts. Members do not meet, and questioning is conducted by formal questionnaires. A central authority evaluates the responses and feeds these back to the experts who are then interrogated in a new round of questions. After several such rounds, the result, generally, is that widely differing opinions increasingly adapt themselves to one another. The system is based on the premise that knowledge and ideas possessed by some but not all of the experts can be identified and **shared** and this forms the basis for subsequent interrogations.

(c) **Scenario planning** might be developed by a specialist writing a detailed account of his or her opinions and views about a particular issue eg, 'The fiscal strategy of a coalition UK government influenced by a minority Liberal balance'. The scenario is then subjected to critical examination, discussion and amendment until the management are satisfied that it represents a constructive dissertation from which decisions can be influenced.

(d) **Brainstorming** is a method of generating ideas. There are different approaches but a popular one is for a number of people (no fewer than six, no more than fifteen) drawn from all levels of management and expertise to meet and propose answers to an initial **single** question posed by the session leader. For instance, they may be asked 'How can we improve product A ?' Each person proposes something, no matter how absurd. No one is allowed to criticise or ridicule another person's idea. One idea provokes another, and so on. All ideas are listed and none rejected at this initial stage. Rationality is not particularly important, but what is essential is that a wide range of ideas emerge and in the ensuing spoken answers for these to be picked up, developed, combined and reshaped. Only after the session are ideas evaluated and screened against rational criteria for practicability. An enlargement on this is for an idea proposed and seen to be promising when matched against criteria, to be subjected to a brainstorming session in which the question 'How might the idea fail?' is asked.

Brainstorming provides a forum for the interchange of ideas without erecting the normal cultural, behavioural and psychological barriers which so often inhibit the expression of ideas.

(e) **Derived demand** exists for a commodity, component or good because of its contribution to the manufacture of another product. For example, the demand for chrome, copper and rubber which are used in the manufacture of many different products, including cars, are derived demands. The forecasting technique involves analysing some aspects of economic activity so that the level of other aspects can be deduced and projected. The principle is simple, but the practice is complex and costly. Take the example of chrome matched with car manufacture. In order to forecast the demand for cars (thus chrome) the forecaster will be faced with the mammoth task of analysing an enormous number of influences and correlated factors. Due to its cost and complexity the technique has a very restricted use.

2.3 Causal techniques

Causal techniques are concerned with constructing and refining mathematical models (usually regression models) of the system for which the forecast relates. This would involve identifying the key variables in the system, and expressing their relationship in mathematical form. Such models can take the form of a series of simultaneous equations which can be revised on the basis of experience. Then data, based on different assumptions, could be fed into the model to generate different forecasts. The model will allow the forecaster to appraise the results of different decisions based on different assumptions.

An example of such a model, albeit a highly sophisticated one, is the Treasury model of the economy which contains hundreds of variables. To handle this complexity, the model is on a computer program. However, the model is not fixed. Besides feeding different assumptions into the model (eg, the level of government expenditure, the level of taxation, interest rates etc.) to generate different forecasts, economists have modified the model by revising or reweighing some of the equations in order to improve its predictive capacity.

3 THE USE OF SCENARIO BUILDING

3.1 Introduction

Definition Scenario building is an attempt to construct views of possible future situations.

Scenario building is used in strategic planning to allow a number of deductions to be made about future developments of markets, products and technology. The aim is to draw up a limited number of logically consistent, but different scenarios so that managers can examine strategic options against the scenarios and ask such questions as 'what should we do if...?, or what would be the effect of..?

Examples of scenarios that are drawn up so that the strategies can be tested against a range include:

(a) an optimistic scenario, where everything turns out favourably in the future;
(b) a pessimistic scenario, which describes the worst possible scenario; and
(c) a 'most likely' scenario, which is likely to be between the other two.

Strategies will need to be developed which help the organisation either to gain a competitive advantage or to minimise the potential damage deriving from the environment.

The issues facing the industry may be influenced by such things as:

- the entry or exit of firms;
- the rate of demand;
- changing buyer needs;
- innovations in products or production processes;
- how easily innovations can be imitated;
- stage in the life cycle.

Another benefit of scenario building is that managers can examine the implications of scenarios so as to challenge the assumptions which are taken for granted in the environment in which they operate. This may be important where there are long-term horizons because operating managers may be so concerned with the short term that they ignore the long-term changes.

3.2 Approach to drawing up scenarios

The main steps in drawing up scenarios are as follows:

(i) The first step is to identify the key assumptions, or forces, that are to be worked on. This may build on a PEST (political, economic, social and technological) analysis. It is best to restrict these assumptions to environmental forces, and not include the strategic action of the organisation or of competitors. It is also important that the number of assumptions is kept relatively low, since the complexity in drawing up scenarios will rise dramatically with the number of assumptions that are included.

(ii) Another step is to understand historically the trend with regard to assumptions being considered, their impact on market conditions and organisational strategies, and what these assumptions themselves depend upon. For example, if fuel is being considered, understanding what affects such things as oil or gas prices.

(iii) As explained in the previous section, scenarios are built by considering possible futures, usually on the basis of an optimistic future, a pessimistic future and a 'dominant theme' or mainline future. Two to four scenarios are appropriate to aim for.

4 AN ENVIRONMENTAL PERSPECTIVE

4.1 Business - an open system

As we now face the rest of the 1990s it is worth considering the forces at work in the business environment. There is over $80 (US) trillion annual trading currency, with $1 trillion in Eurobonds, putting enormous strain on international exchange rates. The price of oil can rise or drop drastically virtually without warning. There is an increase in junk bonds and leveraged buyouts, and $1 trillion in developing-country debt, with an explosion in business start-ups and a record number of bank failures in the industrialised nations. In the market place there is more affluence, but also more poverty. Consumers are demanding superior quality but also expect more choice. Uncertainty surrounds every strategic decision. There is market fragmentation and complexity, with an explosion in products and services, market nichemanship and the use of smaller flexible factory units. Electronic hook-up has reached the consumer, and CAD/CAM and just-in-time systems have drastically reduced design-to-manufacture lead time.

With over one billion people all dressing the same ways, eating the same kinds of food, watching the same television programmes, humming the same songs, and having the same attitudes and behaviour on sex, permissiveness, materialism and *'quality of life'* the world has shrunk to become virtually a *'global village market'*. This market is targeted by companies situated in almost every part of the world. Competitors from the developed nations (eg, UK, US, Japan, Germany), from the newly industrialised nations (eg, Korea and the Philippines) and from the rapidly developing economies like Brazil and China, are battling *'for every inch'* to win a share.

The rules of the business game have changed in response to these forces, and the message is clear. To survive and prosper in the 1990s and into the next century, companies will need to accept new rules and adopt strategies which reflect the competitive nature of the market-place. The strategies of future winners will involve niche oriented market creation, flat, flexible and fast organisation structures, smaller operation units (even if small within large), and a totally consumer oriented marketing philosophy. Environmental management will be a critical aspect of strategic planning.

4.2 Effect of the internal environment on corporate strategy and plans

Definition The environment is defined as the set of elements that affect the system, but are not controlled by it. Though clearly relevant to the system, they are regarded as falling outside its boundary.

Much of the relevant work in this area has been carried out by open systems and contingency theorists, and Burns and Stalker's and Lawrence and Lorsch's research is particularly relevant. Ruth Carter *et al* though provide a useful definition.

Obviously, there are some components within the system over which the management of an organisation have little control and some writers rather confusingly refer to these as forming part of the *internal environment.*

An organisation's environment can be split into:

- **Macro environment**

  Definition Those components of the environment that may potentially affect the organisation but whose relevance is not specific at a particular time. They are the broad forces - demography, economics, law and politics, culture and technology - that exercise a profound influence on the organisation's **microenvironment**.

- **Microenvironment**

Definition The part of the environment that is directly relevant to the organisation in achieving its goals. It varies depending on the domain the organisation has chosen for itself.

- **Domain**

Definition What an organisation stakes out for itself with respect to the range of products or services offered and markets served. (*The Sun* and *The Guardian* are both newspapers but they report news differently, carry different features and appeal to different segments of the newspaper market.)

4.3 The organisation's boundary

An organisation is a complex system with a particular identity and must therefore have some frontiers separating it from its environment. All organisations fall somewhere on a continuum between:

(a) a totally open system where the environment is so important that the organisation merges into it and has no real identity of its own;

(b) a totally closed system which is self-contained and has no environment at all.

The concept of organisational boundaries is not as clear cut and well defined as one would image. Take a public limited company. This could be viewed as being a collection of shareholders, personnel, directors and physical assets; with an environment containing customers, suppliers, competitors and other elements in the 'outside world'. Yet its shareholders probably own shares in other companies too, and, of course, institutional investors such as pension funds or investment trusts will be organisations in themselves. Employees may also be members of trade unions and other external bodies (political parties, for instance, or local government) and could also purchase the products/services of the company - making them its customers, or consumers.

4.4 Environmental influences

The environment exerts three basic forms of influence upon the organisation.

(a) It offers **threats** (to the well-being of the organisation, such as Government legislation, or, say, national action by trade unions) and **opportunities** (for exploitation, such as growth in market demand, or new technological possibilities).

(b) It is the source of organisational resources (human resources come from outside the organisation, as do funds and supplies generally).

(c) It contains interest or 'pressure groups' which have some kind of direct interest in organisational activities (these range from the general public and Government bodies to 'action' groups such as Greenpeace and Animal Rights).

5 A FRAMEWORK FOR ENVIRONMENTAL ANALYSIS

We have seen that the environment consists of those factors that can affect an organisation's operations, but which its management have little or no power to influence or control. An organisation can be thought of as an open system which is influenced by a complex political, economic, social and technological (PEST) structure of variables which can change.

5.1 The political and legal environment

Relevant factors include

- Trading regulations.

- Price controls (eg, EC Common Agricultural policy may result in a minimum price for a product).
- Taxation (eg, the level of corporation tax will affect the amount an enterprise can reinvest).
- Employment legislation.
- Nationalisation/denationalisation.

The problem facing strategic planners is how to plan for changes in the political environment. As change is not predictable, the planner needs to approach the problem by considering what type of political change could affect the enterprise rather than trying to estimate all the political changes that might occur.

The main feature of the legal environment is its increasing complexity. This is typified by company legislation. From 1948 to 1967 there were no major changes to company law; since then there have been four major Acts, plus the consolidating 1985 Act (the *CA 1989* amended certain provisions of the *CA 1985*).

This pattern is repeated in almost all areas. Employee legislation, consumer protection, planning and building regulations are all areas directly affecting business activities in which the legislation has become much more complex.

5.2 The economic environment

An analysis of economic factors should include

- Growth in demand for goods and services
- Availability of finance/level of interest rates
- Availability of manpower/unemployment rates
- Import controls
- Exchange control

The UK economy has been subject to considerable change. Several features characterise this change:

(i) steady, but relatively slow growth in output;
(ii) decline in employment;
(iii) a net oil exporter; and
(iv) rates of inflation often above other Western economies.

These have resulted in major changes in the economic environment faced by most companies.

The 'single market' of the European Community (EC) members in 1992/93 has caused further considerable changes. In essence, the analysis of economic factors will still be split between National and International, but the term National will include all EC member states. The 'domestic' market thus increases from 50 million people to 320 million.

5.3 The social and cultural environment

Business operates within a social framework. Four aspects of this are relevant

(i) Power – who has it, how effective is it, and how is it used?

(ii) Leadership – who are the leaders, what are their qualities and weaknesses?

(iii) Culture – the values and traditions within which the business must operate. One problem facing multinationals has often been a failure to cope with the different cultural values of the countries within which they operate.

(iv) Risk – the attitudes towards risk and risk-taking.

The social environment also covers the study of population trends. The strategic planner will make use of such trends to determine the size, type and location of the market place for products or services.

(i) Size. The expected growth or decline in national and international population.

(ii) Type. Changes in the age distribution.

(iii) Location. The expected drift of population into different parts of the country, eg, the South East of the U.K.

5.4 The technological environment

The technological environment determines the type of products that are made or services that are sold. It also determines the way in which products are made or services are provided.

The frequent effect of technological change is to make redundant an existing product or service. Enterprises that thus do not plan for change will no longer be in business.

Examples of recently developed new products are compact discs and micro computers. The introduction of microchips has changed the type of many home electrical products – eg, stereo systems and washing machines.

Examples of changes in the way in which products are made includes the use of robotics and computers. Their introduction either results in lower costs of production or better quality products or both.

An example of change in the way services are provided would be cash dispensers in banks and building societies.

The strategic planner looks upon the technological environment as part of the *product development* plan.

5.5 Types of business environment

Unless business planners are able to identify the actual and potential forces of change on their businesses, they will have no means of knowing what steps to take to minimise the danger or to cash in on the opportunities which the changes present. It is incumbent on strategic planners to take the steps necessary to collect, analyse and interpret relevant information on the key factors, or segments. It may be a case of closing the stable door after the horse has bolted if historic information only is produced, that is, after the changes have taken, or are taking, place. Information must be made available which shows the magnitude and rates of change of significant events and activities.

Four types of business environment are:

(a) **Simple environment**

Some organisations are fortunate to operate in business environments in which they only have to cope with relatively few uncertainties or change agents. It could be said that these organisations are in simple environments.

(b) **Complex environment**

The more complex an organisation's environment is, in other words the more variables there are that can change, the more uncertainty it faces. Complexity usually relates to the **diversity** of the environmental segments, and the extent to which they are interrelated. For example because of their size, and the diversity of their product-market involvement, the Hanson group of companies are operating in a very complex business environment.

It will be necessary for an organisation operating in a complex environment to try and reduce the environmental complexity, perhaps by structuring the management tasks round specialist operating areas. This would probably involve segmenting the environment into discrete sectors on a basis that reflects the significance of the different environmental influences on the organisation.

(c) **Static environment**

An organisation operating in a static environment faces no change of significance or relatively little change in the variables that give rise to uncertainty. The organisation is thus able to place confidence in its forecasts and assumptions. The business managers will be guided by their experience of the business environment in which they operate. They will be influenced by past events and the impact they had on organisational performance. The forecasting methods will, in the main, be **statistical** by nature based on projecting from past trends. There is, however, still a danger of unanticipated or unpredicted change, which should not be ignored.

For example, the baby-food producers in Europe, companies such as Gerber, and Cow & Gate, failed to anticipate the full impact that the declining birth rates and changing positive attitude of women to breast-feeding babies would have on their market. The European market for baby-foods fell by about 5% in real terms over the five year period 1976 - 1980. Exports to the developing countries had also grown very slowly. By failing to spot and act on these trends the industry was plunged into disorder

(d) **Dynamic environments**

The degree of environmental dynamism relates to the rate and frequency of change of the factors that give rise to uncertainty. An organisation that operates in an extremely dynamic environment is faced by rapid, and probably novel change, and thus plans its future facing a very uncertain business situation.

The business planners operating in this type of environment will need to consider the novelty of future events and not be influenced solely by past events and results. They will need to be very sensitive to change, and forecasting will be based on a mix of statistical and intuitive techniques. There is a danger that the organisational structure, and culture, will be unable to cope with the change required. A dynamic environment is far more risky than a static environment.

We can see from this that different types of environment can be classified into two major groups: (a) by speed and nature of change (static or dynamic), and (b) by convolution (simple or complex).

5.6 Activity

Describe two situations, the first where the environment is simple and dynamic and the second where the environment is complex and stable.

5.7 Activity solution

(i) An example of a simple and dynamic environment is one where the product is only being sold in one market (simple) and where the product is still in the introduction stage and demand might be predicted to increase dramatically (dynamic). Virtual reality games in leisure arcades could fit this description.

(ii) The environment of a group of research scientists working for a pharmaceutical company, funded by an international grant to investigate genetic disorders, might be classified as stable and complex. The stability arises because of the grant which means that they will not be exposed to cuts in funding. The complexity is in the amount of knowledge required which is drawn from different disciplines and is uncertain in its future discoveries.

5.8 Strategic implications of different environments

The practical implications, then, are that each company faces a particular environmental outlook. Building on our previous overview we shall distinguish four such environmental vistas:

- Stable and unchanging;
- Stable with minor fluctuations;
- Gradually changing in a predictable fashion;
- Rapidly changing in an unpredictable fashion.

(a) **Stable and Unchanging**

In this case the organisation can focus its attention on its past decisions and results, and on attempting to correct its past mistakes. Tactical planning is more important than strategic planning. (For example, British Telecom until recent years operated in a stable marketing environment and could safely invest large amounts of resources in the pursuit of achieving a maximally efficient telephone service.)

(b) **Stable with minor fluctuations**

This describes an environment characterised by cyclical and/or seasonal fluctuations within a fairly stable structure. (For example, a **local government education service** will adopt a set of procedures for educating children, only having to adjust its scale of activity to accommodate the changing numbers of children in education.)

(c) **Gradually changing in a predictable fashion**

This is where an organisation recognises that its environment is slowly being changed into something new and predictable. With this recognition it can begin to make the necessary adjustments to its goals, strategic direction, organisation structure, and systems so that it can proceed in a meaningful way for the future. (Thus with the predictable changing values of women the *Girl Guide* movement shifted its programmes toward developing the *'new woman'* rather than the *'future wife and mother'*.)

(d) **Rapidly changing in an unpredictable fashion**

Within this environment an organisation operates in highly turbulent and unpredictable businesses. Strategic planning is much more important than tactical planning, and effectiveness (doing the right things) are just as essential as achieving efficiency (doing things the best way). (Thus **National Health Service hospitals** in recent years have endured a succession of shocks and surprises. Private medicare, rapidly changing medical technology, in-depth appraisal of their activities by the National Audit Office (and Audit Commission), new government policies and constraints, rising costs and consumerism has led to hospitals closing, *'opting out'*, and finding creative ways of adapting to their environment in order to survive.)

6 IDENTIFYING CURRENT AND EMERGING CHANGES

6.1 The economic environment

Every organisation and industry operates within a *business ecosystem.* Consider the textile business. The industry comprises a huge system consisting of cotton, wool, synthetic materials, factories, transportation, the economies of many different national states, the tastes and fashion of the time, and the incomes of millions of people. The industry goes on year after year adapting and balancing with other *ecosystems,* such as the economic system, the political system, the consumer value system, and so on. Irritations do occur, such as recessions, inflation, climatic calamities, sudden changes in people's clothing tastes and industrial disputes. These are dealt with by the built-in homeostatic mechanisms of the textile ecosystem such as budgetary tightening, layoffs, price movements, new product development and labour agreements. However a major trauma within the industry would still pose a serious threat to the textile manufacturers, which through its 'destruction power' would present a tremendous threat to many and a tremendous opportunity to others. For example, the sudden softening of the pound sterling against other major currencies by over 20 percent in the two months following *Black Wednesday* in October 1992 when the British Government withdrew from the European exchange rate mechanism (ERM), was a major trauma for companies within the industry purchasing their raw materials from overseas sources. The economic dimension for companies, then, can be considered by posing a series of questions.

(a) What are the essential economic and technological characteristics of the industry?

(b) What is the level of industrial concentration (ie, what percentage of total capacity is controlled by the five or six largest companies)?

(c) What are the prospects for fundamental changes in the industry's economic and technological structure?

(d) What is the apparent relationship between sales and economic indicators (eg, what degree of correlation exists between industry sales and gross national product)?

(e) What problems are likely to be created by fluctuations in the business cycle?

(f) What are the possible consequences for the company of fluctuations in business activity, government fiscal policy, and/or international events on cost/profit/volume, return on capital employed on new investments or replacements of redundant or obsolete equipment, availability and utilisation of labour resources, cash flow and organisational structure such as its flexibility and adaptability to swift or gradual changes in product output levels.

6.2 The strategic relevance of economics

We have seen that making informed judgements and assumptions about future economic events is often crucially important for planning business strategy. The level of economic activity has a bearing on: input costs, labour costs, interest rates, cost of capital, foreign exchange rates, inflation rates, sales turnover levels, unemployment levels, and so on. Economic factors can:

(a) Induce competition into an industry **or** force companies out.

(b) Encourage foreign investment **or** conversely investment by foreigners.

(c) Prolong **or** shorten product life.

(d) Encourage companies to substitute automation for people, **or** to recruit more people and reduce machines.

(e) Make a very strong market relatively weak.

(f) Turn a safe market, risky.

(g) Turn a *'hard plan'* (high probability of certainty with strong commitment) into a *'soft plan'* (uncertainty and contingent commitment).

6.3 Factors affecting the national economy

The national economy is the vehicle by which its citizens attempt to achieve their economic aspirations. The institutions through which any economic system operates are many and varied and encompass national ideas, attitudes, pressure groups and organisations which individually and collectively determine the direction and effectiveness of the system. Influences are many and varied.

(a) Traditions and codified behaviour patterns.
(b) National habits towards waste and inefficiency.
(c) Corporate structures and international competitiveness.
(d) Price and wage policies.

(e) Government controls.
(f) Market organisation.
(g) Transport systems.
(h) Social welfare policies.
(i) Professional and institutionalised self-regulation.

Most countries now use overall growth as an internal measure of the success or failure of their economic system, but even where there is a high rate of growth there are likely to be areas of high unemployment and poverty. A government assumes responsibility for action in such cases, but if it extends or reduces its present level of commitment and responsibility, the economy will take on a different shape and emphasis.

After growth, stability is generally rated as the most desirable attribute of an economy, provided that stability does not bring with it stagnation. Instability is reckoned to be a pernicious and socially unsettling phenomenon, because it tends to create unemployment, booms and slumps, price and wage fluctuations and provides the opportunity for certain key groups of workers in the economy to gain a greater share of the national income at the expense of the remainder of the population. Thus, the actions of individuals, organisations and the government to achieve stability or to accept instability will have a significant impact on the shape of the economy.

7 INFORMATION SOURCES

7.1 Introduction

In the business world there are very few product or service markets that do not experience some degree of turbulence, competitive hostility and restrictiveness. Marketing managers, in particular, face the *'sharp edge'* of the effects of change. Gordon and Miller (1976) identified three environmental characteristics - *dynamism, heterogeneity* and *hostility* which influence the design of management information systems. The greater the *dynamism* ('rate of change which has force') the more is the need for external non-financial information, and intelligence to be reported at more frequent intervals. The greater the *heterogeneity* of the organisation's product-market (ie, the diversity of the organisation's products and services) the more internal departmentalisation and compartmentalisation is likely to follow, with the information being similarly disaggregated. Finally, the more *hostile* and competitive the market place the more likely it is that the organisation will develop tight systems of cost control that it monitors frequently.

Strategic planners require information covering two broad areas.

(a) **Environmental data.**

McNamee outlines the environmental data that should be included in a database for strategic planners. This data covers:

(i) Competitive data on the five competitive forces facing the industry;

(ii) Economic data;

(iii) Political data about the influence of governments (both domestic and foreign) on the industry;

(iv) Legal data on recent and likely future legislation that affects the industry;

(v) Social data.

In practice, many organisations do not collect much of this information on an internal database as the input time may be high and external databases may be available.

There is an increasing availability of information from external databases. Much of this information may have been available before the advent of computer database systems. For example, a wealth of information is (and was) contained in published government statistics, published financial statements of competitors and economic forecasts. The advantage to the strategic planner in accessing such information from a computer database is the ability to make rapid calculations on the data, and to resort the data.

Many public databases consist of environmental data which has been collected for the specific purpose of a particular type of data user. On line information can be obtained about various aspects of the financial markets - interest rates, foreign exchange rates, and share prices. Some databases supply data on a particular industry.

The main objective in using external databases is to obtain information about the environment within which the organisation has to, or will be expected, to operate.

Examples of public databases

There is a multitude of instant-access or on-line public databases available to meet every need, from very general coverage, such as those offered by *Ceefax* (BBC), *Oracle* (ITV) and *Prestel* (BT) through to specialist information, such as *Who Owns Whom,* a database which shows the ownership of all UK subsidiary and associate companies.

(b) **Internal data about the organisation itself.**

Internal data about the organisation itself should be in plentiful supply. In the initial stages of strategic planning internal data on **resources** of the organisation would be required. The data would enable the planner to:

(i) carry out an **audit** of resources, ie, what resources does the business have in terms of:

- physical resources;
- human resources;
- operating systems; and
- current image in the market place.

(ii) plan the **utilisation** of those resources.

In the later stages of strategic planning internal data (often expressed in financial terms), would be required to determine the **efficiency** and **effectiveness** of the organisation and its business. We will deal with all of these planning aspects later.

7.2 Activity

Draw up a list of the sources of environmental data that is both useful and available to most organisations.

7.3 Activity solution

The list could be very long, but the most popular sources would include the following:

- Relevant environmental information is found in newspapers and periodicals.
- Trade journals contain information about a particular industry and trade associations are another source.
- The government is a source of statistical data relating to the economy and society. The government also gives specific advice to businesses eg, Single European Market information and advice on overcoming trade barriers.
- Published accounts of competitors, suppliers and customers are all available sources of relevant environmental information.

- Technological information can be sought from the Patent Office, universities and specialist libraries.
- Chambers of Commerce have information on exporting to certain countries.
- Various databases can be accessed.

8 CHAPTER SUMMARY

A strategic planning system interacts with its environment, that is, those distinct factors that have actual or potential impacts on the organisation. Among the key environmental segments influencing strategy formulation are the changing national and international characteristics and events, and economic aspects.

The environmental forces impact on business in different ways and with different degrees of strength. Some organisations confront a complexity of environmental forces that are dynamic, and which present opportunities if they are able and willing to grasp them, and serious threats if they do not.

The conclusions we might draw about forecasting are:

(a) There is no one *'best'* forecasting technique. For long-range environmental forecasting where little data is available and/or change is likely to be continuous, intuitive techniques are relevant. For short-term forecasting where data is available and where relationships are relatively stable, statistical techniques are more appropriate. For situations which require a high level of accuracy, or in which there is environmental complexity and dynamism, and where the additional forecasting costs are justified, a mixture of causal and intuitive forecasting techniques is suitable.

(b) The forecast is only as good as the assumptions and data on which it is based. Mathematical sophistication cannot compensate for faulty data or erroneous assumptions, or, more bluntly, *'garbage in - garbage out'*. As Savage and Small write: 'In the practical application of forecasting techniques, predictive accuracy is ultimately more important than over-concentration on the finer points of statistical theory.'

(c) The forecast can only reduce uncertainty; it cannot eliminate it. Thus in addition to management acting in a proactive manner (ie, forecasting and anticipating the future) it needs also to have reactive flexibility (ie, the ability to respond quickly to unanticipated developments).

(d) Forecast results need to be cross-checked as the basis for establishing their predictive accuracy, and if appropriate for deciding on how this accuracy can be improved.

(e) Any forecast is intended as a basis for action and is not simply an academic exercise. Therefore, it needs to be integrated within the planning and control systems.

9 SELF TEST QUESTIONS

9.1 List five methods of statistical forecasting (2.1).

9.2 What is scenario planning? (2.2)

9.3 What is a PEST analysis? (3.2, 5)

9.4 Distinguish between an organisation's macroenvironment and its microenvironment (4.2).

9.5 What is a business's technological environment? (5.4)

9.6 Explain how the dynamism of an environment affects the need for external non-financial information (7.1).

10 EXAMINATION TYPE QUESTION

10.1 Environmental appraisal

It has been stated that the strategic environmental appraisal should be directed towards identifying threats as much as opportunities. Five specific areas are usually included in any such appraisal ie, competitors, political, economic, social and technological. **You are required** to discuss each of these at local, national and international levels. **(25 marks)**

11 ANSWER TO EXAMINATION TYPE QUESTION

11.1 Environmental appraisal

(a) **Competitors**

The company will need to examine what actions its competitors might take over the relevant future that will affect it at the local, national or international level. Their actions may affect its market, its employees, its research, its suppliers and its position within the industry. The majority of companies face a large number of competitors and it would be extremely difficult to analyse them all. It is possible, however, to study a few of the most important ones and to place the others in categories by size or some other relevant classification. In most industries there are a few companies of national or international importance, a few dozen of moderate significance and thousands of small ones. For example, in the vehicle building industry, it may be possible to predict that virtually none of the thousands of lorry manufacturers who employ less than ten people will enter the over 40-ton vehicle building market. Such generalisations serve to concentrate a company's enquiries into those areas that are most relevant to that company's business.

(b) **Political**

A 'political change' is a change inspired by local, national or international governments or government controlled agencies.

Here the company would try to determine whether any political changes at the local, national or international level will affect its business, (eg, anti-trust legislation, taxation, pollution, safety regulations, trade union law, tariff and quota agreements, rising nationalism in developing nations, economic federations of nations, government sponsored research, nationalisation). Such lists can be endless. At the local level changes that may be significant include: opening hours of shops, parking regulations, construction of roads and buildings, etc. It must be remembered, however, that these studies are being conducted at a strategic level and that only those political changes that will materially affect the company over a period of years need to be considered.

(c) **Economic**

At the local level, economic changes affect remuneration rates, availability of labour, purchasing patterns and prices. Clearly the smaller the company is relative to the local community, the more carefully it will have to predict local economic changes, a statement that is also valid in respect of the national level. It should also be noted that certain companies operate from one central factory, but at the same time sell to international markets and local economic changes may, therefore, not be highly significant for its costs, but wholly significant for its prices.

The broad economic changes are well known (eg, primary and secondary industries are now growing rapidly in some of the developing nations, while tertiary industries are growing more rapidly in the developed nations). It is now quite apparent that the size of companies in some industries is increasing, while in other industries there may well be a revival of the small business.

(d) **Social**

Changes in social attitudes, behaviour and composition are critically important to consumer-oriented industries. They are now becoming important to even the heavy end of industry as well, for although consumer needs and buying patterns have an effect on the market for steel or coal only at second or third hand, certain social attitudes are beginning to affect many aspects of industry other than the market. In particular, attitudes to work are changing and these must be taken into consideration when designing the organisational elements of a strategic structure. Again, society is applying increasing pressure on all companies in respect of pollution, noise and environmental aesthetics generally, so that the design of factories, offices, products and equipment must take these changes into account.

Changes in education, wealth, life styles, attitudes to work, changes in society's composition and its attitude to race, colour and religion are some of the areas that most companies need to consider, whether they are operating in consumer-oriented industries or not.

(e) **Technological**

While social changes have to be forecast mainly to identify the changing needs of consumers, technological changes need to be forecast to identify how these needs might be met in the future. Technological changes can threaten a company in two main ways: a substitute product may appear or new methods of manufacture or distribution of the existing product may be discovered. In much the same way, a company's technical knowledge can often be used to invade the markets or production methods of other industries. Technological changes do not only affect companies in areas of high technology, because manufactured products and their processes are subject to technological change as well. It is perhaps less obvious that service industries are affected and yet it can be argued that recent advances in computing and telecommunications have affected the banking industry at least as much as they have affected the manufacturing industry. Presumably the High Street retailing industry will feel the effects of 'television buying' (ie, mail order service linked to television display and selection in the home) in the near future.

It is obviously important that the technological forecast is integrated into the framework of corporate strategy as this is fundamental to its effective use. It is directly analogous with the place of sales forecast in the planning of operational activities for the company in the shorter term.

10 A FRAMEWORK FOR STRATEGY IMPLEMENTATION

INTRODUCTION & LEARNING OBJECTIVES

The preceding chapters outlined the anatomy of the strategic planning system and examined the strategic options open to the company. The task now is to show how the strategic plans are implemented.

We discovered, from our previous discussion of Mintzberg's analysis, that not all intended strategies are implemented. The deliberate strategies often cross over with emergent strategies, which are developed as they are implemented.

It is probably impossible to plan for every eventuality, as some decisions may not be anticipated and implementation may involve adjusting the plan to suit the changed conditions.

When you have studied this chapter you should be able to do the following:

- Explain what is involved in the implementation of strategy.
- Describe the different skills needed for successful strategy implementation.
- Outline the problems that can arise.
- Classify and discuss organisational structures.
- Explain the effect of centralised and decentralised decision making
- Describe Mintzberg's structural configurations.
- Outline the influences on organisational design.

1 IMPLEMENTATION OF STRATEGY

1.1 Requirements

The implementation of a plan requires:

(a) selection of an appropriate strategy;

(b) management planning and control; and

(c) operational planning and control.

To clarify the distinction between strategic planning and management planning and control, it is useful to quote the definitions given by R.N.Anthony.

Strategic planning is the process of deciding on the objectives of the organisation, on changes in those objectives, on the resources used to attain the objectives, and on the policies that are used to govern the acquisition, use and disposition of the resources.

Management control is the process by which the managers ensure that resources are obtained and used effectively and efficiently in the accomplishment of the organisation's objectives.

In other words, strategic planning determines what is to be done and the general policies which will decide how it is done, while management planning and control is concerned with the detail of how resources are to be acquired.

Operational plans are the short-term element of the company's overall plan. They are concerned with the day to day running of the company in the immediate future and usually cover a period of one year.

Operational planning and control can be defined as planning and controlling the effective and efficient performance of specific tasks. It therefore differs from management planning and control in focusing on one task at a time, whereas management planning and control focuses on resource requirements for the whole range of tasks.

1.2 Choice of strategy

In evaluating alternative strategies, the company will have to take into account:

(a) **Objectives**

The chosen strategy must allow the company to achieve each of its objectives.

(b) **Strategic balance**

The chosen strategy should not place too much dependence on one particular area of operations.

(c) **Analysis**

The company needs to analyse its own strengths and weaknesses in relation to its industry and to the general social-economic climate. For instance, 'to be in the leisure and pleasure business' is quite a common strategy nowadays. In selecting such a strategy, companies are taking into account social trends towards greater leisure and towards the concept of spending rather than saving, which, accompanied by higher living standards, are leading to increased expenditure on leisure time activities.

The chosen strategy should build on the company's strengths, eliminate weaknesses, avert or provide for threats, exploit opportunities which are foreseen, and leave sufficient flexibility to exploit any opportunities which may arise but which have not yet been foreseen.

The company must beware of thinking that too abrupt a change can be made. Although it is certainly possible to improve skills within the time-scale of a strategic plan, this can only be done if the financial resources are sufficient to buy-in know-how, engage high calibre staff, etc. Thus, spotting an attractive area of business is not the end of strategy formulation, for the overall resources must be taken into account.

(d) **Feasibility**

Can the individual strategies called for by the overall strategy be carried out in practice? It is important to emphasise that, in thinking how a strategy will be implemented, detailed thought is given to the feasibility of its implementation. There is no sense in proceeding with the implementation if, in planning how it should be done, it becomes clear that the strategy is unrealistic. Because of the generalised nature of strategic decision-making, it may be that detailed consideration of a strategic course of action does not actually take place until the beginning of the implementation plan.

A strategy must not only be workable but be seen to be so, so that all employees will feel fully committed to it.

Ranking alternative strategies will be difficult, because they will contribute different amounts to different objectives and will have different pros and cons under each of the headings above. Unless one strategy emerges that is clearly superior to the others on all counts (or on all the major objectives - short-term profitability, long-term profitability and flexibility), it may be necessary to weight the various factors according to importance, to arrive at an overall best strategy. Argenti suggests that the use of a business model (whether computerised or not) will be useful - perhaps even essential - in evaluating strategies.

1.3 Implementation

More detail is required to implement a plan than to select it. Once approved, the long-term strategy must be used to draw up more detailed plans for the medium-term period, and even more detailed plans for the immediate future (the operations plan). The operations plan will contain a statement of requirements for each department, together with a detailed budget, so that managers know what they are to achieve.

Each action which is taken during the period of the plans must be assigned a time when it is to be taken. This phasing of a sequence of actions turns the plan into what Ansoff calls a programme.

If the plan is proposing a shift from the company's traditional area of business, or if a large growth or change in emphasis is envisaged, it might be necessary to re-think the organisational structure of the company to ensure better lines of communication and better control. Such a change would have to be implemented while the strategy itself was being put into effect (and indeed might form part of the overall strategy if a major change was involved).

2 SKILLS NEEDED FOR IMPLEMENTATION

2.1 Team skills

Organisations need the capability to manage their systems (production and marketing), as well as controlling the financial and human resources aspects properly. They should possess a balance of skills necessary to implement a strategy successfully. The breadth of services or products offered has implications for the types of skill required. A broad scope of services may be dealt with either by competent, adaptable individuals who can turn their hands to a variety of tasks (the 'craftsman' approach), or through a number of specialists brought together in project teams to tackle specific problems (the 'team' approach). Both approaches require highly trained, experienced and probably expensive staff. The team approach would require quite a large scale of business to justify the employment of many specialists. The organisation needs to be able to convince their clients that it can perform better than the competition, not just to get the business but to justify charging premium prices.

A deep understanding of the customer's business and its problems is essential for success, and the ability to communicate how the organisation can solve problems (add value) is an important pre-requisite to securing the business. The way that an organisation's skills are linked together in the value chain can also be a source of competitive advantage and have been referred to as the non-tradable assets of the organisation.

If team working is necessary to carry out the strategy, then the ways that the team behave and communicate are also important. Belbin has looked at the mix of personality types in terms of the balance of skills and human resources required to operate in a team effectively. He suggests a character mix of eight ideal types:

- **the leader** - co-ordinating (not imposing) and operating through others;
- **the shaper** - committed to the task, may be aggressive and challenging, will also always promote activity;
- **the plant** - thoughtful and thought-provoking;
- **the evaluator** - analytically criticises others' ideas, brings group down to earth;
- **the resource-investigator** - not a new ideas person but tends to pick up others' ideas and adds to them; is usually a social type of person who often acts as a bridge to the outside world;
- **the company worker** - turns general ideas into specifics; practical and efficient, tends to be an administrator handling the scheduling aspects;

- **the team worker** - concerned with the relationships within the group, is supportive and tends to defuse potential conflict situations;

- **the finisher** - unpopular, but a necessary individual; he is the progress chaser ensuring that timetables are met.

Strategic change will have a significant impact on the people within the organisation. The issues which are important are manpower configuration, recruitment, training and development.

2.2 Skills to support different strategies

Depending on the type of strategy, there will be different resource requirements and it is important to identify those value activities which are critical to the success of particular types of strategy.

- A strategy of low price will require emphasis on plant and processes which are cost efficient, and possibly on low cost distribution systems. The key skills required are planning the processes and labour supervision, supported by management systems to ensure that cost efficiency actually delivered. Cost leadership requires skills in controlling the sources of costs: the cost drivers. Raw materials, components, labour, machinery, power or storage space could each be the largest component of unit costs. These costs need to be identified and ruthlessly controlled. Where the manufacturing process involves the use of expensive equipment it may well be that scheduling skills are required to achieve maximum utilisation of capacity. In a labour intensive assembly process, where labour forms a large component of costs, then skills in method study, payment by result schemes, supervision, job design and manning are required. Skills in procurement are vital to minimise the costs of bought-in components.

- A strategy of differentiation is likely to need skills in marketing, research and creative ability, with an emphasis on product development. The requirements for systems may not be so stringent, but there should be a strong emphasis on co-ordinating the separate value activities to ensure that they are genuinely adding value in the process of creating and delivering the service or product.

3 PROBLEMS WHICH CAN ARISE

Hrebiniak and Joyce developed a strategy implementation model based on an integrated approach to decision making. They posed two questions:

(i) What decisions and actions can be taken by managers who are implementing strategy?

(ii) How can these decisions be organised to meet the criteria of logic, action and contingent prescription?

From these questions they suggest that guidance can be obtained from the principles of:

- **intended rationality**, which is based on the premise that top management has both limited time and limited capacity to think through decisions fully; and

- **minimum intervention**, which implies that, in implementing strategy, managers should change only what is necessary and sufficient to produce an enduring solution to the strategic problem being assessed.

The decisions that are involved in strategic implementation are identified as:

- planning decisions, which include strategy formulation, operating level objectives and incentives and controls;

- organisational design decisions, which include the decisions involved in moving from one structure to another.

The decision processes are a study of means-end relationships which are designed to break down strategic interventions into manageable actions within the planning horizon of the implementation of the strategy. To do this, interventions need to be broken down into smaller parts for operating units and individuals to manage. The control process must be made clear and the appropriate targets set if managers are to cope with what is required of them and also to help their staff.

4 KEY IMPLEMENTATION ISSUES

4.1 Critical success factors

One of the major problems with strategy implementation in many organisations is a failure to translate declarations of strategic purpose into a practical statement of those factors which are critical to achieving the targets, and the key tasks which will ensure success.

These issues can be addressed systematically:

- The critical success factors for the specific strategy must be agreed and scrutinised to make sure that all the factors are genuinely necessary and the list is sufficient to underpin success.
- The key tasks which are essential to the delivery of each critical success factor must be identified. These may relate to the organisations value activities, identified in the value chain, and include improvements in support activities or changes in linkages within the value system. For example, an office supply company with a critical success factor of customer care would underpin the CSF through the three key tasks of responding to enquiries, supplying accurate information and an efficient and quick breakdown and maintenance service. These tasks are dependent on the office supplies company's infrastructure, particularly the database of customer installations.
- Allocate management responsibility for the key tasks identified. For the office supplies company, the area which could go wrong is the maintenance of the customer database. The responsibility for this is assigned to the maintenance department but there should be linkages established with both the sales and the software department to ensure accurate information.

4.2 Activity

Draw Porter's value chain, identifying the areas which show where the key tasks underpinning the critical success factor of customer care will appear on it.

4.3 Activity solution

Critical success factor of 'customer care' and its fit with the value chain

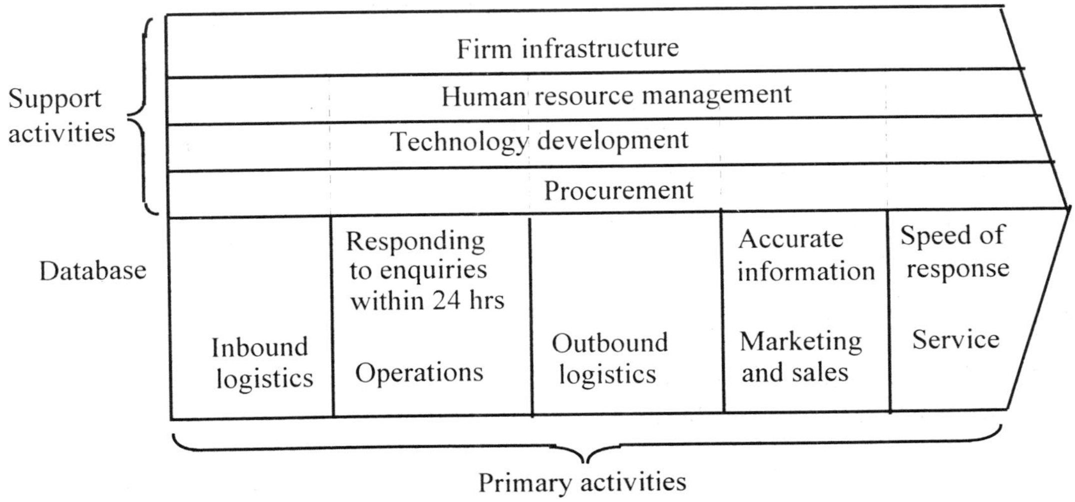

4.4 Implementation and change

There are aspects of implementation which can be changed directly, generally implying physical changes in the way resources are allocated. These include:

- the organisation's structure;
- management systems;
- procedures and policies;
- short term budgets and action plans; and
- management information systems.

Other aspects of implementation which can be changed indirectly are the behavioural aspects, which imply changes in beliefs and attitudes. These include:

- the culture and values of the organisation;
- developing the quality of the business, its people and its products or services;
- internal communication systems which are dependent on the co-operation between parts of the organisation;
- the willingness of employees to search for a better way of doing things.

5 DEVELOPING A FRAMEWORK

5.1 The overall planning system

A (simplified) overall planning system is shown below. The area within the dotted line is the strategic plan. At this stage **resource management** strategies have been grouped together as one because they will be considered in detail later. (It could be argued that at least some of this area should be outside the dotted line, but it is not profitable to try to make too fine a distinction between the types of plan.)

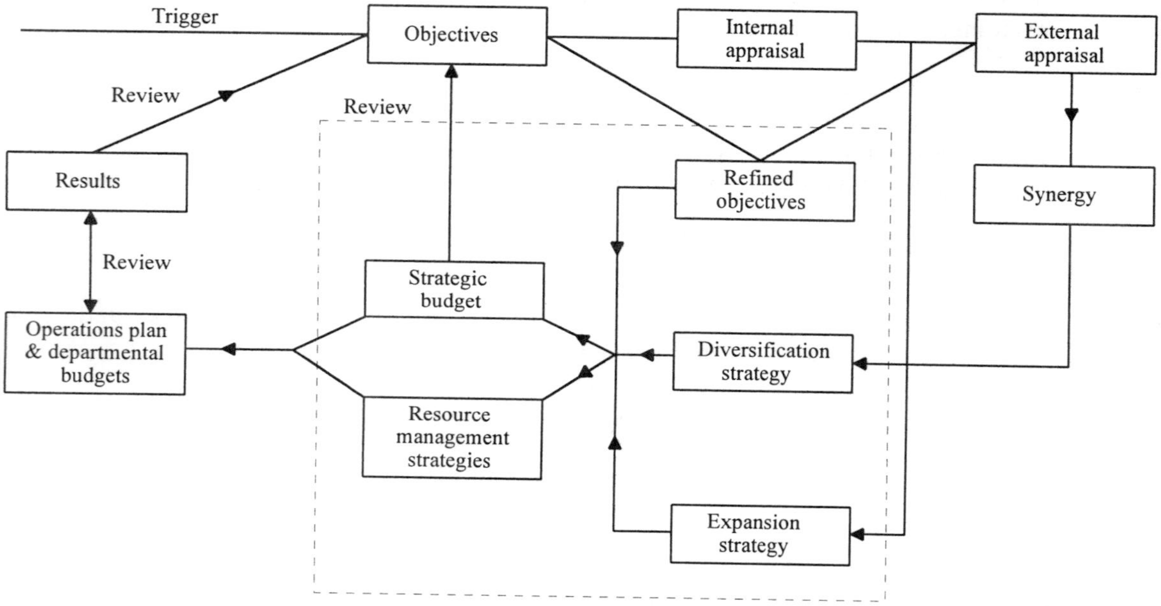

The strategic budget contains the quantification of the strategy - the expected profit, resources to be devoted to expansion and diversification.

You will note that the diagram is simplified to the extent that there is no provision for non- growth strategies in the strategic plan.

The various review points are as follows:

(a) Objectives may have to be reviewed when the strategic plan is drawn up if a strategy cannot be devised which meets all the objectives.

(b) Results will be compared frequently (weekly, monthly or quarterly) with departments' budgets.

(c) Results will be taken into account at least once a year in reviewing objectives and restarting the planning cycle. (Ideally the process should be continuous.)

5.2 Control

You should be familiar with the concept of control by comparison with budget in the short term. An effective procedure is illustrated below:

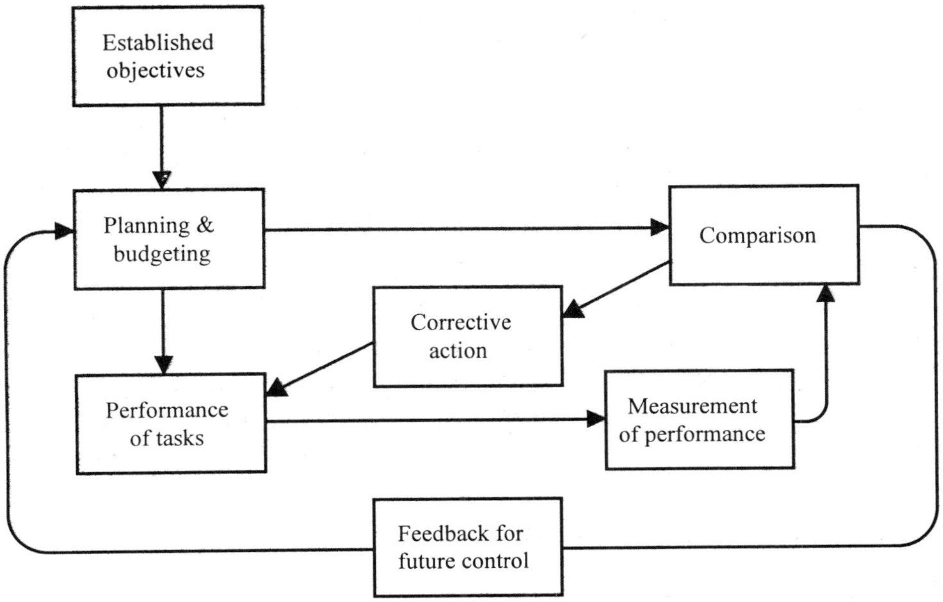

This technique cannot, however, be applied to control strategy, because of the long time interval between the planning of a strategy and its being implemented. Indeed, a strategy might never be fully implemented, because in the meantime the environment will have changed and the strategy will have been reviewed.

Therefore the 'closed loop' feedback system cannot be used, and an 'open loop' (ie, no feedback) has to suffice:

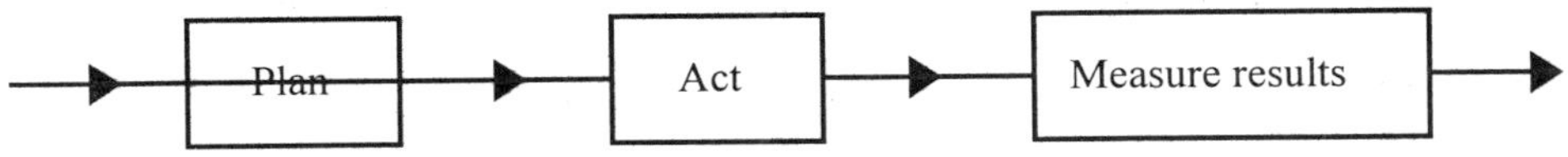

The results which are measured are not the end results of the strategy, but progress towards it, and it must be recognised that progress in the early stages, where long time scales are involved, might not provide any real indication of the eventual outcome.

Because of this lack of effective measurement, plans must be flexible in order that they can be amended to reflect changed circumstances. The ways in which this is achieved (eg, by contingency planning, by maintaining adequate cash reserves, etc) have already been discussed. However, the planning process itself must also be flexible. There has to be provision for the continuous review of objectives, strategy and the forecasts and assumptions on which the plan is based. Objectives should be reviewed during strategy formulation and at least once a year, assuming that planning is carried out on a formalised cyclical basis.

However, there must also be a willingness to review objectives (and hence strategy) each time a major project decision is due to be taken. In other words, we would not plan in January, and evaluate a project within the framework of that plan in October, without enquiring as to whether the strategy is still the appropriate one to be pursuing. All aspects of strategy formulation should therefore be reviewed continuously.

5.3 Review of factors affecting strategy

Review must cover all the areas which were covered in planning. Objectives will have to be reviewed if, for instance, the inflation rate rises, shareholders' aspirations alter, or the attitude of society to large companies changes. Forecasts must be continuously updated, allowing continuous performance-risk gap analysis.

Strengths and weaknesses must be reviewed. They might change unintentionally, eg, a key manager resigns, a number of customers merge so that the company becomes dependent on a single customer, or they might change intentionally - after all, one of the aims of strategy is to correct weaknesses, so the analysis **should** change; or it might be proved that the company's original analysis was incorrect.

Opportunities and threats, in particular, must be reviewed, because these are the most unpredictable - they change rapidly and the company has no control over them. It is important to specify the assumptions on which any decision is based or which are important to the success of a project. These assumptions can then be monitored, and management alerted if they prove incorrect.

Action taken must be reviewed against the programme specified in the plan. If action has not been taken, then the succeeding elements in the plan will have to be reviewed and perhaps rescheduled. Argenti also makes the point that any failure to carry out the planned action is a failing in the original plan, because the plan ought to have taken account of any difficulties which might arise to cause delay. There must have been some weakness or threat which was not identified. If the plan can fail in one area it can fail in others, and therefore such a failing should trigger off a revision of the entire strategy.

6 DIFFERENT TYPES OF ORGANISATION STRUCTURE

6.1 The influence of structure on strategy

The people in an organisation are one of the most important resources and how they are organised is crucial to the effectiveness of strategy.

The tools and techniques of strategic management in implementing plans are theoretically independent of the business organisation. However, the way in which a plan is implemented must in practice be influenced by the type of organisation.

The influences which have a bearing on organisational structure and design include:

- the types of problems the organisation has when constructing strategies;
- a consideration of whether it is operating in a stable environment or in a highly complex or changing environment;
- the diversity of the organisation. The needs of a multinational are different from those of a small company;
- the technology;
- the type of ownership.

Because of all of these different influences, it is not possible to have a simple set of rules which can prescribe organisational structures and systems. The structure of the organisation is only a skeleton on which the flesh of the strategy can be hung and, unfortunately, the structure in itself will not ensure the success of the strategy, although an inappropriate choice of structure could impede success.

Developing the flesh on the structure consists of three elements:

(i) organisational configuration - matching the detailed structure with the context in which the organisation is operating;

(ii) centralisation / decentralisation - where the responsibility for operational and strategic decision-making should lie;

(iii) management systems - how the systems relate to the structure and influence the behaviour of people.

6.2 Classification of organisation structures

There are many ways of classifying organisation structure.

A common analysis views organisation structures which develop in response to the size of the organisation. There is thus:

(a) a small business structure;

(b) a functional structure (which arises when (a) develops beyond a small business); and

(c) a divisional structure (which arises when an organisation grows by diversification into many different products).

6.3 Small business structure

This is illustrated below:

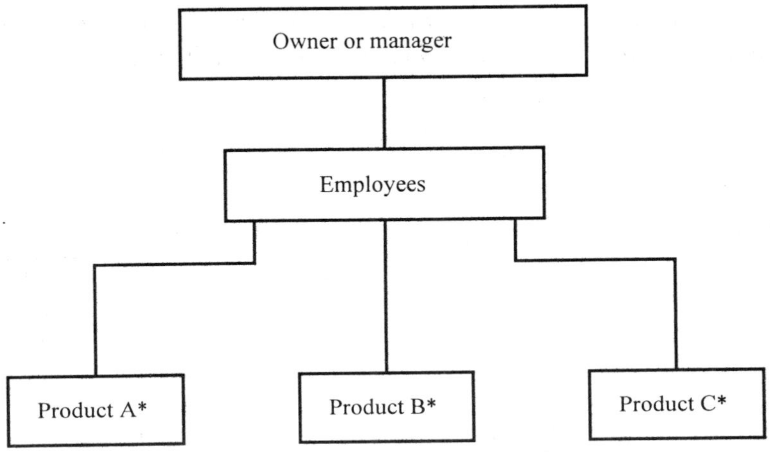

*(Although, throughout, the term 'product' is used to describe the output of a business, this section could apply equally well to companies that produce only 'services'.)

This type of business produces a single product, or a related group of products, and the owner, or manager, is responsible for strategic and operational management. Thus, it is a discrete, self-contained and largely self-controlled business unit. It is equivalent to a strategic business unit in a divisionalised organisation.

6.4 Functional structure

The functional structure is usually chronologically the next stage in the development of a business, and is illustrated below:

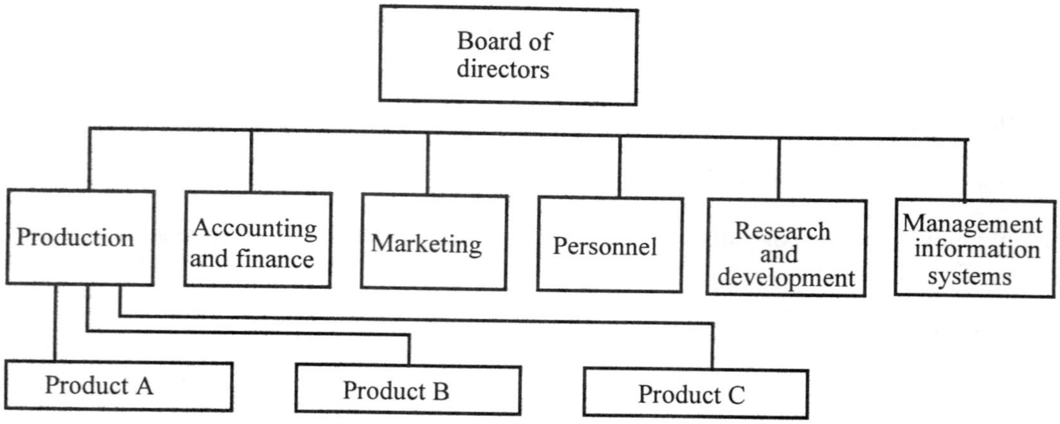

Planning is divided between the corporate and functional levels, with strategic planning being decided at board level and being executed at the functional level.

6.5 Divisional structure

Where the functionally-structured business grows by diversification, the structure will be found to be inappropriate, and the divisional structure illustrated below is likely to be adopted:

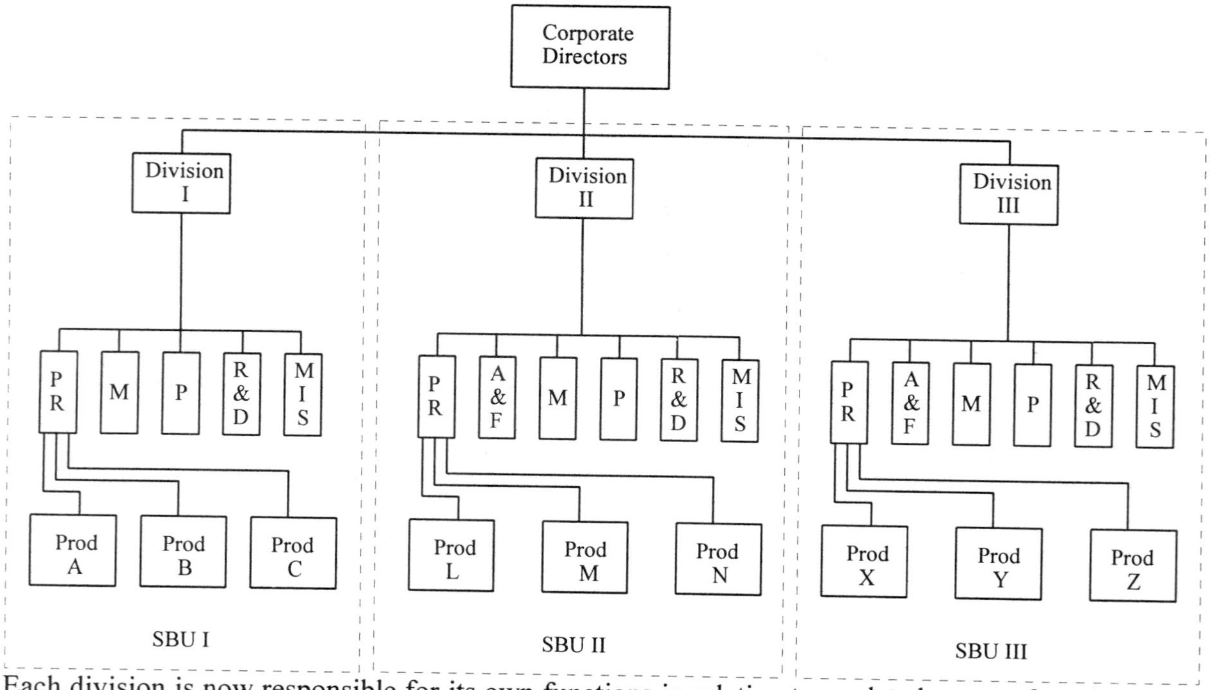

Each division is now responsible for its own functions in relation to a related group of products. Thus, each division may be regarded as a Strategic Business Unit (SBU).

Strategic planning in this environment becomes a complex hierarchical process:

(a) corporate strategic planning takes place at central board level. This is concerned with guiding the divisions so that the competitive advantages of a diversity of business accrue to the company, and encouraging each division to plan to take maximum advantage of its individual position;

(b) divisional planning is concerned with developing a portfolio of products; and

(c) operational planning is at the functional level within divisions.

6.6 Matrix structure

(a) The matrix concept

The grid/matrix approach came into being because the US Government decided it did not wish to deal with a number of specialised executives when negotiating defence contracts and insisted that contractors appointed project managers.

The concept has now been extended to whole organisations (Lockheed Aircraft, British Airways) as well as to major divisions as in ICI and in schools of polytechnics/universities, etc eg:

Course Responsibility (Product)	*BA Business Studies*	*BA European Business*	*MBA*	*etc*
Subject Responsibility (Function)	Mr R White	Miss J Brown	Mrs T Black	
Accounts Miss V Red	Fred	Susan	Simon	
Economics Mr A Green	Ian	Frank	Jill	
Sociology Mr G Blue	Mary	Tony	Alan	

In this approach the course leaders (project/product co-ordinators), responsible for course management, would share their authority with the subject leaders (functional heads), responsible for academic development and research.

The matrix structure may be appropriate where there are at least two significant criteria for success. For example, a multinational company produces three sets of product ranges Product A, Product B and Product C and sells the product in three geographical areas Europe, U.S.A. and South America. The management of each product range is equally important, as is the responsiveness to the needs of the different geographical areas. The product managers and area managers have equal weight. Thus the manager of the U.S. area must liaise with the managers of Product A, B and C but does not have authority over them or vice versa.

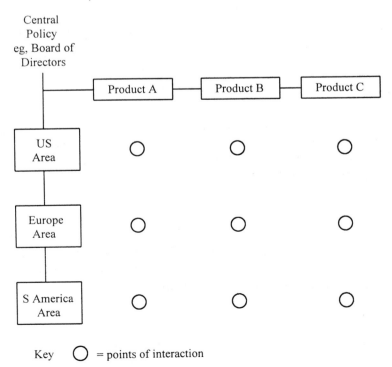

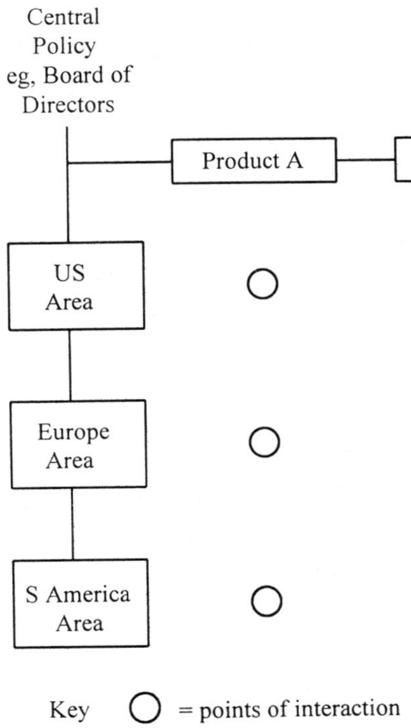

(b) **Advantages of matrix structures**

- Retains functional economies and product co-ordination.
- Is organic - open communications and flexible goals.
- Improved motivation through:
  - people working participatively in teams;
  - specialists broadening their outlook;
- encouraging competition within the organisation.

(c) **Disadvantages of matrix structures**

- Higher administrative costs.
- Conflict between functional and product managers leading to individual stress arising from:
  - threat to *occupational identity*;
  - reporting to more than one boss;
  - less clear expectations.

6.7 Choice of organisation structure

Among the factors to be considered when deciding on the organisation structure appropriate to a particular company are:

(a) **Size**

Clearly a business controlled by one entrepreneur has quite a different structure from a multi-million pound, multi-national giant.

(b) **Chosen strategy**

A company pursuing a growth strategy will probably need a different organisation structure from one pursuing a non-growth, low risk strategy. It must be able to move quickly, so the organisation structure must allow quick decisions. This means that chains of command should not be too long.

A department specifically concerned with promoting change is needed. The Research and Development manager will have a high status in the company. The organisation must be forward-looking it cannot afford to dwell on yesterday's mistakes.

(c) **Management style**

An ideal organisation structure cannot be imposed on an organisation regardless of management style. For instance, a programme of decentralisation, however desirable in other circumstances, will be doomed to failure if the chief executive is an autocrat who is reluctant to relinquish control to any appreciable degree.

(d) **Potential synergy**

The greater the potential synergy, the greater the desirability of integrating a new operation or a new acquisition with the existing operations for if integration is not achieved in some degree, the potential synergy cannot be realised. On the other hand, weak synergy might suggest a holding company/subsidiary company relationship.

(e) **Extent of diversification**

With very diverse operations there might even be negative synergy if top management try to interfere in areas they do not understand. This points to decentralisation.

(f) **Extent of geographical separation**

The greater the geographical distance from the centre, the greater the necessity for decentralised control.

Choice of the best structure is not easy. Each has advantages and disadvantages. For instance, the matrix structure overcomes the difficulties of lack of communication and co-ordination inherent in more traditional structures, but has the disadvantage that a person is trying to serve two masters. However, this may only be admitting a conflict which existed anyway, and if this is true, it is better that the conflict should be brought into the open.

Whatever type of structure is adopted it is essential that the form facilitates communication at and between all levels of management this means that chains of command should not be too long - and that the structure defines clearly the areas of responsibility and authority of different managers. In general, the higher up the organisation tree a decision is taken the longer term its effects will be, the more departments it concerns, and the greater the number of unquantifiable factors which affect the decision.

6.8 Consequences of structural deficiencies

According to Child, the following deficiencies may arise out of weak structure

(a) *Motivation and morale* may be depressed, because of

- (i) apparent inconsistency
- (ii) little responsibility
- (iii) lack of clarity as to what is expected
- (iv) competing pressures
- (v) overloading due to inadequate support systems.

(b) *Decision-making* may be delayed and faulty, because

- (i) information may be delayed in the hierarchy
- (ii) decision-making is too segmented
- (iii) decision-makers are overloaded – no delegation
- (iv) past decisions are not evaluated.

(c) *Conflict* and lack of co-ordination, arising from

- (i) conflicting goals that have not been structured into a single set
- (ii) no liaison – people working at cross-purposes
- (iii) operators not involved in planning.

(d) *No response to change*, because

- (i) there is no established specialist in research and development (R&D) or market research (MR)
- (ii) R&D and MR do not talk to each other
- (iii) R&D and MR are not mainstream activities.

(e) *High administrative costs*, associated with

- (i) 'too many chiefs, too few indians'
- (ii) excess of procedure and paperwork
- (iii) some or all of the other organisational problems being present.

6.9 Effect of structure

(a) *Structure* is affected by various *contingencies*

(i) *Technology* at the operating level
(ii) *Environment* at the strategic level
(iii) *Size* relating to complexity
(iv) *Personnel employed*, be they viewed as X or Y (McGregor).

These contingencies may or may not be interrelated, and may vary from department to department.

However, as stressed by Child, there is a choice of structure available to management in order that they can pursue the chosen objectives for their individual firms, and such a choice does not rest on technical considerations alone – it can be affected by the politics of the situation and by the style of management preferred.

(b) *The effect of structure is limited* – it is a means to achieve objectives and cannot be successful if the organisation

(i) adopts the *wrong strategy*
(ii) does not possess the requisite *skills*
(iii) falls foul of *over-politicisation*
(iv) possesses inherently *bad morale*.

Moreover, structure by itself cannot resolve *conflict*, although it might bring such conflict out into the open.

7 CENTRALISED AND DECENTRALISED DECISION MAKING

7.1 Effect on organisation

Another method of analysing structures is by reference to the level at which decisions are made.

Definition '**Centralisation** is a condition where the upper levels of an organisation's hierarchy retain the **authority** to take most decisions.' John Child

whereas:

Definition **Delegation** is a particular meaning of the term 'decentralisation', and describes a condition when the **authority** to make specific decisions is passed down to units and people at lower levels in the organisation's hierarchy.

Absolute decentralisation of authority is not possible because any delegated authority can derive only from the top, and the activities delegated must conform with the policy decided at a higher level. Also, absolute centralisation of authority is not practical except in very small concerns, because day-to-day decisions must be taken at lower levels.

The choice of organisation will depend to a certain extent on the preferences of the organisation's top management, but equally important is the size of the organisation and the scale of its activities. Thus the small business structure is likely to be centralised, and the divisional structure is likely to be decentralised.

7.2 Advantages of centralisation

Those who support a high degree of centralisation claim advantages such as:

(a) co-ordinated decisions and better management control, therefore less suboptimising;

(b) conformity with overall objectives;

(c) standardisation eg, variety reduction and rationalisation;

(d) balance, between functions, divisions, etc - increased flexibility in use of resources;

(e) economies of scale - general management, finance, purchasing, production, etc;

(f) top managers become better decision makers, because:

- they have proven ability;
- they are more experienced;

(g) Speedier central decisions may be made in a crisis - delegation can be time-consuming.

Conclusion Research shows that **centralisation of strategic decisions** and **delegation of tactical and operating decisions** can be very effective.

7.3 Disadvantages of centralisation

(a) Those of lower rank experience reduced job satisfaction.

(b) Frequently, senior management do not possess sufficient knowledge of all organisational activities. Therefore, their ability to make decisions is narrowed and delegation becomes essential.

(c) Centralisation places stress and responsibility onto senior management.

(d) Subordinates experience restricted opportunity for career development toward senior management positions.

(e) Decisions often take considerable time. This restricts the flexibility of the organisation, as well as using valuable time.

(f) Slower decision-making impairs effective communication. Such communication problems may affect industrial relations.

8 MINTZBERG'S STRUCTURAL CONFIGURATIONS

8.1 Building blocks

Mintzberg has suggested that organisational structure is more complex than just differentiating between hierarchical types. His ideas consist of building blocks and co-ordinating mechanisms which make up the detailed configuration of the organisation.

The six building blocks that he described are:

(i) the **operating core** represents the basic work of the organisation eg, the shop floor;

(ii) the **strategic apex** represents the higher management of the organisation;

(iii) the **middle line** represents the managers between the operating core and the strategic apex;

(iv) the **technostructure** includes the accountants, computer specialists and engineers;

(v) the **support staff** are those that support he work of the operating core eg, secretarial, clerical and catering;

(vi) the **ideology** which represents the organisation's values and beliefs.

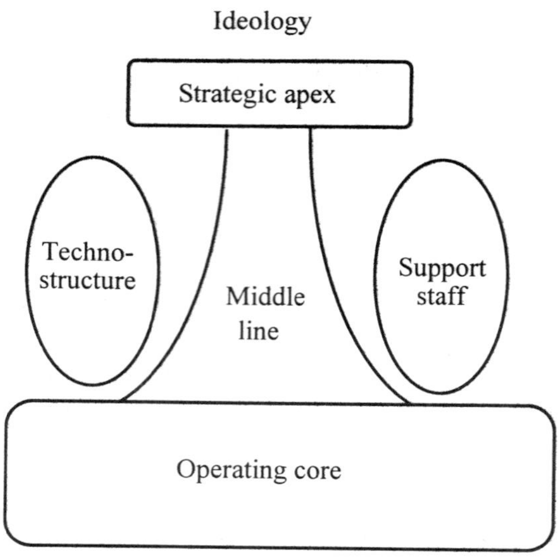

The structure of organisations; H Mintzberg

The importance and relative size of these blocks will vary with organisations

8.2 Co-ordinating mechanisms

Mintzberg lists the ways that co-ordinating mechanisms work:

(i) **Mutual adjustment** is co-ordination through informal contact. This exists in simple structures where people work closely together.

(ii) **Direct supervision** exists throughout the hierarchy where individuals issue instructions and monitor performance.

(iii) **Standardisation of work processes** exists where the work is specified. It is usually the work of the technocrats to design and develop these systems of work.

(iv) **Standardisation of outputs** through such things as product or service specifications.

(v) **Standardisation of skills and knowledge** is an important co-ordinating mechanism in professional activities and specifies the kind of training needed to perform the work.

(vi) **Standardisation of norms** exists where co-workers share the same beliefs.

8.3 Influences on organisational design

The configuration chosen to support the organisation's strategies depends on the mix of building block and co-ordinating mechanism. Mintzberg discusses six configurations which broadly cover the combinations already discussed and also the environment, the type of work and the complexity of tasks facing the organisation.

These are outlined in the chart below:

	Environment	Internal factors	Key building block	Key co-ordinating mechanism
Simple structure	Simple/ dynamic	Small Young Simple tasks	Strategic apex	Direct supervision
Machine bureaucracy	Simple/ static	Large Old Regulated tasks	Technostructure	Standardisation of work
Professional bureaucracy	Complex/ static	Professional control Simple systems	Operating core	Standardisation of skills
Divisionalised	Simple/static Diverse	Very large Old Divisible tasks	Middle line	Standardisation of outputs
Adhocracy	Complex/ dynamic	Young Complex tasks	Operating core Support staff	Mutual adjustment
Missionary	Simple/ static	Middle-aged Simple systems	Ideology	Standardisation of norms

Mintzberg's organisational configurations

9 CHAPTER SUMMARY

All planning must result in action. When implementing plans it is important to stay flexible to cope with changing situations. Progress can be measured using budgetary control, performance monitoring and regular planning.

This chapter has concentrated on structural and design implications of strategic change. It has been argued that strategy implementation is brought about through the people in an organisation, and the way those people are organised is of key importance.

The subdivision of control in a large company can provide the motivation to perform well as a division and thus improve the company performance as a whole. In order to structure an organisation, work needs to be reduced to manageable proportions. This can be done by separating into segments by function, by product or service and by location. Organisation charts may be used to define, in broad terms, an individual's duties and responsibilities.

10 SELF TEST QUESTIONS

10.1 Explain the elements of implementing a plan (1.1).

10.2 Why is it difficult to rank strategies? (1.2).

10.3 List Belbin's ideal types (2.1).

10.4 Outline the specific skills needed to implement a cost leadership strategy (2.2).

10.5 Describe the aspects of implementation which can be changed directly (4.4).

10.6 Draw an effective control procedure (5.2).

10.7 How may organisation structures be classified? (6.2).

10.8 Name the most common organisation functions (6.4).

10.9 List 4 disadvantages associated with divisional structures (6.5).

10.10 Define centralisation (7.1).

10.11 Outline the six building blocks identified by Mintzberg (8.1).

11 EXAMINATION TYPE QUESTIONS

11.1 Frozac Foods Ltd (1)

Frozac Foods Ltd is a medium sized food processing factory situated in an industrial estate in the south east of London. The company which is still owned and managed by its original founders has a diversified market and produces a wide range of cooked, semi-cooked and raw meat packaged products. The company has its own packaging plant and produces several food lines under its own label, two of which are for dessert foods, which is a segment of the food market it entered eight years ago. The company has a good reputation and distributes over 80% of its products through five large supermarket chains. Twice in the last three years the directors of the company have managed to avert acquisition threats from large competitors.

The 1980s were not good for the company. Coming out of recession in the earlier part of the decade and facing stiff competition towards the end, the directors divested from some of their product lines in order to increase overall profitability and reduce inefficiencies. However promotional activity from competing companies caused enormous problems and the company began to lose shares in it's hitherto secure markets. Furthermore the company is now facing considerable pressure from imports, particularly from the Scandinavian countries which have made significant advances in the British processed food markets in recent years. Although input and labour costs steadily increased over the past few years the competitive nature of the market resulted in a period of relatively low increases in market prices, and as a result Frozac's products were marginally over-priced, and its profit margins are down.

Indeed several months ago a senior buyer from an important supermarket chain did intimate that his company, although satisfied with quality standards of the company's food lines was concerned over the recommended selling prices on some lines. He said that his company was beginning to review medium term contracts.

As previously stated the company is operating in highly competitive segments of the food market since it is competing with other small producers and with national and international firms who have well established brands. Several of its competitors squeezed by rising costs and static prices have been taken over by larger firms, mainly to acquire their production plants, since food producing capacity and location are significant factors in the industry, particularly in the London area.

Furthermore the company has been financially cautious, avoiding large scale expenditure which would require borrowing. (The latest processed-meat producing plant which came on stream in 1986 was financed out of retained profits.)

However, it is clear that significant changes are occurring in the industry and Frozac Foods has commissioned a survey of its market segments from SE Management Ltd, a firm of management consultants.

The main findings were:

(1) Forecast market growth likely to continue at the rate of 8% per annum.

(2) Forecast of increased competition after 1992 with firms seeking to establish 'European' brands, and tastes.

(3) Significant costs involved in meeting EC standards in packaging and manufacturing from 1993, particularly for firms operating older plants.

(4) Continuing trend to 'healthier' and 'natural' products, including low sugar/sugar free, and additive-free food and to 'white meat'.

(5) Increased dominance of supermarket chains such as Sainsbury's and Tesco's, selling 'own label' as well as branded products.

Faced with such developments, Frozac Foods Ltd is developing a strategy to see it to the end of this decade aimed at preserving its independence, and increasing both its profitability and sales.

You are required to assume the role of an independent management consultant and prepare a confidential report for the directors of Frozac Foods Ltd covering the following areas:

(a) the strengths and weaknesses of Frozac Foods in light of the forecast trends and developments;
(b) the strategic options open to Frozac Foods;
(c) the strategy you recommend, and proposals for implementation. **(25 marks)**

11.2 Frozac Foods Ltd (2)

Two separate aspects are worrying senior management of Frozac. Details of these are given below:

Industrial relations

Frozen Foods Limited has a full-time working-force of about 110 people. Most of the work is manual with some mechanical assistance. The task force consists of three shifts and the management structure consists of gang supervisors, shop managers and senior managers. The quality inspectors have management status and the company has a small management services unit.

Disturbed by production statistics and consumer research findings, the management decided that it would be necessary to change work systems to increase productivity and reduce costs. SE Management Ltd, the management consultants were commissioned to advise on this matter and their staff conducted an extensive work study project consisting of both method study and work measurement. Resulting from their recommendations Susan Fields, the plant manager decided to introduce a new system of work which would involve job simplification, the purchase of several large modern processing machines and an increase in direct labour productivity by 8%. A new production standard was also decided and a revised group bonus rate set. The consultants were of the opinion that the new standards would result in an overall increase in take-home pay for the staff. Details of the new work systems, performance standards and piece-work rates were explained to the staff collectively on each of the three shifts by representatives of the management consultancy. The rationale behind the changes were explained and details of the company's position described. The staff was assured that although there was to be a planned reduction in staff numbers, this would be achieved by 'natural wastage' and their own jobs were secure. Questions, and there were many, were answered and staff went back to work.

The changes were implemented soon after the meetings with staff, and took effect less than a month ago. There have been disturbing results, the main problems being itemised below:

- On the morning in which the new standards were implemented the employees held an **ad hoc meeting** (during company time), discussed the matter and their nominated representatives informed George Miles, the managing director that all three shifts had **rejected the new standards and bonus rates as arbitrary and unreasonable**. It was noted that representatives from all three shifts were present during the shop-floor meeting.

- The employee representative also informed the managing director that the employees felt that a gesture was required and had decided to call **a one day token strike** which would take place in two weeks' time.

- One week prior to implementation of the revised working methods the official trade union shop-steward informed the managing director that the trade-union (of which most of the employees are members) was concerned about the changes and the manner in which they were to be introduced and **demanded suspension of the new methods** until formal discussion and negotiations had taken place. The very morning of the change the managing director received a letter from the trade union's regional representative, Tom Christie, **demanding reinstatement of the old methods** and discussions.

- Production levels in this first month of change have **dropped significantly** causing a serious delay in fulfilling an order for the same supermarket chain, the buyer of which had only recently intimated concern over the company's performance and contract.

- **Absenteeism** has increased sharply and five manual workers have since tendered their resignations. There are widespread rumours that a number of employees are looking for alternative work.

- Only yesterday there was **open conflict** between a group of meat sorters and the senior quality inspector, Zany Warrick. Ever since the changes were formally announced there has been general hostility and lack of co-operation between the floor workers, the supervisors and managers.

A new marketing manager

A new marketing manager, Jake Vale, has been appointed who has asked what assistance in his work he could expect from the management accountant. Jake is to attend his first senior executives' meeting in a week's time and is putting together some thoughts on a few pressing matters.

He is concerned to try and arrest the declining profitability of different brands, be better positioned in the market with new product launches and carry out a general cost reduction programme.

He has asked you to help on these matters.

You are required:

(a) to describe the 'culture' problems that Frozac Foods Ltd are now experiencing as a result of the changes outlined, and put forward proposals as to how management might try to resolve them;

(b) to suggest approaches that might be used to halt a product's declining profitability;

(c) to put forward proposals as to how a product launch would take account of purchasing behaviour;

(d) to list the areas of information where you feel that as management accountant you could offer help to the marketing manager in his intention to reduce costs. **(25 marks)**

12 ANSWERS TO EXAMINATION TYPE QUESTIONS

12.1 Frozac Foods Ltd (1)

REPORT

To: Directors of Frozac Food Ltd

From: SE Management (Consultants) Ltd

Subject: **Strategic analysis, options and recommendations**

Status: Confidential

1.0 **Summary of contents**

2.0 Introduction
3.0 Strengths of Frozac Foods Ltd
4.0 Weaknesses of Frozac Foods Ltd

5.0 Opportunities
6.0 Threats
7.0 Strategic options and recommendations
8.0 Strategic implementation

2.0 Introduction

If Frozac Foods is to achieve its stated objectives of independence, maintaining its profitability and increasing its sales, it needs to develop and implement a strategy which matches its corporate strengths against the opportunities that are emerging in its environment. It would be a useful exercise to clarify and quantify these objectives, particularly the profitability and sales goals, however this lies outside the scope of this report.

3.0 Analysis of strengths

3.1 Frozac Foods appears to be in a strong financial position, having purchased its meat-processing plant out of retained profits. The case states that '*Frozac Foods has been financially cautious, avoiding large scale expenditure which would require borrowing.*'

3.2 Frozac Foods had a modern food-processing plant, located in the south east, probably with spare capacity. The case states that '*food producing and location are significant factors in the industry.*'

3.3 The company has good brand reputation and has a balanced distribution pattern.

3.4 The company is obviously attractive to its large competitors and has twice in the last three years been targeted for take-over.

3.5 The company has a wide product-mix which is internally and externally consistent providing sales, cost and investment synergies.

3.6 Customers seem satisfied with quality standards of the company. A very positive mark.

3.7 The existence of a national distribution network is potentially a valuable asset.

3.8 The ownership of Frozac Foods is concentrated in the hands of the managers and this is probably a key factor in its survival as an independent company.

3.9 The attitude of the directors, in commissioning a survey of the industry and this report, is indicative of a readiness to face up to the changes that are occurring in the company's environment.

4.0 Analysis of weaknesses

4.1 The company has experienced input and labour costs increases over the past few years.

4.2 The company might be too labour intensive because of it's policy of avoiding large scale expenditures. This would need to be investigated on an industry basis.

4.3 The reliance of the company on the founders who fill the principal posts. (Has '*succession*' been considered?)

4.4 The increased dominance of supermarket chains.

5.0 Opportunities

5.1 Frozac Foods is operating in a market for which there are good opportunities for product development, line filling and brand extension.

5.2 Forecast market growth is likely to continue at the rate of 8 per cent per annum. This is an encouraging statistic. The company may well be able to achieve its objectives within its present markets.

5.3 Although there is the threat of competition from European companies, Frozac foods is geographically positioned to begin marketing in European countries, which from 1993 might make sense.

5.4 The continuing trend to *'healthier'* and *'natural'* products provides as much opportunity as it does threat. The company might do well to consider it's market *'positioning'* and *'mix'*.

5.5 The company might see an opportunity in *'own label'* channel alliances.

6.0 **Threats**

6.1 The company's markets are threatened by both domestic and foreign companies.

6.2 The competitive nature of the market is pushing down selling prices and the company has a relatively high cost structure.

6.3 The company is in danger of losing at least one important outlet. There may be more problems in the pipeline.

6.4 Competitors are concentrating in size and this is going to be a source of concern for Frozac if it remains in the *'volume'* market.

6.5 The company faces significant costs as it deals with European rules and directives.

7.0 **Strategic options and recommendations**

Four strategy options needed to be considered and evaluated:

7.1 **Market consolidation and penetration**

This involves Frozac Foods concentrating on its existing products and markets, but increasing efficiency and effectiveness. It is recommended that Frozac Foods rationalises its product range, by dropping products for which it has low sales volume and low profitability.

7.2 **New product development**

This involves developing new products for existing markets, It is recommended that Frozac Foods researches the potential for extending its product range by introducing environmentally friendly food products.

7.3 **New market development**

This involves developing new markets for existing products. It is recommended that Frozac Foods extends its sales outside the south east and reduces its reliance on main supermarkets by selling to wholesalers and small independents. Additionally, the European market needs to be considered.

Options 7.1, 7.2 and 7.3 involves a significant investment in advertising to promote brand awareness and preference.

7.4 **Complete diversification**

This is a leap in the dark and is the riskiest of options. It is not recommended for Frozac Foods.

8.0 Strategy implementation

8.1 The strategic decisions needs to be fully backed by the board and to be communicated to all staff.

8.2 The strategies needs to be funded and this may involve additional capital which in the case of Frozac Foods can be raised in a variety of ways. These need to be carefully appraised and evaluated.

8.3 The strategies need to be co-ordinated which given the simple structure and the personal involvement of the main owners should not be a problem. At the very least, regular meetings will be necessary to agree and review options and progress.

8.4 If growth is to be managed and organised effectively, new managers will need to be recruited. In a company of Frozac Food's size, such selection decisions are critical, particularly given the need to plan the succession of the existing management team.

8.5 Control and information systems need to be established to monitor the implementation of the strategies. Additional marketing research, including sales analysis, may be desirable. More sophisticated financial control systems, particularly budgets, should be developed, if not already in place.

8.6 In the longer term, growth will require new organisation structures, particularly as the founders become less personally involved.

Signature

12.2 Frozac Foods Ltd (2)

(a) There are behavioural problems associated with change, even when its probable effects seem to favour the long-term interests of the people concerned by it. The problems become more aggravated when people are to be made redundant, or the change results in people suffering a loss in status or income, either actual or perceived. The problems are not solved by a heavy-handed management imposing its will by force.

People are inclined to resist change because of the implicit threat it poses to their job security, friends, work, life style, working relationships, routine, promotion prospects and status. In an era of change, fear becomes a powerful motivator. Fear stifles loyalty and even personal integrity while prompting aggression and resistance.

In this, fear hardens attitudes, affects behaviour adversely, changes the values of people and generally develops a climate which weakens the organisation. The problems become *'shared'* between the people concerned, which generally weakens *'the glue which holds the organisation together'*. The corporate value system and belief system is threatened by this *'paradigm'* or *'mind set'*.

The truth of this behavioural occurrence is reflected from the present industrial climate position of Frozac Foods Ltd. The alacrity with which employees have responded by grouping together and demonstrating in a number of ways their hostility towards the new policy shows the extent of their fear and anger. The actions they have already taken reflect the importance they place on the changes. They probably also feel unfairly dealt with. It is important to recognise the reasons for change resistance. It is apparent that the employees in the company were not *involved* in the decisions which resulted in the change. Involvement, or participation, in decisions of this magnitude can prove difficult, even risky, and requires careful handling, but nonetheless should provide a forum of discussion even if the out turn is not complete mutual harmony of agreement and teamship.

Generous and honest communication of cause/effect and justification to the people likely to be concerned is an important ingredient in successful change. Regular discussions and consultation between employee representatives and management are vital if there is to be any harmony and goodwill arising in the change. Frozac Foods seems to have forgotten this important requirement!

To resolve the present *industrial relations problem* is going to be difficult. both sides, management and employees, seem to be holding entrenched positions. A number of initiatives are called for. First, there is a requirement for urgent, frank and open discussions between the **top** management of the company and the representatives of the employees. Ideas from the employees should be encouraged, evaluated and genuinely considered. The consequences of stoppage or prolonged periods of unproductive work should be spelt out, so that everyone in the company is aware of the good sense of the changes proposed, the direction the company is moving in, its vulnerability, and the threats posed not only to the company, but to the future employment security of people working in it.

Particular complaints, worries or fears of the employees should be considered very carefully. Solutions, if there are any, to alleviate, mitigate or remove these, should be sought urgently. People should know that the management are concerned about their welfare with intentions to do everything possible to make the effects of the change as palatable as possible.

It is possible that the new work systems, performance standards and piece-work rates are essential if the company is to recover from its present position, and if so management must be resolute in its intention to retain its policy, unless a better solution is proposed. Nobody in the company should doubt this fact.

The management of the company should now be planning contingency policy, including financial contingencies, in case disruption does occur. This is going to be a difficult, but not impossible exercise, a discussion of which is outside the requirements of this question.

(b) A product's declining profitability can be due to various factors. Although the main concern occurs at the point in the product's life when saturation has been reached, the organisation will need, in fact, to reformulate its marketing strategy several times in response to changing marketing conditions, and this response is not only required at the point of saturation. Furthermore the shares, and natures, of product life cycles are various. Product life can refer, for example, to: product categories, product forms, brands, style, fashion, trend, technology, industrial and international events and changes.

The major factors calling for a possible major overhaul of marketing strategy to stop a declining profitability of a product are:

- **product life cycle stage** - marketing strategy must be modified to the product's stage in it's life cycle;
- **company's competitive position in the market** - marketing strategy must be adapted to the company's position in the market; and
- **the economic climate** - marketing strategy must be adapted to the economic outlook and climate, such as pressures resulting from inflation, shortages, over capacity, or recession.

Approaches that might, therefore, be used to halt a product's declining profitability would include:

- cost reduction generally;
- conversion of non-users;

- entering new market segments (say, by line stretching by moving down in quality and price);
- winning competitors' customers (for example, by aggressive marketing);
- increasing the frequency of use;
- developing new and more varied uses;
- relaunching the product (say, new packaging, brand and advertising message);
- feature improvement (adapt, modify, magnify, minify, substitute, rearrange, reverse or combine existing features);
- style improvement;
- price modification (for example, by the use of premiums, discounts);
- distribution modification;
- communication mix modification (for example, by increasing sales promotion, with competitions, gifts, premium offers, couponing);
- becoming selective in distribution;
- studying exit costs, deciding whether to withdraw from the market.

(c) One of the major challenges in marketing planning is to develop ideas for new products and to launch them successfully. Organisations need to find replacements for its products that have entered the decline stage, or to be able to exploit opportunities opening in the market. There are a number of problems associated with new product development, the main ones being: **shortage of ideas, social and government constraints, costliness of the new-product-development process, capital shortage, fragmented markets,** and **shorter growth periods for successful products**.

One answer to successful new-product introductions is for the organisation to have organisational arrangements, and screening processes to ensure that the product is developed in line with consumers needs and their purchasing behaviour. The following must be taken into account with regard to customer/consumer purchasing behaviour when deciding on the new product:

- **cultural influences** – values, perceptions, behaviours, and socialisation;
- **sub-cultural influences** – national religious, racial and geographical groupings;
- **social class stratification;**
- **reference group and opinion leader influences** (including aspiration and dissociative grouping);
- **economic circumstances** – spendable income, savings and assets, borrowing power, attitude towards spending versus saving;
- **lifestyles** - activities, interests, opinions, demographics;
- **psychological factors** – motivation, perception, beliefs and attitudes.

The following factors need to be taken into account when launching the new product:

- maximising the power of the brand and brand image;

- carrying out the correct level of consumer survey;
- analysing the business prospects (for example, to estimate 'take-off' volume to ensure that stock is made available);
- test marketing can be used in specific, but representative, areas;
- choosing between slow market penetration (ie low levels of advertising) or rapid market penetration (ie high levels of advertising);
- deciding on the pricing strategy (skimming – fast or slow, low price/low quality, etc);
- deciding whether to use selective distribution;
- designing a promotional message that is informative and educative (more 'long-copy' than 'impulsive symbolic');
- conducting a consumer sales promotion campaign;
- conducting sales promotion aimed at the distribution channels (eg retailers, dealers, jobbers);
- training staff in the new product, particularly staff in the sales field;
- designing intelligence system to collect marketing information regarding the new product.

(d) **How management accounting can help the marketing manager**

- Analysis of costs and profitability (contribution per product).
- Analysis by product/product group to arrive at minimum drop size.
- Analysis of costs by market/type of customer (eg direct sales compared through agents) to arrive at minimum account size.
- Analysis of costs of different distribution methods (eg by mail/road/van salesman, etc). Assessment of validity of using own warehouses.
- Comparison of costs of different distribution channels (eg wholesalers, retailers, agents).
- Comparison of profitability by size of order or size of customer.
- Analysis of salesmen's costs compared with their performance, and the development of control system for these costs.
- Help in compilation of the sales budget and marketing costs budget.
- Calculation of expected costs for any marketing changes being considered.

11 OPERATIONAL PLANNING

INTRODUCTION & LEARNING OBJECTIVES

The key to successful implementation usually lies in identifying specific individual responsibilities and obtaining the co-operation and commitment of the people involved. Many organisations have moved to a variety of participative implementation and budgeting systems, where responsible executives are invited or encouraged to participate in the planning process. A sophisticated approach is to use Management by Objectives (MBO). This method, along with a consideration of different operational planning and control responsibilities is outlined in a later chapter.

There is no foolproof system of implementation, many things can go wrong. Usually companies deal with the complexity of the implementation and control processes by using budgets.

When you have studied this chapter you should be able to do the following:

- Outline specific functional areas of operational planning and control.
- Describe a methodology for effective resource allocation
- Relate budgetary control to strategy.
- Describe some simple aids to planning

1 OPERATIONAL PLANNING AND CONTROL

1.1 Characteristics of operational planning and control

Operational plans are the short-term element of the company's overall plan. They are concerned with the day to day running of the company in the immediate future and usually cover a period of one year.

Operational planning and control can be defined as planning and controlling the effective and efficient performance of specific tasks. It therefore differs from management planning and control in focusing on one task at a time, whereas management planning and control focuses on resource requirements for the whole range of tasks.

A further difference is that management planning and control is essentially a matter of exercising management judgement, with some scientific forecasting and evaluation methods available to assist, while operational planning and control is in general far more scientific.

At the operational level, problems tend to be repetitive: general rules can often, therefore, be laid down as to how to respond to a given situation, though there are of course exceptions requiring management judgement. Anthony uses the terms 'programmable' and 'non-programmable' control: most management control is non-programmable while most operational control is of the programmable type.

Programmable control is applicable where the optimum relation between inputs and outputs can be established in advance and where rules can therefore be used the decide the action which will be most efficient in a given set of circumstances.

Examples are: inventory control, where stock levels can be decided when the storage cost, cost of losing an order etc, are known; the determination of the optimum mix under a set of constraints, which can be solved by linear programming techniques; production scheduling in automated plants. As new techniques are developed, more activities become susceptible to programmable control and the usefulness of computers is enhanced.

Because of the shorter time-scale involved, forecasting at the operational level can be more accurate than at the management or strategic planning levels, and actual data can be quickly obtained for comparison with the forecast or target. Continuous feedback is therefore possible as in the diagram below:

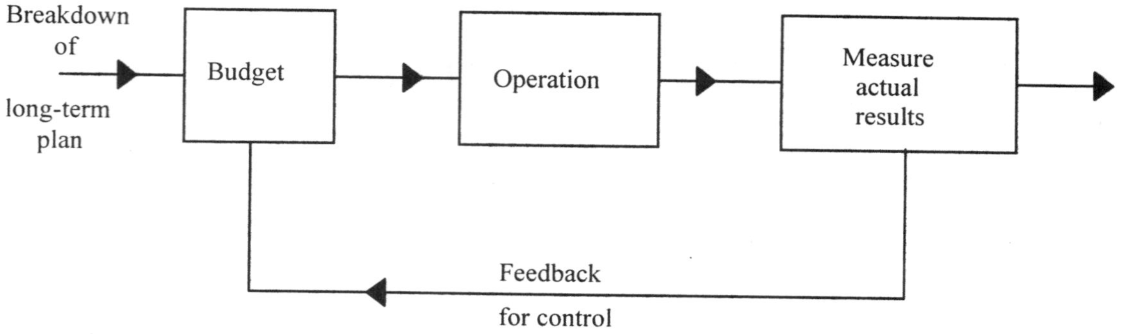

Contrast this with strategic or management control where, because plans are long-term, results may never be available for comparison with targets because plans may never be fully implemented. Only progress towards targets can be measured. Even if results could be measured they would come too late for effective corrective action to be taken. Because operational control does not suffer from such difficulties, it is considerably easier.

A good operational control system should require a minimum of management intervention. The principle of **management by exception** can be applied, the manager intervening only when deviations from the plan are revealed. Nevertheless, success is dependent on good management - a good information system alone will not solve all the problems. Intervention, when it is necessary, must be done promptly to prevent any further deviations, and it takes a good manager to recognise the warning signs early enough. In addition it is only the manager who can take account of human factors - morale, motivation etc. A computer can be used for comparing results with targets and analysing variances, but it cannot explain the variances.

1.2 Characteristics of plans

(a) **Time period** – within the same organisation strategic plans are obviously longer term than managerial and operational plans. However, for some organisations with major capital investments, such as the CEGB, strategic plans can be prepared for periods of 10 to 15 years whilst other organisations, particularly those in the fashion industry, need only plan for a year ahead.

Elliot Jacques stresses that, at higher levels of management, the most significant element of a job is the time that must elapse before decisions taken can be reconsidered – he felt that the 'time span of discretion' should form the basis for remuneration.

Whatever the duration of a plan, it is important that it should be made on a rolling basis and revised and extended annually.

(b) **Timeliness** – with long term commitments it is easy to either leave things too late and risk greater uncertainties or begin planning too early and become inflexible. The annual rolling plan advocated above helps with the resolution of this dilemma.

(c) **Repetitiveness** - plans can be either

(i) **Single use** - 'ad hoc' planning occurs when judgement is required particularly in complex situations and when qualitative factors are involved. They are more common at the strategic level but also occur at the other two levels – repair work, customer complaints, motivation of individual members of staff.

(ii) **Standing policies** - methods and operating procedures are employed for problems of a routine nature - the difficulties described in systems approaches. Many operational control decisions can be programmed and undertaken by computers – using robotics, in stock control and in many other areas.

(d) **Scope** - this increases in accordance with the following classification for which examples have been drawn from the 'construction' of Rutland Water, which was the largest man made lake in the UK.

(i) **Functional plans** - the reservoir's pumping system.

(ii) **Project plans** - the building of the dam at Empingham.

(iii) **Comprehensive plans** - the whole concept of Rutland Water including surrounding land use, recreational facilities, traffic control, effects on local communities etc.

As pointed out by Kast and Rosenzweig

> 'The complexity of broader scope is one of increasing uncertainty'

Strategic planning has a wider scope than managerial or operational control.

(e) **Level of management** – normally the higher a person is within an organisation the more he or she will be involved with planning and spend less time on implementation.

Management commitment to plans at lower levels is normally an essential requirement for their success as is effective communication of plans to all levels concerned.

(f) **Degree of vagueness** – sometimes it is advantageous to have the whole situation in partial focus rather than one part sharply focused and the others unidentifiable. The saying 'you can't see the wood for the trees' can be particularly appropriate.

(g) **Flexibility** – plans can vary along a continuum ranging from

(i) 'Cook's tours' – specific routes from A to B which can be applied in stable and precise situations.

(ii) Branch approaches advocated by Lewis and Clark and linked to logical incrementalism. Managers do not plan but put into hand preparations to adapt when certain occurrences happen.

(h) **Effectiveness** - plans can be evaluated according to their economic effectiveness and by analysis of the various procedures adopted and the resultant characteristics which differentiate good plans from bad ones. Such characteristics include objectivity, degree of structuring, flexibility and ease of implementation and control.

2 ACTIVE PARTICIPATION IN THE PLANNING PROCESS

2.1 Attitudes concerning the need for planning

Many firms claim that long term planning in their particular industry is practical and such organisations are normally operating in areas of rapid change such as in

(a) Taste - fashion companies.
(b) Technology - computer manufacturers.

The arguments for effective planning include

(a) Providing the company with an aim and the direction necessary for long term survival.

(b) Reducing the uncertainty of the future and the need for crisis management.

(c) Engendering an *esprit de corps* and creating a sense of purpose amongst employees.

(d) Producing a positive attitude towards change and encouraging a climate favourable to innovation, initiative and creativity.

Ackoff claims that attitudes towards planning vary greatly amongst organisations be they businesses, government departments or voluntary bodies. The four alternative perspectives discussed below can have a profound effect on who does the planning in an organisation and the planning procedures adopted.

(a) **Inactivists** wish to 'ride with the tide' and undertake no planning nor problem solving. They are conservative satisficers who seek stability and survival within organisations by

(i) Requiring all important decisions to be made at the top.

(ii) Only acting when forced to – normally to avoid change – preferring words to deeds.

(iii) To delay matters – form committees, councils, study groups etc, – unrepresented parties can object and form new groups.

(iv) When decision is eventually taken they make sure it cannot be implemented through being understaffed or under-financed.

Feasibility is of paramount importance and 'ends' are often fitted to 'means'. Inactivists are more concerned with *errors of commission* than *errors of omission* and react only to serious threats and not to opportunities – *'crisis management'*.

Such attitudes prevail within closed systems which are protected from the environment – in the past these have included Universities and nationalised industries and, even in the aggressive 1980s, many monopolies and oligopolies continue to demonstrate inactivist traits.

(b) **Reactivists** try to 'swim against the tide' as they have a preference for a previous state to the one they are in. They try to avoid the undesirable rather than attain the desirable.

In their minds nothing is new and they prefer the *art of muddling through* to the science of management. A high value is placed on seniority as experience is relied on greatly. Reactivists dislike complexity and are *panacea prone* problem solvers.

Such reactionaries are found in organisations that were once successful but are now declining.

(c) **Preactivists** attempt to 'ride in front of the tide' and want more than just survival – they are liberal optimisers. They predict and prepare using scientific methods and are concerned with both errors of commission and omission. Their planners are not involved with the implementation of the plans they prepare.

Such people are hardware (thing) oriented and engage in research and development rather than individual and institutional change. They are preoccupied with the allocation and use of the resources they control.

It is believed that the environment constrains and that organisations have to *compete* to survive. Consequently, preactivists seek change within the system – not change of the system or its environment.

(d) **Interactivists** are radical idealisers who want to *control* their own destinies. They try to prevent and not merely prepare for threats and they like to create as well as exploit opportunities. Experience is not reckoned to be the best teacher – a great deal of experimentation is carried out. *Co-operative* change is encouraged.

Interactivists view science, the search for similarities, and the humanities, the search for differences, as two aspects of the same culture.

2.2 Barriers to effective planning

The following obstacles to planning exist at all levels and most stem from the inappropriate attitudes discussed in the previous sub-section

(a) Plans are never urgent – can easily be put off.

(b) As it is difficult to estimate future payoff of a plan or otherwise measure its effectiveness, planning is avoided by those executives who have a low tolerance for uncertainty.

(c) Planning implies change and this is resisted by many in authority and elsewhere who wish to maintain the 'status quo'.

(d) Planning is a passive affair – 'young tigers' are inspired by the immediacy of operating.

(e) Power groups want decisions their own way including the managing director whose pet projects can be subject to undue influence.

(f) Constraints imposed by unions and others are overpowering.

2.3 Specific areas of operational planning and control

(a) **Sales/marketing**

This department has to analyse sales statistics and salesforce returns in order to build up a file of customer characteristics for each type of customer, and for each product in each market. These statistics will be needed to analyse demand trends over time and to predict latent and incipient demand as an aid to strategic decisions.

The department will be responsible for conducting market research exercises to ascertain customer reaction to new products. Such exercises need to be carefully controlled in order to ensure that an unbiased sample is selected.

It will have to decide on advertising campaigns - which media to use, how long to run the campaign, etc. It will have to try and assess the effectiveness of different media to provide for planning future campaigns. For instance, if advertisements are placed in magazines with enquiry slips which the reader may complete, these should be coded so that the company can tell which magazine brings the best response.

In order to control selling activities, good communications are needed between head office, regional sales offices, and salespeople as they travel around. Data links connecting regional sales offices to a central computer can be very useful - by interrogating the central data bank, each regional office can obtain precise up-to-date information on availability of each product. Others can also be transmitted over such a link.

For example, in 1990 Market Solutions added the Distributed Database module to its SaleMaker Plus range of software. The module allows SaleMaker Plus client records to be distributed between corporate users in up to 999 remote locations. Any time a record on the user company's central database is added to, deleted or updated, the DDB changes the record in the remote locations. Two-way contact can be made by modem at night to take advantage of off-peak call rates, and special monitoring routines are said to guarantee error-free transmission during the process.

(b) **Credit control**

The credit control department needs to analyse overall credit, on a year by year basis, to see if customers are beginning to take longer to pay and therefore whether credit arrangements need to be revised.

In addition, they will have to analyse credit on a product by product basis, on a customer type by customer type basis, and on a credit type basis, in order to see if there is any particular type of customer who is a bad risk, any type of credit which should be discontinued, or any products which should be sold only for cash. The statistics collected by the sales department will be useful in this analysis.

(c) **Production**

The problem of the production department will depend on whether production is on a batch or continuous flow system. Production scheduling will be a particular problem if products are made to customers' specific order. The aim will be to minimise setting-up time and setting-up costs; to minimise machine idle time; to work as near as possible to economic batch quantities; to avoid production bottlenecks or hold-ups. Network analysis will help in scheduling.

When an order is placed, the production department will have to fit it into the production schedule in the optimum manner which allows the delivery date to be met; decide on the materials (type and quantity) to be used, and requisition the stores for same, decide on any overtime necessary to meet the delivery date; finally carry out the work in the most efficient manner possible. On all jobs, the department will have to ensure that material wastage is minimised, that overtime is kept to a reasonable level, and that optimum machine utilisation is obtained.

There will have to be some form of inspection to ensure the quality of the finished product - for instance Quality Control, which is a statistical method for sampling products for inspection and for deciding whether any deviations in quality are random only or are due to a defect in the process which should be investigated. This is a very cost-effective method of controlling quality: it provides the best assurance of quality possible short of inspecting every item, which is usually not feasible.

The production department also has to decide on maintenance methods - should maintenance be primarily on a preventative basis, or only when the machines actually break down? This will depend on the cost of maintenance, the cost of lost production if there is a machine break-down, and the likelihood of machine breakdown. Again, this problem can be solved by statistical techniques. Indeed, the production department provides several very good examples of programmable control Normally however companies opt for preventative maintenance which we touched on previously.

The department should keep records which will form the basis of longer term decisions such as the need for capital investment. Records will be needed of amount of overtime worked or the extent of idle time, machine utilisation (measured by capacity ratio), and deterioration in quality of output over time, wastage of materials, etc.

(d) **Personnel**

This department will be responsible for specific industrial relations issues such as negotiating wage settlements. It is responsible for ensuring that the company complies with such legislation as the Health and Safety at Work Act, Equal Opportunities and Race Relationship legislation, and other relevant labour legislation.

In addition the department plays an important part in helping to plan and operate the company's manpower plan, and is responsible for activities such as advertising vacancies, making arrangements for interviews (probably in conjunction with the relevant functional manager), arranging training, seeing that the staff appraisal exercise is properly conducted, etc.

This is not an area which is easily susceptible to programmable control.

(e) **Accounting**

This department is of course responsible for seeing that accounts are prepared for audit in accordance with statutory requirements, for seeing that budgets are properly prepared and approved in accordance with the agreed timetable, and for seeing that management accounting information is extracted. The particular role of the management accountant is covered later.

(f) **Purchasing and stores**

This department will receive requisitions for stores from the production department and must ensure that the company receives the materials at the time required. Orders must be placed with suppliers in accordance with pre-determined re-order levels and economic order quantities which should be periodically reviewed. This department will be responsible for buying policy - whether to buy in large quantities to obtain discounts, whether to buy from several suppliers to retain flexibility, etc. They will have to decide, in conjunction with the production departments, which items to stock as standard and which to order only when required.

2.4 Activity

Consider carefully the personnel department or function in your own company, or a company that you know of, and then describe its responsibilities.

2.5 Activity solution

(a) **Employment:** ascertaining staffing requirements immediate and long-term; arranging for job descriptions and person specifications to be provided; advertising vacancies; arranging interviews and determining selection procedures; deciding conditions of employment; arranging for transfers of personnel; handling termination of employment; setting up and maintenance of adequate employee records.

(b) **Education and training:** making arrangements for and seeing to the administration and records relating to induction training, operator training, apprentice training, clerical training, external training, management and supervisory training, and further education of employees.

(c) **Wages and salaries:** advising on policy, carrying out job analysis and job evaluation to set up wage and salary structures for different grades; devising and administering merit rating schemes; advice and administration of fringe benefits eg, company housing, company cars, loans for house purchase, assistance with children's education, etc.

(d) **Working conditions:** advising on introduction, improvements and maintenance of adequate lighting, heating, ventilation, washing and change-room facilities, toilets, and other working conditions.

(e) **Health and safety:** making sure that adequate provisions are made for first-aid, maintenance of hygiene standards, company nurse, company doctor (or provisions for seeing a doctor); dealing with sickness and absences; promoting accident prevention and safety at work.

(f) **Employee services and welfare:** adequate provision for transport facilities, canteens, housing (in some cases), sporting facilities social clubs, and other recreational facilities; advice on pension schemes.

(g) **Industrial relations:** advising on policy; setting up the procedures and administering grievance procedures, joint consultation, and works committees; negotiating with the representatives of staff associations and trade unions; giving information to employees; and assisting employees with personal problems.

3 A METHODOLOGY FOR EFFECTIVE RESOURCE ALLOCATION

3.1 Planning at the corporate level

Resource planning encompasses both how resources should be **allocated** between the various functions, departments and divisions and also how they should be **deployed** within any one part of the organisation to support the strategies.

At the corporate level of the organisation, resource planning is mainly concerned with allocation. According to Johnson and Scholes there are two factors which determine the approach to allocation:

- the perceived need for change - whether the level of resources may need to grow, decline or shift between areas; and
- the extent of central direction - whether detailed allocations are dictated from the corporate level or are a response to the plans of the various departments in the organisation.

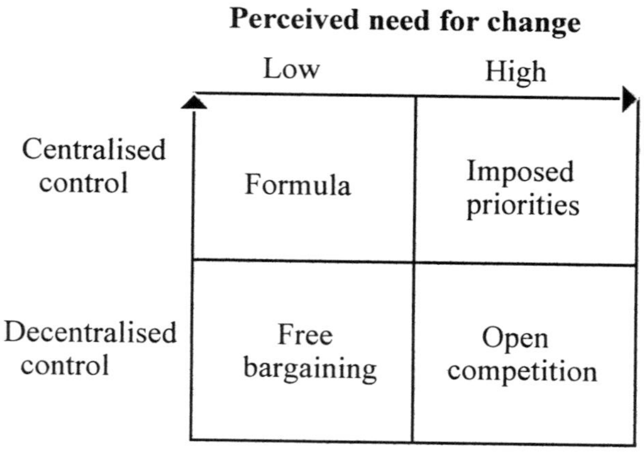

Using this model as a methodology to allocate resources would have the following results:

- If the changes in the level of deployment of resources are perceived to be **low** and the management control is **high**, then formula-driven allocations will be used as a starting point in establishing allocations. For example, allocate the public services revenue on a per capita basis, such as dental patients.
- If the changes in the level of deployment of resources are perceived to be **low** and the management control is **low** (decentralised), the allocation will involve a bargaining process in which managers of different department and units haggle with each other over the resources.
- If the changes in the level of deployment of resources are perceived to be **high** and the management control is **high**, priority areas could be established centrally and the resource allocations could be imposed from the centre.
- If the changes in the level of deployment of resources are perceived to be **high** and the management control is **low**, the centre could allocate resources through a process of open competition, perhaps through an internal investment bank from which departments can bid for additional resources.

3.2 Planning at the business level

The main issues which an organisation's resource plan should address include the following:

(a) **The critical success factors**; where the strategic implementation is fundamentally dependent on these factors for its success eg, reduce product cost.

(b) **The key tasks** which must be undertaken to underpin the critical success factors.

(c) **The priorities** which need to be actioned to get the plan under way. The identification of priorities and key tasks also provides a basis for the allocation of responsibilities. The plan needs to be explicit about:

- who is responsible for each of the key areas;
- where the key areas interlink;
- who is responsible for co-ordination;
- what things can or should be left until later; and
- which of the priorities need to be followed up.

The plan sets out what resources need to be obtained or disposed of. This may take the form of a budget, but might also be expressed as a timetable of priorities, a sequence of actions or a written plan.

The **just-in-time** (JIT) approach to activity scheduling has received considerable attention and proved to be of strategic importance to many manufacturing organisations. This technique has revolutionised the acquisition of resources, with a resultant reduction in costs (of stock) or improvement in lead times. Some organisations have gained a competitive advantage on the basis of JIT.

4 BUDGETS AS A TOOL FOR CONTROL

4.1 Introduction

Because of the characteristics of operational planning and control described in the previous section, it can be effectively decentralised and delegated. Budgets are an essential element of delegated control.

A budget is not the same thing as a plan: rather, a budget is the quantification of the action specified in the plan. Budgets are approved for each department, and all managers are expected to keep within their parts of the budget.

A budget is essentially a short-term planning and control tool. Typically, budgets are prepared one year forward. However, as management has felt the need for longer-term planning, one solution has been seen as to extend budgets further into the future. However, budgets are not suitable for this purpose for several reasons:

(a) The form of budgets relies on forecasts. However, the nature of a forecast changes as its occurrence becomes more remote. A sales budget for next year may be realistic; that for five years is just wishful thinking.

(b) Errors in long-term forecasts can be enormous, but budget reports typically have no error columns, since they were designed for short-term forecasts.

(c) In budgets figures are usually expressed in money terms, in long-term plans it is easier to express them in physical or qualitative terms.

(d) Budgets are both planning and control schedules; a five-year budget is only a planning exercise.

(e) Budgets relate to exploiting existing resources; plans are about creating resources.

Thus, budgets must be seen as distinctive from strategic plans. Rather budgets are the short-term financial plans resulting from a long-term strategic plan.

4.2 Setting budgets

In setting budgets there is always a conflict between the different objectives of budgets:

(a) planning - requires forecasts based on 'most likely' outcome;

(b) motivation - requires forecasts which need some extra effort to be achieved, and are therefore more optimistic than that required for planning;

(c) evaluation - to evaluate manager's performance, a budget should correspond to the best achievable by the managers in the situation in which they are operating.

These conflicts should remind you that the process of establishing budgets is not a pure accounting matter. Important behavioural factors influence the outcome. For a reminder of these you should refer back to your studies of Paper 8 Managerial Finance.

In reality, any budget must be a compromise between these different objectives.

4.3 The budgetary control system

Budgeting is about more than just a budget. It is a whole system which involves preparing budgets, comparing actual with budgets, and taking corrective action. Argenti describes budgeting as 'the most successful and valuable management tool ever invented'.

As such budgetary control systems form an important component of strategic plans. They are the key to detailed short-term monitoring of the achievement of planned objectives. For control purposes, managers will need a report on costs incurred in their department as against budget, in a format similar to the following:

ABC Ltd.

Cost report: Plant Administration.
Manager:
Period:

	Year to date			*May*		
	Budget	*Actual*	*Variance*	*Budget*	*Actual*	*Variance*
Material & supplies Wages & payroll Fringe benefits Travel & subsistence Insurance Telephone Miscellaneous						
Total						

In addition, managers will need a report on costs incurred by their subordinates, typically in the following form:

ABC Ltd.

Cost report: Plant Administration.
Departmental costs

Period:

Dept	*Year to date*			*May*		
	Budget	*Actual*	*Variance*	*Budget*	*Actual*	*Variance*
Plant administration Dept 1 Dept 2						

You will already be familiar with the technique of variance analysis whereby possible causes for variations from budget are identified. Flexible budgets should of course be used for this purpose to take account of variations from the planned level of output, for which the individual manager cannot be held responsible. Ratios should be used to measure productivity and activity levels compared with budget.

Graphical presentation of results is often useful to supplement tables - for instance by means of the *Z-chart* which shows monthly, cumulative and moving average totals, and which can be compared with the previous year's data.

Conformity with budget is not the only performance measurement: other statistical and physical measurements can also be used.

4.4 Monitoring performance

Sometimes it may be desirable to change a planned course of action but this is not a licence for neglect. Managers are expected to fulfil all plans which are still appropriate and to substitute modified plans where plans are inappropriate. The important element is deliberate decision and evaluation and understanding of the implications of the change: it is not action by default. It is not an offence to change, but it is an offence for a manager not to know he has changed.

Monitoring standards should give top management an opportunity to see the effect on the overall plan of failure and changes. Any actions which are rescheduled are entered on to the appropriate agenda sheet for control at a future meeting.

4.5 Monitoring assumptions

All plans are based on assumptions. One important aspect of the control of plans is to continue to study and assess environmental trends so that the company may know whether its assumptions are still correct.

The organisation of a system to monitor assumptions need be little more than an extension of the company's continuous assessment of the environment.

Most companies are likely to prepare their long-range plans on a rolling basis with the opportunity to review annually. When a fundamental change occurs it may be necessary to update a part or all of the plan outside of the normal planning cycle. Recognition of the need to amend the long-range plan is not an indication of failure by the planner: indeed, it is possible to claim it is a success. The ability to identify something that is going wrong before it happens, and the flexibility to react speedily to external influences, are factors which should be incorporated in the approach to planning. There can be no doubt that a certain amount of re-planning may be essential between planning cycles, and there are likely to be a number of circumstances when replanning is advisable.

5 PLANNING AT THE TACTICAL/OPERATIONAL LEVEL

5.1 Simple aids to planning

Network analysis, also known as critical path analysis, is a technique used for planning projects by breaking them down into their component activities and showing those activities and their interrelationships in the form of a network.

It has been used very effectively in all types of activities associated with strategy implementation, such as: new product or service launches; acquisitions and mergers; plant construction; and relocation.

This type of analysis can help in resource planning by:

- breaking down the programme of implementation into its constituent parts by activity, making it easy to build onto the value chain analysis;
- helping to establish priorities by identifying the activities which others depend on;
- representing a plan of action, where the implications of changes or deviations in the plan can be examined.

Another planning tool, the **programme evaluation review technique (PERT)**, allows uncertainty about the times of each activity in the network to be considered.

There are other techniques which can also be helpful in scheduling activities such as **Gantt charts** or **route planning.**

The **just-in-time** (JIT) approach to activity scheduling has received considerable attention and proved to be of strategic importance to many manufacturing organisations. This technique has revolutionised the acquisition of resources, with a resultant reduction in costs (of stock) or improvement in lead times. Some organisations have gained a competitive advantage on the basis of JIT.

5.2 Analysis risk

'Risk' can be defined as 'a situation in which various outcomes to a decision are possible but where the probabilities of the alternative outcomes are known' (Samuels/Wilkes, *Managerial Finance*).

The treatment of risk in the theory of finance is largely based upon the use of subjective probability distributions. Subjective probability can be distinguished from objective probability as follows. Objective probability views probability as the ratio of the number of 'positive' outcomes of an experiment to the total number of outcomes possible – in other words, as the 'relative frequency' of the positive outcomes. The experiment produces results which are objectively verifiable. The results can be used as the basis for a probability statement. Subjective probability involves the assignation of a number to represent the individual decision-maker's degree of belief concerning the likelihood of occurrence of some future event. The normal convention is to employ a 0 to 1 scale; complete certainty that a future event will occur is equated with a probability of 1, and less than complete certainty with a number between 0 and 1. Subjective probabilities can be viewed in terms of betting odds.

The degree of risk is an important measure of acceptability. The degree of risk can be measured in a number of ways:

(a) The level of financial risk created by funding a proposed strategy from long-term loans can be tested out by re-examining the likelihood of the company reaching the break-even point and the consequences of falling short of that volume of business whilst interest on loans continues to be paid. In this respect there is a clear link between the assessment of risk and the feasibility of alternative strategies.

(b) Another method of assessing the degree of risk is to look at the level of uncertainty in the expected performance should the strategy be adopted. It is helpful to speculate what is likely to happen to performance if some of the assumptions behind the forecasts are ill-founded. Sensitivity analysis is a simple and effective method of performing this task.

6 CHAPTER SUMMARY

In designing an environment for the effective execution of strategy the most essential task is to see that purposes and objectives, and methods of obtaining them are clearly understood. People must know what they are expected to accomplish and this is the function of the implementation stage of planning. It is the most basic of all the stages involved in planning strategy. It involves selecting from alternative future courses of action for the company as a whole and every department or work centre within it. Budgets are in the first instance tools for control, but they illustrate the basic actuality that the task of control is to make plans succeed, and therefore control must reflect the plans, and planning must precede control.

By breaking plans into components consistent with the desired organisation structure, budgets correlate planning and allow authority to be delegated without a loss of control by senior management.

Functional departmentation is the most widely employed basis for organising activities and the reality is that many operational plans formulated to implement corporate strategy are departmental plans. Although manufacturing organisations employ terms such as 'production', 'marketing', 'personnel' and 'finance' to describe the different functions there is a variance of terms which relate to the range of different industries and companies. However, notwithstanding, the implementation of strategy involves functional plans, such as 'production plan', 'marketing plan', 'personnel plan' and 'finance plan'.

7 SELF TEST QUESTIONS

7.1 Define operational planning and control (1.1).

7.2 Explain 'management by exception' (1.1)

7.3 Name two industries which operate in areas of rapid change (2.1).

7.4 Distinguish between inactivists and preactivists (2.1).

7.5 In Johnson and Scholes model of resource allocation, what are the two factors which determine the approach? (3.1)

7.6 Explain briefly what a budget is (4.1).

7.7 Outline the benefits of network analysis (5.1)

8 EXAMINATION TYPE QUESTION

8.1 Albert Owens Ltd

Albert Owens Ltd was founded in 1863 as a manufacturer of confectionery. By 1978 the company commanded approximately 8% of the sugar confectionery market, in the United Kingdom, in particular *'OWENS SHERBETS'*, which were marketed to the retail trade in large bottles and sold-on loose in paper bags often on a "pick and mix" basis and accounted for over half the company's sales. The remainder of the company's product range was composed of other boiled sweets sugar confectionery products such as *'BLUE GLACIER MINTS'*, *'WIZ HUMBUGS'* and *'DANDY FRUITIES'*, marketed under one of the company's three house names, 'Johnsons', 'Owens' and 'Younger'.

The company's sales force consisted of three selling units: one a small group of two senior sales managers who sold to large retail charge accounts, and the other two groups which consisted of about 50 salespersons each, and who sold the company's product according to the house-name attributed to each item either 'Johnsons', 'Younger', or 'Owens'. Because all products were sold through similar outlets, this arrangement often led to duplication of sales calls, but the chairman was of the view that it would not be effective for salespersons to sell products operating under three house names at once.

Over the years Albert Owens Ltd had achieved good profits and grown steadily by a process of vertical integration into wholesaling and by consolidating its product range. By the early 1990s the future presented a number of threats such as the instability of sugar prices, an increasing concern about tooth decay caused by sweets, an increase in the popularity of savoury snacks and the possibility of incursions into sugar confectionery by manufacturers of chocolate products. Similarly, there was an increasing concentration of confectionery in supermarkets, at the expense of small shops which were Owens' traditional outlets. Supermarkets demanded prepackaged sweets in a form Owens found difficult to comply with.

Faced with such threats Owens' Board of Directors viewed the future stability of the company as requiring steady expansion. Of the options open to them, two were short-listed for further consideration:

1. To adopt a programme of product development eg, savoury snacks, chewing gums, and so on.
2. To consolidate current positions in present markets and develop sales through supermarkets.

You are required to:

(a) discuss the criteria (including financial) that would be appropriate for evaluating each option and comparing one against the other; **(15 marks)**

(b) outline the competitive environment in which Albert Owens Ltd operates and to indicate which of the competitive forces in it are of greatest importance to the company; **(5 marks)**

(c) suggest ways in which the number of options available to the company could be narrowed down to this short list of two during the preliminary analysis stage. **(5 marks)**

(Total: 25 marks)

9 ANSWER TO EXAMINATION TYPE QUESTION

9.1 Albert Owens Ltd

(a) One of the most difficult tasks undertaken in planning strategy is that of evaluating various options. This must be carried out logically and analytically. Numerous writers have attempted to produce lists of criteria for testing strategy, probably the best known being those of Argenti and Tilles. For example, Argenti lists six criteria by which to test any proposed strategy:

1. Can it be shown that this strategy gives the company a performance risk curve similar to the one selected by its shareholders (and managers, employees, etc)?
2. Has the company the necessary competence to carry it out?
3. Does it eliminate or reduce the company's outstanding weaknesses?
4. Does it allow the company to exploit any opportunities that may occur in future?
5. Does it sufficiently reduce any of the severe threats that may face the company?
6. Does it call for any action that is or may become objectionable on moral or social grounds?

What Argenti and the other writers really say is that any strategy must: (a) be consistent internally and with the environment; (b) be appropriate in the light of available resources as well as being workable; and (c) have a satisfactory degree of risk and an appropriate time horizon. Another way of looking at this evaluation is to see whether the strategy meets the criteria of: (a) **suitability** - consistent with the objectives of the organisation both internally and externally; (b) **feasibility** - within the resources and capability of the organisation; and (c) **acceptability** - in the degree of risk and uncertainty, the time scale, as well as politically, ethically and morally.

This approach could be adopted to advantage in the case of Albert Owens Ltd.

Suitability

Owens must review each option to establish whether it is in line with its objectives. Such criteria might include:

- cost of entry, initial and continuing investment;
- profitability and cash flow objectives;
- fitting into strategic structure and general compatibility, synergy aspects;
- other financial objectives - gearing ratios, etc.

Both options should be examined and then listed according to some agreed rating scale. For example Option 1 (a programme of product development) will not receive as high a rating with regard to cost of entry, etc, as will Option 2, however it may well be rated higher in respect of profitability. Both options must be measured against the twin criteria of internal consistency (Option 2 seems high in this respect), and consistency with the environment (Option 1 might score high points for this). If the strategy meets these criteria it might be considered suitable. The strategy must match up to the overall image of the organisation and its social goals. In addition, it must be suitable for the organisational and employee objectives.

One important fact that cannot be avoided when analysing the position of Owens Ltd is that it has become mismatched with its environment. It is facing threats and its current product/market situation indicates considerable weaknesses. Customer preferences are obviously changing as is the distribution environment. The company needs to consider these factors when assessing the suitability of a particular option.

Feasibility

This is probably the most important criterion which asks the question "What is the company able to do?" A capability profile is a most useful tool - it is simply a declaration of the resources available (actual or potential) to the organisation. This would be in a form of SWOT ('strengths, weaknesses, opportunities and threats') analysis. Factors to be considered include competence of management, availability of finance, company image, manpower, skills and products. Secondly it asks the question, "Is the strategy workable?" For example a good discounted cash flow return might be achieved from Option 1 but can it be supported by the cash flow throughout the period?

Acceptability

After studying the suitability and feasibility of an option, the organisation must consider whether it is acceptable. For example, does the degree of risk and the time span involved in adopting a programme of product development (Option 1) make its worth doubtful? Over the time period, is it acceptable politically, internally and externally? For example is it acceptable for Owens to enter further into an environment where the power of the buyer is so strong as would be the case with Option 2?. Finally the strategy might be satisfactory internally, but what about questions such as social responsibilities and the company's overall image? Albert Owens Ltd has built its goodwill as a manufacturer of confectionery. Will entering into markets of savoury snacks and chewing gum, etc, water down the company's image?

(b) **There are five key forces involved:**

1. The extent of competitive rivalry within the market

   It would seem that Albert Owens Ltd is protected by its brand differentiation, although all the other factors listed suggest that its market is highly competitive. The decline in the market added to the high exit barriers (in terms of committed investment costs) cause particular problems.

2. The threat of substitutes

   The board of Owens has already recognised the very real threat from the substitute offerings threatening its confectionery products. One of the strategic options under consideration is to move into these markets.

3. The threat of entry

   Although there is a threat in the form of large chocolate manufacturing firms looking to maximise their under capacity there seems little threat to Albert Owens Ltd which appears to hold a firm position in a well defined and differentiated niche.

4/5. The power of buyers and suppliers

   The power of suppliers and buyers has an important affect on market conditions. There are numerous aspects involved in these two forces but of particular concern to Owens is the strength of the buyer power. The buyers may restrict the future freedom of Owens in terms of product packaging, product development, advertising and promotion generally, pricing and merchandising policies. In this respect Owens is in a market which is becoming increasingly concentrated and competitive.

(c) The ways in which the number of options available to Owens were narrowed down to two during the preliminary analysis stage could have included:

1. **The use of scenario models** to describe in detail, a sequence of events which could plausibly lead to a desired result. The approach is essentially **qualitative** and is particularly directed to the likely impact of uncertain aspects of evaluation. Scenarios will produce information regarding the relevance or otherwise of different courses of action.

2. **Portfolio analysis** which considers the balance of products within the organisation. Such analysis will highlight the need for one course of action compared to another.

3. **Synergy analysis** measures the extra benefit which could accrue from providing some sort of linkage between two or more activities.

4. **Ranking** which relies heavily on qualitative assessment of the suitability or fit of any strategy with the overall evaluative criteria. Each alternative strategy is assessed against a number of key factors which the strategic analysis identified in the organisation's resources, environment and values.

5. **The use of decision trees** in which options are ranked by the process of progressively eliminating others. Probabilities can be assigned to different outcomes.

6. **Gap analysis** which is used to identify the extent to which different options will fail to meet the needs/requirements of the organisation in the future.

7. **Opportunity matrix analysis** by which strategic options can be assessed against potential opportunities identified within the strategic analysis.

8. **Profitability analysis** by which cost behaviour is analysed and potential profitability measured.

12 SOME PROBLEMS OF CHANGE

INTRODUCTION & LEARNING OBJECTIVES

In this chapter we will consider the nature of change and its effects upon organisations. Management has been defined as 'the management of change' and certainly, change is ever present and occurring at an ever increasing rate.

Organisations inevitably change because they are open systems in constant interaction with their environment. Although the impelling force for change can be attributed to internal or external stimuli (or both), the underlying impetus is the exposure of system boundaries that allow new technologies, skills, values and demands affect the organisation.

When you have studied this chapter you should be able to do the following:

- Appreciate the nature of change.
- List the reasons for change.
- Identify and illustrate the different categories of change.
- Critically examine how change should be introduced.
- Analyse the relationships between the different levels of change.
- Discuss Lewin's 3-step model of change.
- Discuss the views of Kanter and Bennis.
- Understand change management.
- Consider the implementation of change through power politics.
- Define and explain organisational development (OD).

1 THE DYNAMICS OF CHANGE

1.1 Why change is a challenge to management

For managers the management of change is about maintaining a dynamic equilibrium. By diagnosing events and situations and making adjustments which are appropriate for coping with current conditions, the management would ensure that:

- there is enough stability to achieve current goals;
- there is continuity to allow orderly change in either ends or means;
- the organisation is adaptable and can react to external opportunities and demands as well as changing internal conditions;
- there is enough innovativeness for the organisation to be proactive and initiate change when conditions are right.

The managerial role involves coping with accelerating change in both the external environment and the internal subsystems that affect the managerial process.

Accelerating change can lead to increasing complexity, making the job of the manager increasingly difficult. They need a tolerance for ambiguity and an ability to diagnose situations and identify opportunities and problems.

As decision-makers, managers are the ultimate change agents, whether they are centrally involved or merely guiding and co-ordinating activities. Change can stem from adjustments in managerial behaviour eg, leadership style, approach to planning and controlling or degree of participation in decision-making. When the focus is more technical, structural or psychosocial, managers may respond to suggestions from others or actively instigate changes.

There are external or internal consultants that facilitate organisational change. Specialists in economic and marketing research, industrial relations and organisational development are all examples of change agents.

1.2 The role of force field analysis

Force field analysis is a general purpose diagnostic and problem-solving technique, developed by Kurt Lewin. He argued that managers should consider any change situation in terms of:

- the factors encouraging and facilitating the change (the driving forces); as well as
- the factors that hinder change (the restraining forces).

The force field model suggests two ways of dealing with change. The first is by strengthening your own side and the second is by weakening the opposing forces.

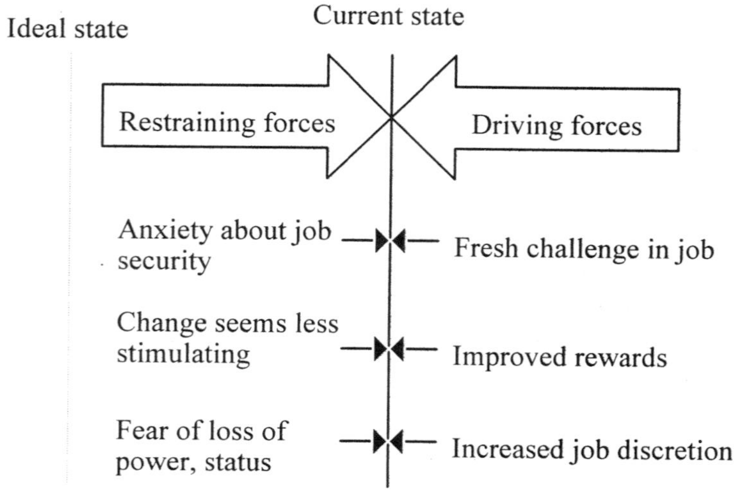

Restraining and driving forces in a change situation

The change process consist of:

(i) Identifying the restraining forces and overcoming/removing/getting round them.

(ii) Carrying out the change.

(iii) Stabilising the new situation by reinforcing the (now changed) behaviour of individuals and work groups with praise and encouragement.

If the forces offset each other completely, it results in equilibrium and status quo. Change can be brought about by either increasing the driving forces or by reducing the restraining forces. New pushing forces can also be added. Reducing the restraining forces is often easier because to increase driving forces without attention to the restraining forces may increase pressure and tension in the system to the point that creative problem solving becomes impossible.

Using a common individual and organisational problem, that of lack of time, we can illustrate the use of force field analysis. To work on the problem effectively we need to state the situation in terms of current and desired conditions, where we are and where we want to be.

Current condition = no time spent on planned change

Desired condition = large blocks of time to critically appraise the organisation.

In order to understand the situation we have to identify the forces that are keeping us in equilibrium, which is no change from the current condition.

Driving forces

- knowledge of theory that says it would be 'better'
- feeling that it would be 'better'
- success stories about increased productivity from current literature
- success stories from acquaintances in similar organisations
- consultants selling the virtues of a new approach

Restraining forces

- programmed activity increases to absorb available time
- current deadlines leave no time to analyse the problem of lack of time
- we seem to be doing satisfactory work, there is no sense of urgency
- reluctance of participants to rock the boat by analysing group processes
- assumption that time is not currently wasted

This list is not exhaustive but it leads to the next step which is to pick one or more of the forces, starting with restraining forces and generating ideas for increasing them or decreasing them.

After alternatives have been evaluated, action plans can be designed and implemented.

1.3 Factors affecting an individual's responses to change

Whilst there is no doubt that change affects all our lives, considerable debate is currently taking place as to the desirability of some of the changes and the necessity for their rapid introduction. Tofler argues that change is out of control and that man is suffering from the increased pace of life and its accompanying transient relationships.

Others argue that change is being introduced too slowly and that organisations, particularly within the UK, are left behind by their major competitors.

Much depends on the organisation's relation with its environment. As a consequence of the environment becoming more turbulent and complex, there is a need for organisations to develop more effective adaptive response systems.

Huczynski and Buchanan claim there are four basic features of organisational change:

Triggers

Change is initiated by some kind of disorganising pressure or trigger arising either within or outside the organisation. Changes may thus be triggered by the discovery that one of the company's machines is old or beyond repair, or by changes in legislation that affect the ways in which employees have to be treated.

Interdependencies

The various facets of an organisation are interdependent. Change in one aspect of an organisation creates pressure for adjustments in other aspects. The introduction of word processing in the typing pool may require authors to alter the style in which they write and present reports and letters for typing.

Conflict and frustrations

The technical and economic objectives of managers may often conflict with the needs and aspirations of employees and this leads to conflicts which in turn create pressures for and resistance to change. The new machine that management want to buy may lead to demands for a new payment system from the people who will have to operate it.

Time lags

Change rarely takes place smoothly. Instead it happens in an 'untidy' way. Some parts of the organisation change more rapidly than others. People and groups may need time to 'catch up' with everyone else. The maintenance staff may still be learning new skills months after that new machine has been installed.

The above characteristics evolve from the open systems perspective and the feedback mechanisms described earlier in the text.

Whether a change does or does not take place within an organisation is dependent on the relative strength of the various positive and negative feedback loops affecting the situation. Positive feedback invokes change whereas negative feedback leads to stable and consistent behaviour.

If we take the above example concerning the introduction of a new machine then, in very simple terms, wear and tear would form part of a positive feedback loop whilst maintenance and repair would be contained in a negative feedback loop. As long as the machine could be repaired equilibrium would persist but when this loop became no longer viable then the positive wear and tear loop would take over and the machine would have to be eventually replaced. Obviously, costs of repair and replacement, together with many other factors, would have to be included in the multiple cause diagram analysing such a situation.

Internal triggers for change are those factors that can cause organisational disequilibrium and include:

(a) questioning authority and intra-organisational conflicts;
(b) adverse organisational climate;
(c) poor performance – unstable labour relations, low output and high costs...;
(d) presence of entrepreneurs and other innovators;
(e) changes in or reordering of organisational goals;
(f) favourable changes experienced in the past.

These internal triggers may, or may not, be related to external forces operating within the organisation's environment which, according to Martino, revolve around:

(a) changes in knowledge both technical and social;
(b) economic opportunities;
(c) distribution of political power;
(d) demographic make-up of the population;
(e) ecological considerations;
(f) ideological and culture factors.

There are varying attitudes to change as Robertson's classification shows:

(a) **Inactivists** could be focused on either of the following:

- **Business as usual** - such people seek stability and survival within the organisation and include those conservative satisficers who make up the establishment at large. They work very hard to keep still - a process termed 'dynamic conservatism.'

  Their efforts appeal to placid and pragmatic people including both moderate reformers and those content with the present situation.

  This attitude attracts defeatists, cynics and the worldly wise.

- **Disaster** - appeals to calm and thoughtful people although it can attract pessimists, preachers and doomsters.

(b) **Reactivists** would be interested in **totalitarian conservation** and would include all those reactionaries who prefer a previous state to the one they are in.

Such people:

- feel there is more to lose from disorder than dictatorship;
- are of an authoritarian, dominating temperament;
- take a low view of other people;
- think they belong to a governing class.

(c) **Preactivists** These liberal optimisers are interested in much more than mere survival and they are generally means oriented.

Their approaches appeal to optimistic, energetic, ambitious, competitive people for whom material growth is more important than personal and social growth. Such persons are often male, toy loving and over intellectual.

(d) **Interactivists** must be interested in a **sane, humane, ecological** future and as radical idealisers they want to control their own destiny. Optimistic, participating, reflective people are attracted to such an attitude together with a number of cranks.

1.4 Why people may resist change

The following sources of resistance can be commonly expected.

Sources of resistance

- fear of the unknown
- need for security
- vested interests threatened
- contrasting interpretations
- poor timing
- lack of resources

Suggested responses

- Information, encouragement, involvement
- Clarification of intentions and methods
- Demonstrate problem or opportunity
- Enlist key people in change planning
- Disseminate valid information, facilitate group sharing
- Await better time
- Provide supporting resources and/or reduced performance expectations.

Such sources of change should be compared with those identified by Schein who differentiated between:

Economic fears

- pay reductions
- redundancies

Social fears

- impaired status
- reduced satisfaction
- implied criticism of past performances
- break up of working group

Resistance to change can be directed against the change itself, the change strategy or the change agent and should be viewed as a form of negative feedback by those managing the change which could be constructively employed to modify their approach.

2 MANAGING CHANGE

2 MANAGING CHANGE

2.1 Planned change

Earlier, the arguments for strategic choice versus determinism were aired including interactivists' belief that people have the potential to control change. Predictions are often **self fulfilling,** (if something is forecast it can be made to happen); or **self defeating,** (undesirable predictions can provoke activities for their avoidance).

Whilst change can never be fully planned due to unexpected problems and follow on effects, many organisations are adopting a positive attitude to the need for change. Theodore Levitt recognised four variables which can be affected by change and claimed that these 'entry points' can become specific targets for managerial efforts to instigate change. The variables are:

(a) **technology** - the processes employed by the organisation to carry out its business.

(b) **business** or 'task' - the activities an organisation undertakes to achieve its overall goals.

(c) **people** - the employees of the organisation whose behaviour has been discussed in detail earlier. Changes in employees' attitudes, beliefs, skills, abilities and behaviour, together with structured changes have been evaluated.

(d) **structure** - the various ways in which organisations can be structured and changes to such structures, together with people changes, have been explored.

The interdependence of these four variables can be illustrated as follows:

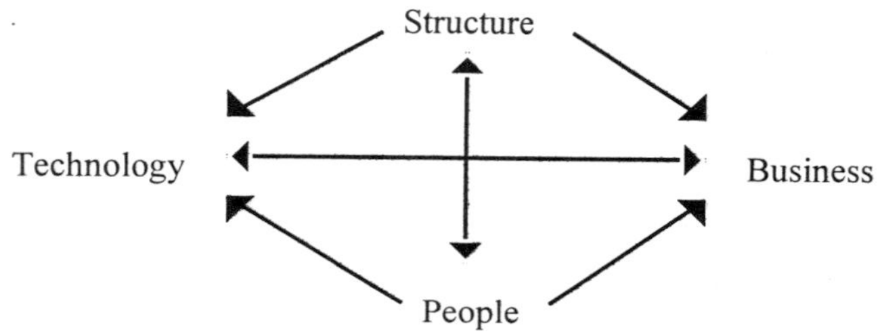

As a result of these interdependencies changes in one variable could lead to unanticipated, and possibly undesirable, changes to other variables. Moreover, it is possible to deliberately change one variable to bring about a desired change in another variable - the increasing adoption of mass production technologies has led to the spread of capitalist structures.

2.2 Key issues in successful change management

The five strategies for managing change are:

- participation;
- education - communication;
- power/coercion;
- manipulation;
- negotiation.

(a) **Participation**

This approach aims to involve employees, usually by allowing some input into decision-making. This could easily result in employees enjoying raised levels of autonomy, by allowing them to design their own jobs, pay structures etc.

Employees are more likely to support changes made and give positive commitment as they 'own' the change. Another advantage of participation is the improved utilisation of employee expertise.

The possible disadvantages include:

- The time element. The process can be lengthy due to the number of people involved in the decision making process.
- The loyalty element. There is a need for a strong trusting relationship to exist between management and workforce.
- The resistance element. Management may suffer from restricted movement as the amount and direction of change acceptable to employees will have some influence.

(b) **Education and communication**

Usually used as a background factor to reinforce another approach. This strategy relies upon the hopeful belief that communication about the benefits of change to employees will result in their acceptance of the need to exercise the changes necessary. The obvious advantage is that any changes could be initiated easily. However, employees may not agree about the benefits of proposed changes as being in their best interests. Also, the process of education and persuasion can be lengthy to initiate and exercise unless there is a firm mutual trust. Without this they are not likely to succeed.

(c) **Power/coercion**

This strategy involves the compulsory approach by management to implement change. This method finds its roots from the formal authority that management possess together with legislative support. When there is a state of high unemployment, management enjoys greater power and is therefore able to use this strategy with more success. The advantages of this method are:

- Changes can be made with speed.
- Adhering to management's requirements is easy when opposition is weak from the work force.

The disadvantages are:

- The lack of commitment of the workforce and determination to reverse policy when times change.
- Poor support resulting in weak motivation, low morale and performance.

Future implications also need to be considered. For example, when employees enjoy a stronger position ie, union representation, they are less likely to co-operate due to their experiences of past management treatment.

(d) **Manipulation**

A manipulative strategy has many of the advantages and disadvantages of the power strategy. It can therefore be viewed as part of a power strategy.

(e) **Negotiation**

This particular strategy is often practised in unionised companies. Simply, the process of negotiation is exercised, enabling several parties with opposing interests to bargain. This bargaining leads to a situation of compromise and agreement.

Branching from this are two strategies:

- Each party involved seeks to negotiate for itself, at the cost of the other parties involved.
- Each party aims to find an agreement with aspects advantageous to all concerned.

Branching from this are two strategies:

- Each party involved seeks to negotiate for itself, at the cost of the other parties involved.
- Each party aims to find an agreement with aspects advantageous to all concerned.

The advantage of negotiation strategy is that it offers the company the opportunity to note possible conflict and allows it to be dealt with in an orderly fashion. This hopefully prevents such problems as industrial action. Also, when an agreement has been made, the outcome can be to encourage commitment, preserve morale and maintain output.

The main disadvantage is that this approach may be time consuming, and should opposition be strong enough the management may choose to adopt a power strategy instead.

2.3 Activity

Changes in organisations can be seen as threatening. You will possibly know this from your own experience. Think about the possible effects of change and then list the reasons why people might fear or resist organisational change. Think further on the matter and then list where resistance might occur in an organisation, and describe what senior management might be able to do to eliminate resistance or reduce its effects.

2.4 Activity solution

People tend to resist change because they fear one or more from the following list:

(a) A loss of job security.
(b) A loss of status.
(d) Possibility of having to work for a different manager.
(c) The loss of work they enjoy.
(e) A break up of working relationships.
(f) Having to work in a different location (moving home, etc).
(g) Having to work at a different time (shift work, etc).
(h) An inability to cope with new duties/responsibilities.
(i) Inconvenience of the change (training etc).
(j) The closing of potential promotion (career implications).
(k) Economic aspects (loss of overtime etc).

Cultural resistance tends to occur in different ways and at different levels of an organisation. Often resistance is confined to a particular coalition. The main types of resistance are:

(a) Organisation-wide resistance.
(b) Hierarchical resistance - at a particular level of management.
(c) Departmental resistance - in a particular department.
(d) Individual resistance - by particular individuals.
(e) Collection (or coalition) of people - by a particular group or trade union group, etc.

Resistance to cultural change be managed or reduced in the following ways:

(a) Total, genuine and visible support for the change by top management.

(b) Positive reinforcement (eg, by first changing in areas where managers approve).

(c) The use of a rewards system, such as promoting managers willing to change.

(d) Good communication/participation systems associated with the change.

(e) Recruiting people already experienced in working in the changed system or environment.

2.5 How organisations can create readiness for change

The senior management group has responsibility for establishing the organisation's vision and objectives and for making sure that the whole organisation pursues the same vision.

The managers are then responsible for creating the conditions that will promote change and innovation. To manage the change process successfully, the culture of the organisation will need to be permissive and flexible. Bureaucracies are very slow to change because they do not have this culture.

Managers need to encourage individuals to use their initiative and must put the emphasis on teamwork. An autocratic management style is not conducive to change because the manager should act as a facilitator of change rather than just telling people what to do.

Ronald Corwin, in his book **Strategies for Organizational Intervention**, argues that an organisation can be changed more easily:

- If it is invaded by creative and unconventional outsiders with fresh ideas.
- If those outsiders are exposed to creative, competent and flexible socialization agents.
- If it staffed by young, flexible, supportive and competent boundary personnel.
- If it structurally complex and decentralised.
- If it has outside funds to lessen the cost of innovation.
- If its members have positions that are sufficiently secure and protected from status risks involved in change.
- If it is located in a changing, modern urbanised setting where it is in close co-operation with a coalition of other organisations that can supplement its skills and resources.

2.6 The role of the leader

There must be a leader of the change process who accepts the responsibility. Such a leader must have certain skills and attributes, such as:

- inspiration;
- interpersonal skills;
- ability to resolve a multitude of interdependent problems;
- ability to plan;
- opportunist;
- gift of good timing.

To maximise the advantages and minimise the disadvantage of the change process, the role of the leader should be to:

(i) Give all staff concerned the maximum possible warning of impeding change to give them time to get accustomed to the idea.

(ii) Explain as far as possible the reasons for change as the provision of both adequate and accurate information scotches rumours before they can be circulated.

(iii) Involve individuals and/or work groups in the planning and implementing of change as much as possible. Employees will be more likely to become committed to change if they feel they can have some influence on the change and its outcome. It also a way of gaining valuable suggestions.

(iv) Keep lines of communication going, monitor progress, giving regular feedback and communicate results.

(v) Try to introduce changes gradually; phased change stands a better chance of success.

(iii) Involve individuals and/or work groups in the planning and implementing of change as much as possible. Employees will be more likely to become committed to change if they feel they can have some influence on the change and its outcome. It also a way of gaining valuable suggestions.

(iv) Keep lines of communication going, monitor progress, giving regular feedback and communicate results.

(v) Try to introduce changes gradually; phased change stands a better chance of success.

(vi) Offer and provide appropriate training.

(vii) Ensure the workforce are aware of the benefits to them of the change eg, increased responsibility, job enrichment.

(viii) Consider the effects of change on individuals, giving counselling where necessary.

(ix) Follow up regularly and be supportive.

(x) Develop a favourable climate for any subsequent changes envisaged.

3 THE CHANGE PROCESS

3.1 Lewin's 3-step model of change

Kurt Lewin demonstrated the effectiveness of using group norms and consensus decision-making to change individual and organisational behaviour. His research programs included Weight Watchers and the effect of group discussion and commitment in changing eating habits. The key findings were that behaviour change is more likely to occur and persist when commitment is on a group basis, rather than an individual one.

The process of change, shown in the diagram below, includes unfreezing habits or standard operating procedures, changing to new patterns and refreezing to ensure lasting effects.

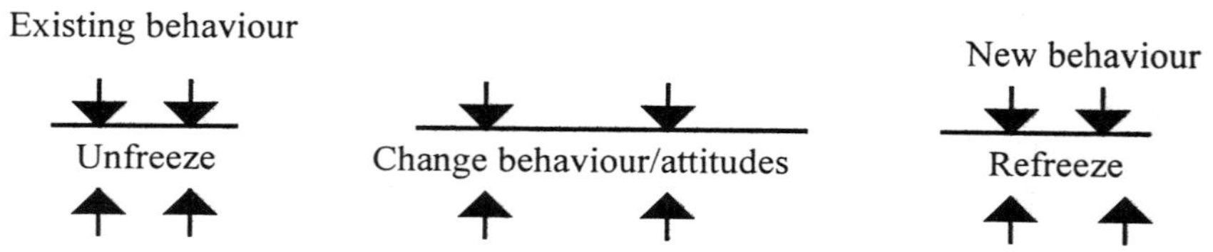

The process of change comprises three stages:

(a) **Unfreezing** - create the initial motivation to change by convincing staff of the undesirability of the present situation.

(b) **The change process itself** - mainly concerned with identifying what the new behaviour or norm should be. This stage will often involve new information being communicated and new attitudes, culture and concepts being adopted.

(c) **Refreezing or stabilising the change** - implying reinforcement of the new pattern of work or behaviour by rewards (praise etc). Develop the belief that the changed situation satisfies organisational and personal values.

3.2 Alternative models of change management

Leavitt argued that approaches to change that succeeded in one organisation were not necessarily successful in another. He suggests that the chosen approach to change in a particular organisation reflects the underlying beliefs within that organisation.

whereas for novel, loosely structured tasks, a more open multi-channel communication network may seem more appropriate.

(c) **Technology** – An early example of a change approach to this category includes method study approaches where an outsider views the work pattern and suggests changes in a technological approach (Taylor). Updating and replacement of equipment is a natural example of an external approach. The essence is that the approach occurs outside of the work group itself.

(d) **People** – Group working, attitude training, changes in styles of management are examples of the people approach.

3.3 Implementing change through power politics

If transformational change is required in an organisation, it is likely that there will be a need for the reconfiguration of power structures. Any manager of change needs to consider how it might be implemented from a political perspective. For example, a critical report by an outside change agency such as market research findings on customer perceptions of service may be 'rubbished' by the board because it threatens their authority and power.

Understanding these systems, there is a need to plan changes within this political context. The political mechanisms include:

(i) **the control and manipulation of organisational resources.** Acquiring, withdrawing or allocating additional resources, or being identified with important areas of resource or expertise, can be an important tool in overcoming resistance or persuading others to accept change. Being able to manipulate the information opposing the changes can also be important.

(ii) **association with powerful groups or elites** can help build a power base. This may be useful for the change agent who does not have a strong personal power base to work from. Association with a change agent who is seen as successful or who is respected can also help a manager overcome resistance to change.

(iii) **handling the subsystem effectively** can achieve acceptance of change throughout the organisation. Building up alliances and a network of contacts and sympathisers may help win over powerful groups.

(iv) **symbolic devices** that may take different forms. To build power the manager may become involved in committees which reinforce and preserve the change model. Symbolic activity can be used for consolidating change by positive reinforcement towards those who most accept change. These rewards include new structures, titles and office allocation.

3.4 Framework for the management of change

The idea of change that is planned assumes that the management can identify gaps between current conditions and desired conditions on the following dimensions:

(i) How can this organisation be more effective?
(ii) Can we operate more efficiently?
(iii) How can we make it a more satisfying place to work?

Whenever the organisation can identify differences between where it currently is and where it would like to be on any of the dimensions, it can pursue planned change or improve the organisation.

Systems would be implemented to identify and diagnose particular problems within these general areas eg, poor morale, inefficient computer programs, lack of quality control or inadequate downward communication. Depending on the problem, a suitable change effort can be designed.

If the process of planned change is to become part of the culture of the organisation, provisions must be made for introspection and self criticism on a routine basis. It should also be followed up as a natural part of the managerial style.

(iii) How can we make it a more satisfying place to work?

Whenever the organisation can identify differences between where it currently is and where it would like to be on any of the dimensions, it can pursue planned change or improve the organisation.

Systems would be implemented to identify and diagnose particular problems within these general areas eg, poor morale, inefficient computer programs, lack of quality control or inadequate downward communication. Depending on the problem, a suitable change effort can be designed.

If the process of planned change is to become part of the culture of the organisation, provisions must be made for introspection and self criticism on a routine basis. It should also be followed up as a natural part of the managerial style.

4 OTHER VIEWS ON CHANGE

4.1 Rosabeth Moss Kanter

Kanter's work on change is contained mainly in her 1984 book **The Change Masters - Corporate Entrepreneurs at Work**. She performed an in-depth case study on 10 major US companies, and drew on research into a further 100 enterprises. As a result of this, she identified two main approaches to change and innovation.

- The integrative approach describes the methods of firms that see change as an opportunity rather than a threat. These firms take an integrated, holistic view of problems and are ready to re-shape the organisation in search of a response.

- The segmentalist approach sees problems as being compartmentalised. The organisation is not a unified whole, but a collection of segments. Managers wish to confine each problem to a particular segment of the organisation and resist any alteration in the balance of the overall structure.

Not surprisingly Kanter's findings suggest that innovation is handled much better by integrative organisations than by segmentalist organisations.

To achieve an integrative approach organisations must develop three new sets of skills.

- Power skills, to persuade others to invest time and resources in new (risky) initiatives.

- Skills in managing problems arising from team working and employee participation.

- An understanding of how change is designed and constructed in an organisation.

Kanter also suggests a number of actions to overcome resistance to change.

- Top management must be committed and must learn to think integratively.

- Management should encourage a culture of pride by highlighting achievements.

- Innovation should be supported by extending access to power sources, such as management committees.

- Cross-functional links should be improved by means of enhanced lateral communication.

- Staff should be 'empowered' in an organisation structure based on devolving authority as low down the hierarchy as possible.

- The plans of the organisation should be communicated widely so as to encourage input from as many people as possible.

4.2 Warren G Bennis

Bennis is an influential American author on leadership and change. He focuses on the need to inspire change rather than merely imposing it. He identifies five 'avenues of change'.

- Dissent and conflict. Top management impose change by mans of their position power, the result being rancour amongst those affected.
- Trust and truth. Management must gain trust, express their vision clearly, and persuade others to follow.
- Cliques and cabals. Cliques have power, money, resources. Cabals have ambition, drive and energy. 'Unless the cliques can co-opt the cabals, revolution is inevitable.
- External events. Forces of society can impose change, eg, by new government regulation or through overseas competition.
- Culture or paradigm shift. Changing the corporate culture is the most important avenue of change.

Bennis also provides advice on avoiding disaster during change.

- Recruit with scrupulous honesty.
- Guard against the crazies. (Innovation may attract people who will distort its ideas.)
- Build support among like-minded people.
- Plan for change from a solid conceptual base.
- Don't settle for rhetorical change.
- Don't allow those who are opposed to change to appropriate basic issues.
- Know the territory.
- Appreciate environmental factors.
- Avoid future shock.
- Remember that change is most successful when those who are affected are involved in the planning.

5 STRATEGY REVIEW AND STRATEGIC ISSUE MANAGEMENT

5.1 The importance of reviewing progress

The success of any change should be reviewed to make sure that it meets the objectives that it was supposed to achieve.

By building into the change process a means of reviewing its progress, the organisation is making strategic change more coherent, which in itself is a way of making the change a success. Being coherent across all aspects of the organisation means that:

- There is a consistency between the intended strategy, the stated strategic objectives, their expression in operational terms, the behaviour of executives in reinforcing the strategy and a means of assessing performance and progress.
- The direction of strategic change is consistent with what is happening in the environment and with what is understood in the organisation.
- The strategy is feasible in terms of the required resources, the structuring of the organisation and the changes that need to occur in organisational culture and operational routines.

- The strategy is feasible in terms of the required resources, the structuring of the organisation and the changes that need to occur in organisational culture and operational routines.

- The strategic direction is clearly related to achieving competitive advantage or excellent performance, and internally it is understood how this is happening.

The key issue is finding an appropriate means of reviewing the progress and success of any strategic change and identifying strategic issues as they arise. Performance measures for strategic change are not easy and, more often, financial results are relied upon. In their book **Strategic control: milestones for long-term performance**, Goold and Quinn suggest that most companies take a pride in fostering a performance-driven culture that emphasises profitability as the key goal for business management, but too much emphasis on budgetary control and short-term profit can disguise strategic problems from senior managers.

5.2 A framework for strategy review

The introduction of a strategic control system to monitor the organisation's strategic position has advantages which include:

- planning realism;
- encouraging higher performance standards;
- motivation;
- ability to intervene when the activity is not going to plan;

Goold and Quinn identify a formal and an informal system of strategic control.

The **formal** process begins with a strategy review where the organisation's key success factors are outlined. A cost leadership strategy would identify cost measures, which are one of the easiest to monitor. Milestones of performance are then identified, both of a quantitative and a qualitative nature. These milestones are short-term steps towards long term goals and act as a way of pulling the organisation towards its goals. Milestones are the means to monitor both the **actions** such as the launching of a new product and the **results** eg, the success of the launch. The areas that milestones cover include:

- market share;
- quality measurement;
- innovation; and
- customer satisfaction.

When setting target achievement levels the targets must be reasonably precise, suggesting strategies and tactics. Competitive benchmarks are targets which are set relative to the competition. It may be difficult to obtain data about the competitor, but a relative advantage is important in competitive terms.

Informal systems of strategic control exist where the organisation does not define explicit strategic objectives or milestones that are regularly and formally monitored as part of the management control system. The argument in favour of informality mainly concentrates on aspects such as flexibility and openness of communication. However, these systems do not always work because they enable managers to ignore important strategic issues.

5.3 The importance of strategic issue management

Goold and Quinn suggest the characteristics of strategic control systems can be measured on two axes.

(i) The formality of the process
(ii) The milestones that are identified for performance

Whilst there may be no optimum degree of formality of the process and no optimum number of milestones identified for performance, the following guidelines are recommended.

- If there are important linkages among businesses, the formality of the process should be low, to avoid co-operation being undermined.
- If there is a lot of diversity, it is doubtful whether any strategic control system is appropriate, especially where the critical success factors for each business are different. Formal processes may not find the right objectives, informal ones may confuse the issue.
- Where an organisation's strategic stance depends on decisions which can, if they go wrong, destroy the company as a whole (e.g. launching a new technology) need strategic control systems which have a large number of performance criteria so that emerging problems in any area will be easily detected. Where there is high environmental uncertainty, a strategic control process monitors some of the background assumptions.
- Fashion-goods manufacturers, and other industries which are prone to many changes, must respond to relatively high levels of environmental turbulence and must be able to react quickly. Where changes are rapid, a system of low formality and few measures may be appropriate, merely because the control processes must allow *ad hoc* decisions to be taken.
- For businesses with few sources of competitive advantage, control can easily focus on the key factors, where market share or quality is the source of success. Where there are many sources of advantage and success covers a wide area eg, market share, sales, mix, pricing policy and distribution, there is the danger that control can be misdirected because it focuses on inappropriate objectives and carries a high cost because measurement of performance is difficult.

6 CHAPTER SUMMARY

The future is going to bring change and at an accelerated rate; if the organisation is to survive it has no choice but to participate in the development of more humane and democratic systems. Much of this accelerated change will be uncontrollable and managers must practise management with incomplete information and little stability. Peters states that managers must welcome and expect chaos since this will prevail under conditions of rapid change.

7 SELF TEST QUESTIONS

7.1 Describe the factors identified by Lewin in his force field analysis (1.2).

7.2 What are the four basic features of organisation change? (1.3).

7.3 What are the main sources of resistance to change? (1.4).

7.4 List the five strategies for managing change (2.2).

7.5 Describe two aspects of an organisation which can manage change successfully (2.5).

7.6 Draw a diagram showing Lewin's 3-step model of change (3.1).

7.7 Explain the four interacting variables identified by Leavitt which give rise to a different approach to change (3.2).

7.8 In a formal review of strategy, what types of milestone can be measured easily? (4.2).

8 EXAMINATION TYPE QUESTION

8.1 Managing change

You are required to explain **four** strategies for managing change, giving the advantages and disadvantages of **each**. **(20 marks)**

9 ANSWER TO EXAMINATION TYPE QUESTION

9.1 Managing change

(a) **Participation**

This approach seeks to involve employees in the decision making process. There are cases where this has been extended to the designing of own jobs, payment systems etc. This has proved successful, as the American Coch and French study of Harwood Manufacturing and the UK experience of Pirelli would suggest. The advantage of this method is that it enhances commitment to change, since the employees have developed their own change. In addition, the wider range of input into the change process will bring in an equally wide range of knowledge and experience.

However, there are a number of significant disadvantages. First of all, there must be the culture and climate to permit participation in change. RC Townsend boasted how change worked in Avis with the same people. However, the type of person who would work for a car-rental firm is likely to be different, and probably more adaptable, than someone who is in a very highly programmed job with little scope for creativity. The cynic would view the Pirelli example in terms of what were the implications upon the shop floor.

Secondly, the greater number of people in the decision making process can give rise to an extremely protracted decision making process. Also, as is evidenced from the Japanese **ringi** approach, no-one is responsible and hence accountable for the decision.

Thirdly, there is a need for a high degree of trust between the management and work people. Again, there may not be the culture and tradition of this, with the result that the invitation to participate will be treated with considerable suspicion.

Fourthly, participation must be honest. Pseudo-participation is always exposed for the sham that it is, and only serves to exacerbate the problem. This can easily happen, since with the wide variety of people being involved, there is a high risk that plans for change degenerate into a talking shop.

(b) **Education**

There is a mistaken view that if people are better educated and trained, then they will be receptive to change. While better education and training may make changes easier, and create an environment where people are prepared to participate in the change process, it will also raise the expectation of the individual. This could mean an increased turnover as people become more marketable, or an exacerbated hostility derived from frustration where enhanced expectations have not been met.

(c) **Communication**

This assumes that if the plans for change are effectively communicated, then people will understand the need for change and accept the changes. This would lay the foundations for change to be implemented fairly easily and painlessly.

Sadly, the communication of the plans for change is subject to misinterpretation and, if the wrong medium is selected, manipulation into disinformation by self-seeking interests. In addition, communication can be a two-edged sword. People may learn of the need for change and morale may drop, exacerbating the current situation. Similarly, the more marketable people may move, and this will also create a situation where change is needed, but the best people to implement it have left.

(d) **Power**

This is where management exerts what is perceived as its 'right to manage' and imposes change unilaterally. Management has the formal authority to do this within the parameters of appropriate legislation, and the de facto situation in relation to the labour market. In periods of high unemployment, management may elect to take this option, knowing that if employees do not like the situation, then they should look very carefully at the alternatives. It is argued that this draconian only in times of high unemployment, but it could be argued that in times of full employment those who are not prepared to go along with the changes can be eased out less painfully.

Such a strategy has the obvious advantage of being easy and quick to implement, especially if the workforce is in a weak and demoralised position. However, there are two significant potential disadvantages. First, in the short term, there is the obvious problem identified by Etzioni that such a coercive strategy will fail to gain the wholehearted support of the workforce, with the result that the desired levels of motivation, morale and output will not be achieved. Secondly, in the long term the company may be building up further problems for itself. Unions have long memories, and a coerced, demoralised workforce provides a fertile area in which confrontation and antagonism will develop. As a result, when the time becomes ripe for a more co-operative approach, the management is unlikely to find the unions and the employees very helpful, or predisposed to comply with managerial wishes.

(e) **Manipulation**

This can be very similar to the power strategy. It is ostensibly less coercive. A management team may use the media of pseudo-participation and pseudo-effective communication to persuade the workforce about the need for change. Ideally it will be done through a mass meeting, similar to union meetings outside the factory gate. Agreement comes from position power and an unwillingness to step out of line. The benefits are the same as from the power strategy, as are the considerable disadvantages.

(f) **Negotiation**

This moves along the spectrum from autocratic styles to a more consultative approach, usually through the media of the unions. The objective is an acceptable compromise solution. Two possibilities exist. First, that one side wins and one loses. Compromises are often unsuccessful, so this approach may be the best way. Secondly, is the possibility to work towards a compromise. This option may not exist or it may be very unpalatable. The obvious example is where rationalisation is required. The unions may resist the closures, but the future of the whole company or even the industry may be at stake. This may mean that the path towards a compromise is really not available. It also means that one party to the negotiations is fighting with a considerable handicap.

The obvious advantage of negotiation is that it recognises potential conflict and seeks a solution without running the risk of creating damaging industrial disputes. It has the further advantage that the resultant agreement will produce a commitment to the changes and maintain the morale of the workforce and the output that management requires. However, it can be a protracted process and if it goes on too long, patience may be lost on both sides. It also depends upon the level of confidence that exists in the union and the negotiating team. If there is a feeling that the unions have sold the employees out, if they could have got a better deal, and if they feel they have been the victims of cynical manipulation, then the whole process will fail.

13 SETTING EMPLOYEE GOALS

INTRODUCTION & LEARNING OBJECTIVES

Resource planning is an essential part in the strategic planning process. All managers, whatever their functional interests should be conversant with the mechanics and implications of the formulation, implementation and control of resources, at least as far as their own activities are concerned.

One of the most important aspects involved in setting work objectives is that they are directed towards the achievement of organisational goals. The term 'Management by Objectives (MBO)' was first discussed by Drucker. It is a system which aims to achieve a sense of common purpose and common direction amongst the management of an organisation in the pursuit of results.

Once the objectives of the organisation are chosen, the means to achieve them must be implemented. Large complex projects may at first seem daunting to management, but when they are broken down into smaller manageable units, these units can be analysed independently of each other. The work can then be planned, estimated and resourced.

There are some planning tools which are available to help project managers schedule activities effectively. Network analysis techniques are a way of finding the best way to schedule activities by highlighting the relationships between them.

When you have studied this chapter you should be able to do the following:

- Discuss the role of individual work objectives in ensuring the achievement of the organisational goals.
- Explain the hierarchy of objectives.
- Describe the differences between top-down and bottom-up strategy setting.
- Evaluate the advantages and disadvantages of Management by Objectives (MBO).
- Describe the procedures for the planning of achievement of objectives.
- Discuss the factors that influence the allocation of resources.

1 SETTING WORK OBJECTIVES

1.1 Introduction

Definition Objectives are time-assigned targets derived from the goals, and are set in advance of strategy.

We have seen that goals and objectives are very loosely used terms and that in this text objectives would normally be the term used to refer to short term **means** employed to attain the longer term goals or **ends** of the organisational members. The degree to which these goals are attained is a measure of the organisation's **effectiveness**. This term should not be confused with the **efficiency** of the organisation which is concerned with the means employed. If inappropriate means are employed the organisation could be very efficient but totally ineffective – conversely an organisation can be very effective but have sufficient organisational slack to be able to operate inefficiently.

Objectives have all or some of the following characteristics:

- They are mainly statements expressed in quantitative terms ('closed') derived from the goals.
- More than one objective may be required to satisfy a goal.
- Objectives are set in advance of strategy.
- They are time-assigned.

One thing which is clear is that objectives must be capable of being quantified, otherwise progress towards them cannot be measured.

1.2 Work objectives

In order to be operational, objectives such as 'to make a profit' or to 'be more efficient' should be translated into more specific terms. When goals can be quantified they can be translated into explicit plans by which performance can be measured.

Planning work means:

- scheduling and allocating routine tasks to be completed within pre-determined time limits;
- handling deadlines and high priority tasks which may interrupt the usual level of work;
- adapting to changes;
- drawing up standards for working, which can be used to measure performance;
- co-ordinating the activities.

Humble defines a work objective as being the condition that will exist when a key area of the job is being done according to accepted performance.

1.3 Hierarchy of objectives

We have already looked at a hierarchy of objectives. At each higher level in the hierarchy the objectives are more relevant to a greater proportion of the organisation's activities so that the objectives at the top of the hierarchy are relevant to every aspect of the organisation. The following diagram illustrates the hierarchical relationship outlined by Argenti.

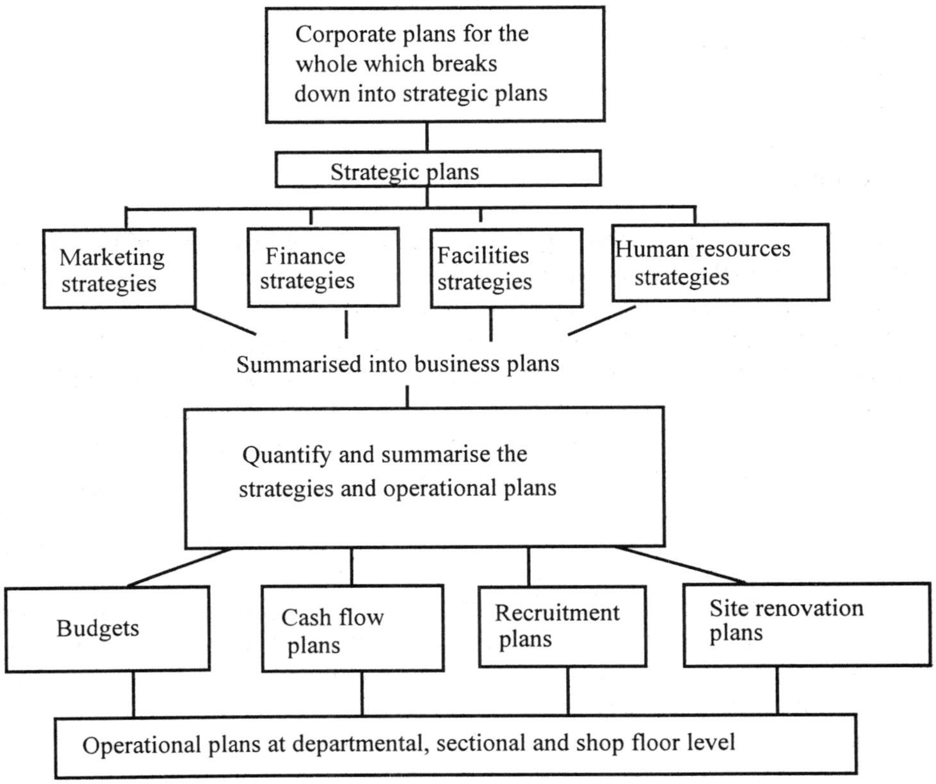

1.4 Top down versus bottom up strategy setting

Objectives can be specified from the top down, ie, the company objectives are broken down into management objectives and specified to the job holders. This is the John Humble approach and is the natural method of implementing a company plan.

Other writers suggest that objectives should be participatively agreed and that in some companies it would be beneficial to start at the lower level and build a hierarchy of objectives upwards from this base.

The bottom up approach maximises the participation of lower level personnel who are closer to the actual operations. However, the top down approach has the advantage of providing clearer guide-lines and parameters for lower level participants in setting their own objectives.

Some companies have discovered that a compromise may be best where the process cannot be exclusively top down or bottom up if it is to be an effective way of managing the business. The communication and planning effort must go in both directions.

1.5 Individual work objectives and organisational goals

Many claim that referring to organisational objectives is an act of rectification but it is very apparent that in some organisations the formalised organisational objectives are paramount and that the goals of individuals are scarcely, if ever, considered important. Hicks stresses

'Organisations exist because persons need them – to do things that they need to do or want to do, and that they either could not do as well or could not do at all without people organisations. The things that people need or want – their objectives – thus are responsible for the existence of organisations. Further, how effective any organisation is (that is, how well it meets its own objectives as an organisation) is ultimately determined by the degree to which it helps its members to achieve these individual objectives.'

There are a number of possible relationships between company objectives and the individual objectives of those working for it; the spectrum covers five categories:

(a) totally opposing;
(b) partially opposing;
(c) neutral;
(d) compatible;
(e) identical.

If the objectives of an individual are diametrically opposed to those of the organisation then conflict will result as long as the person remains with that organisation. If the individual's objectives are only partially opposed to those of the organisation the best outcome for the company is that the individual does not actively hamper achievement of the overall organisational objective. Where a neutral situation exists the individual does not take an active role in the organisation but goes his own way, if allowed to, whilst the organisation pursues its own goals. Where compatibility is achieved then most personal and company goals can be achieved without much harm to either party. This is called Goal Congruence whereby the organisation works in such a way as to encourage behaviour that blends in with top management goals. Occasionally, it is possible that the aims of the individual are identical with those of the company for which he/she works and there should be a complete absence of conflict.

The requirements are not too difficult to meet as far as organisational objectives are concerned but obvious problems of definition exist when the objectives of individuals are being considered. Most people have needs, abilities, skills, aspirations and preferences but their objectives may vary in changing circumstances. Often people's behaviour is difficult to reconcile with their declared objectives and the correct way to motivate them is difficult to find.

2 MANAGEMENT BY OBJECTIVES

2.1 Introduction

Management by objectives (MBO) is undertaken to permit individuals to establish objectives through which they can determine their contribution to the corporate objectives, as well as their own personal ones.

Peter Drucker, in his Practice of Management (1954) and John Humble (writing in the 1960s) are associated with MBO. The ideas of Drucker are based upon McGregor's concept of motivation, in that Theory Y suggests that the individual has untapped reservoirs of intellect, and originality. If an individual receives challenging tasks at work, then the need for self-esteem is satisfied and commitment to the organisation is achieved.

Definition Humble's definition of MBO is that it is:

A dynamic system which integrates the company's needs to achieve its goals for profit and growth with the individual's need to contribute and to develop himself.

2.2 Stages of MBO

Following Humble's approach, the stages for adoption of a scheme for MBO are:

- Senior management (in particular the chief executive) must indicate the nature of the corporate plan and its strategies.
- Subsystem objectives (secondary objectives) are established for departments and smaller work units.
- The key results analysis (KRA) has to be prepared and thus lists the major attainments expected from each manager, in consultation.
- A unit (or subsystem) improvement plan decides about the priorities to be adopted, and job improvement plans derived from this in respect of individual managers.
- Individual managers have to possess sufficient authority and, of course, the opportunity necessary to achieve the job improvement plan, and target periods are set.
- Performance reviews are established and undertaken systematically, with regard to each manager's results, and there must also be an overall review for the total work unit or department.
- An ongoing management development programme must be adopted.
- Review and revision of plans must be on an ongoing basis.

You should note the major characteristics of the MBO concept:

Key results and performance standards are to be achieved by each individual manager. The job improvement plan is established for both the individual and the unit and it allows a measurable, quantifiable contribution to be made to the success of the corporate entity; performance reviews are disciplined and formal assessments of each manager's results, on a regular basis - using key results and performance standards; the **potential review** is held regularly to identify in respect of an individual manager's potential for higher level tasks; management training plans emerge to improve skills; and there are plans to motivate managers in terms of salary, selection and career development.

2.3 Organisational benefits of MBO

The organisation as an entity derives certain advantages from the adoption of the MBO system approaches. If everyone is committed to the principle wholeheartedly, at all management levels:

- Managerial effort is concentrated upon the most important areas in relation to contribution towards the achievement of corporate targets.
- There is an assessment of performance which leads to indication of management potential and establishment of reward criteria.
- 'Team spirit' is encouraged on a corporate basis and therefore a greater contribution of effort is achieved.
- The clarity of objective definition improves effectiveness of managers.

- It facilitates staff appraisal and helps identify needs for development.
- There is the development of a greater commitment from personnel to the corporate objectives.
- Organisational development is facilitated in that new concepts are directly modified as necessary.

2.4 Individual benefits of MBO

MBO introduces personal targets and, because of this, individuals:

- may have an uplift in their morale as unnecessary activities are eliminated in the analysis;
- are able to determine their own level of performance for self-appraisal purposes;
- benefit from the overall team improvements (eg, increased discussion, better relationships);
- find that the work is more clearly delineated so that each person is aware of what action to take;
- are aware of facts they are expected to know about, volumes of work they are to complete, and so on;
- are able to demonstrate their own capabilities because they are free to contribute as they feel able to do, using own initiative, creative talents and so on;
- are faced with new challenges so that self esteem is derived from success, as is group esteem.

2.5 Disadvantages of MBO

Problems occur because:

- Commitment of senior management levels has to be sustained, and personnel may not be appropriately rewarded for their work;
- Eventually, objectives may simply be proposed and then imposed by superiors with insufficient consultation;
- Regular objective reviews and necessary amendments may not be carried out.
- A good deal of organisational effort is deemed necessary by MBO.
- Training, counselling and guidance generally may not always be adequate for staff working towards their own personal goals.
- Individual efforts may be distracted from set objectives by external forces and local differences.
- Higher and higher targets for staff achievement may be introduced, causing stress on the part of those involved.
- The system could evolve into a mechanistic one, resisting any individual ideas of an enterprising or original nature because the plan does not incorporate such innovations for contributions to objectives.
- The objectives may be stated misleadingly and/or ignore some KRAs.

2.6 Setting objectives MBO

A strategy can only be implemented when all the managers involved know what they are to achieve. A 'Management By Objectives' exercise helps to arrive at a situation where all managers do know, and have agreed with, their individual objectives. Each manager will have a range of objectives, some short-term, some longer term, contributing to the overall long-term objective of the company.

Some typical objectives for various managers are now given:

(a) **Sales/Marketing manager**

- Increase the turnover by A% in 6 months at a rate of a% per month.
- Increase our share of the market for Widgets from 15% to 20% in the next 18 months.
- Successfully introduce our new Product Y and obtain sales of £10,000 per week after 3 months.

  Open up the Scottish region, in which we have always been singularly unsuccessful.
- Recruit and train effectively six new sales people.
- Institute a long-term market research survey to analyse trends in customer buying behaviour, and hence to make recommendations as to the type of product likely to be needed in 4 years time.

(b) **Production manager**

- Operate plant at maximum practical operating output.
- Reduce overall costs of manufacturing by 5% over a six month period using the new equipment.
- Improve the performance of junior managers and supervisors by the use of in-plant training courses.
- Contain wage levels to the lowest possible increase but in any case no larger than X% in line with expected domestic inflation.
- Continue to develop new methods of manufacture to achieve future cost savings, particularly from the XYZ project which looks most promising.

(c) **Corporate planner**

- Advise management on objectives.
- Maintain intelligence on the business environment.
- Develop planning systems.
- Make recommendations to the Board about the desirability of acquisitions or divestment and handle negotiations if it is decided to proceed.
- Make recommendations about changes in the organisation structure.
- Work with accountant on reviewing the budgetary control system.

(d) **Accountant**

- Maintain the cash flow in the customary efficient manner so that we always have sufficient cash to meet our immediate needs.
- Progress customers' accounts in conjunction with the Sales Department in order to reduce the average balance outstanding from £150,000 to £100,000 without upsetting any significant customers.

- Maintain the existing planning and control committee and through the office of Secretary to the committee to make impartial assessments of the relative merits of some of the problems discussed.

- Maintain a close watch on the external environment both in the press and from contacts for any factors which are going to significantly affect the company, either favourably or otherwise.

- Collect and disseminate information and data concerning actual performance against plans and objectives.

- Review the implications for the company of a statutory requirement for inflation accounting, and in particular to report on the likely extent of changes needed to computer programs and the requirements for extra staff.

2.7 Relating objectives to mission

A problem with the MBO approach is that the focus on individual objectives may blur the importance of overall organisational mission. Campbell, Devine and Young in A Sense of Mission address this problem by showing how goals can be linked to organisational mission.

The authors refer to two different ways of looking at the organisational mission.

- One view is that a mission is 'the cultural glue that enables an organisation to function as a collective unity'. In other words, mission is a set of values rather than a description of ultimate commercial goals.

- The second view is that mission is above all 'a strategic tool, an intellectual discipline which defines the business's commercial rationale and target market'. This view more clearly shows the links between overall mission and individual goals.

3 PLANNING FOR THE ACHIEVEMENT OF OBJECTIVES

3.1 Introduction

Work planning is necessary to ensure that work is carried out in accordance with the organisation's requirements and needs, whether those requirements are clearly defined or are merely implied. It necessitates planning how work should be done and establishing policies and procedures and work methods and practices to ensure that predetermined objectives are efficiently met at all levels. It includes:

(i) the allocation and scheduling of routine tasks for completion at appropriate times;
(ii) the handling of high priority tasks and deadlines;
(iii) adapting to changes and unexpected demands – being prepared for emergencies;
(iv) devising standards for measuring performance;
(v) co-ordinating individual and combined efforts.

3.2 The role of policies and procedures

Planning is an activity which involves decisions about:

- organisational aims and objectives;
- means or policies; and
- results.

Definition A policy is a general plan of action that guides the members of an organisation in the conduct of its operations.

Once an organisation has established its corporate objectives, it can begin to say in what manner it intends these to be achieved. Policies cause managers to take actions in certain ways, but they are not actions in themselves.

Procedures may be defined as:

Definition The formal arrangements by which the principles stated in policies are put into effect.

Procedures provide a sequence of activities that executives are required to follow when implementing policy.

Northcott has compared rules, procedures and policies to ground, middle and top floors, respectively, of a three storeyed building. 'Policies are broad in content and are the concern and responsibility of top management. Procedures are less detailed; to carry them out is the responsibility of middle and lower management. They prescribe action in respect of situations and thereby govern both management and workers. Rules are detailed, regulating the conduct of all employees'.

The role of policies and procedures is to extend management influence to all organisational levels, creating a uniformity of operations. Once established, understood and accepted the policies and procedures provide similarity of action in meeting certain situations.

3.3 Setting priorities

Activities need to be sequenced and scheduled. There may be conflict between the two planning tasks since the best sequence of activities to put the plan into place might mot be consistent with the schedule of when particular activities need to be completed.

The sequence of activities may be determined by the following:

- An activity must precede another when it is a pre-requisite for later activities. Assembly of a car cannot precede the manufacture or purchase of its components.
- The sequence of activities may be dictated by the ease with which they can be done. New products or services are often introduced into the most receptive parts of the market first.
- An activity may be considered more important than others, eg, in the building industry priority will be given to outdoor work when the weather is favourable to minimise the risk of delays later.

The scheduling of when the activities should be completed may be determined by the following:

- The organisation's operations require proper scheduling of resources to run efficiently and avoid periods of over and under utilisation.
- Some activities must occur at precisely the right time, eg specific day and time slot for advertising a new product.
- The scheduling of tasks can affect customer service in terms of delivery.

In determining priorities, the following should be noted.

(a) Wherever it is possible for a priority to be anticipated, such as in the case of the 'natural order of events' described above, then associated difficulties will usually be overcome by sensible, logical planning.

(b) Where 'emergency-type' tasks arise then normal routine work will automatically take second place. It is here that decisions must be taken to decide which routine tasks should be postponed. Also, plans should be formulated and implemented to ensure that the routine work postponed is carried out as soon as possible, resulting in minimum disruption to the normal routine.

(c) Often there may arise situations where one priority comes into conflict with another. Here the task deemed more important by a responsible individual should take preference. It is to be expected that in being responsible the individual endeavours to ascertain the relevance of the conflicting tasks.

(d) It should be remembered that individuals within one department or section often become blind to the needs of other departments or sections. A task that is classed as low priority within one department or section may be of the utmost priority to another. Thus in arriving at any decision the individual making that decision must ensure that the effect on each department is included in the decision-making process.

(e) The determination of priorities should be made by the appropriate individual. Often, especially in the matter of routine cycles, the individual responsible for that work will be qualified to determine any priority. However, the greater the effect and the wider the span of influence of priority determination, the more responsible the individual should be.

There is, perhaps, a tendency sometimes to look for problems where problems do not really exist. This may be applied to the area of priority determination also. Perhaps it is not at all necessary to follow a determination process. This is often true in the case of routine work where any deadlines are often some time apart.

3.4 Formulating and evaluating work plans

The basic steps formulating and evaluating work plans include the following:

(a) the establishment and effective treatment of priorities (considering tasks in order of importance for the objective concerned);

(b) scheduling or timetabling tasks, and allocating them to different individuals within appropriate time scales (eg. continuous routine work and arrangements for priority work with short-term deadlines), to achieve work deadlines and attain goals;

(c) co-ordinating individual tasks within the duties of single employees or within the activities of groups of individuals;

(d) establishing checks and controls to ensure that priority deadlines are being met and work is not 'falling behind', and routine tasks are achieving their objectives;

(e) agreeing the mechanism and means to re-schedule ordinary work to facilitate and accommodate new, additional or emergency work by drawing up 'contingency plans' for unscheduled events. Because nothing goes exactly according to plan, one feature of good planning is to make arrangements for what should be done if there was a major upset, eg. if the company's computer were to break down, or if the major supplier of key raw materials were to go bust. The major problems for which contingency plans might be made are events which, although unlikely, stand a not-impossible chance of actually happening.

The planning of work involves the allocation of time to the requirements of work to be done. This must be applied to the organisation as a whole, to individual departments and sections and to single employees. An important feature of the principles is the role of time. Planning must be geared to terms of time and the degree of flexibility built into planning will vary according to the length of time being planned for. The principles of planning will revolve around:

(a) the determination of the length of time the plans will be concerned with;
(b) planning by departments and groups of individuals;
(c) planning by individuals;

(d) the implementation of planning principles;
(e) the updating of and alterations to plans.

There are three time ranges which are normally involved in planning work and it is the utilisation of long-term, medium-term and short-term ranges on which the principles of planning are based. These three terms are really only expressions of convenience. Different organisations will include different lengths of time under the same heading. For example, a length of five years might be considered long-term within an organisation producing footwear but short-term in, say, the aviation industry. It must be remembered that all time ranges are relative. It may well be that three years is short-term to an organisation but to a department within that organisation it may be medium-term. Indeed, to an individual employee it may be long-term. It is important that whatever the relevant time span may be to a group or individual, work is allocated accordingly.

The allocation of work to time should be undertaken periodically with the ultimate aim of attaining the objectives of the organisation. These objectives will only be attained if the contribution made by individual departments is enhanced by the application of planning principles at departmental level. Again this contribution at departmental level will be valid only if individual employees function effectively – an action which encompasses sensible planning.

Planning in the long term involves forecasting and as such may be somewhat inaccurate and is, therefore, normally expressed only in general terms. Medium-term plans are likely to be less inaccurate and less forecasting is required. It is likely that plans have already been put into practice, and the likelihood of medium-term objectives being attained may be measured against the results of these plans. In the short term forecasting will be fairly accurate and the plans made will probably be adhered to without alteration.

3.5 Methods of planning work

It is important to recognise and understand that different organisations and different individuals have individual characteristics, tastes, styles, preferences and objectives. These particular objectives may well be attained via different methods and systems. It is thus difficult to state categorically that all methods apply to all organisations. All that can be given are guidelines to the methods available.

The following methods and systems are probably the most common:

(a) checklists;
(b) bar charts;
(c) bring-forward, bring-up and follow-up systems;
(d) activity scheduling and time scheduling;
(e) action sheets;
(f) other systems including planning charts and boards, requisition forms and diaries.

Checklists are often used at individual level and is perhaps the simplest system, being essentially a list of items or activities. The preparation of a typical checklist would involve:

(a) the formulation of a list of activities and tasks to be performed within a given period;

(b) the identification of urgent or priority tasks;

(c) the maintenance of a continuous checklist with the addition of extra activities and tasks as and when required.

A **bar chart** has two main purposes:

(a) to show the time necessary for an activity;
(b) to display the time relationship between one activity and another.

Bar charts are particularly useful for checking the time schedules for a number of activities which are interdependent. They show:

(a) overall progress to date, thus assisting in monitoring;
(b) the progress attained at an individual stage of a multi-stage process.

Bring-forward, bring-up and follow-up systems are all somewhat more sophisticated than check-lists and bar charts. They are particularly useful for coping with documentation and are utilised in many offices. The systems involve the filing of details of work to be done and the dates on which it is to be done. A routine is established with a view to allocating necessary tasks to the precise day.

Activity scheduling is concerned with the determination of priority and the establishment of the order in which tasks are to be tackled. Time scheduling is an extension of activity scheduling by indicating the required time for each task.

(a) *Activity scheduling* – The theory of the establishment of an order of priority is not in practice as easy as it may appear in theory. Some tasks must be completed before others may be commenced. Some may need to be carried out at the same time as others. Indeed some tasks may need to be completed at the same time as others but factors such as finance or manpower may prevent this. A typical problem which is particularly suited to activity scheduling is the arrangement of an interview where, say, three panel members are required and six candidates have been short-listed for interview. Obviously mutually convenient dates must be found when all six parties are available and to add to the burden the room which is to be used for the interview must be available on the days when the six parties are available.

Activity scheduling involves the identification of key factors and their assembling on a check-list. In the example given above the two key factors are room availability and people availability. It may be used for any task which involves a number of actions which must necessarily be undertaken in some sequence.

(b) *Time scheduling* – This follows the preparation of an activity schedule and involves the determination of time required for each activity. Given that within an activity schedule some tasks will be performed simultaneously it should be noted that the time period in which the series of activities will be completed may not equate with the total of the individual activity times.

Effectively a time schedule determines the order in which activities are scheduled on a check list, the time required for each activity also being shown alongside each item.

The process of time scheduling commences with the determination of the time required to perform each activity. This is not as simple and straightforward as it might seem at first. This is because of the interdependence of some activities: some may need to be performed in advance of others whilst some may need to be performed simultaneously. The total of the individual activity times, with allowances for simultaneous activities, will produce the time allowed for one complete group of activities.

Time scheduling is thus particularly useful in the process of planning especially as it enables deadlines to be set, at least initially.

Action sheets are a natural progression from activity and time scheduling. Action sheets really represent a summary of the time each stage of a particular task should take and the relationship of that time both to the total time necessary to complete the task and to the time of individual stages.

3.6 Allocating available resources

Because departmental managers and supervisors have overall understanding of the nature and volume of work to be accomplished, and the resources at their command, it will be their job to divide the duties and allocate them to available staff and machinery.

Planning is essential in this division of labour because, although there are some obvious work allocations, those of specialist tasks to specialists (computer programmers, accountants etc.), others may be more complicated. Some areas that need consideration are outlined below.

(a) Peak periods in some tasks may necessitate redistribution of staff to cope with the work load and there should be flexibility in who does, and is able to do, various non-specialist tasks. It is quite usual for staff to be pulled off one job and asked to help out somebody else who has a backlog of work.

(b) Staff attitudes and status must be considered. A hierarchical organisation structure with job grades and different levels of authority and seniority can work towards efficiency, providing close control, motivation etc. but it can also cause planning problems.

Flexibility in reassigning people from one job to another or varying the work they do may be hampered by an employee's perception of his or her own status. 'Helping out' or 'covering' for others may be out of the question. Planning must take into account seniority and experience when allocating tasks, but it must also recognise that junior employees may need and expect challenges and greater responsibility to avoid boredom and frustration.

(c) Individual abilities and character differ, and work should be allocated to the best person for the job. Planning should allow for flexibility in the event of an employee proving unfit or more able for a task.

(d) Efforts will have to be co-ordinated so that all those involved in a process (eg. sales orders) work together as a team. Where the team is large, sub-groups may be formed according to activity or skill for closer supervision and sense of unity. Work-sharing will also be more flexible for a unit with common skills and experience, so similar skills should be grouped together.

(e) The hierarchy must function efficiently. There should be suitable team leaders, supervisors and management staff to ensure control throughout the organisation, without an unmanageable span of control or waste of managerial time.

3.7 The importance of time management

Time management is fundamental to job performance and effective delegation. In the past the relationship between time and job performance came under the heading of scientific management and applied mainly to manual work. More recently the theories of organisation and methods have been applied to clerical workers.

The main influences on a person's use of time are outlined in the diagram below:

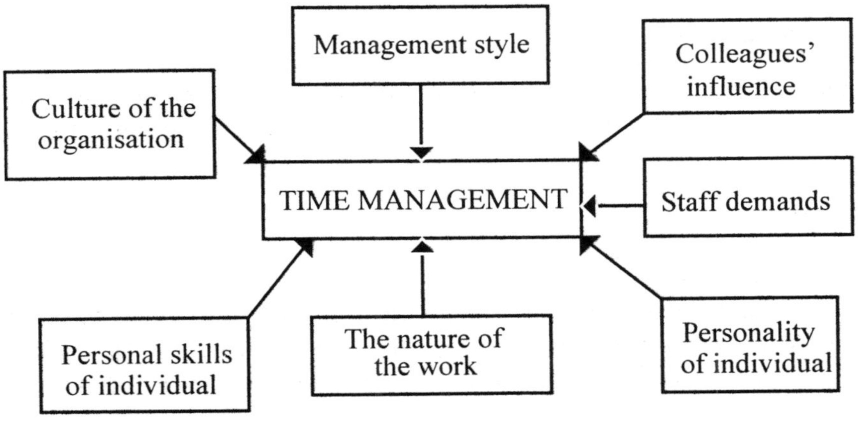

The nature of the work is critical to the amount of control over time management. In established jobs, where the work has become routine and predictable, time management is going to be different from new or developing work. Where a job involves contact with others there is more likelihood of interruptions than a job working with no near contacts. An interfering superior, for example, can be very disrupting whereas a boss who is an effective delegator can be a positive source of help in identifying job priorities.

The physical environment can either help or hinder a person's efforts at time management. Those with offices of their own are able to operate an 'open door' policy for staff communications but a 'closed door' policy when a physical barrier is needed in the interests of personal work efficiency.

Travelling is another major influence on a person's time management. The location of colleagues, customers and suppliers can contribute to time wasted in travelling between appointments.

Culture of the organisation: some organisation's cultures favour strict adherence to protocol and procedures, discouraging informal contacts. Others encourage an open access communications policy which can be stimulating but time wasting.

The organisations which stress accuracy and quality encourage their employees to take time over their work, as opposed to those organisations which work to tight deadlines and have to risk inaccuracy or occasional errors.

An individual's personal work standards are going to be influenced by the type of decision-making in the firm. Decision-making in some organisations is slow and deliberate whilst in others it is much quicker.

Attributes of job holder depends on personality and preferences.

The differences in attributes and style are due to the fact that some people:

- are more assertive and find it easier to deal with colleagues who waste their time;
- have more skills and experience than others;
- work best in the morning, whilst others work best later in the day;
- are untidy and disorganised whilst others are neat and methodical;
- like to concentrate their efforts into short, intensive periods, whilst others pace their work;
- can deal with several tasks simultaneously, whereas others can only cope with one issue at a time;
- are task-oriented as opposed to people-oriented;
- like to delegate as others prefer to keep the work to themselves;

Improving time management

Time management can be improved by personal planning, developing appropriate skills (faster reading, report writing, handling meetings and assertiveness skills), target setting, negotiating and delegating.

4 CHAPTER SUMMARY

In designing an environment for the effective execution of strategy the most essential task is to see that purposes and objectives, and methods of obtaining them are clearly understood. People must know what they are expected to accomplish and how they are going to achieve it. It involves selecting from alternative future courses of action for the company as a whole and every department or work centre within it. MBO and budgets are in the first instance tools for control, but they illustrate the basic actuality that the task of control is to make plans succeed, and therefore control must reflect the plans, and planning must precede control.

By breaking plans into components consistent with the desired organisation structure, budgets and MBO schemes correlate planning and allow authority to be delegated without a loss of control by senior management.

Management by Objectives is best thought of as a system of management or an approach to management. It provides an opportunity for managers to identify the key areas for results and establish performance standards that they can be measured against.

5 SELF TEST QUESTIONS

5.1 Describe the characteristics of objectives (1.1).

5.2 How does Humble define a work objective? (1.2).

5.3 Explain the differences between top-down and bottom-up strategies (1.4).

5.4 List four relationships between company and individual objectives (1.5).

5.5 Define Management by Objectives (2.1).

5.5 List the stages involved in a management-by-objectives scheme (2.2).

5.7 Describe two benefits of MBO to the individual (2.4).

5.8 Outline some typical objectives for a production manager (2.6).

5.9 Define policy (3.2).

5.10 Explain bar charts as a method of planning work (3.5).

5.11 Describe the main influences on a person's use of time (3.7).

6 EXAMINATION TYPE QUESTION

6.1 Management by objectives

You are required

(a) to describe the structure of MBO (Management by Objectives); **(11 marks)**
(b) to assess its advantages over other methods of direction; **(5 marks)**
(c) to suggest reasons for its comparatively rare use. **(4 marks)**

(Total: 20 marks)

7 ANSWER TO EXAMINATION TYPE QUESTION

7.1 Management by objectives

(a) **Management by objectives** has been defined by its initiator, John Humble, as a dynamic system which seeks to integrate the company's need with the manager's personal development needs, in order to define, clarify and achieve specific targets. It contributes both to the organisation and to the self-development of managers.

The key features of MBO are that it

- focuses on results rather than activities or processes,
- develops logically from the corporate planning process by breaking down corporate and departmental objectives into individual management ones,
- seeks to improve management performance and thus organisational performance.

The diagram below is an attempt to represent the main events in the MBO process. ***(Tutorial note:*** *In the examination, it would not be advisable to attempt an elaborate diagram; a narrative account would be less time-consuming.)*

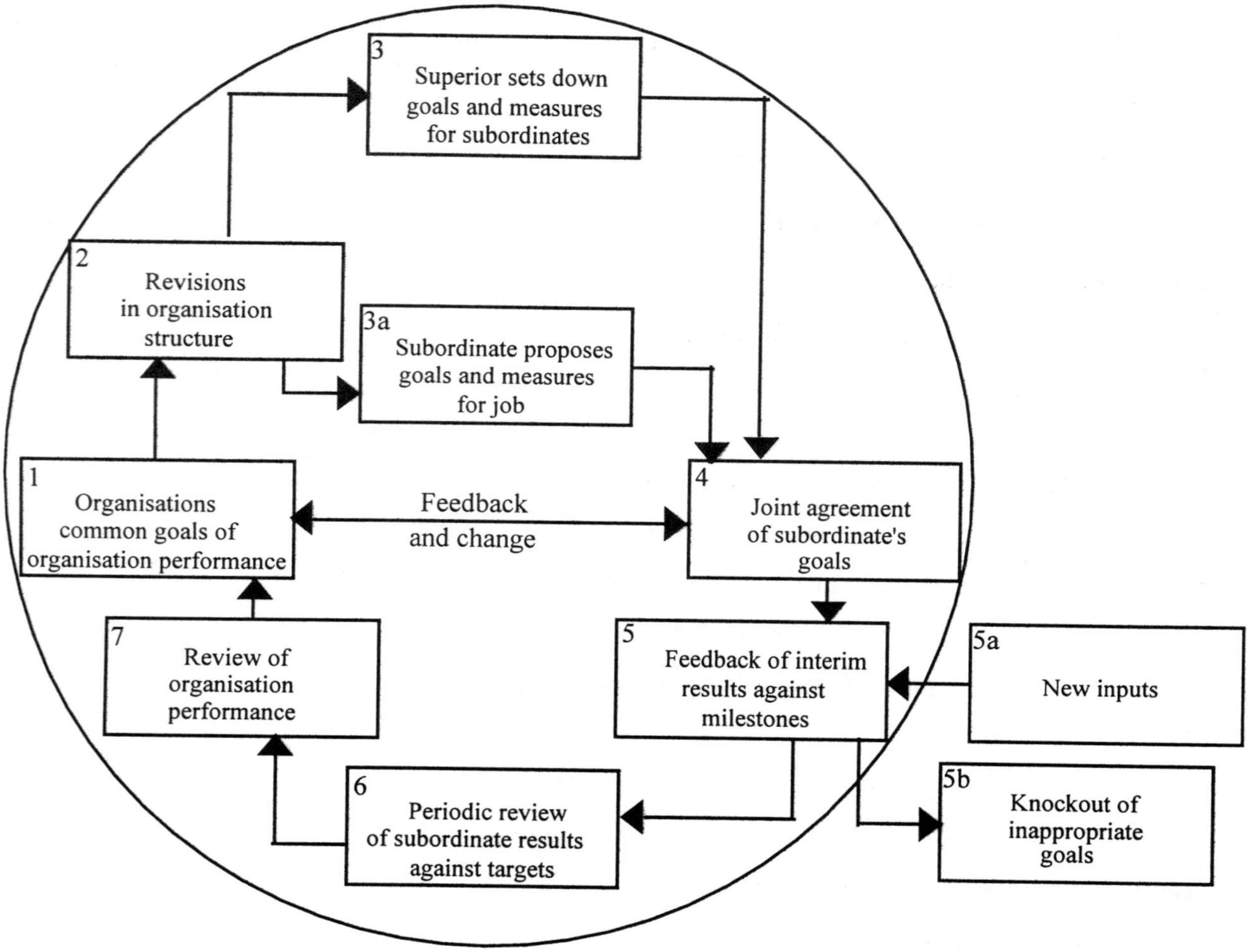

As can be seen from the diagram, the structure of MbO consists of a cycle of events. The start of the cycle is to break down or translate corporate, strategic and unit objectives into individual management objectives. These individual management objectives are then converted or broken down again into key tasks, and a standard is set for the performance of each of these tasks. The next stage is to use the key tasks/performance plan as a basis for job improvement which is an action plan setting out what is required to ensure that the key tasks are fulfilled to an acceptable standard. Periodically the performance of managers is formally appraised. At this appraisal past performance is reviewed, new targets set and training needs and succession/development plans for each individual manager discussed. As can be seen from the diagram, the assessment of performance of each manager is then fed back to those senior managers concerned with meeting the overall objectives of the corporate plan.

(b) **Advantages**

The advantages over other methods of direction claimed for MbO are explained below.

- The individual knows what targets he is expected to achieve and how they will be measured, and where they interact with company goals.

- The targets are clearly expressed in measurable terms and therefore the planning and control functions are made much more effective.

  MbO makes it possible to measure the performance standards of specialist managers as well by the use of quantitative as well as qualitative measures.

- Communications are improved as targets are usually agreed by discussion and this in turn gives better commitment to the success of plans.

- It provides an effective way of monitoring staff's potential and ability and can be linked in with reward systems, thus acting as a motivator.
- Appraisal becomes more meaningful, as it can concentrate on measured performance rather than on matters of opinion.

(c) **The reasons why MBO is not used** by many companies may be due to one or more of the following.

- It can involve time and effort out of all proportion to the perceived benefits.
- If too much stress is placed on individual targets, it can have an adverse effect on co-ordination and teamwork. Targets that are too tight often erase flexibility within the staff.
- It will fail if the commitment from high levels of management is missing.
- Often the culture of a company is not receptive to the changes in attitude required by MbO.
- It requires a high trust relationship between managers and subordinates which is absent in some organisations because of the history of industrial relations in the firm.
- Whenever introducing significant changes to work patterns, the benefits have to be identified, and explained to those concerned. This is especially required in MbO, but many companies just impose them, thus reducing their chances of success.

Conclusion

MbO has many merits, but the above disadvantages are based on experiences of companies who have tried to introduce MbO without success, but the best way to learn is from other people's mistakes.

Success is often achieved when using MbO in a modified version, especially useful when trying to improve a managers performance in any particular management activity.

14 THE WORK TO BE UNDERTAKEN

INTRODUCTION & LEARNING OBJECTIVES

Project management aims first at recognising the stages that all projects go through, and dividing complex stages into sub-tasks, each sufficiently simple for it to be possible to assess the time and resources needed to complete them.

The sub-tasks and the dependencies between them are put into a table or diagram, which is then manipulated to minimise time and cost.

Nearly all projects go through the stages of selection, analysis, feasibility study, specification, design, costing, implementation and testing, installation, evaluation, maintenance and decommissioning.

When you have studied this chapter you should be able to do the following:

- Discuss the project life cycle.
- Explain the objectives of project management.
- Estimate resource requirements.
- Explain what is involved in estimating the time needed for the project.
- Understand a variety of project control tools, such as Gantt charts.
- Explain the use of resource histograms and resource smoothing.

---

1 PROJECT MANAGEMENT

1.1 Introduction

The pressures of accelerating technology and short lead times have made it necessary to establish some formalised managerial arrangement to provide overall integration of many diverse functional activities. Various terms have been used to designate this arrangement, such as systems management, program management, product management and project management.

A project can be defined as:

Definition An activity which has a start, middle and end, and consumes resources.

In this way, project management differs from the normal management functions. The project manager acts as a focal point for the concentration of attention on the major problems of the project.

Projects must be carefully controlled in order for them to be successful. Project Managers are responsible for organising and controlling all activities involved in achieving the ultimate objective eg, the timetabling, budgeting and quality of the project.

Not all projects are internal and before some external projects can be undertaken it is necessary to draw up a project contract. This sets out the requirements and specifications for the project, both from the viewpoint of the purchaser and the vendor.

The project contract will include such things as

- Description of service bought/supplied
- Timescale for project
- Budget for project
- Acceptance criteria of system

- List of deliverables
- Constraints or penalties imposed on either party
- Change control and the responsibility for it
- Payment terms.

It is likely, however, that a 'Risks Limited/Commitment Limited' contract will be signed. This means that the project will be managed in stages and either party can withdraw at the end of each stage and that payments will be in instalments.

Once the project has been agreed and the contract signed, a project plan will be drawn up, probably using a structured diagram to identify the main areas. The function of the project plan is to allow the overall project structure to be clearly defined.

1.2 Project life cycle

Depending on the size of the project, there are many stages in the project's life cycle that are possible. The following diagram could be the stages in a nuclear power station project:

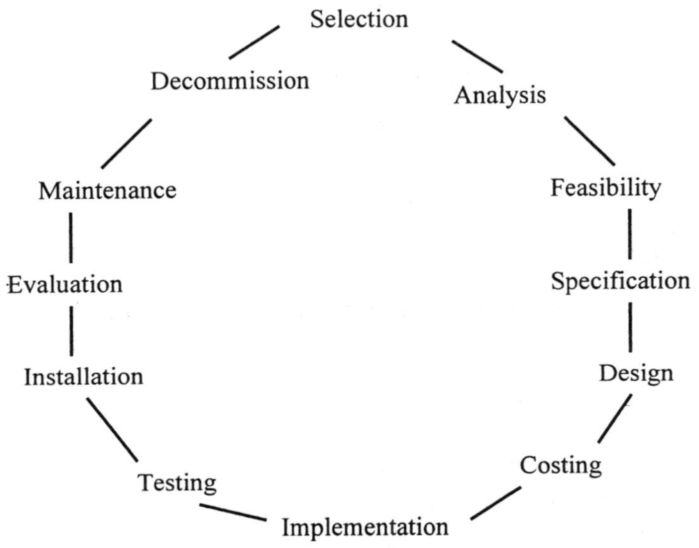

The **selection** of the project must be part of the organisation's overall strategy and the objectives must be clear.

The **analysis** stage of the current situation should identify the possible methods of implementing the project.

The **feasibility study** aims to assess the probability of success and the risk of failure. High risk projects should still be pursued if the expected gain is high enough.

The **specification** of the system is the key to the project. The document produced should be detailed and agreed before the next stage starts, adhered to unless there is a compelling reason to change, and kept up to date when there are changes.

The **design** stage sets out how the project is to be implemented, tested and evaluated. Other decisions to be taken are: who is going to do it; where is it to be done; documentation standards; and training required.

The **costing** stage is where resources are allocated to the tasks in the project, and a budgeted cost determined.

At the **implementation and testing** stages there will be vetting on progress, discussion on milestones achieved or missed, and costs of equipment and manpower will be compared to the budget.

The **installation** phase will include operator training.

Evaluation and **maintenance** produces adequate documentation to find and fix problems or make changes.

Where there is a **decommissioning** stage in the life cycle it may include retraining and relocating staff. Occasionally disposal of equipment and structures is a major problem (eg, nuclear power stations) and necessitates another project initiation.

It must be remembered that no two projects will be the same. However, project managers must work within some type of framework in order to maintain control and achieve standards. They will ultimately be responsible to the organisation and must seek to gain the full support of management throughout each phase of development.

Ideally there should a project co-ordinator. The project co-ordinator will be an employee of the organisation, will be the project manager's contact within the organisation and will have the main dealings with the Steering Committee.

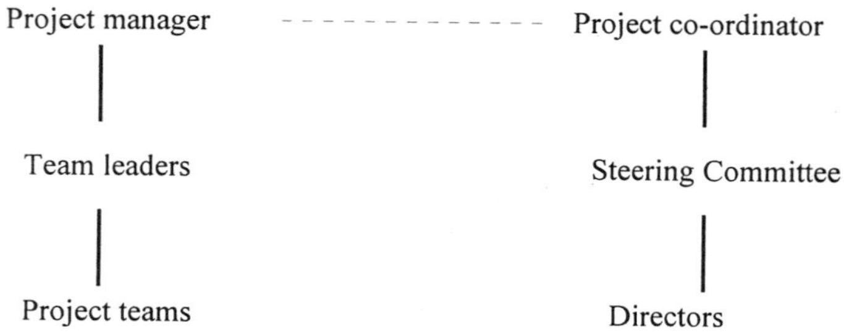

1.3 The objectives of project management

To achieve the project's purpose it is necessary to manage five project objectives, shown in the diagram below:

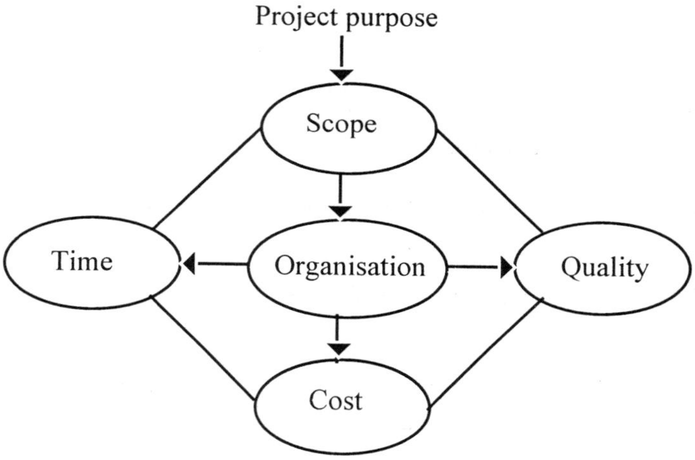

Three of the objectives outlined above, cost, time and quality, are traditional performance measures which are traded against each other to obtain the best, or optimum, result.

The **organisation** objective is at the centre of the diamond because, without the organisation, the project cannot be delivered. The aim of the project organisation must be to assemble the appropriate resources (human, material, technical and financial) to undertake and complete the project successfully.

The aim of the **scope** objective is to:

- ensure that the project's purpose is achieved;
- specify the work that must be done;
- specifically exclude work that is superfluous or otherwise unnecessary.

Developing the scope of the project means planning for **quality**. In project terms this means delivering a project which satisfies the customer and is 'fit for the purpose'.

The **time** objective helps to:

- plan for a firm delivery date which will make the project viable;
- minimise disruption time;
- co-ordinate the availability of resources;
- optimise cash flow.

1.4 Breaking projects down into manageable units

Technical plans will need to be produced to identify the major areas. Each area will be sub-divided into specific activities.

Once the technical plans have been produced then resource planning can take place. This will identify the resources required for each activity – resources include equipment and human skill requirements. The project board, or steering committee, will approve the plans at each stage. From the technical and resource plans, estimates can be ascertained as to timescale and costings.

Every activity will produce an end-product and this must be passed for quality assurance. At the end of each stage or activity the project board will verify the project manager's report on achievements to date. This will be compared against projected achievements. Throughout the project stage there will be weekly reports concerning progress.

Standards should be in place for assessing the managerial and technical activities and also the skills required to perform them.

At each stage throughout the project, all activities would be assessed, evaluated, measured for performance, compared to standards, monitored and reviewed.

2 ESTIMATING RESOURCE REQUIREMENT

2.1 The importance of accurate estimates

There are different classifications to denote the accuracy of project cost estimates:

(i) **Definitive estimates** aim to be accurate to within 5% and are produced after the design stage of the project life cycle.

(ii) **Feasibility estimates** are accurate to within 10%. These are made in the early design stage.

(iii) **Comparative estimates** are made when the project under review is similar to a previous one. The accuracy of this estimate depends on the similarity and the prevailing economic conditions.

(iv) **Ball-park estimates** are a rough guide to the project costs and are often made before a project starts. They may only be accurate to within 25%.

Cost estimation invariably involves some guesswork where the project manager is beginning a new, uncertain project. For projects where there is no margin of safety, then it is crucial that the estimates are definitive. The project manager can improve the accuracy by:

- learning from previous mistakes;
- having sufficient design information;
- obtaining a detailed specification; and
- breaking the project down into smaller jobs and detailing each constituent part.

2.2 Work breakdown structure to identify resource needs

Work breakdown structure (or WBS) is a hierarchical view of the way a project is structured; in other words, a formal version of a project outline.

Identifying the minute stages of a project begins with the whole project, followed by breaking up into smaller parts and then continually breaking down the work until the smallest unit can be identified. This exercise is the best way of discovering the work that must be done, as well determining the resources required. The sequencing of tasks and the priorities and pitfalls also become more apparent as the project is broken down.

The set of plans or forms produced from the work breakdown structure can then be used for estimating. A list of all the tasks, broken down into their constituent parts can be completed and analysed into direct and indirect costs, with columns for all the identifiable expenditure, including labour, materials and the project overhead costs.

WBS codes are a coding system based on the work breakdown structure. A unique code is assigned to each task in a project, based on an outline-style hierarchy. For example:

1. Make tea
1.1 Boil water
1.1.1 Fill kettle.

Where projects require sub-contractors there may be a problem in estimating correctly, especially for the type of contract where fixed penalties are difficult to enforce if the estimates are wrong eg, bricklayers on a building project.

Collecting estimates from the members of the project team can also be fraught with difficulties. If labour time is requested there is the possibility that the person asked wants to please the project manager and therefore estimates optimistically, understating the amount of time needed to complete the task.

There is the opposite problem where the person asked is over-cautious and estimates too high by building in a cushion in case of problems.

Unless extra costs are built into the estimate, problems can arise from:

- design faults;
- an increase in prices over the project's life;
- material or component failure;
- production errors;
- resource delivery delays.

When all the estimated costs have been collected, projections made on future inflation built in and allowances are made for errors in the project team's estimation of time, the estimated total project cost can be calculated.

2.3 Estimating direct and indirect costs

The normal approach to project costing is to use the work breakdown structure in order to produce the cost breakdown structure (CBS) at an increasing level of detail. This CBS will be a complete list of every item that can be classed as expenditure.

Project costs can be analysed into:

- direct costs, including labour and materials; and
- indirect costs, including rent, light, heating and other overheads.

The various costs identified with each part of the work breakdown structure will be collected to provide a useful cost analysis for the various business functions and also to be a mechanism for controlling costs.

A useful means of estimating costs is to design estimation forms, based on the work breakdown structure so that by each work unit number there is a separate column for each of the costs eg, labour and materials.

Another methodology for cost planning, called the C/SPEC, combines the work breakdown structure, the organisation breakdown structure (labour, sub-contractors, materials, overheads, etc) and the cost breakdown structure. This would have to be done using a computer, because of the three dimensions.

2.4 Why estimates may be inaccurate

Collecting estimates may be difficult, especially if many people are involved. Apart from the inconsistency of personal estimates, there are other problems that cause estimates to be inaccurate.

Projects can be delayed due to design errors, mistakes in production, material and component failures. A contingency allowance is sometimes built in by reviewing problems in previous projects.

Material costs can be estimated by the purchasing department but failure to receive materials on time can result in unexpected delays.

Increases in prices will increase costs over the contract's life.

3 PLANNING THE TIMESCALE

3.1 Estimating the time needed

To estimate the time schedule, the project manager will list the work elements, together with estimates for their key time dimensions. These dimensions are:

- The duration; the time taken to complete the task.
- The early start date; the first date at which the task could commence.
- The late finish date; the last date at which the task could be completed.
- The late start date; the last date at which the task could be commenced and still meet the late finish date.
- The float; the buffer time between the early and the late starts.

Mathematical models can be used, although they are not always appropriate. We could use a normal distribution with the formula:

Estimated time =
(most optimistic duration + 4 x most likely duration + most pessimistic duration) / 6

3.2 Network analysis

Network analysis is a general term, referring to various techniques adopted to plan and control projects which are complex and consist of activities that are interrelated. The emphasis of the analysis is upon the sequence of events and activities to co-ordinate them.

There are two major groups of techniques in network analysis

(a) critical path analysis (CPA), and
(b) programme evaluation and review techniques (PERT).

The planning of any big project involves, to a greater or lesser extent, the taking into account of four aspects

(a) logic;
(b) timing;
(c) resources; and
(d) cost.

The network presents graphically, the logic of the project (ie, the sequence of the project activities), and allows the timing of the various parts of the project.

The analysis of the network itself permits information to be obtained by management for *resource scheduling* and making the decisions relating to methods to be used. Stricter control of costs may also be undertaken.

3.3 Network analysis – critical path analysis

This method is applied in a large number of work areas, and it is especially useful where tasks have to be carried out by a number of different individuals. In the simplest version of CPA, the aim is to determine which segments of the project are 'critical' to the completion of activities by the target date, and so which may be delayed or advanced without having any effect upon that date.

First the tasks to be carried out should be listed, and each contribution which needs time is an activity. The point at which an activity begins or ends is an event.

The network reveals all the relationships between the operations. *Activities are represented by continuous lines. Events are represented by circles.* The direction or progress is shown by arrows (conventionally, these will point to the right). All operations which result in an event have to be finished prior to any activity's commencement from that event.

If there is an operation which cannot start until another operation somewhere else is finished, then the link is shown by a dotted line (a 'dummy').

After the logic of the sequence has been established, times are inserted for each operation. 'Critical tasks' contribute directly to the complete duration of the whole project, and the *critical path* is the route they adopt through the whole network. The total times of each operation constituting that path is the length of time the project takes.

Network analysis is an important tool in project control, particularly where the timing of work is critical.

3.4 Network analysis – PERT

Program evaluation and review technique is very similar to CPA. The difference lies in timings. In the PERT network, there are three times allowed for each activity

(a) an optimistic time (assuming all goes well);
(b) a realistic estimate (updating occurring as progress is made); and
(c) a pessimistic time (assuming all possible problems arise).

PERT is generally used for R & D planning, major construction work etc. For small projects PERT is rarely used.

All network planning, irrespective of the technique used, requires a review of the critical path, including comparison with the progress made in fact. This is so that any necessary action can be taken to correct a deviation. Where there is a critical path delay, then the float on the other activities is increased. If the critical path is improved upon, another line could be critical as the float reduces. The review must be undertaken or network analysis cannot be regarded as a successful management technique.

Properly used network analysis provides these advantages to management.

(a) identification of both the duration and critical path;

(b) provision of an analytical device for any project which has an introduction (start) time and a finishing point;

(c) progress control is emphasised;

(d) an early indication is given of crises in the project; and

(e) the technique stresses and encourages careful appraisal of activities and stages of projects on the part of managers.

4 CHAPTER SUMMARY

Projects are directed towards a specified goal, but while the goal may be specific the means of achieving it may involve dealing with the unexpected. The main objectives of project management are to ensure that the end product or service conforms with its specification and is produced on time and within budget.

In this chapter we looked at the steps in the project life cycle. Part of project management is the estimating of resources and the time needed to complete parts of the project. We outlined some of the techniques used for estimating, eg. Gantt charts, network analysis and critical path analysis.

It must be possible to measure progress made in acceptable terms, determine and report any deviations, undertake corrective action as necessary and issue specific reports.

The evaluation of a project takes into account the total costs and total resource usage and assesses problems encountered. Eventually there will be a general appraisal of the whole project results undertaken formally, followed by regular project reviews.

5 SELF TEST QUESTIONS

5.1 What is a project? (1.1).

5.2 List five steps in the life cycle of a large project (1.2).

5.3 Draw a diagram showing the five objectives of a project (1.3).

5.4 Briefly describe the different classifications which denote the accuracy of project cost estimates (2.1).

5.5 Why might project cost estimates be inaccurate? (2.4).

5.6 List the three elements in a network CPA (3.3).

6 EXAMINATION TYPE QUESTION

6.1 Project management

Developing and implementing large-scale administrative computer systems requires a formalised and disciplined approach to project management and control.

(a) Outline an approach to project management suitable for controlling the development of such a system. **(10 marks)**

(b) How can computers be used to help in the administrative support and technical development of a project? **(10 marks)**

(Total 20 marks)

7 ANSWER TO EXAMINATION TYPE QUESTION

7.1 Project management

(a) Project management differs from functional management in that it is the management of resources which are attempting to achieve specific objectives within set timescales and budgets. Functional management, on the other hand, is concerned with providing an on-going service.

A project has boundaries and it is one of the activities of the project management team to set and keep the project within those boundaries.

A project will be initiated to develop or try something new and accurate costs are therefore difficult to estimate. It is also difficult to estimate benefits or eventual outcome and projects must therefore be carefully controlled and monitored.

The project management team would need, first of all, to identify the standards for:

(i) the organisation of the project, including any user involvement;
(ii) estimating, resourcing and scheduling the project including drawing up a project plan;
(iii) quality control;
(iv) the activities performed and their assessments;
(v) the end product produced or developed.

Each project will be different, but it is still necessary to identify suitable technical standards relating to what is being developed.

The development of a computerised administrative system is used to illustrate an approach to project management. The stages are as detailed below.

Organisation

Creating a project board who will be responsible for the project and who will have authority over it. The board will be responsible for:

(i) approving plans;
(ii) monitoring progress;
(iii) allocating resources;
(iv) assessing results; and
(v) recommending continuance or termination.

A project manager will be in charge of the project itself and he will report back to the project board.

The project manager is responsible for:

(i) defining individual responsibilities;
(ii) preparing state or phase plans;
(iii) setting objectives;
(iv) collating information from project teams;
(v) controlling team activities; and
(vi) reporting to the project board.

The project manager would have a number of project teams with team leaders reporting back to him.

Planning

At the beginning of a project outline technical plans will be needed to identify the major technical activities.

When the technical plans have been produced, identification of required resources can then take place. These resources include 'expert' staff who may be required at particular times or for particular activities.

The project itself will be broken down into a number of stages, with each stage being monitored and then assessed at its completion. In this way identification of deviances from the expected plan can be fully analysed.

Controls

At the end of each stage the project manager will report to the project board, who will compare the actual achievements against the expected achievements.

These comparisons will allow the project board to estimate the likelihood of the project being successful, completed within the specified timescale, and completed within the specified budget.

Activities/end products

The activities of the project should result in the end project being quality assured, as each activity is fully monitored throughout.

A quality assurance test would be performed before each stage or before the final project was deemed to be completed.

Review

At the completion of the project the management of that project would be reviewed. Although no two projects are the same, experience gained throughout the course of the project should be fully assessed and documented in order that similar types of projects may benefit in future.

(b) The management of a project is very complex. Activities need to be scheduled and planned in order to make the most effective use of the resources available.

Some activities are reliant upon other activities having been completed before they themselves can be started. All activities therefore need to be properly planned to assess the order in which they need to be undertaken. A critical path will exist throughout the project. Network analysis identifies the dependence of one activity on another.

Computer-based packages now exist which aid the project manager to identify the critical path. If activities differ in their actual time from their estimated time, these differences can be entered into the computer and a recalculation of the critical path takes place.

Project evaluation and review techniques (PERT) allow for probability and risk assessment to be input and resource requirements to be more accurately estimated.

PERT packages aid project management because they allow for fast recalculation of the critical path. Project managers may also perform 'what if' calculations in order to assess possible outcomes for alternative assumptions.

Computer aided software engineering (CASE) is another tool of the project manager. CASE tools incorporate the use of products such as 4GLs which automate part of the programming function. 'Case tools' is the generic term for this support.

Project management is also aided by the use of standard packages such as word-processing, desktop publishing, etc. These packages prove most useful in the rapid preparation of clearly laid out reports and manuals.

15 THE ROLE AND PURPOSE OF MARKETING

INTRODUCTION & LEARNING OBJECTIVES

A corporate strategy is formulated to achieve defined corporate objectives, and to provide guidelines for lower level strategies. Marketing strategy, which is of a lower level, cannot have a decision framework independent of the corporate strategy, although it ought to be flexible enough to combat sudden dangers or to take advantage of opportunities in the organisation's operational environment. Marketing executives need the authority to vary the components in the marketing strategy when they consider it necessary, even if their decisions are temporarily incompatible with the corporate strategy. Marketing is, therefore, a dynamic concept which involves decisions shaped by changes in the organisation's operational market environment.

The marketing concept has advanced over the years from a narrow customer focus resting on a set of generalised principles to an integral component of marketing strategy. The theme is 'customer satisfaction'. Its social justification is the identification and satisfaction of human needs and wants, while its economic justification is that it offers the company the best chance of profitable operations by supplying the defined needs of a target group, provided it possesses the necessary resources.

When you have studied this chapter you should be able to do the following:

- Explain the marketing concept.
- Describe the characteristics of a market-oriented organisation.
- Discuss marketing in non-profit organisations.
- Outline the main activities of the marketing function.
- Describe the main elements in the promotion mix.

1 MARKETING

1.1 Role and purpose of marketing

Marketing is concerned with ensuring that business transactions happen, and that they benefit both the supplier and the user. It is a vital link between the two. The marketing department investigates and interprets the needs of potential customers so that they can be satisfied. At the same time, the effectiveness of a company's marketing determines its sales income and, ultimately, its success as a business enterprise.

1.2 Some definitions of marketing

The American Marketing Association gives a widely-used definition of marketing:

Definition The performance of business activities that direct the flow of goods and services from producer to consumer or user.

Philip Kotler, in Marketing Management, Analysis Planning & Control (Prentice-Hall), one of the most influential marketing authors, says:

Definition Marketing is the set of human activities directed at facilitating and consummating exchanges.

Both these definitions take marketing beyond the point of sale. It should be noted that, although selling is one of the most important aspects of marketing, it is not the only one.

1.3 What is a market?

The word market can be misleading to a student learning marketing for the first time. We are not talking about a market-stall or a shop. One of a number of definitions of a market is:

A number of potential customers

This group may be defined in several ways for example:

(a) Geographically eg, the Middle East market.
(b) By industry type eg, the electronic engineering market.
(c) Demographically eg, the teenage market.

Often, however, markets may be defined in terms of the products or services for sale.

(a) The used-car market.
(b) The property market.
(c) The machine tool market.

2 THE MARKETING CONCEPT

2.1 Concept defined

An organisation which adopts the marketing concept accepts the needs of potential customers as the basis for its operations. Its financial success is seen as dependent upon the satisfaction of those needs.

Such an organisation will evolve a structure which is designed to interpret customer needs, to create goods and services appropriate to those needs, and to persuade potential customers to purchase those goods and services.

This involves integrated marketing that is, the use of all marketing variables in a balanced and co-ordinated manner, and an appreciation that all departments of a firm have an impact on the customer, and are therefore part of a marketing system.

2.2 Marketing orientation and its alternatives

Marketing orientation means exactly the same as the marketing concept; a marketing oriented business is one which has adopted the marketing concept.

The implications of marketing orientation become much clearer when it is compared with alternatives:

(a) **Sales orientation**

Some companies see their main problem as selling more of the products or services which they already have available. They may therefore be expected to make full use of selling, pricing, promotion and distribution skills, but the weakness of such a policy is the absence of a systematic attempt to identify customer needs, or to create products or services which will satisfy them.

(b) **Production orientation**

When a business is mainly preoccupied with making as many units as possible, it is said to be production oriented. The way to profitability lies through economies of scale and production rationalisation. A classic instance is Henry Ford's statement: 'you can have any colour you like, so long as it's black'. Customer needs are subordinated to the desire to increase output. This approach works when a market is growing more rapidly than output, but it offers no security against a reduction in growth rate and changes in customer preference.

(c) Product orientation

It is easy for company employees to fall in love with their product. Many of the businesses that suffer from this tendency are in a high technology sector of industry. Their products may be expected to be fully up-to-date and technically attractive, but they may fall foul of development costs (as did Rolls Royce's Aero Engine division) and miss marketing opportunities which do not call for extreme sophistication.

2.3 Marketing environment

All products for sale in a country such as the UK's share common environmental features. They are sold through established channels of distribution to a population (or companies) influenced by the cultural values which are prevalent in that society. They have a shared scientific and technological basis, even though any manufacturer draws on only a small portion of the techniques or scientific knowledge which is available to it. All British companies have to comply with legislation from the same source, and they co-exist in the same broad economic environment.

The analysis of the environment already covered is as relevant to the marketing concept as it is to the overall strategic plan.

Environmental factors heavily influence the nature of goods and services, and the way in which they are marketed. Changes in the factors create marketing opportunities for new and changed products at the same time as they form a threat to established ones. Factors relating to a company's customers are termed the market environment.

2.4 Marketing in not-for-profit organisations

Non-profit does not necessarily imply non-financial. Many non-profit applications of marketing involve money transactions, eg, charities such as Oxfam have complete marketing operations and organise the manufacture and distribution of products.

In other cases, whilst there is no profit, revenue is sought to enable the organisation to continue to exist. For example, marketing is used by museums and galleries to increase the number of visitors by presenting and promoting attractive exhibitions. Similarly, opera and theatre companies use marketing in the selection and promotion of their productions. Many cultural organisations have used the marketing technique of sponsorship to obtain funds.

At a more localised level, organisations such as tennis clubs and social clubs use advertising to enrol new members.

Where the objective of profit-marketing is, in essence, to make consumers part with money, the objective of social marketing is to increase the acceptability of a social idea, cause or practice. A controversial example is that of political candidates and parties seeking election and support.

However, the most widespread application of social marketing is by governments who use marketing skills in areas such as:

- public health campaigns to promote the use of condoms in the battle against AIDS and campaigns to reduce smoking and obesity;
- environmental campaigns to conserve resources and reduce litter;
- road safety campaigns to reduce drink-driving related accidents, to increase considerate and careful driving in relation to child safety and cyclists; and
- campaigns by the post office to encourage the use of post codes in return for improved service and lower postal rate increases.

Such campaigns have used marketing research skills both to identify the segment indulging most in the behaviour that is sought to alter and to indicate the types of appeal most likely to be effective. These campaigns have used much the same techniques and referred to the same values as campaigns for products.

Anti-smoking advertisements have been targeted at young people of both sexes and attempted to associate smoking with social ostracism. Advertisements to discourage drinking and driving, targeted at young males in particular, have linked drunken driving not simply with financial penalties and imprisonment, but also with the foolishness and inconvenience of losing their driving licence and guilt about killing or injuring their friends.

Anti litter campaigns have been targeted at children and used authority figures relevant to this segment, such as footballers and pop stars.

The extent to which non-profit marketing is the same as profit marketing depends on whether it uses the marketing concept or merely uses the marketing techniques. The techniques and skills used by the marketeers are the same regardless of profit.

Simply using market research to define the target market and then spending large sums on promotion may be no more than a sales-oriented attempt to sell a product or an idea regardless of whether it is wanted by consumers. The techniques of personal selling can be unwelcome whether it is for encyclopaedias or religion.

By following the marketing concept, an organisation would need to replace a product for which there is no demand. With social marketing, however, this may not be possible as the idea or cause is often pre-determined and not susceptible to adaptation. For example, market research might show that a museum is in the wrong business and that it should transfer its resources and activities to more fashionable markets such as discos or fast foods. Whilst the museum management are unlikely to welcome such market-oriented solutions, they may consider the re-design and popularising of exhibits, the introduction of audio-visual guides and extension of opening times.

Similarly, a political party might make electorate-oriented alterations to its policies in order to maintain or increase support. In the USA, soccer has been marketed by modifications to the game rules and by consumer-oriented presentation and ground facilities. In the UK, however, the marketing of soccer has been restricted to product-oriented advertising with no alteration to the fundamental causes of consumer dissatisfaction.

Social marketing such as anti-smoking also appears to be product-oriented. In these cases marketing is used to identify and meet consumer preferences. Only the positive, health, financial and social advantages of not smoking are emphasised, rather than the negative aspects.

Some non-profit organisations regard marketing as a promotion function - a means of increasing and maintaining their activities. Marketing can assist by promoting these activities or by developing a previously under-utilised aspect of the organisation's resources. Since appointing marketing personnel in colleges the finances have been improved by renting the teaching and living accommodation for conferences and summer schools when not in use by the college. City centre colleges have allowed their car parks to be used by the public at weekends to supplement their income.

3 THE MARKETING FUNCTION

3.1 Main activities

The basic functions performed by marketing include the following:

(a) **Consumer analysis**; examining and evaluating consumer characteristics and needs.

(b) **Purchasing**; covering the procurement, the analysis and selection of vendor, the terms of purchase and the buying procedure.

(c) **Selling**; incorporating advertising, sales promotion, sales force management, publicity, warranties, public relations, displays and communication with the consumers.

(d) **Product or service planning**; including the areas of new product development, product management, product mix, branding, packaging and deletion of old products are all included.

(e) **Price planning;** covering the level and range of prices, credit availability and terms, cash flows, budgeting and profits

(f) **Distribution**; including warehousing, physical distribution, stock management, service levels, retail site location, allocation of goods or services, vendor control, transportation, wholesaling and retailing.

(g) **Marketing research** providing the basis for future decisions and planning. It also includes the collection of data and analysis of information in all areas of marketing.

(h) **Opportunity analysis** ie, the appraisal of the benefits and risks inherent in decision-making.

3.2 Marketing plan

Definition The marketing mix is all the marketing elements concerned with a product. **Professor Neil H. Borden**

The marketing plan, or mix, describes the specific combination of marketing elements used to achieve the objectives and satisfy the target market. The plan consists of four major factors:

(i) product or service;
(ii) distribution;
(iii) promotion; and
(iv) price.

One of the most common ways of presenting the marketing mix is by McCarthy's Four P's: **P**roduct; **P**romotion; **P**rice; and **P**lace

(a) Product: Quality of the product as perceived by the potential customer. This involves an assessment of the product's suitability for its stated purpose, its aesthetic factors, its durability, brand factors, packaging, associated services, etc.

(b) Promotion: Advertisement of a product, its sales promotions, the company's public relations effort, salesmanship.

(c) Price: Prices to the ultimate customer, discount structures for the trade, promotion pricing, methods of purchase, alternatives to outright purchase.

(d) Place: Distribution channel decisions, location of outlets, position of warehouses, stock levels, delivery frequency, geographic market definition, sales territory organisation.

Whilst the Four P's are easy to remember, it can confuse some students because of the inclusion of some sales factors in promotion and some in place.

The following 5-part alternative is sometimes preferred:

Product, Price, Promotion, Sales, Distribution.

The 'product' and 'price' variables are the same as before. 'Promotion' is similar, but excludes sales factors. 'Distribution' is the Four P's 'place' without sales factors.

The new 'sales' category includes the size and organisation of the sales force, its management, training, job definitions and objectives, and methods of payment.

Market research is not mentioned in the above market mixes. This does not imply that market research is unnecessary. On the contrary, market research can be regarded as the source of information which is used in setting all the variables in the marketing mix.

3.3 Push and pull

(a) **Pull**

The consumer and the industrial buyer only experience part of the marketing picture. They are aware of advertisements in the press, on the billboards or on television. They may listen to the salespeople as they try to persuade them to purchase, or they might select from supermarket shelves. They are aware of price levels, and of the attractions of the product or services.

All these are pull factors. That is, they consist of marketing variables set to persuade ultimate customers to purchase.

Where a company sells direct (ie, without using a middleman), the ultimate customer is indeed the object of all marketing effort.

Where the distribution system is more complex, and middlemen are used (for example, wholesalers, retailers, dealers, factors) the company must push as well as pull.

(b) **Push**

To push in marketing means to ensure that products or services are available for purchase where and when the ultimate customer requires them.

The middleman may be favourably influenced by pull in other words, he or she will tend to stock a product if it can be seen that their customers will be enthusiastic about the product, and buy large numbers.

The manufacturers cannot rely on this effect, however. Their marketing must take specific account of the needs of the middleman.

As well as an acceptable ultimate price, there must be a pricing discount structure which encourages the middlemen to purchase. The manufacturer can use appropriate media usually the trade press to advertise to the trade, and may use trade-oriented sales promotions. The company's salespeople are therefore part of an integrated marketing package designed to push company products into the distribution system.

Neither push nor pull can be ignored for long. A failure of the former will reduce sales by cutting the number of distributive outlets and causing stockouts. If the latter is inadequate, middlemen will eventually cease to re-order because of declining customer demand.

3.4 Buyer, customer and user

For many products on many occasions, the buyer, customer and user are the same person. Where this is the case, marketing effectiveness depends upon the accurate determination and satisfaction of that person's needs.

In most industrial marketing, and in a significant part of consumer marketing, the buyer is not the user.

For salespeople of grinding wheels, their customer is a company. The buyer is a member of the purchasing department, and the user is a grinding machine operator.

The marketing of the product is affected by all three; by the company, its overall purchasing policy and the latitude it allows its buyers; by the purchaser himself or herself, his or her level of skill in negotiation, his or her attitude towards the supplying company and its salesperson; and by the user, who will soon have clear ideas about the product in use. The manufacturer's product and marketing have to satisfy the company, the buyer and the user.

Similarly, consider a male perfume perhaps an after-shave lotion. The manufacturers would probably describe their customer as male, but the retailer might find that the majority of its customers are female. In the former case, the term customer refers to the user, in the latter to the buyer. The after-shave must be marketed in such in a way as to satisfy both the user who must associate the product with positive attributes such as enhanced sexual attractiveness and freshness and the buyer, who must be persuaded that the product is desirable to the user and who must be encouraged to make a purchase at the point of sale.

Whenever the buyer, customer and user are not the same, the process of need satisfaction is made more complex by the existence of several sets of needs.

3.5 Variations in marketing mix settings

Marketing mix settings vary enormously from product to product, and company to company.

Consider the examples below.

Company products / Marketing mix variance	Mail-order clothes company	Major national soft drinks manufacturer	Computer manufacturer
Product	Similar to those of several other manufacturers.	Similar to those of several other manufacturers.	Very advanced, subject to continual amendment, with a distinct place in the market.
Price	A vital factor, probably rather higher that similar retailed goods.	Similar level and structure to that of several other manufacturers.	Different to that of its broad competitors. Customer looks for 'value for money' rather than cost.
Promotion	Direct mail and newspaper small ads the source of orders and the major marketing expense.	A high percentage of product cost. Use of TV and various press media. Promotions important.	A low percentage of product cost. Use of trade press and up-market magazines and newspapers.
Sales	No salespeople as such.	A large team of selling-oriented well-trained salespeople.	A large team of salespeople trained to combine selling skills with good knowledge of the product and its use.
Distribution	No middlemen. Distribution determined by carrier and postal system.	Extensive use of wholesalers, retailers and licences of premises. Frequent deliveries, regional warehouses, owns its own transport fleet.	No middlemen. Small company owned vehicle fleet. Relatively infrequent deliveries. Little storage of finished items.

It can be seen from this table and from the many other examples with which you may be familiar that different sorts of businesses use the same basic marketing tools in very different ways. Conversely, there is a tendency for companies operating in the same markets and with the same products as their competitors to use the marketing mix in the same way.

3.6 Promoting the corporate image

The selection of corporate symbols, such as the firm's name (brand), logo and trade characters is a significant element in the establishment of an overall company image.

Some large companies use institutional advertising to reassure the public about the company's intentions, and to create an image of progressiveness, reliability, or good service. Whilst not directly aimed at selling a product, this type of advertising could have a pronounced long-term effect on sales.

In the creation of a brand strategy, an organisation needs to be aware of the effect the brand name can have on the product or service. Some fortunate companies have had their name adopted for the product, regardless of the manufacturer eg, Hoover instead of vacuum cleaner, Sellotape instead of sticky tape. Market research in the UK has shown that most people believe that an organisation which has a good reputation would not sell poor quality products. This is a competitive advantage for those companies when it comes to promoting new products.

Many retailers sell grocery and hardware products under a brand name of their own. In some cases, the brand name is the same as that of the store (eg, Sainsbury). In others, it is different (eg, Marks and Spencer, who use the brand name **'St. Michael'**).

The logic behind the use of own brand is similar to that of the manufacturer's brand. The retailer hopes to promote a consistent image about the company and the products it sells - often an image of reliable quality and value for money.

By encouraging a positive attitude to the shop rather than manufacturers, the retailer expects a higher rate of repurchases from the store - in other words, retailer loyalty instead of manufacturer loyalty.

Some retailers use different names to distinguish between different types of products. Tesco, for example, is a supermarket retailer who uses the **'Tesco'** label on groceries and **'Delamare'** on non-grocery goods.

The manufacturers of own-branded products benefit in a number of ways. A long-term contract provides a guarantee of sales at a known price and a predictable take-off rate. Promotion costs are cut (there is no consumer advertising by the manufacturer). Sales force costs are low because sales are negotiated with a small number of customers on a relatively infrequent basis.

On the negative side, the manufacturer often has to tolerate stringent inspection by the retailer's quality control officers. There is some danger also that the manufacturer may depend on a single retailer as the customer for a very high proportion of his or her output. Strategically, this is bad marketing because loss of that customer could lead to bankruptcy.

3.7 Public relations

Many large companies employ full-time public relations officers. Smaller organisations may prefer to use consultants.

There are several objectives which may be pursued in public relations:

(a) **Encourage good publicity**

As stated earlier, an important part of public relations is to obtain media coverage for the company and its products. The media may refer to the company's products, or to broader actions, which illustrate the company's attitude to technological progress, to the local community, or to a government campaign.

(b) **Offset bad publicity**

If products prove to be unreliable, or the company is accused of making excess profits, the task of the public relations staff will be either to admit or to deny the charges levelled against the company, to reassure the public about the organisation's attitude to such problems, and to state the corrective action being taken.

(c) **Influence important figures**

Some public relations practitioners communicate with such figures as Members of Parliament, local counsellors and government officials to ensure that these people are acquainted with the company's view on matters under their influence and which affect the interests of the business.

(d) **Communicate directly with the public**

Big companies are sometimes regarded as bureaucratic and impersonal. It is important that the public should regard them as institutions which act in their interest and will respond to individual comments. Part of the responsibilities of the public relations department, therefore, is to liaise with people who write in with problems or queries.

(e) **Link the company with the community**

Many organisations become involved with community activities such as sport, scout groups, children's homes, educational scholarships, etc. The result of these activities should be that the company is regarded favourably by the public, and that the sales of products and services it offers benefit from that positive attitude.

4 THE THEORY OF COMMUNICATION AND THE PROMOTION MIX

In the context of marketing, the theory of communication is relevant to the techniques by which an organisation gets a customer to purchase its products or services.

Using communication theory terminology:

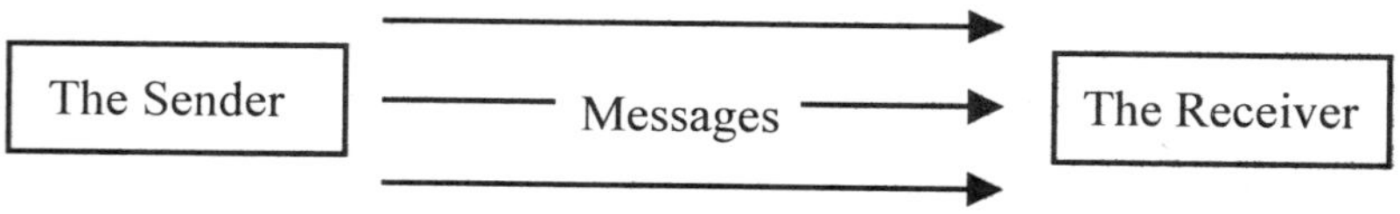

Channels of communication

The sender is the organisation, the receiver is the customer and the processes by which the sender persuades the receiver are messages or channels of communication.

It can be argued that all four Ps of the marketing mix are channels of communication, but the major P is Promotion.

The promotion mix consists of four elements:

(a) **Advertising**

Paid communications in the media which are designed to influence potential customers favourably regarding a company's products or services. Advertising is sometimes called above-the-line promotion.

(b) **Sales promotion**

Non-media promotional activity aimed at increasing sales. Sales promotion includes a variety of techniques such as give-aways, competitions, trading stamps and exhibitions. It is sometimes called below-the-line promotion.

(c) **Public relations**

The creation of positive attitudes regarding products, services, or companies by various means, including unpaid media coverage and involvement with community activities.

(d) **Personal selling**

The techniques by which a sales force makes contact with potential customers.

Each company has a different promotion-mix setting; even companies in the same product area can successfully adopt widely differing promotion policies.

Generally, however, advertising is less important to those selling in the industrial market than to manufacturers of fast-moving consumer goods. In industrial marketing, personal selling is often the most widely used of the above four elements. Sales promotion and public relations are useful in both consumer and industrial marketing: budgets for the former can be as large as the advertising budget for some consumer products.

Techniques of public relations have already been described. The other factors in the mix - advertising, sales, promotion (sometimes called below-the-line promotion) and personal selling - are described below.

5 ADVERTISING

5.1 Stages in the buying process

The AIDA model of buyer behaviour (Awareness, Interest, Desire, Action) is discussed in the following chapter.

The following table, taken from Marketing Theory & Application (Wentz & Eyrich, Harcourt Brace) relates that model to the task and effect of marketing:

Buyer stage	Promotional task	Advertising effect
Awareness	Establish buyer awareness	Inform potential customers about the product or service.
Interest	Create buyer interest	Stimulate interest in the product.
Desire	Create desire	Induce favourable attitude, especially in relation to competing products.
Action	Sell the product	Induce purchase by stressing the immediate desirability of the product.

5.2 Advertising budget

As a percentage of sales, advertising expenditure varies enormously from company to company. Some big pharmaceutical companies spend in the region of 20-25%, whilst organisations such as For and General Motors spend rather less than 1%. A common figure for fast-moving consumer goods is around 8-12%, but it should be stressed that the wide range of alternative promotion mix policies leads to an equally wide range of expenditure policies.

There are a number of ways in which companies may decide their advertising expenditure level:

(a) **Fixed percentage of sales**

In industries with a stable, predictable sales pattern, some companies can be seen to set their level of advertising consistently at a fixed percentage of sales. The policy has the virtue of avoiding an advertising war which could be disastrous for profits, but there are some drawbacks. This kind of rule of thumb assumes that sales are directly related to advertising. This is not the case, since other elements of the promotion mix and of the marketing mix also affect sales levels. If the rule is applied when sales decline, the result will be a reduction in the advertising budget just when promotion is most needed.

(b) **Same level as competitors**

As with the previous example, this approach seems widespread where products are well-established with predictable sales levels. It has similar virtues, too. Its proponents argue that it avoids the development of advertising wars and that, in any industry, the appropriate level of advertising for one company is bound to be similar to that for another. The method is likely to be inadequate, however, because it avoids systematic consideration of the value for money associated with any level of advertising expenditure, and because it could prevent a company from changing its market share by restricting advertising when it needed to increase sales.

(c) **What is left after everything else**

Some companies appear to consider all other expenses before advertising, and then use what they can afford. There is no attempt to associate marketing objectives with levels of advertising. In a good year, large amounts of money could be wasted. In a bad year, the low advertising budget could guarantee a further year of low sales.

(d) **Objective-task method**

This is a more systematic method, and it is preferable to those given above. First, the company defines the objectives of its advertisement campaigns in detail. Then it describes alternative ways in which these objectives can be attained. The cost of each alternative is totalled and the most cost-effective way is selected.

5.3 Some advertising objectives

It is not enough to say that advertising is expected to increase sales. The objective of a campaign must be more precisely stated, eg:

(a) **Introduce new products**

Advertising is the most effective way to acquaint a market with a new or revised product. Some authorities distinguish between informative and competitive advertising. The former type is definitely informative, and is useful in accelerating sales on launch so that profitability is achieved as soon after launch as possible.

(b) **Improve the competitive position**

The company may decide to increase sales by inducing potential customers to switch brands. It may do this by claiming a product feature or benefit which is unique; alternatively, it can claim its product is more efficient than the competition, eg, *'this toothpaste leads to 30% fewer fillings'* or *'this soap powder washes whitest of all.'*

(c) **Sell in to dealers**

If a product is being heavily advertised, dealers and retailers will be more likely to buy it. The effect can be enhanced by advertising to the trade, and by salespeople briefed to refer to the main promotion.

(d) **Develop the company's image**

Many large companies use institutional advertising to reassure the public about the company's intentions, and to create an image of progressiveness, reliability, or good service. Whilst not directly aimed at selling a product, this type of advertising could have a pronounced long-term effect on sales.

(e) **Build or maintain brand loyalty**

For a company with a strong brand and a high market share, a major objective is to keep brand loyalty high, ie, to prevent brand-switching. One of the best examples of this type of advertising was the Coca-Cola campaign with its catch-phrase *'it's the real thing'*. Companies in this position sometimes emphasise the tradition and quality of their product.

(f) **Bring salespeople and customers together**

One of the effects of most advertising is an increase in the morale of sales personnel. Some advertising, however, is specifically designed to put potential customers in touch with salespeople. A good example is the use of return-coupons in industrial advertisements.

There are many other potential objectives in advertising, but the above are among the most important. The objective of a campaign is crucial in determining the message.

Example of how advertising is used to build brand loyalty as a long term strategy:

The 1990 IPA Advertising Effectiveness Awards Grand Prix went to what must be one of the longest-running ad campaigns of all time - the chimps for **PG Tips**. The success of the 35- year-old advertising idea has been its consistency through almost four decades of dramatically changing fashions, social values and mores. The story starts with Pre-Gestive Tea, as PG Tips was known pre-1955, which was re-launched in 1955 under the new name, although this failed to shift its market position in the first year.

That was before the chimps hit the screen with their own very particular endorsement for the brand. Chimps' tea parties at London Zoo were all the rage at the time. By replicating in people's homes, the fun of the zoo, Brooke Bond hoped to establish a stronger relationship between brand, advertising and consumers. It had a dramatic effect. Within two years, PG Tips had knocked Typhoo from the top slot, passing Brooke Bond Dividend and Lyons on its way up. The chimps have been at work ever since.

It is suggested that without advertising, PG Tips would, at best, have remained at its 1955 number four position. On this assumption the chimps have earned the company £2,000 million (at 1985 prices) over the past 20 years alone.

Example of the power of advertising:

The power of advertising is amply illustrated by a 60-second commercial for **Apple Computers** based on George Orwell's 1984. It was shown **once** on network television in the United States during the Super Bowl game on January 22, 1984. Two days later, when the Apple Macintosh went on sale, 200,000 people queued up to see it, and within six hours they had bought $3,500,000 worth of Macintosh computers and left cash deposits for $1,000,000 more. The commercial received editorial coverage on the ABC, CBS and NBS network news, on BBC Television, on 27 local US TV stations and in virtually every major newspaper and news magazine. (Source: Douglas, T., 'The Complete Guide to Advertising'.)

5.4 Advertising message

Some authorities believe that the most effective way to advertise is to stress the USP of a product. The USP (unique selling proposition) is an attribute or benefit which the customer regards as unique to that product. A mint may be seen as *'the strongest'* or a toothpaste as *'the only one with the stripes'*.

A concept similar to the USP is that of added value. While it is accepted that similar products have similar characteristics, some brands are considered to be superior in one respect or another. For example, several detergents could be described as washing white, brightening colours and leaving clothes fresh. Particular brands may acquire added value in the mind of the consumer because of advertising campaigns stressing softness or economy.

The complexity of the message must vary according to the product, the potential customer, and the medium.

The approaches mentioned above, USP and added value, are particularly applicable to fast-moving consumer goods.

Where a product is more complex, there is a tendency for advertisers to use lengthy copy (copy is the term which describes the words and pictures used to convey a message). A motor car could be described by the advertiser as stylish, economical, roomy, safe, and rust-protected in the same advertisement.

The message carried by a television advertisement must be shorter and less comprehensive than that in a medium such as the Financial Times newspaper. Generally, the advertisements seen in the trade press and in 'quality' newspapers are those with longer, more complex copy.

In industrial advertising, the customer is an organisation rather than an individual and several people influence the purchase decision. For this reason, the advertiser must use a more rational, economically-biased approach with copy which will influence a number of key people. The single consumer's needs are individual, based on psychological rather than economic factors; the message is consequently simpler and less economic in content.

The message has to be:

(a) seen;
(b) read;
(c) believed;
(d) remembered; and
(e) acted upon.

5.5 Media

The selection of the right medium depends on several factors:

(a) Size of the audience.
(b) Demographic composition of the audience.
(c) Geographic coverage of the medium.
(d) Frequency with which advertisements can be placed.
(e) Physical factors such as colour, print quality, etc.
(f) Length of time for which the medium exists.
(g) Cost of medium.

The cost of the medium should be measured in terms of the target audience which is that proportion of the total audience which are regarded as prime potential customers. A common measure is cost per 1,000 target audience.

The difference between target and total audience can be illustrated by considering the marketing of a top-price perfume. To advertise this product in one of the mass-market daily newspapers would be futile; although the audience is large, there would be very few potential customers amongst them. A better approach would be to advertise in up-market women's fashion magazines. They have a relatively low readership, but one which includes a much higher proportion of likely customers.

Factor (f) above deals with the difference between, for example, television (in which an advertisement is seen for 15, 30 or 60 seconds only - subsequent viewings have to be paid for) and a monthly magazine. Once the advertisement is placed in the magazine, it may be re-read many times before the next issue is published.

The charges for various media in the UK are shown in BRAD (British Rate and Data).

Some of the media choices available are:

(a) **National daily newspapers**

Television has reduced the importance of national newspapers as an advertising medium. Circulations vary greatly: mass dailies may enjoy sales of around 4,000,000, while quality newspapers (readership consisting of a much larger proportion of AB consumers) may sell only 300,000 - 1,000,000. The selection of the newspapers with an appropriate readership profile is crucial.

Fast-moving consumer goods and consumer durables use these media, whilst some of the 'upmarket' (quality) newspapers read by managers carry a certain amount of industrial advertising.

The position of an advertisement is important - some pages are read more frequently and some more closely than others. The advertiser may vary the size of the advertisement from full-page down to single-column-centimetre, and can pay extra for colour.

(b) **Local newspapers**

These cover a limited region, but tend to be sold to a large proportion of local people or distributed free of charge. They are usually not stratified by socio-economic class in the same way as the national press. Whereas daily newspapers are discarded daily, weeklies last somewhat longer, and may be re-read more. They carry some national advertising, but have a much higher proportion of local (especially retailer) advertising. There is some co-operative advertising; in which a national manufacturer and a local retailer share the costs of advertising the same goods.

(c) **Sunday newspapers**

Some of the mass-market, and up-market Sunday newspapers have a very high readership. They are less stratified than the national dailies. Many Sunday newspapers have colour magazines in which the advertising is mainly for consumer durables. Sunday papers may be re-read several times, and last for several days.

(d) **Consumer magazines**

Some magazines have a broad appeal and are used to promote consumer goods. They sell to various customer groups (eg, women's magazines) and are stratified by age and class. Others are for the specialised consumer, eg, the amateur angler, photographer, machinist, modeller, or collector. These are highly discriminatory media which give the specialised manufacturer access to his or her market segment.

(e) **Trade press**

Most industrial advertising is still carried out in the trade press. Most of these media are highly selective, allowing the advertiser to select media appropriate to the industries in which the best sales prospects exist. An unusual feature is that there is a very large readership in relation to the sales of these magazines.

(f) **Television**

The bulk of TV advertising is for fast-moving consumer goods. The vast majority of British families have a TV. Demographic segmentation and audience size vary by programme: some programmes have a large, relatively unsegmented audience, whilst others are more selective. Television is regionalised, so that advertisers have a choice between national and regional coverage. It is an extremely expensive medium which cannot cope with complex messages and in which every second of advertisement has to be paid for. Its main advantage is audience size.

Examples of television targeting

Television advertising is the key medium for marketers to get their message across to children. But advertisers do not just place ads while children's programmes are being aired. Four to six-year olds may watch *Thomas The Tank Engine* and *Postman Pat* but they also watch *Neighbours. Coronation Street* is still a big favourite for seven to nine-year-old girls while the boys go for *You've Been Framed with Jeremy Beadle*. Ten to 12-year-old boys opt for the more adult *Lovejoy* while the girls remain devoted to Australian soap operas.

(g) **Radio**

Commercial radio is the most recent of the media in the UK. It is regionalised. Daytime listeners are primarily housewives. Advertisements are a mixture of local and national. As with TV, copy must be short.

Amid much activity in the commercial radio sector, top-line results from the first set of Jicar data issued in September 1990, covering the whole commercial network revealed that the independent radio network has increased its adult weekly reach (the percentage of all adults within independent radio regions who tune in at least once during a week) by seven percentage points to 50 per cent. The research was conducted during April-June 1990.

(h) **Posters**

The advertiser controls his or her expenditure very precisely geographically with this medium. There is little selectivity as to the socio-economic class of the audience, and poster advertisements are accordingly used to promote mass-market consumer goods. The medium is relatively cheap, and is often used to back national TV and press campaigns, using the same words and situations to reinforce the TV or newspaper message.

Example

Poster board manufacturer **Multiboard** has claimed to have pushed back the limits of poster board technology with its June 1990 'breakthrough' - a moving triangular board which turns inside out. Baffling though it may be to mathematicians, Multiboard claims that it can offer six advertising opportunities on one site with the bizarre structure. Multiboard 6 has as many advantages as it has sides, the makers insist. They claim that advertisers can now tell a story or show a range of products. Multiboard has patented its invention in 15 international markets including the US and Japan. *(Source: 'Marketing', June 1990.)*

(i) **Transport advertising**

This uses posters on buses, railway sites, etc. Advantages and disadvantages are much the same as for ordinary poster advertising. There is a very high incidence of local advertising.

(j) **Direct mail**

Direct mail used to be regarded as a rather cost inefficient medium. However, the developments in computer technology have significantly changed this position. There are now many list-broking concerns who will supply, relatively cheaply, names and addresses against virtually any geographic, demographic or industrial criteria. So, for example, 'all garages in Glasgow employing more than ten people' is a perfectly viable request. This ability to accurately target potential buyers has led to the appearance of many specialist direct mail advertising agencies and this medium has experienced very considerable growth.

(k) **Cinema**

TV has taken over some of the functions which used to belong to cinema advertising. The medium is especially suitable for younger age-groups, however. There is a mixture of local and national advertising.

Example of the power of cinema advertising:

A very successful commercial which shows just how powerful cinema advertising can be is **Levi's** *'Rivets'*. *'Rivets'* shows the making of the rivet on the front of the Levi jeans, from the mining of the ore, through the stamping of the metal, the transportation by truck to the jean itself. It is made with beautiful photography and has a strong music track. The commercial was also shown on television but it lost much of its impact on the small screen.

(Source: Douglas, T., 'The Complete Guide to Advertising'.)

5.6 Advertising agency

Advertising agencies are usually responsible for the creation and placement of advertisements. The cost of the service is paid for in two ways. Firstly, agencies receive commission from the media. This is the traditional source of agency income. Secondly, the agency bills the client for a further amount. The move towards client payment reflects development in the role of the advertising agency. Rather than being simply selectors of media they have become increasingly involved with market research and other marketing services. The organisation chart below illustrates the structure of an advertising agency.

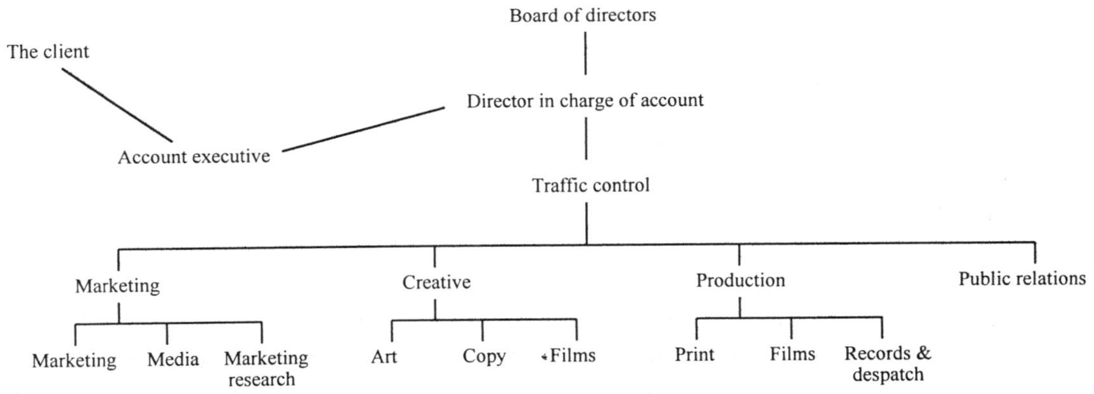

5.7 British Code of Advertising Practice

This is a set of rules which limits the content of advertisements. For example, it excludes misleading or untruthful claims and does not allow for explicit sex in advertisements. It goes beyond government legislation in these respects.

The Code is operated by several bodies, including the Advertising Standards Authority, the Code of Advertising Practice Committee and the Advertising Investigation Department of the Advertising Association.

It is not a body with legal powers, but it has nevertheless caused the withdrawal of offending advertisements. However, it is not unknown for the Advertising Standards Authority to reject claims of the lack of probity of certain advertisements.

Example

Sensuality and ice-cream are an acceptable combination, according to an Advertising Standards Authority report, which rejected 64 complaints about sexy ice-cream ads.

Häagen-Dazs' smouldering press advertising, which used scantily-clad models in erotic poses, provoked the highest number of complaints in the ASA's November (1991) report. However, it said that "while the advertisements could be described as erotic, they were not sexually explicit".

5.8 Activity

So many messages are fired at the general public in commercial television and print advertisements that many are bound to miss their target. Also advertising is very costly. For these reasons management need to formulate and evaluate advertising strategy with great care and attention. What advice would you give management regarding advertising strategy?

5.9 Activity solution

Our advice provides the following guidelines:

(a) **Set clear advertising objectives and strategies.**

Example

Product management recommended that *Fairy Liquid* be advertised to emphasise its cleaning ability first, with mildness as a secondary claim. **Proctor & Gamble's** senior management rejected this and instead approved the reverse - an advertising strategy stressing the product's superior mildness with reassurance on cleaning. The decision proved to be a good one. *(Source: Davidson, H., 'Offensive Marketing')*.

(b) Continuously monitor and evaluate advertising.

(c) Run only effective advertising.

(d) Consider public sensitivity.

(e) Create a climate which encourages creativity.

(f) Run successful campaigns on and on.

Example

When **IDV** moved into the Spanish sherry market in 1966 with *Croft Original*, it faced two main difficulties. To start with, as the first pale Spanish sherry on the UK market, it went against the received wisdom that cream or sweet sherries were dark in colour. Secondly, it faced the mighty brands of the three main shippers - Domecq, Harveys and Gonzalez Byass.

For the first ten years, Croft Original built its share gradually in a growing sector, but by 1976 it was still little more than a brand which appealed to the more experimental sherry drinker.

Jeeves To The Rescue! A new advertising campaign featuring PG Wodehouse's famous duo Jeeves and Wooster served to solve the problem. In five years (1977 - 1981), the niche player had become pretender to Harveys Bristol Cream's crown as number two. Through the 80s, although the Spanish sherry market declined dramatically, Croft Original - supported by the long-running and well-liked Jeeves campaign (and its slogan, *"one instinctively knows when something is right")* - further increased its share and narrowed the gap between the two top brands. *(Source: 'IPA Advertising Effectiveness Awards', 1990.)*

(g) Always seek to improve the advertising.

6 BELOW-THE-LINE PROMOTION

6.1 Objectives of below-the-line promotion

To refer again to the AIDA model, below-the-line promotion is primarily at the action end. It is intended to stimulate the actual purchase, rather than to be informative or interesting.

Sales promotion can be aimed at the ultimate customer, to encourage pull, or at the trade, to push goods into dealerships or the retail system.

The objectives of sales promotion should be considered in more detail, however, because there is a wide range of techniques which are useful in different marketing situations.

Some of the more important objectives are:

(a) 'Sell in' to the trade.

(b) Gain new users.

(c) Counteract competition.

(d) Gain repeat purchase.

(e) Improve display/shelf position.

(f) Clear old stock prior to the launch of a new product.

(g) Add excitement to a well-established product that may be suffering from consumer familiarity.

Example

By the early 80s **Kellogg's Cornflakes** had become commonplace. It was so familiar that it was no longer noticeable, and children considered cornflakes were boring. In 1984 Kellogg's launched a promotion to mark its Diamond Jubilee and replaced the product's regular pack with a 1924 pack design for a limited period. By sending in four packet tops the consumer would get a toy replica of a 1924 Kellogg's delivery van. The offer was supported by a TV commercial and a 10-million door-to-door leaflet drop. There was also a competition in the TV Times as part of a comprehensive PR campaign.

The results were good. Kellogg's had 1.9 million applications for the toy van, and in exchange gained 2.3 million kilos of extra cornflakes business. *(Source: 'Marketing', May 1985.)*

6.2 Sales promotion techniques

To suit objective 6.1 (a) above, appropriate techniques would be: dealer discounts (or *'11 for the price of 10'* offers), trade competitions, or incentive offers to company salespeople.

For 6.1 (b), a company could distribute free samples of the product, offer a trial use, or use a banded pack, in which a sample of a new product is attached to the pack of one of the existing lines.

To achieve 6.1 (c), price discounting is common. Other possibilities are to offer twin packs at an advantageous price, or to run a consumer competition.

Repeat purchase can be encouraged by coupons on the pack which can be traded in at the next purchase, by a series of give-aways in the packs, by send-away offers which require several labels or coupons, or by a competition which requires proof of purchase of several items.

Shelf display may be improved by the use of free on-pack premiums (gifts attached to the pack), by container premiums (in which the container is attractive in its own right), by consumer competitions, or by competitions in which retailers are given prizes for the best window display.

There are some types of below-the-line activity not listed above. For example, trading stamps are issued to encourage loyalty to retail outlets. One of the most important below-the-line activities in industrial marketing is attendance at exhibitions. This is intended to gain new users, but afterwards it is difficult to determine whether a sale resulted from an exhibition or another source.

Examples

Types of **immediate** consumer promotion incentives

(a) **Home couponing** where a coupon with monetary value, redeemable against a specified brand, is distributed to homes.

(b) **Magazine or newspaper couponing** where the coupon is cut from magazine or newspaper.

(c) **Reduced price packs** with a price reduction marked on package by producer. Value of typical price reduction varies between 3% and 12% of retail price.

(d) **Bonus (or free) packs** where the consumer is given an extra product at no additional cost (eg, four for the price of three).

(e) **Free merchandise packs** where the consumer is given a gift which is attached to brand package.

(f) **Re- usable container packs**. The product is packed inside a special container which has an intrinsic value. The container may be free or involve the consumer paying extra for it.

(g) **Home sampling** (distribution by hand or mail to individual homes). Usually a free sample is delivered to the home.

(h) **Cross-ruff sampling** where a free sample of one brand is attached to another brand which is retailed at normal price.

Types of **immediate** consumer promotion incentives

(a) **Buy 'X' number and get one free** where the consumer sends in packets or labels and will receive a coupon inviting him/her to a free pack or product. (There are a number of variants of this scheme).

(b) **Free premium** where the customer mails in a specified number of packet tops or labels and will then be sent a free gift by the producer of the product.

(c) **Self-liquidating promotion** where the consumer mails in one or more labels plus some money (normally the cost of the premium item) and receives a specified gift item in return.

(d) **Charity promotion** where for every label or packet top sent in, the manufacturer will donate a specified amount or percentage of product value to a named charity.

(e) **Contests**:

- card and stamp game
- rub-off cards
- skill competition
- sweepstake, (or draw) contest.

6.3 Activity

Promotions tailormade by a supplier for an individual retailer are one of the most complex form of sales promotion activity. They are complex to create, since the needs of two different 'brands' have to be accommodated:

(a) The **supplier's brand**, positioned in competition with other brands in the same product category.

(b) The **retailer**, pursuing policies and communicating a proposition designed to compete successfully against other retailers.

They are complex to implement, since many people are likely to be involved:

(a) Marketing, sales promotion and key account managers on the supplier's side.

(b) On the retailer's side, a buyer, a marketing/merchandising/pro motions department and individual store managers.

(c) Possibly also a sales promotion agency employed by the supplier, and another employed by the retailer.

Consider what is involved in sales promotion ('below-the-line) activities and then:

(a) describe the main stages you think would be involved in developing a promotion;

(b) state the advice you would give management regarding promotion development; and

(c) explain how a sales promotion could be controlled.

6.4 Activity solution

(a) The stages in developing promotion typically require management to:

- determine the objectives and strategy for the promotion;
- evaluate the different promotion techniques and draw up a short-list of those which fit the strategy and the budget;
- think up creative ideas, stemming from the half-dozen or so techniques short-listed;
- pick out the best idea and develop it in detail.

(b) Our advice to management includes the following:

- Set clear objectives and strategy.
- Get the balance right between promotion and advertising. (Sales promotion is rarely used as the sole promotional activity and is probably most valuable when supplementing advertising.)
- Aim to innovate new promotion techniques.
- Ruthlessly prune ineffective promotions.
- Monitor promotions and analyse the results.
- Plan long term.

(c) Evaluating the response to promotion is very difficult, although it is generally recognised to be easier than trying to assess the return gained from advertising. Different aspects of sales promotion can be monitored and if possible controlled. Examples are given below:

- Time : laying down a date on which the promotion will end.
- Area : limiting the area, or outlets, through which promotions will run.
- Products : limiting the promotion to special goods.
- Budget : establishing financial budgets of expenditure.
- Objectives : coupon returns, competition entries, sample issued, gifts taken up, sales results.

It is not easy to control promotion costs because results are often not easily identified with costs. However there are ways which help management to establish the success of a promotion. These include the following:

- retail audits,
- consumer panels,
- retail feedback-questionnaires etc.,
- coupon/competition count,
- sales force feedback,
- sales analysis.

Example

At the end of 1990 AMRA and Nielsen Consumer Research launched *Spotcheck* - a package to test the impact of promotional activities. The service can be used to test such variables as advertising impact, copy, weight and style. It is said to be able to measure the take-up of coupons and response promotions, and test the uptake, trial and repeat purchase of new products.

6.5 Merchandising

Merchandising is a form of sales promotion concentrated at the point-of- sale and is especially concerned with the display of products within shops. It is, therefore, very much linked with the *"silent salesmen"* aspects of packaging, store display and window presentation.

The main factors involved are:

(a) packaging
(b) display of products
(c) ideal use of shelf or floor layout
(d) window displays
(e) point-of-sale (POS) advertising
(f) lighting
(g) traffic flow (the movement flow of people through a shop).
(h) the shopping environment

Example of merchandising at work

When you enter a large supermarket what is the first category of goods you see? It is normally shelves and displays of fruit and vegetables. What feeling does this conjure up? Is it one of freshness, variety, brightness and colours, internationalism and aroma?

7 SELLING

7.1 Some different ways to sell

There are several alternative selling methods to consider:

(a) **Door-to-door**

This type of sales person has, in the eyes of some customers, a poor image. Door-to-door salespeople are sometimes regarded as hard-selling, partly dishonest peddlers of dubious products. Several modern companies, however, use advertising and point-of-sale material with good quality merchandise to back up a door-to-door sales team. Avon Cosmetics is an example in the UK.

(b) **Telephone selling**

The main drawback of this method is that it only gives access to telephone users. It is widely used by locally-based teams selling home-improvement products such as double glazing and house insulation, and is a fast and relatively inexpensive way of contacting large numbers of people.

The telephone is often used by industrial and trade suppliers to take orders from regular customers.

(c) **Mail order**

Selling by means of direct mailings and small advertisements - in the UK they appear in special publications and in weekend editions of daily papers - avoids expenditure on sales force, and allows the use of relatively inexpensive premises. Packing and postage/distribution costs are, however, expensive.

(d) **Catalogue selling**

Catalogue selling companies, sometimes part of the same company as retail chain stores, use part-time (usually female) agents who show the catalogue to their friends and neighbours. Sales are made partly because of the 'free' credit, partly because of the bond of friendship. As well as packing and postage, the cost of the catalogues is high.

(e) **Party selling**

Such goods as lingerie, children's clothes, plastic containers and jewellery are frequently sold at 'parties' held by housewives for friends and neighbours. As with the previous selling method, an important factor in securing sales is the personal relationship between potential customers attending the party, and the party-holder.

(f) **Retail selling**

Appropriate for consumer goods with large numbers of potential customers. There are more retail sales employees than any other kind of sales person.

The above list is not exhaustive, but it illustrates some of the alternatives available in sales management. Methods (a), (b), (c), (d) and (e) above use part-time sales forces, paid by results only.

7.2 Different kinds of sales person

Apart from the part-time sales personnel mentioned above, there are many sorts of sales person. Each company describes its sales jobs differently, but there are sufficient shared characteristics to consider the following:

(a) **Travelling sales representatives**

Widely used in both consumer and industrial marketing, this is a creative, demanding job calling for extensive training and skill in dealing with individual customer requirements.

(b) **Technical sales representatives**

In industrial selling, the sales person may need a high degree of product knowledge and a good understanding of the customer's problems in using the product. Technical sales representatives, or sales engineers, can sometimes be called upon to assist customers in the installation or fitting of the items they sell, and in planning for operation and maintenance.

(c) **Retail sales persons**

There is great variation in the role of sales persons in shops. In supermarkets and many other types of outlet, the person at the till or counter does no more than total the bill, take the money, and wrap the goods. For expensive durable goods, such as hi-fi equipment and furniture, there is much more scope for constructive selling.

(d) **Van salespeople**

Where consumer products are highly perishable and are sold through a large number of small outlets, van salespeople are used. They are partly salespeople, partly a physical distribution system. Most of their deliveries are to regular, repeat orders, which limits their selling to order-taking.

8 SELF-TEST QUESTIONS

8.1 List three alternatives to a marketing orientation (2.2).

8.2 Contrast 'pull' and 'push' marketing strategy (3.3).

8.3 List the four main elements making up the promotion mix (4).

8.4 Discuss the ways in which companies may decide their advertising expenditure budgets (5.2).

8.5 Describe the different objectives of advertising (5.3).

8.6 The selection of the right advertising medium depends on several factors. What are they? (5.5).

8.7 There are several different objectives of below-the-line (sales promotion) activities depending on the company's situation and aims. What are they? (6.1).

8.8 What are the main factors involved in merchandising? (6.5).

9 EXAMINATION TYPE QUESTION

9.1 Marketing Mix Decisions

You are required to:

(a) describe the role of advertising as an element in the marketing communications mix for companies manufacturing and marketing:

(i) chocolate confectionery, and
(ii) fork-lift trucks; **(10 marks)**

(b) describe how 'below-the-line' promotional activity differs from advertising as such, and explain what major factor must be considered when planning an advertising campaign;

(10 marks)
(Total: 20 marks)

10 ANSWER TO EXAMINATION TYPE QUESTION

10.1 Marketing Mix Decisions

(a) For both types of product, advertising is one of four main elements of the **promotion mix.** The other three are personal selling, sales promotion and public relations. We shall accept, to depict the way in which promotion works, the model AIDA:

A	=	awareness
I	=	interest
D	=	desire
A	=	action

Advertising can be effective in making people aware of products, in generating interest in them, in encouraging desire for them, and in stimulating the actual purchase. Sales promotion is effective mainly at the action end. Sales forces are more successful if advertising has been used to promote awareness and interest, and public relations is concerned with improving attitudes to the product and to customers.

(i) A manufacturer of chocolate confectionery may well spend as much as, say, 6-7% of the sales price of the product on the advertising budget. Much of this may be spent on TV and daily press advertising. The message would be designed to promote brand preference. The message would be simple and clear, and might exploit psychological characteristics such as the need for 'belongingness' or friendship. If the product were already well-known, the advertisement would be expected either to improve customer preference ('desire') for the brand or to stimulate interest in it in some other way.

(ii) A fork lift truck manufacturer would probably spend a lower proportion of the goods' price on advertising, with trade magazines and perhaps up-market newspapers selected as the media. In industrial advertising, it is common to find advertisements designed more explicitly as an aid to the sales force (for example, the use of a return coupon). The message would be more complex, to persuade economically-conscious managers about claimed product advantages. The promotion mix in industrial marketing is more sales-force oriented than in consumer marketing, and sales promotion also is less important.

(b) Whereas 'advertising' refers to promotional messages transmitted through the media (TV, radio, press, posters, cinema), below-the-line' promotion refers to the use of non-media methods, such as competitions, free gifts, retail displays, etc.

The major factors to be considered in planning an advertising campaign are the advertising budget, the message to be communicated, the media to be used, and the location and timing of the advertisement.

The budget size should be considered in relation to the resources available, the effect on company profitability, and the estimated advertising expenditures of competitors. Advertising expenditure is often fixed by companies as a proportion of the sales for each line, but his criterion, and the others mentioned, may be overridden in order to achieve a particular objective.

Message design involves the creation side of advertising – what is said, what images appear on the TV screen, the layout and pictorial features of press advertisement. Creative factors must be appropriate to the market segments at which they are aimed, catering for the tastes and needs of that segment.

Media selection depends upon the viewing, reading or listening habits of the potential customer. Cost-effectiveness is the major criterion, and the ratio used is cost per thousand of the target audience. The decision as to which media are actually used generally rests with the advertising agency; there is no 'either-or' choice, since many products use several media in integrated campaigns.

Location and timing (in TV and radio advertisement placing), and frequency of placement must be decided. The placement of the advertisement should be next to items or programmes of particular interest to the target audience, and the size or duration of the advertisement must be decided in relation to the budget, the required response, and the complexity of the message.

16 ANALYSING MARKET NEEDS

INTRODUCTION & LEARNING OBJECTIVES

Management will try to minimise the risks inherent in marketing an existing or new product by analysing information available about the following aspects:

(a) whether there is a gap in the market which the product can fill and, if so, whether it will appeal to a sufficient number of customers;

(b) the pricing policy which will yield the best returns, the sale/volume/selling price relationship and the price elasticity of demand;

(c) the advantages which it will have over competitive products, how long these advantages might continue and whether competitors will be motivated to enter improved versions;

(d) the level of support dealers are prepared to offer the product, and the most effective form of dealer organisation;

(e) whether there might be the environmental objections to its use; such as the danger of atmospheric pollution;

(f) the advertising and sales promotional campaign which will have maximum impact;

(g) the prospects for market segmentation and price discrimination; and

(h) the design of the physical product.

In this chapter we shall examine the elements in the marketing mix and consider how they might be used to achieve the company's marketing goals.

When you have studied this chapter you should be able to do the following:

- Discuss the theories of buyer and consumer behaviour.
- Describe the characteristics of the industrial market.
- Describe the principles of market segmentation.
- Describe methods of consumer and market research.
- Understand the basic strategy behind product development.

1 MARKET ANALYSIS

1.1 Objectives

Market analysis will use information gathered in the strategic planning process and in the everyday running of the organisation. This information will be about:

(a) The environment in which the organisation finds itself and the forecast environment.

(b) The present state of the products/markets eg, analysis of the product life cycle, and the Product Market Portfolio (cash, cows, dogs, etc).

(c) The consumers and how the market is segmented.

The purpose of the analysis should be to identify gaps in the market where consumer needs are not being satisfied and to look for opportunities which the organisation can benefit from in terms of sales or development of new products or services.

1.2 A framework for analysing the market

In order to analyse the market, an organisation must first address the following questions:

What business are we in?

What share of the market do we have?

What business do we want to be in?

Do we have the products or services to achieve this objective?

To answer these questions the organisation would have to carry out an analysis of the market. This analysis will include the following:

(a) Appraisal and understanding of the present situation. This would include an analysis for each product showing its stage in the product life cycle, strength of competition, market segmentation, anticipated threats and opportunities, customer profile.

(b) Definition of objectives of profit, turnover, product image, market share and market position by segment.

(c) Evaluation of the marketing strategies available to meet these objectives. Such strategies as pricing policy, distribution policy, product differentiation, advertising plans, sales promotions, etc.

(d) Definition of means of control to check progress against objectives and provide early warning, thereby enabling the marketing strategies to be adjusted.

1.3 Sub-dividing a market

Marketing managers often find the term 'market' too imprecise for their purposes. When they plan to sell to an identified customer type, the term target market is used so as to eliminate people or organisations for whom the product is not primarily intended.

Frequently, marketing effort is more effective if different groups of customers within the target market are treated differently. This process is called market segmentation, and it will later be described more fully.

1.4 Industrial and consumer markets

One of the most commonly-used divisions between types of market is that between consumer and industrial markets.

The consumer market is the market for products and services bought by individuals for their own use or for that of their family.

The industrial market consists of organisations (and individuals) which buy goods or services so as to use them in creating the goods or services they offer for sale.

Industrial and consumer marketing sometimes differ widely in the emphasis they place on various factors in marketing. Bearing in mind that it is easy to over-generalise, consider the following table:

Marketing factor	Industrial	Consumer
Product characteristics:		
Complexity	Often greater	Often less
Reliability	Crucial	Important, but less so
Running costs	Must be minimised	May be less than optimal
Utilisation	Usually higher	Usually lower
Aesthetic factors	Less important	Very important
Price factors:		
Initial cost	Important, but other factors scrutinised	Often the major factor
Alternatives to purchase	Rent, lease or hire	Mainly hire-purchase
Price level determined by	Usually the manufacturer	Usually the retailer
Average order value	Higher	Lower
Promotion factors:		
Budget as % of turnover	Lower	Higher
Primary message	Economic	Emotional
Complexity of message	More	Less
Media	Much use of trade press	Newspapers, TV, etc.
Sales factors:		
Sales person's technical knowledge	Greater	Usually less
Sales person's payment	Higher basic salary	Greater use of incentives
Sales person's job	Selling, plus	Selling technical advice
Distribution factors:		
Numbers of customers	Fewer	Greater
Unit volume purchased	More	Less
Order frequency	Lower	Higher

This table is by no means comprehensive and there are many exceptions to it. Nevertheless, it shows clearly some of the major differences between industrial and consumer marketing.

1.5 Classification of goods

(a) Consumer goods

There are several categories of goods sold in both consumer and industrial markets.

Familiar to most people are fast-moving consumer goods, which are of low unit value and which are subject to frequent repurchase.

Consumer durables have higher average unit prices, are not used up but wear out and are replaced at longer intervals.

The American term soft goods is sometimes used to describe items made from natural or synthetic textiles. Some examples are given later, although these goods can be regarded as a type of consumer durable.

(b) Industrial goods

Industrial goods may be categorised as follows:

- Raw materials, which have been extracted from the natural state, but subject to little processing.

- Processed materials and components, which have been transformed into a condition in which they can be incorporated into either finished goods or more complex processed parts. Americans often refer to the former as semi-manufactured goods.
- Capital goods, which consist of equipment used in the creation of goods and services and in their marketing, but are not consumable.
- Supplies, which is the industrial equivalent of fast-moving consumer goods, and covers all industrial consumables.

Services, also, can be classified in ways similar to goods, in both consumer and industrial markets. Such classifications are not widely used, however, and the following tables are therefore confined to the categorisation of tangible goods:

Consumer goods

Fast-moving consumer goods	Consumer durables	Soft goods
Toothpaste Make-up Washing powder Canned foods Shoe polish Razor blades	Refrigerators Vacuum cleaners Lawnmowers Motor cars Furniture Liquidisers	Handkerchiefs Towels Shirts Skirts Sheets Jumpers

Industrial goods

Raw materials	Processed materials and components	Capital goods	Supplies
Iron ore Timber Coal Crude oil	Steel Textiles Car trim panels Packing materials	Machine tools Computers Buildings Lorries	Stationery Carbide tips Lubricants Fuel oil

2 ANALYSING BUYER AND CUSTOMER BEHAVIOUR

2.1 Rational economic behaviour

A crucial element in the marketing process is understanding why a buyer purchases or does not purchase an organisation's goods or services. If the organisation does not understand the process, it will not be able to respond to the customer's needs and wishes.

Traditional views of marketing tend to assume that people purchase according to the value-for-money that they obtain. The customer considers the functional efficiency of the alternative products, and arrives at a decision by comparing this with the price. This set of beliefs is demonstrably inadequate in explaining consumer behaviour. In industrial purchasing, it is somewhat closer to the truth. The organisation places constraints on the freedom of the industrial buyer, causing subordination of the individual's needs and preferences.

Due to the differences that often exist between 'consumer buyers' (those who purchase items for personal consumption), and 'industrial buyers' (those who purchase items on behalf of their organisation), it is traditional to split buyers into these two broad group for the purpose of analysis.

2.2 Consumer buyers

Abraham H. Maslow proposed a hierarchy of needs which he used to explain human motivation. Conventionally used to explain the motivation to work, his hierarchy can also be applied to customer motivation.

The five-part hierarchy is arranged in the order in which human needs must be satisfied. Thus, a 'safety' need is a motivating factor only when 'physiological' needs have been satisfied. When the 'safety' need is satisfied, 'love' needs become important, and so on:

Maslow's need hierarchy

(a) Physiological needs - heat, air, light, etc.
(b) Safety needs - the need for the familiar, the secure.
(c) Love needs - the need to be loved by family, friends.
(d) Esteem needs - the need to be regarded as important, having prestige.
(e) Self-actualisation needs - the need to initiate, to achieve for oneself.

Products and services could be considered against this hierarchy. For example, insurance and banking are involved with safety needs; cigarettes and alcohol are frequently dependent upon love needs in their promotions; a fast car exploits customers' esteem needs.

2.3 Cognitive dissonance

Leon Festinger introduced the theory of cognitive dissonance. Dissonance is said to exist when an individual's attitudes and behaviour are inconsistent. One kind of dissonance is the regret which may be felt when a purchaser has bought a product, but subsequently feels that an alternative would have been preferable. In these circumstances, that customer will not repurchase immediately, but will switch brands. It is the job of the marketing team to persuade the potential customer that the product will satisfy his or her needs, and to ensure that the product itself will not induce dissonant attitudes.

2.4 Personality and product choice

The personality of individuals is their psychological make-up. It is shown in their beliefs and attitudes, and in their lifestyle. Products, and their brand-names, tend to acquire attributes in the mind of the potential customer; indeed, this is one of the primary functions of branding. When considering goods or services for a purchase, customers will invariably select those which have an image consistent with their own personality. Thus, in a public house, the relatively staid middle-aged drinker will prefer mild or ordinary bitter; the young bachelor may choose lager; the sophisticated businessperson could opt for gin and tonic. Personality and value systems are important determinants of choice.

2.5 Influence of other people

So far we have considered customers as individuals. This is unrealistic, however, because each customer is a part of larger social groupings. When people make purchase decisions, they reflect the values of their social and cultural environment. In fact, the form of products and services for sale has been determined by that environment.

Among the more obvious influences are those of family and of reference groups.

The family is often important in engendering brand purchasing habits in grocery lines, although it also has a far broader influence in forming tastes in its younger members.

Reference groups which may be school-friends, working colleagues, fellow club members etc. exert a strong normative influence. That is, they cause members of the group to buy similar things and tend to disapprove of those who behave in too individualistic a manner. It is a bold person who reads the Sun in an office of Financial Times readers, and groups of teenagers can be seen to dress with almost identical styles.

2.6 Stages in the purchase decision

It is the function of promotion to bring people to the point at which they actually purchase a product. Some potential customers might be completely unaware of a product, others could be vaguely interested in it, whilst the remainder may want to own it. There are several complex models which illustrate the stages through which people pass on their way to a decision, but one of the simplest and easiest to remember is commencing with awareness:

A - awareness
I - interest
D - desire
A - action

The customer must be made aware of the product, should become interested in it, then desire it, and finally act by purchasing.

The use of the promotion mix to achieve these ends is dealt with later.

2.7 Consumer adoption model

The people who first buy one type of consumer goods are frequently the same people who first try others. Customers can be divided into groups according to the speed with which they adopt new products. Everett M. Rogers, in his **Diffusion of Innovations** (Macmillan), has produced a useful diagram illustrating this point. His graph closely resembles a normal curve.

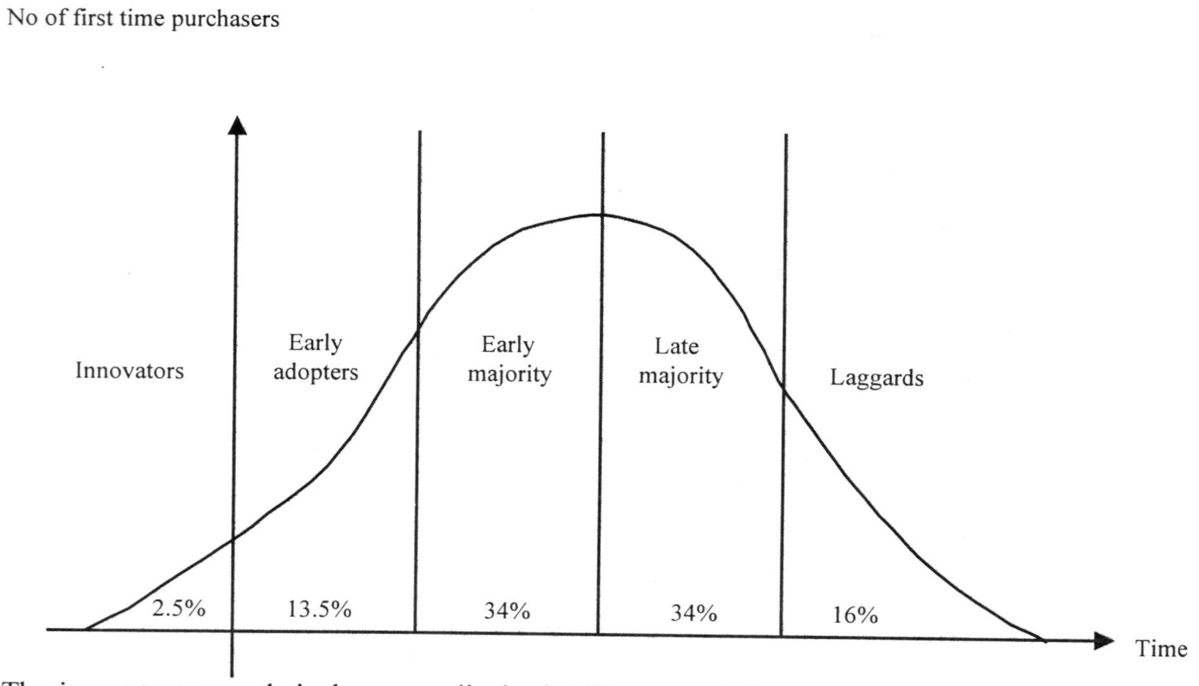

The innovators are relatively young, lively, intelligent, socially and geographically mobile and of a high socio-economic group (largely AB).

Conversely, the laggards, who are slow to accept new products, are older, less intelligent, fixed in their job and residence, less well off, and lower on the socio-economic scale.

It can be seen that, when a company launches a new product, its early customers are likely to be significantly different from its later ones.

3 INDUSTRIAL BUYERS

3.1 Introduction

In industrial marketing, the buyer is frequently not the customer or the user. For example, a salesperson of grinding wheels may have a company as a customer. The buyer is a member of the purchasing department and the user is a grinding machine operator.

As a result there may be major differences between consumer and industrial selling.

3.2 Features of industrial buyers

(a) **Motivation**

An industrial buyer is motivated to satisfy the needs of the organisation rather than his or her individual needs. Often, purchases are repeat orders when stock of items have fallen below a certain level and thus the buying motive is clear, ie, avoiding nil stocks. With significant one-off purchases, the motivation will be the achievement of the organisation's goals or targets. Thus a profit target may mean the buyer placing an emphasis on cost minimisation. A growth target expressed in terms of sales motivates a purchase that will promote that goal.

(b) **The influence of the individual or group**

An industrial purchase may be made by an individual or group. The individual or group are buying on behalf of the organisation but the buying decision may be influenced by the behavioural complexion of the individual or group responsible. The behavioural complexion will be influenced by the same influences on consumer buyers already discussed.

(c) **General organisational influences**

Each organisation will have its own procedures and decision-making processes when purchases are made. Large centrally controlled organisations will often have centralised purchasing through a purchasing department. The purchase decisions will tend to be formal with established purchasing procedures. In small organisations there will not be a purchasing department. Purchasing decisions will tend to be made in a personal basis by persons who have other functions as well in the organisation. Personal relationships between the supplier and the buyer will often be very important.

For (b) and (c) above the salesperson must therefore identify and understand the buyer in the organisation. As the buyer may be a department, the term decision-making unit (DMU) is sometimes used. The DMU is the group of people (there may only be one in the group in some instances) who has some influence on the purchasing process.

(d) **Reciprocal buying**

A feature in many industrial markets is the purchase of goods by organisation A from organisation B only on condition that organisation B purchases from organisation A.

(e) **Purchasing procedures**

An industrial buyer appraises a potential purchase in a more formal way than a consumer buyer. Written quotations, written tenders and legal contracts with performance specifications may be involved. The form of payment may be more involved and may include negotiations on credit terms, leasing or barter arrangements.

(f) **Size of purchases**

Purchases by an industrial buyer will tend to be on a much larger scale.

3.3 Activity

Kotler suggests that 'the industrial market consists of all the individuals and organisations that acquire goods and services that enter into the production of other products or services that are sold, rented, or supplied to others.' The industries making up the industrial market are the public sector, banking, insurance, transportation, manufacturing, agriculture, and so on. Consider the industrial market that a brick manufacturer operates in and describe its characteristics.

3.4 Activity solution

A brick manufacturer's industrial market has characteristics that contrast sharply with consumer markets. These are described below:

(a) **Fewer buyers**

There are fewer buyers in the industrial market than in the consumer market. Although the ultimate users of houses and structures built from using bricks number in the millions, the company's fate critically depends on getting orders from perhaps only a few thousand property developers.

(b) **Large buyers**

Even in popular markets, a few large buyers normally account for most of purchasing. The buyers can thus exert some power over suppliers in terms of price fixing, distribution and product design. These buyers are often geographically concentrated.

(c) **Fluctuating demand**

The demand for industrial goods, such as bricks, tends to be more volatile than the demand for consumer goods and services. A certain change in consumer demand can lead to a much bigger percentage change in demand for the industrial good. Sometimes change in industrial demand can be over twenty times that of the consumer demand change. Economists refer to this as the **acceleration principle.**

(d) **Derived demand**

The demand for bricks is ultimately derived from the demand for houses and structures built using bricks. If the demand for these declines, so will the demand for bricks decline.

(e) **Inelastic demand**

The total demand for many industrial goods and services is not much affected by price changes. Property developers are not going to buy many less bricks if the price for bricks rises, unless they can find suitable substitutes such as glass, metal and wood. However, construction companies will use price to decide which suppliers to purchase from, although price levels will have less impact on the quantity purchased.

(f) **Rational buying**

Industrial goods are usually purchased by professional buyers, who are continually learning new methods of how to make better purchasing decisions. Consumers on the other hand are not so well trained in the art of careful buying.

(g) **Direct purchasing**

Industrial buyers often buy direct from producers rather than through middlemen.

4 SEGMENTATION

4.1 Market segmentation

Definition Market segmentation is the division of the market into homogeneous groups of potential customers who may be treated similarly for marketing purposes.

Kotler provides a similar meaning:

Definition Market segmentation is the subdividing of a market into distinct subsets of customers, where any subset may conceivably be selected as a market target to be reached with a distinct marketing mix.

Market segmentation allows companies to treat similar customers in similar ways, whilst distinguishing between dissimilar customer groups.

Each customer group has slightly different needs, and these can be satisfied by offering each group, or segment, a slightly different marketing mix setting. In addition to superior satisfaction of customer needs, segmentation encourages better analysis of marketing opportunities.

Some companies, and some products, do not require the use of segmentation techniques. Two alternatives are undifferentiated marketing and concentrated marketing.

(b) **Undifferentiated marketing**

Segmented marketing is sometimes referred to as differentiated marketing because it differentiates between customer groups. Undifferentiated marketing is the opposite, in that it treats all customers and potential customers as identical.

(c) **Concentrated marketing**

Some businesses have become specialised in single segments of the market, and do not attempt to market in others. They acquire a great deal of expertise in their market segment, which must be large enough to sustain profitability.

Examples of companies with a clear segmentation policy are Proctor & Gamble and Lever. in the household detergents market. Sugar is a product which is sold in a relatively undifferentiated way. Morgan cars are a good example of concentrated marketing.

4.2 Consumer segmentation

There are several different ways of dividing up markets.

(a) **Geographic**

Markets are frequently split into regions for sales and distribution purposes. Many consumer goods manufacturers break down sales by television advertising regions.

(b) **Demographic**

Customers are defined in terms of age, sex, socio-economic class, country of origin, or family status. The most widely used form of demographic segmentation in the UK is the socio-economic classification shown in the table below:

Socio-economic class	Social status	Job descriptions	Approx % of UK population
A	Upper middle class	Higher managerial, administrative and professional	3
B	Middle class	Middle management, administrative and professional	11
C_1	Lower middle class	Supervisory, clerical, junior management, administrative staff	23
C_2	Skilled working class	Skilled manual workers	33
D	Working class	Semi and unskilled manual jobs	22
E	Subsistence	Pensioners, widows, lowest grade workers	8

This form of segmentation is particularly useful in advertising. Socio-economic class is closely correlated with press readership and viewing habits, and media planners use this fact to advertise in the most effective way to communicate with their target audience.

Another useful form of demographic segmentation is to divide customers by their position in the family life cycle.

Family life cycle segmentation

Life cycle stage	Characteristics	Examples of products purchased
Bachelor	Financially well-off. Fashion opinion leaders. Recreation oriented.	Cars, holidays, basic furniture, kitchen equipment.
Newly married couple	Still financially well-off. Very high purchase rate, especially of durables.	Cars, furniture, houses, holidays refrigerators.
Full nest (i)	Liquid assets low. Home purchasing at peak. Little money saving.	Washers, TVs, baby foods, toys, medicines.
Full nest (ii)	Better off. Some wives work. Some children work part time. Less influenced by advertising.	Larger size grocery packs, foods, cleaning materials, bicycles.
Full nest (iii)	Better off still. Purchasing durables.	New furniture, luxury appliances. Recreational goods.
Empty nest (i)	Satisfied with financial position. Home-ownership at peak.	Travel, luxuries, home improvements.
Empty nest (ii)	Drastic cut in income. Stay at home.	Medicines, health aids.

(c) **Psychological**

Consumers can be divided into groups sharing common psychological characteristics. One group may be described as security-oriented, another as ego-centred and so on. These categories are useful in the creation of advertising messages.

A recent trend is to combine psychological and socio-demographic characteristics so as to give a more complete profile of customer groups. Appropriately called life style segmentation by one of the companies originating the method, this kind of segmentation uses individuals to represent groups which form a significant proportion of the consumer market. These individuals are defined in terms of sex, age, income, job, product preferences, social attitudes, and political views.

(d) **Purchasing characteristics**

Customers may be segmented by the volume they buy (heavy user, medium user, light user, non user). They may be segmented by the outlet type they use, or by the pack size bought. These variables, and many others, are useful in planning production and distribution and in developing promotion policy.

(e) **Benefit**

Customers have different expectations of a product. Some people buy detergents for whiteness, and are catered for by Daz or Persil. Others want economy, for which Surf may fit the bill. Some customers may demand stain removal; one of the biological products is appropriate.

It can be seen that, within the same product class, different brands offer different perceived benefits. An understanding of customers' benefits sought enables the manufacturer to create a range of products each aimed precisely at a particular benefit.

(f) **Other classifications of social grades**

Three other well known market segmentation classifications are (i) 'The National Readership Survey', (ii) Acorn and (iii) Research Bureau Ltd's classification of housewives.

1 The National Readership Survey (UK)

In the UK, the Nation Readership Survey's classification of the population is one of the most basic definitions of a target group.

A - Higher managerial, administrative or professional (3%)

B - Intermediate managerial, administrative or professional (13%)

C - Supervisory or clerical, and junior administrative professional (22%)

D - Skilled manual (31%)

E - Semi and unskilled manual (19%)

F - Those at the lowest level of subsistence: pensioners, widows, casual workers, and the unemployed (11%)

2 Acorn

Acorn is a 'marketing segmentation system' which classifies consumers by the type of residential area in which they live. There are 11 ACORN neighbourhood groups: Group A - agricultural areas; Group B - modern family housing, higher incomes; Group C - older housing of intermediate status; Group D - poor quality older terraced housing; Group E - better-off council estates; Group F - less well-off council estates; Group G - poorest council estates; Group H - multi-racial areas; Group I - high status non-family areas; Group J - affluent suburban housing; Group K - better-off retirement areas.

3 Research Bureau Ltd's classification of housewives.

Research Bureau Ltd a leading British marketing research agency, conducted a study of 3500 housewives under the age of 45. As a result it classified housewives into the following eight groups.

The young sophisticates (15%)

Extravagant, experimental, non-traditional, young, well educated, affluent, owner occupiers, full-time employed, interested in new products, sociable, and with cultural interests.

Cabbages (12%)

Conservative, less quality conscious, not obsessional, demographically average, more are full-time housewives, middle class, average income, average education, lowest level of interest in new products, very home centred, and partake in little entertaining.

Traditional working class (12%)

Traditional, quality conscious, unexperimental in food, enjoys cooking, middle-aged, less educated, lower incomes, council house tenant, sociable, husband and wife share activities, and keen on betting.

Middle-aged sophisticates (14%)

Experimental, not traditional, less extravagant, middle-aged, well educated, affluent, owner occupiers, full-time housewives, interested in new products, and sociable cultural interests.

Coronation Street housewives (14%)

Quality conscious, conservative, traditional and obsessional, live relatively more in Lancashire and Yorkshire ITV areas, less educated, lower income, lower level of interest in new products, and not sociable.

The self-confident (13%)

Self-confident, quality conscious, not extravagant, young, well educated, owner occupiers and average income.

The homely (10%)

Bargain seekers, not self-confident, house proud, Tyne Tees and Scotland ITV areas, left school at early age, part-time employed, and partake in average level of entertaining.

The penny pinchers (10%)

Self confident, house proud, traditional, not quality conscious, 25-34 years old, part-time employment, less education, average income, betting, saving, husband and wife share activities, and sociable.

4.3 Industrial segmentation

Three of the following types of segmentation are as used in consumer marketing; the other two are different:

(a) **Geographic**

The basis for sales-force organisation.

(b) **Purchasing characteristics**

The classification of customer companies by their average order size, the frequency with which they order, etc.

(c) **Benefit**

Industrial purchasers have different benefit expectations to consumers. They may be oriented towards reliability, durability, versatility, safety, serviceability, or ease of operation. They are always concerned with value for money. Two advertisements illustrate the benefit concept in industrial marketing. Coventry Climax fork-lift trucks were advertised as very durable, and Colt factory air-conditioning systems were promoted as reducing industrial and human relations problems.

(d) **Company type**

Industrial customers can be segmented according to the type of business they are ie, what they offer for sale. The range of products and services used in an industry will not vary too much from one company to another. A manufacturer considering marketing to a particular type of company would be well advised to list all potential customers in that area of business.

(e) **Company size**

It is frequently useful to analyse marketing opportunities in terms of company size. A company supplying canteen foods would investigate size in terms of numbers of employees. Processed parts suppliers are interested in production rate, and cutting lubricants suppliers would segment by numbers of machine tools.

4.4 Activity

Think about what market segmentation is and then write down the reasons why a company would want to use it.

4.5 Activity solution

The reasons why a company will differentiate a market into segments are:

(a) It can develop marketing programmes and budgets based on a clearer idea of the response characteristics of specific market segments.

(b) It is in a better position to spot and compare marketing opportunities.

(c) It can make finer adjustments to its product and marketing appeal.

(d) It develops expertise within segments.

(e) It develops intelligence systems within segments enabling it to establish product-life cycle positions and forecast with more accuracy.

4.6 Activity

Give reasons why demographic segmentation, by itself, is not a successful basis for car manufacturers targeting their customers.

4.7 Activity solution

Reasons include the following:

(a) A car manufacturer may use buyers' age in developing its target market and then discover that the target should be the psychologically young and not the chronologically young. (The Ford Motor Company used buyers' age in targeting its Mustang car, designing it to appeal to young people who wanted an inexpensive sporty car. Ford, found to its surprise, that the car was being purchased by all age groups.)

(b) Income is another variable that can be deceptive. One would imagine that working class families would buy Ford Escorts and the managerial class would buy Ford Granada, or BMWs. However, many Escorts are bought by middle income people (often as the family's second car) and expensive cars are often bought by working class families (plumbers, carpenters etc.)

(c) Personal priorities also upset the demographic balance. Middle-income people often feel the need to spend more on clothes, furniture and housing which they could not afford if they purchased a more expensive car.

(d) The **upgrading urge** for people trying to relate to a higher social order often leads them to buy expensive cars.

(e) Some parents although 'well off' pay large fees for the private education of their children and must either make do with a small car, or perhaps no car at all.

4.8 Objectives

The objectives of the marketing plan are really the same as the objectives of the organisation. The objective may be expressed as an objective which is subsidiary to the overall objective eg, the overall objective may be a profit target, with the subsidiary marketing objective stated in terms of market share.

4.9 Strategy

The selection of a strategy is the first step in the implementation of a plan to achieve the stated objectives. The alternative strategies for developing products and markets have already been stated in the text. The key points are repeated here. In addition, the next section provides a more detailed analysis of the product mix of the organisation.

4.10 Marketing growth

We have already seen that the product/market matrix provides a simple and logical presentation of marketing growth. At the same time as creating growth, the alternative policies also have implications in avoiding the product obsolescence illustrated by the product life cycle.

		PRODUCTS EXISTING	PRODUCTS NEW
MARKETS	EXISTING	Market penetration	Product development
MARKETS	NEW	Market development	Diversification

(a) **Market penetration**

Increasing sales of present products or services in the same markets. This policy entails little risk. Additional expenses primarily caused by extra promotional expenditure. The policy is attractive because of its cheapness and low risk, but does not give security against changes in market structure or in quantitative aspects of demand.

(b) **Product development**

New or improved products are made available for unchanged markets. Initially, the company faces expenses of marketing research and product research/development. Later, all the expense of a marketing launch will be incurred. However, the company is familiar with the market and the distribution system appropriate to it. The changing needs of the market are satisfied by new or changed products.

(c) **Market development**

The manufacturer attempts to sell existing products in new markets. This is usually taken to mean new geographical markets but it could refer to new potential customers within present geographical limits. The company is unfamiliar with the new markets and their distribution systems. It may have to increase its sales force, and will incur expensive promotion bills. This policy gives production economies of scale, and provides against a decline in the company's traditional market.

(d) **Diversification**

Although this term is often loosely used to describe any change in a company's area of business, Ansoff uses it specifically to represent marketing of new products/services to potential customer groups who are not in the company's existing markets. If executed rapidly, the policy may be risky, expensive (especially as takeover/merger are often the tactics used to acquire new products or customers) and disintegrative to management. A slower, carefully planned approach would spread the expense and reduce the risk, whilst improving security of profits by broadening both customer and profit base.

4.11 Integration

Horizontal integration is the merging or acquisition of competing businesses. In marketing terms, this may be a good way to reduce competition, and it is sometimes done so that a larger organisation may gain access to the products or markets of a smaller one.

Vertical integration occurs in two directions, backwards and forwards. Backwards vertical integration refers to, for example, the acquisition of a supplier by a manufacturer, or of a wholesaler or manufacturer by a retailer. In this way, companies may guarantee that their sales are not restricted by supply shortages. Forwards vertical integration is the acquisition by a company of one of the destinations for its products. A manufacturer might acquire its dealers, or some retail outlets. In effect, such businesses are improving their distribution by gaining control over middlemen.

5 PRODUCT MIX

5.1 The concept of product mix

Definition The product mix is the composite of products offered for sale by a firm or business unit (American Marketing Association).

This definition could be amended to allow for services, since such organisations as banks and insurance companies face similar mix decisions to those of manufacturers. A useful way of presenting the product mix is pictorially, like an organisation chart. If we consider a fictitious tool company which manufactures spanners, adjustable spanners, sockets and screwdrivers, the diagram on the following page might apply.

5.2 Product line

For a definition of the term product line, it is best to turn once again to the American Marketing Association:

Definition A group of products that are closely related either because they satisfy a class of need, are used together, are sold to the same customer groups, are marketed through the same type outlets or fall within given price ranges.

In the example shown over page, sockets are a line, spanners are a line, etc. All the products within each line satisfy the same general need, although there are small differences between each item.

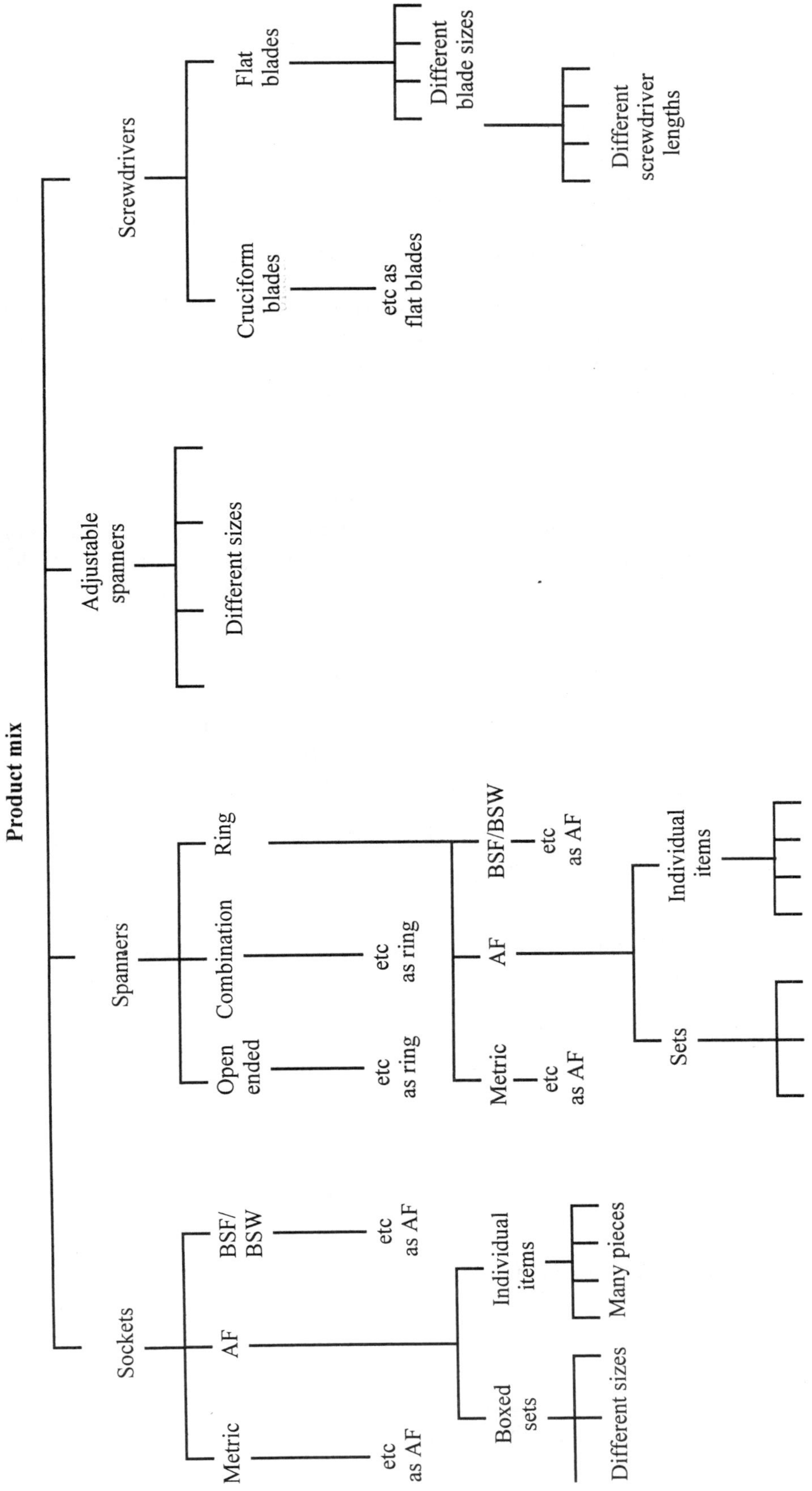
Product mix
Sockets
Metric
etc as AF
AF
Boxed sets
Different sizes
Individual items
Many pieces
BSF/ BSW
etc as AF
Spanners
Open ended
etc as ring
Combination
etc as ring
Ring
Metric
etc as AF
AF
Sets
Individual items
BSF/BSW
etc as AF
Adjustable spanners
Different sizes
Screwdrivers
Cruciform blades
etc as flat blades
Flat blades
Different blade sizes
Different screwdriver lengths

5.3 Width, depth and consistency

Philip Kotler, in Marketing Management, Analysis, Planning & Control, considers the product mix in terms of its width, depth and consistency.

The **width** of a product mix is the number of different lines it contains. In our example there are four: spanners, adjustable spanners, sockets and screwdrivers.

The **depth** of the product mix is the number of different product items in each line. In the tool company example, the product mix is deep because, as in the case of ring spanners, there are different items to suit different types of thread, different items to suit different sizes of thread, and different ways of presenting the items as either individual pieces or sets. The company's product mix is fairly deep in spanners, sockets and screwdrivers but not very deep in the case of adjustable spanners.

The **consistency** of the product mix is the extent to which the company's products are closely linked. In the example we are considering, the mix is fairly consistent because all the lines are hand tools. The odd man out is screwdrivers. All the other products are concerned with tightening or loosening nuts and bolts. If the product mix consisted of spanners, adjustable spanners and sockets, it would be even more consistent.

5.4 Product mix policy

Manufacturers adopt different product mix policies in many situations to suit their overall marketing strategy. Heinz product mix is both wide and deep, with many different lines (considerably more than 57) and many product items in several of the lines (for example, the varieties of canned soup).

Some companies, however, prefer to specialise and consequently offer fewer lines and products in a small, highly consistent mix. The Kiwi Shoe Polish Company is an example.

The former policy is used where the company has acquired expertise and experience which can easily be applied to new products and, sometimes, new markets. It has the advantage of causing expansion and of providing for change by putting the company's eggs in several baskets.

In the latter case, the organisation has a more conservative view, preferring to maximise its efficiency in a single market. This can be a sound policy where the market is not declining, and where the competition is not too fierce.

Generally, as business organisations become older and larger, they increase the width and depth of their product mix and reduce its consistency.

6 METHODS OF CONSUMER AND MARKET RESEARCH

6.1 Marketing research defined

The American Marketing Association describes marketing research as:

Definition The systematic gathering, recording and analysing of data about problems relating to the marketing of goods and services.

Many people use the terms marketing research and market research in the same way, although strictly the latter refers to markets, their sizes, structures, and characteristics.

6.2 Desk research

One of the simplest ways to collect marketing research data is to use all the information which is already available in written form. This is desk research, or secondary research.

There are many sources of secondary data:

(a) **The company itself**

Every business, in its sales records or customer records, has information which can be useful to the marketing department.

(b) **Government information**

Government data is available in many forms, for example, monthly and annual abstracts of statistics, and Customs and Excise returns. Information available includes production details covering many different categories of products, imports and exports, and population demographic data.

(c) **Press**

Newspaper and trade press articles can sometimes be relevant.

(d) **Trade associations**

These organisations frequently collect and publish data about their industry.

(e) **Specialist publications**

Several organisations regularly produce marketing research publications, particularly in the consumer goods area.

The above are some of the most important sources of secondary information. This form of marketing research has several drawbacks:

(a) The information is always historical and sometimes several years out of date.

(b) Accuracy can be suspect.

(c) Data is rarely available in the exact form required by the researcher.

Secondary research is very useful, despite these disadvantages. If existing published data appears to be up-to-date, accurate and appropriate it can avoid the need for an expensive survey. Secondly, it can reduce the scope of a marketing research exercise by providing some of the answers, and by assisting in the drafting of lists from which samples may be drawn.

6.3 Primary research methods

When a research problem cannot be solved by using secondary research methods, the company must resort to primary research. This means that it must itself initiate an investigation.

The three basic methods in primary research are:

(a) experimentation;
(b) observation; and
(c) survey.

6.4 Experimental method

Users of the experimental method attempt to investigate only one variable at a time, keeping all other factors constant.

Examples of the experimental approach can be found in advertisement testing, where alternative advertisement designs can be assessed in otherwise identical marketing situations, and in package testing.

Theoretically, any marketing mix variable could be tested. The method for setting up a test would be similar to that set out below, which describes how to carry out a sales area test in the market place.

(a) Select areas which are as nearly identical as possible and which represent the market for the tested product.

(b) Ensure that all factors except that being tested are as nearly identical as possible. In a sales area test, this means using similar distribution outlets in comparable positions within the area.

(c) Record sales in each area before the variable is introduced.

(d) Set up the new variable in all except one or two areas. These are the control areas, in which previous marketing mix settings are maintained.

(e) Measure sales while the tested variable is set up, and afterwards. Differences between the test-variable areas and the control areas are due to the effects of the test variable.

In practice, it is difficult to find test areas which resemble each other closely, and non-tested variables tend to alter during the test due to factors beyond the researchers' control.

6.5 Test marketing

(a) **Objectives**

Test marketing is usually associated with new product development. After management is satisfied with the new product's functional performance and the product's packaging has been designed, a brand name fixed and a preliminary marketing programme determined, it is often considered appropriate for it to be tested under authentic consumer conditions. The purpose of test marketing is for management to learn how consumers, middlemen and dealers react to handling, using and repurchasing the actual product and to be able to estimate the potential size of the market. Not all companies choose the route of test marketing, however it is widely accepted that test marketing can yield valuable information about buyers, dealers, market programme effectiveness (in terms of pricing, distribution channels, advertising and other forms of promotion), market potential, and other matters.

Test marketing can also be used when management wishes to relaunch a product, change any of its features or alter it's market programme (particularly in terms of pricing and promotion).

The amount of test marketing is influenced by the investment cost and risk on the one hand, and the time pressure and research cost on the other. High investment/risk products warrant test marketing so as to reduce the possibility of error with the cost of the test marketing being an insignificant percentage of the total cost of the project itself. In other words new-product categories (particularly those that are innovative and have novel features), warrant more test marketing than product relaunch or product or market programme modification. However the amount of test marketing may be curtailed if the company is under pressure to introduce the product, or make changes to an existing product, quickly because competitors are just about to launch their new brands or the season is just starting. Management would then need to balance the risk of losing market penetration on a highly successful product.

(b) **Methods of consumer-goods market testing**

In testing the actions of consumers to a product, management wants to estimate the main determinants of sales, namely, trial, first repeat, adoption, and purchase frequency. There are a number of different buying behaviours, such as high first repeat but rapid **'wear-out'**, or high permanent adoption but low frequency of purchase and so on. In market-testing **'the trade'**, management will endeavour to learn how many and what types of dealers will handle the product, under what terms, and with what shelf-position commitments.

The major methods of consumer-goods test marketing, from the least to the most costly are:

- sales wave research,
- simulated store technique,

- controlled test marketing, and
- test markets.

- Sales wave research

  This is a research technique by which selected consumers who initially try the product offered by free sample, are re-offered the product at slightly reduced prices. They may be re-offered the product as many as three to six times (sales waves), the company noting the repeat purchases pattern and reported levels of satisfaction. Sales wave research can also include exposing consumers to different advertising concepts in rough form to see what impact the advertising has on repeat purchases. This method of research enables the company to estimate the repeat-purchase rate under conditions in which consumers spend their own money and choose among competing brands. On the other hand it does not provide details about the trial rates, nor does it indicate the brand's power to gain distribution and favourable shelf position from the trade.

- Simulated store technique

  This is a research technique by which thirty to forty shoppers are found (often randomly in a large shopping centre) and invited to a brief screening of some television advertisements. Included in a number of well known commercials is one advertising the new product, but it is not singled out for attention. The consumers are given a small amount of money and invited into a store where they may use the money to buy any items or keep the money. The company records how many consumers buy the new product and competing brands. The consumers are asked the reasons for their purchase or non purchase. Some weeks later they are interviewed by phone to determine product attitudes, usage, satisfaction and re-purchase intention. This method of research has several advantages, including the projection of trial rates (and repeat rates if extended), advertising effectiveness, speed of results, and competitive comparisons. The results are usually incorporated into mathematical models to project ultimate sales levels.

- Controlled test marketing

  This is a research technique by which a controlled panel of stores agree to carry new products for a certain fee. The company offering the new product carefully selects the number of stores and geographical locations. The company delivers the product to the participating stores and controls shelf location, number of facings, displays and point-of-sale promotions, and pricing according to pre-specified plans. Sales results can be audited both from shelf movement and from consumer diaries. The company can also test small-scale advertising in local newspapers during the test.

- Test markets

  Test markets are used to test the total marketing mix for a product in a small area of a national market. Test markets are often used prior to the national launch of a new product or where an established product is to be re-marketed. For consumer products, test markets areas are often linked to television areas especially where consumer advertising emphasises the use of television. In industrial marketing, depending on the product concerned, test marketing is likely to be much less formal, involving sales personnel and key customers.

(c) **Decisions facing management in setting up test markets**

In spite of the benefits of using test markets, some experts question their value. Alvin. A. Achenbaum, ('The Marketing Concept in Action') lists the following problems:

- the problem of obtaining a set of markets that is reasonably representative of the country as a whole.
- the problem of translating national media plans into local equivalents.
- the problem of estimating what is going to happen next year based on what has happened in this year's competitive environment.
- the problem of competitive knowledge of your test and of deciding whether any local counter activities are representative of what competition will do nationally at a later date.
- the problem of extraneous and uncontrollable factors such as economic conditions and weather.

The points made by Achenbaum relate in part to the decisions facing management in setting up test markets. Test marketing can cost the company several hundred thousand pounds, depending on the extent of the testings, the duration of the test, and the amount of data the company wants to collect. The major decisions called for in test marketing are:

- How many geographical areas are to be included in the test?
- Which geographical areas? No area is a perfect microcosm of the nation as a whole, some however typify aggregate national characteristics better than others. A company would look for cities or towns that have diversified industry, good media coverage, chain stores, average competitive activity and no evidence of being over tested.
- Duration of test? Test markets last anywhere from a few months to several years. The longer the product's average repurchase period, the longer the test period necessary to analyse repeat-purchase rates. On the other hand, the test duration should be shortened if competitors are rushing to the market.
- What data is required? Management will need to decide on the type of data to collect in relation to its value and cost.

(d) **The test marketing area**

Test marketing is the marketing of a limited quantity of a new or revised product in a relatively small market, to determine whether it should be launched in the total market.

It cannot be described as a classic use of the experimental method because several factors at once are tested eg, the product, its price and its promotion may all be new.

A test market area should be:

- Representative in consumption and demographic patterns of the total market.
- Served by a similar distribution system.
- Served by similar promotional media. This means that, for consumer products, TV regions are often selected as test markets. As far as possible, the distribution for the test market should coincide with the boundaries of the media and with the catchment area for shoppers.
- Reasonably close to the factory at distribution point.
- As small as is consistent with reliable results.

The longer the test period, the more reliable the results.

Test marketing is suitable for products which have a high rate of re-purchase (generally consumables with a low unit value) and for which a small-scale production system can be cheaply established.

The results of the test market can be useful to the manufacturer in several ways. It can avoid costly investment in a product which has inadequate potential, and it can provide valuable budgeting data by indicating likely sales levels. There may be useful feedback as to the incorrect setting of marketing variables, and the test market is a useful training period for the final launch.

6.6 Research by observation

The most common use of observational methods is in the investigation of retailing. For example, traffic counts in retail outlets are used to determine the numbers of people passing particular points in the store at various times of day, and during different days of the week.

Shoppers can be observed, or even photographed, at point of sale to investigate the effectiveness of a store's merchandising.

The observation of customers is a research method which is relatively free from bias, but it has limited uses and gives no indication as to customer motivation.

6.7 Research using surveys

Surveys are conducted using questionnaires, and the design of the questionnaire is therefore important in reducing bias.

In designing a questionnaire, the following points should be borne in mind:

(a) The questionnaire should include information about the interviewer, respondent, and date, time and place of the interview.

(b) Language should be colloquial, but avoid slang.

(c) Language and structure should be simple.

(d) Questions should be clear and unambiguous.

(e) Jargon should be avoided.

(f) The questionnaire should never ask more than one question at once.

(g) Questions about the same general topic should be grouped together.

(h) There should be no 'leading' questions.

The initial design of a questionnaire may be tested by carrying out a pilot survey. This will indicate the results likely from the main survey, and will allow the correction of any faults in the questionnaire or survey method.

The researchers must decide whether the questionnaire is to be completed by the respondent alone, or by an interviewer. The former choice requires a simpler questionnaire with a full explanation of every stage.

The questionnaire may be sent by mail, completed by interview on the telephone or by personal interview.

Use of the mail is cheap and allows a broad geographic coverage. However, the response rate may be low, and the addressee may delegate completion of the form to a subordinate. The questionnaire needs to be short and simple, and it is difficult to assemble a good mailing list.

Telephone interviews limit the researchers to those respondents who have a telephone. This is not a significant disadvantage in industrial marketing research, but the method discriminates against lower socio-economic groups in consumer surveys. Telephone interviewing can be relatively fast and cheap, and the interviewer can explain questions to assist the respondent.

Personal interviews may be held:

(a) In the street or other public place. Here the interviewer may have difficulty categorising the respondent. The questionnaire should be fairly short and simple.

(b) At or near the point of purchase. This is a useful method if the questionnaire is concerned with a particular type of product or retail outlet.

(c) At home. Socio-economic stratification can be achieved by selecting appropriate households in identified areas of towns and cities. Long interviews can be conducted in this way.

(d) At work. This is used in industrial research. It can be difficult to obtain an interview with a busy manager, but long and complex questionnaires can be completed in this way. A prior appointment is advisable.

Selection and training of a team of interviewers, their supervision and the checking of their work, are most important.

6.8 Activity

A company's strategy - the concept of its business - provides an idea of the sort of area where it ought to look for new opportunities. You will recall that we previously discussed forecasting and analysis of opportunities open to the company. However, neither of these is quite the same as looking for market opportunities - forecasting assesses what is likely to happen and can only take account of known or likely circumstances; analysing opportunities assumes that the market opportunities have already presented themselves.

Reflect on your own organisation, or any other experience you have, and describe the different ways by which an organisation can look for opportunities.

6.9 Activity solution

The organisation can look for opportunities in one of four ways:

(a) **Undirected viewing**

Here the organisation maintains general contacts, keeps an eye on general literature, general trends etc, with no particular purpose but in the hope that some useful information will emerge.

(b) **Conditioned viewing**

Here the organisation maintains contacts in more specific areas (eg, City lunches). General literature is still scanned but the 'scanner' is pre-disposed towards certain areas. He is not looking for anything in particular but will be more likely to find it in, say the Financial Times than the Guardian. When he comes across a piece of information of the type to which he has been 'conditioned' he will assess the significance of it.

(c) **Informal search**

This differs from conditioned viewing in that the organisation has decided in advance what sort of information it is looking for. However, the methods used are fairly formal and unstructured. If, for instance, a company has begun to think about the possibility of taking over another company, it will make tentative soundings to discover companies likely to be in the market.

(d) **Formal search**

This differs from informal search in that a more deliberate effort is made to obtain the right sort of information. Thus if a company has decided that a take-over is desirable, it will seek expert opinion on potential candidates.

7 PANELS AND ADVERTISING RESEARCH

7.1 Use of panels

Panel research is continuous research, that is research which is conducted over a considerable length of time at regular intervals.

Panels are groups of respondents who are selected to represent particular markets, and are individually researched on several occasions.

An example of panel research is the retail audit. Samples of various categories of retailer are visited by the auditor at regular intervals. The auditor notes the following:

(a) Products available for sale, different pack sizes, flavours, etc.
(b) Prices of each.
(c) Stock levels of each.
(d) Purchases of each since the previous audit.
(e) Any special promotions.

The auditor can calculate sales since the preceding visit by the following means:

Sales = Previous audited stock + Purchases - Current audited stock.

Retail audits are useful to both manufacturers and retailers by providing the following information:

(a) Geographic region sales patterns.
(b) Sales levels of all manufacturers' products.
(c) Details of any current promotions.

The home audit is a continuous panel research activity which can provide information complementary to that of the retail audit.

The housewife is visited by researchers at regular intervals. Stocks in the house are noted, together with details of the goods she has purchased since the previous visit. The latter have been recorded in a 'diary' of purchases (alternatively, the wrappers or containers of grocery goods can be stored after emptying in a plastic bag or similar container; this is the 'dustbin' method).

The results of a home audit differ from those of a retail audit in that they give a socio-economic breakdown of customers.

Home audit techniques are used to carry out audience and readership research in the media.

To maintain a representative panel, members have to be replaced after they have been researched several times. This is known as mortality.

7.2 Advertising research

There are two main types of advertising research:

(1) Pre-testing, which is carried out to determine the effectiveness of a trial advertisement before it is run, and

(2) Post-testing, which measures the effect of advertisements which have run.

(a) **Pre-testing can use several techniques:**

- Depth interviews with individuals about draft advertisements, to give an initial idea of the way the advertisement will work. The same approach can be adopted with groups of respondents.

- Folder tests for press advertisements. Respondents are given a folder containing a series of advertisements, including the one being tested. After the folder has been handed back, the respondent is asked to complete a questionnaire testing detailed recall of the advertisement. A modern alternative is to publish a special magazine or newspaper for use instead of the folder.

- Theatre testing. This is used to pre-test TV advertisements. A representative audience is collected into a room in which it is shown a series of films, including the tested advertisement and other advertisements. After the showing, the audience is asked to complete questionnaires which will reveal the effectiveness of the tested advertisement.

- Technical devices. An example is the tachistoscope, which is a projector that is adjustable to allow the image of a trial advertisement to be shown for variable, extremely short periods of time.

  Alternative designs are shown to respondents, initially for a very short duration. The duration of the image is increased until the respondents recognise the words on the advertisement. The design which has greatest visual impact is that which is recognisable during the shortest exposure.

  Another gadget is the psycho-galvanometer. This device measures changes in the electrical resistance of the skin, which is affected by perspiration. The higher the reading of the psycho-galvanometer, the greater is the arousal caused by the advertisement being shown.

  There are many other pieces of equipment which can be used for similar purposes in pre- testing.

(b) **Post-testing can be carried out in three basic ways:**

- Sales of the product during and after the advertising campaign, when compared with sales levels before the advertisement was run, should give a good indication of effectiveness.

- A survey can be conducted to establish the extent of consumer recall about the advertisement, and detailed aspects of it.

- Questionnaires designed to evaluate attitudes about the product can be issued before and after the advertisement campaign. The difference between the two sets of responses should be mainly attributable to the advertisements.

We have looked in detail at panel research and advertising research because they are important examples of marketing research. However, research can be carried out into all areas of the marketing mix, and into all market variables including customer attitudes and motivation.

8 DEVELOPING NEW PRODUCTS AND SERVICES

8.1 Product development

An organisation may decide that consolidation in its present markets/products does not present enough opportunities. This will lead them to search for alternatives which build upon their present knowledge and skills. In the case of product development the organisation will maintain the security of its present markets while changing or developing products.

Retailing organisations follow the changing patterns of customer needs by a policy of continually introducing new product lines. If a company is particularly good at research and development, it will also try to bring new products or services onto the market. Product development becomes an essential requirement when product life cycles are short eg, in consumer electronics.

8.2 Strategies

Attempting to gain market dominance by being first to launch a new product is known as an offensive strategy. This strategy can be successful and result in the market being captured by the first entrant eg, VAX produced a combination floor cleaner for domestic use. This strategy is the high risk strategy and careful market analysis is important in order to reduce the risk of launching a product that is not currently wanted.

The defensive strategy involves a more cautious approach to the market, often allowing a competitor to test the demand and build up a consumer response before launching their own product. The approach is to ensure that the company adopts a strategy which makes use of developments. The exploitation of developments may make use of product innovations of competitors, seeking to improve on them or at least differentiate from the original merchandise.

9 CHAPTER SUMMARY

Marketing is the sum total of activities that keep a company focused on its customers and with good management ensure that the company's offerings are valued by its customers. The marketing concept has such a potent force that a company's basic strategic vision is relevant to its marketing concept, although in some cases the reverse is true as well.

Marketing management is the sustained effort to achieve desired exchange outcomes with target consumers. The marketer's basic skill lies in analysing and segmenting markets, determining the needs and wants of target consumers, and regulating the level, quality, timing and character of the organisation's offerings. For this reason marketing information is a critical input into effective marketing, and marketing research is an essential activity. Marketing research uses both secondary and primary data collection methods, and panels are often used as part of the latter. Test marketing is an important aspect of marketing research and provides very meaningful management information.

10 SELF-TEST QUESTIONS

10.1 Distinguish between consumer goods and industrial goods (1.5).

10.2 List the five levels in Maslow's need hierarchy (2.2).

10.3 What are the stages in the purchase decision? (2.6).

10.4 Define market segmentation (4.1).

10.5 List the different bases by which a consumer market may be segmented (4.2).

10.6 List the main sources of secondary data (6.2).

10.7 Describe the major methods of consumer-goods test marketing (6.5).

10.8 Describe the techniques used in both the pre- and post- testing of advertising effectiveness (7.2).

11 EXAMINATION TYPE QUESTION

11.1 MARKETING CONCEPT

You are required to:

(a) explain the 'marketing concept' and its implications for an organisation; **(9 marks)**

(b) distinguish between 'customer' and 'consumer' and indicate the importance to a marketing executive of the distinction; **(8 marks)**

(c) explain to what extent, and why, an organisation offering a service (as opposed to a physical product) would require marketing research. **(8 marks)**

(Total: 25 marks)

12 ANSWER TO EXAMINATION TYPE QUESTION

12.1 MARKETING CONCEPT

(a) The idea behind the 'marketing concept' is that the consumer is the vital factor ('the consumer is sovereign') and it is the satisfaction of his or her needs which is paramount. For this reason, the enterprise is in direct communication with the consumers, using the techniques of marketing research to ensure that all production is founded upon the needs which have been identified in accordance with characteristics determined.

Demand and supply are thus optimised (balanced) in such a way that economies of scale are able to be undertaken - resulting in 'mass production'.

The opposite to this concept lies in the idea of 'production orientation', where major problems are defined as problems of production and the majority of effort is devoted to techniques of production. This arose from the arrival of the industrial revolution and mass markets in which there was usually no direct manufacturer-consumer link.

However, the acceptance of the marketing concept gives rise to a number of organisational changes and, for one thing, the 'drive' of the enterprise is altered. The organisation now understands that it exists in order to satisfy consumer needs. The unsuccessful organisation is one which does not do this. There must thus be effort on the part of the enterprise to identify and satisfy such needs.

The function of marketing is created in order to identify needs and therefore is seen to possess a major influence for corporate performance and corporate strategy. Production - working to marketing needs - has to produce products in accordance with identifiable needs.

However, the marketing concept is not the exclusive preserve of firms. Any type of organisation which allows its users to make the decision as to the nature of the service offered (eg, opening hours) has adopted the concept.

Therefore, the organisation which follows this approach becomes consumer-oriented, produces products to satisfy a demand which is known, and usually is able to adopt mass production as its manufacturing technique.

(b) Irrespective of the customer or consumer role, as such, executives in marketing are directly involved in the processes of customers buying and consuming the products of their organisation which are being put on to the market. Any buying decision involves:

- the influences which affect the decision to buy;
- the buying decision itself;
- the act of buying (by the customer); and
- the consumption of the goods/services (by the consumer).

The customer role is the purchasing role, and the user role is the consumer role. On many occasions, someone buys something to be used by someone else (as in the case of, say, a birthday present).

In industrial markets (where the customers themselves are organisations) the person actually buying is the purchasing manager (or whoever has this role) and sometimes the individual could be a relatively junior member of the hierarchy. But the actual consumers (users) may well be occupying different grades in that hierarchy. In the consumer markets (where the buyers are individual persons, not organisations) the purchase of some products may be differentiated. In the case of, say, washing-up liquid, the person who does the washing-up is likely to be the buyer.

A clear instance of the importance of the distinction being discussed here lies in the purchase of, say, a tin of meat from the corner shop. The customer may well be the user (or only one of the users) whereas the shop may have obtained the tin through a wholesale unit (so the shop is a customer here but not, obviously, the consumer). The middleman may have a similar relationship in relation to the producers of the tin of meat. This means that there have been three steps in this buying-selling process – and in two of these the customer is not the consumer.

The point is that the marketing executive has to deal with markets and demand. To be effective, the executive has to be able to identify each specific need/demand. It is not sufficient to look only at the actual buying role. The market must be segmented.

(c) The concept of marketing relates to the organisational awareness that it is necessary to know every factor of the organisational activity which is concerned with customer-attitude to the current/future output of the enterprise. Marketing is an entity which is incorporated in the activity which creates viability of production, and which includes the selling activity.

Service-producing organisations need to consider specific marketing attributes in particular, and these are:

- Opportunity analysis must be carried out carefully - the 'target markets' need to be assessed and market segments determined. This enables needs of different customer groupings to be considered and suitable services generated for each.
- The service offered will have the elements of:
  - the offering itself;
  - the terms of sale (contract);
  - the manner in which the service is to be distributed;
  - the communication with the market and potential customers.

However, in marketing a service it must be realised that there is no way in which the service can be stored and warehoused:

- it is produced and consumed at once;
- services cannot be generated and held back for future sales.

Services are also directly linked to human beings and offered (sold) directly by the person providing the service. There is therefore no 'middleman'.

The many different types of service-providing organisation (churches, circuses, car hire firms, theatres, cinemas, TV companies, governments, and so on) all require the marketing approach.

17 MAINTAINING SERVICES - QUALITY

INTRODUCTION & LEARNING OBJECTIVES

'Quality' and 'quality management' are widely used business terms which can be interpreted in different ways. The terms could mean that the organisation operates a formal and comprehensive quality control system, or they may merely signify that the aim of the organisation is to produce quality products or services without any formal method or process to achieve it.

One of the problems with the term 'quality' is that it is a relative measure and often difficult to quantify; one person's judgement of quality is very unlikely to be exactly the same as another person's.

By developing the right approach to quality, organisations can benefit by 'getting it right first time' and avoiding the problems that faulty goods and dissatisfied customers can bring.

The Japanese commitment to total quality management (TQM) is widely held to be one of the main reasons for the success of Japanese companies in achieving international competitive advantage.

Although quality is subjective, as far as business is concerned it needs to be measured. We will be discussing the International and British standards and the role that they play.

The publication of **In Search of Excellence** by Peters and Waterman challenged the conventional thought of the time and the research findings focus on the excellence factors of companies in the USA.

When you have studied this chapter you should be able to do the following:

- Explain the concept of quality.
- Discuss the ideas of Deming, Crosby, Juran, Feigenbaum, Ishikawa and Taguchi.
- Outline the difference between 'quality control' and 'quality assurance'.
- Analyse the role of total quality management .
- Discuss the characteristics of a successful organisation.
- Describe how quality is monitored and maintained.
- Explain what the barriers to quality might be.
- Discuss the role of quality audits, assessments and reviews.

1 THE CONCEPT OF QUALITY

1.1 Introduction

In recent times a great deal of attention has been devoted to quality issues. Although there has always been a general awareness of the need to ensure the satisfaction of the customer, it is the worldwide nature of competition that has focused attention on the need to act. Competitor pressure has often come from the Japanese, whose basic premise is that poor quality is unacceptable.

The term 'quality' is difficult to define because it has a wide range of meanings, covering a large and complex area of businesses and processes. Quality is also a matter of perception and relative measure. For example, if you asked a group of people to each nominate a 'quality sound system', it could be that you would get a different suggestion from each of them.

The Japanese have shown, with their highly competitive products, that high quality does not always mean high cost. The response in the West to improve quality is still really in its infancy.

Before we consider various approaches to improve quality, it is useful for us to consider the extent of **quality related costs**. Such costs exist because resources are wasted as a result of errors, poor workmanship, poor systems and poor communication. A recent statement from an executive from IBM stresses the importance of understanding the costs of quality. He suggests that '..measurement is the heart of any improvement process. If something can't be measured, it cannot be improved'.

1.2 Quality related costs

A report *'The effectiveness of the corporate overhead in British business'* Develin & Partners 1989, estimates that the average cost of waste and mistakes in the UK represents 20% of controllable corporate overhead.

(a) **Quality related costs**

Definition Cost of ensuring and assuring quality, as well as loss incurred when quality is not achieved. Quality costs are classified as prevention cost, appraisal cost, internal failure cost and external failure cost.

(b) **Prevention costs**

Definition The cost incurred to reduce appraisal cost to a minimum.

(c) **Appraisal costs**

Definition The cost incurred, such as for inspection and testing, in initially ascertaining and ensuring conformance of the product to quality requirements.

(d) **Internal failure costs**

Definition The cost arising from inadequate quality before the transfer of ownership from supplier to purchaser.

(e) **External failure costs**

Definition The cost arising from inadequate quality discovered after the transfer of ownership from supplier to purchaser such as complaints, warranty claims and recall cost.

2 QUALITY MANAGEMENT

2.1 Management role

Quality management suggests a concern that the organisation's products or services meet their planned level of quality and perform to specifications. Management has a duty to ensure that all tasks are completed consistently to a standard which meets the needs of the business. To achieve this they need to:

(a) set clear standards;
(b) plan how to meet those standards
(c) track the quality achieved;
(d) take action to improve quality where necessary.

(a) **Setting standards**

To manage quality everyone in the organisation needs to have a clear and shared understanding of the standards required. These standards will be set after taking account of:

- the quality expected by the customers;
- the costs and benefits of delivering different degrees of quality;
- the impact of different degrees of quality on:

(i) the customers and their needs;
(ii) contribution to departmental objectives;
(iii) employee attitude and motivation.

Having decided on the standards these must be communicated to everyone concerned to ensure that the right standards are achieved. Documentation of the standards must be clear, specific, measurable and comprehensive.

(b) **Meeting the standards**

Having decided on appropriate quality standards management should then:

(i) agree and document procedures and methods to meet the standards;

(ii) agree and document controls to ensure that the standards will be met;

(iii) agree and document responsibilities via job descriptions and terms of reference; and

(iv) prepare and implement training plans for employees to ensure they are familiar with the standards, procedures, controls and their responsibilities.

(c) **Tracking the quality**

After the process to achieve quality has been set up, an information system to monitor the quality should be set up. This is called quality control.

When a good system to track the quality has been achieved, it can be used constructively to improve quality and work on problem areas.

Employees within the organisation have a huge influence on the quality of their work and to gain their commitment and support the management should:

(i) publish the quality being achieved;

(ii) meet regularly with the staff involved to discuss the quality being achieved as well as the vulnerabilities and priorities as they see them and also agree specific issues and action points for them to work on to improve quality;

(iii) encourage ideas from the staff about improvements and consider introducing short-term suggestion schemes.

2.2 Quality revolution

Tom Peters in his book *Thriving on Chaos*, concentrates on the twelve attributes of a quality revolution.

(i) Management obsessed with quality.

(ii) A guiding system or ideology.

(iii) Quality is measured.

(iv) Reward for quality.

(v) Training in technologies for assessing qualities.

(vi) Teams involving multiple functions or systems are used.

(vii) Concentration on small improvements.

(viii) Constant stimulation.

(ix) Creation of a shadow or parallel organisation structure devoted to quality improvement.

(x) Everyone is involved. Suppliers especially, but distributors and customers too, must be a part of the organisation's quality process.

(xi) Quality improvement is the primary source of cost reduction.

(xii) Quality improvement is a never-ending journey.

These are traits which companies like IBM, Ford and Federal Express share in their quality improvement programs.

Peters argues that most quality programs fail for one of two reasons: they have a system without passion, or passion without a system. The type of system to follow, and the results obtained, causes some controversy. There are many ideologies used in quality processes. Should one follow Deming via statistical process control or Phil Crosby, author of *Quality is free* or Armand Feigenbaum's Total Quality Control or Joseph Juran's 'fitness for purpose'?

2.3 W Edwards Deming

In the 1920s and 1930s in America, statistical quality control methods were used to monitor and control the quality of output in flow line production processes. These methods, the origins of modern quality management, were introduced into Japan by American consultants like Deming, who were involved in the aid program to rejuvenate the industry in Japan after the war.

Some companies (and governments) blame unions for having a negative impact on worker productivity. Deming insists that management is 90% of the problem. Organisations need to address the problems of the quality of direction being given to the workforce, the resources available to get the job done efficiently and the opportunities for workers to contribute ideas about how to do the job better.

Deming, in his book *Quality, Productivity and Competitive Position*, suggests that improving quality leads to improved productivity, reduced costs, more satisfied customers and increased profitability. His system for management to improve quality and competitiveness covers the following main areas.

- The organisation should have a constant purpose of improving their product or service.
- Quality objectives should be agreed and action taken to accomplish them.
- Systems for production and service delivery should be improved, eliminating all waste.
- Consideration of quality and reliability should be just as important as price when choosing a supplier.
- Attention must be paid to training people so they are better at their jobs and understand how to optimise production.
- Mass inspection of goods ties up resources and does not improve quality.
- Education and self improvement should be encouraged in all members of the organisation. Management should enable staff to take a pride in their work.
- Barriers between staff areas should be broken down.

2.4 Phil B Crosby

Crosby is another theorist on quality. He is so prominent in America that General Motors bought a 10% stake in his firm. His thinking is based on his background working on the Pershing missile programme, where the main objectives were zero defects. The zero defects concept and his assertion that a product should not have to be corrected once it is built (right first time) are embodied in his four standards.

(i) Quality is conformance to standards.
(ii) Prevention is the system for advancing quality, not appraisal.
(iii) The goal should be zero defects.
(iv) The importance of quality is measured by the cost of not having quality.

The problem for Crosby's standards is that quality must be judged as the customer perceives it, as we discussed earlier. He asserts that his process is customer-oriented but companies, such as Milliken and IBM in the USA, after pounding away at quality for many years, have found that a second revolution is required - to become more responsive to customers. Crosby firmly believes that quality is not comparative, it either conforms to customer requirements or it is unacceptable. It is the role of management to make sure that the customer's needs are reflected in the specifications set within the organisation. Quality is, therefore, an attribute and not a variable.

2.5 Joseph Juran

Juran defines quality as 'fitness for purpose'. This can be described loosely as 'that which relates to the evaluation of a product or service for its ability to satisfy a given need'. The elements of this theory are:

- **quality of design**, which can include customer satisfaction which is built into the product;
- **quality of conformance**, or a lack of defects;
- **abilities**; and
- **field service**.

Because customers incorporate such things as 'value for money' in their 'fitness for purpose' equation, Juran's theory is looking at quality from the point of view of the customer and is a more practical concept.

2.6 Armand Feigenbaum

Feigenbaum emphasises the relevance of quality issues in all areas of the operation of a business. He believes that 'prevention is better than cure', stressing the importance of identifying the costs of quality in economic and accounting terms.

Organisations adopting his ideas are encouraged to change the role of the quality control function from inspecting and rejecting output to one in which quality is given a planning role, involving the design of systems and procedures to reduce the likelihood of sub-optimal production.

2.7 Kauro Ishikawa

Although modern quality management practices have their roots in the USA, some of the best Japanese principles offer significant lessons to Western organisations. Studies have shown that the success of some Japanese companies has been due to progress in design quality, especially in miniaturisation, rather than conformance quality.

The late Ishikawa is noted for his proposals on quality circles and quality control. The Ishikawa cause and effect diagram, known as the 'fishbone diagram' because of its shape, illustrates the relationship between possible causes and effect and helps to discover the source of the problem.

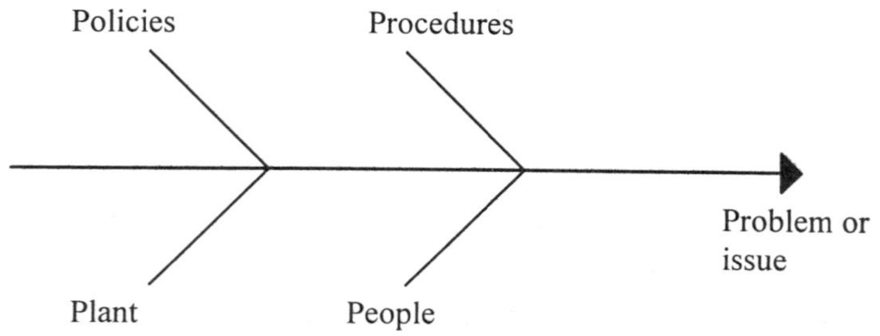

The diagram above follows the 4P pattern of policies, procedures, people and plant of non-manufacturing areas. The 5M pattern has branches comprising machinery, method, material, manpower and maintenance.

After the initial diagram has been drawn, the major causes of problems can be further expanded and treated as separate branches.

2.8 Genichi Taguchi

Taguchi developed a mathematical model of loss, measuring costs incurred or profits forgone relative to some baseline of performance. In his terms loss is more than cost. Quality is 'the loss imparted to society from the time the product is shipped'. Because goods use up time and resources in production, a measure of quality is the fact that this 'loss' is minimised.

Taguchi identifies two aspects of quality control; off-line and on-line.

(a) Off-line quality control incorporates systems design, parameter design and tolerance design. Systems design should reflect appropriate technology.

(b) On-line quality control aims to minimise the loss due to variations between goods produced, weighing the cost of the variation against the cost of correcting the variation. Examples of these variations could include slight differences in weight between identical parts or slight differences in time to produce something.

3 QUALITY CONTROL AND QUALITY ASSURANCE

3.1 The difference between quality control and quality assurance

Quality control is the title given to the more traditional view of quality. It may be defined as the process of:

(a) establishing standards of quality for a product or service;

(b) establishing procedures or production methods which ought to ensure that these required standards of quality are met in a suitably high proportion of cases;

(c) monitoring actual quality;

(d) taking control action when actual quality falls below standard.

Quality assurance, however, is the term used where a supplier guarantees the quality of goods supplied and allows the customer access while the goods are being manufactured. This is usually done through supplier quality assurance (SQA) officers, who control the specification of the goods supplied.

Some companies follow Japanese practice and use supervisors, work people or quality circles to control suppliers' quality. These representatives or the SQA officer may enter the supplier's plant, to verify that production is to the correct specification, working tolerances, material and labour standards. For example, the Ministry of Defence would reserve the right to ensure that defence contractors produce to specification, since defective work could mean the failure of a multi-million pound aircraft, loss of trained pilots and possibly ground crew as well as damage to civilian life and property. Likewise, a weapons system failure could have disastrous consequences.

One great advantage of SQA is that it may render possible reduction of the in-house quality control headcount, since there will be no need to check incoming materials or sub-assemblies or components.

3.2 Quality control

Quality control is concerned with maintaining quality standards. There are usually procedures to check quality of bought-in materials, work-in-progress and finished goods. Sometimes one or all of these functions is the responsibility of the research and development department on the premise that production should not self-regulate its own quality.

Statistical quality control through sampling techniques is commonly used to reduce costs and production interruptions. On some occasions, where quality assurance has been given, customers have the contractual right to visit a manufacturer unannounced and carry out quality checks. This is normal practice with Sainsbury's and Tesco's contracts with manufacturers producing 'own label' goods (eg, Tesco Baked Beans).

In the past, failure to screen quality successfully has resulted in rejections, re-work and scrap, all of which add to manufacturing costs. Modern trends in industry of competition, mass production and increasing standards of quality requirements have resulted in a thorough reappraisal of the problem and two important points have emerged:

(a) It is necessary to single out and remove the causes for poor quality goods before production instead of waiting for the end result. Many companies have instigated 'zero defects' programmes following the Japanese practice of eradicating poor quality as early in the chain as possible and insisting on strict quality adherence at every stage – as Crosby points out in his book *Quality is Free*, this is cost effective since customer complaints etc. reduce dramatically.

(b) The co-ordination of all activities from the preparation of the specification, through to the purchasing and inspection functions and right up to the function of delivery of the finished product, is essential.

It is accepted that it is not possible to achieve perfection in products because of the variations in raw material quality, operating skills, different types of machines used, wear and tear, etc. but quality control attempts to ascertain the amount of variation from perfect that can be expected in any operation. If this variation is acceptable according to engineering requirements, then production must be established within controlled limits and if the variation is too great then corrective action must be taken to bring it within acceptable limits.

3.3 The role of standards

The British Standards Institution, through its Certification and Assessment Services, provides industry with first class product certification and company quality assessment schemes. When an organisation operates to the quality standard BS5750 it is a way of demonstrating that the organisation is committed to quality and has been assessed accordingly.

There are three parts to the BS5750 standard:

(a) specification for design;
(b) specification for manufacture and installation;
(c) specification for final inspection and test.

In 1987 the ISO 9000 series of international standards on quality systems were published by the International Organisation for Standardisation.

This series consists of five individual standards, ISO 9000-9004. Two of them are guideline standards and the others are reference standards.

- ISO 9000 is the *Guide to Selection and Use,* which is the guide to other standards in the series.

- ISO 9001 is the *Specification for Design/Development, Production, Installation and Servicing,* covering organisations concerned with all activities from conceptual design to after-sales service.

- ISO 9002, the *Specification for Production and Installation,* concerning organisations with product and service quality in production and installation only.

- ISO 9003 is the *Specification for Final Inspection and Test.* This is for activities which can only be quality assured at final inspection and test.

- ISO 9004 is the *Guide to Quality Management and Quality System Elements*. This is a guide to good quality management practice.

Note that it is now standard practice to refer to BS5750 by its 'international' title - BS EN ISO 9000 - though the older term is often heard in conversation.

4 TOTAL QUALITY MANAGEMENT (TQM)

4.1 Approaches

Total quality management (TQM) is the name given to programmes which seek to ensure that goods are produced and services are supplied of the highest quality. Its origin lies primarily in Japanese organisations and it is argued that TQM has been a significant factor in Japanese global business success. The basic principle of TQM is that costs of prevention (getting things right first time) are less than the costs of correction.

This contrasts with the 'traditional' UK approach that less than 100% quality is acceptable as the costs of improvement from say 90% to 100% outweigh the benefits. Thus in the analysis of quality related costs there may be a trade-off between a lowering of failure (internal and external) at the expense of increased prevention and appraisal costs.

Which view is correct is a matter of debate but the advocates of TQM would argue that in addition to the cost analysis above the impact of less than 100% quality in terms of lost potential for future sales also has to be taken into account.

4.2 Features of TQM

The philosophy of TQM is based on the idea of a series of quality chains which may be broken at any point by one person or service not meeting the requirements of the customer. The key to TQM is for everyone in the organisation to have well-defined customers - an extension of the word, beyond the customers of the company, to anyone to whom an individual provides a service. Thus the 'Paint shop' staff would be customers of the 'Assembly shop' staff who would themselves be the customers of the 'Machine shop' staff. The idea is that the supplier-customer relationships would form a chain extending from the company's original suppliers through to its ultimate consumers. Areas of responsibility would need to be identified and a manager allocated to each, and then the customer/supplier chain established. True to the principle outlined above the quality requirements of each 'customer' within the chain would be assessed, and meeting these would then become the responsibility of the 'suppliers' who form the preceding link in the chain.

Quality has to be managed - it will just not happen. To meet the requirements of TQM a company will probably need to recruit more staff and may also need to change the level of services on offer to its customers, which includes 'internal' customers. This would probably entail costs in terms of the redesign of systems, recruitment and training of staff, and the purchase of appropriate equipment.

Thackray indicated the following features of companies which follow TQM:

(a) There is absolute commitment by the chief executive and all senior managers to doing what is needed to change the culture.

(b) People are not afraid to try new things.

(c) Communication is excellent and multi-way.

(d) There is a real commitment to continuous improvement in all processes.

(e) Attention is focused first on the process and second on the results.

(f) There is an absence of strict control systems.

The last two points appear to go against the central thrust of UK management accounting. The point being made is that concentrating on getting a process right will result in an improved result. A process is a detailed step in the overall system of producing and delivering goods to a customer. Improving a process without worrying about the short-term effects will encourage the search for improvement to take place, the improvement will more likely be permanent, and will lead to further improvements. A concentration on results and control generally means attaching blame to someone if things go wrong.

Therefore employees would not have an incentive to pick up and correct errors but rather would be encouraged to try and conceal them.

4.3 Analysis and restructuring of resources

In many businesses, employees' time is used up in **discretionary activities**. Discretionary activities are activities such as checking, chasing and other tasks related to product failures. Some/most of this time may be capable of being redeployed into the two other categories of work:

(a) Core activities, and
(b) Support activities.

Core activities add direct value to the business. They use the specific skills of the particular employees being examined and are the reason for their employment. Support activities are those activities which clearly support core activities and are thus necessary to allow core activities to add value. The importance of this analysis can be seen in a quote from a US Chief Executive some years ago: 'The only things you really need to run a business are materials, machines, workers and salesmen. Nobody else is justified unless he's helping the worker produce more product or the salesman sell more product.'

Analysis of employees' time will provide a clearer view of the costs of poor quality and whether efforts in other departments could reduce the amount of time spent by a department further down the product chain on discretionary activities. For example, suppose there are seven processes from purchasing of raw materials through various stages of production to delivery of the product to the customer. If each process is 90% effective then there will be only a 48% success rate at the end of the seventh stage (90% x 90% x 90% etc). What happens in practice however may be that personnel employed in stage 4 of the process spend a lot of their time on discretionary activities trying to remedy the effect of defects at earlier stages. It is suggested that it would be more sensible for departments in the earlier stages to get things right the first time.

An example has been quoted of an office equipment supplier which analysed employees' time into core, support and discretionary activities. It was found that half of the salesmen's face-to-face selling time with customers consisted of listening to their complaints about poor customer service.

4.4 Quality circles

Quality circles consist of about ten employees possessing relevant levels of skill, ranging from the shop-floor through to management. They meet regularly to discuss the major aspect of quality, but other areas such as safety and productivity will also be dealt with.

The main aim is to be able to offer management:

(a) ideas connected with improvement and recommendation;
(b) possible solutions and suggestions;
(c) organising the implementation of (a) and (b).

The development of Quality circles allows the process of decision making to start at shop floor level, with the ordinary worker encouraged to comment and make suggestions, as well as being allowed to put them into practice. Circle members experience the responsibility for ensuring quality, and have the power to exercise verbal complaint. quality circles may be applied at any level of organisational activity, being used to cover all aspects and could conceivably involve all employees.

Jaguar, the established motor company, has effectively used this system resulting in the involvement of ten percent of the workforce. A notable point here is that in one decade the number of quality inspectors required has been roughly halved. Clearly, quality circles are a practical means of gaining employee participation, they are not mainly for reducing costs although this aspect will be a major topic for discussion. Other benefits are, increased awareness of shop-floor problems, members gain confidence over problem solving etc, greater output, improved quality and shop-floor participation.

Equally, putting this system into practice can prove difficult. The well established system of hierarchical management is difficult to penetrate, and to some organisations it would present extreme changes. Some systems may not be able to accommodate such change, eg, the armed forces or Police Force where a powerful hierarchy has developed.

5 THE PURSUIT OF EXCELLENCE: CHARACTERISTICS OF A SUCCESSFUL ORGANISATION

5.1 Peters and Waterman

Tom Peters and Robert Waterman, in their book *In Search of Excellence*, identified certain core values that were associated with 'excellent' organisations. These have already been discussed in an earlier chapter, but are repeated here for convenience.

(a) **A bias for action:** the excellent companies get on with it. They are analytical in their decision making but this does not paralyse them as it does some companies.

(b) **Close to the customer:** they get to know their customers and provide them with quality, reliability and service.

(c) **Autonomy and entrepreneurship:** leaders and innovators are fostered and given scope.

(d) **Productivity through people:** they really believe that the basis for quality and productivity is the employee. They do not just pay lip service to the notion 'people are our most important asset'. They do something about it by encouraging commitment and getting everyone involved.

(e) **Hands-on, value driven:** the people who run the organisation get close to those who work for them and ensure that the organisation's values are understood and acted upon.

(f) **Stick to the knitting:** the successful organisations stay reasonably close to the businesses they know.

(g) **Simple form, lean staff:** the organisation structure is simple and corporate staff are kept to the minimum.

(h) **Simultaneous loose-tight properties:** they are both centralised and decentralised. They push decisions and autonomy as far down the organisation as they can get, into individual units and profit centres. But, as Peters and Waterman state, 'they are fanatic centralists around the few core values they hold dear'.

Though Peters and Waterman stress the positive benefits of having a strong organisational culture there are also potential drawbacks.

(a) Strong cultures are difficult to change.

(b) Strong cultures may stress inappropriate values.

(c) Where two strong cultures come into contact, eg in a merger, then conflicts can arise.

(d) A strong culture may not be attuned to the environment, eg a strong innovative culture is only appropriate in a dynamic, shifting environment.

Despite these problems it is still possible to agree with Alan Sugar, Chairman of Amstrad, who said in 1987 'It is essential to retain a strong corporate culture and philosophy, otherwise the business can drift and become confused and lost in direction'.

5.2 Goldsmith and Clutterbuck

Other studies on excellence have followed Peters and Waterman. Goldsmith and Clutterbuck in *The Winning Streak,* made some observations on the characteristics of top British companies. They showed a similarity to those quoted for American corporations.

The factors in the British companies were:

(a) **leadership**, with visible top management and clear objectives;
(b) **autonomy,** with encouragement to take 'controlled initiative';
(c) **control**, with detailed planning but an ability to deal with the unexpected;
(d) **involvement**, which is a commitment and a positive attitude at all levels;
(e) **market orientation**;
(f) **zero basing**, or keeping in touch with the fundamentals;
(g) **innovation**, a recognition that innovation and change is the norm;
(h) **integrity**, with everyone knowing where they stand.

5.3 The end of sustainable excellence?

Because the performance of some of the excellent organisations of the 1980s has deteriorated, the issue of sustainable excellence has been raised. The problems that they face is that their markets are changing faster than before and as companies grow larger it becomes more difficult to maintain the flexibility needed to match the changes.

Excellence may be difficult to sustain for other reasons, such as:

- the successful company leader may retire or run out of steam;
- the leaders may grow away from their customers and staff as the business grows;
- 'Empire building' can limit flexibility and creativity;
- loss of customer focus can be the outcome if companies assume that they dominate the market.

The key to maintaining excellence seems to be continuous improvement and the ability to recognise complacency throughout the organisation.

6 MONITORING AND MAINTAINING QUALITY

6.1 Quality and reliability

Quality itself must be regarded as relative to other factors such as price, consistency and utility. The market for a product or service will accommodate itself to various degrees of quality.

A concept met today is that of a quality and reliability system, including the following elements:

(a) A study of customer requirements, particularly as they relate to performance and price.

(b) The design of the product or service.

(c) Full specification of the requirements of the design, clearly understood by everybody concerned with production.

(d) Assurance that operational processes can meet the requirements of the design.

(e) Acceptance by everybody of responsibility for meeting standards. Many people share in this responsibility. The manager plays a part by declaring what quality standards are to be. Design engineers must work within the parameters which give satisfaction to the customer. Production controllers make sure that output of the right quality is produced on time. Purchasing officers must find reliable suppliers. Operatives must be trained to achieve standards.

(f) Checking that the product or service conforms to the specification.

(g) Instructions on the use, application and limitation of the product or service.

(h) Study of consumer experience of the product, feedback to the departments concerned and immediate remedial action if necessary, otherwise praise all round.

6.2 Barriers to quality and excellence

It has been shown that it is much easier to achieve quality and excellence in a new business, where the principles are built in from the start. It is much harder to develop and improve quality and excellence in an existing company because it may be necessary to overcome a series of barriers. These barriers may be human, technical or financial.

(a) Human barriers exist because people are naturally resistant to change. Some kind of revolutionary process is usually necessary to provide the momentum and incentive for change. This transformation of attitudes needs total commitment from the top and requires one or more champions as well as involvement at all levels.

(b) Technical barriers concern the knowledge and skills that are required to plan, implement and control the best performance practices.

(c) The finance required to sustain excellence and improve quality may be yet another barrier for the company to surmount.

It takes commitment to quality and excellence. Tom Peters's advice to managers is: 'Starting this afternoon, don't walk past a shoddy product or service without comment and action - ever again!'

In his seminars on quality he poses a situation where a brochure is going out to customers. The deadline is missed; five thousand have been printed, inserted into envelopes, addressed and sealed. They are packed and ready to take to the post office. The unit you are in charge of has a not-too-healthy cash flow. You then discover a single typo on page two, in the small print. Should you walk past it or act?

He argues that you should act and throw it out. If you knowingly ignore a tiny act of poor service or quality, you have destroyed your credibility and any possibility of moral leadership on this issue.

6.3 A total quality programme

The characteristics of a total quality programme should include the following:

(a) Everyone in the organisation is involved in continually improving the processes and systems under their control and each person is responsible for his or her own quality assurance.

(b) A commitment to the satisfaction of every customer.

(c) Employee involvement is practised and the active participation of everyone in the organisation is encouraged.

(d) There is an investment in training and education to realise individual potential.

(e) Teamwork is used in a number of forms eg, quality circles.

(f) Suppliers and customers form an integrated part of the process of improvement.

(g) Process re-design is used to simplify processes, systems, procedures and the organisation itself.

7 ASSESSING THE QUALITY OF SERVICES

7.1 The nature of quality assessment

Quality assessment is a process of identifying business practices, attitudes and activities that are either inhibiting or enhancing the achievement of quality improvement.

The purpose of assessment is to:

- supply proof that quality improvement measures are necessary;
- provide a base for future measurement;
- build support for quality measures; and
- convince senior management that the issue is important.

7.2 Quality audits, assessments and reviews

The quality control function looks at the process as a continuous operation, a series of trends and rejection rates. Reports from the quality control department to management include:

(a) analysis of defects by cause;
(b) comparisons between processes and departments;
(c) comparison of defect levels with previous levels and standard levels;
(d) longer term trends in quality;
(e) reports on customers' complaints;
(f) developments in quality control practice; and
(g) special reports.

Apart from receiving reports, management may also commission a quality control audit to find answers to the following questions:

(a) What is the actual level of rejects?

(b) Are the standards fairly set?

(c) Are the standards achieved at the expense of excessive costs?

(d) What is the number of customer complaints?

(e) Has the quality control system been modified in accordance with changes in processing policies, materials and products?

(f) What are the costs of quality control?

(g) What is done to improve performance by eliminating causes of poor performance?

(h) Should a personnel audit on efficiency and knowledge be carried out?

Assessments and reviews of the systems and procedures are an ongoing activity in excellent companies. The responsibility for quality control cannot be isolated as we have seen and can only be effective when it is the result of joint effort. The advantages lie in the fact that quality control points out why faulty work is being produced and the extent of it. Action taken as a result can reduce scrap and the amount of necessary re-work. It shows where a design modification could raise efficiency in manufacture. It minimises the chances of poor materials being processed.

The requirements of the customers must be continually reviewed and the sales department and market research can advise on this. They will be aware of competitors' prices and qualities and a decision must be taken whether or not to increase quality. To increase quality may mean increasing costs and establishing the point at which the customer will decide that the quality is more than he or she can afford.

8 CHAPTER SUMMARY

A combination of high quality products and services being provided by new, especially foreign, competitors with quality being increasingly demanded by industrial and individual customers, means that organisations must adopt quality measures in a big way.

This chapter has considered quality, its management, practices and procedures. In an increasingly competitive world, tolerances and quality levels must be acceptable to customers and in line with those used by competitors. There are, however, financial and technical constraints when designing for quality and the producer's costs of achieving certain standards must be balanced against the value attributed to quality by the consumer.

9 SELF TEST QUESTIONS

9.1 How are quality costs classified? (1.2).

9.2 What should management do to gain employees' commitment to quality? (2.1).

9.3 Explain Crosby's four standards of quality (2.4).

9.4 Outline the elements of Juran's theory (2.5).

9.5 Draw a 5M 'fishbone diagram' (2.7).

9.6 Explain quality assurance (3.1).

9.7 List the three parts of the BS5750/BS EN ISO 9000 standard (3.3).

9.8 What are the six features of companies which follow TQM, according to Thackray? (4.2).

9.9 Explain the main aims of quality circles (4.4).

9.10 Outline the core values associated with excellent companies (5.1).

9.11 Why might a company find it difficult to sustain excellence? (5.3).

9.12 Discuss the type of questions that quality control audits might need to ask (7.2).

10 EXAMINATION TYPE QUESTION

10.1 QUALITY ASSURANCE

You have just been informed by the MD that 'something drastic has to be done about quality'. In his view, quality is the responsibility of your department and he has suggested that you take a tougher line with those responsible for quality problems, raise quality standards, increase inspection rates, and give greater authority to quality control inspectors.

You are required

(a) to evaluate the suggestions made by the MD. **(10 marks)**

(b) to state what additional or alternative proposals you would offer. **(15 marks)**

(Total: 25 marks)

11 ANSWER TO EXAMINATION TYPE QUESTION

11.1 QUALITY ASSURANCE

In general terms, the suggestions made by the MD reflect a mistaken view of quality and how it is assured. His emphasis is 'reactive' rather than 'pro-active', is 'feedback' based rather than 'feedforward', and is concerned with quality control rather than quality assurance.

(a) Specifically:

(i) His initial statement that 'something drastic has to be done about quality' does not seem to be based on any kind of systematic analysis or measurement. Nor does it suggest that the MD understands the meaning of quality, which according to Crosby is 'conformity to requirements'.

(ii) His statement that 'quality is the responsibility of your department' ignores the fact that quality is the responsibility of all staff at all stages, in all departments and at all levels.

(iii) The 'tougher line' suggests a punishment-oriented approach which contradicts the advice of Deming 'to drive out fear', and to seek co-operation.

(iv) 'Raising quality standards' without targeting particular areas, and without understanding why such quality improvement is necessary, is likely to be a costly and unproductive exercise.

(v) 'Increasing inspection rates' and 'giving greater authority to quality control inspectors' reinforces the 'control' approach, and the 'specialist' emphasis discussed earlier.

(b) An alternative approach involves viewing quality control as part of a more strategic approach to quality - quality assurance. This requires:

(i) An analysis of existing quality performance and problems. Such an analysis should involve all levels and all departments, and should concern itself with the customers, with the competition, and with suppliers as well as the activities of the firm itself. Crosby advocates the creation of 'quality committees' composed of members drawn from different departments.

(ii) Calculating the 'cost of quality', which involves measuring the costs of not 'getting it right first time', and includes 'prevention costs', 'appraisal costs', and 'failure costs'. Such an analysis should identify a sizeable potential cost saving (or to quote Crosby 'quality is free').

(iii) The careful selection and monitoring of suppliers, perhaps involving an 'active' rather than a passive relationship.

(iv) The design of the product, to ensure an appropriate level of quality.

(v) The installation of quality information systems which measure and feedback quality performance to those involved, and which can serve as the basis for targets.

(vi) Quality improvement, perhaps involving the creation of quality circles.

(vii) Quality staff, which involves investment in recruitment, selection, training, development, appraisal and reward.

In conclusion, such an approach is essentially long term, and requires a shift in thinking about quality at all levels. The essential ingredient in this cultural shift is a 'right first time' mentality which encompasses all activities that impinge on quality. In short, the MD and other staff need to be educated in 'total quality management'.

18 PURSUIT OF COMPETITIVE ADVANTAGE

INTRODUCTION & LEARNING OBJECTIVES

Famed American baseball player Satchel Page was often quoted as saying 'Don't look back; someone may be gaining on you.' But in business it is essential to know who's gaining on you, and it is not just a matter of looking back, but looking forward and sideways as well. It is far better to know who your competitors are, what strengths they possess and how they are likely to react to your own strategic initiatives and to environmental changes, than to be surprised when suddenly your market share begins to fall.

When you have studied this chapter you should be able to do the following:

- Comprehend what is involved in the pursuit of competitive advantages.
- Discuss the military dimensions of business and the main competitive manoeuvres used in the market-place.
- Describe the importance to strategic planning of the competitive perspective.
- Appreciate the difficulties of identifying and studying competitors.
- Classify the competitive positions within a market and describe strategies of the main players.

1 PURSUIT OF COMPETITIVE ADVANTAGES

1.1 Competitive advantage

This is the special characteristic which a company seeks for in a strategy which will enable it to obtain a special sphere of influence or a strong competitive position. Kotler suggests that a company needs to pay attention to its distinctive competence, ie, 'those resources that the organisation is especially strong in'. The view is that a company will generally find it easier to build on its existing strengths than trying to build from a new position. The company therefore needs to plan strategy that fully utilises areas where it enjoys distinct advantages, that is 'it can outperform competitors on that dimension'.

1.2 Strategies

We have already seen that companies attempt to achieve competitive advantages through cost leadership, product differentiation and/or market focus. There are other strategies that can also achieve this goal.

(a) The erection of strong defensive positions or barriers to entry. We already know that barriers to entry may be in the form of low market prices, high levels of advertising investment, technological know-how requirement and so on. Large companies with significant resources may opt to enter markets with high entry requirements in order to build a competitive position over the medium to long term.

(b) Another game-plan that is closely aligned with a strategy of cost leadership is market dominance. Achieving market dominance not only provides the company with a competitive advantage in terms of cost and thus price determination, but also allows it to reduce the adverse influence of its business environment. In other words to have more control over its environment. Often a market leader is a major part of the environment for other companies in its markets.

(c) In situations where demand outweighs capacity a low cost position often obtains a very competitive position. However in these markets other companies have more scope to build special spheres of influence or competitive advantage based on their differentiated position. During periods of recession or slump inefficient companies fall into liquidation and thus leave the market. Their removal frees discrete amounts of the market allowing efficient companies to gain sales volume, often quite considerably. Furthermore, when the market picks up, the number of participants is less, reducing the competition for the market upsurge which ensues.

2 THE STRATEGIC ROLE OF MARKETING

2.1 The competitive perspective

Competition is the existence of rival products or services within the same market, and in addition to analysing all the company's critical competence and resources, strategic planners need to survey competition in its totality, including such critical strategic elements as the company's competitors' R&D capabilities, sales, services, costs, manufacturing and procurement (including all the other businesses in which competitors may be engaged). Strategists need to put themselves mentally in the place of planners in rival companies and to persistently search out the key perceptions and assumptions on which the competitors' strategies are formulated.

Example

Suppose you were an accountant involved in helping to formulate a two-year strategy for a maturing product. Here's what your competitive analysis might turn up:

- an existing UK competitor has drastically reduced overhead and input costs by a policy of rapid decentralisation and global sourcing;
- another existing UK competitor has just fended-off a hostile takeover bid by selling off the division that competes with you to another strong competitor who will use technological synergy to reduce costs, and who has a distribution system better than yours;
- a competitor has just installed a computerised customer on-line system hooking-up to each of its 1,800 distributors, reducing order-to-delivery time by 75%;
- another competitor has recently introduced a just-in-time assembly system at the centre of which is a computerised manufacturing resources planning (MRP) system, enabling the company to tailor-make the product to the specifications of its customers;
- an existing Japanese competitor continues to add product features, improve quality and reduce prices;
- a new Korean competitor has just entered the UK market;
- a new company, led by a team of breakaway managers from a large competitor, has claimed a technological breakthrough.

It is because this scenario is now **commonplace** - for every industry and every segment of industry - that your company is not alone in requiring major strategic surgery.

2.2 Identifying the competitor(s)

The first problem in analysing competitors is to establish **who** exactly is the competition? This is a simple-to-understand but difficult-to-answer question. Too often companies have focused on the wrong adversary, by being obsessed with old rivalries.

Examples

By concentrating its attention on its cross-town rival Kodak, and its new, and good, high-price copiers, **Xerox** effectively ignored the **'small timers'** Savin and Canon who were operating in unimportant market segments. Then suddenly, or so it seemed, these mice turned into lions, and Xerox lost more than half its market share before it stemmed the tide.

While the two Detroit giants of **General Motors** and **Ford** were looking over their shoulders at each other, Toyota stormed into both their markets.

So seeking an answer to the **'who'** is no easy task. Strategists will need to check out:

- obvious **majors** in the market;
- the **next best** competitors, region by region;
- new, big companies, with troubles of their own likely to **intrude** into their market;
- **small domestic companies** perhaps operating in small premium market niches;
- **foreign companies**, with special emphasis on the first unobtrusive move into small domestic niches;
- **oddball forays** from unexpected competitors.

2.3 Need to focus beyond brand

Kotler suggests that companies are myopic if they focus attention only on their brand competitors, and gives the example of confectionery companies whose real challenge, he says, is to expand their primary market, namely the sweet market, and not simply to battle for a larger share in a reducing market. Sweet manufacturers have to be concerned about megatrends in the environment, such as people eating less in general, and eating less sweets in particular, and switching to substitutes, other forms of confectionery, and dietetic confectionery, and so on. Indirect competitors are often overlooked because they are not apparent. Cadbury's and Rowntree's presentation boxes of chocolates were once the main personal gifts in a variety of social situations, now they have been replaced by flowers, plants, wine and gift-vouchers. There is a danger for companies only concentrating on their **brand competitors** and neglecting the opportunities to build the whole market or failing to make moves to prevent it from declining. Kotler supports this view by distinguishing four types of competition:

(a) **Desire** competitors: other needs and wants that a consumer may desire to satisfy.

(b) **Generic** competitors: alternative ways in which the consumer can satisfy a particular desire.

(c) **Form** competitors: other forms of product (or service) that can satisfy the consumer's particular desire.

(d) **Brand** (or **enterprise**) competitors: other brands (or enterprises) offering the same product (or service) that can satisfy the consumer's particular desire.

The consumer decision process follows the path shown in the diagram below:

Figure 1 Kotler's classification of four types of competition*

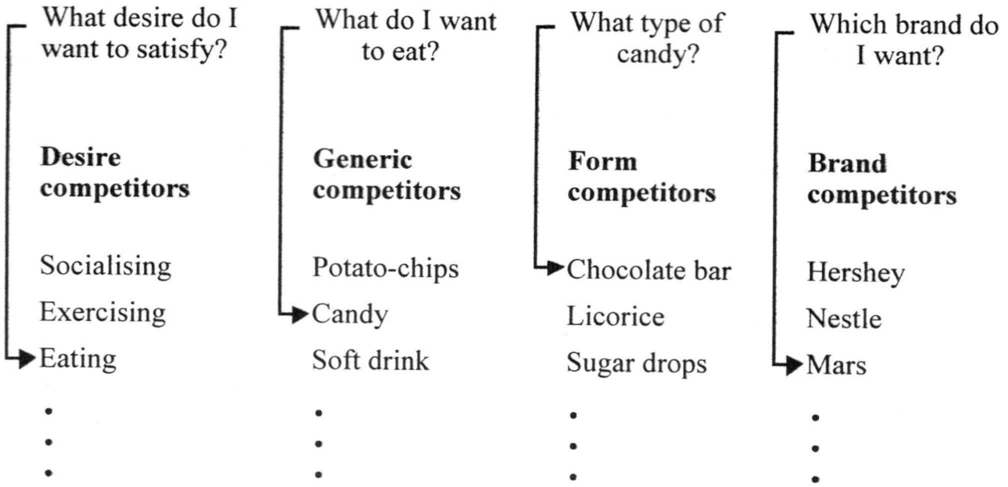

(* Kotler, P. 'Marketing Management: Analysis, Planning and Control', Prentice-Hall, 1984.

2.4 Example

The competition facing a private college offering education for the qualifying examinations of professional accountancy institutions provides another example. A student, say female, after graduation from university could decide to travel the world, get a job, carry on with full time education, or study for an accountancy qualification (**desire competitors**). Suppose she favours getting a job and studying for an ACCA qualification. She then considers how best do this (**generic competitors**), choices are to purchase a correspondence course, read books, enrol on an college evening course, or enrol on a college weekend course. She decides in favour of joining a weekend course. Next she needs to consider what type of college (**form competitors**): private college or state college. She favours a private college. This leads her to compare the offerings of the private colleges and to consider which one to use: Accountancy Tutors, and so on. Thus the planners in the private college face at least four types of competitors in attempting to enrol this student on a course of study. Managers planning competitive strategy for a college would therefore need to be involved in trying to build their market as well as attempting to build their brand share in that market.

2.5 The fallacy of 'perfect competition'

There is also the problem of the competitive state of the market. Economists refer to the state of **perfect competition** which is the only market form which can be considered as a comprehensive self-contained system.

However one of the objectives of the marketer is to distort perfect competition in the interests of the company by differentiating its product, and deterring potential competition from entering the market, thus making the company's product a quasi-monopoly in the market. (In other words aiming to make the product become **a big fish in a small pond**, rather than **a small fish in a big pond**.) Marketing techniques for this include: adding product features, advertising, sale promotion, pricing, merchandising and personal selling.

Example

The colour-generating system behind **Sony's** Trinitron television tube, with its single electronic- beam gun, challenged the industry which had always used three electronic guns for the three primary colours: red, blue and green. It gave Sony virtually a two-year monopoly in the market.

2.6 Activity

You will perhaps remember from your studies of economics the main characteristics of a perfectly competitive market. Try to list these characteristics now.

2.7 Activity solution

The main characteristics of a perfectly competitive market are listed below.

(a) A large number of buyers and sellers, none of whom is large enough to affect the total supply or demand, nor powerful enough to dictate or influence market price.

(b) The market price is determined by the equilibrium point resulting from the combined pressures of the aggregate demands and supplies of all buyers and sellers in the market and will change when the forces of demand and supply change.

(c) Barriers to entry are low and potential entrants find no difficulty in competing if they so choose. Ease of entry to and exit from the market in response to movements of market prices ensures that over the long term companies produce up to the point where marginal cost is equal to market price. Although in the short term, the market price may be pushed up above the marginal cost, this will not persist over the long term, as potential entrants would be attracted by the higher profit and their additional capacity would soon bring prices and profits down. By contrast, if market prices fell below marginal costs, the less efficient companies would be forced to leave the industry until the price level increased.

(d) The product is standardised so that buyers are indifferent from whom they purchase. Promotional activity such as advertising is pointless, because price is the sole purchasing determinant.

(e) Buyers and sellers are fully informed of the market conditions, so that no one can buy or sell at an advantageous price.

(f) As the demand curve forced on an individual supplier is perfectly elastic and the market price is known, the theoretically optimum for the supplier is to produce at that volume where marginal cost equals marginal revenue.

3 SUSTAINABLE COMPETITIVE ADVANTAGE

Michael Porter argues that an organisation gains competitive advantage from within an industry. Its position, relative to the competition, determines whether its profitability is above or below the industry average.

Strategic planners need to make reasonable predictions of what the competitive state of their market(s) will be in the future. There is always an ongoing dynamism within a market, with new competitors entering, and sometimes established competitors dropping out. Planners need to know who their new competitors are likely to be and what threats they are likely to bring to the market.

Although there are barriers to entry, from a practical view few barriers last very long, particularly in new and emerging markets and fields. Laws change, patents do not always provide the protection expected, differentiated positions can be weakened, and costs often reduce. Thus, planners need to estimate how long barriers will remain before they are breached by new competitors.

Porter notes that the fundamental basis of above-average performance in the long run is sustainable competitive advantage, based on cost or differentiation in the whole market or focus strategy concentrating on a few segments.

- A cost leadership strategy is where a firm sets out to become the low-cost producer in its industry.

- A differentiation strategy is where the organisation seeks to be unique in its industry along some dimensions that are widely valued by consumers.
- A focus strategy is based on the choice of a narrow competitive scope within an industry.

4 TACTICS OF COMPETITIVE ADVANTAGE

4.1 The military dimension of business

Any study of competition also involves the perception of conflict. Nobody can doubt that the underlying reason for the upkeep of a military force is the probability of combat, and similarly it is difficult to see how conflict can be avoided in the market-place. The instruments used, and application of strategies for both armies and companies are parallelisms, as can be evidenced from their systems, structures and even language. Very briefly the similarities of armies and business organisations are discussed below looking mainly from the business view.

(a) **Objectives**

- War breaks out in the market place when one company considers it will gain from aggression.
- Any challenge to the security, and sovereignty of a company is a declaration of war. (A company's security is its market position, and company sovereignty relates to it's customers.)

(b) **Principles**

Both companies and armies:

- are goal oriented;
- acknowledge that taking the advantage can give a crucial result;
- recognise the power of concentration of resources;
- use security to prevent surprises;
- consider co-ordination to be essential;
- deem economy to be essential;
- avoid the pressures of complexity by using simplicity of objectives, systems and instructions.

(c) **Manoeuvres**

The deterrence, attack, defence and alliance strategies undertaken by companies in response to actual or perceived moves by competitors in the market place, are analogous to those taken by the military in the battle-field.

(d) **Functions**

Companies, like armies, require:

- weapons to fight with (design, brand names, manufacturing, marketing and human resources);
- the skills to fight;
- intelligence on both the market environment and competitors;
- logistics - to move products and services to the consumer;
- internal and external communications (the first for information transfer, the second for propaganda reasons);
- leadership and organisation - to direct and motivate employees.

(e) **Training**

Companies and armies both use in-house specialist skills courses and management development programmes as an integral feature of organisational development. Basic training in Matsushita, GEC, British Rail, and so on has its parallels in army recruit training. Specialist skills developed in Ford's apprenticeship programme have their equivalent in the army trade schools. Middle management programmes at McDonalds' **Hamburger University** emulate those at infantry schools, and senior management programmes at IBM or Burton's can be compared to army staff-officer courses.

4.2 Activity

Much of the language of armies which describes the nature of conflict, and military terminology has been widely adopted by business. Try to think of at least five business terms that have military connotations.

4.3 Activity solution

There are many examples, and you will probably be able to think of terms not included in this short answer. However business vocabulary such as **'advertising campaigns', 'battle for market share', 'price wars', 'promotional blitz'** and **'sales force'** describe a few of the military expressions adopted by business to describe market conflict.

4.4 Deterrence strategy

Deterrence is a business strategy used by a company to prevent conflict, by convincing rational competitors, or potential competitors, that because of it's strengths and determination to use them, peace is more acceptable then war. It depends on psychological pressure rather than physical combat. Conflict hardly every occurs when a competitor anticipates that the risk is high in relation to the gain from a planned aggressive move, or impulsive action. Four key elements are present in all effective business deterrence strategies.

(a) **Credibility**

When a company convinces a competitor that it is willing to fight to maintain its position or further its aims, and the competitor regards this threat as potentially damaging and credible.

(b) **Competence**

Where a company convinces a competitor company that in addition to being determined to fight, it has the means and the resources necessary to carry out the threat of retaliation. Competence consists of marketing (such as Proctor and Gamble with its $500 million media budget), production (such as Texas Instrument's high-volume, low-unit-cost position), finance (such as the cost to build and work a VLSI RAM chip producing plant), and technology (such as Kodak's previous monopoly on it's Disc camera).

(c) **Rationality**

Where because of the company's capability the competitor company can be persuaded to act in a rational, reasonable, and objective manner.

(d) **Signal of intention**

Where a company clearly signals to a competitor its intention to retaliate if needs be.

4.5 Attack strategy

Offensive strategy plans for the physical assault on a competitor to change the status quo in favour of the aggressor. Companies use five basic offensive strategies.

- Frontal attacks
- Flanking attacks
- Encirclement
- Bypass attacks
- Guerrilla attacks

(a) **Frontal attacks**

By which an aggressor launches a **'head-on'** attack by massing its forces right up against those of its opponents. It attacks the opponent's strengths rather than its weaknesses. For a frontal attack to succeed, the aggressor needs a strength advantage over the competitor. (An example was the way IBM attacked Apple when entering the personal computer market, a strategy we looked at previously.)

(b) **Flanking attacks**

By which an aggressor attacks at a point in the defence of the enemy where it has weak spots and is less secure. The major principle of modern offensive warfare is **'concentration of strength against weakness.'** The element of surprise is an important ingredient in the strategy. If a company cannot overcome a strong competitor with brute strength, it might be able to outmanoeuvre it with subterfuge.

Examples

German and Japanese car manufacturers chose not to compete with the American majors by producing large, petrol-expensive and **'flashy'** car models, even though research suggested they were the preference of American buyers. Instead they recognised a growing need for small, fuel-efficient cars and moved to fill this unserved segment of the market. This segment grew to be a substantial part of the market.

Casio a small electronic toy manufacturer launched a frontal attack on Citizen and Seiko by using its extensive computer and electronics know-how to drive the price of electronic quartz watches to a very low level of about £8 each. Citizen and Seiko repositioned themselves by abandoning the low cost segment of the electronic quartz watch market.

(c) **Encirclement**

Encirclement is the complete envelopment of the enemy's force on both flanks thus forcing the enemy to capitulate or face annihilation. This strategy involves launching a grand offensive on several fronts simultaneously, thus forcing the enemy to protect its front, rear and sides simultaneously. Envelopment (or encirclement) makes sense as a marketing strategy where the aggressor commands superior forces to those of the competitor and believes that the encirclement will break the opponent's will to resist.

Example

Boeing adopted an encirclement strategy by developing a family of jet airlines to offer a full product range:

Short range	:	737 (versus BAC111, DC-9, F-28)
Medium range	:	727 (versus Trident 1-3)
Continental	:	720 (versus Comet 3, DC-8 10/20, Convair 880)
Intercontinental	:	707 (versus VC-10, Comet 4, DC-8 40/50, Convair 990)
Larger capacity	:	747 (versus DC-8 60)

Despite heavy competition, by 1980 Boeing was taking almost two of every three civil jets ordered world-wide as a result of a family of products covering virtually the full range of market segments.

(d) **Bypass attack**

Where strong points are isolated and then bypassed by the main forces and left to surrender or be mopped up by later waves of troops. In effect the aggressor is widening its base of operations. In business terms bypass strategy can involve three lines of approach: jumping into new technologies, diversifying into unrelated products, and diversifying into new geographical markets.

For example, by the early 1970s Colgate came to recognise that any head-on battle with Proctor and Gamble was futile. It was 'outgunned' 3 to 1 at store level and the opposition had three research people to every one employed at Colgate. Colgate's strategy was simple - increase its involvement overseas and bypass P&G at home by diversifying into non P&G markets. The company diversified (by acquisition) into a number of industries: textiles, hospital products, cosmetics, food products and a range of sporting goods. The result: in 1971, Colgate was underdog to P&G in about 50 percent of its business. By 1976, in 75 percent of its business it was well placed against P&G or did not face it at all.

(e) **Guerrilla attack**

Which is a form of combat used by irregular forces fighting limited, small scale actions, against orthodox military forces.

> 'The enemy advances, we retreat.
> The enemy camps, we harass.
> The enemy tires, we attack.
> The enemy retreats, we pursue.'
>
> Mao Tse Tung

Normally guerrilla warfare is a form of combat used by a smaller company against a larger, stronger one. Being unable to mount an effective or frontal attack the smaller company launches selective price cuts, intense promotional bursts, supply interferences, executive raids in unobtrusive corners of the larger opponent's market with the goal of gradually weakening the opponent's grip on the market. Guerrilla warfare is not necessarily **'low cost'** often requiring a high expenditure of resources. Furthermore guerrilla warfare often develops into full war.

Example

On the basis that most people who hire cars merely want to get from A to B, the US company, Rent-A-Wreck built a network of 250 car hire outlets in the US, achieving a turnover of $30 million a year by 1982, by renting old cars, sometimes over 25 years old. Because of low costs - inexpensive cars with low depreciation, the company is able to hire out at about half the price of Avis and Hertz.

4.6 Activity

The example we have used to illustrate **'encirclement strategy'** is Boeing's product-market positioning. Try to think of another company that you know of that has carried out a policy of market encirclement.

4.7 Activity solution

The Burton Group with their many different chain-stores ('Principles', 'Principles For Men', 'Champion Sport', 'Dorothy Perkins', 'Evans', 'Top Shop', 'Debenhams', etc) have certainly attempted to envelop their targeted area of the fashion market. However an even better example is Seiko which markets over 2,000 different models of wrist-watch. There are many more examples of this strategy for you to choose from.

4.8 Defence strategies

Defensive strategies are used to resist assault and to inflict such losses on an aggressor that he will either provide the defender with the opportunity to counter-attack or will retreat from the field of battle. Companies use six basic defensive strategies.

- Position defence
- Mobile defence
- Pre-emptive defence
- Flank strengthening
- Counter attacks
- Strategic withdrawal

(a) **Position defence**

By which a company erects fortifications, or barriers to entry, around a product or service to protect its position against assault. A number of sub-strategies are used in business as a means to defend market position including: product differentiation, cost advantages, promotion, line-extension, supply ownership, acquisition of competitors.

(b) **Mobile defence**

By which a defender plans for flexibility of response against attack. The key to mobile defence is to strike hard and fast at an attacker before he secures a viable position, and by reducing the effect of the attack, secure defence.

(c) **Pre-emptive defence**

Where a strike is initiated against the (expected) aggressor before he starts his attack against the company, in the belief that a first-strike will cause such a physical or psychological blow that the aggressor, caught by surprise, will be either forced to sue for immediate peace, or will be incapable of launching the attack that was imminent. In business, pre-emptive strikes can take numerous forms.

- Resource strikes.

  For example, in 1981 **Coca-Cola** introduced high-fructose corn sweetener to replace up to half the sugar in coke. (The price of high-fructose was then about 20% less than refined sugar.) To defend itself against competitors following suit, Coca-Cola signed long-term purchase contracts buying-up most fructose capacity.

- Market strikes.

- Financial strikes.

  HBO the leading cable and TV network in the US, successfully applied financial strike strategy by funding the production of films in return for exclusive pay TV viewing rights. This pre-emptive financial strategy enabled HBO to secure access to quality films, defend its position in the pay TV market and increase its profit margins.

- Technological strikes.

  Genentech, Cetus and Genex invested heavily to acquire access to the new biotechnologies developing in the late 1970s to protect their markets.

- Distribution strikes

  Timex, in the early 1950s, innovated by distributing low cost watches through a variety of retail outlets rather than through the traditional jewellery store system.

- Customer strikes.

(d) **Flank strengthening**

Where a defender plans to guard its market position by erecting some flanks or outposts to serve as a defence to protect a weak front, or possibly to use as a launch-pad for counterattacking if appropriate. In business the strategy normally takes the form of **repositioning a product** in the market place

Armstrong Rubber, (the sixth largest US tyre manufacturer) was faced by competitive pressures from Firestone, Goodrich, Goodyear, General Tire and Uniroyal and a declining demand for tyres caused by OPEC oil price increases, inflation, a stagnating US economy and unemployment, Armstrong repositioned from primarily marketing tyres to the manufacturers of new cars to take up a strong niche in the **replacement** type market which it serviced through 1,000 independent distributors, and an agreement with Sears Roebuck which purchased up to 40% of Armstrong's tyres. The environment, including quite substantial increases in new car prices, forced motorists to keep their cars longer which increased the market for replacement tyres. Armstrong was thus able to increase unit sales by 11% although the total US unit market only increased by 2%.

(e) **Counter-attack**

The classic response to attack, where the initiative is taken by the defender attacking back. Counter-attack strategies include:

- product counter-attack,
- production counter-attack,
- financial counter-attack,
- promotional counter-attack, and
- combination counter-attack

In 1979, McDonalds the world's largest fast food restaurant chain was faced with reducing sales due to increasing costs of petrol (which meant that people were reluctant to drive out to eat), soaring costs, and increasing and diversity of competition including pizza houses, fish and chip shops, fried chicken and Chinese take-aways, which began to make inroads into McDonalds' prime business - the hamburger. The company counter-attacked by introducing a **chopped steak sandwich** (1979) and its chicken sandwich and **Chicken McNuggets** (1981). By 1983 **Chicken McNuggets** earned 12% of the company's $8.2 billion sales. At an earlier time (1976) the company had flank-positioned by introducing a new product **Egg Muffin** to close a **'breakfast segment'** gap in its product range to defend itself against the US breakfast companies Chock Full O'Nuts and Dunkin' Donuts. By 1982 McDonalds' was earning $3.2 billion turnover from its breakfast line extension.

(f) **Strategic withdrawal**

Which has the object of extricating the maximum amount of resources from an untenable product position to provide an opportunity to use these resources in some better way.

4.9 Alliance strategy

(a) **Forms of alliances**

In business, alliances are common combat strategies which are entered into to serve common interests such as preserving the balance of market power, controlling spheres of influence and protecting the corporate interests. These alliances combine marketing, production, technological or financial resources in such a way as to serve common objectives. There are many forms of alliances.

- Licensing
- Marketing agreement
- Joint venture
- Franchising
- Consortium
- Private label
- Seller-buyer
- Research

(b) **Rationale of alliance strategy**

Alliances are used to serve various business objectives.

- To preserve the balance of market power.
- A means of controlling spheres of influence of competitors.
- For deterring new entrants.
- A way by which a company's spare (unused) capacity can be utilised.
- An approach for breaking into new technology/markets.
- A sharing out of high investment cost and resultant risks.
- For companies to gain the advantages of **'the joint effects of synergy'**.

(c) **Drawbacks associated with alliance strategy**

Alliance strategy carries with a number of potential disadvantages.

- Alliances can form an organisational structure in which the decision making process is slow (often **ad hoc**), accountability is imprecise and communications are weak - all of which cause significant operating problems.

- Temporary alliances designed to protect long-term independence may weaken rather than strengthen a company's competence since it can lose the ability and capacity to independently produce a fully integrated product in the future.

- Proprietary information can easily flow to allies, who may at some future time again be competitors.

- A company may become too dependent on a partner for essential components or market outlets.

- Business alliances are frequently short term since they are designed to satisfy a common interest which may be difficult to sustain over a longer period, or a threat which may only be relevant in the short time span. Any organisation relying totally on an alliance as core strategy, without developing an independent strategic structure, will be at risk when circumstances change.

5 GAINING POSITIONAL ADVANTAGE

Companies operating in a market pursue different competitive strategies and hold different competitive positions. The competitive positions of companies, (or the market structure), can be described in different ways. For example, Arthur D. Litt, in the book **'A System for Managing Diversity'**, sees companies occupying one of six competitive positions in their market, as **dominant, strong, favourable, tenable, weak** or **non-viable**. Each company will be able to place itself in one of these competitive positions, which along with an analysis of its product life cycle and resource balance between its product-markets, will help it decide whether to build, hold, harvest, or withdraw from the market. We will look at these four product-market strategies later.

Philip Kotler in his book, 'Marketing Management: Analysis, Planning and Control', develops a different classification of competitive positions. He bases this on the behaviour, or market strategy, of different companies and suggests that ideas for strategies can be generated by classifying a company's situation in one of four positions:

(a) market leader,
(b) market challenger,
(c) market follower, or
(d) market nicher.

6 NICHE MARKET STRATEGY

6.1 Characteristics

A niche market strategy involves entering markets or segments which are too small or specialised to attract large competitors, ('small harbours which the supertankers cannot enter'). Almost every industry includes minor companies, or small units within big organisations, that trade in parts of the market which do not interest large operating units because they lack volume or require specialist skills which are not available without uneconomic expenditure. Almost without exception niche products are **premium-priced,** to compensate the suppliers for lack of scale of economy with the coincident problems in recovering overheads at normal price levels. Also they usually command above average profit margins.

Morgan Cars is a niche company. It offers a product ('with a ride as hard as rock, offering minimal comfort and space and with noise levels deafeningly high') for enthusiasts seeking the nostalgia of a 1930s sports car. The limited appeal of this vehicle would not interest the majors (such as General Motors, Ford or Toyota) and yet the current order-to-delivery time for a new Morgan is six years.

For a number of reasons, which are listed below, we are rapidly moving into a marketing era of the flexible specialist.

(a) An explosion of new and relatively small business enterprises, encouraged by government venture investment policy.

(b) Foreign companies are increasingly searching for toeholds in every European market.

(c) There has been no let-up in the technology revolution.

(d) The cultural move away from mass identity, and thus undifferentiated markets.

An ideal market niche would have particular characteristics.

(a) Large enough to be profitable.

(b) Has demand growth potential.

(c) Sufficiently **differentiated** to allow premium pricing strategy.

(d) Sufficiently small so as not to attract large-scale operators.

(e) The company has the competence and resources required to take full advantage of the opportunities offered by the niche.

6.2 Types of niche market

The key factor in niche marketing is flexibility and specialisation. The niche company will normally take on a specialist role along market, consumer, product or marketing-mix lines. There are a number of directions a niche market can take.

- Customer-needs specialist
- Geographical specialist
- Product, or product feature, specialist

- Jobbing specialist
- Quality/price specialist
- Vertical-level specialist

(a) **Customer-needs specialist**

The company concentrates on servicing the needs of particular customers. For example, Rowntree was up against the tremendously strong Cadbury image (the leading brand name in UK chocolate). Early on the company determined that its main marketing strategy would be market creation by identifying specific market niches and developing products and marketing-mix that would have strong appeal to the particular consumer groups involved. Out of this strategy came products such as Aero, Smarties, Black Magic and Yorkie.

Now there are even niches in the credit card business with the emergence in the US of **'affinity cards'.** For instance, Ducks Unlimited of Reno, Nevada, markets a Visa card bearing a picture of a duck in its wildlife habitat; and pledges some of the interest paid in by account holders will go to preserve marshland for ducks.

(b) **Geographical specialist**

The company limits its activities to a certain locality or region. For example, British Airlines is one of the largest aircarriers in the world, covering most major international air routes. But it is also involved in small geographical niches. For example it operates services to Aberdeen thus building the customer loyalty of oilmen in transit between UK and US.

(c) **Product, or product feature, specialist**

The company produces only one product or product line. For example, British Caledonian aware that it could not compete against the major aircarriers, concentrated on the special requirements of the business traveller and developed a distinctive service package which would appeal to that type of passenger.

(d) **Jobbing specialist**

The company supplies, or manufactures, customised products according to the design specifications of the customer.

(e) **Quality/price specialist**

The company operates at the premium price/high quality or discount price/low quality end of the market. (Rolls Royce cars are positioned at the top end, and Lada cars at the low end, of their respective markets.)

(f) **Vertical-level specialist**

The company specialises at some particular link in the manufacturing- distribution chain.

6.3 The rationale of market-niche strategy

A niche strategy can lead in a number of directions. The niche may be an end in itself, as in the example of Morgan, and the company will be content to settle and prosper in it. The niche may also be a means of the company establishing a toehold in a larger market, by using the small corner of the market as an entry point and building it into a beachhead for subsequent launch across the large market.

Niche marketing may also be important for large organisations (usually by decentralising responsibility to a small division or **'Strategic Business Unit (SBU)'**) who may need to protect their flank positions against incursions of new, but potentially dangerous, competitors in seemingly unobtrusive parts of their market. Niche markets may also be of interest to large organisations who want to adapt and stretch their brands across a number of different segments to reach optimum scale of operating economy. Also niche markets, because of the ability to charge premium price levels, often give outstanding investment return.

Beecham, a large chemical and food processor, has the knack of creating markets which it often does at niche level. It takes an established brand, such as **Ribena,** and identifies niches with different needs. It then designs different product versions in terms of taste, flavouring, packaging, and product versions which will appeal to the different types of consumer involved (babies, schoolchildren, old people, and so on).

The whole point about a niche market is that it is often small and easily defended. The needs of its customers differ in some way from those in the market at large. Niches can open and close rapidly.

6.4 Beachhead strategy

A beachhead is a military term which defines, 'an area held on an enemy's shore for purpose of landing' (Chambers 20th Century Dictionary). The military manoeuvre is planned with the objective of taking and holding an area (or areas) of an enemy's shore and building strength within this area for subsequent attack using the beachhead as a launchpad. In 1944 the Allies planned an invasion on the shores of France. The plan involved organising three million men, 12,000 aircraft and 4,600 vessels to support the landing of 150,000 troops and 1,500 tanks on the beaches of Normandy.

Companies use niche markets as beachheads and this presents danger for the existing brands. Companies already existing in markets probably need to respond by also niche marketing. It is a almost a case of, **'Niche or be niched.'** The fast changing macro- and micro-economic environment of the early 1990s lays down a warning to even large organisations, that marketing should focus on market creation, not market sharing. Tom Peters writes, "If you are not reconfiguring your organisation to become a fast-changing, high-value-adding creator of niche markets, you are simply out of step."

7 CHAPTER SUMMARY

The pursuit of competitive advantage and dedication to achieving the leading market position generally delivers the best profit in an industry. This is why organisations actively plan for the attainment of excellence.

Following on from the previous sections we find that excellence in organisations is difficult to create, yet we know when we are receiving quality service or products. Many companies get away with poor service and shoddy goods and their customers tolerate it because there is no competitor to offer a better option. Once a new competitor comes into the market, the whole industry is transformed; the casualties being those companies which offer no real competitive advantage.

8 SELF-TEST QUESTIONS

8.1 Describe Kotler's four types of market competition (2.3).

8.2 Explain why barriers to entry might not last for a long time (3).

8.3 What are Porter's suggested strategies for sustaining competitive advantage? (3).

8.4 State the 4 main manoeuvres used in competitive strategy (4.1).

8.5 Name 5 different attack strategies (4.5).

8.6 Name at least 5 different defence strategies (4.8).

8.7 Name at least 6 different forms of business alliance (4.9).

8.8 Describe Kotler's classification of competitive positions (5).

8.9 Describe the characteristics of a niche market (6.1).

9 EXAMINATION TYPE QUESTION

9.1 Generic strategies

Michael Porter suggests that there are three generic strategies for creating and sustaining superior performance. These strategies are:

(1) overall cost leadership;
(2) differentiation;
(3) focus.

Required

(a) Describe each of these strategies and indicate how each strategy will result in competitive advantage. **(8 marks)**

(b) What factors are important in achieving 'overall cost leadership'? **(9 marks)**

(c) Discuss the risks faced by an organisation which adopts the strategy of 'overall cost leadership'. **(8 marks)**

(Total: 25 marks)

10 ANSWER TO EXAMINATION TYPE QUESTION

10.1 Generic strategies

(a) Porter argues that the most crucial strategic aim of all companies is to obtain and maintain competitive advantage. He defines three generic strategies, and argues that only one of these may be employed at any time.

(i) **Overall cost leadership**

Companies usually achieve cost advantages by entering into efficient, high volume production, typically employing capital intensive 'high-tech' equipment. The Japanese are the masters of this type of production. It is argued that this type of production results in industry's 'critical mass' (low volume, inefficient producers remain uncompetitive largely due to their small size). In the car industry, the high critical mass means that the market is virtually impenetrable for newcomers.

The economies of scale which result from large scale producers mean that certain activities, such as research and development, treasury management, and efficient distribution systems will only be possible for a sufficiently high volume producer.

The learning curve factor will be more applicable to the more automated production techniques of larger companies.

Discretionary costs such as advertising will be lower for larger companies. For instance Coca-Cola, despite its incessant advertising, has a considerable advantage over its competitors, in that it has the lowest unit advertising costs in the soft drinks industry.

(ii) **Differentiation** presents the product in a unique way, and in this way shields itself from competition by shedding (or hiding!) the product's commodity status. It is vital that potential buyers should be aware of the differentiating factors.

Differentiating can be achieved by branding, or more substantially by improved quality, design, technological benefits, etc.

(iii) A **focus** strategy involves concentration on particular products, well defined demographic segments, and possibly distinct geographics. Success is achieved by specialising in providing a particularly efficient and effective product or service to a small market segment. Such products may be niche products. The Morgan sports car would fall into this category.

The focus strategy enables an 'expert' image to be credibly relayed.

(b) Given that a company has effective, reliable distribution channels and a comprehensive marketing apparatus to reach its customers, the cost leadership strategy critically hinges on the following resources.

(i) **Capital** – As high volume production tends to be capital intensive in nature, companies have vast capital requirements to pay both for the equipment and for the vastly increased working capital requirement to support the increased sale of operations.

(ii) **Manpower** – The new computerised techniques will require well trained and committed employees, in large numbers. Thus an effective personnel department would typically be required.

(iii) **Product design and quality** – It is crucial that the product will be so apparently 'crammed' with added value as to prove irresistible to the end consumer. The product benefits should be obtained using efficient working practices. (For instance, Japanese car factories are able to make several different products on one production line.)

(iv) **Distribution channels** – These should be sufficiently comprehensive to cover consumers in as many countries as possible. The channels should be capable of carrying a high intensity of product, and should be as short as possible to achieve this end (with the minimum number of 'middle men').

(v) **Cost control** – This is crucial, and inefficiency should be able to be detected by a comprehensive budgetary control system.

(vi) **Sales and marketing** – Should be sufficiently expert, and employ enough talented resource, to steer the corporation towards new world markets (and service existing customers).

(c) The risks involved in attaining 'overall cost leadership' include the following.

(i) The low unit cost of product may result in compromising safety.

(ii) The larger organisational size may prove too complex for the current management.

(iii) There may be an over-emphasis on efficiency, not considering the market characteristics in enough detail.

(iv) Technological advances can quickly erode the competitive edge of large companies (when the transistor was invented, many value producers were obliterated overnight).

(v) Larger companies will be less adaptable to other environmental changes, for instance violent swings in the economy.

19 HUMAN RESOURCE MANAGEMENT

INTRODUCTION & LEARNING OBJECTIVES

It has become fashionable to speak of the human assets of the organisation, rather than staff, personnel or manpower. It is also useful because it reminds us that although people only appear as costs in the formal accounts, they are assets in the sense that they are, or should be, a productive resource which needs maintenance and proper utilisation and that has a finite life and an output greater than its cost.

Manpower planning is a strategy to maintain and improve the ability of the organisation to achieve corporate objectives, through the development of strategies designed to enhance the contribution of manpower at all times in the foreseeable future.

Expanding this idea, we see that manpower (personnel) planning deals with human activity directed towards a specific economic aim, and so provides the organisation with the right number of employees who have the skills to achieve the organisation's objectives.

When you have studied this chapter you should be able to do the following:

- Assess the role and nature of Human Resource Management (HRM) and Human Resource Development.
- Explain how an organisation integrates HRM into its strategic plans.
- Compare the traditional views of human resources and their development with the more modern approach.
- Define and explain the need for, and methods of, individual, team and management development
- Evaluate the importance of career management.
- Analyse the internal and external factors that might affect an individual's or a team's performance.

1 THE CONCEPT OF HUMAN RESOURCE MANAGEMENT

1.1 Overview

Human resource management (HRM) can be viewed as a strategic approach to acquiring, developing, managing and motivating an organisation's key resource.

The people in most organisations are of central importance, and human resource management should be in a position to complement and advance the organisation's objectives.

Most cynics will say it is only a new name or modern approach for personnel management with an involvement in the strategic planning process. We will contrast the modern approaches, emphasising the need for empowerment or passing authority down the line as far as is sensible, with the traditional approaches.

1.2 The role and purpose of HRM and human resource development

The role of personnel departments in most large organisations is well established, and their operations, although not often clearly understood, are very wide ranging. Many of their activities are seen to be critical to the success and reputation of the company. This is because their basic responsibilities are all concerned with the human resource of a company, from recruitment to retirement.

The Institute of Personal Development (formerly the Institute of Personnel Management (IPM)) has defined the personnel management role as:

Definition 'That part of management concerned with people at work and with their relationships within an enterprise. Personnel management aims to achieve efficiency by bringing together the men and women who make up an enterprise, and developing them into an effective working group, thus enabling each to make their own best contribution to its success both as an individual and as a member of the working group.'

Many modern management writers tend to question the credibility of personnel departments. Douglas McGregor for instance suggested that it was impossible to carry out the dual role of 'helper' and 'policeman', as these roles were seen to be incompatible. Peter Drucker suggested that personnel management, as a specialist function, was 'bankrupt'.

A more modern view of human resources management is expressed by Michael Armstrong.

Definition A strategic and coherent approach to the management of an organisation's most valued assets: the people working there who individually and collectively contribute to the achievement of its objectives for sustainable competitive advantage.

Michael Armstrong

This definition sees the role of HRM as:

- suggesting a strategic approach to the personnel function;
- serving the interests of management;
- dealing with gaining employees' commitment to the values and goals laid down by the strategic management;
- aiding in the development of the human resources which helps the organisation add value to their products or services.

1.3 The integration of HRM into strategic planning

The activities of the personnel function, culminating in manpower planning, have to be integrated with the corporate planning process. The organisation cannot, in every case, simply adjust manpower to match the needs of the corporate plan; in some instances the current and probable future availability of the human resource (especially in terms of managerial and technical abilities) must be taken into account **before** the plans are outlined.

For this clear reason, there must be direct communication between the corporate planners and the personnel function.

It is often the case that technical change is planned in anticipation or response to market demand. At the strategic level, the introduction of technical change usually requires major investment decisions. These traditionally concentrate on the technical analysis of competing proposals and on the financial return on them.

The staffing implications of strategic technical change should be part of the corporate planning process, but are often not considered because the managers of personnel functions do not have the information which would be useful in reaching these corporate decisions.

At the management level, the costs of technical change are smaller but are still allocated to 'capital expenditure' or 'wages' budgets. In the minds of most operating managers, these budgets occupy separate pigeonholes. Personnel issues are often not considered until the help of the personnel department is needed to sort out problems that have arisen.

Personnel specialists should seek to increase their involvement at the strategic level by putting themselves in a position where they can make a useful contribution to the corporate planning process.

1.4 Human resource plans

New themes in planning are concerned with the improvement of competitive performance. We are in the middle of an industrial revolution based on a wave of new technologies: electronics, computers, robotics and automation, biotechnology, and various new materials. The success of Japanese industry has encompassed all of the above, but another competitive edge is their manpower strategies and their ability to engage, involve and motivate people, thus tapping their energy and ideas. This success has encouraged many western firms to re-examine their approaches to personnel. Multinational companies are now investing as much in human resource programmes on leadership, competitive bench marks, quality improvement and employee involvement as they are spending on new equipment. We are seeing the emergence of flexible organisational arrangements such as short-term contracts, part-time working and the use of consultants and bought-in services.

2 MANPOWER PLANNING

2.1 Introduction

Manpower planning has been defined by the IPM Edinburgh group as **'a strategy for the acquisition, utilisation, improvement and preservation of an enterprises' human resources'.** It is through manpower planning that a company can determine its recruitment and selection needs, and can assist in the planning of its training needs.

Its purpose is to reduce uncertainty in the environment and assist in shaping a company's personnel policies.

A better definition is perhaps provided by Angela Bowey in her book **A Guide to Manpower Planning**.

Definition The activity of management aimed at co-ordinating the requirements for, and the availability of, different types of employee. Usually this involves ensuring that the firm has enough of the right kind of labour at such times as it is required.

Manpower planning is an integral part of corporate strategy. Neither can be accomplished without the other. Corporate strategy is a reconciliation process between what an organisation might do (opportunities) and what it can do (resources). This is an impossible process without consideration of manpower requirements. Similarly, manpower planning needs, as its base data, predictions of future output and some indication of available finance. Within this framework, manpower planning serves two functions

(a) It fulfils a problem-solving role by identifying manpower requirements, controlling the flow of labour, developing skills and increasing adaptability.

(b) It also has a strategic role in contributing towards the shape of the organisation as required by external and internal changes.

In both cases, manpower planning represents an important flow of information to aid decision making and the formulation of policies.

2.2 Predicting manpower

Manpower is a crucial resource, and therefore long-term plans are needed to ensure availability of the right type of skills.

The main problem with manpower planning is that with the speed of change in technology it is difficult to predict not only how many workers will be needed in n years' time, but also what type of skills they will need. Some jobs which now form a major part of the work content may be completely automated within a few years. In addition the rate of growth of the firm's business cannot be accurately predicted. There is thus considerable uncertainty on the demand side.

In addition, people cannot be treated like other resources. They are unpredictable and might leave the company. There is therefore uncertainty on the supply side also.

Nevertheless, an attempt must be made to assess the numbers which will be required in each type of work for some years ahead, even though the estimates will be subject to wide error. Demand and supply must then be reconciled, with decisions being taken as to the level of recruitment required, the extent of internal promotion, the amount of internal training needed, etc. This in turn will lead to decisions about the size of the personnel department needed to handle interviews, training, etc.

2.3 Management succession

One of the most important aspects of manpower planning is ensuring the management succession. It is, of course, both possible and desirable to bring in top managers from outside the company, thereby adding a breadth of experience to the top management team, but it is still necessary to have people at the top who have come from within the business. They bring specialist knowledge of different aspects of the firm itself and provide an inspiration for more junior managers who can aspire to the same position. It is thus essential that people with management potential are identified early in their careers.

Good training schemes must be provided for such people to integrate with planned career patterns including a number of development moves, to widen experience. However, care must be taken that grooming the chosen few does not take precedence over everyone else's career: if certain people are known to have been singled out, resentment will be caused and the company may miss out on spotting late developers. This points to the need for a thorough appraisal system throughout the organisation. Everyone should be made to feel that his actual and potential contribution is of value.

Management succession planning will probably entail compiling:

(a) for each post, a list of perhaps three potential successors; and
(b) for each person (at least from a certain level upwards) a list of possible development moves.

These lists then form the basis for long-term plans and development moves, and in addition supply a contingency plan to provide a successor for any post which becomes suddenly and unexpectedly vacant (eg, through death).

The most difficult post to plan for is of course that of Chief Executive: there are plenty of examples of power struggles within organisations. However, the situation where there is more than one potential successor and therefore a power struggle which can be very disruptive is not as serious as that where the present Chief Executive is so over-dominant that none of his or her subordinates is able to take over from him, because they are all 'yes men'.

2.4 The manpower plan

No manpower plan today can ignore the changing attitudes to work. There is increasing pressure for job enrichment and for worker participation and industrial democracy.

One problem which remains to be settled if industrial democracy boards are introduced is the precise roles of worker directors: are they to be representatives of the workers or directors in their own right with the same responsibility as any other director? How will their seat on the Board affect their trade union status?

On the job enrichment front, it is interesting to note that some car manufacturers have reverted from the production line system where each line-employee adds one part to each car to a group working system where each group makes a complete car. The same trend is apparent in some office situations. The fact that people prefer to work in a certain manner cannot be ignored - they will, after all, vote with their feet if they are dissatisfied. Management must recognise that some jobs will be seen as anti-social to the extent that people might eventually refuse to do them.

Thus, questions need to be asked at an early stage in the corporate planning process: what manpower does this strategy require; will it be available? Management must attempt to involve the unions in the planning process to secure co-operation (though not all issues will be negotiable).

Acquiring adequate numbers of staff of the right grades is not the end of manpower planning. Good industrial relations must be promoted. This begins, as outlined above, with participation at the planning stage, and perhaps eventually at Board level. It also involves a continuous review of working conditions by comparison with other organisations: pay, wage relativities between different grades, pensions, holiday and sickness pay, physical working conditions, safety aspects, sports and social facilities, other fringe benefits.

Manpower planning cannot, of course, be considered in isolation. It is related to all other resources strategies and particularly to capital investment. Capital investment often means less manpower. It can, however, lead ultimately to an increased manpower requirement, but with a change in the mix of grades required.

Capital investment brings economies which lead to lower prices, leading to growth, leading to greater manpower requirement. The mix of grades will tend to change from unskilled to skilled, from production to maintenance, from technical operating to planning, researching, marketing, purchasing, accounting. Such changes must be planned for as far in advance as possible. Re-training schemes must be organised.

If an overall drop is going to be necessary an attempt should be made not to build up too much only to be cut back later. (The 'hire and fire' attitude is definitely 'out' these days.) If any cuts are necessary, planned use should be made of early retirement schemes, voluntary redundancy etc. What one wants to avoid is the sort of situation which occurred at **The Times** newspaper, where workers were reluctant to accept new technology because they saw it as a threat to their jobs, while management believed that this was the only way to obtain efficiency.

2.5 Objectives of human resource strategy

An effective human resources strategy must include realistic plans and procedures. The objectives will include the following:

(a) Identifying, in precise terms, the kinds of talent the organisation will need in order to achieve its strategic goals in the short, medium and long term.

(b) Recruiting an adequate supply of young entrants with the potential to become outstanding performers, allowing for wastage and for the actions of competing organisations.

(c) Developing people's potential by training, development and education.

(d) Retaining as high a proportion as possible of those recruited in this way whose potential is demonstrated in the early years in employment.

(e) Ensuring that everything possible is done to prevent poaching of talent by competitors.

(f) Recruiting an adequate number of talented people of proven experience and accomplishment and easing their adjustment to a new corporate culture.

(g) Motivating the talented personnel to achieve high levels of performance and to build ties of loyalty to the organisation.

(h) Searching for ways of improving the performance and productivity of the most talented.

(i) Creating an organisational culture in which talent is nurtured and can flourish and in which different streams of talent can be integrated within a framework of shared values so as to form a winning team.

3 PERSONNEL POLICIES AND PROCEDURES

The personnel policy is decided at board level and establishes the way in which personnel procedures for the organisation should be actioned. Clear definitions of standards are expressed and these are usually detailed in a written policy statement. When formulating these policies it is quite usual for the employee representatives to be involved, and note taken of the recommendations of the Advisory, Conciliation and Arbitration Service Codes of Practice. The policy statements would not be expected to be presented in vague general terms. Clear information must be the order of the day.

There are many definitions of policy but the essence of them is that a policy is a general principle laid down for the guidance of executives in handling their jobs.

(a) **Policies should be distinguished from objectives, plans and strategies.**

Objectives which state an aim or goal are ends.

Plans provide a framework within which action to achieve an objective can take place ie, they are means.

Strategies which formulate action plans to achieve objectives are also means. Policies are neither ends nor means, but guidelines for action. They are not, however, actions in themselves.

(b) **Policies find expression in procedures and rules.**

Procedures may defined as 'formal arrangements by which the principles stated in policies are put into effect.' They provide a sequence of activities that executives are required to follow when implementing policy.

Rules or regulations are the laws with penalties attached by which procedures are enforced.

(c) **Policies are based on principles.**

A principle is a fundamental truth or assumption forming the basis of a chain of reasoning. Many such principles could be stated, but some fundamental concepts include those of co-operation, human dignity and justice.

(d) **Policies are both general and consequential.**

General policies are broad statements of the principles underpinning the actions to be taken in implementing policies.

Consequential policies are derived from the general policies and thus form the basis for procedures. An example of a statement of general policy is 'The company desires that your life here in the factory should be spent under the happiest and best working conditions and that the goods you are helping to produce shall be pure and wholesome'. From these two general policies relating to employment and production consequential policies can be derived.

(e) **Policy is a collective noun.**

What is termed the policy of an organisation is the total of all the policies, general and consequential, of the organisation. The policy of an organisation comprises financial, marketing, personnel, production, purchasing, research and development etc. Each of these areas can then be broken down such that personnel policy includes policy relating to industrial relations, promotion, recruitment, welfare etc. In turn welfare policies lay down principles and guidelines concerning holiday provision and retirement courses for employees nearing the end of their working lives.

(f) **Policy statements, when written, should consist of two parts:**

 (i) a preamble stating the general principles upon which the policy is based;

 (ii) statements of consequential policy derived form the principles in the preamble. (An example of a written policy statement will be shown in the section on Training and Development).

The usual contents of a personnel policy would be expected to include:

(a) **Security** – An assurance that there will be an acceptable level of security for the employees. Reasons for dismissal will be stated and reviewed regularly with full consultation.

(b) **Negotiation** – A statement giving an outline of the procedures for negotiation and fixing of the salary structure and merit systems.

(c) **Grievance** – An assurance of access to management for all employees in cases of grievance, with specified time scales for action.

(d) **Development** – The provision of satisfactory opportunities for training and promotion to posts fitting the abilities and reasonable ambitions for the individual, as well as regular appraisal and counselling.

(e) **Conditions** – A commitment to provide and maintain a high standard of working conditions appropriate to the work environment, and always at a level that satisfies the relevant statutory obligations.

(f) **Consultation** – An acceptance to recognise the need for democratic joint consultation on a range of matters which affect employees.

(g) **Industrial relations** – The recognition of trade union membership as a right of employees. Without this element in policy there is a probability of conflict sooner or later. This would also include the recognition of time off for trade union and other community duties.

(h) **Procedures** – A clear statement of disciplinary and grievance procedures, easily available to all employees. These procedures to be agreed by joint consultation with employee representatives.

(i) **Benefits** – Acceptance of the need for the provision of accident benefits, and for absence through sickness or other reasons. Policy on retirement pensions should be clearly stated and consideration for portable pensions should be made.

(j) **Welfare** – An awareness of the need for a high standard of welfare provision with outlines of the types of benefits available to staff.

(k) **Recruitment** – Implementation of recruitment of disabled people and ethnic minorities in line with government legislation.

Policy statements in writing will nevertheless be worthless if management does not carry them out effectively, and humanely. A bureaucratic approach cannot succeed with policies that are dealing essentially with people. Management and employee representatives will, at times, have to show a little flexibility to resolve an individual's unique problems.

4 THE TASKS OF HUMAN RESOURCE MANAGEMENT

4.1 Traditional view

The functions of the traditional personnel department are normally regarded as:

(a) Recruitment and selection

   (i) Human resource planning
   (ii) Job analysis
   (iii) Job descriptions
   (iv) Interviewing
   (v) Schools liaison

(b) Training

   (i) Induction
   (ii) Appraisal
   (iii) Day release
   (iv) In-house training
   (v) Supervisory training

(c) Industrial relations

   (i) Collective bargaining
   (ii) Joint consultation
   (iii) Grievance and discipline
   (iv) Incentive schemes
   (v) Job evaluation

(d) Welfare

   (i) Sick pay
   (ii) Counselling
   (iii) Recreation facilities
   (iv) Social outings
   (v) Community activities

(e) Health and safety

   (i) Upholding relevant Acts
   (ii) Accident audits
   (iii) Safety committees
   (iv) Emergency procedures
   (v) Accident records

(f) Administration

   (i) Personnel records
   (ii) Statistical information
   (iii) Co-ordinating committee

By examining the general activities of a personnel department given above, the specific functions of the department should be identified, and typically these would be:

(a) manpower planning;
(b) recruitment;
(c) selection;
(d) placement and termination;
(e) training and career development;
(f) grievance and discipline procedures;
(g) welfare;
(h) legal aspects of employment;
(i) terms of employment;

(j) working conditions and services;
(k) retirement;
(l) record maintenance;
(m) communication and consultation;
(n) negotiations on wages and other matters and procedures for avoiding disputes;
(o) management development.

The traditional view of 'personnel management' includes activities which are described by Michael Porter as 'maintenance' functions. They are necessary but the more modern approach is that the functions will add value and be strategic. The traditional role offers scope for specialisation and the personnel function is increasingly being carried out by people who spend their entire careers in the personnel field. They may start by specialising in job analysis and end up as company personnel manager or personnel director, but only in rare instances with a seat on the board.

4.2 Modern view

The more modern approach of human resources development can be defined as the process of achieving outstanding organisational performance through empowering people to achieve and give of their best. As such, it is directed at building a sustainable competitive advantage and is a strategic activity. Because of this approach it is not the exclusive province of the specialist in the personnel area. It is an activity which should actively involve not only line managers but all those responsible for the strategic direction of the organisation.

Human resources development can be a powerful force in improving the performance of organisations. In talent-intensive organisations, such as ICL, such an approach is important as a part of the organisation's competitive strategy. The value, which can be added by means of fully exploiting the potential of the most talented, is unequalled.

'Our attitude to people is created by the fact that we are in a knowledge industry. Our business success will therefore be led by people first and products second. We are no longer mainly selling boxes of computer equipment. We are selling creative solutions to business problems. If we are to be successful, to excel in all we do, to win rather than merely compete, then the full capabilities of all ICL people must be realised and released into action. That is the business of our managers, who are expected to cultivate employees' skills continuously and systematically'. (From **The ICL Way.**)

5 INDIVIDUAL AND TEAM DEVELOPMENT

5.1 Development objectives

Human resource development is the process by which the knowledge, skills and attitudes of the employees are enhanced to the benefit of the organisation, the individual, the teamwork and the community.

Any development activity would be integrated with the strategic objectives and the organisational culture and would also be subject to the environmental constraints or social responsibilities.

A measurement of how the human resource development function is given a high profile within the strategic objectives of the organisation can be seen in times of recession. A car manufacturer in Detroit USA, during the recent recession, reluctantly laid off a large proportion of its skilled workforce, leaving the remaining employees anxious and demoralised and the community angry about the increase in unemployment. A Japanese manufacturer, in the same industry and suffering the same economic downturn, instead of laying off staff that they had invested in and would need when the upturn came, used the time available to train the car workers in maintaining the manufacturing equipment. This strategy meant that, not only did they retain their staff and keep the morale of the workforce high, but when the recession lifted the Japanese plant could benefit from reduced maintenance costs and machine down-time and a co-operative workforce.

The culture within the organisation is also an important factor in the development of employees. Introducing an elaborate programme of self-managed learning into an organisation where there has previously been no formal training policy would require a revolutionary change that needed some powerful persuasion by management.

Personal objectives exist, and individual decisions to join, stay with, or leave the organisation will relate to these. The same constraint applies to decisions concerning the extent of co-operation with particular management strategies, and whether to accept transfer to other work and so on.

The environmental constraints and social responsibility factors must also be taken into account. Government policy on training and development, as well as grants available from different sources would be built into the organisation's strategy; the human resources manager would be aware of the strategic benefits and competitive advantages which might accrue to the organisation.

Legal aspects arise, together with social and ethical considerations, which determine the manner in which manpower may be utilised, the controls imposed, replacement, rates of pay, and also standards used in selection for recruitment and promotion.

External influences affect the demand for manpower (eg market conditions, government policy) and its supply (eg education policy, competing employment opportunities).

5.2 Development methods

The methods available for individual and team development include: training courses, both external and in-house; on-the-job training; mentoring; coaching; business games, computerised interactive learning and planned experiences; and self-managed learning.

A summary of development methods and their advantages and disadvantages follows:

Methods	Advantages	Disadvantages
On-the-job instruction	Relevant; develops trainee-supervisor links	May get bad habits of trainer. Distractions and pressures of workplace
Coaching	Job-related; develops supervisor-subordinate relationship	Subject to work pressures; may be done piecemeal
Counselling	Supervisor provides help when employee needs it	Counselling skills have to be developed
Delegation by supervisor	Increases scope of job; provides greater motivation	Employee may make mistakes or may fail to achieve task
Secondment	Increases the experience of employee; creates new interest	Employee may not succeed in new position
Guided projects/action learning	Increases knowledge and skills in work situation, but under guidance	Finding suitable guides and mentors
Lectures/talks	Useful for factual information	One-way emphasis; little participation
Group discussions	Useful for generating ideas and solutions	Require adequate leadership
Role-playing exercises	Useful for developing social skills	Requires careful organising; giving tactful feedback is not easy
Skill development exercises	A safe way to practise key skills	Careful organisation required

College courses (long)	Leads to qualification; comprehensive coverage of theory; wide range of teaching methods	Length of training time; not enough practical work
College courses (short)	Supplements company training; independent of internal politics	May not meet clients' needs precisely enough. Trainers may lack practical experience.
Consultants/other training organisations	Clients' needs given high priority; fills gaps in company provision; good range of teaching methods.	Can be expensive

6 CAREER MANAGEMENT

6.1 Purpose

If the organisation does not address the problem of career development it will have to rely on filling vacancies by **ad hoc** methods either from internal or external sources. The risks are great that the correct manpower will not be available or that current managerial resources will be wasted, with consequent effects on commitment and morale.

The questions raised by this area are:

(a) What basic job and professional training needs to be provided to prepare new and existing staff to fulfil their roles satisfactorily?

(b) Should we concentrate on in-service training or external courses?

(c) How can induction procedures be improved?

(d) What special programmes need to be developed to deal with re-training and updating?

(e) How can internal procedures be improved to aid the movement of staff to jobs where they can exercise greater responsibilities?

(f) What new succession plans need to be drawn up for key management and supervisory roles?

(g) How well is training linked to career development?

Manpower planning also requires a method of plotting career progression so that the organisation can ascertain at what rate employees progress, and whether factors such as age-spread will lead to promotion blockages or the over-promotion of inexperienced employees.

Managing careers is a difficult part of manpower planning. Expectations of employees seem to change and higher levels of education may add to the difficulty.

A key decision is whether careers are expected to fall within specialist areas, such as the professions, or in departments, or whether a broader base is required.

6.2 Objectives

Many organisations have elaborate schemes for planning the career progression of all, or most, of their managerial staff. This is generally done with the objectives of:

(a) providing each individual with a satisfactory career; and

(b) ensuring that the organisation makes the best use of its managerial resources.

Charles Handy argues that career planning in many organisations is not a development process so much as a weeding-out process. Because career development is a series of hurdles – appointments and levels of authority – only the strong survive to the end. The need to provide a large number of hurdles, or promotion possibilities also leads to clutter in the organisation, with many more levels of authority than often necessary.

6.3 Role

The majority of managers are not just interested in their current job but are concerned about where this job is going to lead to in the future. The objective of many managers is to ensure that they 'grow' during their career. This objective can obviously benefit the organisation as well as the individual.

The growth is triggered by a job that provides challenging, stretching goals. The clearer and more challenging the goals, the more effort the person will exert, and the more likely it is that good performance will result. If the person does a good job and receives positive feedback, he or she will feel successful (psychological success). These feelings will increase a person's feelings of confidence and self-esteem. This should lead to the person becoming more involved in work, which in turn leads to the setting of future stretching goals.

If an organisation does not wish to lose its good managers, it must consider how to satisfy their needs of growth and challenging work. In addition organisations have to become more flexible if they are to adapt to changes and uncertainty in the external environment. One way in which an organisation can achieve this is by cross-functional or location moves.

Cross-functional moves often occur at the beginning of a person's career. It is argued that this type of move keeps a person fresh and open to new learning opportunities. It also gives them a broader perspective on the company as a whole.

6.4 Activity

Compare and contrast a management training course and a management development programme.

6.5 Activity solution

(a) Both the training course and the development programme are aiming to improve management performance. However, the training course will present ideas and techniques to all course delegates, whereas a development programme will relate to one individual alone.

(b) A development programme will involve the planned introduction of a delegated responsibility, appointments for specific experience. Selective training will therefore form a part of a management development programme.

(c) Training may relate to present skills (eg, company accountant being trained on tax regulations changes). A development programme, on the other hand, concentrates on the future.

7 FACTORS AFFECTING PERFORMANCE

Many factors affect an individual's or a team's performance, ranging from the personal through the organisational and the social variables.

(a) **Individual factors** include personal circumstances, age, sex, physical characteristics, education, experience, intelligence, aptitude, personality, motivation and interests.

(b) **Job factors** include the physical environment, immediate work space, design and condition of machinery and equipment, methods and hours of work.

(c) **Organisational and social factors** include the type of organisation, pay, attitude to overtime, supervision, training, incentives, colleagues, welfare and social facilities.

(d) **Economic factors** include unemployment, recession, inflation, constraints on hours worked.

8 CHAPTER SUMMARY

Human resource management accepts that an organisation's employees are a key resource. An acknowledgement of this reflects on the strategic business objectives and planning within the organisation and empowers decision-makers down the management line.

HRM should have clear and consistent policies and encourage all employees to be committed to the organisation's goals. It must be flexible and responsive to internal and external change and work within the framework of constraints and opportunities whilst still contributing to the overall corporate aims.

Human resource training and development is the process by which the knowledge, skills and attitudes of the employees are enhanced to the benefit of the organisation, the individual, the teamwork and the community.

Management development, in particular, is the finding, tracking and developing of people for positions of responsibility in the organisation. It is based on providing training and experience to enable an individual to assume progressively more challenging and senior positions.

9 SELF TEST QUESTIONS

9.1 Define the modern view of HRM (1.2).

9.2 Explain why there must be direct communication between the corporate planners and the HRM (personnel) function (1.3).

9.3 What is the purpose of planning human resources? (1.4).

9.4 List and explain the objectives of a human resource strategy (2.5).

9.5 What would the usual contents of a personnel policy contain? (3).

9.6 Make a list of the functions of the personnel department (4.1).

9.7 Describe six development methods and outline their advantages and disadvantages (5.2).

9.8 Explain Charles Handy's views on career planning (6.2).

9.9 List some of the internal and external factors which might affect an individual's or a team's performance (7).

10 EXAMINATION TYPE QUESTION

10.1 Installing a training and development system

(a) Describe the steps that should be taken to set up a training system in an organisation. **(10 marks)**

(b) Identify five ways in which such a system would benefit the accounting function. **(10 marks)**

(Total 20 marks)

11 ANSWER TO EXAMINATION TYPE QUESTION

11.1 Installing a training and development system

All firms, whatever their size and level of complexity, will need some form of training if staff resources are to be used properly. Even smaller firms who tend to recruit staff ready trained will need to train existing staff to cope with new systems and to teach new staff the finer details of their working practices. The main difference between the different types of firm is likely to be the degree of formality involved in the training system.

The steps that should be taken to set up a training system will depend on its formality, but would normally include:

(a) An analysis of the organisation's training needs, based on a comparison of the skills possessed by its employees with those needed for its smooth operation;

(b) A decision on the scale and type of training system needed, and whether it can best be provided by the organisation's own staff or by external consultants;

(c) The allocation of responsibilities for training within the firm, including a co-ordinator for any external training;

(d) Planning specific training courses and ensuring that they are properly timed to allow normal operations to continue; and

(e) Reviewing the system on a regular basis to ensure that it is still satisfying the organisation's training needs.

In particular, the most likely benefits of a training system for the accounting function of an organisation are:

(a) More efficient use of staff resources as staff understand their duties more clearly, so that, for example, difficult accounting entries will be dealt with more intelligently;

(b) Greater flexibility of operation as more staff acquire more skills, allowing for replacement of those concerned with maintaining one set of records by those working on others if workload or absences demand it;

(c) Greater ease in introducing new techniques as a training system will exist to help with the changeover, particularly useful if the accounting records are being computerised;

(d) Greater capability for dealing with staff turnover as the training programme automatically provides for career succession; and

(e) General improvements in efficiency and staff morale.

20 RECRUITMENT AND SELECTION

INTRODUCTION & LEARNING OBJECTIVES

The consequences of good selection are often clear, whereas those of poor selection are not always obvious. The cost of advertising, the management time involved in selection and training and the expense of dismissal are easy to calculate but the longer term effects such as lowering of morale, reduced business opportunities and reduced quality of product or service are possibly more serious.

Recruitment is concerned with finding the applicants; it is the process of contacting the public and encouraging suitable candidates to come forward for final selection. Because it naturally precedes the need for training and development, effective recruitment can, to some extent, reduce the need for expensive training, although in a fast-developing environment most people need to acquire new skills or update old ones.

Selection is the process of choosing between applicants for the job and of eliminating unsuitable applicants.

When you have studied this chapter you should be able to do the following:

- Discuss the process by which personnel requirements are determined.
- Outline the different forms of employment.
- Explain the use of cost-benefit analysis in evaluating and determining the benefits of additional or new personnel.
- Explain the purpose of job and personnel specifications in the recruitment and selection of staff.
- Discuss the methods of recruitment
- Explain the use of application forms, CVs, interviews and selection tests as part of the selection process.
- Explain the usefulness of references.

1 RECRUITMENT

1.1 The importance of recruitment

Recruitment and selection are part of the same process and some people often refer to both as the recruitment process. This is not entirely accurate; the process of recruitment as distinct from selection involves the attraction of a field of suitable candidates for the job. Once this has been achieved, the selection processes begin; these are aimed at selecting the best person for the job from that field of candidates. An effective recruitment policy is important for a number of reasons; these are

(a) It is an activity which affects the shape of a firm's manpower, and therefore has a direct bearing upon the effectiveness and in some cases the ultimate survival of an organisation.

(b) Ineffective recruitment policies may result in labour shortages, and when coupled with ineffective selection procedures can lead to the hiring of unsuitable employees. This in turn may lead to work inefficiencies, individual dissatisfaction and labour turnover. On the other hand, the **Employment Protection Acts** and specifically 'unfair dismissal' legislation may mean it is difficult and perhaps costly to dispense with an unsuitable employee who remains with the organisation.

(c) The effectiveness of recruitment is particularly important, since recruitment itself has become very costly. A block advertisement in a prestigious daily newspaper can cost over £1,000 per insertion.

1.2 Determining requirements

The whole process of recruitment entails deciding whether and how to recruit, job analysis and attracting candidates. In his article **Recruitment and Selection** 1989, P Plumbley identified the following questions that should be asked before recruiting:

(a) What is the purpose of the job? Is it necessary? Is it fulfilling its purpose?

(b) Could it be combined with another job or jobs or could tasks be allocated to make better use of other people in the department?

(c) Can we learn any lessons from the record of the last incumbent?

(d) Could the vacancy be used as a temporary training position eg. Youth Training Scheme, or to accommodate a redundant employee elsewhere, to provide easier work for an employee approaching retirement or in failing health, or as an opportunity for promoting someone?

(e) Are we certain that no existing employee would be suitable? Could we afford to train someone?

(f) Is the required type of person easier to recruit locally? Are there aspects of the job analysis (eg. hours of work) or of the person specification which could be adjusted to attract a wider choice of candidates?

In conjunction with these questions, the choice is between:

(a) recruitment from outside the organisation;
(b) recruitment from other divisions within the organisation;
(c) promotion from within the division;
(d) promotion from within the department;
(e) secondment of existing staff;
(f) closing the job down and sharing the duties among existing staff;
(g) rotating jobs so that the vacant post is filled by different staff on a systematic basis;
(h) not recruiting or considering the job at all.

1.3 Different forms of employment

Most organisations are adopting a flexible approach to manpower planning. Different forms of employment are used to allow the organisation some adaptability in a changing environment.

There are three broad levels of employment:

(a) **Prime employees**. These are direct employees on permanent contracts.

(b) **Secondary employees**. These are also direct employees, but on temporary or part-time contracts. Job sharing is a peculiar mixture of both prime and secondary employment. Allied Carpets have recently introduced a zero-hours contract where suitable staff can be contacted at the eleventh hour to help with busy periods.

(c) **Outworkers**. These are not employees at all but contractors, agency staff, consultants and so on.

1.4 Activity

There are some types of jobs which lend themselves to all of the above types of employment and others which fit only one type. Identify some jobs to each category.

1.5 Activity solution

There are many types of job that you could have identified; the following are a small selection.

Lecturers can be employed as prime employees, secondary employees or outworkers. Other jobs which lend themselves only to one category include:

MPs as prime employees are on permanent contracts for the duration of the government's term of office.

Weekend staff in retail stores are only part time staff; the stores use them to cover the busy periods but manage with their full time staff during the week.

Outworkers are generally used to deliver leaflets or catalogues at certain times of the year.

2 COST-BENEFIT ANALYSIS

Manpower remains the only area of some company management where investment decisions of enormous cost can be made with little or no attempt at financial evaluation and post investment appraisal. The analysis of the personnel department as a force working against company profitability led Robert Townsend to recommend the disbandment of the personnel department (**Up the Organisation**).

Some attempt must be made to cost manpower planning and the technique of cost benefit analysis can be used as it takes account not only of financial costs and benefits but also of indirect social costs and benefits. If these can be quantified in financial terms then they should be discounted in the same way as for a DCF (discounted cash flow) calculation to arrive at a NPV (net present value).

Initially the cost of additional or new personnel can be weighed against the increase in output. The costs include:

- recruitment costs in terms of the advertising, management time and fees;
- salaries and related costs of employing staff;
- Training and development costs, both in money and in learning and training time;
- Additional costs of equipment, space and facilities.

The results of this comparison can then be used to compare the cost of the alternatives eg, contracting out, buying capital equipment or altering work processes to enhance productivity.

3 JOB AND PERSONNEL SPECIFICATIONS

3.1 The process of recruitment

The process of recruitment involves several stages; these are

(a) An analysis of the need for recruitment. This is determined by manpower planning and a full analysis of the job or jobs.

(b) A decision as to whether jobs will be filled from within or outside the organisation.

(c) Choosing the most appropriate method of recruitment.

(d) Evaluation of the recruitment procedures.

3.2 The importance of job analysis

According to the British Standards Institution, job analysis is:

Definition 'The determination of the **essential** characteristics of a job' (BSI 1979).

Describing the job requires a precise and descriptive vocabulary. It demands writing skills of a high order.

Job analysis is a vital preliminary to any recruitment activity and involves three main aspects; these are

(a) An analytical study of a job to determine accurately the work done.

(b) Achieving an understanding of the work in relation to other tasks in the organisation.

(c) An identification of the qualities required of the job holder.

Such an exercise is frequently necessary since all too few organisations have a precise picture of the work that people do to achieve organisational objectives. It has often been said that discrepancies occur between what superiors believe is taking place, what job-holders believe is taking place, and what subordinates believe is taking place and all these can differ from what is actually taking place.

3.3 The uses of job analysis

Effective recruitment depends upon accurate job analyses. Precision in identifying the type of person required by an organisation can save time and money and avoid unwanted personnel. For instance, if the exact nature of the job is known, then it facilitates precisely worded advertisements, which assist in attracting a suitable field of candidates. If the advertisement is loosely worded, based upon an insufficient analysis, then totally unsuitable candidates may be attracted to apply, thereby causing an increase in the costs of recruitment. Job analysis is helpful to the recruitment process in another way, since it may establish that the job is no longer necessary or that it can be done elsewhere in the organisation or that it can be shared amongst other employees. Thus, job analysis may eliminate the need for recruitment. However, apart from its value in the recruitment process, job analysis as a technique is useful in many areas of personnel work. The list below gives an indication of its many uses

(a) To assist in determining the most appropriate method of selection.

(b) To help identify the need for training and the most appropriate training method.

(c) As part of a job evaluation exercise. Job analysis is the first step in establishing differences between jobs so that wage and salary differentials may be determined.

(d) As an important preliminary to any job redesign exercise, as in work improvement through job enrichment.

(e) It may be useful in the field of industrial relations by providing information vital to negotiating exercises.

(f) It is an important part of manpower planning at the micro-level; one aspect of this has been mentioned already, namely the re-allocation of jobs when they fall vacant.

3.4 Methods of job analysis

Various methods may be used, all with advantages and disadvantages depending upon the nature of the task to be analysed.

The main methods are as follows

(a) **Observation**

This may be carried out by a manager or, in some cases, a job analysis specialist. While this technique is adequate for simple repetitive jobs it is generally poor for more complex work. However, for jobs involving a number of different operations at different times, activity sampling may be used. This involves making observations at regular or random intervals over a period of time until a complete picture is built up. Even this may be inappropriate for jobs where key tasks are performed very infrequently as in the case of teachers marking examination scripts. General observation has been found to be a particularly useful method of identifying the learning difficulties of new recruits.

(b) **Interviews**

Inevitably, the interview will be used at some stage. 'The main difficulty with interviews, however, lies not so much with the technique itself but with the quality of the interviewer'. (Edwards and Paul 1978). This is why the skill of the interviewer is of prime importance.

(i) **Interviews with the job-holder**

This is probably the most popular method of job analysis, and the most acceptable to job-holders themselves who may resent being observed without participating in the exercise. It is based on the notion that no one in the organisation knows more about the job than the actual job-holder. Its accuracy depends upon a full interview, a trained interviewer and a lack of bias on the part of the job-holder. Some job-holders may exaggerate the difficulty of their work or inflate its importance; this can occur especially in a job evaluation exercise where job analysis is being used as a basis for wage negotiation.

(ii) **Interviews with management**

This method is helpful to gain an overall picture of the relationship of the tasks to other jobs in the work process. It is also a useful check on the accuracy of the job-holder's account. It may, however, lack the precision of the previous method since the manager may not be aware of all the intricacies of every job under his supervision.

(c) **Questionnaires and checklists**

These are useful adjuncts to the interview methods and may be designed to enable relatively inexperienced managers to carry out an accurate job analysis.

(d) **Procedure manuals**

Many jobs already have written accounts and such manuals often abound in training departments where they were specially devised to assist in the training process. These existing accounts are an obvious starting point in any analysis, but they should be treated with caution, since for most jobs they will be sadly out of date. This raises an important issue for job analysis; it should never be regarded as a once-for-all process. Many jobs change frequently and the process of job analysis should be continuous.

An accurate job analysis should identify the tasks and duties that are being performed; the decisions that need to be made and the equipment that is used; how the job fits in with other jobs in the organisation; and the degree of complexity and difficulty involved in the job. These are the what, why and how questions of job analysis and are the basis of the job description and the personnel specification

3.5 Job descriptions

After a full job analysis has been carried out, job descriptions can be drawn up identifying the precise nature of the jobs in question. There are various methods of classification but most include all of the following points

(i) The title of the job and the name of the department in which it is situated.

(ii) The purpose of the job identifying its objectives in relationship to overall objectives.

(iii) The position of the job in the organisation indicating the relationships with other jobs and the chains of responsibility. For this purpose, many firms refer to existing organisation charts.

(iv) Principal duties to be performed, with emphasis on key tasks, and limits to the job-holder's authority. Usually under this heading is included an indication of how the job differs from others in the organisation.

(v) A further breakdown of principal duties is made identifying specific tasks in terms of what precisely is done and in what manner, and with some explanation, both in terms of quantity and quality.

(vi) Aspects of the 'job environment' should be considered. Descriptions should be made of how the organisation supports the job in terms of management and the provision of key services. The working conditions should be considered in terms of both the physical environment and the social environment (is the job part of a group task?). The opportunities offered by the job should be identified; these are especially important in a recruitment exercise. Such opportunities should be those offered by the job, and not those open only to talented individuals and may include such factors as promotion prospects and general career development. The rewards offered by the job should be taken into account, including not only the wage rate but bonuses, the amount of expected overtime and the related fringe benefits. Finally, some assessment should be made of the temperamental demands placed upon the job-holder such as the uncertain nature of the work and the amount of stress involved.

(vii) No job description is complete without a full identification of the key difficulties likely to be encountered by the job-holder.

3.6 Personnel specification

This is variously referred to as the job specification and even the man specification. Its aim is to construct a blueprint of the qualities required of the job-holder. It is based firstly on the job description and secondly upon an analysis of successful as well as unsuccessful job-holders. Such a specification is of obvious value in framing recruitment advertisements and as a guide to the selection process. The main problems involved with all types of specification are detail and flexibility. Some writers feel that over-specification is as bad as being too vague, in that too detailed a specification may be aimed at the ideal candidate who just does not exist; it may, therefore, prove to be too limiting in the recruitment and selection exercise. Probably the most appropriate policy is to apply a detailed specification with a certain degree of flexibility. Several classifications have been produced, the most famous of which is undoubtedly the **Seven Point Plan** devised by Alec Rodger in the 1950s. Rodger's classification involves the following factors

(i) **Physical make-up**

This can be extremely precise, as in the case of listing minimum height requirements for recruits to the police force, or refer to more general attributes such as a pleasant appearance, a clear speaking voice and good health. A good example can be found in broadcasting where requirements are often set relating to appearance (in the case of television) and microphone voice (more particularly in the case of radio).

(ii) **Attainments**

These relate to both job attainments and educational attainments. It is quite common for organisations to stipulate minimum entry requirements in terms of the number of GCSEs, A-levels or a degree, and in some cases, as with jobs in the Civil Service, the class of degree. People aspiring to the professions, as in the case of accountancy, must have minimum educational qualifications to enable them to tackle the required professional examinations. Many jobs require applicants to possess specific work experiences such as typing speed, experience of working with certain types of computer language or have proven ability at operating a certain machine.

(iii) **General intelligence**

Many attempts have been made by psychologists to link measured intelligence levels with the ability to do certain jobs. Research in this area is, however, somewhat inconclusive. Many jobs do, nonetheless, require such abilities as a good memory, verbal and numerical skills and problem-solving.

(iv) **Special aptitudes**

Some jobs carry specialised requirements such as the ability to drive a car or bus, the ability to type, or the ability to speak a foreign language.

(v) **Interests**

Certain interests may be appropriate to certain jobs, such as an interest in practical work or socialising. The latter might be important where jobs require a fair amount of 'off duty' entertaining. Any interest in helping people may be considered a necessary requirement for social work. Candidates for certain teaching posts may be favoured if they express an interest in such extra-mural activities as drama or running a soccer team.

(vi) **Disposition**

All firms require their employees to be honest and reliable. A friendly disposition is usually essential in jobs which involve a great amount of contact with the general public as in the case of a receptionist. Jobs without close supervision invariably call for employees who are self-reliant and can make decisions.

(vii) **Circumstances**

These may include such factors as the availability for working irregular hours or the home address of the candidate. For example, if a firm requires its employees to be on regular call, it may be difficult for someone living in an isolated rural community. Some firms may expect employees to stay a minimum number of years and the individuals' circumstances must be compatible with this.

A similar blueprint to the Seven Point Plan was devised by Munro-Fraser. He referred to it as the **Five Point Plan**, to include the following considerations

(1) The impact on others.
(2) Qualifications.
(3) Brains and abilities.
(4) Motivation.
(5) Adjustment.

Thomason criticises both the Seven and Five Point Plans on the basis of the fact that while it is relatively easy to allocate qualifications, the qualities required are often a matter of personal judgement. Even qualifications, which Thomason refers to as having a superficial objectivity in that they are more readily measurable, are subject to a certain amount of personal interpretation. Thomason does, however, suggest that the categories which might be expected to vary with job performance, can be identified. He lists these categories as

(1) Intellectual requirements – in terms of training, skills and experience.

(2) Physical requirements – in terms of muscular or sensory abilities and health.

(3) Personality requirements – in terms of such factors as memory, speed of reaction, temperament, co-operation, perseverance, initiative, and so on.

3.7 The purpose of specifications

Whichever classification system is used it must be adapted to the job in question. It may be useful to distinguish between essential and desirable attributes. Plumbley suggests that it is also important to identify contra-indications: those attributes which would disqualify a candidate. Such contra-indications may include such factors as shyness or, in the case of a Liverpool retailer requiring Saturday shop assistants, disqualifying candidates who expressed a strong support for one of the city's soccer teams. It can clearly be seen that a personnel specification can be helpful in not only the recruitment process but also as a template by which candidates may be selected. It is important to reiterate an earlier point about the need to be flexible and to draw up the specification in terms that can be recognised and measured – not a list of abstract human qualities. Finally, care must be taken not to transgress one of the recent laws relating to discrimination, as in the case of a job advertisement seeking 'a female Scottish cook and housekeeper', which was barred both on the grounds of race and sex discrimination.

4 METHODS OF RECRUITMENT

4.1 Introduction

Apart from the preliminary decision as to whether the job needs filling and the determination of the job description and personnel specification, a decision must be reached as to whether the firm is seeking to recruit from within its own organisation or from outside. Each has its own advantages and disadvantages.

4.2 Internal recruitment

This occurs when a vacant position is filled by one of the existing employees. It generally applies to those jobs where there is some kind of career structure, as in the case of management or administrative staff. Most firms invariably recruit supervisors from their own shop floor staff. If a policy of internal recruitment is to be pursued the following points should be noted:

(a) Recruiting from within by promoting existing employees can act as a source of motivation and may be good for the general morale of the workforce.

(b) In dealing with existing staff, selection can be made on the basis of known data. The old adage of 'better the devil you know' applies here.

(c) The internal recruit may be fully conversant with the work involved and will certainly know the people with whom he will be dealing; he may even have been carrying out the duties either as part of his own job or as the understudy to the incumbent.

(d) It can save considerable time and expense in recruitment and selection.

(e) If training is required this can be costly, but generally no induction is needed, and the firm may be able to train employees to its own specifications.

(f) One of the problems caused by internal recruitment could be the ill-feeling it creates among those not selected or the difficulty of promoting someone to supervise ex-workmates. This latter problem has been considered by both the Army and the Ford Motor Co., both of whom usually transfer staff when promoted, although this normally only applies for the first levels of supervision.

(g) It sometimes necessitates a planned programme of career development and talent spotting. While some may consider this essential to the running of an effective organisation it can be as costly and time-consuming as external recruitment procedures. As part of this policy some firms deliberately over-recruit trainees at the lower levels of management to fill more senior positions in later years. This can cause frustration for those denied promotion opportunities.

4.3 External recruitment

This occurs when an organisation seeks to bring in someone from outside the organisation to fill a vacancy. In general its advantages and disadvantages are opposite to those of internal recruitment, but the following specific points should be noted

(a) External recruitment may be essential if an organisation is seeking specific skills and expertise not available. At some stage external recruitment is necessary to restore manning levels, depleted by employee wastage and internal promotion policies.

(b) It may be necessary to inject new blood into an enterprise. People from outside the firm often bring with them new ideas and different approaches to the job, gleaned from their experience working in other organisations. With internal promotion policies there is a real danger of producing a succession of employees all with the same ideas; indeed, this may be a barrier to progress in the organisation. On the other hand, it should be remembered that newcomers can be equally set in their ways and have difficulties of adjustment to new techniques and approaches.

(c) Although training costs may be reduced since there is the opportunity to recruit personnel with the required expertise, external recruitment does add to replacement and selection costs, and induction is still necessary.

(d) Bringing in someone from outside may create dissatisfaction among existing employees.

(e) In order to attract people to change their jobs a firm may have to pay initially higher wages.

There are no hard and fast rules concerning internal and external recruitment. It is largely a policy decision on the part of each individual firm as to which suits it best for different jobs. If internal recruitment is used, then a limited number of methods are available. The most usual is really a form of direct invitation. Assessments are made of employees, and on the basis of these, management decide who will be offered a promotion opportunity. Some firms, however, allow employees to compete for vacancies by advertising internally, either through newsletters or by using notice-boards; normal selection procedures then follow. In some concerns it is obligatory that all promotion opportunities be open to competition, although this does not preclude management inviting certain chosen candidates to apply. Even where external recruitment is the main policy it does not prevent an existing employee from applying. The remainder of this chapter will focus on the techniques of external recruitment beginning with an assessment of recruitment advertising.

4.4 Recruitment advertising

This is an extremely important method of recruitment. Plumbley notes that significant changes have taken place since 1958 when restrictions on newsprint were lifted and newspapers could devote a great deal more space than hitherto to job advertising. This led to the development of display advertising not merely to attract the active job seeker but also to attract those not consciously seeking alternative employment. In some instances this placed job advertising in the same category as product advertising. In most cases, however, advertising is a costly business and care must be taken to ensure that it is money well spent. This section will look not only at press advertising but also at the growing use of radio and television as methods of recruitment advertising.

4.5 The preliminaries of recruitment advertising

Before embarking upon an advertising exercise, an organisation must be clear about its objectives in so doing, ie, precisely what to say and how to say it and a choice must be made as to the most appropriate media.

(a) **Defining the objectives**

Plumbley identifies three objectives of recruitment advertising. These are

(i) To produce a compact field of suitable candidates and deter the unsuitable from applying.

(ii) To achieve a balance between coverage and cost.

(iii) To facilitate future recruitment by presenting an attractive image of the organisation.

(b) **What to say**

This is based on a careful job analysis, followed by a selection of those key aspects that provide necessary information to prospective job candidates. Several research studies have been carried out to determine the type of information required and there is a measure of agreement that the most important factors are a succinct description of the work involved, the location, the remuneration, and a brief indication of the type of person required. Plumbley suggests that the information should be **factual, relevant and unambiguous**. Examples abound in most newspapers of evasive advertising making statements such as **the job will be located in the North of England** or **the salary will be commensurate with the seniority of the position**. Such statements do nothing to attract candidates and may actually deter potentially suitable applicants.

(c) **How to say it**

Generally advertisements should be concise and attractively written. Unfortunately in some organisations the job of writing the advertisement is given to an inexperienced personnel officer or is the product of a committee; both can result in poor advertisements. The following factors may be of importance

(i) an attractive eye-catching heading, possibly incorporating a company symbol or logo;

(ii) a job title that will leave the applicant in no doubt as to what the job entails;

(iii) a written style that holds interest; and

(iv) the offer of further information, perhaps inviting applicants to telephone for further information and to discuss their suitability.

All these factors are important considerations before actually placing an advertisement. Some companies employ management consultants for the entire undertaking, although this incurs a consultancy fee as well as the cost of the advertisement. The advantages and disadvantages of various forms of advertising are discussed below.

4.6 Press advertising

(a) **The national press**

The main advantages include the following

(i) There is regular publication, so space is usually available for an immediate insertion.

(ii) The layout is usually attractive.

(iii) There is a wide circulation and readership, thereby increasing the field of potential candidates.

(iv) Many British newspapers are sold in other countries, so that overseas coverage is achieved at no extra cost. This may be important in recruiting for jobs requiring the experience of working in another country, as in some marketing posts.

(v) Certain newspapers such as **The Times** have a certain status which may enhance the reputation of the firm.

(vi) Some newspapers have regular job features. **The Guardian**, for instance, devotes particular days to certain types of job advertisements; Monday is devoted to media appointments, Tuesday to teaching appointments and so on.

The main disadvantages include

(i) The fact that approximately 95% of the circulation is wasted.

(ii) The advertisement has a relatively short life; many people do not keep daily newspapers beyond the day of issue.

(iii) Since national papers are popular sources of recruitment, competition is fierce. A firm may find that its advertising is surrounded by others of a similar nature, perhaps offering more attractive jobs.

(iv) The national press is very expensive. A column centimetre can cost anything from £10 – £20 and a large block display can be £1,000 or more; and these rates apply for only one issue.

The national press is probably more suitable in the case of recruitment for managerial, some professional and senior technical staff. More popular daily papers such as the **Daily Mirror** may be used where large numbers of skilled or semi-skilled workers are required, and incentives are offered for moving area.

(b) **The local press**

The main advantages include the following

(i) It is usually much cheaper than the national press (but it still may constitute a considerable expense for some firms).

(ii) It can reduce recruitment and selection costs by eliminating the costs of resettlement in that readers are usually from the local area.

(iii) The firm may already be well known so that the length of advertisements may be reduced.

(iv) The use of local papers has the added advantage of contributing to good public relations and vacancies may attract editorial coverage.

(v) Most local papers have a longer life than their national counterparts.

The main disadvantages include the following

(i) A sufficient number of people with the necessary requirements may not be available in the local area.

(ii) Circulation is usually limited and issues are often only on a weekly basis.

(iii) The quality of layout is very variable.

Local newspapers are probably most suited for the recruitment of skilled manual, clerical, local authority and lower management positions.

(c) **Specialist journals**

These include the publications of the professional bodies and various trade journals. As such they are most suited for recruitment in the professions and specialist trades.

The main advantages include the following

(i) The readership is particularly homogeneous; there is already a degree of pre-selection which may reduce eventual recruitment and selection costs.

(ii) Many, because of their small circulation, have relatively cheap advertising rates, although this may not be the case for the more popular accounting journals.

(iii) It may be assumed that likely readers are those who wish to keep up-to-date with developments in their field.

The main disadvantages include the following

(i) Closing dates for advertisements usually occur well before publication; this can inhibit speedy recruitment.

(ii) Because they are so specialised there is considerable competition from other advertisements.

(iii) Many give little space to job advertisements.

(iv) Circulation can be slow and haphazard, particularly where it involves subscription readership.

4.7 Radio and television

The use of radio and television is increasing in popularity particularly since the advent of commercial radio. Whilst there is wide exposure, the desired audience may not be listening or watching. In some case firms using television have been overwhelmed by the response which creates significant problems of selection. It should also be remembered that television advertising can be more expensive than the national press, although the use of television, along with the cinema, may be appropriate for mass-recruiting in situations of severe labour shortage.

4.8 Other methods of recruitment

It has been noted that while advertising has a number of distinct attractions, it does have drawbacks, notably cost. Some practitioners feel that advertising should only be used when all other avenues of recruitment have been exhausted. This is rather a sweeping statement, but certainly other methods do exist that are of low cost to the organisation. This section will explore the advantages and disadvantages of those other methods.

(a) **Nomination by existing employees**

This can be a selective method of recruitment, since generally only suitable applicants are recommended. In times of severe staff shortages incentives can be offered to existing employees who recommend a recruit who stays for more than six months. It is a very unpredictable method in terms of response but can be useful for certain manual jobs. At the other extreme, personal recommendation is often a popular form of recruitment for the most senior executive posts.

(b) **Casual enquiries**

This form of recruitment places the onus on job candidates and as such is unpredictable and offers the firm no control over the process. Some firms see it as an indication of motivation on the part of the job-seeker and some facilitate enquiry by posting notices of vacancies outside the premises. Even when jobs are not available this can be a useful method for building up dossiers of potential employees to be contacted at some later date.

(c) **Government employment services**

The unemployed register presents firms with a reservoir of potential employees categorised according to skill and pre-selected according to suitability. The separation of the benefit and employment functions by the creation of Job Centres also provides details of vacancies to people already holding a job. In general terms, the Government service is most used by firms when seeking manual workers, although unemployed managers, technical and professional staff are available on the Professional and Executive Register. The main disadvantages of using the Department of Employment seem to come from the fact that unemployment is still seen by many employing managers as a social stigma and indicative of poor work records and there are constant complaints from firms that too many unsuitable applicants are sent for interview. These criticisms may be lessened by the high rates of unemployment in the 1980s. As well as providing the above services, the Department of Employment offers firms advice on recruitment and has specialist services for youth employment and careers guidance. In terms of recruitment it has one obvious advantage in that services apart from Professional and Executive recruitment are provided without cost to the employing organisations.

(d) **Private agencies**

There are several types of these:

(i) **Employment agencies**

There has been a tremendous increase in the numbers of such agencies offering a recruitment service. They tend to specialise in clerical, secretarial and domestic jobs and operate by charging a recruitment fee (usually one week's wages) to the firm for introducing an employee. One of their biggest advantages is that they are often a valuable source of temporary staff; this is particularly true in the area of secretarial skills, but this service has spread to other areas, notably nursing. As Plumbley points out, they flourish when demand exceeds supply.

(ii) **Candidate registers**

These operate in a similar way to employment agencies but tend to specialise in professional and technical jobs. Potential job-seekers participate in this scheme by putting their name and qualifications details on a register which is then circulated to firms who subscribe to that particular register.

(iii) **Advertising agencies**

These assist a firm by taking over responsibility for its recruitment advertising and gain substantial income not only from the fee charged but the discounts they receive from the press and journals.

(iv) **Management consultants**

As with employment agencies there has been a considerable increase in the numbers of consultants specialising in recruitment and selection. Such firms specialise in the recruitment of senior management and senior technical staff. There is often an overlap with the role of advertising agencies and candidate registers. In the latter case some consultants offer firms an **executive search service** which entails the pre-selection of a group of likely candidates.

The main disadvantage with all forms of private agency is that they are expensive. This is particularly true of management consultants.

(e) **Recruiting direct from schools and colleges**

This is often a cheap method of obtaining trainees and sometimes involves pre-selection by the schools and colleges themselves. A feature of management trainee recruitment for a number of years has been the **milk-round**, where firms seeking employees visit a number of universities and other colleges, working in liaison with the appointments boards in those institutions. Most large organisations have a long history of graduate recruitment. As the nature of work changes and the economy develops, there is an increasing need for organisations to recruit high calibre staff.

Selection techniques should ensure that the most suitable applicants are chosen. In the interview the applicants should be encouraged to talk freely about their interests and aspirations.

Direct recruitment, particularly from schools, is often associated with problems of induction and labour turnover. It should also be remembered that while initial wages will be relatively low, training costs will be high.

4.9 The evaluation of recruitment

There is no best method of recruitment; a firm must choose the most appropriate method to suit its own particular recruitment needs and the type of job involved. Since most forms of recruitment are expensive both in terms of time and money, it is important to make a constant evaluation of the entire process. Such evaluation should consider the following factors

(a) The total cost of the exercise including staff time, the cost of advertisements and the use of external services.

(b) The extent of coverage of the method of recruitment used.

(c) The level of response from suitable applicants.

(d) The subsequent work records of those engaged.

(e) The length of service of those engaged.

By keeping records of these factors with respect to both the type of job and method of recruitment, information may emerge which may point to a more efficient use of recruitment resources.

5 SELECTION

5.1 Introduction

Selection is the process at the end of which a decision is made as to whether an individual is offered and takes up employment with an organisation. While this chapter will focus upon management policy concerning selection, the opening statement suggests that selection is really a two-way process. Not only is the firm selecting the individual but invariably the individual is making decisions as to the suitability of the job offered, the terms of employment and the firm. For individuals, this is part of a process known as **occupational choice** which is concerned with the way individuals make and implement decisions about pursuing a particular type of work. It is a complex process which has been the subject of a great deal of research into such influences as family background and education and the nature of the decision-making process itself. Many texts on personnel management imply that the candidate for a job has a purely passive role and that 'the decision rests solely with management'. Research has shown this can lead to ineffective staffing and subsequent problems of job dissatisfaction and labour turnover. Several writers take the view that the more a candidate is allowed to participate in the selection process and the more information the employing organisation imparts, the more successful the subsequent employment will be for both the firm and the individual.

5.2 Key aspects of selection

(a) Who makes the decision?

The ultimate decision, as indicated above is in the hands of the prospective employee when he decides to accept or reject the offer. The decision to make an offer may be taken by a variety of people in the organisation. The main debate revolves around whether the decision should be made by the manager for whom the employee will eventually work, or whether selection should be carried out by specialists. Most managers would argue the right to select their own employees based upon their local knowledge of the type of work to be carried out and of the nature of the working environment. This method of operation reinforces the authority of the individual manager and makes him responsible for the consequences of faulty selection. However, in some organisations managers only act in an advisory role and the decision is taken by some form of centralised senior management. The argument here is that the employment decision is made on behalf of the entire firm, since individual workers may move from department to department and a suitable employee in the eyes of one manager may not be so suitable for another. In addition, centralised staff may be more experienced in selecting staff than the individual manager. Some firms opt for a strategy of collective responsibility where the decision rests with a selection board. A good example of this is the selection of teachers, which is usually made by a panel consisting of head teachers, other teachers, senior employees of the local Education Authority and members of the school governors. The advantages and disadvantages of the panel method will be discussed later. The method of decision-making used will depend largely on the type of job. The selection of semi-skilled machine operators will usually be made by the department manager concerned or by the personnel department. The selection of middle or senior managers will be made invariably by a centralised group of senior managers drawn from a variety of functions. The role of the personnel department in the selection process will vary from firm to firm. In some cases, particularly the selection of large numbers of workers at the shop floor level, the personnel department may have sole responsibility for the entire process. In most cases the personnel manager will operate in an advisory capacity offering specialist knowledge and carrying out specialist techniques, such as testing, when required.

(b) What to look for

This is indicated to a large extent by the job analysis process. However, in some cases a decision must be made regarding the employment of fully trained personnel as opposed to selecting untrained personnel with potential to develop. This decision will obviously vary according to the nature of the job and the supply factor of the labour market. In general, the selection of trained personnel reduces training costs but remuneration costs will be higher. It does have the advantage of ensuring a predicted level of output and the possible introduction of new ideas. The selection of trainees will carry high training costs and possible increased costs of a higher level of labour turnover and a higher rate of materials wastage. Some of these can be offset by lower payroll costs and it may be a useful strategy when recruitment fails to attract sufficient numbers of qualified candidates.

(c) Selection methods

In general these should be tailor-made for a particular organisation and job. The thoroughness of the procedure will depend on a number of factors

(i) The consequences of faulty selection; obviously an organisation will take more care in selecting its Financial Director than it will in selecting its car-park attendant.

(ii) The time and finance available; these are both constraints on the process. A firm may have neither the time nor the money to invest in lengthy, complicated selection methods.

(iii) The company policy, which may lay down certain rules for the composition of selection panels or the use of certain tests. Some companies have policies of over-hiring certain types of trainees, to ensure that the most able graduate is available for all positions. This will often offset losses through labour turnover.

(iv) The selection process becomes more important the longer the length of the training period, since this represents a considerable investment on the part of the organisation.

(d) **Screening process**

Before selection can take place the number of applicants must be reduced to manageable proportions. There are two methods available:

(a) **Telephone screening**. This can considerably shorten the time of selection because interview dates can be arranged immediately for suitable applicants.

(b) **Letters, CVs or application forms.** People responding to the job advertisement will be most often be asked to complete a job application form or to send details of previous job experience and qualifications together with personal details (ie, CV – curriculum vitae).

5.3 Application forms

The application form usually seeks information about the applicant on several fronts, namely:

(i) personal details of address, age, family background, nationality;
(ii) education and experience history;
(iii) present employment terms and experience;
(iv) social and leisure interests.

The application form should be regarded by the applicant as an opportunity to qualify for the interview. It usually includes a general section enabling the applicant to express career ambitions, personal preferences, etc. in his own words. This can be an important section in gauging an applicant's ability to express himself in writing and perhaps even aspects of motivation, ambition and character.

The application form has advantages over the personal CV in that:

(i) it allows for standard comparisons between applicants;
(ii) it includes all areas of interest to the company.

The purpose of the application form, from the point of view of the company, is to enable an initial sifting of suitable from unsuitable candidates; a standardised form speeds the sorting and short-listing of applicants and can be most useful where the ratio of applicants to vacancies is high. At a basic level it is a test of literacy and the ability to understand simple instructions. Since interviewing is an expensive and time-consuming business, it is important that candidates who are unlikely to be successful should not reach the interview stage.

Most firms use application forms as a useful preliminary to selection interviews. Basic information can be gained which would otherwise take up valuable interview time. Some interviewers use the form as the framework for the interview itself; it can be a particularly useful guide for inexperienced interviewers. Some organisations have extended the role played by the application form, compared to the interview, by asking for much more detailed information, sometimes asking candidates to answer questions relating to their motivation towards applying. This extension of the use of application forms is undoubtedly related to the relatively recent lack of confidence in the interview as a means of selection but must itself be viewed with suspicion, as selection decisions may be based more on the standard of literacy rather than job ability or potential.

If the applicant is eventually employed, the information on the application form is kept as the personal record. A well designed application form contains all the relevant data relating to address, age, qualifications, previous experience and so on. This should be updated at regular intervals.

5.4 Interviews

The interview is an extremely popular method of selecting employees. However, there are many different types of interview. In some case it is merely a ritual to explain to workers their terms of employment whilst in other cases it is the real basis upon which selection decisions are made.

There are many different types of interview, including the following:

(a) **The face to face interview**

This occurs when the candidate is interviewed by a single representative, usually of the employing organisation. It is considered the best situation for establishing rapport and is certainly cost effective in terms of people employed. While it does have the advantage of placing candidates at their ease the selection decision relies heavily on the judgement of one individual.

(b) **Successive interviews**

This type of interview consists of a series of face-to-face interviews. A fairly large manufacturing company in Britain has a standard procedure for this type of interview, which it uses in selecting management trainees. The candidate is interviewed first of all by an ex-trainee, then by a department head and finally by the director in control of the particular function to which the candidate has applied. Obviously this type of exercise is more costly and can be more wearing on the candidate, but it may enable a more balanced judgement to be made.

(c) **Panel interviews**

In this situation candidates are interviewed before a panel of two or more people, in some cases as many as six or seven. For some senior posts in some local authorities in Britain, panels of twenty or more can be found. The usual panel size is between two and six interviewers, depending upon the nature of the job and the customs of the employing organisation. Panel interviews have the advantage of sharing judgements and most panels have the authority to reach immediate decisions. Their main drawback is the question of control: with so many people, irrelevancies can be introduced and a particular line of questioning can soon be destroyed. The success of a panel interview often depends upon careful planning and effective chairmanship. While they can be impressive in terms of ritual, panel interviews can be particularly unnerving for some candidates.

All the interview types above usually operate to the same format; questions are asked relating to the biography of the candidate and his or her motivation for the job in question. The following two types of interview deviate from that format.

(d) **The problem-solving interview**

In this situation, the candidate is set a hypothetical problem. For example, a problem may be posed to a prospective industrial relations trainee concerning the action he would take following a fight between a foreman and a shop steward where both participants told a different version of the incident and a work stoppage had ensued. The drawback with such interviews is that the quality of the answers is very difficult to assess and compare to those given by other candidates.

(e) **The stress interview**

In this case the candidate is put under deliberate stress usually by an aggressive interviewer, who attempts to disparage the candidate's answers at every opportunity. This method of interviewing proved successful during the war for selecting undercover agents and was in vogue a few years ago for selecting managers, based on the theory that their ability to handle stressful situations was the best test of their ability. Research evidence concerning stress interviews suggests they are of dubious value and can actually cause harm by alienating favourable candidates.

5.5 Activity

Outline the limitations of interviews.

5.6 Activity solution

Factors such as time limitation, interviewer bias and the fact that the impression made by a candidate at the interview is not always reflected in job performance have highlighted the limitations of the interview as a valid and reliable selection instrument. Because of this, interviewing is often supplemented by some form of further testing.

5.7 Selection tests

The majority of tests used in selection procedures are generally forms of psychological test such as intelligence tests, tests of motor ability, personality tests and so on. The use of tests in selection is a relatively recent concept. The types of tests used in selection include the following:

(a) **General intelligence tests**

These attempt to arrive at an approximation of a candidate's overall intelligence, unlike aptitude tests which attempt to measure a specific component of intelligence such as mechanical or spatial ability. Such intelligence tests usually assess both verbal and non-verbal skills. The use of general intelligence tests is based on the assumption that intelligence is related to the general occupational level. Research work in this area has revealed that the general validity level is poor but the greatest correlations are found between intelligence and skilled work. Many large organisations, such as the Civil Service, use intelligence tests in the selection of management trainees.

(b) **Aptitude tests**

These tests aim to indicate a level of future performance in some specific component of intelligence. They can include assessment of clerical, numerical, mechanical, spatial and even creative capacities. Research work by Vernon led him to the conclusion that the general image of the aptitude test is poor. Nevertheless aptitude tests of one type or another are used by many firms for a variety of jobs. For example, many bus companies use tests of numerical ability when selecting bus conductors or drivers on one-man operated buses; these tests are considered important in assessing the ability of the applicant to calculate fare returns. Many firms use tests of manual dexterity for certain semi-skilled manual jobs.

(c) **Attainment tests**

These tests are devised to measure an applicant's range and depth of knowledge in a particular area and are particularly useful when formal qualifications were obtained some time ago. Typical attainment tests for clerical work would cover vocabulary, spelling, punctuation and arithmetic.

(d) **Performance tests**

These attempt to measure current performance levels at a given task. A good example would be sample work assignments given to applicants for shorthand and typing posts.

(e) **Personality tests**

Such tests aim to establish whether replies are typical or untypical of particular groups. There is little agreement on the value of such tests and they are usually only applicable to management posts as in the case of the Post Office which uses tests of personality for their more senior grades. Some organisations do use such tests when selecting salesmen. There are a number of personality tests in use and the most popular take the form of an interest or attitude survey. The main drawbacks in the use of such tests are the interpretation of the answers and a tendency for candidates to give socially desirable answers.

(f) **Situational tests**

These are developed to meet the criticism of most other types of test, where answers are either right or wrong. Those in favour of situational tests argue that most work situations are probabilistic and the most useful tests are those of problem-solving and creative thinking in a simulated work setting.

(g) **Assessment centres**

The concept of the assessment centre was developed in the USA and is becoming more popular in the UK. It is really a combination of all forms of selection previously mentioned, but at present its use is confined more to the selection of employees for promotion. Groups of employees attend the centre for a number of days and are subjected to a number of tests, group exercises and interviews.

5.8 References

The reference check is usually the last stage in the selection process and is often used to assist the manager to make a decision about the suitability of the candidate. References can operate as a factual check on information provided by the candidate and as a character reference. Good referees are almost certain to know more about the applicant than the selector and it would be foolish not to seek their advice or treat the reference check as a mere formality. As well as the applicant's suitability for employment, the reference may provide information on strengths and weaknesses, training needs and potential for future development.

The type and number of references taken up varies with different organisations. Some rely on the use of the informal reference given over the telephone, whereas others require written references going back five years or two previous jobs. An applicant's present employers are contacted only after a decision has been made to make an offer of employment.

However, the value of references may be somewhat limited by three factors.

(a) The degree of knowledge the referee has of the candidate.
(b) Their ability to communicate this information fully and clearly in a reference.
(c) Their capacity to give an unbiased assessment of the candidate.

Research has indicated that many firms place little weight on references in the selection process, many using them only as a search for negative information.

6 CHAPTER SUMMARY

Recruitment and selection will be approached differently by most organisations and will also differ depending on the job vacancy. The key is to choose those elements which are the most suitable for the organisation.

Regardless of the method and approach chosen, good selection will ultimately rest on the firm understanding of the requirements of the job and job holder and a sensible use of techniques which will objectively measure the extent to which the candidates possess those qualities and skills.

7 SELF-TEST QUESTIONS

7.1 Explain why an effective recruitment policy is important (1.1).

7.2 List the questions that should be asked before recruiting (1.2).

7.3 Explain the three broad levels of employment (1.3).

7.4 List the costs which may be incurred by additional or new personnel (2).

7.5 What are the stages in the process of recruitment? (3.1)

7.6 Define 'job analysis' (3.2).

7.7 Describe the main methods of job analysis (3.4).

7.8 What should be included in a job description? (3.5).

7.9 Outline the advantages of recruiting internally (4.2).

7.10 Explain the three objectives of recruitment advertising (4.5).

7.11 What are the factors to be considered when evaluating recruitment? (4.9).

7.12 Explain why the application form may be better than the CV (5.3).

7.13 List and briefly describe the types of interview methods available (5.4).

7.14 Compare and contrast general intelligence tests and aptitude tests (5.5)

7.15 Explain why references may be limited in their use (5.8).

8 EXAMINATION TYPE QUESTION

8.1 Recruitment and selection

What is the objective of the recruitment and selection process? Describe the main stages of this process, once authorisation has been received by a departmental manager to proceed, for example, with the recruitment of graduates and part-qualified staff into a large accounting and finance department. Illustrate your answer with examples from your own knowledge or experience. **(25 marks)**

9 ANSWER TO EXAMINATION TYPE QUESTION

9.1 Recruitment and selection

(Tutorial note:

Students should be able to describe the objectives of the recruitment and selection process. Illustrations and examples from the student's own knowledge and experience should be given.*)*

Recruitment and selection objectives and the stages of process

The main aim or objective when appointing is to achieve the closest match between applicant and the vacancy. This match has two aspects, firstly matching the suitability of the candidate to the post and secondly matching the post to the most suitable candidate.

The management should possess a clear picture of the type of person required, as well as the requirements of the job eg, the nature of the work, operational and social performance. It is, therefore, vital that these requirements are stated within the job description and specifications. The process of recruitment and selection should piece together an ever clearing picture of the relationship between the characteristics of the applicants and the demands of the vacancies available. The degree of effectiveness of the selection process will rest upon the closest possible match between these two aspects.

Once management authority has agreed to commence, the course of selection and recruitment can be divided into the following stages.

(a) **The compilation of the job description**

This is where the main aspects of the vacancy become obvious eg, particular responsibilities, duties expected, the level of discretion etc.

(b) **The compilation of personnel specification**

Such aspects as qualities, characteristics, skills, experience, qualifications and training may be sought here. It is vital to relate personnel specifications to the job description when a candidate of limited work experience eg, new graduate is considered. The management involved with deciding who to appoint has limited information with which to assess accurately the suitability of the applicant.

(c) **The choice of recruitment supply**

There will be two choices available, the internal source and the external. The internal sources will comprise of centralised personnel files or internal advertisements. However, when considering this particular question, the external sources are more likely to be considered. If the company forge close links with universities, polytechnics etc. it is possible to notify suitable graduate applicants through the educational establishment and interview systematically from within. Media advertisements will also be spotted by finalist but their main aim is to encourage part-qualified accountants to consider application. The use of recruitment agencies or placing an advertisement direct also are available choices.

(d) **Releasing information and forms of application**

Naturally, interested parties will require detailed information and it will be necessary for them to complete the application form. A well structured, efficiently organised form, is better than asking for a curriculum vitae from each individual. The curriculum vitae method is beyond company control. A typical application form should request the following points of information from the interested party:

(i) qualifications gained, both educational and professional;
(ii) history of employment;
(iii) personal aspects such as interests, background; and
(iv) career ambitions and aspirations.

The management are able to assess each applicant's form and compile a 'short list', to be interviewed. The process of choosing will use both personnel specification and the job description already compiled.

(e) **Acquiring references etc.**

Frequently the use of references or testimonials is put into practice. These are used to support the application received and are usually written by persons of some standing or in a position of authority eg, university tutors or the present employer.

(f) **Objective testing of applicants chosen for interview**

This aspect may be used by some companies. The tests are usually geared towards such aspects as literacy, numeracy etc. Results are compared against a standardised sample at the particular level of each candidate's age, intellect or qualification. The testing procedure is also used to measure the candidates potential capacity within a particular task whilst under some form of pressure eg, completing a number of questions within a set time limit. The tests help to predict areas of performance and should relate to the work or nature of the post to be filled. As application forms or interviews do not explore specific attributes, these tests help the deciding management panel to form a clearer picture of each applicant tested.

(g) **The interview**

The main aim is to finalise all the information and establish the suitability level. Applicants may be interviewed by a panel or by one person. There may also be time spent on group discussion or presentations made by the applicant. The nature of the interview may be a relaxed approach or take a more serious form and be highly structured. A good interviewer should help place the candidate at ease, stimulate natural conversation whilst extracting skilfully any aspects about the applicant the interviewer needs to know.

The technique of the interviewer is vital to the effectiveness of the interview process. All information carefully extracted helps with the final decision making process.

(h) **Selecting the successful applicant**

At this point all aspects of information and assessments should be gathered to form a clear view of the applicant. This must be compared and related to the personnel specification and the job description. Once an appointment has been made, such aspects as the checking of qualifications through to the completion of contract arrangements should be implemented.

21 MOTIVATION, APPRAISAL AND DISCIPLINE

INTRODUCTION & LEARNING OBJECTIVES

One of the most important aspects of human resource management is making sure that the people within the organisation are motivated to perform their jobs effectively and efficiently. This motivation should accord with the objectives and culture of the organisation.

Motivated people are those who have made a conscious decision to devote considerable effort to achieving something that they value, although this will differ from one individual to another. Effective management will recognise this fact and will be aware of the techniques available to keep the employee interested and keen to achieve.

Performance appraisal within an organisation can be informal or by some formal and regular system. One of the advantages of appraisal is that both the employees and the management are interested in their progress and want to see how well others see them as performing.

When you have studied this chapter you should be able to do the following:

- Describe Schein's models of motivation.
- Define the needs, expectancy and goal theories of motivation with reference to Maslow, Herzberg, McClelland, Vroom, Porter and Lawler.
- Compare the methods of improving motivation.
- Explain the purposes of staff appraisal and the appraisal process.
- Outline the role of the assessment centre in assessing participants' competences.
- Identify the importance of congruence between an organisation's appraisal system and its objectives, strategy and culture.

1 MOTIVATION

Definition Motivation can be defined as the will to do, the urge to achieve goals, the drive to excel.

Motivation is concerned both with why people choose to do one thing rather than another and also with the amount of effort or intensity of action that people put into their activities. This important examination topic is examined in more detail later. Here we shall confine the coverage to a consideration of five major motivators as outlined below.

Definition Motivators are forces that induce individuals to perform, forces that influence human behaviour.

(a) **Values**

The values a person holds can influence motivation in two particular ways. First they affect the types of activities the person will find appealing and secondly, values influence a person's motivation towards specific outcomes such as money, power and prestige.

People with different values tend to end up in different jobs. Different values are held by people in social work professions, for example, from those held by people in the armed forces. Even within organisations patterns of values held by different groups can vary considerably eg, between levels (senior management as compared with shop floor workers) and between functions (production versus research and development).

On a more specific level, the way in which people value particular organisational rewards has a major effect on their motivation. If a person values monetary rewards highly and finds his/her self in a situation where effective performance leads to greater income they are likely to be highly motivated. On the other hand if, in the same situation, a person values friendship above income this person might be poorly motivated. People will hold different values and this variety of values has to be taken into account by management in attempting to motivate others. Understanding an individual's values is a crucial element in determining a motivation approach.

(b) **Beliefs**

There are two ways in which beliefs are particularly important to motivation. Employees must believe that what the organisation requires of them is possible to achieve. If they believe work demands to be impossible they are going to be poorly motivated. Also employees need to believe that by performing well they will personally benefit from their efforts. Again poor motivation is the outcome if a person believes that effective performance will not bring personal rewards.

Beliefs may be correct or incorrect. In terms of the impact on motivation this does not matter. A person who mistakenly believes he or she is not capable of doing the job will be as poorly motivated as the person who is correct in his or her belief. The problem of incorrect beliefs is that they often lead to irrelevant or inappropriate behaviour. Managers must make sure that people hold realistic beliefs, both about their own capacities and the likely consequences of effective performance.

(c) **Attitudes**

Definition Attitudes refer to persistent feelings and behaviour tendencies directed towards specific persons, groups, ideas or objects.

Attitudes are important to our understanding of motivation because of the links that exist between them and behaviour. A person with a negative attitude to another department in the organisation may be unlikely to behave in a friendly or co-operative way with members of that department. A person with a positive attitude toward the company will be more likely to come to work regularly and stay with the company even if offered a job in another organisation.

However, it should be remembered that people sometimes act in ways that are inconsistent with their attitude, ie, the person says one thing and does another. We should not be too surprised by this because, while the concept of attitudes is valuable, a full understanding of why people actually behave the way they do requires us to take into account the many additional factors that influence individual motivation and behaviour.

(d) **Needs**

People can be thought of as having a variety of different needs that influence their motivation. As we shall see later a number of theories, notably Maslow's, have identified needs as the key feature of all human motivation. Needs are seen as varying from basic needs such as food and shelter to more complex needs such as the needs for friendship, self-esteem and self-realisation. Motivation is said to relate to need in that a person with a particular need will be motivated to engage in behaviour that will lead to the gratification or satisfaction of that need. The implication for organisations is that to motivate employees it is necessary to set up situations in which people are able to satisfy their most important needs by engaging in behaviour most desired by the organisation for effective performance.

There is no generally agreed, comprehensive list of human needs. It is very easy to become confused in distinguishing what a person wants and what a person needs. The very simplicity of need theories of motivation which makes them initially attractive may also be their greatest weakness. Motivation is a complex process and needs are but one component of that process.

(e) **Goals**

Goals influence motivation in two ways. First, a goal provides a target to aim at, something to aspire to. This means the existence of a goal generates motivation in a person to work towards the achievement of the goal. Second, goals provide a standard of performance. A person is doing well if they have achieved a goal or are on the way to achieving it. On the other hand failure to achieve a goal or at least to make some progress toward it is evidence of unsatisfactory performance.

Research has investigated the importance of goals in motivation and concludes that for goals to be significant motivators they must be specific, sufficiently difficult to be challenging and they must be accepted by the person as their own particular goals and not as something imposed from outside.

2 MOTIVATION MODELS

2.1 Introduction

Various research has been undertaken in an attempt to answer

(a) what motivates individual employees at work?
(b) how managers can improve motivation of employees.

The motivational strategy that is decided upon will depend on the beliefs held, and the culture that prevails, in an organisation. There are radically different views held in different organisations about people's nature, the influence of work and what motivates them to work harder and more effectively.

2.2 Schein's model of motivation

In 1965 Professor Edgar Schein published a classification of the assumptions about what motivates people, based on management's assumptions about people. He identifies four sets of assumptions as follows:

(a) **Rational-economic man**

This view states that the pursuit of self-interest and the maximisation of gain are the prime motivators of people. It lays stress on man's rational calculation of self-interest, especially in relation to economic needs. According to Schein this set of assumptions places human beings into two categories: (a) the trustworthy, more broadly motivated, moral elite who must organise and manage the mass, and (b) the untrustworthy, money-motivated, calculative mass. In practice the rational-economic approach was an important assumption in the minds of Frederick Taylor, the Scientific Managers and the entrepreneurs of mass-produced technology.

(b) **Social man**

This view draws heavily on Mayo's conclusions from the Hawthorne experiments. This sees people as predominantly motivated by social needs and finding their identity through relationships with others. Acceptance of this view by managers concentrates on people's needs rather than task needs. Studies have shown that productivity and morale can be improved by fostering social relationships in order to improve co-operation and teamwork.

(c) **Self-actualising man**

This concept is based on Maslow's theory of human needs which sees not social needs but self-fulfilment needs as being the prime driving force behind individuals. 'Self-actualising man' needs challenge, responsibility and a sense of pride in his work. The managerial strategy which operates under this set of assumptions provides challenging, demanding work aiming for greater autonomy at work. Studies have shown that this model of motivation appears to be strong amongst professional and skilled grades of staff. However, it is less clear whether it applies as strongly to lower graded employees.

(d) **Complex man**

As you would imagine, this view sees people as being more complex and variable than the previous ones. The requirement for management is an ability to diagnose the various motives which may be at work with their staff. A consequence of this is that managers need to be able to adapt and vary their own behaviour in accordance with the motivational needs of particular individuals and teams.

Schein himself sees motivation in terms of a 'psychological contract' based on the expectations that the employee and employer have of each other, and the extent to which these are mutually fulfilled. Ultimately, the relationship between an individual and the organisation is an interactive one.

2.3 Douglas McGregor –Theory X and Theory Y

Like Schein's classification of man, McGregor's Theory X and Theory Y are essentially sets of assumptions about behaviour.

In his book **The Human Side of Enterprise**, published in 1960, McGregor presented two opposite sets of assumptions implicit in most approaches to supervision. He called these two sets of assumptions **Theory X** and **Theory Y**, which are the opposite extremes. Within these two extremes there are a number of possible combinations of the two. Theory X assumptions are

(a) The average human being has an inherent dislike of work and will avoid if it he can.

(b) Because of this human characteristic of disliking work, most people must be coerced, controlled, directed and/or threatened with punishment to get them to expend adequate effort towards the achievement of organisational objectives.

(c) The average human being prefers to be directed, wishes to avoid responsibility, has relatively little ambition, and wants security above all.

This is the traditional approach greatly influenced by the results of specialisation, standardisation and mass production techniques. Jobs have been sub-divided to such an extent that initiative and discretion have been reduced; conformity, obedience and dependence have been demanded from the members of the organisation. This appears to be the approach of the scientific managers and classical theorists and the supporters of Weber's type of bureaucracy. The theory may provide an explanation of some behaviour patterns in industry, but McGregor regards it as an extreme and unacceptable set of assumptions about human beings. Unfortunately, it can often be a self-fulfilling prophecy, since people tend to behave in the way expected of them.

McGregor derived a new set of assumptions which he called Theory Y

(a) Expenditure of physical and mental effort in work is as natural as play or rest. The average human being does not inherently dislike work which can be a source of satisfaction.

(b) External control and the threat of punishment are not the only means of bringing about effort towards organisational objectives. People can exercise self-direction and self-control to achieve objectives to which they are committed.

(c) Commitment to objectives is a result of the rewards associated with their achievement. The most significant of those rewards is satisfaction of the self-actualisation needs.

(d) The average human being learns, under proper conditions, not only to accept, but to seek, responsibility. Avoidance of responsibility, emphasis on security and low ambition are the results of experience and are not inherent in man's nature.

(e) Capacity to exercise a relatively high degree of imagination, ingenuity and creativity in the solution of organisational problems is widely, not narrowly, distributed in the population.

(f) Under conditions of modern industrial life, the intellectual potential of the average human being is only partially utilised.

McGregor felt that Theory Y assumptions provided a better explanation of human nature and indicated that the need for a different managerial strategy in dealing with people if they were to be correctly motivated.

Lupton sounds a note of caution regarding McGregor's work; managers should approach all prescriptions, whatever their origins, sceptically and critically. He believes there is insufficient evidence to support the view that the adoption of Theory Y is, in itself, followed by an improvement in the indicators of organisational performance. Much more research needs to be carried out on this, and other, prescriptions.

Other criticisms of the theory include

(a) Not all people want self-direction, individual freedom and autonomy; many could not cope with such freedom.

(b) It over-emphasises the workplace as the primary source of the satisfaction of needs. With the accent on a shorter working week and greater leisure time, it is more important to seek off-the-job satisfaction.

(c) Theory X is not necessarily the cause of the conflict between the individual and the organisation; the universal conflict may be inherent in all organisations, not just in modern industry. If this is the case, then Theory X may not be the cause and Theory Y, therefore, not the cure.

3 MOTIVATION THEORIES

3.1 The needs, expectancy and goal theories

The subsequent theories can be categorised as follows:

(a) **Content theories (needs)**

Which offer ways to profile or analyse individuals to identify their needs. Often criticised as being static and descriptive they appear to be linked more to job satisfaction than to work effort. Maslow, Herzberg and McGregor take a universalistic approach whereas McClelland and Argyle list forces and drives that will vary in relation to different individuals.

(b) **Process theories (expectancy and goal)**

Offer a more dynamic approach and try to understand the thought or cognitive processes that take place within the minds of people and which influence their behaviour. Adams' equity theory and various expectancy and goal theories adopt such an approach and complement rather than compete with content theories.

Motivation can be either positive or negative. Positive motivation, sometimes called anxiety-reducing motivation or the carrot approach, offers something valuable to the individual such as pay, praise or permanent employment for acceptable performance. Negative motivation, often called the stick approach, uses or threatens punishment by dismissal, suspension or the imposition of a fine if performance is unacceptable.

Douglas McGregor, in his book **The Human Side of Enterprise**, believed that 'Mature, self-disciplined persons do not require external discipline from others, or the stick. But it seems certain that our world is still populated by many persons who must depend upon others for their discipline'

4 CONTENT THEORIES

4.1 Principles

According to these theories motivated behaviour has the following characteristics

(a) **Sustained** – it persists for a relatively long time.
(b) Directed towards achievement of a **goal**.
(c) Results from a perceived **need**

(i) Drive.
(ii) Aspiration.
(iii) Desire.

Motivation can be viewed as **tension reducing**

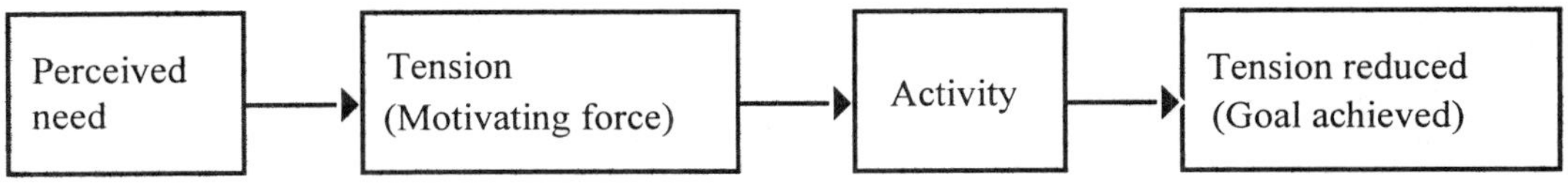

If efforts to motivate employees are to be successful management must either

(a) **Create** needs within an individual; or
(b) **Offer means** of satisfying individual's existing needs.

Needs vary between individuals and within individuals according to the situation, the time of day and the stage reached in their life cycle.

4.2 Maslow's hierarchy of needs

In the mid-1950s, Maslow advanced the following propositions about human behaviour

(a) Man is a wanting being – he always wants, and wants more; what he wants depends upon what he already has. As soon as he satisfies one need, another takes its place and the process is unending. Although one particular need may be met and satisfied, needs in general cannot be.

(b) A satisfied need is not a motivator of behaviour, only unsatisfied needs motivate.

(c) Man's needs are arranged in a series of levels; a hierarchy of importance. As soon as needs on a lower level are met those on the next, higher level will demand satisfaction. Maslow believed the underlying needs for all human motivation to be on five general levels from lowest to highest. Within those levels, there could be many specific needs, from lowest to highest.

(i) **Physiological** – the need for food, drink, shelter and relief from pain.

(ii) **Safety and security** – once the physical needs of the moment are satisfied, man concerns himself with protection from physical dangers with economic security, preference for the familiar and the desire for an orderly, predictable world. Safety needs also include the desire to know the limits or boundaries of acceptable behaviour.

(iii) When man's physiological and safety needs have been met, **social** needs, the next level, become important motivators of his behaviour. The individual wants to belong, to be accepted, to give and receive friendship and affection. These are held to be dominant needs in Western society.

(iv) The next level deals with **esteem or egoistic** needs. There is a need both for self-esteem and the esteem of others, which involves self-confidence, achievement, competence, knowledge, autonomy, reputation, status and respect. This fourth level is of increasing importance today, especially among managers and professional people.

(v) **Self-fulfilment or self-actualisation** – is the highest level in the hierarchy; these are the individual's needs for realising his or her own potential, for continued self-development and creativity in its broadest sense. It is a feeling of accomplishment and of being satisfied with the self.

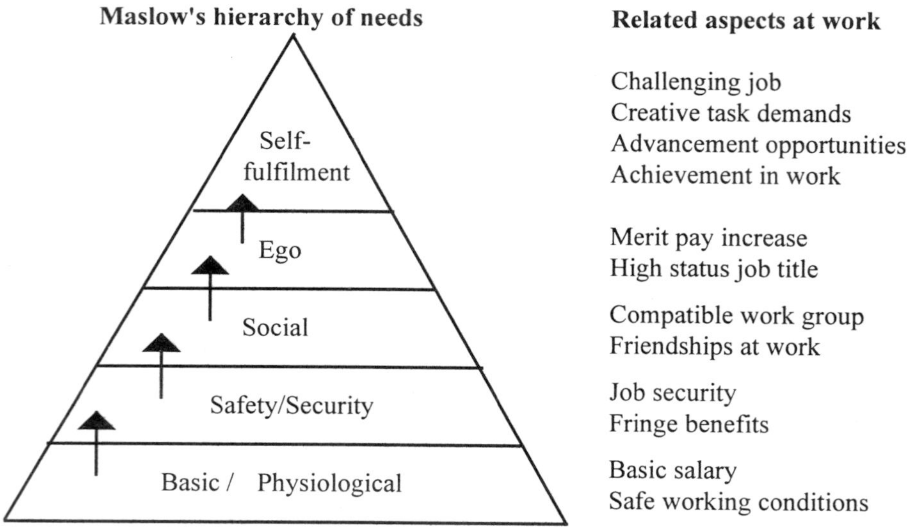

The peak of each level must be passed before the next level can begin to assume a dominant role. Needs do not have to be completely satisfied before higher needs emerge: as Simon puts it 'they only need to be satisfied'. In other words, a sufficient level of satisfaction is acceptable as opposed to the maximum or optimum level.

To be of use, Maslow's basic theory needs qualification to include the individual as a determining factor in motivation and behaviour. These qualifications include

(a) Levels in the hierarchy are not rigidly fixed: boundaries between them are indistinct and overlap.

(b) There are individual exceptions to the general ranking of the hierarchy. Some people never progress beyond the first or second level (for example, many inhabitants of the third world), others are so obsessed with the higher needs that lower ones may go largely unnoticed.

(c) Variables apart from individual needs may motivate, eg social standards and a sense of duty.

(d) An act is seldom motivated by a single need; any act is more likely to be caused by several needs.

(e) The same need will not give rise to the same response in all individuals, who have different characteristics.

Substitute goals may take the place of a need that is blocked.

4.3 Herzberg's theory of motivation

In the late 1950s F. Herzberg published his original research from interviewing 200 engineers and accountants about events at work, events which had brought them marked job satisfaction or marked loss of job satisfaction.

Five factors stood out as strong determinants of job satisfaction which he regarded as **motivators**

(a) Achievement.
(b) Recognition for work well done.
(c) Attraction of the job itself.
(d) Responsibility.
(e) Advancement.

Lack of these intrinsic factors was only rarely mentioned in regard to dissatisfaction with the job.

Hygiene factors (or dissatisfiers) are

(a) Company policy and administration.
(b) Supervision.
(c) Salary.
(d) Interpersonal relations.
(e) Working conditions.

Such extrinsic factors attract people to the job and persuade them to remain – the 'Golden Handcuffs' of many organisations.

As distinctly separate factors are associated with job satisfaction and job dissatisfaction, Herzberg concluded that the two feelings are not the opposite of one another, but that they are concerned with two different ranges of man's needs.

Hygiene factors are purely preventive: if the organisation provides them it will prevent the workers from being dissatisfied with their job, but they will not motivate positively. To help them to do creative, satisfying, responsible work the organisation must provide motivators.

Since the initial study, Herzberg has carried out further investigation involving over 1,600 employees in a variety of different jobs in different countries and that investigation confirms his findings regarding motivators and hygiene factors. Herzberg believes that jobs should be enriched to include more motivators in order to increase job satisfaction.

Professor Lupton, Deputy Director of the Manchester Business School, echoes Herzberg's own initial caution that not all research has supported the original theory. The ideas are apparently common sense, but they are over-simple and incomplete because they do not take into account factors such as size, technology, product and labour market which might make the redesign of the organisation for job enrichment very difficult.

4.4 D McClelland

This researcher, together with J Atkinson, emphasised three fundamental needs as motivators: achievement; affiliation; and power.

(a) **Achievement**

This need is to attain something related to a specific set of standards. There are two extremes: some people want to achieve something which has only a limited chance of success, whereas others want to undertake work in which chances of being a success are highly rated. The majority lie somewhere in between.

(b) **Affiliation**

Here, there is a need to develop interpersonal relationships on a friendly basis – some people want this at all costs and most enjoy working in an environment in which friendly co-operation is possible.

(c) **Power**

This is the need to influence others and lead them into behaving in a way in which they would not normally behave.

Writing in the early 1950s these researchers showed that managers have a high level need for achievement, a relatively high need for power, but a low need for affiliation. The general idea is that the entrepreneurs have a high need for achievement, and relatively high need for power; chief executives of larger organisations tend to have a high need for power, but because they have reached their sought-after level they are less in need of achievement.

4.5 M Argyle

This writer produced another listing of 'drives' which affect motivation. The idea here, however, is that they are on a provisional basis, because individuals may be unaffected by some of them and would in any case be affected differently by each one.

(a) **Biological drives;** those which affect social behaviour, eg hunger and thirst.

(b) **Dependency;** assistance, guidance and counselling obtained from those in power. New situations at work can give rise to dependency upon people who have the relevant facts.

(c) **Affiliation need;** the need here is to socialise – which can be carried to the extreme and allow work to be neglected as a secondary activity.

(d) **Dominance;** this drive is to achieve influence and to control other people's actions. People with this drive attend meetings and do most of the talking.

(e) **Sex;** on a social level this drive is generally directed to people of the opposite sex, eg colleagues at work.

(f) **Aggression;** this is the need to cause harm to others – usually on a verbal basis (including rumours).

(g) **Self-esteem;** this drive varies between individuals.

(h) **Additional drives;** include needs for achievement and money. Persons who rank highly in this area tend to be those most concerned with the work which is being done – others may have an affiliation drive which makes them much more concerned with 'getting on' with other people.

4.6 Adams' equity theory

Adams argues that inequities exist whenever people feel that the rewards obtained for their efforts are unequal to those received by others. Inequities can be negative or positive.

When people sense inequities in their work they will be aroused to remove the discomfort and restore a state of felt equity to the situation by

(a) Changing work inputs.
(b) Changing rewards received.
(c) Leaving the situation.
(d) Changing the comparison points.
(e) Psychologically distorting the comparisons.

People who feel overpaid (feel positive inequity) have been found to increase the quantity or quality of their work, whilst those who are underpaid (feel negative inequity) do the opposite.

Feelings of inequity are determined solely by the individual's interpretation of the situation – the fact that a manager feels that the annual pay review is fair is immaterial.

5 PROCESS (EXPECTANCY) THEORIES

5.1 The V H Vroom Model

Vroom believes that people will be motivated to do things to reach a goal if they believe in the worth of that goal and if they can see that what they do will help them in achieving it.

Vroom's theory is that people's motivation toward doing anything is the product of the anticipated worth that an individual places on a goal and the chances he or she sees of achieving that goal. Vroom's theory may be stated as

Force	=	valence x expectancy
Where force	=	the strength of a person's motivation;
valence	=	the strength of an individual's preference for an outcome; and
expectancy	=	the probability that a particular action will lead to a desired outcome.

When a person is indifferent about achieving a certain goal, a valence of zero occurs. Likewise, a person would have no motivation to achieve a goal if the expectancy were zero. The force exerted to do something will depend on both valence and expectancy. For example, a manager might be willing to work hard to achieve company goals for a promotion or pay valence.

Vroom's theory recognises the importance of various individual needs and motivations, and avoids some of the simplistic features of the Maslow and Herzberg approaches.

5.2 The Porter and Lawler Model

Porter and Lawler derived a more complete model of motivation. They have applied this model primarily to managers. It is summarised in the following diagram

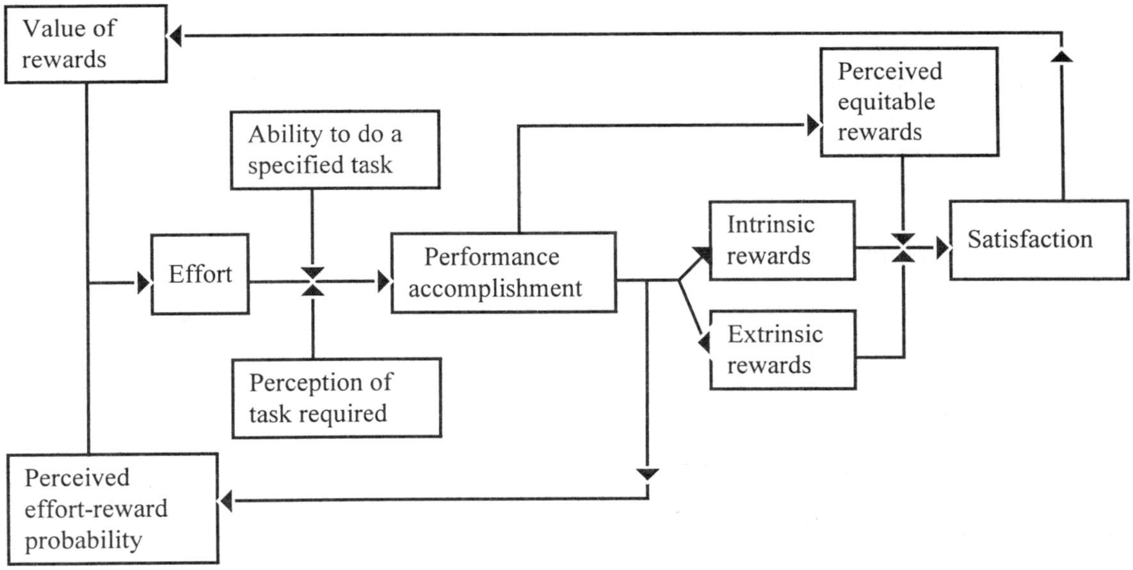

This model indicates that the amount of effort exerted depends on the value of a reward plus the amount of energy a person believes is required and the probability of receiving the reward. The perceived effort and probability of actually getting a reward are, in turn, also influenced by the record of actual performance.

Actual performance in a job is determined principally by effort expended. But it is also greatly influenced by an individual's ability to do the job and by his or her perception of what the required task is. Performance is seen as leading to intrinsic rewards (such as a sense of accomplishment) and extrinsic rewards (such as working conditions and status). These rewards lead to satisfaction. What the individual sees as a fair reward for effort will affect the satisfaction derived. Likewise, the actual value of rewards will be influenced by satisfaction.

To the practising manager, this model means that motivation is not a simple cause and effect matter. It shows that managers should carefully assess their reward structures and that through careful planning, and clearly defining duties and responsibilities, the effort-performance-reward-satisfaction system can be integrated into an entire system of managing.

6 METHODS OF IMPROVING MOTIVATION

6.1 Psychological contracts

Psychological contracts exist between individuals and the organisations to which they belong, be they work or social, and normally take the form of implied and unstated expectations. According to Handy, the individual has a set of results that he expects from the organisation, results that will satisfy certain of his needs and in return for which he will expend some of his energies and talents. Similarly, the organisation has its set of expectations of the individual and its list of payments and outcomes that it will give to him.

An individual belonging to more than one organisation will have more than one psychological contract. Only if each contracts is perceived identically by all parties to it will conflict be avoided.

Psychological contracts can be classified as follows

(a) **Coercive contracts** which are not freely entered into and where a small group exercise control by rule and punishment. Although the usual form is found in prisons and other custodial institutions, coercive contracts exist also in schools and factories.

(b) **Calculative contracts** where control is retained by management and is expressed in terms of their ability to give to the individual 'desired things' such as money, promotion and social opportunities. Most employees of industrial organisations 'enter into' such a contract.

(c) **Co-operative contracts** where the individual tends to identify with the goals of the organisation and strive for their attainment. In return the individual receives just rewards, a voice in the selection of goals and a choice of the means to achieve such goals. Most enlightened organisations are moving towards such contracts but it must be emphasised that if they are to be effective then the workers must also want them – if such a contract is imposed on the workforce it becomes a coercive contract.

In all cases the employees must know the results of their increased efforts and the management must understand the individual's needs.

6.2 Money as a motivator

Money in the form of pay is a powerful motivator and can be viewed as all-embracing, as a basis for comparison or as a reinforcement. The multiple meanings of pay can be related to the motivational theories examined as follows

(a) **Maslow** – pay is unique in that it can satisfy all types of need – directly in the case of lower level needs and otherwise indirectly, for example the prestige of being on a high salary level can be a source of ego-fulfilment.

(b) **McClelland** – high-need achievers view pay as performance feedback and as a measure of goal accomplishment; group bonuses are attractive to high-need affiliators; those seeking power could view pay as a means of buying prestige or as a way of controlling other people.

(c) **Herzberg** – pay is normally viewed as a hygiene factor but it can be a motivator when it occurs as a merit increase that gives special recognition for a job well done.

(d) **Equity theory** – pay is an object of social comparison and is a major reason for felt inequity.

(e) **Expectancy theory** – pay is only one of many work rewards that may be valued by individuals at work. When instrumentality and expectancy are high, pay can be a source of motivation.

Money is a complicated motivator, associated with several levels of needs, not just the basic level. Economists, accountants and many managers tend to regard money as a prime motivator (Bernstein 1985, *inter alia*), however, behavioural scientists tend to place it low on the scale of motivators. Probably, neither view is correct as an all embracing approach: it depends on the individual.

6.3 Payment by results

The most direct use of money as a motivator is payment by results schemes whereby an employee's pay is directly linked to his results. All such schemes are dependent upon the belief that people will work harder to obtain more money. Whyte carried out extensive research on incentive pay schemes for production workers. He concluded that 'money is not an almighty' motivation and estimated that only 10% of production workers would ignore group pressure from workmates and produce as much as possible in response to an incentive scheme.

6.4 Power and status

In discussing money as a motivator it is necessary to recognise its effects at two levels.

(a) Money in absolute terms, as an exact amount, is important because of its purchasing power. It is what money can buy, not money itself, that gives it value. Saul Gellerman (**Motivation and Productivity**) sees the main significance of money in its power as a symbol. Because money can be exchanged for satisfaction of needs, money can symbolise almost any need an individual wants it to represent. The next increase in salary could mean affording a better car, or an extra holiday.

(b) Money is also important as an indication of status. Increasing differentials between jobs creates feelings of a senior status in the person enjoying the higher salary. Money is a means of keeping score.

6.5 Performance-related pay

In both these aspects it is only true that money will motivate if the prospective payment is significantly large in relation to the normal income of that person. Small increases can prevent feelings of dissatisfaction but to create motivation in a person who will be motivated by money it is necessary for the amounts to be large. Jay Schuster in a well-known article in **Management Review** in 1985 argues the case for a large motivating element in a worker pay package which would be dependent upon meeting agreed objectives. It is interesting to cite the experience of the NHS which has introduced a payment system, starting with senior managers, in which up to 20% of the salary is dependent upon achieving short-term and long-term objectives. Performance is evaluated according to results achieved against these objectives and classified in five grades. The amount of bonus, which can be nil and has to be re-earned each year, is dependent upon the grade allocated. This approach has become common practice amongst senior managers in large companies since the mid-1980s. Such practice relates to the two aspects of money as a satisfier of needs and as a status/ego measurement.

6.6 Non-financial motivators

We have already noted the content theories of Herzberg etc. which point to the job itself as a source of motivation. The job content can be interesting and challenging. It can meet needs for advancement, social standing, professional recognition, self-esteem etc. This can sometimes compensate for lower earnings and cause people to hold back from pursuing a higher paid position because the job content is seen to be less interesting.

Some methods of non-financial motivators follow:

(a) **Participation**

The use of participation is frequently quoted as a means of stimulating motivation. There is no doubt that people are motivated by being involved in the actions and decisions affecting them. Participation is also a recognition of the value of staff, since it provides a sense of accomplishment and 'being needed'. A manager seeking to raise performance by increasing motivation could involve staff in the planning and inspection aspects of the work encouraging staff to participate in the design of the work planning schedules. Staff would be motivated to achieve the targets that they had helped establish.

The use of participation is not an automatic recipe for increased motivation. Hopwood writes that it is 'naive to think that participative approaches are always more effective than authoritarian styles'. It depends upon the individual people and circumstances involved. There are certain guidelines that must prevail if participation is to be effective in raising motivation.

(i) The matters for participation must be meaningful and relevant. If staff believe that the items are trivial or outside of their scope then there will be an adverse reaction that will damage existing levels of motivation.

(ii) The participation must be seen as part of a continuing approach not just a 'one-off' exercise.

(iii) Staff must be fed the results of their involvement as quickly and fully as possible. Herzberg said 'a manager cannot motivate staff in a vacuum'. Feedback is essential if motivation is to grow.

(iv) The participation must be genuine. It should be defined for staff in the first stage whether their participation is limited to consultation 'where staff's ideas are sought but management makes the decision' or whether there is a sharing of authority in that staff are involved in the final decision.

(v) People must have the ability, equipment and will to be involved. For example, you cannot motivate someone to do a job for which they have not been trained. Also, if staff feel dissatisfied in work because of deficiencies in the maintenance/hygiene factors, then participation will fall on deaf ears.

(b) **Quality of work life**

An interesting approach to motivation is the recent development of 'quality of work life programmes'. Introduced as a concept by Davis and Cherns (1975), one of the main advocates in the UK has been Eric Trist. There are many case studies published in such companies as General Motors, Proctor and Gamble etc. Basically the approach is a very wide-ranging application of the principles of job enrichment.

The intention is to improve all aspects of work life, especially job design, work environment, leadership attitudes, work planning and industrial relations. It is an all-embracing systems approach which usually starts with a joint management and staff group looking at the dignity, interest and productivity of jobs.

(c) **Job design**

Herzberg defines three avenues that management can follow in attempting to improve staff satisfaction and motivation.

(i) **Job enrichment** – a deliberate, planned process to improve the responsibility and challenge of a job. Typical examples include delegation or problem solving as in:

- adding query-solving to a clerk's routine duties;
- staff signing own letters instead of passing them through for manager's signature.

Job enrichment, in this sense of improving responsibility and challenge, has been called 'vertical job enlargement' by Argyris and other authors. Although Herzberg's term 'job enrichment' is the more descriptive and commonly accepted, it is important to note the alternative term which will be mentioned in many textbooks and could occur in an examination question.

(ii) **Job enlargement** – widening the range of jobs, and so developing a job away from narrow specialisation. There is no element of enrichment. Argyris, Seashore etc. term this as 'horizontal job enlargement'. Herzberg contends that there is little motivation value in this approach.

(iii) **Job rotation** – the planned rotating of staff between jobs to alleviate monotony and provide a fresh job challenge. The documented example quotes a warehouse gang of four workers, where the worst job was tying the necks of the sacks at the base of the hopper after filling; the best job was seen as being the fork lift truck driver. Job rotation would ensure that equal time was spent by each individual on all jobs. Herzberg suggests that this will help to relieve monotony and improve job satisfaction but is unlikely to create positive motivation.

7 THE APPRAISAL PROCESS

7.1 Introduction

Performance appraisal may be defined as:

Definition 'The regular and systematic review of performance and the assessment of potential with the aim of producing action programmes to develop both work and individuals'.

7.2 Assessment

In all organisations the performance of each employee is assessed by someone. Often this is a casual, subjective and infrequent activity but, increasingly, many organisations (particularly larger ones) have decided to formalise the assessment process and use it to improve performance, assess training needs and predict the potential of employees.

Such a formal process is considered necessary for three main reasons:

(a) Organisations are becoming increasingly aware of the growing financial investment in human resources; in many service industries, labour costs represent over 50% of total costs and rise faster than other costs.

(b) The social responsibility objective of the organisation leads to an increased concern for the growth and development of employees.

(c) The use of quantitative or 'objective' measures of effectiveness such as output, sales or materials wastage may not reflect accurately on the performance of individuals.

An organisation's performance appraisal system must generate fair, accurate and valid information that can serve as a sound basis for organisational decision making regarding salaries, promotions and so on. At the same time appraisals must assist and encourage open sharing of information regarding employee strengths and weaknesses in order to ensure that the process will aid employee motivation and development.

7.3 The purposes of appraisal

Different organisations will use performance appraisal for different purposes. The following list is a comprehensive summary of potential purposes though it is doubtful whether all these purposes could be successfully pursued in any one organisation:

(a) General feedback on individual performance, as information for management and motivation for the individual employee.

(b) To identify potential in the employee and assist in career counselling.

(c) To identify training needs of individuals and help in the evaluation of training programmes.

(d) To provide evidence to justify unpopular decisions such as dismissal or deviation from 'last in first out' redundancy policy.

(e) To assist in the selection process by identifying the performance criteria of job holders and possibly by indicating why some people are unsuitable.

(f) As part of the manpower planning process appraisal can help in succession planning and provide information on the flexibility of the workforce.

(g) As part of the management planning process, performance appraisal can help in the setting of realistic targets.

(h) To provide incoming managers with useful information on their subordinates.

(i) As an aid in the construction of accurate job descriptions.

(j) To assist in problem-solving by giving valuable information on trouble spots.

Torrington and Hall, in a recent survey of 350 companies, give the following results of how the companies actually use performance appraisal.

Uses	Blue collar	White collar	Management
To set performance objectives	35	125	164
To assess past performance	72	189	208
To help improve current performance	77	197	214
To assess training and development needs	65	200	215
To assess increases or new levels of salary	35	92	104
To assess future potential	63	175	200
To assist in career planning decisions	35	139	168
Others	6	11	9

The table shows the distinctive uses made of performance appraisal by different organisations and the fact that performance appraisal is used differently with different categories of employee.

7.4 The appraisal process

(a) Who is appraised?

It is clear that appraisal schemes have been developed in the most part for the evaluation of managerial performance. Though they are increasingly used for other groups, the traditional focus is on management.

In practice who is appraised will vary from those organisations who do not have an appraisal system (and hence no one is appraised) to those where appraisal is a central feature of the organisation's culture and applies to every employee. In their survey Torrington and Hall also revealed not only that over a quarter of those surveyed carried out no appraisal whatsoever, but also a diverse range of answers to the question 'who is appraised?' as shown in the table below:

Categories of staff	Number of organisations appraising this category
Manual, unskilled and semi-skilled	92
Manual skilled and technical	119
Clerical/secretarial	189
Supervisory	215
Middle management/administrative	251
Technical/professional specialists	240
Senior management	229

(b) Who does the appraising?

In any organisation there are a number of alternative individuals or groups who might be involved in the appraisal of others. In this section we shall briefly examine the alternatives.

- **Appraisal by the immediate superior**

  This is the most common arrangement. The advantage of this is that the immediate superior usually has the most detailed knowledge of the tasks and duties carried out by the subordinate and the most intimate awareness of how well they have been carried out. The formal appraisal session should also be seen as part of the continuous appraisal and feedback process that goes on all the time between a superior and subordinate.

- **Appraisal by superior's superior**

  The superior's superior may be involved in the appraisal process in two ways. First, they may be required to countersign the appraisal of the immediate superior in order to legitimise it and show that it has been carried out fairly. Secondly, the superior's superior may directly carry out the appraisal. This is felt to offer a fairer appraisal in many situations, reducing the chances of 'victimisation' and ensuring that common standards are applied.

- **Appraisal by the personnel department**

  Frequently the personnel department is responsible for the administration and organisation of the appraisal system but this does not normally mean that it actually carries out appraisals. However, it can happen in situations where there is no logical immediate supervisor to do the job, as, for example, in a matrix organisation.

- **Self-appraisal**

  How people rate themselves is of crucial importance to the realisation of many of the objectives of an appraisal system. If a person feels the present system is unfair and that criticisms of performance are ungrounded then the individual is not going to be concerned about self-improvement and development. Self-appraisal as the sole form of appraisal is very rare but an element of self-appraisal is quite common. This may consist of getting individuals to prepare for the appraisal meeting by filling out a self-appraisal form or perhaps to complete one section of the superior's assessment form. This differs from full self-appraisal in that it is always the superior who has the final say.

- **Appraisal by peers**

  It can be argued that a person's peers will have the most comprehensive view of the appraisee's performance and hence will be able to make the most acceptable and valid appraisal. However, this method is not often accepted by managers.

- **Appraisal by subordinates**

  Though not widely used certain benefits may be claimed for this approach. In particular, subordinates are likely to be very closely aware of the performance of their boss. As part of a more comprehensive appraisal method an appraisal by subordinates can play a useful role.

- **Assessment centres**

  Assessment centres are used to appraise the potential of employees as supervisors or managers. They use tests, group exercises and interviews to assess this potential.

(c) **The openness of the appraisal process**

This is one of the most crucial issues in performance appraisal and it concerns the extent of participation by the job-holder in the assessment of his/her own performance. However, what is meant by participation in appraisal? In many cases it is used only to denote that the employee has been allowed to see the appraisal. In only a minority of cases does the appraisee actually participate in assessing their performance as an integral part of the appraisal system.

Several systems of appraisal have been identified involving different degrees of participation:

- The appraisal is totally closed and nothing is revealed to the job-holder.
- Most of the appraisal is closed and only adverse comments are made known to the job-holder.
- The assessment of performance is revealed but the assessment of potential is not.
- All aspects of the appraisal are made known to the job-holder.
- The job-holder is allowed to participate in the exercise by making a self-appraisal an integral part of the process ie, job-holder and boss will complete the appraisal form jointly in discussion.

There are arguments for and against open performance appraisal.

Arguments against open appraisal:

- Some individuals may feel that to disagree with a superior's appraisal may jeopardise their career prospects.
- Superiors may tend to overrate the performance of subordinates not wishing to appear over-critical.

- Where appraisal is exposed it may raise false hopes in the individual in terms of early promotion or an increase in pay.
- Where job-holders have been asked to assess their own performance there is evidence that people tend to over inflate or deflate their achievements.

Despite these arguments there is evidence that open appraisal is increasing and plays an important part in many appraisal interviews. The main reasons for this are:

- The prevailing social and organisational climate places more emphasis on participation. In Germany and the USA there is now legislation enforcing open appraisal.
- Union pressure and particularly the growth of white collar unions has led to demands for more openness.
- Where Management by Objectives is adopted it is essential for subordinates to know strengths and weaknesses and the targets they are expected to reach.
- It is generally recognised that closed appraisal, though it may be franker, offers little chance for the job-holder to improve performance.
- Many of the problems of open appraisal can be successfully met by improved training and counselling.

It may be concluded that the case for open appraisal is strong and there is every reason why an organisation should adopt this approach.

7.5 General principles of appraisal

The following list represents the generally agreed set of criteria which should be fulfilled for an appraisal scheme to be effective:

(a) It should be systematic in that all relevant personnel should be appraised using the same criteria.

(b) It should be objective. Critical remarks that are factual may be acceptable but citing personality defects or subjective judgements is not.

(c) It should be based on factors that are relevant to the performance on the job and not consider those factors which may relate more to the personal prejudices of a particular assessor.

(d) It should be carried out on a regular basis so that the assessment of any individual is based on current information.

(e) Wherever possible it should be mutual and there should be a large amount of agreement between superior and subordinate about the subordinate's performance. This is seen as essential for motivation purposes if the subordinate is to improve performance.

(f) It should be constructive, helping the improvement of performance. Destructive appraisals will lead to resentment and a worsening of superior/subordinate relations.

(g) Before an appraisal scheme is established there should be an agreement between management and the trade unions involved concerning the need for appraisal, the uses that will be made of it and the method of operation.

(h) There should be adequate training given to those responsible for carrying out the appraisal.

(i) The standards should be consistently applied in all functions at all levels.

7.6 The methods of appraisal

What should appraisals measure?

A key issue in performance appraisal is determining what constitute valid criteria or measures of effective performance. The problem is made more difficult because almost all jobs have many dimensions so that performance appraisal must employ multiple criteria or measures of effectiveness in order to accurately reflect the actual job performance of the employee.

Although it is impossible to identify any universal measures of performance that are applicable to all jobs, it is possible to specify a number of characteristics that a criterion of job performance should possess if it is to be useful for performance appraisal:

(a) A good criterion should be capable of being measured reliably. The concept of reliability of measurement has two components. Firstly, stability which means that measures taken at different times should yield the same results. Second, consistency which means that if different people use the criterion or a different form of measurement is used the results should still be more or less the same.

(b) A good criterion should be capable of differentiating among individuals according to their performance. If everyone is rated the same the exercise rapidly becomes pointless.

(c) A good criterion should be capable of being influenced by the job-holder. If a person is to improve performance after appraisal then it must be about matters over which the individual has discretionary control.

(d) A good criterion should be acceptable to those individuals whose performance is being assessed. It is important that people feel that their performance is being measured against criteria that are fair and accurate.

A key issue that has to do with the criteria of effectiveness is the question of whether they should focus on the activities (tasks) of the job-holder or the results (objectives) achieved. For example, a salesman might be assessed in terms of activities eg, number of cold calls or speed of dealing with complaints or in terms of results eg, total sales volume or number of new customers. Measures of results pay no attention to how results were achieved.

There are advantages and disadvantages of using either results or activities as criteria. Appraisal based on results has the advantage of encouraging and rewarding the results desired by the organisation. However, it has the disadvantage that it might encourage people to break rules or go against company policy to get the desired results. It may lead to frustration if the failure to achieve results is due to factors beyond the control of the individual. Assessment in terms of results also has the shortcoming that it does not generate information about how the person is doing the job and hence has limited value in suggesting ways of improving performance.

A major advantage of appraising in terms of activities is that it helps in generating information that can help in the training and development of poor performers. However, it may only encourage people to concentrate on their activities at the expense of results achieved. This can result in excessive bureaucratic emphasis on the means and procedures employed rather than on the accomplishments and results. There are then problems in incorporating the successful non-conformist into the appraisal system.

An effective appraisal system needs to have a balance of both measures of results and measures of activities.

7.7 Techniques of appraisal

(a) **Employee ranking**

Employees are ranked on the basis of their overall performance. This method is particularly prone to bias and its feedback value is practically nil. It does, however, have the advantage that it is simple to use.

(b) **Rating scales**

Graphic rating scales consist of general personal characteristics and personality traits such as quantity of work, initiative, co-operativeness and judgement. The rate judges the employee on a scale whose ratings vary, for example from low to high or from poor to excellent. It is called 'graphic' because the scale visually graphs performance from one extreme to the other.

The main problem associated with rating scales is the 'clustering' of results around the 'average' or 'satisfactory' level with little use made of the extreme levels. This negates the whole purpose of an appraisal scheme. To overcome this, some specialists replace terms like 'poor', 'satisfactory' or a numbering system with a series of statements. Each statement is tested for best match with appraisee's performance.

Despite their popularity there are problems with the use of rating scales. They provide little information to the individual as to how to improve his/her performance. There is no identification of training needs so it is difficult to design training programmes on the results of rating scales. Frequently rating scales will induce resistance on the part of superiors doing the rating because they are required to assess on factors where they do not feel they have adequate information. For the person being assessed, rating scales can readily provoke resistance, defensiveness and hostility. Telling someone that they lack initiative or that their personality is unsatisfactory can strike at the heart of their self-identity and self-esteem.

Current practice is to separate pay discussions from the appraisal procedure.

Bias can occur when using rating scales for a number of reasons:

- **Halo effect**

  This refers to the tendency of people to be rated similarly on all of the dimensions or characteristics being assessed. Thus if quality of work is rated as fair then there will be a likelihood that all other factors in the assessment will be rated as fair. The term halo is used because all of the ratings fall within a narrow range or within a halo.

- **Recency bias**

  Though appraisal should normally relate to a person's performance over the whole period since the last appraisal it is found that, in fact, assessors tend to be most strongly influenced by their most recent observations. Thus what is supposed to be an annual review is actually based on performance only in recent weeks.

- **Bias through the contrast effect**

  This can happen when appraising a number of subordinates within a short space of time. A manager's appraisal of an individual can be affected by the evaluation of the preceding subordinate. For example, a poor performance by one individual can make the next person to be appraised look excellent in comparison even though the performance is really only average.

- **Attribution errors**

  Since we are appraising a person, good and bad performance will be explained in personal terms. Success or failure will be attributed to factors in the individual rather than any situational factors that have had major effects on performance.

7.8 Reducing rating errors

Though it is difficult to eliminate all sources of error it is possible to minimise them by applying the following general guidelines:

(a) Superiors should be encouraged to observe performance regularly and keep records of their observations.

(b) Rating scales should be constructed so that each dimension on the scale is designed to measure a **single, important** work activity or skill.

(c) Appraisers should not be required to appraise a large number of subordinates at any one time.

(d) Raters should be made aware of the common sources of error and helped to avoid them.

(e) There should be training in the effective use of performance appraisal techniques and in the conduct of an appraisal interview.

7.9 Behaviourally anchored rating scales (BARS)

These differ from the common rating scale in two major respects. First, rather than rate personality, BARS evaluate employees in terms of the extent to which they exhibit **effective behaviour** relevant to the specific demands of their jobs. Secondly, each item to be assessed is 'anchored' with specific examples of behaviour that correspond to good performance, average performance, poor performance and so on.

A simplified example is given below which relates to performance in communicating and co-operating with others in a production control environment.

Rating	**Behaviour**
Excellent	Reports, oral and written, are clear and well organised; speaks and writes clearly and precisely; all departments are continually informed; foresees conflict and handles with initiative.
Good	Conveys necessary information to other departments; does not check for misunderstandings, but willingly tries to correct errors.
Unacceptable	Does not co-operate with or inform other departments; refuses to improve on reports or to handle misunderstandings.

To arrive at the behavioural examples for all jobs in an organisation is a complex task which involves the collection of much data and the discussion and participation both of management and of those who are to be appraised.

(a) **Advantages of BARS**

- Rating errors can be reduced because the choices are clear and relevant.
- Performance appraisal can become more reliable, meaningful and valid for both the appraiser and the appraisee because of their participation in establishing the scheme.

- The degree of conflict and defensiveness is reduced because people are being assessed in terms of specific job behaviour and not their personalities.

- The feedback that is generated can clearly identify deficiencies and identify needs for training and development activities.

(b) **Disadvantages of BARS**

- Decision making, inventiveness and resolution of problems are difficult to incorporate.

- The time, effort and expense involved is considerable and the investment may only be worthwhile if there are a large number of people doing the same or similar jobs.

- Since BARS are concerned with **observable** behaviours then jobs with a high mental content such as a research scientist or a creative writer do not lend themselves to evaluation using BARS.

- There is an inevitable level of generalisation involved so that BARS cannot hope to cover all examples of employee performance at all levels.

Overall it is felt that BARS are superior to graphic rating scales and they are increasingly popular.

7.10 Activity

If an appraisal session does not include a discussion on salary, then what is its relevance?

7.11 Activity solution

Current practice suggests that involving pay matters in appraisal sessions inhibits discussion on other aspects. The appraisee is reluctant to be open in case it affects the salary award and will react defensively to criticism

Without pay discussions, the appraisal session can fulfil its key purpose of staff counselling and development. This would involve such matters as:

(a) Feedback on performance and problems encountered;
(b) Career development;
(c) Identifying job interests and likely development areas;
(d) Defining performance targets;
(e) Reviewing promotability;
(f) Enabling individuals to appreciate where their jobs fit in the overall company scheme.

8 THE ROLE OF THE ASSESSMENT CENTRE

These are centres where groups of around six to ten candidates are brought together for one to three days of intensive assessment. They are presented, individually and as a group, with a variety of exercises, tests of ability, personality assessments, interviews, work samples, team problem solving and written tasks.

This type of assessment is particularly useful in the identification of executive and supervisory potential, since it uses simulated but realistic management problems to give participants opportunities to show their potential in the kind of situations which they may be promoted to but currently have no experience of.

Traditionally, the main purpose of assessment centres has been to contribute to management decisions about people, usually the assessment of management skills and potential as a basis for promotion decisions. Assessment centres are better at predicting future performance than are judgements made by unskilled managers, and it is the combination of techniques which contributes to their apparent superiority over other approaches.

Clearly the performance and potential of any member of management will be considerably influenced by his/her interaction with the organisation. Consequently management development programmes are important and require investigation.

9 CONGRUENCE WITH OBJECTIVES, STRATEGY AND CULTURE

Appraisal systems are procedures where managers or supervisors discuss the work of their subordinates. The manager sees each person individually and considers the progress they have been making in their job, their personal strengths and weaknesses and whether they need further training. This could be one of the problems with appraisal systems because they reinforce hierarchy and may be unsuitable in organisations where the relationship between managers and their subordinates is fluid or participatory.

Graeme Salaman suggests that a number of assumptions about organisational structure and functioning lurk behind the claimed common sense approach of modern appraisal systems. His argument is that both staff appraisal and management development schemes take the structure of the organisation as fixed and unchangeable and accept that the individual should change, or be made to change, to fit the structure and culture.

His criticism of appraisal schemes is that most of them regard the problems in an organisation, as well as the successes it achieves, as being entirely attributable to the personal qualities of the people involved. They ignore the organisational and systems context that the employees are subject to. In army terms this would assume that a defeat in battle, because of poor leadership, was the fault of the disciplined and brave troops.

Likert theorises that the objectives of the entire organisation and of its component parts must be in satisfactory harmony with the relevant needs and desires of the great majority, if not all, the members of the organisation and of the persons served by it.

Goals and assignments of each member of the organisation must be established in such a way that he or she is highly motivated to achieve them.

Methods and procedures used by the organisation and its sub-units to achieve the agreed-upon objectives must be developed and adopted in such a way that the members are highly motivated to use these methods to their maximum potential. Members of the organisation and the persons related to it must feel that the reward system of the organisation – salaries, wages, bonuses, dividends, interest payments – yields them equitable compensation for their efforts and contribution.

10 CHAPTER SUMMARY

Understanding individual behaviour in work is a key element in improving staff performance. Since people are individuals it is dangerous to apply any single theory to all people.

There is a fundamental difference between job satisfaction (contentment) and motivation (will to do) and a worker can be high in one but low in the other. There is a clear link between improved motivation and higher performance but no such link exists between job satisfaction and work performance.

The types of motivation theory include:

(a) content theories; and
(b) process theories;

Management development is the finding, tracking and developing of people for positions of responsibility in the organisation. It is based on providing training and experience to enable an individual to assume progressively more challenging and senior positions.

Staff appraisal sessions enable subordinate and boss to focus on past performances and future realisation of potential. The use of factual objectives can provide appraisal schemes with clear indicators of performance and identify areas for improvement.

11 SELF TEST QUESTIONS

11.1 Define and distinguish between motivation and motivators (1).

11.2 Describe Schein's model of motivation (2.2).

11.3 What are the assumptions of Theory X? (2.3).

11.4 Explain how motivation can be positive or negative (3.1).

11.5 Draw a diagram showing motivation as tension-reducing (4.1).

11.6 Explain Maslow's hierarchy of needs and the related aspects of work (4.2).

11.7 Name the five factors which are strong determinants of satisfaction (4.3).

11.8 What are hygiene factors? (4.3).

11.9 What are McClelland's three classes of needs? (4.4)

11.10 Explain intrinsic and extrinsic rewards (5.2).

11.11 Classify and describe psychological contracts (6.1).

11.12 What are the advantages of performance related pay? (6.5).

11.13 Define performance appraisal (7.1).

11.14 Who does the appraising in an organisation? (7.4).

12 EXAMINATION TYPE QUESTIONS

12.1 Influences on motivation

Discuss some of the major influences on people's motivation and discuss the implications for the management process. **(20 marks)**

12.2 Management view of behaviour

Many writers on management believe that the attitudes which managers have towards their employees and the assumptions they make about their behaviour directly affect the policies and practices which those managers provide and initiate.

Discuss the accuracy of this observation, quoting examples to support your views. **(20 marks)**

13 ANSWERS TO EXAMINATION TYPE QUESTIONS

13.1 Influences on motivation

Abraham Maslow identified five sequential needs that man as a wanting animal requires, starting at the base and moving upwards in a progression.

(a) The **physiological** or **basic** level, the need for food, shelter, warmth and other bodily wants.

(b) The **safety** need, the provision of security and protection, which motivates individuals to seek an orderly, predictable environment.

(c) The need for **love and belonging,** involving the desire to both give and receive love and friendship. In the working environment, this means recognition of being part of a team.

(d) **Esteem** ego, can be satisfied outside the purely working environment in the wider social sector; eg, individuals need to be respected in the community, to have their own professional self respect, and the satisfaction of being useful and necessary in the world.

(e) Finally, there is **self-actualisation**. Each individual has his own set of potentialities and his own internally defined goals. It can mean that a person becomes involved in the creative expression of those things he finds most gratifying.

Maslow argues that people's motivation, once they have satisfied their basic needs, depends on satisfying the appropriate level of need. The first two need levels are well satisfied in most companies. They have to satisfy the esteem and self-actualisation levels. Townsend puts it down to having fun on the job - since most fringe benefits (sick pay, pensions, social activities) cannot always be enjoyed on the job. Principally people are activated by satisfaction of unsatisfied needs.

Thus, management must ensure that all levels achieve the appropriate esteem that goes with the job. This will require identifying the appropriate satisfiers which motivate people to work: job satisfaction arising from the nature of the job.

Secondly, to satisfy self-actualisation requires identification of the individual goals so that goal congruence can be worked out between the company goals and the individual goals. Once these effective motivators have been identified, they can be used to give the individual a sense of personal accomplishment through the challenge of the job itself.

The major problem that still remains with management is that automation has reduced much of the work people have to do to way below their mental capacities and in many cases their ambitions. Consequently, to cope with this situation is to identify how the jobs can be matched to the levels of intellect and potential ambitions and position in the hierarchy of needs.

This is further complicated by the fact that people can move up and down the hierarchy and therefore their attention to a particular needs level will change; ie, different motivation 'satisfiers' now become more important

13.2 Management view of behaviour

Management is the process of influencing people towards desired ends, goal achievement, etc, taking into account the needs of the organisation, the task, the group and the individual. The stance taken will also to some extent depend upon the type of group and nature of the work for which the manager is responsible (an observation made back in 1928 by Mary Parker Follett).

The attitude towards staff that either senior management or individual managers adopt is strongly indicative of the type of leadership that can be anticipated. McGregor, in his Theory X - Theory Y exposition suggests two totally opposing viewpoints.

Theory X concerns the manager who considers that people are reluctant to work, are lazy and will do the minimum possible for as much gain as can be achieved. Actions would therefore be likely to move through persuasion, coercion, force - either through direct, continual giving of orders/instruction or through the use of any sanctions that may be within the manager's power. Overall leadership will certainly tend to be autocratic, with decision-making practices polarised and remote in relationships.

In contrast, in Theory Y the manager looks positively at staff, viewing them as people who have an interest in and are willing to work, capable of and desiring to achieve maximum potential. This is more consistent with a democratic, consultative and even participative approach towards those under one's control. Co-operation, rather than compulsion, will be the keyword. Decision-making is likely to be shared or at least be more on a consensus basis.

The trait approach to leadership suggests that there are certain qualities and personality characteristics which make good leaders - hence good managers. However, the human relations school (Stodgill) contends that leadership does not arise simply from a combination of the above factors. Henry Ford, for instance, showed considerable 'charisma' in getting his employees to respond but he combined personality strength with a number of scientific management concepts. He expected the workforce to do the job for which they were paid and not to ask questions. Personality traits are linked with many other 'desires' ranging from aggression, desire for power/achievement (McClelland), self-assurance, initiative, background/education, etc. The 'manager' in the military sense regards subordinates as people to be trained and disciplined and will expect obedience on the spot.

A manager in charge of a number of highly skilled, professional experts, ie, research workers or a senior doctor in charge of a practice, is more likely to exercise a virtually *laissez faire* attitude. Colleagues are seen as co-professionals able to organise their own section of activity with the minimum of supervision and control.

Fiedler's contingency theory focuses attention on the relationship between the manager who psychologically distances himself from the group and those who are psychologically close. He suggests that the psychologically distant manager (PDM) prefers subordinates who are ambitious and tends to be reserved in inter-personal relationships. This manager will be more task oriented, judge his subordinates more on performance and prefers to work in isolation from his superiors as much as possible. 'Distant' supports the view that a manager cannot exercise satisfactory control and discipline if he is too close emotionally. There is truth in this contention but a midway relationship can be achieved.

People generally need a sense of direction and respond favourably to firm but fair control. If the manager is liked and trusted by the group then this fact alone has a positive effect.

In practice it is consistency in style that employees find important. The Ashridge Studies reported that employees spoke of being disconcerted by rapid changes of attitude ie, autocracy, persuasion, consultation, democracy, charisma. Most preferred the consultative approach but it is interesting to note that they still considered their manager 'consultative' when he combined this with the 'tells' and 'sells' techniques.

22 A LEGAL FRAMEWORK

INTRODUCTION & LEARNING OBJECTIVES

In this chapter we look at legislation on recruitment and employment. Because of the concern to avoid exploitation and discrimination, the whole area of human resource management is surrounded by a legal framework that organisations must work within.

Employment law deals almost exclusively with civil law, where a plaintiff takes action against a person who committed a wrongful act. This means that the outcome of any case, if successful, will result in an award for damages or compensation, as opposed to imprisonment under criminal law.

If an employee can show that he or she was dismissed without just cause or excuse, they may bring a claim before the Industrial Tribunal under the Employment Rights Act 1996, and may qualify for compensation or other remedies.

The problems attached to dismissing incompetent employees include the unpleasantness of the task, combined with the fear of being taken to an industrial tribunal. To avoid some of the difficulties the personnel department should design written procedures for discipline and dismissal.

Discrimination may operate in all kinds of areas including: sex; sexuality and marital status; race and colour; religion; politics; disability; and conviction of a criminal offence. Forward-looking organisations will have a positive attitude to equal opportunities and apply non-discriminating procedures to all aspects of human resource management.

The examiner has stated that questions will not be set which specifically refer to existing UK legislation and/or require candidates to quote or describe the content of specific Acts. However, the legislative framework is a useful structure around which to describe the **principles** that you must learn, and for that reason we often refer specifically to provisions of UK legislation.

When you have studied this chapter you should be able to do the following:

- Explain what is involved in the drawing up of a contract of employment.
- Describe the different types of termination of employment.
- Distinguish between unfair and fair dismissal.
- Outline the legal provision for redundancy and maternity rights.
- Discuss equal opportunities in terms of pay, sex and race discrimination.
- Describe the needs for the promotion of non-discrimination and managers' responsibility for developing good practice.

1 CONTRACTS OF EMPLOYMENT

1.1 Introduction

It is important to differentiate the contract of employment (sometimes referred to as a 'contract of service') from other contracts under which one person agrees to perform work for another. Many new statutory rights are conferred only on persons employed under contracts of employment.

When a person is newly employed a contract of employment is usually made expressly (oral or written). This is of considerable significance in the determination of the legal rights and obligations of both parties. In some parts of the world, this individual contract is not so significant since the obligations, rights and remedies of the parties involved in it are determined by collective agreement. However, in the UK these collective agreements themselves create legalities only if and when they are specifically incorporated into the contract.

1.2 Sources of the contract

The contract of employment normally derives from several different sources - some express, some implied. Examples of these sources are:

(a) an agreement between the parties;

(b) an agreement between unions and employers which the parties agree to operate;

(c) a term being implied from common law;

(d) the custom of a trade;

(e) a statutory provision which requires the parties to the contract to observe a certain term (for example, the Employment Rights Act 1996 provides for employees who are laid off to get guaranteed payments).

1.3 Terms of the contract

Note that there are two kinds of terms to a contract of employment, express and implied.

(a) **Implied terms**

The contract does not have to be in writing. There are implied terms and conditions which are established by custom or general usage in the industry or in the organisation.

What is **implied** is that the employer should pay the agreed wages/salaries, and adopt reasonably safe procedures in the workplace. But, as a rule, the employer is not **obliged** to provide work. Also, on the part of the employee, he or she must co-operate with the employer, use skill and care in obeying lawful instructions, and give a faithful service.

(b) **Express terms**

The present trend is for contracts of employment to be in writing. Indeed , UK legislation requires an employer to give employees a written statement which sets out information on the employee's terms and conditions.

There are, in addition, certain statutory conditions laid down in respect of particular industries (eg for road haulage, hotel and catering, etc) and these cannot be in any way limited by any employer-employee agreement.

Additionally, the written statement must have a note stating what disciplinary rules are applicable, to whom the employee can appeal against a disciplinary decision or to whom the grievance can be taken. Any appeals procedure must also be stated.

Furthermore, there are **working rules** which have been established by employers and unions, and these are normally issued in booklet form and set out agreements reached on issues such as

(a) public holidays
(b) night work shifts
(c) conditions payments (eg for dirty work)
(d) bonuses
(e) tea breaks; etc.

This does mean that employers are, overall, restricted as to the conditions of service statements by industrial agreement – the union usually supporting the idea that both employer and employee must abide by these.

Organisational regulations also exist, especially in very large firms, and these are usually set out in pamphlets or booklets which are available to employees. The broad rules are usually indicated to the new recruit upon engagement. The topics these cover will include

(a) the suggestions system;

(b) punctuality;

(c) special leave of absence for, say, local councillors who are employees, or for Territorial Army members;

(d) complaints procedure;

(e) medical examinations; and

(f) parking.

Finally, there are, always, informal rules and regulations which have arisen as conventional, acceptable standards of behaviour in the organisation. These have a very wide range, from the unofficial inferences drawn concerning some official (formal) rules which have arisen over the years, to understood ways of going about things. The recruit has to learn of these from colleagues, usually by experience.

The important point to grasp is that, wherever possible, the employee should be given a statement of the conditions and the regulations of service in writing. This should be completely understood by the employee and he or she should be able to ask for any clarification – which should be offered willingly. Only in this way can there be a clear understanding and the avoidance of conflict in these issues.

1.4 The employer's duties

Imposed upon the parties to a contract of employment are various implied obligations. Though common law based, these obligations have been considerably elaborated upon by statute.

(a) **Duty to pay wages**

The payment of wages is sometimes described as the employer's primary duty – in that a failure to pay on the part of the employer will be regarded as breach of a fundamental term of the contract, entitling the employee to leave immediately.

(b) **Provision of an itemised pay statement**

UK legislation entitles every employee to an itemised pay statement containing the following details:

(i) gross pay;

(ii) variable and fixed deductions and their purposes;

(iii) net pay;

(iv) where different parts of net wages are paid in different ways, the amount and method of payment of each part.

(c) **Payment during sickness**

Where a contract of employment is silent regarding wages during the employee's absence through sickness, the employer is not liable to continue paying wages unless the contract so provides.

(d) **Equal pay for equal work**

UK legislation requires employers to pay men and women equally.

(e) **Duty to indemnify**

It is implied in every contract of employment (unless the contrary is expressly stated) that the employee who incurs expense on his employer's behalf is entitled to be indemnified. The expense or payment must have been made in the course of the employee's duties.

(f) **Duty to provide work**

It is sometimes said that an employer is under a duty not just to pay wages but also to provide work. The accepted view is that an employer will not be failing in his contractual duties by not providing work, provided he continues paying wages except:

(i) in the case of a piece-worker who requires to be given work to earn wages;

(ii) in the case of public performers who require the opportunity of work to maintain and enhance their reputation;

(iii) where failure to provide work extends over such a length of time as to indicate a deliberate intention not to carry out the contract.

Also an employer who agrees to employ an employee for '40 hours per week' is required to pay the employee for 40 hours whether work is available or not. The employer has no right unilaterally to reduce the working week.

(g) **Duty to provide for the employee's safety**

It is the duty of every employer at common law to take reasonable care for the safety of his employees, and failure to do so will render the employer liable in damages to an injured employee or his dependants. Other duties regarding the health and safety of employees and others (non-employees) are laid down by various statutes. Some of these statutes or regulations made under them create specific duties for particular types of work.

1.5 The employee's duties

There is an underlying duty of faithful service implied into every contract of service. Often, of course, contracts of employment will contain express provisions regarding the employee's duties and these may provide additional or supplementary obligations.

(a) **Duty of care**

There is implied into every contract of employment a duty that the employee performs his contract with proper care.

(b) **Duty of co-operation**

Even where the employer promulgates a rulebook containing instructions for the execution of the work, the employee is under an obligation not to construe the rules in a way designed to defeat the efficiency of the employer's business.

(c) **Duty of obedience**

In the absence of express provisions an employee is required to carry out all reasonable and lawful orders of the employer. Some orders clearly do not require obedience eg, falsify sales records on employer's instructions; drive an unroadworthy vehicle which may lead to his prosecution under the Road Traffic Acts.

(d) **Loyal service**

This duty may be expressed, in general, as follows:

(i) To use all reasonable steps to advance his employer's business within the sphere of his employment.

(ii) Not to do anything which might injure the employer's business.

2 TERMINATION OF EMPLOYMENT

2.1 Termination by notice

At common law the contract of employment may be terminated by either party for any reason or for no reason upon giving notice of a reasonable length, unless the contract is one for a fixed term or unless it specifically restricts the reason for which it may be terminated.

Proper notice may be either:

(a) what the contract provides;

(b) what is reasonable if there is no contractual term regarding notice;

(c) what is provided by statutory rules. A contractual term providing for notice shorter than the statutory minimum is void and therefore unenforceable.

UK legislation lays down minimum periods of notice for both employer and employee. A contract of employment may not permit either side to give less than the minimum period of notice. However, either party may waive his right to notice or take a payment in lieu, and there remains a right to terminate a contract without notice in the event of gross misconduct.

2.2 Summary termination

At common law either party may lawfully terminate the contract summarily eg, sacking without giving any notice, if the other party has committed a serious breach of the contract. The general principle justifying summary dismissal is that the employee's conduct prevents further satisfactory continuance of the employer-employee relationship eg, misconduct including disobedience, insolence and rudeness, committing a criminal act such as stealing or causing injury through practical jokes.

2.3 Disciplinary procedures

In the UK, the **Advisory, Conciliation and Arbitration Service (ACAS)** operates services of conciliation, both on an individual and group basis, arbitration, mediation and enquiry. In addition ACAS offers advice to organisations, particularly in its preparation of Codes of Practice, eg in the area of disciplinary procedures. The code proposes that disciplinary procedures should follow certain guidelines as follows:

- should be in written form;
- must identify to whom they apply (all, or some of the employees);
- should be able to deal speedily with disciplinary matters,
- should indicate the forms of disciplinary action which may be taken (eg, dismissal, suspension or warning);
- should specify the appropriate levels of authority for the exercise of disciplinary actions;
- should provide for employees to be informed of the nature of their alleged misconduct;
- should allow employees to state their case, and to be accompanied by a fellow employee and/or union representative;
- make sure that every case is properly investigated before any disciplinary action is taken;

- must inform employees of the reasons for any penalty they receive;
- should state that no employee will be dismissed for a first offence, except in cases of gross misconduct;
- should provide for a right of appeal against any disciplinary action;
- should specify the appeals procedure.

A model disciplinary procedure should aim to correct unsatisfactory behaviour rather than punish it. Employees should be aware what constitutes 'misconduct' and 'gross misconduct' and know the most likely penalty for these categories.

3 DISMISSAL

3.1 Introduction

Dismissal is usually seen as the last step, the ultimate sanction in any disciplinary procedure. However, dismissals occur most frequently in the form of redundancy. Statistics published by the Department of Employment in the UK list the major reasons for dismissal as redundancy, sickness, unsuitability and misconduct in that order. Legislation in Britain makes it a difficult and costly business to dismiss employees. There are now provisions for employees to challenge the employer's decision. However, in recent statistics published by the Department of Employment it was revealed that only a proportion of cases of unfair dismissal actually reach Industrial Tribunals. The majority are dealt with by some form of conciliation and arbitration.

3.2 Fair dismissal

There is a statutory obligation for an employer to show that a dismissal is fair. In this case a dismissal is fair if it is related to

(i) **A lack of capability or qualifications**

This involves cases where the employee lacks the qualifications, skill, aptitude or health to do the job properly. However, in all cases the employee must be given the opportunity to improve the position or in the case of health be considered for alternative employment.

(ii) **Misconduct**

This includes the refusal to obey lawful and reasonable instructions, absenteeism, insubordination over a period of time and some criminal actions. In the last case, the criminal action should relate directly to the job; it can only be grounds for dismissal if the result of the criminal action will affect the work in some way.

(iii) **A statutory bar**

This occurs when employees cannot pursue their normal duties without breaking the law. The most common occurrence of this is the case of drivers who have been banned.

(iv) **Some other substantial reason**

This is a separate reason and will include good work-related reasons for dismissal (eg a need for the business to change and the employees refusing to adapt to the change required).

3.3 Unfair dismissal

In most cases of unfair dismissal there are two stages of proof. Firstly, the circumstances which represent fair grounds for dismissal must be established, and secondly, the tribunal must decide whether dismissal is fair in the circumstances of the case in question.

If the dismissal is for an 'inadmissible reason' the dismissal is automatically unfair (ie, the second stage of proof does not arise). There are two further consequences of an inadmissible reason dismissal:

- the two qualifying conditions for making of claim for unfair dismissal (minimum of two years employment and under the normal retiring age) do not apply;
- the Tribunal may make a higher monetary award.

The inadmissible reasons for dismissal are:

(a) Trade union membership or non-membership;
(b) Pregnancy and/or exercise of maternity leave rights.
(c) Unfair selection for redundancy.
(d) Employee complained about health and safety.

The following reasons also cannot be relied on to justify a dismissal as fair:

- sex discrimination;
- race discrimination; and
- spent criminal conviction.

3.4 Provisions for unfair dismissal

Where employees feel that they have been unfairly dismissed they have the right to take their case to the Industrial Tribunal. The tribunal will normally refer the case to ACAS (Advisory Conciliation and Arbitration Service) in the hope of gaining an amicable settlement. Most cases are settled by some form of conciliation and arbitration. The possible solutions or remedies for unfair dismissal are set out below.

(a) **Withdrawal of notice**

By the employer. This is the preferred remedy.

(b) **Reinstatement (order of Industrial Tribunal)**

This treats the employee as though he had never been dismissed. The employee is taken back to his old job with no loss of earnings and privileges.

(c) **Re-engagement (order of Industrial Tribunal)**

In this case, the employee is offered a different job in the organisation and loses continuity of service.

(d) **Compensation (order of Industrial Tribunal)**

If an employer refuses to re-employ then the employee receives compensation made up of a penalty award of 13-26 weeks' pay (more in the case of discrimination), a payment equivalent to the redundancy entitlement and an award to compensate for loss of earnings, pension rights and so on. Some form of compensation may also be appropriate in cases of reinstatement and re-engagement.

4 REDUNDANCY

4.1 Statutory definition

Redundancy is defined as occurring when

...the employer has stopped or is about to stop carrying on business in the place or for the purpose for which the employee in question was employed, or where the requirements of the business for work of a particular kind, or in a particular place, have ceased or diminished or are likely to do so.

4.2 Reasons

Redundancy arises when the employer

(a) has ceased to carry on business at the place at which the employee was employed.
(b) no longer has a requirement for the work that the employee was employed to carry out.

The most frequent causes of redundancy at the present time are

(a) organisations taking advantage of technological advances to reduce staffing levels. This is a significant factor in both blue and white collar employment. However, new technology does not necessarily always lead to conspicuous manpower savings.

(b) organisations taking initiatives to reduce overmanning in industries where trade unions had maintained unrealistic staffing levels or industries which required streamlining to meet new economic conditions.

(c) changes in the structure of employment with the increased use of 'peripheral' workers at the expense of 'core' workers.

(d) 'cut backs' in public expenditure with resultant enforced redundancies.

(e) shedding of employees unable to deal with the necessary changes taking place in the organisation.

(f) changes in the structure of organisations with fewer lower level workers and consequently, fewer middle managers.

The pace of changes in our society is increasing. Economic, social and technological change will influence dramatically all organisations and as such stable employment patterns, where forty-five years of employment in a single organisation was possible, will be unknown. The future pattern of work is uncertain and is likely to remain so, but it would be true to say that organisations are being forced to make more intensive use of manpower. They have also resorted to unusual employment practices as an alternative to redundancies – job sharing, networking, consultancy contracts, part-time and temporary assignments, use of manpower agencies. However, it is fair to say that redundancy will continue to play a large part in the work of personnel specialists.

4.3 Redundancy pay

In most cases, employees who are made redundant will be compensated by redundancy pay from the employer. In addition firms making more than ten employees redundant must notify the Secretary of State for Employment and consult the trades unions involved at **the earliest opportunity**. Employees who are being made redundant are expected to be given a reasonable amount of time off with pay to seek alternative employment.

Many firms go beyond the statutory requirements and offer redundancy payments in excess of the minimum required. Some personnel departments have instigated a redundancy counselling service whereby employees who are to be made redundant are given advice on how to cope with their changed status and also offered facilities including contacts with other employers in the area.

4.4 Selection for redundancy

When companies devise redundancy policies or agreements they often spend much time and effort on drawing up a detailed list of selection criteria and order of discharge

(a) The practice of last-in-first-out is not necessarily the starting point for declaring redundancies. Indeed in many cases it is the final stage when all else has failed. If a company has insufficient volunteers, whether for redundancy or early retirement, part-time staff and so on, then the last criterion usually used is last-in-first-out. Two points have to be taken into consideration:

(i) the need to retain a balanced staff; and
(ii) the length of company and departmental service.

(b) Any hint of discrimination either negative or positive should be avoided. Perceived 'favourites' will have an adverse effect on the workforce preserved. There is always the danger in 'value to the organisation' of subjective judgement entering into the equation. However, justification can be made even in breach of an agreement where the special skills of the employee can be shown to be necessary for the continued functioning of the department, process, etc.

(c) Most agreements provide for the acceptance of voluntary redundancy before any attempt is made to terminate employment compulsorily. Companies prefer to use voluntary severance as it avoids problems over selection, also hardship and resentment. The most common combination of voluntary terms are indeed large lump sums for those with little service (and therefore little entitlement under the statutory scheme) and early retirement for those aged over fifty-five or sixty.

Companies can face two problems when asking for volunteers – maintaining a balanced workforce and selecting from volunteers when they get a massive oversubscription. The bulk of organisations get round the problem of a balanced workforce by reserving the right to refuse a volunteer.

(d) Early retirement is probably the first method to be used by most companies in a situation which requires the workforce to be reduced. The plea of a company for individuals over a certain age to take early retirement is nowadays construed as the 'thin end of the wedge.' However, there are those to whom this form of 'redundancy' might appeal. If the compensation and pension rights are generous and available to those within five years of retirement, there is every possibility that there may be acceptors. For those aged fifty-five, however, the scheme would involve further employment which could be difficult in the present climate.

In making any redundancy decisions, many factors have to be taken into account. Early retirement, under reasonable terms, does seem to be the least harsh way to deal with such a situation, but the organisation has to be careful to preserve a balance of age and experience. Failing a satisfactory result on early retirement, voluntary redundancy opens the way to individual choice. It is only when both methods have proved ineffective that organisations resort to compulsory redundancies under whatever guise.

5 MATERNITY RIGHTS

5.1 Statutory rights

UK legislation gives protection for employees in connection with a wide variety of matters. It should be noted that these are minimum standards which can be exceeded by agreement or negotiation, but they cannot be denied to an employee. In particular, statute provides protection to female employees who become pregnant.

5.2 Right not to be dismissed on grounds of pregnancy

The dismissal of a woman because of pregnancy, for a reason connected with pregnancy, or because she exercises any maternity rights, is regarded as unfair dismissal in UK law.

Dismissal of a woman because she is pregnant also ranks as unlawful sex discrimination.

5.3 Right to maternity pay

A woman is entitled to maternity pay if she is absent from work wholly or partly because of pregnancy or confinement. Any maternity payments made under the contract of employment for the period covered by the statutory maternity pay will reduce the employer's liability to make the full statutory payment. Maternity pay is provided by the employer, though some small businesses may recover such payments from the state.

5.4 Time off

Every pregnant woman is entitled to time off for ante-natal care (eg, doctor's appointments). She must still receive her normal remuneration.

In the UK, pregnant women are entitled to 14 weeks maternity leave. During the 14 weeks employees are entitled to the benefit of the terms and conditions of employment (except remuneration) which would have been applicable had they not been absent.

There are also provisions entitling pregnant women to return to work after their maternity leave has finished.

Only if the job previously done has become redundant is the employer permitted to offer 'alternative employment'.

Many employees will have contractual rights in respect of maternity. If this is the case she may choose to take advantage, in any particular respect, of her contractual rights or the statutory rights. The effect is that she can pick and choose the most advantageous parts of both sources of rights.

6 EQUAL OPPORTUNITIES AND DISCRIMINATION

6.1 Legislation

A number of statutes in the UK aim to prohibit forms of discrimination based on sex or race. They also seek to create work opportunities for disabled persons and for rehabilitated offenders, as well as regulating equal pay.

6.2 Equal pay

The terms of a woman's employment (eg, pay, holidays etc) must be no less favourable than those of a man's who is or was at the same establishment if she does similar or equivalent work, or work of the same value.

The employer may justify differential terms between men and women if he can show the differential is due to a 'genuine material difference' (eg, that the male comparator is in fact more productive than the particular woman).

6.3 Sex discrimination

It is unlawful to make any form of discrimination in employment affairs because of marital status or sex. This applies especially to the selection process as it offers protection to both sexes against unfair treatment on appointment.

Note that there are two kinds of discrimination, direct and indirect (see also below):

(a) **Direct discrimination**

This occurs when someone is treated less favourably than someone of the opposite sex – perhaps by being banned from applying for a job because of being a woman. This type is not difficult to discover.

(b) **Indirect discrimination**

In this case, an employer may relate a condition to an applicant for a job which does not actually seem relevant to it, but which suggests that only one sex would be acceptable. An example of this may be advertising so that only men are encouraged to apply.

6.4 Disabled persons

Employers are obliged to employ a percentage (standing now at 3%) of people handicapped by disablement. It is an offence to employ additional non-disabled persons if the quota has not been reached.

6.5 Racial discrimination

It is unlawful to discriminate on grounds of

(a) race;
(b) colour;
(c) nationality; and
(d) ethnic or national origin.

Direct and indirect discrimination (as in section above) are included. There is also a **code of practice** to eliminate racial discrimination and to establish equal opportunity in employment, published by the Commission for Racial Equality. As a result of this code, employers are able to adopt anti-discriminatory policies – ensuring that management is aware of the legal position.

6.6 Rehabilitation of offenders

Although UK law declares that former convictions are not relevant and do not have to be stated at interviews for jobs, many exceptions are given and no remedy is forthcoming where someone is discriminated against during selection.

7 PROMOTION OF NON DISCRIMINATION

7.1 Equal opportunities

'Equal opportunities' is a generic term describing the belief that there should be an equal chance for all workers to apply and be selected for jobs, to be trained and promoted in employment and to have that employment terminated fairly. Employers should only discriminate according to ability, experience and potential. All employment decisions should be based solely on a person's ability to do the job in question, no consideration should be taken of a person's sex, age, racial origin, disability or marital status.

7.2 Developing good practice

A number of employers label themselves as **equal opportunity employers**, establishing their own particular kind of equal opportunity policy. However, a report in **Management Today** stated in 1982 that financial institutions employ a very large proportion of women, and yet 96% of these are not in management gradings.

While some protection is afforded by employment legislation, the majority of everyday cases must rely on good practice to prevail.

Developing and applying good working practice should cover all of the aspects of human resource management including the following:

(a) recruitment;
(b) terms and conditions of employment;
(c) promotion, transfer and training;

(d) benefits, facilities and services; and
(e) dismissal.

The main areas where good practice can be demonstrated are:

- **Job Analysis**. Person specifications must not be more favourable to men or women.
- **Advertisements and Documentation**. Advertisements must not discriminate on sex or marital status grounds. This means that job titles must be sexless eg. 'salesman' becomes 'sales person'.
- **Employee Interviewing and Selection**. Questions must not be asked at interviews which discriminate by implication eg, asking a woman whether or not she intends to have children.
- **Redundancy**. If a redundancy situation becomes inevitable management must:

  (a) indicate the reasons for the situation, and what steps they have taken to avoid it;

  (b) indicate the numbers and categories of people likely to be affected;

  (c) indicate the timetable in accordance with the legislation;

  (d) identify a manager to be responsible for the implementation and to have executive responsibility on behalf of the company.

  (This will be important, since redundancy is always news, and there will be all kinds of people who will be asking questions about what is going on.)

8 CHAPTER SUMMARY

In this chapter we have been concerned with the legal requirements and restrictions surrounding employment in the UK. These are contained both in statute and in common law.

Legislation and codes of good practice concerning sex and race discrimination were discussed as well as other aspects of the legislation, including: the employment of ex-offenders and disabled; maternity rights; and dismissal.

Throughout the chapter it is broad principles that matter for examination purposes, and not the detailed legislative rules.

9 SELF TEST QUESTIONS

9.1 Give five examples of the sources of the contract of employment (1.2).

9.2 List some issues that might be covered in a booklet on working rules (1.3).

9.3 Describe the employer's and employee's duties which are implied in the contract of employment (1.4).

9.4 Discuss fair dismissal (3.2).

9.5 Describe the possible solutions or remedies for unfair dismissal (3.4).

9.6 How does redundancy arise? (4.2).

9.7 Describe the rights of a pregnant woman to time off work (5.4).

9.8 What are the grounds of racial discrimination in UK law? (6.5).

9.9 As part of the development of good practice, what should management do if a redundancy situation becomes inevitable? (7.2).

10 EXAMINATION TYPE QUESTION

10.1 Legal framework

You are the newly appointed Chief Accountant of the subsidiary of a publicly quoted company. You have just had a meeting with John Harrison, the senior Management Accountant, about a problem in his department. Your notes from that meeting are set out below.

Notes

Eileen Skinner joined the Accounts Department 4 years ago from Watt and Armitage, a local firm of accountants. She had already passed the final examinations of the Association of Accounting Technicians and came with excellent references. Her performance until recently has been good. She has scored well in every annual review, never getting an overall performance rating of less than 7 out of 10, and has been viewed as a strong candidate for promotion to a higher grade.

In recent weeks the quality of her work has deteriorated and she has taken to arriving late and leaving early. She has also begun to take days off, sometimes without offering a proper explanation. Her immediate superior has tolerated the situation because of Eileen's past record. However. other members of staff are beginning to complain that Eileen is not pulling her weight and, as one colleague put it, 'if she can get away with it, why can't we?'

John doesn't want Eileen Skinner to be dismissed but he can see no other way out if morale in the department is to be maintained. The parent company has a policy of being a " good" employer and of meeting its legal obligations in full.

Required

Prepare a Memorandum for John Harrison setting out your proposals for dealing with the problem.

(a) Set out the legal framework covering the situation **(15 marks)**

(b) What procedure would you follow if Eileen is to be disciplined or dismissed? **(10 marks)**

(Total: 25 marks)

11 ANSWER TO EXAMINATION TYPE QUESTION

11.1 Legal framework

MEMORANDUM

To: John Harrison

From: Chief Accountant

Date: 15th April 199X

Subject: Eileen Skinner

(a) **Legal framework**

There are a number of points to raise on the legal situation.

From the notes it is not clear whether Eileen is employed by the company ie, has a contract of employment or is self employed and has a contract for services. Assuming she is an employee, working full time under a degree of supervision for a salary, Eileen has a contract of employment.

UK law requires that all employees receive a statement of their terms and conditions of employment. As well as details of pay, this statement should outline the normal working hours, holiday entitlement, sickness procedures and periods of notice to be given by both the employee and employer. Where disciplinary and grievance procedures exist, these should be detailed in the statement. As a new recruit Eileen should have been informed of the following:

- disciplinary procedures, including the number of warnings, oral or written, which will be given before suspension or dismissal;
- grievance procedures, outlining who is responsible for dealing with complaints about any aspect of employment which the employee is not satisfied with;
- what constitutes a disciplinary offence;
- how many stages there are to the disciplinary procedure;
- what the rights of appeal and representation are.

A contract of employment places duties on both employer and employee. The employer's duties include provision of remuneration and work, holidays, sick pay and maternity provision. The employee's duties under the contract include fidelity, skill and care and obedience in carrying out lawful and reasonable instruction.

A contract of employment can end by either mutual agreement, by giving notice, by passage of time in the case of a fixed term contract, by dismissal or by redundancy.

Dismissal will be unfair if:

(i) it relates to trade union membership or activities;

(ii) the employer fails to prove the reason for dismissal relates to:

- the capability of the employee to perform the work;
- the conduct of the employee;
- redundancy;
- the employee contravening a restriction imposed by law by continuing employment;
- some other substantial reason;

(iii) a female employee is dismissed because of pregnancy.

Acts of gross misconduct include the refusal to obey lawful and reasonable instructions, absenteeism, insolence and rudeness, committing a criminal act such as stealing or causing injury through practical jokes.

(b) **Recommendations**

Eileen seems to have problems which she is not sharing with either her colleagues or her superiors. She has not committed any gross misconduct, which would justify immediate dismissal and her behaviour is only recently changed.

The company's disciplinary code follows the guidelines laid down by ACAS and I suggest that we initiate this procedure. The steps, which should be agreed with Eileen and formally written down are as follows:

(i) Investigate and record the frequency of Eileen's late arrivals, early departures and days off work. Have an informal talk with Eileen to establish the cause of her recent change in behaviour. There may be problems at home or she may be unwell. She may be experiencing some difficulties in the office, such as sexual harassment or discrimination, which is making her behaviour different. Explain the feelings of the rest of the department and express your concern about the situation, using the results from the investigation.

Eileen may have decided that she would like to work fewer hours or in a different department and the company may be able to help her, if this is the problem.

If the poor conduct continues the disciplinary procedure will continue.

(ii) An oral warning given to Eileen reminding her that her conduct is not acceptable. T quality of work and conduct we expect should be brought to her attention.

(iii) A written warning, outlining the consequences of her continuing misconduct.

(iv) A second written warning.

(v) Dismissal or other disciplinary action (which will be agreed with the personnel department after her oral warning).

23 MANAGING THE WORKING ENVIRONMENT - LEGAL BACKGROUND

INTRODUCTION & LEARNING OBJECTIVES

In this chapter we will be looking at UK health and safety regulations which are designed to ensure reasonable safety in all places of employment.

We examine the roles and responsibilities assigned to employers and employees under the Act, as well as those allocated to safety representatives appointed by trade unions.

When the organisation is devising its health and safety policy, it should apply good practices to every area that is affected. The policy should cover provisions for health and safety made in job descriptions, design of work systems, patterns of work, training and development, accident prevention and counselling.

We remind you once again of the examiner's stated intention **not** to set questions requiring knowledge of specific legislation. Throughout the chapter you should concentrate on broad principles only.

When you have studied this chapter you should be able to do the following:

- Explain the legislation that applies to the working environment.
- Explain the reasons for health, safety and security requirements.
- Outline the principal legislation affecting employers and employees.
- Describe the key elements of a health and safety programme.
- Assess the effect of the environment on work performance.
- Describe some guidelines for good office design.
- Describe the responsibilities of management and the role of the office manager.

1 LEGISLATION AND THE WORKING ENVIRONMENT

1.1 The reasons for health, safety and security requirements

Every year in the United Kingdom there are thousands of accidents in the office which result in injury. The latest estimates amount to around 50,000 office accidents each year, 5,000 of them being serious. Health and safety at work should be a concern for not only ourselves but our colleagues, and if we are managers or employers we also have a responsibility for the health and safety of our employees.

Typical hazards in an office might include:

(a) desks/chairs too near to doors;
(b) unsafe electric plugs;
(c) trailing wires, cables and leads;
(d) torn carpets and other floor coverings;
(e) unlit or poorly lit corridors and stairs;
(f) top-heavy filing cabinets;
(g) untrained operators using machines;
(h) unmarked plate glass doors;
(i) projecting door and drawer handles;
(j) wet floors.

There are of course potentially many others; this list is not intended to be comprehensive.

The consideration, design and implementation of the working environmental factors will be governed by appropriate legal regulations.

1.2 Employers' Liability

Other legislation requires employers to insure employees against injury, ill health and disease arising from their duties. The insurance must be covered by reputable insurance companies and the certificates of insurance must be visibly displayed within the premises. Employers who do not meet these requirements may be subject to heavy fines.

Unfortunately, on occasions, employees are injured or maimed at work as a result of using defective machinery or equipment.

Any employee injured at work by defective machinery or equipment may claim against the employer in the first instance. If the employer feels aggrieved then it is the employer who must claim against the vendor or manufacturer.

2 THE PRINCIPAL LEGISLATION AFFECTING EMPLOYERS AND EMPLOYEES

2.1 The Health and Safety at Work Act 1974

This Act was designed to have far-reaching consequences upon employers' premises and methods of work. It applies in four general areas.

(a) Employee's responsibilities present under common law are restated, namely:

- (i) to take reasonable care of himself and others;
- (ii) to allow the employer to carry out his duties and responsibilities;
- (iii) not to deliberately or recklessly alter or operate any machinery or equipment.

(b) The replacement of many of the provisions of an earlier Act which listed environmental first aid and fire prevention provisions, many of which are now superseded by the general codes of practice recognised by the Health and Safety at Work Act. Some detailed rules which are specified include:

- (i) an allocated allowance of floor area per person;
- (ii) temperature to be 16°C within one hour of work commencement time;
- (iii) sanitation, washing facilities and fresh drinking water must be provided;
- (iv) first aid facilities and named, trained first aiders available.

(c) Fire Precautions Act 1971:

- (i) presence of effective fire alarm system, fire lighting equipment and fire drills – these must be known to employees;
- (ii) regulations regarding fire exits.

(d) General aspects for the employer involve:

- (i) Provision of a safe working environment with minimum risk to health. The extent of this liability is being tested with cases of employees suing their employers for health problems arising many years later, as in the case of the asbestos workers and the recent case of passive smoking-induced cancers. This general provision covers such areas as heating, ventilation, lighting, noise, pollution, sanitation and washing.
- (ii) To ensure the proper and safe operation, handling, storage and movement of all goods, materials (including dangerous substances). There is also a requirement to provide protective clothing free of charge.

(iii) Reporting certain injuries, diseases and dangerous occurrences to the enforcing authority.

(iv) To supply information, training and supervision regarding training matters.

(v) To provide and publish a safety policy.

(vi) To appoint safety representatives to check on safety matters.

(vii) To provide and maintain safe machinery.

(viii) To provide first aid facilities and trained personnel.

(ix) To extend these safety provisions to cover members of the public, as well as employees, so that they will not be at risk on company premises. An example would be the requirement for visitors to wear a 'hard hat' when visiting a construction site.

The Health and Safety at Work Act 1974 is an umbrella statute under which regulations are being made to strengthen and gradually replace the provisions under the earlier statutes such as the Factories Act 1961. Enforcement of safety regulations is now made under the 1974 Act by Health and Safety Inspectors.

2.2 Employers' obligations under the Act

Except where fewer than five people are employed there is a duty on employers to prepare and, as appropriate, revise written policy statements relating to the health and welfare of employees. These statements and their revisions must:

(a) be brought to the notice of all employees;

(b) give details of the organisation and arrangements that are in operation for the implementation of the policy;

(c) be incorporated into appropriate procedures and rules.

Policy statements should, before issue, be approved by the recognised trade unions.

2.3 Safety representatives

The Act introduced Safety Representatives to achieve maximum employee involvement in safety matters. The safety representative must come from a recognised trade union. Certain functions of the safety representation have been identified; these are

(i) to investigate potential hazards

(ii) to investigate complaints

(iii) to make representations to the employer

(iv) to carry out inspections

(v) to represent the employees

(vi) to receive information from inspectors.

A safety representative must be permitted to take time off with pay for the purposes of performing these functions.

2.4 Enforcement of the Act

The enforcement comes within the control of the Health and Safety Commission and Executive, which were set up to administer the provisions of the Act. These bodies now control the inspectorate whose powers include the issuing of improvement and prohibition notices.

(i) An **improvement notice** is served by an inspector on a person who is contravening a requirement of the Act. The person is required to remedy the contravention within a specified period.

(ii) A **prohibition notice** is served where, in the opinion of the inspector, an activity gives rise to risk of serious personal injury.

2.5 First Aid

The Health and Safety (First Aid) Regulations cover employers and self-employed persons. Minimum equipment and facilities are established – where there are 400 employees or over there must be a first aid room, for instance, but boxes have to be established where there are fewer employees. The boxes must contain

(a) guidance notes on a card;
(b) sterile dressings (individually wrapped);
(c) eye pads;
(d) safety pins; and
(e) bandages (triangular).

There must also be enough persons who have had adequate training in first aid (ie, holding an appropriate certificate from the Red Cross, St. John Ambulance Brigade, etc, or having attended a special course).

3 APPLYING GOOD PRACTICE

3.1 The key elements of a health and safety programme

An idealised statement of health and safety policy was made by M Armstrong in his book **A Handbook of Personnel Management Policy**. Its provisions are

(a) The safety of employees and the public is of paramount importance.

(b) Safety will take precedence over expediency.

(c) Every effort will be made to involve all managers, supervisors and employees in developing and implementing procedures.

(d) Legislation is to be complied with in the spirit as well as to the letter of the law.

Within this idealised framework, some or all of the following courses of action may be appropriate

(a) **Job descriptions** which stress health and safety aspect of the job.

(b) **The design of work systems** to reduce health and safety hazards; using engineering design to build in safety controls.

(c) **Creating patterns of work** to reduce accidents directly, eg the introduction of rest pauses, or indirectly, eg by reducing stress by introducing flexitime, job enrichment and so on.

(d) **The training of employees**, identifying what employees must know concerning health and safety and then devising the most appropriate method of instruction. The actual training is comparatively simple; the real difficulty is in ensuring that workers comply with the safety regulations once they have been trained. Follow up campaigns using posters, films, discussion groups and the like have been shown to have a limited effect only and need to be repeated at regular intervals. However, safety training may be handicapped by unfavourable images of the safe worker. Recent research by Piriani and Reynolds concluded that the safe worker was perceived by management as being slow and overcautious and by his workmates as being unsociable.

(e) **Formal procedures** are set up by most organisations. They range from employing a safety officer and a medical officer, to establishing disciplinary procedures to deal with rule-breaking.

(f) **Accident prevention** by carrying out an analysis of accidents. Two measures are commonly used

The frequency rate

$$\frac{\text{Number of injuries} \times 1{,}000{,}000}{\text{Number of employee hours of exposure}}$$

The severity rate

$$\frac{\text{Total number of days lost through injury} \times 1{,}000{,}000}{\text{Number of employee hours of exposure}}$$

However, such measures only involve incidents resulting in some kind of injury. A far more useful exercise from the point of management control is for each manager to carry out a survey in his own department to identify

(i) recurring incidents likely to cause accidents;
(ii) the consequences of such incidents;
(iii) the types of job behaviour involved; and
(iv) the categories of personnel involved.

In this way a study of circumstances can be identified which relates to special and typical kinds of accidents.

(g) **Participative management** is an attempt to involve the workforce in the question of health and safety. We have already seen that involvement has been institutionalised in the Health and Safety at Work Act by the introduction of safety representatives. In some industries, such as mining, there is an obvious commitment on the part of employees toward a shared objective of safe working. In other firms, involving the workforce in safety matters is a problem that no amount of committees or publicity has yet solved. The problem may lie in an attitude generated by management who may see safety work as having a low status.

(h) **Employee counselling** has met with some success, particularly in reducing stress, an area of a great deal of current concern and research.

3.2 The welfare function today

The Shops Offices and Railway Premises Act laid down a law as to the minimum amount of space for an individual worker to occupy. It also addressed such basic issues as washing and toilet facilities and working temperatures. All of this is now expected and accepted by employees and employers and today's welfare issues concern such things as the handling of hazardous substances.

Social issues are also now regarded as a welfare concern; these include things such as smoking within the working environment.

Due to this increase in complexity, the modern role of welfare in organisations is less easy to define. Thomason sees it as **concern for people as individuals**. However, the welfare function today is typified by a movement away from the individual to a more institutional approach through collective bargaining, legislation or company-wide policies. There has been a recent return to individual techniques through developments in employee counselling.

In addition, every Head of Department ought to take into account the way in which his or her plans and ideas impact upon the **welfare** of human beings working there. It must be remembered that the purpose of any specialist welfare unit in the organisation is not to take away from managers their responsibility for staff welfare, but simply to organise certain general activities.

The term **welfare** does not cover state insurance schemes of various types – even though it does include matters of worker security, well-being and health.

3.3 Welfare provisions

In its widest context, welfare, as the concern for people as individuals, can be seen in most personnel management policies, in selection interviewing, counselling, appraisal schemes and so on. In a narrow context welfare can be viewed as a set of provisions that have a great deal of overlap with fringe benefits.

These provisions have been identified by Thomason as

(a) canteen facilities;
(b) recreational facilities;
(c) information services such as legal aid;
(d) the provision of houses, nurseries, transport and the like;
(e) further education provision; and
(f) medical services.

Thomason feels that such provisions may enable people to work better within the normal functioning of the enterprise and may have an effect on such factors as recruitment, loyalty and length of service. The evidence, however, is far from conclusive. A study carried out in the United States in 1970 by Metzger found that most employees preferred higher wages to welfare provisions which they had to accept irrespective of whether they suited individual needs.

3.4 The role of the specialist welfare officer

Specialist welfare officers can offer a unique role where they are neither part of senior management, nor line employees. They possess a neutrality which makes them valuable as helpers and advisers on social problems for all members of the company.

The scope of the welfare officer's work can be summed up in the following list of functions which can be allotted to him

(a) Advice and help on personal problems of company employees.

(b) Medical problems resulting in frequent absenteeism or early retirement.

(c) Advice to those about to retire.

(d) Advising management on safety at work and following up the reports of safety officers.

(e) An advisory first aid function.

(f) Administration of sports and other recreational facilities.

(g) Helping with employee accommodation problems.

(h) Reporting to general management on all welfare matters.

(i) Knowledge of all relevant legislation, eg state social security provisions, landlord and tenant law, health and safety at work legislation.

(j) Advising on matters such as pension schemes, loans, insurance provisions and so on.

4 OFFICE DESIGN

4.1 Office premises

The costs of office accommodation are now so high that management is forced to look very critically at the returns on the capital they invest in this direction. Thus, many aspects must be studied closely

(a) The investment in the building itself.

(b) The location of the office.

(c) The layout of the departments within the office to achieve optimum performance

  (i) open plan
  (ii) panoramic
  (iii) principles of office layout.

(d) The environment

  (i) lighting/heating/ventilation
  (ii) noise reduction
  (iii) furniture.

4.2 Factors determining investment in the building

The way in which an organisation acquires a new building will be determined very largely by the amount of capital it has available for investment. It may also be able to arrange mortgage facilities and offset the interest against tax in order to purchase a suitable property.

Renting or leasing a property may be a good alternative if there is a small amount of capital readily available. One disadvantage in renting is that it is considered 'dead' money. There is no way that the rent can be turned into an investment.

4.3 Factors determining the location of the office

The choice between city, suburban or rural setting for the office will be affected by

(a) **The prestige value of the building**

Although city sites are generally considered to be more prestigious, there is now much to be said for the quality of working life in more rural areas, especially with the greater mobility of the workforce.

(b) **Cost of land**

Cost comparisons between the three types of location must be carefully analysed. City costs tend to be very high because of the demand.

(c) **Expansion possibilities**

Extensions and modernisation can be more difficult in the city areas because of the very strict town planning laws. There tends to be more flexibility for out-of-town locations.

(d) **Transportation**

Costs and difficulties of travel for the staff, and of moving goods and equipment are paramount considerations in the location exercise. This factor alone can affect staffing, and though cities are generally more favourably endowed with transport facilities, the costs tend to be high.

(e) **Parking**

Parking space in cities is difficult to find. All space is of such high value that it tends to be turned into building space wherever possible. Vandalism and theft of parked cars is an increasing problem in the cities.

(f) **Rates of pay**

Rates of pay tend to be higher in cities but the travelling time and costs often militate against employment in a city. This is one of the factors that causes staff to move around much more in an attempt to better their rates of pay.

4.4 Office layout

(a) **Open plan offices**

The main choice in office layout is between the division of the available space into small offices for up to three or four people and the open plan office with all staff working in the same, undivided, area. Generally, there is a trend towards open plan offices since they tend to be cheaper. However, it is not a simple either/or choice. It is likely that some departments such as cashier and internal audit will require individual offices for security and confidentiality while other departments may be grouped in an open plan office. Additionally, an open plan office may contain low-level divides, generally four to five feet high, giving some privacy to individuals or departments without cutting them off from the general atmosphere of the room. Finally, there can be an enormous difference between a normal open plan office, often with desks in rows all facing the same way, and a panoramically planned or landscaped office.

The benefits of the open plan office are

(i) A high proportion of space is saved by dispensing with corridors and dividing walls.

(ii) Communications can be improved as it is easier for staff to consult one another.

(iii) Work flows can be better designed and the layout of the desks or work stations much more easily positioned to suit the staff.

(iv) Supervisors are located with the staff they control, so making supervision more effective.

(v) More effective lighting, heating and ventilating systems can be installed and monitored.

(vi) Machines and equipment can be located in positions that ensure that the maximum potential use is obtained by all staff.

(vii) Cleaning and maintenance costs tend to be more economic.

(viii) Informal supervision can occur as other members of staff will more easily notice if an individual is reading a newspaper, arriving late or not working very hard.

The disadvantages of the open plan office can be said to be:

(i) Staff can be easily distracted by noise or movement and this affects their efficiency. Typewriters and telephones can cause the worst noise problems.

(ii) There can be a lack of privacy, especially for confidential conversations. Often small rooms are provided for this purpose.

(iii) Infectious illness can spread much more quickly since staff are not isolated.

(iv) Staff can lose a sense of 'belonging' in the larger office and this sometimes causes morale problems.

(v) Ventilation can cause disagreements between staff near windows and in the centre of the office.

(vi) An open plan office can look untidy and inefficient, especially to visitors.

(b) **Panoramic office planning**

Panoramic office planning, or office landscaping, requires a very intensive study of the work in the office and the organisation of the communication pattern. This analysis determines the grouping of the staff, machines and equipment. The furniture appears to be grouped casually, the environment is pleasing to the eye and is also efficient. Sound-deadening materials are used for floors and ceilings, and screens and potted plants provide interest and atmosphere.

Many companies are deterred from this kind of exercise in view of the expense incurred but the greater efficiency achieved may compensate in the long run.

(c) **Principles of office layout**

Several points should be considered when planning the use of office space. Limitations in the size and scope of the building, together with the types of offices required, determine how the office should be laid out to achieve the greatest efficiency.

The major factors which should be taken into consideration are

(i) **Space**. The statutory requirements must be complied with. Special needs for machinery and document storage should be noted.

(ii) **Health**. Adequate storage should be available for, eg, damp, outside clothing. Toilet facilities should be hygienic.

(iii) **Services**. Power outlets should be sufficient in number and conveniently placed, as should telephone points. If computer terminals are used they should be placed so that all staff who use them have easy access.

(iv) **Work flow.** Work is generally passed from one person to another for processing before it is completed. This flow should be in one direction with the minimum feasible distance between the staff concerned so that queries can be easily dealt with and time is not wasted walking with documents from one end of the room to the other.

(v) **Financial considerations.** The cost of room dividers, and possibly moving them in the future if needs change, should be borne in mind. Also, the cost of landscaping an open plan office should be considered. On the other hand, the financial benefits, in terms of high productivity and low staff turnover, of a well planned, efficient office with good morale may compensate for any initial costs.

(vi) **Physical considerations.**

Decor: attractive, bright decor can improve productivity and encourage tidiness.

Cleanliness: the attractive decor must be maintained by cleaning, so the office should be made easy to keep clean by careful choice of the finishes and style of furniture.

Ventilation: it should be possible to ventilate the room without making certain areas draughty.

Heating: the ideal office temperature is about 65°F. A uniform heat should be maintained.

Lighting: this should be adequate, with as much natural light as possible.

Noise: invasive external noise should be counteracted with double glazing. Internal noise can be reduced by suitable furnishing materials. Particularly noisy machinery may need to be placed in a separate room.

(vii) **Safety.** Machines should be inspected regularly. Telephone and power cables should not trail across the floor. Floors should not be slippery with high polish. Heaters should not be near paper storage facilities because of the fire risk.

(viii) **Staff movements.** Desks and machinery should be arranged to give clear pathways to points such as toilets, fire escapes, drinks machines and stairways. Also desks should be positioned so that these movements are not distracting.

4.5 The environment

(a) **Lighting/heating/ventilation**

It is not always possible to use the natural daylight. When this is the case, the alternative system should give as good a quality of light as possible to avoid mental fatigue and eyestrain. The lighting system will be designed to take into account the size of the office, the height of the ceilings, the types of work being undertaken by staff and the situation of the work stations.

Employers have a responsibility to ensure that windows are kept clean, and that interior decorations are sensibly chosen so as to reflect the light.

Heating and ventilation systems can be costly, and should be designed to conserve energy. The use of cavity insulation and double glazing helps in this respect. It should be remembered that too much heat, as well as stale air, can affect performance ratings as much as the cold, and a sensible balance must be achieved.

(b) **Noise**

The reduction of noise is important for health. Continuous noise can impair efficiency, so the benefits in reducing it affect health, efficiency and output.

To reduce the internal noise level in the office, acoustic ceilings and carpeting can be installed. A sensible choice of consumables and equipment such as wastepaper bins can also help. The elimination of metals and the introduction of rubber or felt to deaden sound will be appreciated by all personnel.

Sound baffles to windows and double glazing will restrict outside interference. Telephone ringing can be eliminated by using an alternative method such as flashing lights.

Noise consciousness is a habit to be developed. Once management is aware of the problems and hazards, much can be done to encourage a sensible approach by the staff.

(c) **Furniture**

Staff work more efficiently if they are comfortable. The selection of office furniture should take into account the normal characteristics of the human body and the principal characteristics of the type of work. The British Standards Specification for desks and tables and seating is BS 3893, and the measurement and basic requirements of office furniture are also contained in BS 3893.

5 GOOD OFFICE PRACTICE

5.1 Working conditions

Productivity and working conditions can be improved if office workers adhere to a set of guidelines, such as:

(a) **Making the best use of available space**

Space is always at a premium for: doing the job; storage of work in progress; reference material; equipment and furnishings; and for a better environment (plants, open spaces etc.).

Obsolete and unused material should be removed. Completed work should be moved on quickly to its next destination. Material should be stored compactly (eg, in filing cabinets, or held on a computer database).

(b) **Safeguarding the working area**

Personal possessions, confidential documents and equipment should be protected against loss or damage. Secure containers (fireproof safes, etc.) should be available. Staff should know who has reason to be in the area, and strangers should be challenged (but in a friendly way - 'How can I help you?' or 'Who do you wish to see?').

(c) **Exercise**

Office work is largely sedentary, and regular exercise should be promoted. In Japanese offices there are usually set times when everybody in the office will stop work for a period of exercise, though the desks there are often so close that acting in harmony is essential.

(d) **Cleaning**

Efficient use of space will make cleaning easier, and furniture should be such that it is easy to clean underneath and behind it. Loose papers and equipment should be put away each night.

(e) **General Appearance**

Customers and the general public will get a more favourable impression if the office is tidy and looks efficient, and if the staff are well dressed. The reception area is particularly important in this respect. Staff should be trained to handle all the interfaces to the outside world, such as answering the telephone and receiving visitors. Also the staff spend a large amount of their time in the office, and it is their own interests to be in a pleasing environment.

5.2 Management responsibilities and the role of the office manager

It is obviously part of the office manager's role to encourage good office practices such as those outlined above, but this must not be done in dictatorial manner. It is vital that staff feel they have control over their own environment. In a recent experiment carried out by Yale University at an American nursing home the residents were divided into two groups. The individuals in one group were encouraged to make their own decisions about their living conditions and to look after their own areas themselves. The second group was cared for much more directly and the nursing staff attended to all their needs. The mortality rate in the first group was roughly half that of the second.

People deprived of control soon develop feelings of helplessness. They are happier, healthier and more productive if they feel they have power over their surroundings. It is the difficult task of the office management to lead from behind, to give control to the staff yet still ensure that objectives are met.

6 CHAPTER SUMMARY

In this chapter we discussed the management of the working environment, in terms of management responsibilities and the role of the office manager. There are aspects of the work environment which impinge on performance and various groups have different needs, all of which should be considered when designing the office.

We also covered the reasons for health, safety and security at work and outlined the principal legislation affecting employers and employees.

7 SELF-TEST QUESTIONS

7.1 List some typical hazards found in an office (1.1).

7.2 Under common law, what are the employee's responsibilities? (2.1).

7.3 Describe the activities of a safety representative (2.3).

7.4 In a written health and safety policy, describe what actions are appropriate (3.1).

7.5 Why is there an overlap between welfare provisions and fringe benefits? (3.3).

7.6 Outline the disadvantages associated with open plan offices (4.4).

7.7 Describe the factors to be taken into account when designing office layout (4.4).

7.8 What range of working conditions would a manager need to consider? (5.1).

8 EXAMINATION TYPE QUESTION

8.1 Safety and health at work

In 1972 the Royal Commission on Safety and Health at Work reported that unnecessarily large numbers of days are lost each year through industrial accidents, injuries and diseases, because of the 'attitudes, capabilities and performance of people and the efficiency of the organisational systems within which they work'.

To what extent has the situation changed? **(20 marks)**

9 ANSWER TO EXAMINATION TYPE QUESTION

9.1 Safety and health at work

The work of the Royal Commission in 1972 led to the passing of the Health and Safety at Work Act in 1974. This Act, which extends cover to categories hitherto exempted, e.g. the self employed, the general public, those in the educational sector, etc, places the emphasis on the wider, more positive duties of employers and provides for greater and faster flexibility by leaving much to regulations and codes of practice. The detailed standards of the earlier Acts remain, unless specifically revoked, but it is no longer possible for an employer to plead that any act or omission of his was not in contravention of a defined requirement. At the same time, the powers of the Factory Inspectorate have been increased and heavier penalties provided.

The Robens Committee recognised that real progress was impossible without the full co-operation and commitment of all employees. It went on to say that if working people were to accept their full responsibilities, they must be able to participate fully in the making and monitoring of safety arrangements. In consequence, the Act lays stress on training, instruction and consultation and gives certain rights to organised labour.

The responsibilities set out in the Act are twofold. The employer has the general duty of care, covering, in particular, working systems, handling and transport of materials, plant and machinery, premises (including means of access and egress) and the environment. He must provide adequate training, instruction and information. He must issue a written policy statement on safety and consult generally with employees, recognise safety representatives and set up safety committees, when requested to do so by a recognised trade union. In addition, under an amendment to the Companies Act in April 1975, he must give information in the annual report about the measures taken. The employee, for his part, must take reasonable care for his own safety and that of his colleagues and others who may be affected. He must co-operate with the employer and not interfere with or misuse anything provided in the interest of health and safety.

Operation of the Act comes under the direction of the Health and Safety Executive, which is the employer of the Factory Inspectorate. The Executive reports to the Health and Safety Commission. Factory Inspectors are given the right to enter premises to carry out their function at any time and have rights of investigation, questioning and search. They are able to serve Improvement Notices where, in their opinion, remedial action must be taken and Prohibition Notices if they see the situation as so dangerous that it must be stopped immediately. The employer has the right to appeal against these notices within seven days. Pending the appeal, an Improvement Notice will be suspended but a Prohibition Notice will remain in force unless and until the employer wins his case.

A fine of up to £5,000 may be imposed in the Magistrates Courts for breaches of the Act, or, where there has been a conviction on indictment, an unlimited fine or imprisonment for up to two years.

Individuals may be named and held liable for an offence as well as organisations.

The Employment Advisory Service (EMAS) is also part of the Health and Safety Executive, and advises on occupational health problems generally. It carries out, or oversees, medical examinations of those engaged on hazardous processes and works with career officers to ensure that young people with health defects have suitable medical supervision. Employers must therefore advise the Careers Office on Form 2404, obtainable free from the Careers Service, EMAS or the Factory Inspectorate, when they recruit staff under 18 years of age.

Employers must prepare a written statement and outline the organisation set up to carry it out. The only exception, made under the Health and Safety Policy Statement (Exception) Regulations 1975, is for those establishments where fewer than five are employed. The policy must also be brought to the notice of employees but will not supersede the need to issue more detailed safety rules and procedures.

The Safety Representatives and Safety Committee Regulations 1977 give recognised independent trade unions the right to appoint safety representatives with whom employers have a duty to consult. Representatives, who should have two years' service in the organisation or in a comparable job elsewhere, must be given facilities for independent investigation and to inspect relevant documents.

24 THE ACCOUNTANT AS COMMUNICATOR

INTRODUCTION & LEARNING OBJECTIVES

Communication is supremely important in any large industrial organisation for the direction, co-ordination and motivation of all levels involved in its various areas of operations.

Despite the advance in computer systems and communication technology, most large companies would still cite 'communication problems' as a common, major, area of concern.

Communication is an area which all companies recognise can be improved. Many companies devote great effort to improving communication skills, particularly in areas of experts talking to non-experts. This is most significant when staff specialists (eg. computer division, management services, accounts) are working with line departments, customers, etc. In particular, the accountant is seen as an information provider and, as such, is expected to be a good communicator.

It is difficult to overstate the importance of good communications. The 1986 NASA space shuttle disaster was principally caused by a failure in upward communication which failed to transmit results of testing and component standards to top management. Many strikes have been caused by a failure in downward communication where staff have made invalid assumptions about management's intentions.

When you have studied this chapter you should be able to do the following:

- Explain the communication process, both oral and written.
- Clarify information.
- Describe the importance of good listening.
- Summarise information.
- Present information in writing and verbally, using visual aids.
- Begin developing ideas for persuading others to your point of view.
- Describe the different types of negotiating situation.
- Develop negotiation skills.

1 SEEKING AND CLARIFYING INFORMATION

1.1 Introduction

Definition Communication in business can be defined as the transmission of information so that it is received, understood and leads to action.

This definition enables us to understand some of the key aspects of business communication:

(a) Information, and not data, should be communicated. Information is active, relevant and prompts action; data, on the other hand, is passive, maybe historical or irrelevant and does not lead to action.

Information can be classified as 'hard' or 'soft'. Hard information includes documents, reports and facts, whereas soft information covers less tangible information such as feelings, points of view, morale and body language.

(b) Clearly, if information has not been received or is not understood by the receiver, then communication has not taken place.

(c) The communication should lead to action. This action may take the form of a positive decision or may be a change in attitude. If the communication does not lead to any action then, probably, it ought not to have taken place.

Communication means transmitting messages to people in a manner which stimulates response. In some cases, the response will be direct to the sender, as when two people are engaged in debating the merits and demerits of some proposition. In other cases the response will be indirect as when transfer of the information gives rise to some independent action on the part of the recipient or when he merely stores it for future reference.

1.2 The communication process both oral and written

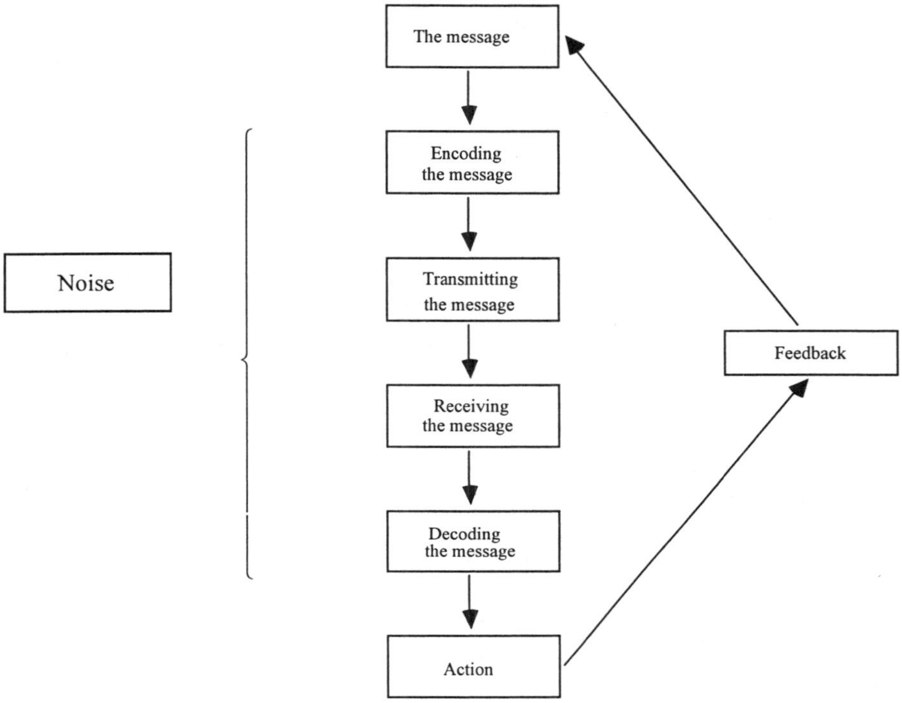

Explanation of stages:

- There must be some idea or thought to be conveyed. The sender has to have a message that he wishes to transmit to another party.
- Next, the message must be encoded and put in a form suitable for transmission. At this point the sender must organise the material of the message into the most coherent and appropriate device. Matters such as: whether it should it be written or verbal, whether it needs illustrations or just text, whether it should be translated into some foreign language; are the sort of issues to be considered at this stage.
- The means of transmission has to be decided. Some messages should be conveyed orally because speed is essential and face-to-face feedback is desirable. Other messages will be best suited to the written form eg, formal announcements for the notice-board.
- The message needs to be received by the other party. The receiver needs to be alert and attentive ('tuned-in'), aware that a message has been transmitted and of the need to receive it.
- The transmission must be correctly decoded. Receivers have to reconstruct the signs, symbols and language in a form that makes sense to them and which is, hopefully, in line with the intentions of the sender.
- Action should follow. Communication is carried out to bring about a response in the receiver. Sometimes this response involves direct action whilst in other cases it may be a matter of

giving information which may or may not involve action at a later date. Even so, registering the new information is to be seen as a form of action resulting from effective communication.

- The final element in the process is that of feedback. It is crucial, though it is sometimes overlooked, for the person sending the communication to get feedback from the receiver. Not only does this confirm that the message got through, it also enables corrective action to be taken in the event of some breakdown of communication. Feedback can take different forms; it can be immediate, as in a conversation or delayed while waiting for the post.

From the diagram illustrating the communication process it is also important to note that communication takes place in a specific environment and that a characteristic of most environments is 'noise'. The good communicator will take into account the specific environment adjusting their communication to the demands of the situation. The problem of 'noise' ie, anything in the environment that impedes the transmission of the message, is significant. Noise can arise from many sources eg, factors as diverse as loud machinery, status differentials between sender and receiver, distractions of pressure at work or emotional upsets. The effective communicator must ensure that noise does not interfere with successful transmission of the message.

1.3 Formal and informal communication systems

All organisations have formal, acknowledged, and often specified communication channels. There will be lists of people who are to attend briefings or meetings, and distribution lists for minutes of meetings or memos. There will be procedures for telling people of decisions or changes, and for circulating information received from outside the organisation.

In addition, an informal 'grapevine' exists in all organisations; people talk about their work, their colleges, and about the state of their firm, whenever they meet: in corridors; over lunch; after work. They swop rumour, gossip, half-truths and wild speculation.

To fulfil these purposes, communication flows exist with the company in three main directions:

(a) downwards, or superior-subordinate communication;
(b) upwards or subordinate-initiated communication;
(c) horizontal or lateral.

1.4 Superior-subordinate communication

Superior-subordinate, or downward, communication has traditionally received the greatest emphasis in organisations, yet the existence of an active downward flow of information does not mean that it is accurate, understood, received or even accepted by subordinates. Katz and Kahn (1966) identified five general purposes of superior-subordinate communication:

(a) to give specific task directives about job instructions;

(b) to give information about organisational procedures and practices;

(c) to provide information about the rationale of the job;

(d) to tell subordinates about their performance;

(e) to provide ideological-type information to facilitate the indoctrination of goals.

In the light of these points it will be apparent that the lack of the appropriate downward communication is likely to result in poor understanding of working instructions and responsibilities, poor awareness of corporate objectives (particularly at lower management levels) and poor morale among junior managers because they have not been informed about changes which affect them or their working conditions.

Chester Barnard (1938) listed seven communication factors which he regarded as especially important in maintaining objective authority between superior and subordinate in an organisation:

(a) Channels of communication should be definitely known.

(b) There should be a definite formal channel of communication to every member of the organisation.

(c) Lines of communication should be as direct and as short as possible.

(d) The complete formal line of communication should normally be used.

(e) Persons serving as communication centres should be competent.

(f) The line of communication should not be interrupted while the organisation is functioning.

(g) Every communication should be authenticated.

1.5 Subordinate-initiated communication

Unlike downward communication, which tends to be of a directive nature, upward, subordinate-initiated communication is non-directive in nature. There are essentially two types of upward communication: personal information concerning, for example, personal problems or suggestions for improving the organisation's performance; and technical feedback information for control purposes (such as product or sales figures).

1.6 Lateral or horizontal communication

The typical hierarchical organisation structure formally recognises only vertical (ie, upward and downward) communication. Yet as organisations become larger, more complex and subject to environmental changes, the need for horizontal or lateral communication becomes increasingly apparent. In particular, lateral communication is essential in the corporate planning process if efforts are to be successfully co-ordinated in order to achieve organisational objectives. Four of the most important reasons for lateral communication are:

(a) **task co-ordination** – for example, department heads may meet periodically to discuss how each department is contributing to organisational objectives;

(b) **problem solving** – for example, members of a department may meet to discuss how they will handle a threatened budget cut;

(c) **information sharing** – members of one department may meet with the members of another department to explain some new information or study;

(d) **conflict resolution** – members of one department may meet to discuss, for example, duplication of activities in the department and some other department.

Formally, lateral communication takes the form of committee meetings, departmental or interdepartmental meetings, and the distribution of written reports. Informal types of lateral communication can be just as important, however. Chester Barnard identified several functions of informal communication:

(a) to communicate intangible facts, opinions, suggestions and suspicions;

(b) to minimise excessive cliques of a political nature arising from too great a divergence of interests and views;

(c) to promote self-discipline of the group;

(d) to develop important personal influences in the organisation.

Lack of lateral or horizontal communication, as will be apparent from the above, can lead to divisions in the management team, lack of co-ordination, rivalry between sections and departments, and inefficiency.

2 CLARIFYING INFORMATION

2.1 Consequences of poor communication

The consequences of poor communication are lack of, poor, or inadequate control, as well as faulty co-ordination.

Lack of **downward communication** is likely to result in:

(a) poor awareness of corporate objectives at lower management levels;

(b) poor understanding of working instructions and responsibilities;

(c) poor morale of junior managers because they are not consulted about changes which affect them or their working conditions.

Lack of **upward communication**, including 'feedback', has the following undesirable consequences for management:

(a) early warning of troubled areas is not received;

(b) benefit of creative ability in subordinates is lost;

(c) participation of subordinates is limited;

(d) need for change is not appreciated because management is isolated from the operation areas;

(e) control becomes difficult;

(f) introduction of change is difficult.

Lack of **lateral communication** often leads to:

(a) divisions in management teams;
(b) lack of co-ordination;
(c) rivalry between sections and departments;
(d) lack of advice and involvement by staff specialists.

A company's policies, plans, instructions and information are required to be known and comprehended if the corporate plan is to be a success. This communication is only seen by some companies to be necessary from the top echelon downwards to lower ones. It is, however, equally essential, as we saw above, for information, ideas and experiences to flow upwards from the lower levels. If communication is only one way, there is no feedback and this is a severe disadvantage. Apart from anything else, employees will not feel a real part of the company. The management that plans and controls positively, and at the same time pays attention to what people feel and think, will be participative and considerate, and more certain of success.

2.2 Barriers to communication

Poor communication in any of the above three areas can be the result of barriers and breakdowns which should be analysed to prevent continuing occurrence. Typical problems are:

(a) lack of preparation and planning before communication;

(b) unstated or incorrect assumptions;

(c) wrong method of communication;

(d) poorly phrased message;

(e) loss in transmission or poor retention by receiver;

(f) biased interpretation;

(g) poor listening skills (Newstrom has demonstrated that people are often not listening in a meeting, even when quiet, because they are thinking about the next point that they will be raising rather than following the arguments of the present speaker);

(h) mistrust and fear (can be clearly seen in many widely publicised trade union and company confrontations);

(i) natural reserve and status barriers can result in reluctance to pass information upwards for fear of incurring criticism;

(j) information overload means that individuals receive too much information to be able to assess what is and what is not important.

2.3 Overcoming barriers to communication

The barriers to effective communication can be removed if all members of an organisation understand the channels and methods available.

This can be achieved by setting up and publicising adequate information channels, which might include briefing groups, joint committees and specific project groups with members from the various sectors of the organisation.

Management can also reduce communication barriers by being aware of their existence and always actively encouraging their subordinates to communicate.

In addition, all employees should be trained how to use communication techniques.

3 ORAL AND WRITTEN COMMUNICATION

3.1 Oral communication

Oral communication can range from **speech without visual contact** – radio, tannoy, personal pager and telephone to **speech with visual contact** – television presentation, television link and face-to-face conversation.

The advantages of oral communication include the following.

(a) It is a quick, direct and cheap medium with little time lapse between sending and receiving.

(b) The meaning of an oral message can be underlined by using stress, timing and pitch.

(c) It has the potential for informality and the sensitive handling of some communications eg, bad news, reprimand, sympathy, or encouragement.

(d) Instant feedback is possible, so that misunderstandings can be cleared and messages can be received and acknowledged.

(e) In face-to-face communication the meaning can be reinforced by facial expression or gestures.

The disadvantages may include the following.

(a) Noise can interfere with the message.

(b) Less time is allocated to the planning the communication and this can lead to inferior decisions being made.

(c) The communication may be distorted because the listener interprets the facial expression or body language wrongly.

(d) Communications that require memory are better written down than spoken.

(e) Clash of personalities may be a barrier to conversation.

3.2 Written communication

Written communication can range from permanent hand-written, typed or printed documents, through semi-permanent output such as screen displays to transient outputs such as written information on television screens and electronic bill boards.

Permanent records have

(a) **advantages** in avoiding personal contact, assisting with long and complex messages and being able to reach a large audience. They have the potential for formality and their permanence enables them to be used as records.

(b) **disadvantages** in that their permanence can lead to rigidity. Moreover they demand considerable linguistic skills, are time-consuming to produce, slower to transmit and can be expensive.

4 GOOD LISTENING

4.1 Learning to listen

Without effective listening there can be no effective communication. It has been discovered that people forget most of what they have heard within a couple of days. This can be improved by better messages, repeated messages and also by helping the receiver to learn to be a more efficient listener. Among the many ideas for maximising your effectiveness as a listener are the following:

(a) Concentrate on the message itself, not on who is saying it. Not all senders of messages are effective communicators, but the information may be relevant.

(b) Provide feedback for the sender by asking for a repeat, requesting clarification, summarising the main points to confirm your understanding.

(c) Try to concentrate on the meaning of the message. Follow all ideas through to their logical conclusion and listen 'between the lines' to what is not being said because it may be as important as what **is** being said.

(d) Avoid distractions and give the communication your full attention. If you are preoccupied with a more pressing matter, try to postpone the unconnected communication until you can avoid mind wandering.

(e) Do not become emotionally involved.

(f) Remember that thoughts are quicker than words and you can evaluate what is being said without missing anything.

(g) Do not take many notes, just the key points.

(h) Stereotyping can get in the way of good listening. Whether this is based on the personal characteristics of the sender or from previous experience of their ideas, you should listen first and decide later.

Listening is not the same as hearing. It involves a more conscious assimilation of information and requires attentiveness on the part of the interviewer. Failure to listen properly to what someone is saying will mean that probing questions (in an interview) may become a worthless exercise. In preparing to listen you should ask 'What new things can I learn from this person?'

4.2 Barriers to listening

Barriers to listening include the following:

(a) scoring points – relating everything you hear to your own experience;

(b) mind reading;

(c) rehearsing – practising your next lines in your head;

(d) cherry picking – listening for a key piece of information then switching off;

(e) daydreaming – you can think faster than people can talk; the temptation is to use the 'spare' time to daydream;

(f) labelling – putting somebody into a category before hearing what they have to say;

(g) counselling – being unable to resist interrupting and giving advice;

(h) duelling – countering the other's advances with thrusts of your own eg. 'Well at least this department is never over budget';

(i) side-stepping sentiment – countering expressions of emotion with jokes or hollow clichés, such as 'Well it's not the end of the world'.

There are also health factors that may cause difficulties in concentrating on what is being said. People who are suffering from stress, who are in pain or are anxious about something will not be at their best when it comes to effective communications.

5 SUMMARISING INFORMATION

The summary is a compact restatement of points which have been made in a discussion, or in a written report so that the principal features are recorded.

The objective of summarising in a discussion or meeting is to check on the level of understanding and give an opportunity to sort out misunderstandings. A summary of a report is often the only part that is looked at by some managers and therefore it should put the reason for the report and the findings quite succinctly so that a decision could be made based on its contents.

Summarising is a key behaviour in effective meetings where it is usually an important part of the chairing role. There are two different ways doing this:

(a) At intervals in the conversation, to give a list of the salient points as you have understood them.

(b) To test understanding by inviting someone else to summarise and check that their summary accords with the one that you would have given at that stage in the proceedings. If a number of people are present, invitations to summarise can be shared around rather than become the prerogative of one person. This is a splendid incentive for people to listen hard since they never know when they might be called upon to paraphrase what they have heard.

Summarising reduces ambiguity by pointing things out explicitly and helps to reduce the likelihood that people are agreeing to different things.

6 PRESENTATION AND PERSUASION

6.1 Factors affecting choice of method

These can be categorised as follows

(a) Nature of audience:
general education and culture
communication skills
knowledge of subject
attitude towards subject and transmitter
expectations regarding method
desire to communicate
role in organisation
general fears, insecurities, prejudices
existence of disabilities.

(b) Importance of ensuring a feedback.

(c) Desire for consultation – written then verbal.

(d) Cost – speed – convenience – methods available.

(e) Need for accuracy – written v real-time feedback.

(f) Degree of coverage required.

(g) Need to catch attention – desire for dramatic impact.

(h) Need for security/confidentiality.

(i) Desire for informality/formality.

(j) Complexity of subject matter/message.

6.2 Business letters

In every organisation, administrative staff must cope with a good deal of correspondence. In the small firm, it may be the secretary who deals with all correspondence. However, in the large business, the functional managers – marketing director, production director, etc, – usually have to cope with correspondence relevant to their own specialist department, the secretary dealing with more general matters.

The specific business letter layout points are:

Name and address of organisation	THE TRAINING FIRM 123 Lecturer Row London NW2 4LR Tel: 071 323232 Fax: 071 232323	logo
Our ref. *Their ref.*	REF NM/WPP Your ref MK/LM	
Date	25 January 19X8	
Recipient's name, Position, and Address	Mr S Brown Office Manager First Line 22, Plain Street Swindon S42 7KJ	
Salutation	Dear Mr Brown	
Subject heading	Business letter layout	
Opening paragraph	Acknowledge any previous letter and introduce the subject	
Main body of letter	In a logical manner, give or ask for the required information	
Closing paragraph	Conclude the letter in a suitable manner	
Complimentary close	Yours sincerely	
Signature of writer		
Name of writer *Designation (position)*	John Jones Sales Co-ordinator	
Enclosure mark	Enc	
More details may be printed here	Reg office: Brick House, Mill Lane, Bromley Kent	

6.3 Reports

A report is any written or oral communication in which, according to the nature and purpose of the report, the reporter presents a collection of facts or a number of alternative propositions, states his conclusions and submits his recommendations.

General rules have been put forward for the writing of reports. One important aspect here is that reports are presented to management and should therefore appear to be directed to that level – being neat, orderly, comprehensive and well-formatted.

Higher levels of management rarely have time to carry out their own detailed investigations into the matters on which they make decisions, and, therefore, people are often instructed to carry out investigations on their behalf and submit a report. A report may consist of some or all of the following

(a) information, retrieved from files or other sources

(b) description of one-off events or procedures

(c) analysis or the processing of information

(d) evaluation and recommendations.

Reports are also used as a permanent record and source of reference and such, and thus need to be clear and concise.

There is, therefore, an obligation on the part of the report writer to communicate information in an unbiased way. Information should be communicated impartially, and any evaluation and recommendations should be given under those specific headings.

The types of report

(a) **Routine reports** – submitted at regular intervals and likely to be purely factual in content, ie, containing no recommendations. Examples are sales, orders, production.

(b) **Special reports** – these may be specially commissioned, or originate from the reporter himself, analysing a situation and giving advice or recommending certain action. Equally, special reports may be the results of the findings of a committee and, depending on the terms of reference, may or may not contain recommendations.

(c) **Statutory reports** – reports required by law. Contents are dictated by the governing statute.

(d) **Technical reports** – prepared by specialists on a technical matter. Again, these may or may not contain recommendations.

A formal report should have the following headings

Title; at the top of every report should be the title of the report; this should include who has prepared it, for whom it is intended and the date of completion.

Terms of reference; this is the scope and purpose of every report and should contain details of what is to be investigated, the kind of information required, and whether recommendations are to be made. It places the contents of the report in context.

Procedure or method; this outlines the procedures carried out to make the investigation.

Findings; this section sets out the information found or required and should be clearly structured in order of importance.

Conclusions; this section summarises the main findings of the report.

Recommendations; if required, in this section the writer may suggest possible solutions to the problem investigated in order to aid the recipient in the decision making process.

6.4 Oral presentations

The following points should be considered before making a presentation.

(a) **Number of people attending;** people are often embarrassed by asking questions in front of a large audience. If the presenter is aiming on feedback and participation from the audience which is not forthcoming then the overall effect of the presentation may fail.

(b) **People hear what they want to hear;** when a familiar subject area is being presented, certain members of the audience may become prematurely disinterested and might not thereafter pay attention. Also, if what the presenter is saying conflicts with set beliefs, the audience may not choose to hear what is being said.

(c) **People hear what they expect to hear** ; instead of hearing what is actually said people often hear what they expect to hear, or interpret what they hear in their own way.

(d) **Words are not objective;** the emphasis placed upon words can alter their meaning. The presenter should choose his words with care in order to avoid mis-interpretation of the message.

(e) **Words are ambiguous;** many words in the English language have more than one meaning. The presenter should avoid the use of words and phrases that are ambiguous.

(f) **Physical factors impede communication;** physical factors can impede the effect of the presentation. For example, if the room is too cold or too hot, if there is noise from heavy traffic.

(g) **Technical noise;** technical noise can also impede the presentation, for instance if the presenter has a very strong accent which is not perhaps easily understandable to all of the audience. Also, the presenter's voice must carry to the furthest corners of the room.

(h) **Emotional factors;** if anyone in the audience is worried or anxious then it is unlikely that they will be able to concentrate on the message being said.

(i) **Retention;** people only retain about 10% of what they hear and the usual attention span is about 20 minutes. It is therefore necessary to alter the delivery of the presentation in order to keep the audience's attention for the majority of the time. The presentation should be summarised regularly. Handouts will reduce the amount of note-taking the audience has to do.

(j) **Coding may not be good;** the presenter may not be very good at coding his message. If the message is not coded in a way that is understandable to the audience then the effect of the message will be lost.

(k) Before making a presentation it is necessary to ensure that all equipment is available and in good working order.

(l) The injection of humour into the presentation might be called for, although some audiences would not appreciate an attempt at humour in certain situations.

(m) The venue of the presentation should also be checked to ensure that sufficient seating is available, that sockets for the overhead projector are within easy reach etc. It may be advisable to run through the presentation with a few colleagues to ensure that all possible problems have been highlighted and dealt with.

The presenter should also be clear about the objectives of the presentation. In order to assess the overall success of a presentation there are a number of factors which can be looked at.

(a) Did the presentation achieve its objectives? Was the system adopted as a result of the presentation?

(b) Was everyone attentive during the presentation?

(c) Did anyone leave during the course of the presentation?

(d) Did the presentation run to time?

(e) Were pertinent questions asked were they competently answered?

(f) Were there any problems with equipment or material during the course of the presentation?

6.5 Graphics and visual aids

Examples of visual communication include:

(a) posters, charts, graphs;

(b) video, TV, slide projection;

(c) product demonstration.

The main advantages are:

(a) Impact – you will notice and remember the picture long after you have forgotten the words and figures.

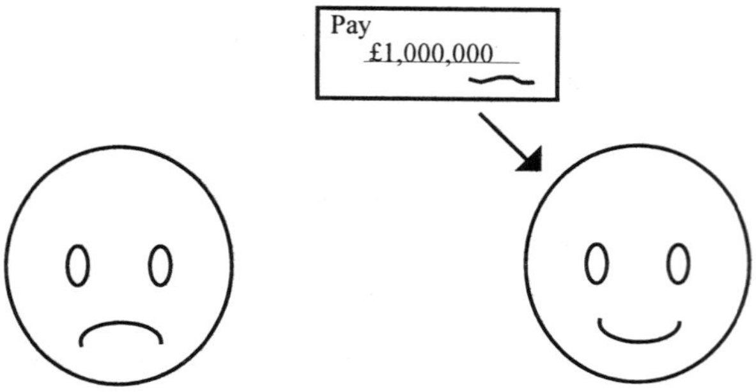

(b) Visual has the highest retention rate (ie,. recall after the event).

(c) The availability of colour and moving images enables the communicator to add drama and grab attention.

(d) They facilitate the understanding of complex material and are comprehensive to those of poor linguistic ability - they can be international in their meaning.

The disadvantages are mainly that:

(a) It is a limited method, in that the amount of content that can be included on one slide, poster etc. is restricted.

(b) Just as in advertising where you may remember the advert clearly but forget the product, so with visual communication, the receiver may be interested by the illustration to the extent that the facts become secondary.

(c) Their worth lies in their simplicity, however cultural connotations may make this simplicity confusing eg, a triangle on the roadside is a cautionary sign in Europe, but represents a helicopter landing point in the USA and a birth control clinic in India.

6.6 Meetings

There are various **purposes** of meetings – to give information
to obtain information
to solve a problem
to secure certain attitudes.

Arrangements for meetings can be split into three stages and the following points are common to all meetings whatever their purpose of form

(a) **Preparation**

(i) Establish valid purpose of meeting and consider whether this could not be achieved by other means.

(ii) Consider the day on which meeting should be held

- Not after the date decision has to be taken.
- Able to give appropriate notice.
- Fridays are popular for day conferences etc.

(iii) Determine who should attend – ensure quorum for decisions.

(iv) Book room with due regard for ventilation, noise, refreshment, seating and security.

(v) Prepare agenda – even if informal for own purposes itemise with most controversial matters neither at beginning nor end.

(vi) Publicise. Inform participants well in advance (if possible) – giving details of the time, venue and purpose of the meeting.

(b) **Conducting meeting (as chairperson)**

(i) Start on time.

(ii) Put members at their ease and focus minds on purpose of meeting – informal call to order.

(iii) Outline procedure to be followed (if irregular) and define technical terms.

(iv) Direct a general or specific question to get meeting started.

(v) Ensure fair play – link speakers and deter verbosity.

(vi) Summarise at appropriate times and at end but do not impose your own views.

(vii) Try to finish on time – if impossible get agreement to continue but never drift.

(viii) Thank those present for attending.

(c) **After meeting**

(i) Have contact memo or minutes prepared by secretary and approved by chairman – these form basis of next meeting.

(ii) Follow up decisions taken.

6.7 Interviews

It should be remembered that interviews are not the preserve of the personnel function and are very useful devices for collecting information for all manner of problem solving, including marketing research.

Information seeking interviews are advantageous because they are

(a) **Flexible** – the balance between a structured and unstructured interview can be determined for each individual informant and questions can be adjusted as the interview develops.

(b) **Enjoyable** for the informant if skilfully handled. As was seen in the Hawthorne experiments, people were motivated when others took an interest in their work.

6.8 Persuading

We have all been in positions where we want to persuade or influence someone to do what we want them to do. In meetings we may have a point of view that we want our colleagues to agree with or adopt. Success in persuasiveness depends on three interrelated factors:

(a) the starting position of the people you wish to influence;
(b) what you say;
(c) how you behave.

Clearly the subject of the matter of the persuasion is going to influence the outcome. If it is inappropriate or if you are not prepared then the likelihood of success is reduced. The sequence of what you say may be crucial. You should start with an initial statement to catch the other party's interest, followed by your idea and the potential benefits of the idea, along with the rationale to back up the benefits. Possible objections should be anticipated and dealt with. Then summarise the idea and its main benefits.

The way you behave is just as important as the content of what you have to say. Persuasive behaviours include: speaking fluently, without hesitations, in a strong and enthusiastic voice; looking at the other person and maintaining eye contact for a complete thought; using gestures with hands and arms to emphasise the points and using open ended questions that avoid yes/no answers.

7 NEGOTIATION

7.1 Effective negotiation skills

Negotiating is an activity that seeks to reach agreement between two or more starting positions.

The skills of a negotiator can be summarised under three main headings:

(a) Interpersonal skills – the use of good communicating techniques, the use of power and influence, and the ability to impress a personal style on the tactics of negotiation.

(b) Analytical skills – the ability to analyse information, diagnose problems, to plan and set objectives, and the exercise of good judgement in interpreting results.

(c) Technical skills – attention to detail and thorough case preparation.

There are behaviours that are typical of successful negotiators and distinguish them from the less successful:

Successful negotiators	Less successful negotiators
Skilled negotiators avoid criticising or attacking the other person and concentrate instead on 'attacking' the problem in a no nonsense but constructive way.	Less skilled negotiators are more likely to get locked into an attacking spiral where one side attacks the other which provokes a counter attack and so on.
Skilled negotiators ask many more questions than the less skilled. The skilled negotiator asks questions not only to gain more information and understanding but also as an alternative to disagreeing bluntly, and as a means of putting forward suggestions.	The less skilled tend to assume that they understand the other person's point of view and that the other person has the same basic information. This makes asking questions redundant.
The skilled negotiator summarises and tests understanding, knowing that being explicit aids common understanding and leads to quality agreement that is more likely to stick.	
Skilled negotiators keep the emotional temperature down by sticking to the facts.	Less skilled negotiators are inclined to exaggeration, using expressions such as 'an offer you can't refuse' and 'mutually beneficial'.
The skilled negotiator is more likely to say things that reveal what he or she is thinking, intending and feeling than the less skilled.	The less skilled negotiator feels vulnerable to losing the argument and is more likely to 'keep his cards close to his chest'.

Disagreements are inevitable during the course of a negotiation. The skilled negotiator gives the explanation first and rounds off the explanation by saying that they were in disagreement. This has a more constructive effect because the explanation becomes the focus for the other person's reaction rather than the fact of a disagreement.	Less skilled negotiators disagree first and then go on to give reasons. This often provokes a negative reaction from the other person who bridles at the explicit disagreement and therefore fails to listen to the reasons.

7.2 Types of negotiating situation

The techniques adopted will depend on the type of bargaining situation. Walton and McKersie in **A Behavioural Theory of Labour Negotiations** identify two main types of negotiation, distributive and integrative bargaining.

Distributive bargaining is that which is aimed at resolving pure conflicts of interest on, for example, hours of work and rates of pay, in other words the substantive issues.

In most bargaining situations it is usual to find that there are some topics that are best discussed on the basis of an integrative, or joint, approach aimed at finding a solution from which both sides will benefit substantially.

The good negotiator must thoroughly prepare the background to the case. A clean vision of the objectives of the negotiations should be established and form the basis for planning.

Appreciation of the costs resulting from failure should enhance the desire for a successful outcome.

7.3 Strategies and tactics

The strategies will vary depending on issues and circumstances under negotiation. An awareness of the history of the conflict and the implications for the future is essential.

Negotiation attempts to resolve and accommodate differing interests by moving towards an end point which is acceptable to both sides - a 'win-win' situation. A 'win-lose' situation culminates where one group has achieved its objectives at the clear expense of the other. This solution tends to cause dissatisfaction and the situation could deteriorate into a 'lose-lose' position where the benefits originally gained by the winner are continuously eroded by resistance and a lack of commitment.

The types of strategy could be classified as follows:

(a) **Power strategy;** where the two sides are unequal, one possessing a kind of sanction over the other. This type of strategy is likely to cause resentment and dissatisfaction, at best resulting in compliance without a shift in attitudes. The worst scenario may result in sabotage, resistance or further dispute.

(b) **Consultation strategy;** involves encouraging the relevant parties to express their ideas, concerns and opinions on the subject under negotiation. However, this does not necessarily mean that these views are taken into consideration; the strategy may be no more than a PR exercise.

(c) **Resolve strategy;** where agreement and conciliation is achieved, even if it means that neither party has achieved the perfect result. One of the problems frequently encountered in negotiating is that sides take up positions which are incompatible. Skilled negotiators concentrate on the interests that lie behind the positions as they are more likely to provide footholds for finding common ground and moving ahead.

8 CHAPTER SUMMARY

Poor communications can be the cause of poor morale, industrial unrest, and inadequate management performance. This chapter has covered the methods and channels of communication within organisations . We have considered the importance of good information and how the barriers to communication can be overcome.

Communication is the basis of group dynamics, allowing the interactions that are necessary in carrying out the group's activity. Two-way communication, feedback and 'checking for meaning' are ways to facilitate mutual understanding.

We looked at the forms of communicating in organisations, through meetings, interviews, presentations, letters and reports.

The communication skills that are important are oral and written, as well as listening, presenting, persuading, negotiating and summarising.

9 SELF TEST QUESTIONS

9.1 Define communication in business (1.1).

9.2 Draw a diagram showing the communication process (1.2).

9.3 Describe an informal communication system (1.3).

9.4 List the consequences which may occur as a result of a lack of upward communication (2.1).

9.5 Outline the typical barriers to communication (2.2).

9.6 Describe the advantages and disadvantages of face-to-face communication (3.1).

9.7 List at least six barriers to listening (4.2).

9.8 Outline the types of business report (6.3).

9.9 Give some examples of visual communication (6.5).

9.10 Describe the various outcomes of negotiation (7.3).

10 EXAMINATION TYPE QUESTION

10.1 Communication skills

Sam Browne is a sole trader. He runs a very profitable newsagents in a leafy town in the English midlands. His shop is very close to the railway station. His customers are the many people who commute daily into Birmingham and the executives who park their cars at the station before catching the early morning express trains to London. Sam is a good salesman, whatever the weather he has a cheery smile for his customers, and he has a shrewd notion of what to stock and the margins available. His weakness is that he can't keep records. His idea of record-keeping is sticking everything into a shoe box.

Not surprisingly, Sam's accounts are in a mess, his tax affairs are getting out of hand and he ignored the need to make a Return last year. There is a risk that the Revenue will start an investigation and Sam has come to you, as an Accountant in practice, for help. You feel the accounting problems are straight forward if only you can get the full background information from Sam.

You are meeting Sam next Saturday afternoon, when Mrs Browne can look after the shop. First you need to think about how you should approach the meeting.

Required

Draft some notes for the meeting with Sam showing:

(a) The types of information you require **(8 marks)**

(b) How you will manage the communication process **(8 marks)**
(c) The skills you will contribute to the process **(9 marks)**
(Total: 25 marks)

11 ANSWER TO EXAMINATION TYPE QUESTION

11.1 Communication skills

(a) Types of information

There is a substantial amount of information that can be gathered before the meeting. Sam Browne's business is hardly unique; a firm of accountants which deals with sole traders could provide services to a number of newsagents. The accountant visiting Sam should already be aware of the nature of Sam's business, the types of supplier, the likely turnover and the expected profit margins on newspapers and journals, sweets and cigarettes.

The types of information which must be solicited at the meeting could be divided into:

- hard information, dealing with facts and documents, which will all be necessary to put Sam's chaotic affairs to rights, especially in relation to tax;
- soft information, such as feelings, point of view and morale. This information could include finding out about Sam's attitudes to the record keeping process, as this will affect the reliability of any additional information which he gives. If Sam is merely incompetent at keeping records, simpler procedures might help him overcome his problems. He might regard an accountant's presence there as an unnecessary waste of time, and this might attract some of the force of his resentment which would be more appropriately directed at the tax authorities.

(b) The communication process

Communication is a way by which information is exchanged, which is the purpose of the meeting with Sam Browne. It can also involve instruction, encouragement or persuasion. Because his co-operation is required the purpose of the meeting will also be to establish a relationship with Sam, building trust and understanding, so that he responds with useful information. The communication model shown below demonstrates the elements in the process, emphasising that it is a two-way exchange in which the recipient is as important as the transmitter.

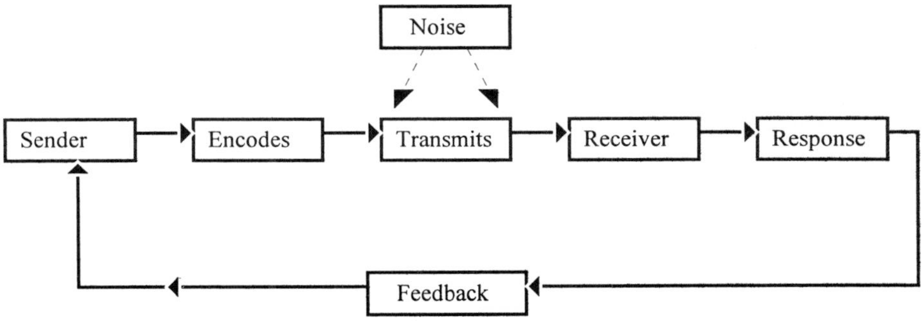

The hurdles to communication (in this case it may be Sam's attitude) may be overcome if:

- the communication is planned effectively. Prior knowledge of similar businesses will be of assistance here;
- direct, simple language is used;
- maximum feedback is obtained. This includes the acknowledgement that both the message and the response is understood, the proposal and clarification of ideas,

checking up on any misunderstanding and further questioning and response to avoid confusion.

(c) The skills contributed to the process

While giving the appearance of a friendly chat, rather than an inquisition, interviewing skills must be used to put Sam at ease so that the two-way process of communication can go as planned.

Information given by Sam should be written down. A pre-planned sheet of questions and the types of response required would make this task easier and ensure that nothing is missed. Unless a tape recorder is used as a method of recording the information, skills in note taking and summarising will be used in the recording process and include the following:

(i) noting key facts, perhaps using a mind map;

(ii) questioning areas of uncertainty.

(iii) noting any follow-up questions;

If the summary is to be communicated to someone else then an assessment of Sam's approach to the record keeping problem should also be made.

The main skills required will be in effective listening to elicit the maximum information from the meeting. These include:

(i) being prepared to listen, not just simulating attention;
(ii) keeping an open mind and not assuming the expected;
(iii) providing Sam with feedback;
(iii) trying to grasp the gist of the matter rather than getting bogged down with Sam's problems.

Effective listening can be impeded by a low level of interest and other worries about the situation. Even worse, fixed ideas of what Sam is expected to say may prevent appreciation of the full situation. Effective listening will also help to reveal any gaps in Sam's logic.

25 EVOLUTION OF IT APPLICATIONS

INTRODUCTION & LEARNING OBJECTIVES

In this chapter we will be dealing with the role of information technology in modern organisations. To appreciate how we have arrived at the situation where the computer is seen as an irreplaceable tool for the conduct of business, we look at the historical development of systems.

Some of the research into information systems distinguishes between the use of computers for data processing, for providing management with information (MIS) and progressing to the provision of information for decision-making and support, decision support systems (DSS) and executive information systems (EIS).

Because of the escalating costs of information technology, which was not always matched with effectiveness, Nolan and Gibson studied the development of IT in US corporations and devised a model of DP growth. This was further developed by Nolan to his six stage model, with the stages ranging from initiation, through contagion, control, integration, data administration and maturity.

Another researcher, McFarlan, developed a grid showing how critical information systems and information technology are to the success of many companies. The four roles of IT he devised are: support; factory; turnaround; and strategic. We describe the use of the grid to assess how much an individual organisation depends on its information systems and then show the effect of IT as a catalyst in encouraging or introducing change.

When you have studied this chapter you should be able to do the following:

- Describe the phases of development of information systems application
- Explain Nolan's six stages of evolution.
- Describe the implications of the evolutionary process.
- Evaluate the importance of IT and the criticality of IT spending.
- Describe McFarlan's strategic grid and the forces that drive an organisation round it.
- Discuss the formulation of an IT strategy and its elements and development.
- Explain the liaison between IT managers and users.

1 PHASES OF DEVELOPMENT

1.1 Information systems

An information system is a set of organised procedures, which, when executed, provides information to support decision-making. Information can be defined as an entity which serves to reduce uncertainty about some future state or event. The basic functions of an information system are outlined below.

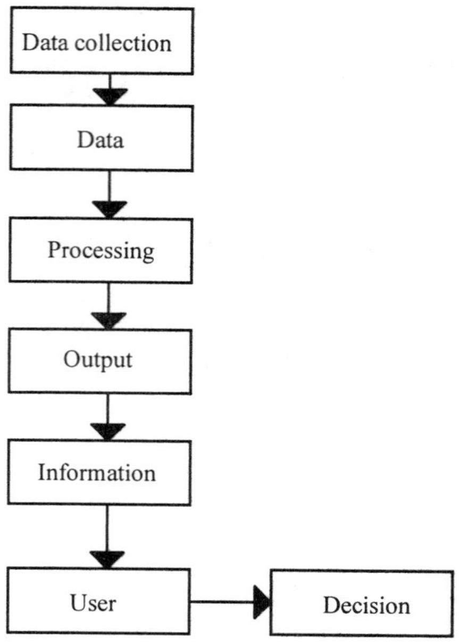

Early information systems were informal and involved the exchange of news, stories and anecdotes. As economies progressed, information on the changing value of goods and services became important. Formal organisations have always needed information to operate successfully. Production, accounting, financial and external data on consumers and markets are vital to most modern organisations. The explosion of information and the need to process large amounts of data to extract small amounts of information have contributed to the importance of computer-based information systems.

1.2 Levels of management

The development framework for information processing was based on the three levels of management and their planning and decision-making role, which all needed different types of information. These levels, shown in the diagram below, are strategic planning, tactical management and operational management.

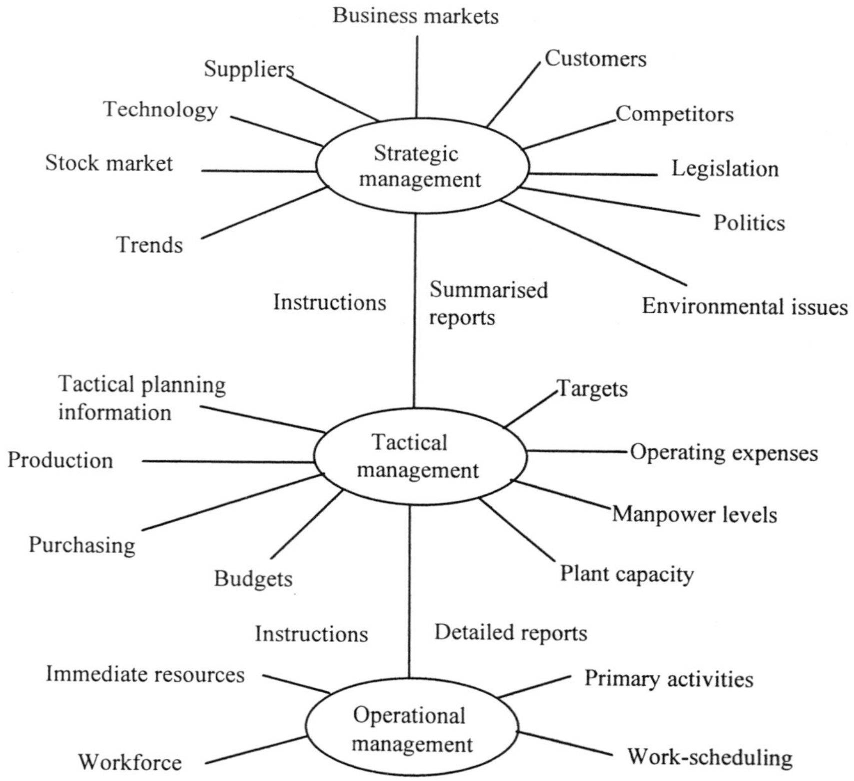

1.3 Data processing

The transaction processing tasks undertaken by the early data processing departments in the late 1950s tended to be routine, repetitive and data-focused office activities. It was seen as addressing the operational control applications, mainly processing and accumulating data which could later be retrieved as information.

The types of activities which were seen as suitable for computerisation were clerical procedures such as accounting, stock control, order processing and payroll.

1.4 Information systems

The improved processors, data storage facilities and communication systems which became available in the 1960s, fulfilled the information needs of managers. The management information systems (MIS) concept recognised that computer systems would continue to process transactions but could produce appropriate reports to satisfy the information needs of management.

Unfortunately, the managers at the tactical management level lacked sufficient knowledge of computers and the data processing staff were equally ignorant of the management role in the organisation. This meant that the management information systems were less integrated than they could have been and were implemented without much enthusiasm or ambition.

1.5 Support systems

The concept of providing systems to support higher levels of management was proposed in the 1970s. The decision support system (DSS) was directed at unstructured business problems. These systems were information models which could be manipulated to help in the decision-making process.

By the 1980s the concept of executive information systems (EIS) was developed to make more use of the information in the planning and control processes of the organisation.

2 NOLAN'S SIX STAGES OF EVOLUTION

2.1 Growth of DP expenditure

Strategic planning for information systems and information technology is now becoming an important topic for most organisations. However, as long ago as the mid-seventies research was still being carried out into the development of computing in business.

As the development of information systems increased, so did the costs, and questions were raised about the escalating costs of effectiveness. Because promises were not being fulfilled, some managers were frustrated and became 'anti-computers', threatening to apply the brakes on further expenditure. In an attempt to analyse the situation Gibson and Nolan studied the DP expenditure in a series of American corporations.

The results of their observations showed that data processing expenditure followed an S-curve of increasing costs, expenditure being gradual at first but increasing dramatically before adopting a more gradual slope again. This curve also represented a path of organisational learning about DP and its uses within the corporation. These findings were modelled and in 1974 Gibson and Nolan produced a 'four stage growth model' which Nolan later expanded into a six stage growth model in 1979, shown in the diagram below:

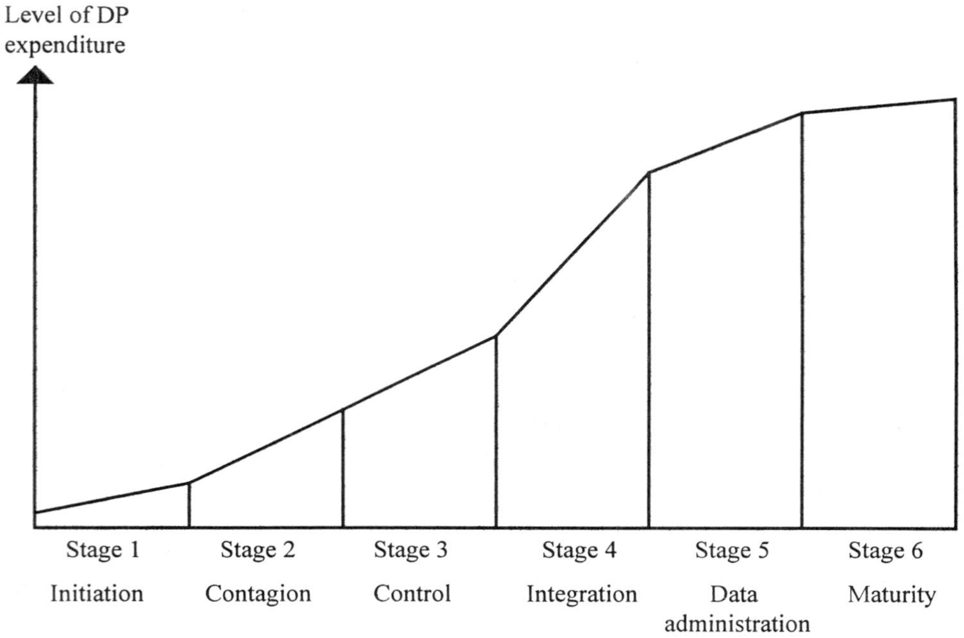

2.2 Stages of evolution

(i) **Initiation stage**; automation of clerical operations, where some more technically-minded employees use technology because they are keen, rather than use it for cost effectiveness.

(ii) **Contagion stage**; rapid growth as users become more familiar with applications and demand more and where the wider benefits of technology are perceived by more staff.

(iii) **Control stage**; planning and methodologies are introduced in order to assert control over developments and ensure investment in technology is taking place in a planned manner. Controls may be introduced by setting up steering committees and project management teams.

(iv) **Integration stage**; the integration of the various computing functions within the organisation; user involvement in the development stage of information technology.

(v) **Data administration stage**; emphasis is placed on information requirements rather than just processing requirements and there is sufficient information available to support the appointment of a database administrator.

(vi) **Maturity stage**; the IS/IT planning is brought into line with the business planning and development. The data resources are flexible and the information flows mirror the real-world requirements of the firm. The firm will be using a variety of applications to support their information needs.

2.3 Activity

Identify a type of organisation for each of the stages outlined by Nolan.

2.4 Activity solution

Nolan identified six stages:

(i) Initiation stage; a social club or a farm.
(ii) Contagion stage; breweries or construction organisations.
(iii) Control stage; the health service or small chain of retail store.
(iv) Integration stage; publishing, travel agencies and libraries.
(v) Data administration stage; banks and large retailers such as Tesco.
(vi) Maturity stage; airlines, shopping catalogues and football pools.

2.5 Benchmarks

Nolan intended that management would use benchmarks to identify their position in the process. Using the strategy guidelines laid down by him, a manager would be able to understand the growth that was ahead and the knowledge would help in the formulation of the best course of action. It was a model for identifying problems and controlling the growth of data processing activities.

The benchmarks comprised:

- a comparison of the annual growth rate of expenditure on DP with the organisation's sales and the type of technology;
- analysis of user awareness, planning and control.

3 IMPLICATIONS OF THE EVOLUTIONARY PROCESS

3.1 Alternative views

A number of researchers have, however, questioned the validity of the six stage model.

Drury (1983) concluded that 'Categorising of DP from initiation to maturity may no longer be feasible with the diffusion of new technologies and functions being introduced'.

King and Kraemer (1984) believe that the model is weak in a number of areas, but basically that the model is too simplistic to be useful.

Wiseman, in his book **Strategy and Computers** (1985), suggests that the influential combination of the Anthony three-tier structural approach (see diagram below) to define organisational systems and the Nolan stage model inhibited the strategic use of IS/IT until quite recently.

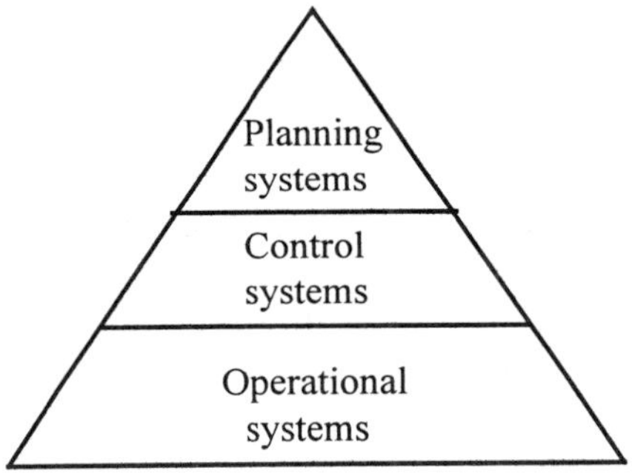

However, despite criticism of the Nolan model, it is generally accepted that a model of the evolving role of IS/IT in an organisation is of value and that the Nolan model is a good starting point.

3.2 Uses for the model

Uses for Nolan's stage hypothesis include

(a) being able to classify organisations into the stage they are presently at, thereby being able to predict their future reactions to technology,

(b) being able to identify how the organisation passed through the earlier stages and the problems they specifically encountered,

(c) understanding the current status of the organisation in terms of technology and being able to produce strategic plans that are not too ambitious for the stage they have reached,

(d) being able to develop plans that will avoid the pitfalls of the later stages in the hypothesis.

3.3 Waves of innovation

Nolan was interested in the evolution of DP expenditure and showed how it escalated through the stages. While the stage hypothesis described the experiences of many businesses in the use of IT, the rapid growth of IT and its pervasive nature will change the management issues.

Arguably the hypothesis has no future implications because the technology described by Nolan has been overtaken in both performance and price. Nolan did not identify the wave-like expenditure as new technologies appear, and his model provides no guide to how new technologies affect the organisation's ability to compete.

McFarlan, McKenney and Pyburn likened the emergence and use of new technology to a wave. Examples of these waves could start with batch processing and progressing through on-line systems, database management systems to personal computers. As each new technology emerges and is assimilated into the organisation, a new wave of expenditure is experienced. Although the cost of the technology may decrease over time, the overall expenditure continues to increase with each subsequent new wave of technology.

McFarlan suggests that there are four stages in the introduction of technologies which affect the planning and managing of the innovation.

(i) The first stage is focused on the technology identification, the initial investment and the development of skills

(ii) The second stage is where the users experiment with the technology and become interested.

(iii) The third stage is the rationalisation and management control phase where planning is dominated by short term efficiency, organisational considerations and cost-effective implementation.

(iv) The last stage demonstrates widespread technology transfer and longer term planning in the use of technology.

The outcome of this study is that the planning approach must evolve along with each new technology and may vary with different innovations. An example of this model would be where an organisation had little experience with DBMS, phase two may involve a pilot project to assess the user satisfaction with a new type of database. At another level of familiarity, a different type of user with more experience might be given the latest technology in DBMS to gain renewed interest and identify new 'tricks' or uses for it.

3.4 The importance of IT

Primozic and Leben recently identified waves of technology describing the evolution of systems, how the technology is used and the importance of IT at each level.

(i) First wave; covers the DP era with the focus on reducing costs and increasing productivity.

(ii) Second wave; concentrates on making effective use of assets to increase productivity. This stage is seen as saving money by better management of processes.

(iii) Third wave; is concerned with enhancing products and services to gain strategic advantage or create new business.

(iv) Fourth wave; is about changing the structure of the organisation and using the technology to enhance the executive decision-making.

(v) Fifth wave; is about reaching the consumer and restructuring the industry. This stage leads to new marketing, distribution and service strategies

Primozic is of the opinion that most firms are still only at the top of the second wave and have not started to build information systems that make money because they are concentrating on saving money.

There is a division between the second and third waves with those above two being more involved with organisational effectiveness and those below concentrating on operational control. Crossing the 'line' from wave two to wave three is achieved by market leaders who are concentrating on profitability and remaining competitive.

3.5 Criticality of IT spending

Information systems have different degrees of importance for all organisations, although they are critical for some. Many organisations invest large amounts of money in IT, some of it spent unwisely. The importance is not how much is spent but how well the funds are used.

Despite all the expenditure there may be a lag before the new facilities are exploited, the benefits of the expenditure being delayed until the users have caught up with its potential.

It is important for organisations to understand whether IT is critical to them or not. If the management can make a case for investing then they should ascertain whether the structure of the organisation can take advantage of the opportunities, decide on an appropriate approach to the management and planning of the information system and then determine the level of expenditure.

4 McFARLAN'S STRATEGIC GRID

4.1 Existing and future systems

The organisation will identify many different types of application that they need. However, it is not always feasible to develop all the applications at the same time and therefore it will be necessary to prioritise the applications.

One way of doing this is by building an application portfolio. The applications in the applications portfolio will need to be managed and in order to do this they are best categorised according to their existing and future contribution to the company.

The grid, shown below, was devised as a framework for classifying the strategic use of IT (information technology). It arrays an organisation's existing applications against those currently under development.

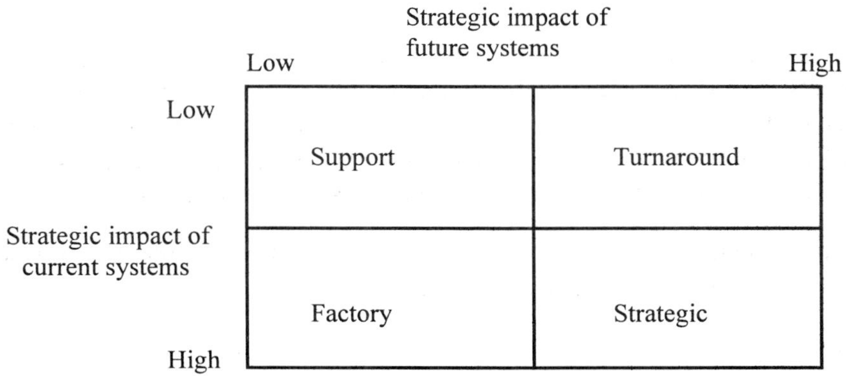

Information systems strategic grid (from McFarlan and McKenney, 1983)

(a) **Support**

Where IT has a support role and is a necessity to the working of the organisation, information systems have little relevance to the organisation's existing or future success. The current information system may include accounting operations and payroll but there are no new developments which can contribute significantly to the competitiveness of the organisation.

There is usually a low level of senior management involvement in this situation because the commitment to information systems planning is low and any development would rely on localised management.

Michael Earl in **Management strategies for information technology** gives a cement manufacturing company as an example in this sector. Information technology may be used to speed up administration and make occasional improvements to the processes but it is not vital or critical to the manufacture or distribution of cement.

(b) **Factory**

If information technology has a factory role, the organisation depends heavily on information systems support for smooth operations. Future IT developments are not likely to add to their competitive edge. Some airlines and retailers would come into this category; Earl mentions a steel works with an on-line real time system for controlling production. Even one hour of disruption to these organisation's booking systems or order processing systems could fundamentally damage their competitive performance.

McFarlan and McKenney maintain that strategic goal setting and linkage of information systems to the corporate plan are not too important if IT has a factory role.

(c) **Turnaround**

Information technology's turnaround role is where existing IT is not too important, but future development is likely to have a significant impact. In these organisations the applications under development have a high potential to contribute to the organisation's strategic objectives. Many supermarket chains have relied on routine information systems for accounting, stock control and ordering. However, most of the chains, to reduce wastage on perishable items and to maximise sales, are investing heavily in communication systems to link their suppliers and stock control systems. They are also installing electronic funds transfer (EFT) at the point of sale.

The performance of firms in a turnaround situation is often inhibited by lack of support from the information processing department. There is a need for planning in this cell because the firm cannot maintain control over its rapidly expanding operations without the new computer applications.

(d) **Strategic**

In some organisations the strategic role of information technology is where existing and future developments are at the heart of the organisation's future success. Banks and insurance companies are typical of this sector. They have applications which they rely on for the smooth running of their day-to-day activities and they have future developments which are vital to their competitive success and are integral to the organisation's strategic objectives.

These firms need significant amounts of planning as the firm would be at a disadvantage if the information processing did not perform well.

4.2 Application portfolio

Each application of information technology in the business eg, payroll or sales analysis or capacity planning, etc, can be positioned in one segment of the matrix according to its existing and anticipated contribution to the business. Then each application can be managed in accordance with that contribution.

A possible application portfolio for a manufacturing company is shown below:

SUPPORT

- Time recording
- Budgeting
- Expense reporting
- Cost accounting
- General accounting
- Payroll
- Word processing

TURNAROUND

- Electronic data interchange (EDI) with wholesaler
- Manpower planning
- Electronic mail
- Decision support
- Expert diagnostic systems
- Image processing

FACTORY

- Employee database
- Maintenance scheduling
- Inventory management
- Shopfloor control
- Computer-aided design of products
- Product (bill of material) database
- Accounts receivable/payable

STRATEGIC

- Computer-integrated manufacturing
- MRP II (manufacturing resource planning)
- Links to suppliers
- Quality control
- Sales forecasting
- Product profitability analysis

The McFarlan Strategic Grid was devised as a way of plotting the overall expected contribution of IS/IT to the business success. This is of limited value since every enterprise is likely to have some strategic, some factory, some support and some turnaround applications. This model has, however, proved effective in providing a framework by which agreement on the portfolio of business application available and required can be reached from the often divergent views of senior management, functional line managers and the IS professionals. It is a simple concept which enables consensus to be achieved, both when a strategy is initially conceived, and later as the business and its requirements evolve.

4.3 Forces that drive an organisation round the strategic grid

Companies may be driven from one part of the strategic grid to another depending on the industry sector and the need to stay competitive. Forces which drive an organisation round the strategic grid may be internal or external.

Internal forces will be concerned with matching the potential of information technology to the organisation's operations and strategy, such as a decision to improve productivity

External forces will be associated with changes in the competitive environment, such as actions of competitors, suppliers or customers.

As a **Support** firm grows it will become increasingly concerned with production and distribution. The need for efficient production, generally using standard IT techniques, will force the company to the **Factory** position. The IT packages, once established, will be fairly static.

If the same firm develops products with high sales potential, and it chooses to market them itself, then it must become more involved with the volatile consumers and in direct conflict with competitors. The environment is likely to change rapidly and novel IT systems will be required to cope with the situation.

4.4 Activity

In the past, ShoeMaker's spending on IT has been strictly controlled and used mainly for accounting, processing sales orders and printing invoices. One of its major customers has sent a letter with the following passages in it: 'We have always valued speed and responsiveness, and this has been the main reason behind our sourcing from domestic suppliers of shoes. However, we have recently had offers from suppliers in the Far East offering a wider ranging flexibility in design with new production technology. Can you offer anything similar?' One of the suggestions from the customer was that ShoeMaker should automate their sales order processing system to become interlinked with their purchasing systems to increase responsiveness.

(i) Explain which position on the grid ShoeMaker currently occupies.

(ii) If the managers decide to introduce new ordering systems and production technology, will their position change?

(iii) Are there any forces driving it round the grid?

4.5 Activity solution

(i) ShoeMaker are currently in the support sector of the McFarlan grid. The commitment to information systems planning is low and IT seems to have below average investment. IT is perceived as having little relevance to the company's existing or future success.

(ii) If the new ordering system and production technology is introduced, it will be as a result of the customer's suggestion and the fact that it is critical to ShoeMaker's success. The introduction of the changes would place them in a turnaround role. This is where existing IT is not important but future developments are likely to have a significant impact. The role of IT is being enhanced.

(iii) The forces driving it round seem to be: the competitive environment shaped by the producer from the Far East and the customer's demands; and the management decision to adopt an IT based strategy in response to the threat.

5 FORMULATING AN IT STRATEGY

5.1 The plan

A plan for information technology should be co-ordinated with corporate strategy. The plan will show the direction of the systems effort and lay down the basis for later evaluation of its performance.

Many organisations agree that a plan is needed but do not develop one. A frequent reason is that the 3–5 year information systems planning horizon is not compatible with the planning horizon of the organisation. It is both possible and highly desirable to develop an information processing plan even without a formal corporate plan.

A typical plan will describe the activities and resources required for the development of the new application of technology. One of the key tasks is to identify new application areas in order to gain strategic advantage.

5.2 Why is it important?

Definition Information technology can be defined as: 'the use of computers, microelectronics and telecommunications to help us produce, store, and send information in the form of pictures, words or numbers, more reliably, quickly and economically.'

It is in effect the fusion of developments in both computing and telecommunications, including the use of fibre optics as cables and transmissions via satellites. The coming together of these two areas (the French have coined the word 'telematique' for them) has begun to transform business communications and, indeed, the very pattern of our lives. A former Minister for Information Technology, pointed out:

'IT is the fastest developing area of industrial and business activity in the Western world. Its markets are huge, its applications multitudinous and its potential for efficiency immense.'

Not only are developments in IT of immense importance to those companies engaged in the industry, they also have considerable influence on all other businesses who must therefore recognise the need for a clear information technology strategy. Perhaps the most fundamental concept in the development of such a strategy is the recognition that information is a valuable corporate resource.

The importance of information as a resource cannot be overstressed. As pointed out by Diebold: 'Information, which in essence is the analysis and synthesis of data, will unquestionably be one of the most vital of corporate resources. It will be structured into models for planning and decision- making. It will be integrated into product design and marketing methods. In other words, information will be recognised and treated as an asset.'

5.3 Elements of a strategy

The structure of the plan is:

(a) **Executive summary** – a statement containing the main points of the scheme. The document should have a section on the **goals**, specific and general, of information processing in the organisation.

(b) **Goals** – a general goal might be to provide a different customer service, whilst a specific goal could be to completely update the database enquiry system.

(c) **Assumptions** – the plan will be based on certain assumptions about the organisation and the current business strategy. It is essential that this plan is linked to the organisation's strategic plan.

(d) **Scenario** – sometimes it is helpful to draw up a scenario of the information processing environment that will result from executing the plan.

(e) **Application areas** – the plan should outline and set priorities for new application areas being planned and for those applications which are in the process of development. A report on their progress and status should be produced. For major new applications there should be a breakdown of costs and schedules.

The plan should outline and set priorities for the application areas. A corporate steering committee containing high level representation should set the priorities as this committee can make the trade–offs among functional areas.

(f) **Operations** – the current systems will be continuing and the plan should identify the existing systems and the costs of maintaining them.

(g) **Maintenance** – the plan should incorporate the budget for the maintenance of, and enhancements to, the existing system.

The resources required for maintenance and enhancement of existing applications should also be planned if the operation of existing systems is to continue.

(h) **Organisational structure** – the plan should describe the existing and future organisational structure for the technology, in terms of location, and human and financial resources.

(i) **Impact of the plan** – management is interested in the impact of a plan on the organisation, particularly its financial impact.

(j) **Implementation** – the plan should identify implementation risks and obstacles.

5.4 Developing the strategy for information technology

When developing an overall information technology strategy the following aspects should be taken into consideration:

(a) What are the key business areas which could benefit most from an investment in information technology, what form should the investment take and how could such strategically important units be encouraged to effectively use such technology?

(b) How much would the system cost in terms of: software; hardware; management commitment and time; education and training; conversion; documentation; operational manning; and maintenance. The importance of lifetime application costs must be stressed. According to Roger Lee, a management consultant: 'Most companies try to assess how much it will cost them to install an information technology function, but all too few measure the costs and benefits after implementation. Yet this is the area of greatest potential loss.'

(c) What criteria for performance should be set for information technology systems? Again quoting Roger Lee: 'The quality of an information technology application should be measured in two ways: the technical standard it achieves and the degree to which it meets the perceived and often changing needs of the user.'

(d) What are the implications for the existing work force; have they the requisite skills; can they be trained to use the systems; will there be any redundancies?

(e) Whether such a strategy is based on a database approach. This will depend on a number of factors. According to the US Department of Commerce (1980) a database approach is called for when:

    (i) Application needs are constantly changing, with considerable uncertainty as to the important data elements, expected update or processing functions, and expected volumes to be handled.

    (ii) Rapid access is frequently required to answer *ad hoc* questions.

    (iii) There is a need to reduce long lead times and high development costs in developing new application systems.

    (iv) Many data elements must be shared by users throughout the organisation.

    (v) There is a need to communicate and relate data across functional and department boundaries.

    (vi) There is a need to improve the quality and consistency of the database and to control access to that resource.

    (vii) Substantial dedicated programming assistance is not normally available.

5.5 Liaison between IT managers and users

Because the existing portfolio of IT applications will influence future policy, there should be an evaluation of the efficiency of current systems. The types of question that managers need to ask are about the satisfaction of the users and the reliability of the system.

The evaluation is a bottom-up exercise, depending vitally on the contribution of the users. The benefits of the exercise are:

(i) users may suggest evolutionary add-ons to systems;

(ii) users and systems specialists can indicate the technical quality of the current system in terms of its reliability, ease of maintenance and cost efficiency;

(iii) users can rate a system on: its business impact (how would we manage without it?); its ease of use and user-friendliness; and the frequency of its use, giving an indication of its importance and value.

Michael Earl has devised a grid to analyse an organisation's information system use:

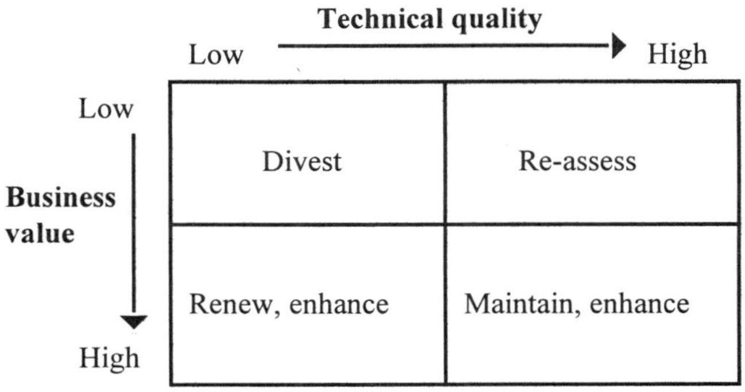

- A system of low quality and little business value should be divested;
- A system with high business value and low quality should be enhanced because the low quality aspects might make it a risk, or might damage the business if it failed;
- A system of high quality and low business use should be re-assessed. If the users had complained about user-friendliness, modifications to this aspect of the system might increase its business value;
- A system of both high quality and high business value must be maintained and possibly enhanced as newer features are introduced.

5.6 Activity

Backwater is a company with an established base of IT applications. The finance department has a fully computerised accounting system. The marketing department has a customer modelling package and the production department does not see the need for technology.

The Finance Director is in charge of IT and he is proposing a 12% increase in IT expenditure to upgrade systems in the relevant departments, based on last year.

Comment on the situation at Backwater..

5.7 Activity solution

There is no strategy for information technology at Backwater. The Finance Director is still treating it as a cost, rather than a way of achieving competitive advantage. The only strategy that exists is directed to enhancing its existing base, which seems to be mainly in the Finance Director's domain, rather than areas where it may prove to be of strategic value and help the company gain strategic advantage.

6 CHAPTER SUMMARY

In this chapter we have looked at the forces that have shaped and influenced information technology and information systems in organisations. In particular we have discussed several models which are used to analyse the status of the technology in organisations. The models we concentrated on were those of Nolan and McFarlan's strategic grid, although other models were used in our discussion.

The importance of planning was also outlined. Because of increasing expenditure on IT, there is a need to make sure that costs do not exceed the benefits. The planning approach needs constant evaluation and must also be flexible to adapt to the assimilation of new technologies.

7 SELF-TEST QUESTIONS

7.1 Draw a model of the levels of management and their decision-making role (1.2).

7.2 What type of business problem is the DSS directed at? (1.5).

7.3 Describe Nolan's six stages of evolution (2.2).

7.4 List the uses of Nolan's stage hypothesis (3.2).

7.5 Describe McFarlan's four stages in the introduction of technology which affect the management and planning of the innovation (3.3).

7.6 Draw an IS strategic grid for classifying the strategic use of IT (4.1).

7.7 Explain the turnaround role of IT and give an example (4.1)

7.8 List six applications which may hold a support role in the organisation (4.2).

7.9 Draw and describe the elements in Earl's grid which analyses the organisation's use of IS (5.5).

8 EXAMINATION TYPE QUESTION

8.1 IS strategy

Many major organisations use formal strategies to identify development priorities for information systems (IS).

(a) Discuss the reason for this **(8 marks)**

(b) What are the major stages in the development of an IS strategy? **(8 marks)**

(Total 16 marks)

9 ANSWER TO EXAMINATION TYPE QUESTION

9.1 IS strategy

(a) There is now a growing recognition amongst organisations of the importance of information as a business resource and it follows, therefore, that the systems manipulating, storing, processing and distributing this resource must not be left to chance.

Information has in the past been collected, stored, processed and dispersed during the course of an organisation's operational activities. However, organisations have seen the introduction of Information Technology and such systems as management information systems, decision support systems and executive information systems as the means to gain a competitive advantage.

Previously, organisations used computers to perform the mundane tasks and computerised data processing has become a routine function. Generally organisations are now more computer literate and this, together with the low price of hardware and new technology has made organisations more aware of the competitive advantages to be gained by the correct application of technology and its related systems.

For an organisation to invest in information technology and information systems it will require some sort of information strategy. The IS/IT strategy should be based upon the corporate strategy, which can be defined by a study of the mission statement.

The mission statement is a statement of purpose by the organisation and from this the aims and objectives can be ascertained. The aims and objectives state what needs to be achieved and the strategy outlines how to achieve them.

Therefore, before an IS/IT strategy can be drawn up, the corporate strategy must be studied to ensure that they are aligned.

An information strategy will comprise two parts:

(i)	organisational -	this is the systems management which is concerned with the collecting, processing and distribution of information.
(ii)	technical -	this is concerned with the means by which the information will be collected, processed and distributed.

Strategic planning for IT ensures:

(i)	compatibility -	between the various systems under development and hardware purchased within an organisation.
(ii)	commitment -	from the strategic level of management.
(iii)	resource allocation -	the monetary commitment from the organisation.

(b) Strategies have to address three major questions:

(i) Where are we now?
(ii) Where do we want to be?
(iii) How are we to get there?

In order to develop an IS strategy the following stages would be completed:

Scoping study

This determines the boundaries of the IS strategy, plus its scope and a timescale for its development and review. At this stage it is essential that the commitment to an IS strategy is sought from, and given by, senior management. It may be the case that more than one IS strategy is necessary if the organisation is very large. The scoping study should prioritise the strategies and clearly identify links.

Strategy study

At this stage a review is made of any existing strategy and progress made towards its aims. The study would provide evidence in support of a selected strategy.

Strategy definition

At this stage the options and findings from the strategy study are fully assessed. Future requirements of IS are laid down together with any resource constraints. The main purpose of this stage is to achieve agreement of a strategy statement underpinning management and technical policies. The technical policies should include such things as hardware architecture, network architecture, provision of manpower, security aspects.

Implementation stage

Progression of the strategy will be achieved by a series of projects. These projects will be IT- and non IT- based. Detailed plans should be produced providing a timetable for strategy progression and an estimation of resource requirements.

Monitoring and review

As with any strategic planning, careful monitoring should take place. This ensures that progress is continuous and any deviations can be brought back to plan. It must be remembered that organisations are themselves dynamic, and therefore alterations may have to be made to the strategic plans. Reviews should take place on an annual basis to ensure that the strategies being followed are still aligned with the corporate strategy.

26 IT AND STRATEGIC ADVANTAGE

INTRODUCTION & LEARNING OBJECTIVES

We continue with our investigation of information technology in this chapter. For many businesses, IT and information processing are critical to their operations. For instance, without computing, banking would break down completely. Processing power is needed to handle cheques and account processing, and to control the nation-wide network of automatic teller machines.

It is necessary that management understand whether, why and how IT is crucial to the organisation. In some cases information technology may have little effect on the overall operations, whereas in other companies IT is critical to current operations but not necessary to strategic planning. In companies where IT is necessary to current operations and strategic operations the IT can be termed as a truly strategic resource, eg a credit card company.

In many cases IT is rapidly changing its nature within the company and becoming critical to survival and growth rather than providing a supportive role.

There are three major factors in the changing IT role which are

(i) the matching of the potential IT with the strategic plans
(ii) the strategic choices which a company's management must make about IT
(iii) changes in the competitive environment.

IT can be used as a strategic weapon in a number of ways. It can pursue competitive advantage; be used to disturb, enhance or limit competitive forces; be used to enhance a product or service; or be used in the distribution and supply in order to change the basis of competition against rivals.

In the traditional era, productivity and performance was often the target, but the scope and potential benefits are much greater in the IT era. Examples include the use of CAD/CAM in manufacturing. There are now new ways of managing and organising by using microcomputers, local area networks and electronic mail, thus enabling employees to work from distant locations. This can have economical as well as social benefits. Space and time constraints are being removed from the working environment.

It is possible to create new business through telecommunications, mass storage and software engineering advances. Examples include the information services provided for the financial markets, expert systems for professionals and data analysis services for market research companies.

When you have studied this chapter you should be able to do the following:

- Describe how IT can be used to support strategic decision-making.
- Give an example of a strategic planning package, and outline any limitations.
- Discuss the effect of IT on management processes in the future.
- Discuss how IT can be used to gain a strategic advantage.
- Describe IT as a strategic weapon.
- Describe how information technology permeates the value chain.
- Identify other frameworks to help identify options to use IT strategically.

1 USING IT TO SUPPORT STRATEGIC DECISION-MAKING

1.1 IT and the five competitive forces

Michael Porter identified the five forces, as shown in the diagram below, that determine the extent of competition in an industry.

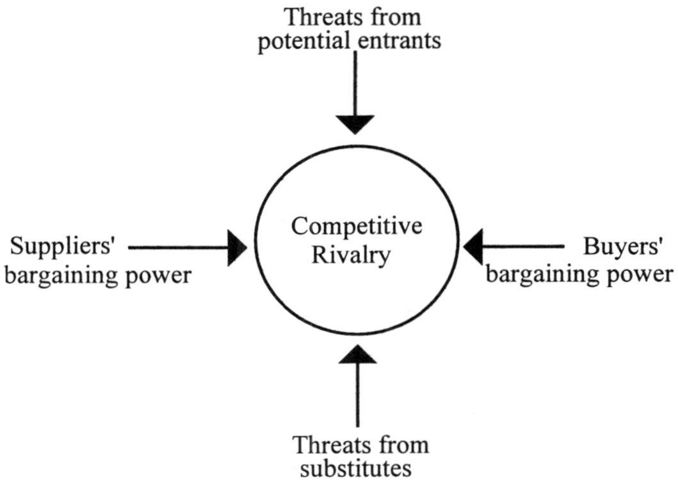

1.2 Threat of entry

New entrants into a market will bring extra capacity and intensify competition. The strength of the threat from new entrants will depend upon the strength of the barriers to entry and the likely response of existing competition to a new entrant.

IT can have two possible roles to counteract the threat:

(i) **Defensively**, by creating barriers that new entrants to the market find difficult to overcome. IT can increase economies of scale by using computer-controlled production methods, requiring a similar investment in the technology of new entrants.

Another defensive move is to colonise the distribution channels by tying customers and suppliers into the supply chain or the distribution chain. The harder the service is to emulate, the higher the barrier is for new entrants.

(ii) **Offensively**, by breaking down the barriers to entry. An example is the use of telephone banking which reduces the need to establish a branch network. Automated teller machines (ATMs) created new distribution channels enabling 'bank branches' to be set up in airports, by out-of-town supermarkets and other areas where there are many potential customers. These machines provided not only expansion of the total market, but also a low-cost method of overcoming the barriers to entry in the areas where the cost of entry was high and space was at a premium.

1.3 Intensity of competitive rivalry

This is rivalry between firms making similar products, or offering the same services, and selling them in the same market. The most intense rivalry is where the business is more mature and the growth has slowed down.

IT can be used to compete. Cost leadership can be exploited by IT, for example, where IT is used to support just-in-time (JIT) systems. Alternatively, IT can be used as a collaborative venture, changing the basis of competition by setting up new communications networks and forming alliances with complementary organisations for the purpose of information sharing. When Thomson Holidays introduced their on-line reservation system into travel agents' offices, they changed the basis of competition, allowing customers to ask about holiday availability and special deals and book a holiday in one visit to the travel agent.

1.4 Threat of substitute products

This threat is across industries (eg, rail travel with bus travel and private car) or within an industry (eg, long life milk as substitute for delivered fresh milk). In many cases information systems themselves are the substitute product. Word processing packages are a substitute for typewriters.

IT-based products can be used to imitate existing goods as in electronic keyboards and organs. In the case of computer games, IT has formed the basis of a new leisure industry.

Computer-aided design and computer-assisted manufacture (CAD/CAM) have helped competitors to bring innovative products to the market more quickly than in the past.

Interactive information systems add value by providing an extra service to an existing product. An example of this is provided by ICI's 'Counsellor', an expert system which advises farmers on disease control. It analyses data input by the farmer on areas such as crop varieties grown, soil type and previous history of disease and recommends fungicides or other suitable ICI products to solve the farmer's problems.

1.5 Bargaining power of buyers

The bargaining power of customers can be affected by using IT to create switching costs and 'lock' the buyer in to your products and services. The switching costs may be in both cash terms and operational inconvenience terms. Until the introduction of PCs, most computers used their own software. Generally speaking this meant that you could not run IBM software on ICL mainframes, making a switch in supplier both costly and inconvenient.

Another form of locking customers in is to develop customer information systems which inform the organisation about the customer's behaviour, purchases and characteristics. This information enables the organisation to target customers in terms of direct marketing and other forms of incentive such as loyalty schemes, where methods of rewarding customer loyalty by giving them 'preferred customer' status are used. If a clothing retailer is launching a new collection it can offer its loyal customers a private viewing. Habitat have special evening showings of their new stock, with added attractions such as drinks and discounts, and only Habitat card holders are invited. Some airlines have deals such as frequent flyers and air miles as incentives.

1.6 Bargaining power of suppliers

The bargaining power of suppliers, and hence their ability to charge higher prices will be influenced by:

- the degree to which switching costs apply and substitutes are available;
- the presence of one or two dominant suppliers controlling prices;
- the products offered having a uniqueness of brand, technical performance or design, which is not available elsewhere.

This power can be eroded by reducing the suppliers' power to control the supply. Where an organisation is dependent on components of a certain standard in a certain time, IT can provide a purchases database which enables easy scanning of prices from a number of suppliers. Suppliers' power can be shared so that the supplier and the organisation both benefit from performance improvements. The Ford Motor Company set up CAD links with its suppliers with the intention of reducing the costs of design specification and change. The time taken and the error rate was reduced because specifications did not have to be re-keyed into the suppliers' manufacturing tools.

1.7 Using the five forces model

Porter's model may be used to help clarify the overall business strategy. The model provides a framework to discuss areas where information technology and systems can yield competitive advantage. The advantages may be in defending the organisation against the forces or by attacking and influencing them in its favour.

Management should use the model to determine which of the forces poses a threat to the future success of the organisation. By ranking these threats in terms of intensity and immediacy, the most critical can then be considered in terms of how information technology or systems can be used to gain advantage or avoid disadvantage.

1.8 Examples of strategic planning packages

Porter emphasises that tomorrow's successful organisation will be a collection of skills and capabilities ever ready to pounce on brief market anomalies. He argues that any useful strategic plan or planning process must focus on the development and honing of these skills, which translates into a readiness to seek and exploit opportunities.

An example of the use of computers in the strategic planning process is ENSCAN, a system for monitoring the environment. Information on the external environment is often the most uncertain and disorganised and generally takes a long time to collect and analyse.

ENSCAN is a type of expert system with the inputs being executive and management opinions on environmental issues at three levels:

- megatrends;
- microtrends; and
- minitrends.

The environmental issues cover a variety of influences including social, technological. ecological, political and economic. The current economic trend both in the national and international market would probably show that it was slowing down, with unemployment showing the only growth rate.

1.9 Limitations of strategic planning packages

Although this type of package has some advantages, it is also limited in that the views that are input may not necessarily be correct or may lack creativity. They may identify relevant issues for the strategic planning process but these issues are general issues which all your competitors will know as well, and their actions would need to be built into the scenario. They identify social trends so that management can be in tune with society, but if your organisation is interested in the Far East, then the trends turned up by a package are unlikely to be the ones which will help your organisation form a strategic plan.

Inaccuracies in strategic planning packages arise from the following causes:

(a) The definition of the current state. Good information gathering can reduce the errors, but modern mathematics 'chaos' theories have shown that minute errors in initial measurements can soon cause enormous differences between what is predicted and what actually happens. Huge amounts of data collection and some of the most powerful computers in the world fail to predict the weather for more than a day or two ahead.

(b) Past experience with a model is the best guide as to how far ahead it can predict the future.

(c) The rules and formulae which are used to 'turn the handle' of the prediction machine are not based on proven, or even generally agreed, theory. Economists hold few views in common, and it is unlikely that any of them are right.

(d) There should be a clear statement of the assumptions that a planning package is based on, and this statement should accompany any results from the package. Results in isolation are meaningless.

(e) Because nearly all the variables of sales and costs are given as probabilities or as distributions, there will be multiple outcomes predicted, each with a probability. The further into the future the package attempts to predict, the more outcomes there will be. The probabilities of each will be lower and the picture less clear.

2 EFFECT OF IT ON MANAGEMENT PROCESSES IN THE FUTURE

2.1 Decision-making

We have already shown that, in general, information systems exist to support decision-making. A person must be aware of a problem, or a range of alternatives, before a decision can be taken. In finding and solving a problem the decision-maker must gather information about it. The need for more and more information has led to the evolution of systems to process data quickly and efficiently.

There are three types of decision made in organisations:

(a) Strategic planning decisions, where the decision-maker develops objectives and allocates resources to achieve these objectives. Decisions in this category are characterised by long time periods and usually involve a substantial investment and effort.

(b) Managerial control decisions which deal with the use of resources in the organisation and often involve personnel or financial problems. For example, an accountant may try to determine the reason for a difference between actual and budgeted costs. In this case the accountant is solving a managerial control problem.

(c) Operational control decisions which deal with the day to day problems of the organisation.

A management information system can provide the information to support all of these types of decision. A model is shown below:

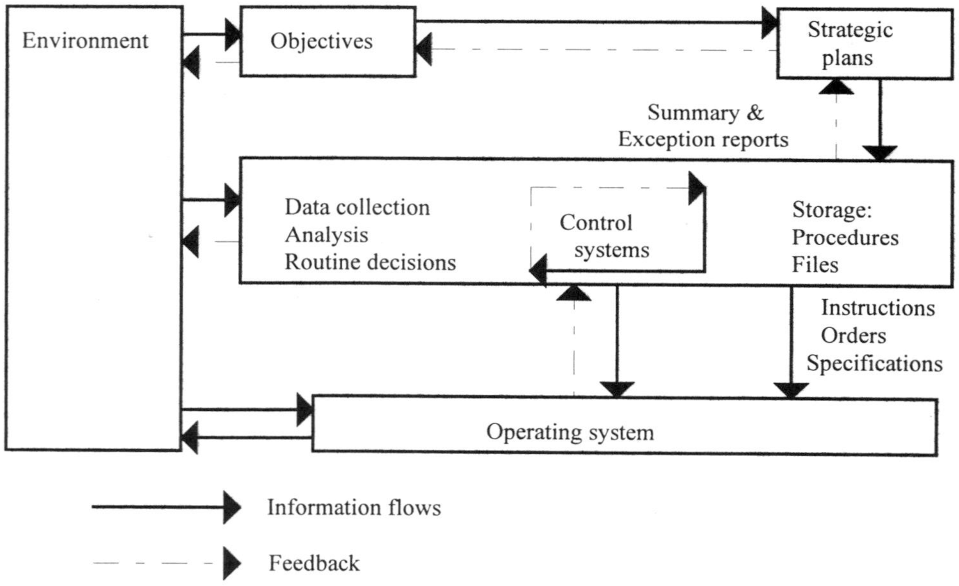

2.2 Information flows

Management considers both internal and environmental information in the process of establishing objectives at strategic level. Assumptions with regard to political conditions, competitors, customer needs and desires, internal capabilities and other factors form a frame of reference for strategic and comprehensive planning. Plans for the organisational activities are transmitted to the operating system and to storage in the control and co-ordination systems for later comparison with operating results. Detailed orders, instructions and specifications flow to the operating system.

Feedback is obtained on the output of the system in terms of quality, quantity and cost. The operating system is monitored to maintain process control and input inspection provides feedback at the earliest stage in the operating system. Information flow is an integral part of the control system because it provides a means of comparing results with plans. Feedback data from various phases of the operating system are collected and analysed.

The analysis involves processing data, developing information and comparing the results with plans. Decisions are also made within the control system itself because routine adjustments can be pre-programmed in the set of procedures or instructions.

Within the control system there is a flow of information to implement changes to the program based on feedback from the operating system.

Summary and exception reports are generated by the control system and become part of a higher level process of review and evaluation that may lead to an adjustment or innovation of goals. Subsequent planning activity reflects such feedback and the entire process is repeated.

Although some information exchange with the environment is evident at each level, the boundary is more pervasive where top management is concerned. The strategic subsystem is primarily responsible for interacting with the environment and maintaining the organisation in a dynamic equilibrium. Nevertheless, some interchange of information occurs between the environment and the managers in the operating and co-ordinative subsystems. Such information is mixed with the internal flows to provide the total picture for managers at all levels.

In an age of increasingly sophisticated computerisation it may be possible to include all data from all subsystems in a management information decision system. But even if it were possible it is not clear that it would be an efficient use of resources. The system should be evaluated on the basis of cost benefit analysis. A balance should be held between the cost of the system and the value of the information generated.

It is important to assess the total incremental cost of equipment and programming as well as the continuing expense of system development. Such costs should be analysed in terms of potential benefits from better information and improved managerial decision making. This type of analysis should be made for any information system. We should be concerned with both effectiveness and efficiency. The system should be geared towards the needs of the decision makers in the organisation.

2.3 Management and decision-making

An integral element of the managerial task is organisational decision making: choosing an overall strategy, setting specific objectives, designing structures and processes, selecting people, delegating responsibility, evaluating results and initiating changes.

Our understanding of management can be enhanced by viewing it from a decision-making perspective and recognising that managerial decision making is a sequential process, rather than distinct actions where problems are resolved once and for all. Subsequent decisions are affected by previous decisions and developments over time. It is a process that includes searching out and recognising problems as well as analysing them and choosing courses of action to be implemented.

A wide spectrum of decision-making methods are relevant to the managerial system. Within the operating subsystem there is relative certainty; hence well-defined problems can be solved via straightforward computational techniques. For long range strategic problems, the board of directors and top management are faced with considerable uncertainty and novel, ill-structured problems. Computational approaches are less appropriate for decision-making at the strategic level except for small parts of some problems.

2.4 Activity

Strategy is the organised development of resources to achieve specific objectives against competition from rival organisations. It is the use of all the entity's resources, financial, manufacturing, marketing, technological, manpower etc, in the pursuit of its objectives.

It is a set of policies adopted by senior management which guides the scope and direction of the entity. It takes into account the environment in which the company operates.

'Scope' used in this context relates to size and range, and **'direction'** describes product/market positioning. In simple terms, an entity's **'environment'** relates to the uncontrollable factors that influence it.

Consider carefully the above explanation of strategy and then try to relate it to either a strategy that you have read about or one from your own organisation. Your example should bring out, or emphasise, the importance of the following words included in the explanation: entity objectives; resources, scope, direction and environment.

2.5 Activity solution

Although the example of strategy given here was implemented by IBM over a decade ago, it is still considered to be a classic example of competitive strategy, and one that exemplifies our explanation of strategy.

In August 1981, **IBM** launched a massive attack on the $1.4 billion US personal computer market, which had been planned in scrupulous detail to take market leadership away from the market creator, Apple. The strategy was in response to the falling mainframe computer market of which IBM was market leader, and the fast developing personal computer market in which the company did not then have a presence. IBM's strategy was based on a simultaneous three- pronged thrust.

First, at the core of the IBM's new PC architecture was an Intel 16-bit microprocessor providing speed and memory size with much superior processing power than obtained from the market's existing 8-bit microprocessor based products.

Second IBM publicised its PC specifications well ahead of its product launch and permitted Microsoft, the supplier of its PCs' basic operating systems, to licence its software to other manufacturers, a strategy which very soon made the IBM microcomputer equipment, and the software produced for it, the industry *de facto* standard.

Third, IBM launched a massive $40 million advertising campaign which it supported with 800 carefully selected computer retailers, at the same time using its experience, goodwill and enormous sales force to penetrate the office segment. Within one year IBM had secured 16% of the PC market. The second wave of the IBM attack, a massive 20% price reduction, took place in the following year, April 1983, securing for it another 10% share, and leadership, of the market.

When implementing this strategy IBM was attempting to respond to its changing business environment by using its considerable resources and distinctive competence to outmanoeuvre its opponents in order to achieve its objective of gaining a superior position in a new market, and to achieve specific financial objectives. Explained simply the company was involved in the process of planning a way by which it could utilise its resources to achieve specific results in a hostile and dynamic business environment.

3 USING IT TO GAIN A STRATEGIC ADVANTAGE

3.1 IT as a strategic weapon

Information technology can be used as a strategic weapon in a number of ways.

(a) It is a potential supplier of competitive advantage to an organisation. We have seen this in travel agents where choosing and reserving a holiday can be done in much less time and more conveniently when the agent is on-line to the suppliers.

(b) Information technology and systems can be used as a strategic weapon to improve productivity and performance. CAD and CAM are two examples where this might be the case.

(c) IT can be used in the development of new business. For example, selling the analysis of a large supermarket's sales to market research companies so that they can identify trends in product purchasing.

(d) Information systems can be used to change the management and organisational structure of the organisation to achieve competitive advantage. Computers with modems enable people to work from home, reducing the cost of travel and office space. Teleconferencing and video conferencing are available to managers, reducing the necessity for them to travel to meetings and making their time more productive.

3.2 How IT permeates the value chain

Organisations carry out a range of primary activities and/or support activities which are concerned with producing the end product or service.

All the activities of the value chain have a potential to enhance or impede the organisation's success in adding value to their product or service.

Porter's value chain model, shown in the diagram below, can be used to analyse these activities for the purpose of identifying IT opportunities. It can be used to suggest areas where IT can interpret activities.

The value chain

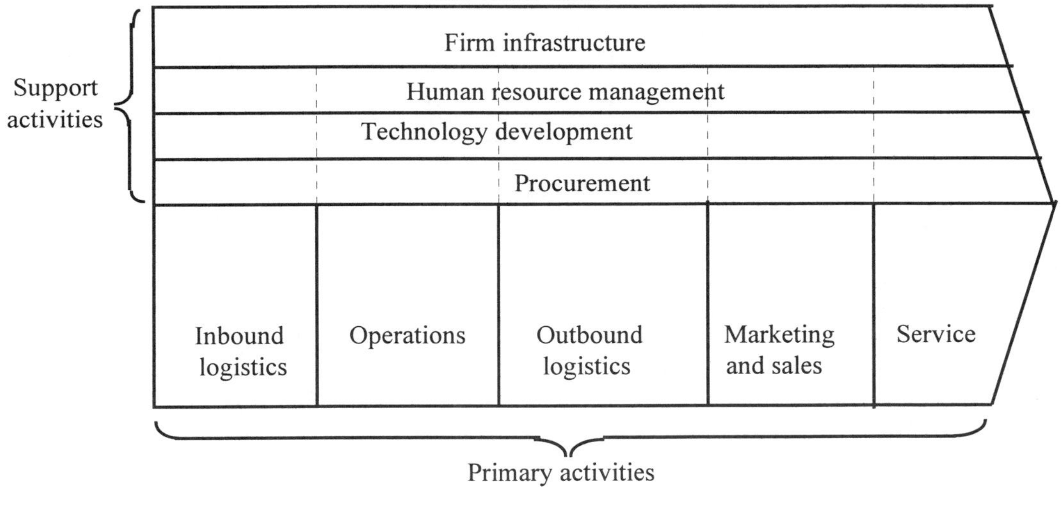

The value chain model divides an organisation's activities into nine generic activities, five primary activities and four support activities. The value an organisation creates is measured by the amount that buyers are willing to pay for a product or service. An organisation is profitable if the value it creates exceeds the costs of performing all the activities involved in producing the product or service.

To gain competitive advantage an organisation must either perform some or all of the generic activities at a lower cost or perform them in such a way that leads to differentiation, depending on which of the generic strategies is being used in the organisation.

In the primary activities of inbound and outbound logistics, IT can be used to advantage. Materials planning systems can help capacity and production scheduling. Warehousing can benefit from bar-codes to identify information about stock held.

Physical tasks in the operations activities can be automated. Examples are process and machine tool control. Also robots can be used for tasks which are either monotonous or dangerous for people to do eg, paint spraying in the manufacture of cars.

Marketing and services activities can be made more effective by databases such as mailing lists or the information provided by EPOS systems.

In the support activities, IT can be used in procurement activities with electronic data interchange (EDI) to link purchasing with sales order systems.

CAD and CAM is an important influence on the technology development activities.

3.3 Linking IT with the value chain

Information systems can provide linkages within and between value chains. The example outlined in the diagram below shows how an information system could provide a competitive advantage. The aim is to:

(a) identify customer needs and values in the market, defined either broadly or by market segment;

(b) consider and establish which of the generic strategy routes is most appropriate;

(c) operate this route in such a way that customer needs are being met by a mix of activities which is distinctly different from that of the competitors, and which achieves a coherent set of linkages between the activities;

(d) achieve cost stability or reductions through experience in these crucial activities, especially where they give cost advantages over the competition.

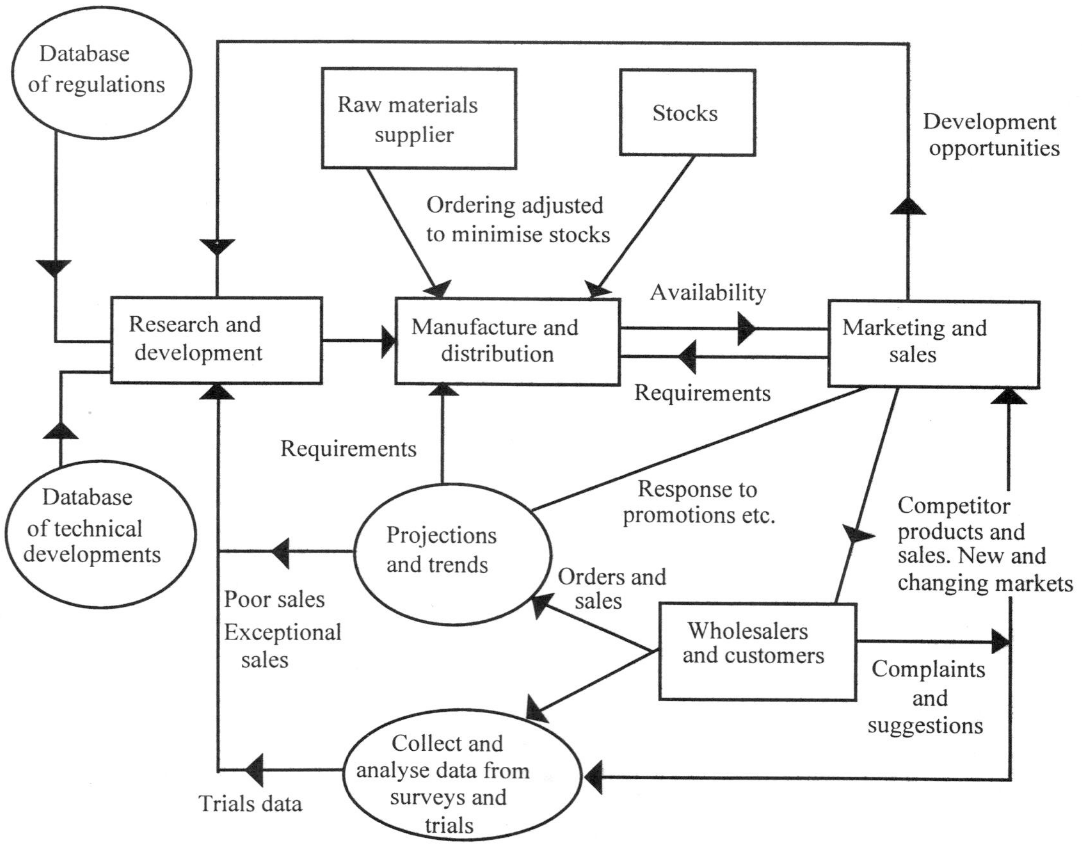

3.4 Other frameworks to help identify options to use IT strategically

Michael Earl developed a number of frameworks for assessing the strategic implications of IT. These are:

- awareness frameworks;
- opportunity frameworks; and
- positioning frameworks.

(a) **Awareness frameworks** are a series of models which help managers assess the general impact of IT on the organisation.

One of the awareness frameworks, the refocus framework, exists to help change 'mind sets' or to challenge assumptions about the use and value of IT, asking questions such as 'Should the organisation use IT to improve access to the market place or use it to improve the organisation's existing operations?' A building society might question access into European ATMs against improving its existing operations to reduce the time it takes to clear a cheque.

An example of an awareness framework is the information intensity matrix developed by Porter and Miller. This is based on a 2-by-2 grid, in which the axes represent:

- the degree of information in the product itself (low or high)
- the degree of information in the value chain (low or high)

This leads to four possible classifications; a product's position on the matrix helps to indicate its potential for exploiting information to secure a competitive advantage.

(b) **Opportunity frameworks** are tools designed to analyse whether an organisation has the opportunity of strategic advantage in a particular area. One of these tools, the applications search tool, was used by Ives and Learmouth to develop a customer resource life cycle. This identifies the steps taken by a customer when acquiring a product or service. The phases they identified in the life cycle were:

(i) requirements; covers what and how much of it?

(ii) acquisition; includes where it is bought, order and payment methods and acceptability testing

(iii) stewardship; covers how is it cared for, repaired or enhanced?

(iv) retirement; incorporates the return or disposal of the product or service.

The life cycle is then used to design applications around actual customer behaviour. After studying a customer resource life cycle for kitchen replacements, a kitchen furniture manufacturer might use a CAD package, installed in a portable computer, to help their field sales staff to 'design to fit' the customer's requirements. The software could be used to simulate the look of a new kitchen and several alternatives can be shown to the customer in the comfort of their home.

(c) **Positioning frameworks** help managers to assess the strategic importance of the current situation of IT for their organisation and their industry. This framework is similar to Nolan's stage hypothesis.

(d) **Strategic options generator**

Wiseman developed a strategic options generator. It is essentially a checklist which guides the manager through all the parameters that must be considered when seeking strategic opportunities. In a systematic way it encourages the search for IT opportunities. The steps are shown in the following diagram:

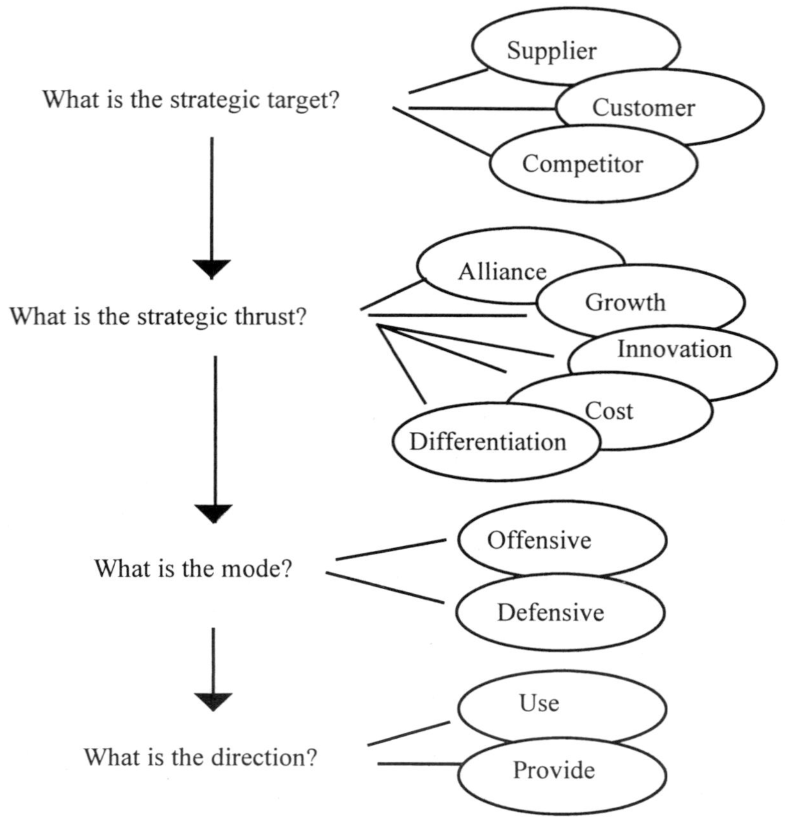

The generator directs its attention towards the strategic targets, the thrust is then used to 'hit' them, either aggressively or defensively and the direction describes whether the organisation is using the strategy for itself or providing it for the target's use.

3.5 Activity

How can hospitals and doctors use expert systems to gain strategic advantage?

3.6 Activity solution

Hospitals which can boast a 99% certainty of abdominal pain being treated correctly because of their medical diagnostics expert system have a strategic advantage over those that have to rely on doctors alone.
Expert systems can also be used to identify illnesses and prescribe the correct drug for a patient.

4 CHAPTER SUMMARY

This chapter has presented a number of business models which are used to help determine strategy. IT's strategic role can be assessed by its abilities in dealing with the five competitive forces. These forces represent the bargaining power of existing suppliers and buyers (or customers), the threat of substitutes and new entrants and the intensity of existing rivalry. Using this model identifies where IT can be used strategically eg, to set up barriers, to enhance a generic strategy.

The value chain can also be used to show where an organisation can benefit from the use of information technology and information systems.

Other frameworks for assessing the strategic options include Earl's awareness framework (for assessing the general impact on an organisation), opportunity frameworks and positioning frameworks, such as McFarlan's grid and Nolan's stage hypothesis. Wiseman also developed an options generator model which can be used when assessing the strategic options available.

5 SELF TEST QUESTIONS

5.1 Describe the two possible IT roles which can counteract the threat of entry (1.2).

5.2 Examine the threat that IT poses on substitute products (1.4).

5.3 Describe two ways of locking customers into products or services (1.5).

5.4 List the three levels of environmental trends (1.8).

5.5 Outline the types of decision made in organisations (2.1).

5.6 Describe the ways that IT can be used as a strategic weapon (3.1).

5.7 Analyse the ways that IT can be used to advantage in three of the primary activities of the value chain. (3.2).

5.8 List the three frameworks developed by Earl to help identify options to use IT strategically (3.4).

5.9 What does Wiseman's options generator do? (3.4).

6 EXAMINATION TYPE QUESTION

6.1 Competitive edge

Using examples show how information technology can be used to give an organisation competitive edge. **(20 marks)**

7 ANSWER TO EXAMINATION TYPE QUESTION

7.1 Competitive edge

The strategic and competitive value of information technology has advanced in recent years to be a critical factor in systems planning issues. The high capital expenditure that new systems command, together with the greatly enhanced information processing capacity provided by technological developments, has meant that organisations are reviewing in detail the positive commercial advantage that can accrue from an imaginative application of information technology to their activities as a whole.

Much depends on the organisation's perception of the future strategic and competitive value of its information systems and on the role of the current information systems. If management simply see the function of information systems as the provision of support for other production or managerial structures, then the strategic and competitive value of future systems will not be regarded as particularly important.

Alternatively, information systems might by viewed as a means to 'factory' produce its information to enable the organisation to produce its goods or services efficiently. The systems might be felt to be vital in providing a competitive edge in existing products or markets, and to make new kinds of products possible.

Michael Porter emphasises that tomorrow's successful organisation will be a collection of skills and capabilities which are ready to pounce on any market opportunity. Possessing competitive edge means having those factors which lead customers to consistently prefer your products. He has suggested three overall competitive strategies which an organisation can implement.

(i) **Overall cost leadership**

This means becoming the most efficient producer. The objective to achieve overall cost leadership in the market is generally held by organisations in very competitive price-sensitive markets, where any means of reducing costs, or maintaining margins on lower prices, can lead to price reductions in goods and services offered to clients or customers. Information systems can reduce staff time spent on clerical work, allowing more to be spent on business development. Information technology can help not only by mechanising production systems but also by making the planning of production more efficient and using effective accounting control systems eg, activity based costing (ABC). Cost containment measures can include detailed control of stock levels and an information system might allow a company to tie up its purchasing services directly with its suppliers by the use of computerised just in time (JIT) systems, reducing stock-holding costs and delays in processing orders.

(ii) **Product differentiation**

This means having unique products or varying them in such a way that they appear to be different from those offered by competitors. IT can help in the design of products eg, computer-aided design. Information systems can enhance an organisation's ability to compete by providing it with up-to-the-minute information as to customer needs and in tailoring their products or services to a customer's specific requirements. IS can also be used to compare customer purchases of the organisation's goods with those of other suppliers, allowing an organisation to differentiate its products on factors other than price.

(iii) **Market niche**

A niche market is a relatively small section of the overall market where customer needs are not fully satisfied. Information technology may be used to identify or exploit such a market niche by the analysis of market research data and other sales statistics. An example of the competitive value of information technology is the introduction of automated teller machines.

Additional to the provision of competitive advantage in the market place, internal changes in an organisation's structure can enhance its competitive edge, by encouraging more effective use of its human and material resources. Sometimes changes can be radical eg, a distribution organisation may get rid of one of its warehouses and employ a more efficient computerised distribution system.

Information systems might be used to foster innovation, by encouraging a free flow of ideas in a large organisation. A computer conferencing system, where individuals communicate their ideas with relative informality is an example of such a system.

Information technology does not guarantee an enhanced competitive ability for the simple reason that any advantage due to information technology alone is likely to by temporary as competitors can also use it. Moreover, improved information does not necessarily lead to better decision making.

27 MANAGING INFORMATION SYSTEMS

INTRODUCTION & LEARNING OBJECTIVES

Until the late 1970s computers were largely confined to the data processing departments of larger organisations. The people who had direct contact with computers were the specialists who often worked in isolation from the rest of the organisation. Contrast this with the current situation where most office staff use a PC at some point throughout the course of their day. Many people will use a PC for the majority of their work yet still not consider themselves either a computer specialist or operator.

Over the same time period there has also been a convergence of office technologies. There used to be a clear distinction in the management of office systems, computing and communications. Office systems would be managed on a decentralised basis with the manager of an individual function being responsible for the purchase of any new equipment. The computer department would have been controlled centrally by computer specialists and communications was also a separate centrally controlled function.

The proliferation of computers, and their use in carrying out simple office functions such as typing and manipulation of figures, has brought about an increasing need for communications between them, so that most organisations recognise that the areas of office systems, communications and computing are all managed as a single technology.

When you have studied this chapter you should be able to do the following.

- Explain the deployment of resources in terms of centralisation and decentralisation.
- Describe end user computing.
- Evaluate the role of the information centre.
- Describe the responsibilities of the IS department.
- Explain the challenges facing IS departments.
- Discuss the role of the IT director.
- Describe the role of steering committees

1 DEPLOYING INFORMATION SYSTEMS RESOURCES

1.1 Trends in IS departments

The information systems function has altered over time and certain trends have emerged which have changed the way that the resources in IS are deployed. When computers were first introduced into organisations, the data processing function was a centralised operation. A single DP department catered for all the processing needs of the other functions. The trend away from centralised DP was accelerated with the introduction of cheaper computers and more packaged software.

Because of the developments in communications, there has also been a trend towards decentralised processing using local and wide area networks.

Growth in the usage of application software packages and development of management information systems has increasingly meant end user involvement in systems decisions, for example, buying a new PC, developing a new spreadsheet or database application.

All of these changes within IS departments pose problems for the deployment of resources, because the traditional structure of the DP department, with particular jobs allocated into different compartments, is no longer viable and the IS resources are spread throughout an organisation.

2 DECENTRALISATION OR CENTRALISATION

2.1 Processing alternatives

Information technology offers considerable flexibility in developing patterns for the structure of the information services function. The firm must identify possible processing patterns, evaluate them and choose an alternative for implementation. Processing alternatives can be divided into three broad groups. These are:

(a) completely centralised processing where all systems analysis and design is performed by a central group and all the equipment is operated centrally;

(b) distributed processing where local sites are tied together in some type of communication network;

(c) completely decentralised processing where all the equipment and processing is resident at local sites and these sites have their own staff for analysis and design work.

The task of managing either a centralised or decentralised configuration is complex and will depend on the existing information processing organisation.

The challenge of a centralised system is to make it responsive while that of a distributed or decentralised system is to make the various parts co-ordinated. Management must trade off the benefits perceived by users in having and controlling their own computer equipment against the need for overall co-ordination in the organisation.

Allowing a proliferation of small computers can lead to high costs if the organisation decides to connect diverse equipment through a network.

2.2 Concepts of centralised processing

(a) **The computer as a centralised service in a single operating unit**

When a business comprises only one factory or office as opposed to a group of factories or other business units, and a computer is implemented in the organisation, then the way in which it is used requires careful consideration. Sometimes it may be used only for processing routine accounting applications such as payroll, sales ledger, stock control and purchase ledger etc.

To obtain the maximum benefit however, the computer should be used to aid management in problem-solving and decision-making by the use of quantitative application packages for linear programming, statistical stock control, production planning, network analysis and discounted cash flow, etc. When a computer is used for all the functions within the business it is a centralised facility in the form of a data processing and information system.

(b) **The computer as a centralised service in a group of operating units**

When a business organisation is a widely dispersed conglomeration of various types of operating unit, including factories, warehouses and sales offices and a computer is in use, it is usually based at head office. In these circumstances the objective would be to provide the best possible service for the data processing and information needs of all functions and operating units in the group.

The benefits to be derived from a centralised service may be summarised as follows:

(a) Economy of capital expenditure due to the relatively high cost of computers through having only one computer for use by the group instead of several located in various units.

(b) If one powerful computer is installed, the resultant advantages are increased speed of operation, storage capacity and processing capability.

(c) Economy in computer operating costs due to centralisation of systems analysts, programmers, operators and other data processing staff as compared with the level of costs that would be incurred if each unit in the group had its own computer on a decentralised basis.

(d) Centralisation would also facilitate the standardisation of applications but this would depend upon the extent of diversity in the dispersed operations regarding payroll and invoicing structures etc.

If the computer is also communications-oriented, whereby all operating units are equipped with transmission terminals connected to the central computer, then basic data may be speedily transmitted for processing by remote job entry and the results transmitted back and printed on a local printer. This would reduce any time delay in receiving computer output through the post or messenger service. The possibility of an integrated management information system then becomes feasible, as data from dispersed units is speedily processed for local use and information becomes available at head office by means of computer files for corporate planning.

Such a centralised computing service should be structured in the organisation at the level which enables the IT manager to report to a higher level of management than the department level or functional level for which he is providing a service. This enables policy matters to be established at board level, rather than at functional level, to secure the use of the computer on a corporate strategic basis in order to optimise its use.

2.3 Concepts of distributed processing

(a) Systems architecture

Distributed processing must not be confused with decentralised processing, even though decentralisation is a feature of distributed processing. Prior to the advent of the computer, different companies in a group may well have used their own data processing installation (a decentralised facility). The centralisation of data processing, as outlined in the previous paragraphs, was the trend of the 1960s but recent trends have reversed this situation, largely due to the development of workstations and PCs. These cost much less than mainframes, which makes it a viable proposition to install them in departments and branches on a distributed processing basis. This is the philosophy of providing computer power where it is most needed, instead of concentrating all processing in a single centralised computer system. Systems architecture is a design philosophy whereby small computers in dispersed operating units may be connected by a communications network to each other and also to a large, centrally-located mainframe. The mainframe may support a large database, which would allow information of a strategic nature to be retrieved on demand for corporate planning. This would be a distributed network.

The micros may be dedicated machines being used for a single main purpose and, in some instances, may be used as stand-alone processing systems when appropriate. This situation allows a high degree of autonomy at the local operating level which encourages motivation, flexibility and a greater acceptance of responsibility by the local management.

(b) Co-ordinating influence of distributed processing

Simplicity of gaining access to a computer by relevant operating personnel at all levels of an organisation is not an easy matter to accomplish even within a single unit business organisation equipped with terminals. The problem is accentuated when there are many dispersed units within the organisation, many of which may be interdependent (marketing and manufacturing), as all units must be fully aware of the operational status of each other's sphere of operations.

With the implementation of distributed processing systems, this is not so much of a problem because it is of no consequence whether the small computers are located in the same building or overseas. Distributed processing allows a business to select the level of processing autonomy in respect of depots, factories, warehouses or sales offices.

Distributed processing also includes the use, on a decentralised basis, of intelligent terminals ie, terminals with processing capabilities which may be used on a local basis for off-line operations or for on-line operations linked to a host computer. The choice of terminal may be selected according to the local needs and may include badge readers and data collection terminals in factory departments, tag readers and point of sale terminals in retail sales outlets and visual display units for offices.

2.4 Impact of information systems on the organisation

Leavitt and Whisler (1958) presented one of the best-known sets of predictions for the impact of computers on organisations. These authors suggested that firms would re-centralise as a result of new computer technology; the availability of more information than previously possible would allow management to centralise. The trend until the development of computer systems had been towards decentralisation because centralised management could not cope with the amount of information and the number of decisions required in a large organisation. Computers offer the power to make centralised management possible so the organisation can be tightly controlled by a group of top managers.

There has been little evidence to support this early prediction. In a few cases, researchers have found examples of re-centralisation after computer systems were installed; however, there is no overall trend evidence.

Another problem in validating predictions of computer impact occurs in defining variables such as centralisation and decentralisation. No one has developed an acceptable definition or a technique to measure it.

There is no real reason why computer systems lead naturally to centralisation. Management should specify the goals of the organisation and the degree of centralisation desired. Given the sophisticated communications capabilities of on-line computer systems and large database systems, computer systems can be designed which provide information for decision-making at any level or geographical location in an organisation.

2.5 Arguments for centralisation

(a) All financial and operating data would be available to the strategic level of management immediately, thereby ensuring more up to date and timely information for decision making.

(b) It might be cheaper to have just one computer rather than to have many. Also, it might produce a saving in costs of computer personnel, and would most certainly produce a saving by reducing duplication of data input.

(c) Better promotional prospects for the computer personnel which will lead to more loyalty and to stability of staff in the computing department. Often in decentralised systems computer professionals have more loyalty to their profession than to the organisation they work for and will often follow jobs that will broaden their computing experience. If the organisation has a centralised system then it will be able to offer a wide range of computing experience itself.

(d) Better control by management over its operations. Also, there will be uniform reporting and this will ensure that each operating unit can be monitored on its performance against other operating units.

2.6 Arguments for decentralisation

(a) Local units are more familiar with local problems and are better able to meet the needs of their customers.

(b) Decentralised units are able to respond faster to changes in their operating environment. A decentralised computing facility would be able to develop specific systems for its unit thereby increasing its efficiency and effectiveness.

(c) The decentralisation of profit and loss responsibilities will make users more aware of their equipment and more sensitive to the cost/benefit considerations of the development of computing systems.

2.7 IT location

It can be said that centralisation offers more efficiency and control to the corporate managers whilst decentralisation allows more flexibility to users.

However, whether a company uses a decentralised or a centralised system will depend upon the type of business they are in.

Centralisation tends to favour situations where

(a) information systems are needed for top-level management decision making
(b) certain functions in all the business units are exactly the same and need the same systems
(c) the processing required is not urgent and can be done more economically at one central point
(d) the organisation is too small to justify setting up a number of decentralised computing systems
(e) centralised processing is essential to the operation, eg on-line airline bookings.

Decentralisation is best suited in situations where

(a) rapid response is required by the system
(b) processing systems differ for each local unit
(c) it is essential to minimise the impact of computer downtime.

The information technology administration could be located in

(a) The department which initially introduced computers into the organisation. This is usually the accounts/finance department. This location is suitable where the information produced relates in some way to the department where it is located. Once processing requirements are needed that have no relation to the department then this might produce conflict or lack of commitment from the people within the department.

(b) A separate service function. In this case the computing people would report directly to top-level management and this would overcome the problems of objectivity in setting priorities for development. However, this sometimes appears as if the computing facility is an outside function and the manager has little or no impact upon the organisation structure.

(c) A separate independent department. This is probably the most favoured of the options because it affirms that information technology is viewed as a corporate function of the organisation. It also ensures that the department has organisational status and it encourages innovation/integration of systems.

However, most organisations end up with a federal arrangement which means that decentralised units exist alongside a centralised unit which is responsible for overall policy and architecture.

The financial control of the function could be dealt with in one of the following ways

(a) As a unallocated cost centre. This is where the IT department is set up as a free resource to users. Problems which could occur include: unrealistic user requests, and no competitive pressure which would ensure that the service offered was effective and efficient. However, with this type of system there is no conflict over IT charges as none are paid.

(b) As an allocated cost centre. This means that the annual budget of the IT department is worked out and the cost shared proportionately between user departments. Problems which occur here tend to relate to the amount of charges each department is expected to pay out of individual budgets. Some departments use very little IT and so their contribution is small, whereas other departments have no option but to use IT and this is often not reflected in their overall budget.

(c) As a profit centre. This means that the internal IT services are bought in the same way as they would be from an external supplier. The centre itself must be profitable and can sell its services outside of the organisation. Problems which arise here include

- the corporate entity losing control of the IT function
- too much time spent in developing systems for the external market
- conflict over higher user costs because the centre is adding on a profit cost.

2.8 Activity

Where is the IT located in a large retail group of stores such as Sainsbury?

2.9 Activity solution

Most large stores like Sainsbury will have both a centralised unit and decentralised units. The local stores have their own system where prices can be adjusted locally to match local competition and analyse shopper spending patterns. At least once a day the information will be sent to the Head Office system, which is centralised, where the information is needed for top level decision making.

3 END USER COMPUTING

3.1 Introduction

Definition 'The direct, hands-on use of computers by users; not indirect use through systems professionals or the data processing staff. End-users include executives, managers, professional staff, secretaries, office workers, salespeople and others'

Sprague and McNurlin in **Information systems management in practice**

End user computing has spread because of a number of developments, which include:

- the increased use of personal computers in user departments;
- user-friendly software;
- increased computer awareness;
- applications backlog on mainframe computers;
- shortage of specialised resources in IS departments.

These end users utilise the computers for a variety of reasons and applications, including:

- word processing;
- spreadsheets for accounting and calculations;
- finding and retrieving information on databases;
- communications such as networks and electronic mail;
- presentation of information in graphical format;
- project management;
- routine processing of transactions;
- computer based training;
- developing new programs;
- booking systems eg, tickets, appointments, sales visits;
- diary facilities.

3.2 Activity

More responsibility for information processing has been transferred to end users because of such things as increased use of micros and the wide availability of general purpose packages.

Outline some of the most important problems faced by organisations which have a significant amount of end user computing.

3.3 Activity solution

The following are some problems associated with end user computing:

- lack of user education and training about personal computing;
- requests for assistance which overwhelm the IT department;
- lack of user concern about equipment security;
- lack of knowledge or concern about control measures such as saving and backup;
- mismatching of user problems and computing alternatives for systems development;
- lack of integration in IT management of personal computing and mainframe end user computing;
- lack of centralised management of corporate data resources that support personal computing;
- poor maintainability of user-developed systems;
- lack of integration in data exchange and control.

4 THE ROLE OF THE INFORMATION CENTRE

4.1 Background

The term information centre describes a department within an organisation, the function of which is to provide help and assistance to other departments in the organisation that use computers. Information centres do not develop application packages.

Information centres came about because of a combination of factors. The first was that the traditional data processing departments could not keep up with the demand for applications packages. In the late 1970s and early 1980s it was not uncommon for data processing departments to have waiting times of three years to start larger projects. This obviously caused frustration in end user departments. The second factor was the availability first of minicomputers and then micro computers. These relatively cheap and simple to operate computers could be purchased and operated by end user departments.

The combination of demand for applications and cheaper computing meant that end user departments purchased hardware and developed their own applications. However there was a need on the part of the users to have access to in-company expertise. Also there was a need on the part of the organisation to exercise some control over the proliferation of technologies and information systems. All of these factors combined led organisations to set up information centres.

4.2 Services offered

Information centres responded to the organisation's need to control technology by:

- Establishing hardware standards;
- Approving a range of suppliers of hardware;
- Establishing software standards;
- Becoming a central point for the release of updated software.

Services offered by information centres

- Training in the use of high level languages and software development tools
- Help when searching for reference publications on software, hardware, development methods etc.
- Specific help with identifying the location of data in the corporate database.
- Technical assistance in dealing with particular problems when writing applications in high level programming languages.
- Guidance when purchasing hardware, software, application packages or external support services.

4.3 Personnel

Information centre personnel usually act as consultants and trainers to computing users in departments. They will need a wide range of skills as the end users may be varied in the extent of their computer knowledge. It is therefore possible to find that the information centre provides guidance to a manager purchasing personal computers to be used for word processing and also gives specific technical assistance to a programmer working in an end user department.

Information centres try to keep their staff to a minimum by training end users to carry out any function which would otherwise cause the numbers of staff in the centre to grow. Take for example a centre that found that it received a large number of calls for assistance from end users when setting up laser printers. The information centre would organise a course on configuring laser printers, run the course at regular intervals and then only accept calls for assistance from staff who had attended the course.

4.4 Problem areas

Problem areas in information centre operations include

(a) opposition from the IS department (if it is a separate department)
(b) cost-benefit difficulties
(c) resistance from non-computer oriented users
(d) problems of who controls the information centre
(e) lack of senior management support
(f) staffing with unsuitable individuals.

5 INFORMATION SYSTEMS DEPARTMENTS

Because IT has permeated throughout most departments in organisations, the information systems department may be seen as a generalised function, similar to finance.

As with the finance department, the specialised responsibilities of the IS department may be identified and shown in a hierarchical diagram, even though the personnel may not actually be in a separate IS department.

The division and types of responsibilities within an IS department are shown in the diagram below:

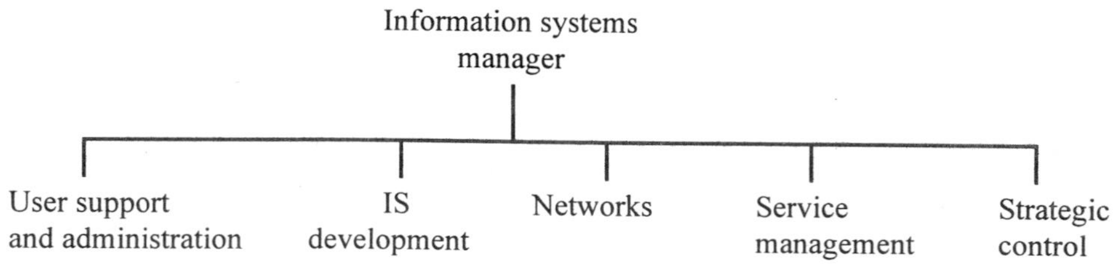

The responsibilities of each of the sections include the following.

- **User support and administration**

  We have already discussed user support (information centre) in some depth in the previous section. Administration covers secretarial, accounting and library services of the IS function.

- **Information systems development** staff include analysts and programmers.

- **Network management** has become important since the growth of networking and distributed processing has necessitated a linking between the technologies of telecommunications and computing.

- **Service management** includes all the responsibilities that used to be associated with the computer operations and data centre.

- **Strategic control and planning** includes the development of procedures and standards for guidance, assigning development work and liaising with users to ascertain their needs.

6 THE ROLE OF THE IT DIRECTOR

6.1 Skills required

Some organisations are large enough to warrant an information director, whilst others cope with an IS department manager with access to the Board, so that IT issues relating to strategy and planning can be represented at Board level.

In his book **Introducing information systems management,** Malcolm Peltu describes the skills that the IT director should possess. These are:

- good management ability;
- good understanding of how the organisation operates and the organisational activities; and
- good technical expertise in developing and running information systems.

It is easy to see that this range of skills might not always be balanced in an organisation by envisaging where such a person would come from. If the person has a background in management and those skills have been developed, then the first area may be covered. People who make good managers, unfortunately do not always have the technical wizardry to have an IT vision for the future, as well as an understanding of the day-to-day computing problems that can crop up. Whilst it may be possible to find a manager with technical ability, it would seem much more difficult to find one that also knew how the organisation operates and all of the activities.

6.2 Context of the role

The role of the information director is likely to include the following:

(a) Developing the information systems strategy to tie in with the overall organisational strategy. This aspect of the role covers the purchase and use of the technology to fit with the organisation's goals and objectives.

(b) Ensuring that there is interaction with the environment. This aspect covers:

- information systems flexibility and connections between other organisations, eg, electronic data interchange (EDI), shared databases and communications links with customers and suppliers. It also entails looking constantly at the trends in new technology and the new systems enhancements that are being marketed;

- the legal environment of IS, which involves the data protection legislation, transborder flows of information and systems security matters covered in the Computer Misuse Act 1990;

- the public relations required to convince suppliers, customers and employees of the benefits of the IS.

(c) Responsibility for the information infrastructure, which incorporates the technical and software standards, the establishment of databases and the provision of a systems service function.

(d) Setting up and servicing links between the IS staff and the rest of the organisation. This part of the role involves the provision of technical assistance, informal discussion with users about their needs, discussion with finance and management accounting about the payoff of IS investments.

(e) Participating in a steering committee to oversee the general direction of IS policy and take decisions on individual IT projects.

6.3 Challenges facing IS departments

Many user and management problems with information services revolve around the manager of this department. Understanding the manager's position helps in developing a relationship between the information services department and users. Nolan (1973) has described the plight of managers of information services departments.

(a) They have a wide variety of subordinates reporting to them, ranging from highly technical computer professionals to clerical personnel.

(b) The department is responsible for a broad range of activities from creative systems design work to routine clerical chores.

(c) The department has an impact on many, if not all, areas of the organisation.

(d) The manager controls a large budget and is responsible for a major investment in equipment.

As the department becomes larger and needs become less technical, the emphasis shifts more towards managerial problems. Unfortunately we often find managers of information services departments with no managerial background because their expertise is all on the technical side of computing.

The IT manager will draw up a plan for information processing, which should be co-ordinated with corporate strategy. The plan will serve as a guide to show the direction of the systems effort.

A typical plan describes the breakdown in activities and resources required for the development of new applications and the operation of existing systems. A key task for the organisation is to identify areas for new applications of technology. What are the applications areas with the highest return? What applications will most further the strategic goals of the organisation? What new opportunities does the technology provide?

A critical area of the plan is the new application areas being planned. Some systems will be in the process of development and they should be identified, along with a report of their status. For major new application areas there should be a breakdown of costs and schedules. The plan should outline and set priorities for application areas, such as marketing promotions and production control. An appropriate organisational structure for processing must be developed, for example, centralised or distributed processing.

The manager and users must select a particular alternative for a given application that is to be developed, such as an on-line system, a system based on a minicomputer or an applications package. Operations of a computer facility also need to be carefully managed. The organisation should measure service levels and establish performance criteria that are meaningful to users.

A manager responsible for information processing must also be sure that there are adequate staff and equipment. Charging for services is generally instituted to help allocate computer resources. Finally, management must control information processing to see that performance is in line with plans.

The diagram below presents a framework for viewing management decision areas involved in information processing:

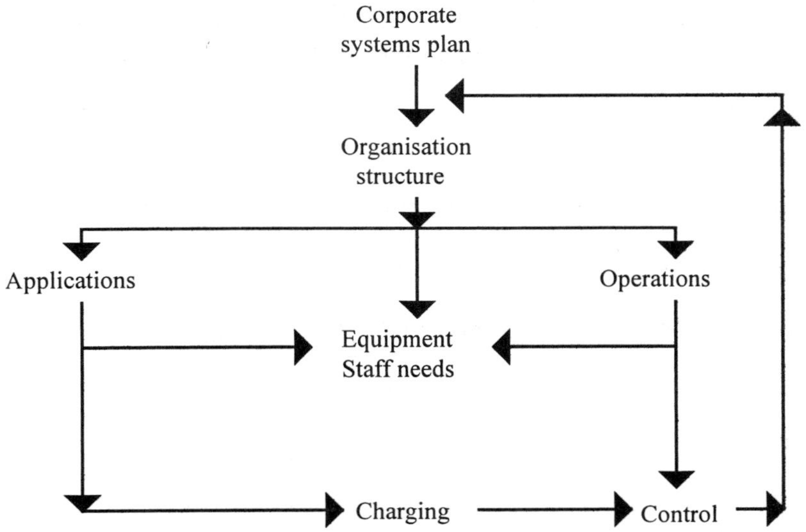

6.4 Implications for systems design

Existing computer-based systems often provide too much data; users frequently have felt overloaded with information that could not possibly be analysed. Managers need to concentrate on selecting the information necessary for decision-making rather than on providing more and more data. The implication of these problems from a systems design stand-point is that the manager should consider the following action steps, which are intended to produce high levels of systems use and successful implementation.

(a) Urge the formation of a steering committee of users and information services department staff members to determine the priorities for the development of new applications.

(b) Encourage training sessions for the information services department staff to help its members adopt a role as catalyst in the development process.

(c) Insist that a user be placed in charge of the design team for a new system.

(d) Provide sufficient resources so that staff can spend time on systems design.

(e) Work personally with the design team to show interest and commitment.

(f) See that decisions and not just data flows are considered in systems design.

(g) Ask probing questions to see if designers have considered the multiple roles of information for the organisation and different decision-makers.

(h) Review all proposed output from a new system, be selective, and avoid system overload.

(i) Examine the user interface with the system; see that users have experimented with the input and output and find it acceptable.

(j) Plan how subordinates and colleagues will use the system, consider different personal and situational factors, and prepare for changes.

(k) Ensure that adequate resources have been devoted to training and user documentation.

7 THE ROLE OF THE STEERING COMMITTEE

Because of the size of the investment involved and the importance of key systems to the organisation, many firms are establishing committees to help manage information processing activities.

A steering committee is a collection of members from the various departments within the organisation and are not, therefore, biased toward one particular functional area of the business. The purpose of a steering committee is to decide how to allocate scarce IT resources and to plan for future system developments. Other activities of the steering committee include

(a) ensuring that all the IT activities are in line with the strategic plans of the organisation as a whole

(b) providing leadership at senior level for the exploitation and management of IT

(c) ensuring that resource allocation decisions are effective

(d) co-ordinating requirements in any organisational restructuring

(e) creating the terms of reference for the project teams

(f) monitoring the progress of the various projects.

Some firms establish a corporate level steering committee for information processing whose objective is to review plans and determine the size of the firm's investment in information processing. The corporate committee reviews division plans, organises and approves education about systems, and seeks areas for the development of common systems serving two or more sub-organisations, such as two different companies with common information processing requirements. The purpose of a common system is to avoid the cost of developing a tailored application at each site.

Each division has a local steering committee that is charged with the responsibility of developing and approving long-range plans for information in that sub-organisation. The local committee also reviews and approves short-term plans and the annual budget for information processing activities in the division. This committee serves to review proposals for new systems and to assign priorities to them. Finally, the local committee reviews and approves staffing requirements for information services.

The problems that arise with steering committees are

(a) the experience and skills of the members do not match the purpose of the committee

(b) the level of operation of the committee is wrong, eg it is either too high in the organisation or too low, and the discussions that take place are not relevant to the issues that need addressing

(c) having the wrong balance of people on the committee, for example, having those that feel they should be represented rather than those with the actual knowledge required

(d) a failure in the communication process from the committee to the rest of the organisation

(e) meetings become too frequent and this leads to a concentration on tactical matters and a possible loss of commitment from some of the members.

8 CHAPTER SUMMARY

In this chapter we have discussed the deployment of IS resources in an organisation, looking at the alternatives of centralised, distributed and decentralised processing.

End user computing has become the norm in most companies, with employees using PCs in a variety of applications. Because of the proliferation of technology throughout the organisation, there has been an increasing need for the information centre and we looked at services offered, the personnel involved and the problem areas associated with the information centre.

We continued by discussing the IS department and the role of the IT director and offered some explanation of the challenges facing an IS department. We ended the chapter by outlining the role of the steering committee in the organisation, looking at the activities and also some of the problem areas.

9 SELF-TEST QUESTIONS

9.1 Explain centralised, distributed and decentralised processing (2.1).

9.2 Describe four arguments **for** centralisation (2.5).

9.3 Outline the situation where decentralisation is best suited (2.6).

9.4 List the reasons given for the spread of end user computing (3.1).

9.5 What are the services offered by the information centre? (4.2).

9.6 List possible problem areas in information centre operations (4.4).

9.7 Explain the skills required by the IT director (6.1).

9.8 Discuss the plight of managers of IS departments (6.3).

9.9 Describe the main activities of the steering committee (7).

10 EXAMINATION TYPE QUESTION

10.1 Thane

Thane Engineering plc is an industrial company serving international markets from factories in France, Germany and Spain, in North America and the UK. The company is a recognised leader in the manufacture of equipment for the automobile and aircraft industries; it also makes a wide range of engine mountings, hoses, plastic mouldings and rubber components. Turnover shown in the last published accounts was £390 million, of which £130 million was contributed by the UK companies.

All the overseas subsidiaries are wholly owned and operate principally in their own country. There is little transfer of goods across national boundaries. The group is managed from a small London headquarters and a great deal of autonomy has been given to the operating units. As a result each subsidiary has evolved its own information systems strategy.

In recent months the London headquarters has begun to press for a more centralised management structure. They argue it will enable more efficient use of resources and so cut costs. The Finance Director has asked you to investigate the options and report to him.

Required

Prepare your report, including the references to key literature you feel appropriate, for the Finance Director setting out:

(a) the advantages of centralising the IT structure; **(8 marks)**
(b) the disadvantages of centralising the IT structure; **(8 marks)**
(c) Include any non-IT factors which might affect your final recommendation. **(9 marks)**
(Total: 25 marks)

10 ANSWER TO EXAMINATION TYPE QUESTION

10.1 Thane

REPORT

To: Finance Director

From: A Consultant

Date: 20 April 19X4

Subject: **Information technology management structure.**

Introduction

This report was compiled for Thane Engineering PLC to recommend a management information structure within the group. It contains an appraisal of the advantages and disadvantages of centralising the management of information technology and includes other relevant, but non IT factors.

Advantages of centralising the IT structure

The benefits to be derived from a centralised service include:

(i) Improved central control with overall co-ordination in the organisation.

(ii) Company wide information systems to support and exploit business opportunities, with a common approach to systems development.

(iii) Centralisation enhances the authority of IT staff and the overall quality of management, establishing company wide technical standards and work procedures.

(iv) Career paths for IT specialists help attract and retain high quality staff.

(v) Economy of capital expenditure due to the relatively high cost of computers through having only one computer for use by the group instead of several located in various units.

(vi) If one powerful computer is installed, the resultant advantages are increased security, speed of operation, storage capacity and processing capability.

(vii) Economy in computer operating costs due to centralisation of systems analysts, programmers, operators and other data processing staff as compared with the level of costs that are incurred with each unit in the group having its own computer on a decentralised basis.

(viii) Centralisation would also facilitate the standardisation of applications but this would depend upon the extent of diversity in the dispersed operations regarding payroll and invoicing structures etc.

(ix) Centralisation will give greater bargaining power with suppliers of hardware and software. The company may also benefit from a better quality service from suppliers if its purchases are perceived as high value.

Disadvantages of centralising the IT structure

(i) It may take longer to get something carried out by a centralised resource over which the user has no direct control.

(ii) Concentration of resources means that the organisation is more vulnerable to sudden breakdowns than it would be if resource were available in its separate units (which would have enough spare capacity to help one another out in emergencies).

(iii) Because the centralised staff are taking a broader view, or because they are less attuned to the circumstances of an individual unit, their contribution may be less focused than that of an insider might have been.

(iv) Users may feel that they lack influence and become unable or unwilling to commit time and resources to developing computer applications.

(v) The reduced expertise at local level may result in delays in processing system enhancements.

Implications for Thane Engineering PLC

Clearly, the disadvantages of the centralised approach are the advantages of the decentralised approach and vice versa.

The centralised facility can reduce costs and excess capacity, can produce career opportunities for staff, and ensure consistent standards across the organisation. But the decentralised approach may give faster and more relevant service to the users and customers and is less vulnerable to problems involving an equipment failure.

Unfortunately, the group is not starting from scratch as far as structure is concerned, because they already have a substantial information system structure in place. This is a decentralised structure where managers are used to taking their own decisions and forming their own IS strategy. It will be expensive and disruptive to change it, especially when the benefits of doing so are uncertain.

The organisation needs to assess the criticality of information technology to them. McFarlan's strategic grid could be used to identify their current dependence on information systems. If the subsidiaries' use of information systems is of strategic importance to current or future operations, falling in the strategic or turnaround sectors of the grid, then they are likely to object to centralisation of these aspects of their business. However, if the usage of information technology is in the factory or support section of the grid, then the subsidiaries may not mind the IT operations being taken over by the London headquarters.

The existing structure, each subsidiary developing and implementing its own IT strategy to suit the local needs and culture, has not been unsuccessful and might be more advantageous in its use of IT to gain local competitive advantage. The trans-border locations of the subsidiaries, with little transfer of goods across national boundaries, would make it difficult to argue for a centralised IT structure with centrally controlled databases of information. Changing the structure of the information technology management, in the hope of reducing costs, would need to be part of the overall IT strategy and its alignment to the structure, taking into consideration the diversity of styles and rate of change throughout the group.

A change to centralisation will result in a different management style of objective setting, that of top-down as opposed to bottom up. Mintzberg suggests that the top down objectives and strategies are intended strategy and the bottom up proposals result in emergent strategy. The management's job is to deliver the overall objective required by the organisation in a way that offers the best chance of success - which is that contributed to, supported and believed in by the employees concerned- bottom up.

28 CONTROLLING IT

INTRODUCTION & LEARNING OBJECTIVES

This last chapter is a culmination of many of the ideas, theories and methodologies that have been studied throughout the study pack.

We continue to develop the concepts of information and examine the difficulties of valuing and costing information at the organisational level. To demonstrate the problems we compare investment appraisal techniques applied to older data processing systems with the current environment of information systems, where projects do not have the same measurable objectives.

If information technology is to be properly integrated with the organisation's strategy, the management will have to formulate a long term plan for it. The development of this plan, the strategic information systems plan (SISP), is a project in its own right and the earlier chapter on project management is very relevant to it.

Any one of several methodologies may be adopted when developing the SISP; some of these are proprietary systems developed by consultancy companies. The methodology we will be focusing on is based on information engineering and can be broken down into six activities, which are not necessarily carried out sequentially. The activities are: initiation; clarifying business strategy; modelling the business; reviewing current information systems; building the information system architecture; and developing the SISP.

When you have studied this chapter you should be able to do the following:

- Explain control and responsibility accounting.
- Describe the measurement and evaluation of the value of information systems.
- Describe how the development of an information system is managed.
- Outline a framework for managing the development of IS.
- Describe the role and composition of the steering committee.
- Explain how a project may be selected.
- Outline the planning and control of projects.

1 CONTROL AND RESPONSIBILITY ACCOUNTING

1.1 Responsibility accounting

The basic principle of responsibility accounting is the existence of a cost reporting system by which costs are accumulated and analysed according to departmental or divisional management responsibilities. These costs are then compared with the budgeted or standard costs over which the manager has effective control.

Any responsibility accounting system requires a planned, logical approach. This has three main aspects:

(a) Firstly, each departmental head or project centre manager must have clear responsibility, as well as agreed authority, for completion of specified tasks. The technique of 'management by objectives', defined by John Humble in his book **Improving business results**, shows how corporate objectives can be filtered down through the lower levels of management. The larger objectives are broken down into a set of smaller objectives which relate specifically to the responsibility level of the relevant manager. Hence, if the lower levels of management achieve their objectives then the overall corporate objectives will be achieved. This vertical interlinking and dependency of objectives must follow the authority chain of the organisation so that the objectives for which a junior manager is responsible will be directly relevant to the objectives of his/her direct line manager.

(b) Secondly, there has to be a proper understanding and agreement concerning the factors over which the manager can be said to have control. This will vary according to the time scale used, ie, costs that are fixed in a one-year cycle may be variable over a five-year period since, in the long term, all fixed costs are variable. Hence, the degree of responsibility accounting will be directly influenced by the planning periods chosen.

(c) Thirdly, there must be a system which reviews the manager's performance regularly. The management by objectives approach specifies responsibility review reports – it is important that these reflect only the costs and performance over which the manager has direct control.

1.2 The main issues concerning control of information technology

Management control is concerned with the broad question of whether information technology is making a contribution to corporate strategy. The contribution could be in the form of independent systems, policy support systems for planning or through a close linkage between strategy formulation and technology. One reason top management may feel uneasy about information processing is the realisation that it is not controlled.

To be successful any system must produce outputs that meet its objectives. To do this, planning must take place and, when the plans have been implemented, control must be exercised to ensure conformity to the plans. A vital element in any planning process is consideration of the controls and control systems necessary to ensure adherence to the plan.

On an operational level a control mechanism is needed to compare actual results with the information processing plan. On a more frequent basis, user reactions to service levels can be measured and reported and progress on individual systems development projects monitored. Management should establish performance criteria and the information services department should report on them.

The basic elements of control are:

(a) a standard specifying expected performance. This can be a budget, an operation procedure or a decision rule;

(b) a measurement of actual performance;

(c) report of deviations.

1.3 Performance and evaluation

It must be appreciated that a management information system has no intrinsic value of its own; it can only come from the users of the system and not from the producers of the information. There is a tendency to assume that more information, earlier or more up to date information or more accurate information is all better information. It may be better information but only if it improves the resulting decisions, otherwise it has no additional value.

The users (management and at all levels and functions) can only cause value to be attributed to the management information systems as a result of actions following decisions taken using the information provided. Actions may:

(a) increase profits

(b) reduce costs

(c) utilise resources more effectively or in some way increase the present or future efficiency of the organisation.

A typical relationship between cost and values is shown in the diagram below:

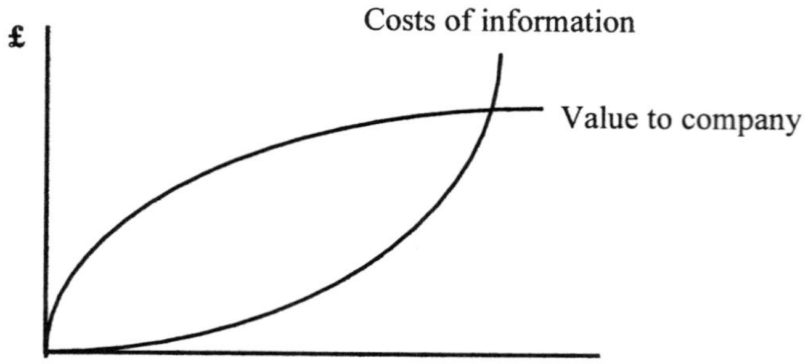

Evaluation of a management information system involves a comparison of the costs of producing the information against the benefits to be obtained from the improved actions resulting from the information. The evaluation should take the form of 'Will the increased volume of information or the more timely information enable better decisions to be made?' If not, the only thing we can say with certainty is that producing the information will incur extra costs.

In most organisations business planning is carried out by a multi-disciplinary team reporting to the chief executive. It is important to remember that qualitative, as well as quantitative, factors are crucial in developing meaningful plans.

1.4 Charging for the use of information technology

The costs of developing and maintaining IT systems can be considerable. How should such costs be accounted for?

One possibility is simply to regard the costs as a general corporate overhead. User departments are unaware of, and unaffected by the costs, because these are all absorbed within a 'head office' budget. Such an approach has the merit of simplicity, and can also help to reduce conflicts between user departments and information systems personnel. However, there are also significant disadvantages.

- The principles of responsibility accounting suggest that departmental heads should be accountable for all the resources they consume. Hiding the cost of the IT resource within a corporate overhead budget obscures the real cost of running user departments, as well as encouraging indiscriminate and irresponsible use of a costly resource.

- It is demotivating for the IT staff themselves. Their expenditure - and hence the scope of their activities - will have been determined in a budget established perhaps many months ago, leaving them little opportunity to respond to changing circumstances.

To overcome these drawbacks, an alternative approach is often adopted. The basic idea is that user departments should bear a fair share of IT costs, but there are various different mechanisms for achieving this.

- One possibility is to treat IT services as a pure cost centre, but to allocate the total costs to user departments on the basis of usage levels. These could be measured by criteria such as cost per transaction processed, cost per hour of staff time etc. This encourages user departments to be discriminating and responsible in their use of the resource, but does little to encourage efficiency within the IT department.

- Another possibility is to establish the IT department as a profit centre, incurring costs as before but recouping them (and perhaps making a profit too) by charging user departments for its services. This approach is particularly valuable where external suppliers offer similar services; in effect, the IT department faces competition from such suppliers and is encouraged to control costs and improve efficiency.

2 MEASURING AND EVALUATING THE VALUE OF IS

2.1 Information economics

Information economics describes an approach to appraising investment in information systems. This approach differs from methods not specifically aimed at information systems in that it attempts to deal with the aspects of information systems which are difficult to quantify in simple monetary terms. Studying the limitations of the conventional methods of investment appraisal when applied to information systems investment appraisal will help when examining how the approach can be enhanced to reflect the nature of what it attempts to measure.

It would appear that information systems have value to organisations because firms continue to invest in new systems and upgrades to established systems. Assuming organisations act in a rational manner seeking to make profits and secure the long term viability of the organisation, then they must see a positive relationship between the cost of the systems and the benefits accruing from their use. How do organisations go about identifying these costs and benefits? This is the question that information economics addresses. The increasing complexity of organisations and information systems makes answering this question considerably more difficult now than ten years ago.

2.2 Conventional investment appraisal techniques

In deciding if a particular project of any kind is worthwhile, an organisation will be seeking to establish what the costs and benefits of the project are. From these two basic pieces of information, investment appraisal can begin. The degree of sophistication of the investment appraisal technique normally applied within a particular organisation will dictate the precise level of detail required under the two general headings of cost and benefit. For example if projects within a firm are decided using a capital rationing system, where projects are ranked by their net present value per pound outlay, then additional detail regarding the time profile of costs and benefits will be required. Historically, it was possible to apply these investment appraisal disciplines to information systems.

Establishing the costs and benefits in monetary terms was relatively straightforward. This was a reflection of the nature of the information systems' applications. Systems proposals would have been to automate an existing manual task. This made the evaluation of the benefits fairly easy because the project would have been able to identify the existing labour cost of carrying out the task manually and an estimate of the labour cost of carrying out the task with the aid of the new system. The saving between the two costs represented the benefits. Benefits could also include the reduction in other resources required to operate the organisation such as more rapid cash collection or lower stock levels.

Establishing the cost of the project was relatively straightforward as the information system to be developed would typically be well defined and logically proven. This was because it would be a copy of an existing manual procedure. It can be seen that there is a relationship between the nature of the application and the certainty with which its costs and benefits can be established.

2.3 The changing environment

The kind of projects that managers now have to decide upon has changed from the automation of existing manual procedures towards projects which aim to change the way the organisation functions, services its customers or deals with it suppliers.

For example, companies which service passenger lifts in offices and other buildings use information systems to monitor the functioning of lifts so that when a defect occurs, the service control centre knows: the nature of the fault; the type of service engineer to despatch; and the tools and spare parts which are required. The system then establishes which of the engineers on duty could travel to the site the quickest. All of this may be accomplished before the client realises that the lift has developed a fault.

Some of these functions would have previously been carried out manually, or more probably mentally, by the service controller. Other functions, such as the monitoring of the lifts, are new. The combination of automating all of the manual tasks into one system will produce changes which are different from the sum of the savings on each of the individual manual tasks, making it difficult to assess the costs and benefits of this kind of information system.

2.4 Cost and benefits assessment

Information systems which are designed to significantly change the way in which an organisation or department operates will, by definition, have no pre-existing manual counterpart upon which they can be based. Therefore the process of development has a greater element of exploration and the unknown, and the cost of developing is less certain than it was with systems installed ten years ago, which typically copied an existing manual system.

The new type of system will rarely be conceived with the aim of reducing the cost of carrying out administrative tasks. The objectives for these systems is frequently to improve the organisation's ability to compete. This may be achieved, for example, by improving customer service or reducing the time taken to develop new products. It is clear that the benefits arising from these kinds of information systems will be difficult to quantify in precise financial terms even assuming that the system has the effect originally envisaged. Furthermore, the technical solution proposed, as part of many information systems' projects, often has considerable capacity to meet additional information requirements on projects yet to be explicitly identified. As such there are further hidden benefits which cannot be quantified.

In making investment decisions managers are asking 'is it worth it?' In this context the definition of worth is 'will the benefits be greater than the costs?' To answer this question, in the environment created by modern technology, requires a broader definition of cost and benefit.

Cost -The concept of cost is expanded to recognise the full range of negative effects that the introduction of an information system could have on an organisation. For example when a new system is planned, the departments affected will operate below their normal levels of productivity because of the concerns that managers and staff will have about how they will be affected.

From benefits to value -Whilst benefit measurement remains an important concept in assessing the worth of an information system, a larger more encompassing concept is required to fully assess the economic impact of the system on the organisation.

Information economics defines value as:

Definition '..the sum of the discrete benefits and of improvements in business performance factors'.

The concept of benefit still remains as an important measure of the various discrete financial gains that the organisation enjoys as a result of implementing the system. In addition the concept of improved business performance is introduced. In doing this, questions about the strategy of the business are raised. By improving the business and competitive performance of the organisation, substantial economic gains may be made. These gains will often dwarf the kind of savings which apply to reductions in costs to carry out administrative tasks. This means that the focus of the manager attempting to measure value will be towards business factors and away from technology.

In the exploration of the worth of information systems the manager will be looking beyond the traditional definitions of costs and benefits into the area of business performance. The focus of the manager will shift from the information system to the effect that the system will have on the business. This implies that the relationship between planning information systems and business planning must be understood.

2.5 Business planning and information systems planning

A business planning system will have a number of objectives. One of the central ones will be to establish a basis upon which the organisation's scarce resources are allocated. Another important aspect of business planning systems is to create an environment where the established resource allocation methods are continually challenged.

Business planning will also identify alternative strategic paths that the organisation may follow. Managers establish criteria by which they can measure the attractiveness of alternative courses of action. These criteria will include:

- The improvement to the firm's competitive position.
- The organisation's capability to carry out the internal steps needed to make the changes to the firm's position possible ie, the internal risks.
- The availability of resources needed to carry out the implied organisational changes and the alternative uses for those resources.

This has two implications for information systems. Firstly, if information technology is introduced in the business planning process it will affect the range and nature of alternative courses of action identified for consideration. Secondly, where an information system is a major component of a strategic course of action, then the managers will be compelled to judge the attractiveness of the strategic path rather than focus on the technology itself or some narrow definition of cost and benefit.

3 MANAGEMENT OF INFORMATION SYSTEMS DEVELOPMENT

3.1 Strategic information systems plan (SISP)

The outcome of this plan should be a document which defines the part that information technology will play in the overall business strategy, describing the IS development effort required to support the business direction over the next three to five years. The process involved in producing the SISP is the information systems planning (ISP).

3.2 Framework

There are a number of methodologies for strategic planning, providing the information systems planning (ISP) project manager with a structured approach and a battery of techniques. It is then the responsibility of the project manager to select the appropriate techniques for the project, adding to the collection as new ones are developed.

The information engineering (IE) methodology is defined as a set of inter-related formal techniques in which business models, data models and process models are built up in a comprehensive knowledge base and are used to plan, create and maintain information systems. Branded products based on IE include:

- Navigator System Series (NSS), developed by Ernst Young;
- Information engineering methodology (IEM,) developed by James Martin Associates;
- Business system planning (BSP), from IBM; and
- Strategic planning, from the London Business Management School.

The six stages of an ISP project, based on an IE methodology, will normally include the following:

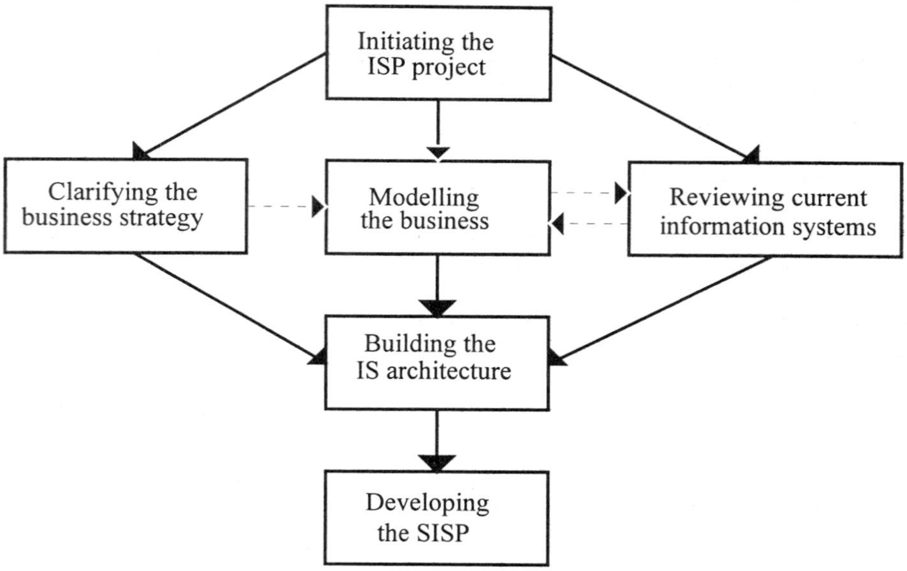

3.3 Initiating the ISP project

This stage includes understanding the scope of the project, the approach to be adopted and how it is going to be organised, resourced and managed.

At this stage it is important to identify and document the scope, goals and objectives of the project.

In determining the scope, the project manager should ascertain whether there are any previous or current planning activities, as the relationship with other ISP projects is important. It would be unwise to duplicate effort or produce conflicting plans. The sequence in which ISP projects are carried out may also impact on the strategic advantage gained. For example, spending money on a SISP for a business which fell into the dog category in the BCG matrix would not be sensible when the continuing profitability of the organisation would presumably depend on those business units in the star or problem child categories.

3.4 Clarifying the business strategy

The purpose of this stage is to develop an IS strategy which is aligned to the business strategy, in a way that can give the greatest benefit.

Developing a picture of the organisation using a SWOT analysis can give valuable insight into the business. The range of models which can contribute to this process include:

- Porter's five forces;
- Porter's generic strategies;
- Wiseman's strategic option generator;
- Porter's value chain and value system; and
- Growth share matrix (Boston Consulting Group).

The preferred approach in IE methodologies is to express the business strategy by identifying the goals of the business and the business objectives set to meet those goals.

These can be modelled on a hierarchy diagram, shown below:

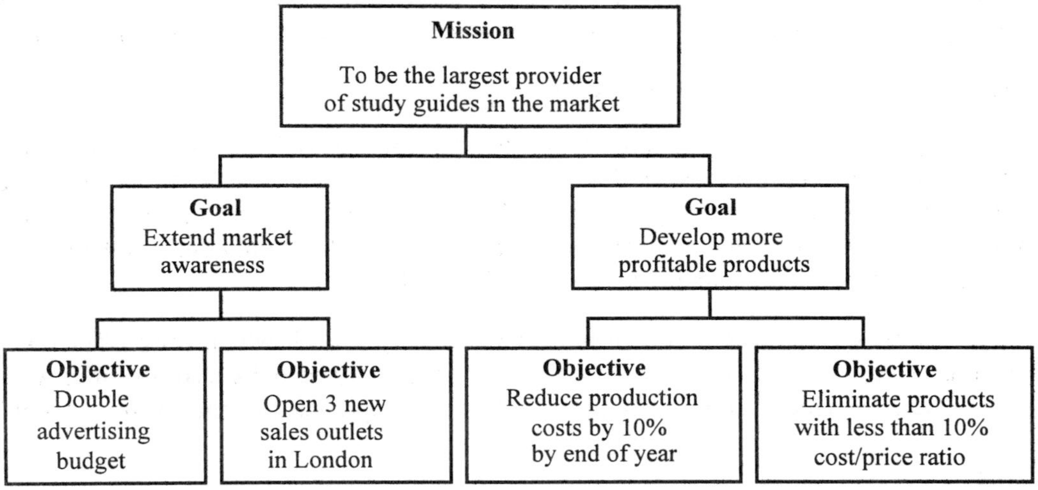

3.5 Modelling the business

Models provide a means for the project team to develop, confirm and present their understanding of the business in a form that is verifiable by the business users and the business management. The four areas that can be modelled successfully are the strategy, functions and processes, data and organisation.

(i) The previous diagram shows how the strategy of a business can be modelled with goals and their dependent objectives.

(ii) Functions and processes can be modelled by drawing a functional decomposition. This show the functions that support the business eg, finance, personnel and marketing, and then breaks down the main business activities (or processes) which form part of those functions.

(iii) The data can be modelled using a variety of modelling techniques, such as dataflow diagrams, entity relationship models and entity life histories.

(iv) The structure and hierarchy of the organisation can be modelled in an organisation chart.

3.6 Reviewing current information systems

It is probable that the organisation will have some IT facilities already in place and these must be recognised as a major building block for the future information systems. The IS review must take into account the views of the people in IT areas who support and keep the IS application running and maintained and also the business users who have to operate the applications.

During the review, it is important to distinguish between investment in the application and investment in the means of delivery, so that the review covers not only the current and planned information systems but also the technology, the management organisation and the control of information systems.

One of the activities in the review of the current IS is documenting resources. These resources can be divided into the following categories:

(i) **Information technology**; a complete inventory of the IT resource should include the technical details, the costs of maintenance, upgrades and financial commitment.

(ii) **The IS infrastructure** review document should cover the personnel, their function and skills, the space they occupy and the facilities they use. The costs, financial commitment, revenues and expenditure, where appropriate, form a part of the review. The models that can help with this review are: Nolan's six stages of growth; McFarlan's phases of technology assimilation and also his strategic grid; and Primozic's waves of innovation.

(iii) **The IS applications and data collections** review document identifies all of the major applications as well as any enhancements to them. The data collections are the physical groupings of data maintained by the organisation eg, computer-based files and databases.

3.7 Building the information systems' architecture

Before the strategy can be prepared, it is necessary to describe the 'vision'. This vision encompasses: the data collections; the applications; a description of the technology; and the management and organisation required to deliver and support them. This is generally called the architecture and is a framework which drives, shapes and controls the IS requirements. It not only defines the vision for the future but it must identify the costs and risks associated with that vision.

The architecture must cover the new opportunities yielded by the IT which may offer competitive advantage or create new strategic options. These opportunities may be enhanced use of an existing IS or a completely new IS which supports an entirely different approach to some business problem or strategy.

There are four interdependent components to the architecture, as shown in the diagram below:

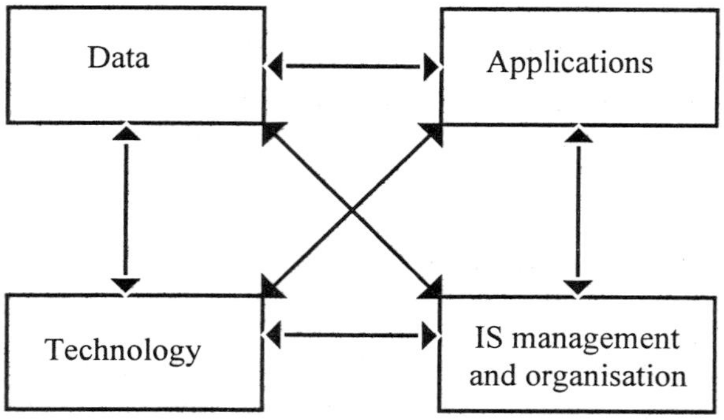

The type of hardware, its capacity and location are influenced by the application needs and the requirement to share data. The IS management and organisation will be influenced by the location of the hardware and the type of data communications required, and vice versa. Each of the components of the IS architecture, whilst being interdependent on the others, is also an architecture in its own right.

Each of the architectures will comprise the same components: parameters; principles; schema; and assessment.

- The parameters are concerned with the essential needs and constraints; they are assumptions which are made so that alternative architectures may be evaluated.
- The principles are the policies which guide decision-making during the development of the architecture.
- The schema describes the architecture, its requirements and how it will work. This description will be based on the business models developed.
- The assessment is the comparison of the current IS situation with the vision described in the schema.

Application architecture

The activities associated with drawing up the schema for the application architecture will include not only identifying the information systems and their applications, but also describing, classifying and assigning priorities to each application. For example, cash management, accounts receivable and general ledger applications may form part of the financial information management system.

Applying the parameters and development principles a decision must be taken on which application or applications to develop or redevelop. The development decision should include whether to build or to buy, or whether re-engineering is appropriate for existing applications. Alternative application architectures can be considered and selection will be based on a cost-benefit analysis.

Data architecture

The schema for the data architecture should include descriptions of the data collections required to support the application architecture. The costs and benefits, return on investment and payback period of the proposed architecture should be analysed and estimated.

Technology architecture

This architecture describes the platform and facilities needed to realise the IS vision of the organisation. It will include:

- the type of processing architecture: mainframe, PC, client server etc;
- the processor configuration: hardware, software, development tools etc;.
- the communications network: LAN and WAN;
- the facilities needed to support both the hardware and the staff.

IS management and organisation architecture

This will describe the infrastructure that will be required for the application, data and technology architectures. It includes an identification of:

- the staff and skills required to support the development, operation and maintenance of the future IS;
- the IS management practices eg, reporting structures, data administration, backup, recovery, security, quality assurance, change control and training;
- the organisation design eg, resource placement, staffing levels, charging structures and the outside services required.

3.8 Developing the strategic information systems plan (SISP)

This plan is inevitably a set of compromises between development and maintenance, risks and returns, infrastructure and applications and long term and short term benefits. There are three sections to the plan: architecture migration strategy; schedule; and maintenance and evolution of the SISP.

Architecture migration strategy

This describes how the move from the current IS position to the vision that is defined in the architectures should be implemented. It shows the phases for implementation, along with an assessment of time, organisational impact, risks, resources, costs and benefits. It also defines the dependency between phases.

Schedule

Each architecture migration phase is reviewed and divided into manageable projects. The projects are then reviewed alongside the application portfolio and the priorities and dependencies are determined.

Maintenance and evolution of the SISP

The SISP will need to be monitored and updated like all plans. Similarly the architectures will also need to be revised as the migration moves forward. The roles and responsibilities for the maintenance of both the plan and the architectures will need to be decided and the procedures to accomplish this maintenance should also be considered. Major reviews of the plan should be defined and the policies concerning them established.

4 THE STEERING COMMITTEE

4.1 Composition and role

The information systems steering committee forms a co-ordinating mechanism at a corporate level and is responsible for IS policies. The members of the committee will include heads of all key business functions and the IT director. The chair person will normally be a Board member.

The committee's objectives for guiding and approving the IS strategy cover:

- ensuring that all ISP projects are co-ordinated and properly carried out;
- formalising and publishing the SISP;
- initiating reviews of the SISP.

In addition to the IS strategic issues, the committee will also be responsible for the IT strategy. The focus will be on the approval and delivery of the architectures defined in the SISP. This gives technical direction to the business and to the method of supply and development of IS.

Overall the committee provides strategic and long range plans, ensuring that IS development plans are fulfilled, the benefits are delivered and the objectives met.

4.2 Project selection

Projects arising from the SISPs have probably already been prioritised and other projects with sources other than the SISP will need to be evaluated and put into place on the list.

When setting priorities for projects, three factors need to be considered:

(i) benefits - what gives the most?
(ii) resources - what can be done?
(iii) risks - what is likely to succeed?

One approach to prioritising is to relate the projects to their position on the strategic grid.

Support Project may be evaluated by the traditional cost/ benefit analysis (based on cost displacement) of a more efficent way of carrying out a task	**Turnaround** Benefits tend to be unknown. They can be termed innovative or R&D projects and justified on the same basis as any other R&D project
Factory Consideration may not be financial but based on the risk of not investing or of failure to invest reducing the ability to achieve future objectives	**Strategic** This project is essential for achieving business objectives and for business strategy

4.3 Planning and controlling projects

The IS steering committee will not be concerned with the management of individual projects; these will be the responsibility of a project steering committee whose objectives will be to:

- initiate formal communication procedures between various groups involved in the project;
- help ensure that all planned outcomes are on time and within budget;
- review and approve project plans;

- authorise commitment to resources;
- approve or disapprove continuance of the project;
- evaluate the post-implementation review.

One of the most important tasks of a manager of an information systems project is project planning and control. Projects which take longer than scheduled cause a loss of money, as well as embarrassment, particularly if they are unexpected or cannot be explained easily.

A survey by Peat Marwick in 1989 showed that for IS projects:

- 60% overran their budget or timescale, or both;
- 33% were abandoned due to rising costs;
- 52% had their timescales extended;
- 15% had more people assigned to them.

Although there were many factors contributing to these problems, the largest single factor was identified as inadequate project management.

5 CHAPTER SUMMARY

The aspects of formulating a strategic information systems plan (SISP) was explained using the six stage IE methodology. In particular we showed how business strategy and analysis models could be used within the methodology.

The process of managing IS development is still an area that organisations can improve. We have outlined a framework in which some of the issues associated with managing the development of IS can be discussed

6 SELF TEST QUESTIONS

6.1 Outline the basic elements of control (1.2).

6.2 How does information economics describe value? (2.4).

6.3 Describe the criteria that managers use to measure the attractiveness of alternative courses of action (2.5).

6.4 Draw a model of the six stages of an ISP project (3.2).

6.5 List the range of models which can help in clarifying the business strategy (3.4).

6.6 Draw a personal strategy hierarchy where the mission is 'To be healthy and look good' (3.4)

6.7 Describe the resource categories which are included in the current IS (3.6)

6.8 Draw a model of the four components of the architecture (3.7).

6.9 What factors need to be considered when setting priorities for projects? (4.2)

7 EXAMINATION TYPE QUESTION

7.1 Meeting the information needs of an organisation

R&C are motor traders in partnership and have been recommended to purchase an IBM-compatible 16-bit microcomputer with a Winchester disc and a daisywheel printer to assist them in the management of the business. It has also been suggested that they purchase software for word processing, spreadsheet modelling, database and business graphs and also that they use the services of PP, a local software house, to write some applications software to assist in the running of the business.

At present the business has a manual system recording details of 3,000 customers and potential customers maintained as hand-written cards in a filing cabinet. Included on a card for a customer are his/her name and address, the make, year, model and registration of his/her car or cars, date of last service and a section for notes to be added by either sales or service staff.

In the case of existing customers, they are sent reminders when the service manager thinks cars are due for their routine service and the sales manager has plans to send selective mailshots to customers who could be due to change their cars or who may be interested in a particular second-hand car taken into stock or in any new model launched. One of the office secretaries is responsible for sending a standard letter to every customer who has not had his/her car serviced for six months reminding him/her of the benefits of routine maintenance and inviting him/her to make an appointment. If the customer fails to respond within a further six months a second letter is sent, this time with a voucher offering £5 off the next service if booked within a month. If there is no response to this letter, the card is removed from the file and held with the 'potential customers'.

Regular customers are offered account facilities and on the back of the card is recorded a credit limit, the date and amount of each invoice, and the date paid.

One application being considered is to use the computer in Service Reception for the booking of appointments; each booking for a service or repair would be entered into the computer and it is intended that enquiries would be handled by displaying the day's bookings on a VDU screen showing the customers and vehicles booked in, the estimated time for each job, and the total workshop hours available for that day.

You are to put yourself in the role of R&C's financial advisor, who, having heard of their plans, offers to give them some impartial advice based on his/her own experience.

You are required to prepare a report with the sub-headings listed below:

(a) Meeting the information needs of the organisation. **(4 marks)**
(b) The effects of automation and change on individuals within the organisation. **(4 marks)**
(c) Criteria for justifying the introduction of a computer-based information system. **(4 marks)**
(d) Dealing with suppliers of hardware and software. **(4 marks)**
(e) Post-implementation maintenance. **(4 marks)**

(Total: 20 marks)

8 ANSWER TO EXAMINATION TYPE QUESTION

8.1 Meeting the information needs of an organisation

(Note: The question asks for a report, as if from R&C's financial advisor, and the format should reflect that as far as possible, and should refer to the circumstances of their decision.*)*

Report to R&C motor traders

Following our discussions of your plans to computerise your information systems, I am now able to provide detailed comments on the areas on which you requested advice:

(a) **Meeting the information needs of this organisation**

It is important to identify your organisation's information needs before making any decision on the acquisition of a computer. Your existing systems will provide a basis, but it is important to consider any shortcomings that they may have and to be aware of the extra information that a computer system may be able to produce. All aspects of the organisation should be considered, including routine daily operations, the maintenance of accounting records for the production of annual financial statements, overall management of the organisation and planning future operations.

(b) **The effects of automation and change on individuals within the organisation**

Most problems in this area stem from fears caused by a lack of awareness of future plans, and all employees who will be affected by the changes should be informed about the development of the new system as early as possible and involved in it as far as is appropriate. General anxiety and hostility among staff who will be operating the new system can best be overcome by a comprehensive training programme which should start as early as possible. It is also important to remember that the conversion of your existing customer records will be a major operation and will cause a great deal of extra work, and to plan the changeover adequately.

(c) **Criteria for justifying the introduction of a computer-based information system**

The new system should be assessed on the basis of its costs and benefits over its expected life, or at least the next three or four years. It is important to ensure that all identifiable costs and benefits are included so that the effect of the changeover can be properly evaluated, and this will include all the staff costs caused by the changeover, such as redundancy, training, etc., and the benefits that the new information will bring. Information benefits may arise because the new system can provide more detailed information or because it can provide it more promptly. Such benefits are difficult to quantify, but it is important to try to include them in the calculations.

(d) **Dealing with suppliers of hardware and software**

It is particularly important when selecting suppliers of software and hardware to consider both their stability and the range of products that they can offer. The computer business is extremely volatile and it is vitally important to ensure continuing support for the system. The more firmly established a product is the more likely it is that such support will be available, and it is worth obtaining details of users of similar systems and contacting them to discuss any problems they may have encountered.

(e) **Post-implementation maintenance**

To minimise the difficulties and expense that may be incurred from any problems with the new system once it is running, it is important to provide for post-implementation support for both the hardware and software.

This may take the form of a service contract covering an agreed period from the date of implementation with the possibility of extension if required, and should include the correction of any faults in the system as specified and arrangements for amendments to the system to cover new information requirements within agreed limits.